P · O · C · K · E · T · S

SPANISH DICTIONARY

SPANISH ENGLISH
ENGLISH SPANISH

DK PUBLISHING, INC.

A DK PUBLISHING BOOK
www.dk.com

First American Edition, 1997

4 6 8 10 9 7 5

Published in the United States by
DK Publishing, Inc.
95 Madison Avenue
New York, New York 10016

ISBN 0-7894-2195-X

This edition revised by Dorling Kindersley

Printed and bound in Italy by LegoPrint

THE IMITATED PRONUNCIATION

Our Imitated Pronunciation will be understood provided each syllable is pronounced as if it were part of an English word; but the exact sounds of the Spanish language can be achieved by remembering a few simple rules:

th	is pronounced like **th** in "thin," not like **th** in "they"
H	is pronounced gutturally, like the Scottish **ch** in "loch"
s	whether represented in the imitated pronunciation by a single or a double **s**, is always pronounced like the **ss** in "missing ," not like the **s** in "easy."
a	the Spanish **a** is pronounced like "ah," but shorter than in "harm." We imitate by "ah " because the sound is never like **a** in "hat," but the "ah" must be pronounced short and sharp.
o	the Spanish **o** resembles the sound of **o** in "not " and even slightly approaches the **aw** in "law." It is not as long as the **o** in "go."
r	is rolled (on the tip of the tongue) more then in English, especially at the beginning of a word or syllable.

STRESS

The stressed syllable is indicated in our imitated pronunciation by bold type, thus: **ploo**-mah, **pah**-pel.

In general, words ending in a consonant stress the last syllable; words ending in a vowel stress the last syllable but one. But the consonants (always n or s) that are merely added to for the plural do not then affect the stress. This is always the same in the plural as in the singular.

When the stress does not follow this rule, an acute accent is placed on the emphasized vowel; allí (there) = ah-l´**yee**, hábil (clever) = **ah**-bil.

VOWELS

a	is pronounced like "ah" (**pluma** = **ploo**-mah)
e	is pronounced like "ay" (**me** = may)
i or **y**	is pronounced like "ee" (**prima** = **pree**-mah)
o	is pronounced like "o" (**toro** = **to**-ro)
u	is pronounced like "oo" (**uno** = **oo**-no)

Each vowel sound has only one sound in Spanish; this is not quite so long and broad as the English equivalent given above. The pronunciation of the vowels is shortened, as in other languages, when they occur in an unstressed syllable, or precede a consonant.

CONSONANTS

z	is pronounced like **th** in "month" or "thick": **luz** = looth, **zapato** = thah-**pah**-to.
j	is pronounced like the German guttural **ch**, or as in the Scottish "loch"; it is merely the English **h** pronounced in the throat. If you find this hard to sound, simply pronounce it like an aspirated **h**. Examples: **ojo** = o-Ho, jugar = Hoo-**gar**.

z and **j** are the only Spanish consonants that are pronounced quite unlike their English equivalent, but there are others that differ in various lesser ways. The following points should be noted:

c	before **e** or **i** is pronounced like the Spanish **z**: **cena** = **thay**-nay, **cinco** = **thin**-ko.
g	before **e** or **i** is pronounced like the Spanish **j**: **general** = Hay-nay-**rahl**.
g	before any other letter is like **g** in "go": **gato** = **gah**-to, **gigante** = He-**gahn**-tay.
gu	before **e** or **i** is like **g** in "go"; before any other vowel it is like **gw** or **goo**: **guerra** = gairr-rah, **guía** = ghee-ah, **guarda** = goo'ar-dah.
h	is not pronounced at all: **hijo** = ee-Ho
ll	is pronounced nearly like **ll** in "million": **calle** = kah-l'yay.
ñ	is almost like **ni** in "companion": **niño** = nee-n'yo, **señor** = say-n'**yor**.
qu	is pronounced like **k**: **que** = kay; **quince** = **kin**-thay.
ch	is pronounced as in "cheap" or "much": **muchacha** = moo-**chah**-chah.
r	is rolled on the tip of the tongue more then in English, especially at the beginning of a word or syllable: **raro**= **rrah**-ro.
s	is always pronounced sharp, as in "see" or "last", never like a **z** as in "easy": **casa**= **kah**-sah.

ACCENTS, SIGNS OF PUNCTUATION, ETC

The acute accent (´) is the only accent used in Spanish. It indicates that the stress or emphasis is to be laid on the syllable containing the vowel over which it is placed: **médico** = **may**-de-ko. It is also used to distinguish between words spelled similarly, but of different meaning: **te** (thee), **té** (tea), both of which are pronounced **tay**. It never alters the pronunciation of a letter.

The accent is also used in such words as **cuando** and **donde**, when they actually ask a question: **¿Cuándo llega el barco?** (When does the boat arrive?), but **¿Sabe él cuando llega el barco?** (Does he know when the boat arrives?).

The dieresis (¨) is placed over u (ü) preceded by **g**, to indicate that the **u** must be pronounced: **agüero** = ah-goo'**ay**-ro.

Question marks and exclamation marks are placed at both ends of the phrase, the first one being inverted (¿)

ADVERBS

Spanish adverbs end generally in "mente" which corresponds to the English "ly" and are formed by adding this termination to the feminine ending "a" of adjectives in **o**, or to the last letter , whether the vowel "e" or a consonant, of the other adjectives. Ex. **raro** (m.), **rara** (f.), **raramente**; **pobre**, **feliz** (m. & f.), **pobremente**, **felizmente**. Adjectives from which adverbs can thus be formed are marked with an asterisk (*).

THE SPANISH ALPHABET

	A	B	C	CH	D	E
F	G	H	I	J	K	L
LL	M	N	Ñ	O	P	Q
R	S	T	U	V	W	X
Y	Z					

NB: In Spanish, ch, ll and ñ represent separate letters; they therefore appear at the end of the C's, L's, and N's as in other Spanish dictionaries. Similarly, where ch, ll or ñ occurs in the middle of a word, that word is to be found after -cz-, -lz-, or -nz-.

VARYING PRONUNCIATION

The lisping pronunciation of **z**, and **c** before **e** or **i**, is usual in Castile, and as Castilian is considered the most correct Spanish we have used it in this dictionary. But in South and Central America, as well as in some parts of Spain, it is usual to pronounce these letters like the English "s." In the following examples, the Castilian pronunciation comes before the variant: **izquierdo** = ith-ke-**air**-do, iss-ke-**air**-do; **cerca** = **thair**-kah, **sair**-kah; **cielo** = the-**ay**-lo, se-**ay**-lo.

The letter **ll** is pronounced in several ways; we imitate it as "l'y . . . " but in some areas and in Latin America it has a strong gutteral sound, with the "l" virtually disappearing. Thus **mantilla**, mahn-**tee**-l'yah, becomes mahn-**tee**-yah. In Andalucia and Argentina it is even stronger, the "l" sound being replaced by something like a soft "j" or the "si" in "occasion."

You are advised to pronounce the Spanish **d**, **b**, and **v**, exactly as in English, not making the final **d** too sharp and distinct.

NB: The imitated pronunciation in the Spanish-English section is for English-speaking people only. Similarly, the imitated pronunciation in the English-Spanish section is for Spanish people only.

ABBREVIATIONS USED IN THIS DICTIONARY

a	adjective	*naut*	nautical
adv	adverb	*pp*	past participle
art	article	*pers pron*	personal pronoun
conj	conjunction	*photog*	photography
eccl	ecclesiastical	*pl*	plural
elec	electric	*pop*	popular
f.	feminine	*poss adj*	possessive adjective
fam	familiar	*prep*	preposition
fig	figuratively	*pron*	pronoun
interj	interjection	*refl*	reflexive
m.	masculine	*s*	substantive
mech.	mechanics	*s & a/s y a*	substantive and adjective
med	medical	*s pl*	substantive plural
mil	military	*v*	verb
mus	musical	*vulg*	vulgar
n.	neuter		

LA PRONUNCIACIÓN FIGURADA

Cada sílaba de la pronunciación figurada debe pronunciarse como si formara parte de una palabra española. En inglés hay sonidos que no existen en español. Es imposible, por tanto, imitarlos exactamente con sílabas españolas. Las siguientes aclaraciones ayudarán a conseguir la pronunciación exacta de los sonidos.

VOCALES

Es muy importante distinguir las vocales largas de las breves. Las vocales largas se representan en la pronunciación figurada duplicando la vocal. Por ejemplo **cheap**, chiip: **boot**, buut. En algunos casos, la vocal larga se indica con un acento, como en **chair**, chér. Las vocales largas se pronuncian como un **solo sonido**.

A — representa un sonido breve, entre **a** y **e**, parecido al de la **e** en "sello."

oa — debe prooonunciarse como la **o** en "monte" , pero mas alargado, casi como la **oa** en"loa."

ŏ — representa un sonido corto y medio, entre la **eu** y la **a** de las palabras francesas "fleur" y "lac"

a, e, i, o, u – Estos signos representan vocales no acentuadas que tienen un sonido obscuro y breve que apenas se oye, parecido al de la **e** en las palabras francesas "de" y "le", y que va casi siempre al final de la palabra. Algunos ejemplos son **doctor**, doc'-ta; **partner**, part'-na. En algunas terminaciones, este sonido indistinto se indica omitiendo la vocal no acentuada: **useful**, ius'-fl; **candle**, kan'-dl. **El sonido verdadero de la vocal no ha de oirse.**

Hay que tener en cuenta esta observación, sobre todo con respecto a las numerosas terminaciones indicadas por *a*, (en inglés *er* no acentuado), en las que la *a* tiene el sobredicho sonido e -vago e indistinto- .

ei, ou – Estas sílabas tienen respectivamente el sonido largo de la **e** y la **o**. La **i** y la **u** se pronuncian con rapidez y tan ligeramente que apenas se oigan.

ĕr — como la **eu** en las palabras francesas "peur", "fleur ."

El mismo sonido, aunque mas rápido y ligero, se oye también detrás de las vocales largas **é, í, ó, ú**, en las terminaciones **ér, ír, ór, úr**, de la pronunciación figurada.

CONSONANTES

z   como en Castilla, nunca como la **s**.
D   mayúscula; (véase página viii).
k   siempre como la **c** en "casa", "como."
j   lo mismo que la **j** española, pero menos gutural.
s   en la letra gruesa itálica indica un sonido suave, el mismo que **s** en la palabra francesa "chaise."
sh   como **ch** en las palabras francesas "chat" y "affiche."
CH   mayúsculas representan un sonido parecido pero mas suave que la **j** francesa en "jamais" precedido de **d**.
sh   gruesas como **j** en la palabra francesa "jamais."
g   (itálica) no suena separadamente, puesto que es un sonido nasal.
r   (itálica) no se pronuncia sino muy ligeramente.
b   se pronuncia siempre lo mismo que la **b** francesa, nunca como la **v**.

LOS DOS SONIDOS DE "TH"

El sonido agudo o fuerte de **th** en inglés se corresponde exactamente con la pronunciación castellana de **z** en la palabra "vez" o de la **c** en la palabra "once." En la pronunciación figurada indicamos este sonido con una **z**. Los hispanos-hablantes que pronuncian la **z** diferente de la manera castellana (andaluces, sudamericanos etc), deben pronunciarla como la castellana al leer nuestra pronunciación figurada.

El sonido llano o suave de la **th** en inglés se parece al sonido agudo, precedido por una **d** débil. Si se pronuncia como la **d** española en las palabras "padre," "admirar," podra comprenderse, pero no es absolutamente correcto. Este sonido se representa con una D (mayúscula).

El sonido llano se pronuncia también con la lengua entre los dientes, lo mismo que cuando se cecea, pero forzando el aliento para que salga fuera por **debajo** de la lengua, en lugar de por encima, como sucede en la pronunciación aguda de **th**.

LOS SONIDOS DE "S"

La **s** inglesa, como la francesa, tiene dos sonidos diferentes. Siempre es aguda al principio de una palabra, como en español (castellano) en "seis" y "sobre." Pero a menudo suena como la **z** inglesa o francesa, sobre todo entre dos vocales. La **s** suave (suena como algunos españoles pronuncian la **s** en "risa" o "rosa") se representa con una **s** gruesa en itálica. Este sonido inglés es como la **s** francesa de "chose" y "église."

"H" ASPIRADA

La letra **h** aspirada se representa con j. Se pronuncia con una respiración fuerte, detrás de los dientes y no detrás de la garganta como la **j** gutural española o la **g** de "gente" o "giro."

"WH" ASPIRADA

En nuestra pronunciación figurada, ju pronunciada muy ligeramente y apoyándose sobre la vocal que sigue, representa exactamente el sonido de **wh** aspirada, que aparece en palabras como "who ," juu; **whom** , juum; o **whose**, juus.

LA LETRA "R"

Salvo que vaya seguida inmediatamente de un vocal, se puede decir que al final de una palabra o sílaba es muda o se pronuncia muy flojo, en Londres y en casi todo el sur de Inglaterra. Por ejemplo, **scholar** y **popular** suenan casi como scol'-*a* y pop-**iu**-*la*. Pero la letra **r** modifica a menudo, y a veces cambia completamente, el sonido de la vocal que la precede.

Ejemplos:

español	inglés	pronunciación figurada
te	tea	tii o ti
rasgar	tear	ter
el	he	ji o jii
ella	her	jer

Casí en todo el resto del Reino Unido la **r** se pronuncia más fuerte.

ACENTO

La señal ´ indica que la sílaba precedente debe pronunciarse con mas énfasis que las demás.

ADVERBIOS

El asterisco indica los adjetivos a los cuales basta añadir la terminación "**ly**" para convertirlos en adverbios. Por ejemplo: **wise**, sabio; **wisely**, sabiamente. Esta terminación "**ly**" tiene un sonido intermedio entre "le" y "li."

Advertencia: Como la pronunciación figurada en la parte inglés - español es sólo para uso de los españoles, los sonidos ingleses están representados por letras y grupos de letras de origen español (castellano). De la misma manera, la pronunciación figurada de la parte inglés-español solo interesa a las personas de habla inglesa.

EXPLICACIÓN DE LAS ABREVIATURAS

a	adjetivo	*n.*	neutro
a po	adjetivo posesivo	*nau*	náutico
adv	adverbio	*pp*	participio pasado
art	artículo	*photog*	fotografía
conj	conjunción	*pl*	plural
eccl	eclesiástico	*pop*	popular
elec	eléctrico	*prep*	preposición
f.	femenino	*pron*	pronombre
fam	familiar	*pro pers*	pronombre personal
fig	figuradamente	*refl*	reflexivo
interj	interjección	*s*	substantivo
m.	masculino	*s y a.*	substantivo y adjetivo
mech	mecánica	*s & a*	substantivo y adjetivo
med	médico	*s pl*	substantivo plural
mil	militar	*v*	verbo
mus	musical	*vul*	vulgar

SPANISH · ENGLISH
ESPAÑOL · INGLÉS

a, ah *prep* at; to; in; on; by; for; as

abad, ah-**bahd** *s* abbot

abadejo, ah-bah-**day**-Ho *s* codfish; yellow wren

abajo, ah-**bah**-Ho *adv* below; under; underneath

abalanzar, ah-bah-lahn-**thar** *v* to balance; to dart; to rush

abalear, ah-bah-lay-**ar** *v* to winnow; to sift

abandonar, ah-bahn-do-**nar** *v* to abandon; to give up; to forsake

abandono, ah-bahn-**do**-no *s* abandonment

abanico, ah-bah-**nee**-ko *s* fan

abarca, ah-**bar**-kah *s* sandal

abarcar, ah-bar-**kar** *v* to embrace; to clasp; to include

abarrotar, ah-bar-rro-**tar** *v* to stow; to overstock

abastecedor, ah-bahs-tay-thay-**dor** *s* caterer

abastecer, ah-bahs-tay-**thair** *v* to supply; to provide

abastecimiento, ah-bahs-tay-the-me-**en**-to *s* provisions

abate, ah-**bah**-tay *s* abbé

abatido, ah-bah-**tee**-do *a* dejected; abject

abatimiento, ah-bah-te-me-**en**-to *s* depression

abatir, ah-bah-**teer** *v* to throw down; to discourage, to be depressed

abdicar, ahb-de-**kar** *v* to abdicate

abeja, ah-**bay**-Hah *s* bee

abejón, ah-**bay**-Hon *s* hornet; drone

abellacado, ah-bell-yah-**kah**-do *a* mean-spirited

aberración, ah-bair-rrah-the-**on** *s* aberration

abertura, ah-bair-**too**-rah *s* opening; overture

abierto*, ah-be-**air**-to *a* open; frank

abigarrar, ah-be-gar-**rrar** *v* to variegate

abismar, ah-biss-**mar** *v* to think deeply; to depress

abismo, ah-**biss**-mo *s* abyss

abjurar, ahb-Hoor-**ar** *v* to abjure

ablandamiento, ah-blahn-dah-me-**en**-to *s* softening

ablandar, ah-blahn-**dar** *v* to mollify; to relent; to soften

ablución, ah-bloo-the-**on** *s* ablution

abnegar, ahb-nay-**gar** *v* to renounce

abobado, ah-bo-**bah**-do *a* silly; stupid

abobamiento, ah-bo-bah-mee-**en**-to s stupefaction

abobar, ah-bo-**bar** v to stupefy

abocarse, ah-bo-**kar**-say v to meet; to have a conference

abofetear, ah-bo-fay-tay-**ar** v to slap; to hit (in the face)

abogado, ah-bo-**gah**-do s advocate; lawyer; barrister

abogar, ah-bo-**gar** v to advocate; to plead

abolengo, ah-bo-**len**-go s ancestry, lineage

abolición, ah-bo-le-the-**on** s abolition

abolir, ah-bo-**leer** v to abolish; to repeal

abollar, ah-bo-l'**yar** v to emboss; to dent

abominable, ah-bo-me-**nah**-blay a abominable

abominar, ah-bo-me-**nar** v to abhor; to abominate

abonado, ah-bo-**nah**-do s subscriber; a creditable; fit for

abonador, ah-bo-nah-**dor** s guarantor

abonar, ah-bo-**nar** v to bail; to fertilize; to pay; to credit; to subscribe

abonaré, ah-bo-nar-**ay** s promissory note; IOU

abono, ah-**bo**-no s guarantee; subscription; receipt; manure

abordaje, ah-bor-**dah**-Hay s boarding a ship

abordar, ah-bor-**dar** v to board a ship

abordo, ah-**bor**-do s attack on a ship

aborrecer, ah-bor-rray-**thair** v to abhor

aborrecible, ah-bor-rray-**thee**-blay a hateful; abhorrent

abortivo*, ah-bor-**tee**-vo a abortive

aborto, ah-**bor**-to s miscarriage; abortion; monster

abotonador, ah-bo-to-nah-**dor** s buttonhook

abotonar, ah-bo-to-**nar** v to button

abovedado, ah-bo-vay-**dah**-do a vaulted

abra, ah-**brah** s bay; creek; haven

abrasamiento, ah-brah-sah-me-**en**-to s burning

abrasar, ah-brah-**sar** v to burn; to set on fire

abrazar, ah-brah-**thar** v to embrace; to hug

abrazo, ah-**brah**-tho s hug; embrace

abrebiatura, ah-bray-ve-

ah-**too**-rah s abbreviation

abrelatas, ah-bray-**lah**-tahs s can opener

abreviación, ah-bray-ve-ah-the-**on** s abbreviation

abreviar, ah-bray-ve-**ar** v to abridge; to cut short; to abbreviate

abridor, ah-bre-**dor** s opener

abrigar, ah-bre-**gar** v to shelter; to cover

abrigo, ah-**bree**-go s shelter; overcoat

abril, ah-**breel** s April

abrimiento, ah-bre-me-**en**-to s opening

abrir, ah-**breer** v to open

abrochar, ah-bro-**char** v to button

abrogar, ah-bro-**gar** v to abrogate; to repeal

abrojo, ah-bro-Ho s thorn; thistle

abromado, ah-bro-**mah**-do a dark; hazy

abrumado, ah-broo-**mah**-do a weary; overwhelmed

abrumar, ah-broo-**mar** v to crush; to overwhelm

abrutado, ah-broo-**tah**-do a brutish

absceso, ahbs-**thay**-so s

abscess

absolución, ahb-so-loo-the-**on** s absolution

absoluto*, ahb-so-**loo**-to a absolute

absolver, ahb-sol-**vair** v to absolve

absorber, ahb-sor-**bair** v to absorb

abstemio, ahbs-tay-me-o a abstemious

abstenerse, ahbs-tay-**nair**-say v to abstain

abstinencia, ahbs-te-**nen**-the-ah s abstinence; temperance

abstinente, ahbs-te-**nen**-tay a abstinent

abstraer, ahbs-trah-**air** v to abstract; to remove

abstraido, ahbs-trah-ee-do a retired; absentminded

absuelto, ahb-soo-el-to a absolved

absurdo, ahb-**soor**-do s absurdity; a absurd

abuela, ah-boo´ay-lah s grandmother

abuelo, ah-boo´ay-lo s grandfather

abultado, ah-bool-**tah**-do a bulky

abundante, ah-boon-**dahn**-tay a abundant

abundar, ah-boon-**dar** v to abound

aburrir, ah-boor-**reer** v to weary; to bore

abusar, ah-boo-**sar** v to abuse

abuso, ah-**boo**-so s abuse

abyección, ah-be´ayk-the-on s abjection

abyecto, ah-be´ayk-to a abject

acabado, ah-kah-**bah**-do a perfect; complete; worn out

acabamiento, ah-kah-bah-me-**en**-to s end; completion

acabar, ah-kah-**bar** v to finish; to end

academia, ah-kah-**day**-me-ah s academy

acaecer, ah-kah-ay-**thair** v to happen

acaecimiento, ah-kah-ay-the-me-**en**-to s occurrence; event

acallar, ah-kah-l´**yar** v to quiet

acalorar, ah-kah-lo-**rar** v to warm; to inflame

acampar, ah-kahm-**pahr** v to camp

acantilado, ah-kahn-te-**lah**-do s steep cliff

acantonar, ah-kahn-to-**nar** v to quarter (troops)

acariciar, ah-kah-re-the-**ar** v to fondle; to caress

acarreador, ah-kar-rray-ah-**dor** s porter; carrier

acarrear, ah-kar-rray-**ar** v to carry; to cause

acarreo, ah-kar-**rray**-o s cartage

acaso, ah-**kah**-so adv by chance; s chance

acceder, ahk-thay-**dair** v to accede; to agree

acceso, ahk-**thay**-so s access

accesorio, ahk-thay-**so**-re-o a accessory

accidentarse, ahk-the-den-**tar**-say v to have an accident

accidente, ahk-the-**den**-tay s accident

acción, ahk-the-**on** s action; feat; battle

accionar, ahk-the-o-**nar** v to gesticulate; to set off

accionista, ahk-the-o-**niss**-tah s shareholder

acechar, ah-thay-**char** v to waylay; to pry; to watch

aceite, ah-**thay**-e-tay s oil

aceitería, ah-thay-e-tay-**ree**-ah s oil shop

aceitoso, ah-thay-e-**to**-so a oily; greasy

aceituna, ah-thay-e-**too**-nah s olive

aceleración, ah-thay-lay-rah-the-**on** s

acceleration

acelerador, ah-thay-lay-rah-dor *s* accelerator

acelerar, ah-thay-lay-rar *v* to accelerate

acendrar, ah-then-drar *v* to refine metals

acento, ah-then-to *s* accent

acentuar, ah-then-too-ar *v* to accentuate

acepción, ah-thep-the-on *s* acceptance; meaning

aceptable, ah-thep-tah-blay *a* acceptable

aceptación, ah-thep-tah-the-on *s* acceptance

aceptador, ah-thep-tah-dor *s* acceptor

aceptar, ah-thep-tar *v* to accept

acepto, ah-thep-to *a* acceptable, agreeable

acequia, ah-thay-ke-ah *s* canal; drain

acerado, ah-thay-rah-do *a* made of steel

acerbidad, ah-thair-be-dahd *s* acerbity; rigor

acerbo*, ah-thair-bo *a* harsh; cruel

acerca, ah-thair-kah *prep* about; relating to

acercar, ah-thair-kar *v* to approach

acero, ah-thay-ro *s* steel

acérrimo, ah-thair-rre-mo *a* staunch; stalwart

acertado*, ah-thair-tah-do *a* proper; fit; correct

acertar, ah-thair-tar *v* to hit the mark; to hit upon; to guess; to succeed

acertijo, ah-thair-tee-Ho *s* riddle

acervo, ah-thair-vo *s* heap

aciago, ah-the-ah-go *a* unfortunate; sad

acíbar, ah-thee-bar *s* aloes; bitterness

acicalar, ah-the-kah-lar *v* to polish; to dress; to embellish

acidez, ah-the-deth *s* acidity

ácido, ah-the-do *a* acid; sour

acidular, ah-the-doo-lar *v* to acidulate

acierto, ah-the-air-to *s* good hit; good guess

aclamación, ah-klah-mah-the-on *s* acclamation

aclamar, ah-klah-mar *v* to acclaim; to applaud

aclaración, ah-klah-rah-the-on *s* explanation

aclarar, ah-klah-rar *v* to explain; to clarify

aclimatar, ah-kle-mah-tahr *v* to acclimatize

acné, ahk-nay *s* acne

acobardar, ah-ko-bar-dar *v* to daunt; to intimidate

acocear, ah-ko-thay-ar *v* to kick; to ill-treat

acodiciar, ah-ko-de-the-ar *v* to long for; to covet

acoger, ah-ko-Hair *v* to receive; to admit someone; to shelter someone

acogida, acogimiento, ah-ko-Hee-dah, ah-ko-He-me-en-to *s* reception

acometedor, ah-ko-may-tay-dor *s* aggressor

acometer, ah-ko-may-tair *v* to assault; to attack

acometida, ah-ko-may-tee-dah *s* assault

acomodado*, ah-ko-mo-dah-do *a* convenient; fit; wealthy; reasonable

acomodar, ah-ko-mo-dar *v* to accommodate; to reconcile; to supply

acomodo, ah-ko-mo-do *s* employment; situation; lodgings

acompañar, ah-kom-pah-n´yar *v* to accompany

acondicionado, ah-kon-de-the-o-nah-do *a* conditioned

acondicionar, ah-kon-de-the-o-nar *v* to dispose;

to prepare

acongojar, ah-kon-go-*Har*
v to oppress; to afflict

aconsejar, ah-kon-say-*Har*
v to advise

acontecer, ah-kon-tay-
thair *v* to happen

acontecimiento, ah-kon-
tay-the-me-**en**-to *s*
event; happening

acopiar, ah-ko-pe-**ar** *v* to
gather; to store up

acorazar, ahh-ko-rah-**thah**
v to armor; to harden
oneself

acorcharse, ah-kor-**char**-
say *v* to shrivel

acordado*, ah-kor-dah-do
a agreed

acordar, ah-kor-dar *v* to
resolve; to agree; to
remember

acorde, ah-**kor**-day *s*
accord; *a* conformable

acorrer, ah-kor-**rrair** *v* to
run to; to succor

acortamiento, ah-kor-tah-
me-**en**-to *s* shortening

acortar, ah-kor-tar *v* to
shorten

acosamiento, ah-ko-sah-
me-**en**-to *s* relentless
persecution

acosar, ah-koh-**sar** *v* to
pursue closely; to harass

acostar, ah-kos-**tar** *v* to lay

down

acostumbradamente, ah-
kos-toom-brah-dah-
men-tay *adv* customarily

acostumbrar, ah-kos-
toom-**brar** *v* to accustom

acotación, ah-ko-tah-the-
on *s* limit; annotation

acotar, ah-ko-tar *v* to set
limits on; to survey

acre*, ah-kray *a* acrid;
sour

acrecentamiento, ah-kray-
then-tah-me-**en**-to *s*
increase

acrecer, ah-kray-**thair** *v* to
increase

acreditar, ah-kray-de-tar *v*
to prove; to credit

acreedor, ah-kray-ay-**dor** *s*
creditor; *a* deserving

acribar, ah-kre-**bar** *v* to
sift

acriminar, ah-kre-me-**nar**
v to accuse

acrimonia, ah-kre-**mo**-ne-
ah *s* acrimony

acrisolar, ah-kre-so-**lar** *v*
to refine

acritud, ah-kre-**tood** *s*
sourness; acrimony

acróbata, ah-**kro**-bah-tah
s acrobat

acta, **ahk**-tah *s* act; record;
minutes

actitud, ahk-te-**tood** *s*

attitude

activar, ahk-te-var *v* to
push; to hurry; to
activate

actividad, ahk-te-vi-**dahd**
s activity

activo*, ahk-**tee**-vo *a*
active

actor, ahk-**tor** *s* actor

actriz, ahk-**treeth** *s* actress

actuación, ahk-too-ah-
the-**on** *s* law
proceedings; actuation

actual*, ahk-too-**ahl** *a*
actual; present

actualidad, ahk-too-ah-le-
dahd *s* present time

actuar, ahk-too-**ar** *v* to
act; to prosecute; to
perform judicial acts

actuario, ahk-too-ah-re-o
s clerk; actuary

acuarela, ah-koo´ah-**ray**-
lay *s* watercolor

acuario, ah-koo-**ah**-re-o *s*
aquarium

acudir, ah-koo-**deer** *v* to
come; to turn up; to run
to; to have recourse

acueducto, ah-koo´ay-
dook-to *s* aqueduct

ácueo, ah-koo´ay-o *a*
watery

acuerdo, ah-koo´**air**-do *s*
resolution; accord;
recollection; agreement

acumular, ah-koo-moo-**lar** *v* to accumulate

acuosidad, ah-koo-'o-si-**dahd** *s* wateriness

acurrucarse, ah-koor-rroo-**kar**-say *v* to squat; to curl up

acusación, ah-koo-sah-the-**on** *s* accusation

acusar, ah-koo-**son** *v* to accuse

acusón, ah-koo-**son** *s* (*fam*) sneak; tattletale

acústica, ah-**kooss**-te-kah *s* acoustics

achacar, ah-chah-**kar** *v* to impute

achacoso, ah-chah-**ko**-so *a* sickly; ailing

achaparrado, ah-chah-par-**rrah**-do *a* dwarfish

achaque, ah-**chah**-kay *s* ailment; malady

achatar, ah-chah-**tar** *v* to flatten

achicar, ah-che-**kar** *v* to diminish; to lessen; to humble

achicoria, ah-che-**ko**-re-ah *s* chicory

achispado, ah-chis-**pah**-do *a* tipsy

achuchar, ah-choo-**char** *v* to flatten; to jostle; to crush

adalid, ah-dah-**leed** *s* chief; leader

adamascado, ah-dah-mahs-**kah**-do *a* damasklike

adán, ah-**dahn,** *s* Adam; (*fig*) slovenly man

adaptación, ah-dahp-tah-the-**on** *s* adaptation

adaptado*, ah-dahp-**tah**-do *a* adapted; fitted

adecuado*, ah-day-koo-'ah-do *a* adequate

adecuar, ah-day-koo-'ar *v* to fit; to adapt

adefesio, ah-day-**fay**-se-o *s* extravagance; ridiculous attire

adelantado, ah-day-lahn-**tah**-do *a* advanced; forward

adelantar, ah-day-lahn-**tar** *v* to advance; to anticipate; to accelerate

adelante, ah-day-**lahn**-tay *adv* farther; forward

adelgazar, ah-del-gah-**thar** *v* to make thin

ademán, ah-day-**mahn** *s* gesture; look; manners

además, ah-day-**mahs** *adv* moreover; further; besides

adentro, ah-**den**-tro *adv* within

adepto, ah-**dep**-to *a* adept; *s* follower

aderezar, ah-day-ray-**thar** *v* to adorn; to dress

aderezo, ah-day-**ray**-tho *s* adorning; dressing (food)

adeudado, ah-day-oo-**dah**-do *a* indebted

adherir, ah-day-**reer** *v* to adhere; to stick

adhesión, ah-day-se-**on** *s* adhesion

adición, ah-de-the-**on** *s* addition

adicto, ah-**deck**-to *a* addicted

adiestrar, ah-de-ess-**trar** *v* to guide; to teach; to train

adinerado, ah-de-nay-**rah**-do *a* rich; wealthy

¡adiós! ah-de-**os** *interj* good-bye; farewell; adieu

aditivo, ah-de-**tee**-vo *s* additive

adivinar, ah-de-ve-**nar** *v* to foretell; to conjecture; to guess

adjetivo, ahd-**Hay**-tee-vo *s* adjective

adjudicar, ahd-Hoo-de-**kar** *v* to adjudge; to adjudicate

adjunta, ahd-**Hoon**-tah *s* enclosure

adjunto, ahd-**Hoon**-to *a*

enclosed

administración, ahd-me-niss-trah-the-**on** s administration

administrar, ahd-me-niss-**trar** v to manage; to administer

admirable*, ahd-me-**rah**-blay a admirable

admirar, ahd-me-**rar** v to admire

admisible, ahd-me-**see**-blay a admissible

admitir, ahd-me-**teer** v to admit; to accept

admonición, ahd-mo-ne-the-**on** s admonition; warning

adobar, ah-do-**bar** v to fertilize; to pickle; to cook

adocenado, ah-do-thay-**nah**-do a common; vulgar

adoctrinar, ah-dok-tre-**nar** v to instruct

adolecer, ah-do-lay-**thair** v to be ill; to suffer

adolescencia, ah-do-less-**then**-the-ah s adolescence

adolescente, ah-do-less-**then**-tay a adolescent

adonde, ah-**don**-day adv whither; where

adoptar, ah-dop-**tar** v to

adopt

adoquín, ah-do-**keen** s paving stone

adorable*, ah-do-**rah**-blay a adorable

adorador, ah-do-rah-**dor** s worshipper

adorar, ah-do-**rar** v to adore; to worship

adormecer, ah-dor-may-**thair** v to cause sleep; to fall asleep; to lull

adornar, ah-dor-**nar** v to adorn

adquirir, ahd-ke-**reer** v to acquire; to get

adrede, ah-**dray**-day adv purposely

adscribir, ahds-kre-**beer** v to appoint

aduana, ah-doo-**'ah**-nah s customs; custom house

aduanero, ah-doo-**'ah-nay**-ro s customs officer

aducir, ah-doo-**theer** v to cite; to adduce

adueñarse, ah-doo-'ay-n´**yar**-say v to take possession of

adulación, ah-doo-lah-the-**on** s adulation

adulterar, ah-dool-tay-**rar** v to adulterate

adulto, ah-**dool**-to a adult

adusto, ah-**dooss**-to a sullen; gloomy; austere

advenedizo, ahd-vay-nay-**dee**-tho s immigrant; upstart; foreigner

advenimiento, ahd-vay-ne-me-**en**-to s advent

adverbio, ahd-**vair**-be-o s adverb

adversario, ahd-vair-**sah**-re-o s opponent

adversidad, ahd-vair-se-**dahd** s adversity

advertencia, ahd-vair-**ten**-the-ah s warning; notice; advertence

advertido*, ahd-vair-**tee**-do a warned; clever

advertimiento, (see **advertencia**)

advertir, ahd-vair-**teer** v to warn; to observe

adyacente, ahdfyah-**then**-tay a adjacent; contiguous

aerobic, ah-ay-ro-**bek** s aerobics

aerodromo, ah-ay-ro-**dro**-mo s airport

aeronave, ah-ay-ro-**nah**-vay s airship

aeroplano, ah-ay-ro-**plah**-no s airplane

aeropuerto, ah-ay-ro-poo-**'air**-to s airport

aerosol, ah-ay-ro-**sol** s aerosol

afabilidad, ah-fah-be-le-

dahd s affability
afable*, ah-**fah**-blay a affable
afamado, ah-fah-**mah**-do a celebrated; famous
afán, ah-**fahn** s anxiety; solicitude; desire
afanar, ah-fah-**nar** v to toil; to be oversolicitous; to press
afear, ah-fay-**ar** v to deface; to disfigure; to decry
efección, ah-fek-the-**on** s affection
afectado, ah-fek-**tah**-do a affected
afectuoso, ah-fek-too-**o**-so a affectionate; kind; loving
afeitar, ah-fay-**e**-tar v to shave; to trim
afeminado, ah-fay-me-**nah**-do a effeminate
aferrar, ah-fair-**rar** v to grasp; to grapple
afianzar, ah-fe-ahn-**thar** v to guarantee; to make secure; to set bail
afición, ah-fe-the-**on** s liking; inclination; interest
aficionado, ah-fe-the-o-**nah**-do s amateur
afijo, ah-**fee**-Ho s affix
afilado, ah-fe-**lah**-do a

sharpened; sharp; keen
afilar, ah-fe-**lar** v to sharpen; to whet
afín, ah-**feen** s relation by affinity; close by
afinar, ah-fe-**nar** v to complete; to polish; to tune
afincarse, ah-fin-**kar** v to acquire real estate
afinidad, ah-fe-ne-**dahd** s affinity; analogy
afirmar, ah-feer-**mar** v to affirm; to secure
afflicción, ah-fleek-the-**on** s grief; sorrow; anguish
afligir, ah-fle-**Heer** v to afflict; to grieve
aflojamiento, ah-flo-Hah-me-en-to s relaxation; slackening
aflojar, ah-flo-**Har** v to loosen; to relax; to debilitate
afluente, ah-floo-en-tay a affluent; copious
afluir, ah-floo-eer v to flow into; to congregate
afortunado, ah-for-too-**nah**-do a fortunate; lucky
afrenta, ah-**fren**-tah s affront; insult
afrentar, ah-fren-**tar** v to affront; to insult
afuera, ah-foo-**ay**-rah adv

abroad; away; outside
afueras, ah-foo-**ay**-rahs s environs; outskirts; outer suburbs
agacharse, ah-gah-**char**-say v to crouch; to stoop
agallas, ah-gah-l´yahs s glands; gills; galls; guts
agarrada, ah-gar-rrah-dah s row; argument
agarrar, ah-gar-**rrar** v to grasp; to seize
agarro, ah-**gar**-rro s grasp
agasajar, ah-gah-sah-**Har** v to treat kindly; to regale; to entertain
agasajo, ah-gah-sah-**Ho** s kind treatment; gift
agazaparse, ah-gah-thah-**par**-say v to hide oneself
agencia, ah-**Hen**-the-ah s agency
agenciar, ah-Hen-the-**ar** v to solicit; to negotiate
agente, ah-**Hen**-tay s agent
agigantado, ah-He-gahn-**tah**-do a gigantic
agilidad, ah-**He**-le-dahd s agility; nimbleness
agio, ah-**He**-o, **agiotaje**, ah-**He**-o-tah-Hay s speculation
agitación, ah-He-tah-the-on s agitation
agitar, ah-**He**-tar v to

agitate; to stir

aglomerar, ah-glo-may-**rar** v to agglomerate

agobiar, ah-go-be-**ar** v to bow; to oppress

agobio, ah-go-be-o s burden; oppression

agolparse, ah-gol-**par**-say v to crowd; to rush

agonía, ah-go-**nee**-ah s agony

agorar, ah-go-**rar** v to prognosticate

agosto, ah-**goss**-toe s August

agotamiento, ah-go-tah-me-**en**-to s exhaustion

agotar, ah-go-**tar** v to exhaust

agraciado, ah-grah-the-**ah**-do a graceful; genteel; attractive

agradable, ah-grah-**dah**-blay a agreeable

agradar, ah-grah-**dar** v to be pleasing; to please

agradecer, ah-grah-day-**thair** v to thank for

agradecido, ah-grah-day-**thee**-do a thankful; grateful

agradecimiento, ah-grah-day-thee-me-**en**-to s gratefulness

agrado, ah-**grah**-do s affability; pleasure; liking

agrandar, ah-grahn-**dar** v to enlarge

agrario, ah-**grah**-re-o a agrarian; rustic

agravar, ah-grah-**var** v to aggravate; to become grave or worse

agraviar, ah-grah-ve-**ar** v to offend; to injure

agredir, ah-gray-**deer** v to attack; to assault

agregación, ah-gray-gah-the-**on** s aggregation

agregar, ah-gray-**gar** v to aggregate; to gather; to add; to heap

agresión, ah-gray-se-**on** s aggression

agreste, ah-**gress**-tay a rustic; rude

agriar, ah-gre-**ar** v to make sour; to irritate

agricultor, ah-gre-kool-**tor** s farmer

agrio, ah-**gre**-o a sour

agrupación, ah-groo-pah-the-**on** s cluster; group

agrupar, ah-groo-**par** v to cluster; to group

agua, ah-**goo**-ah s water

aguacate, ah-goo-ah-**ka**-tay s avocado

aguacero, ah-goo-ah-**thay**-ro s shower; downpour

aguado, ah-goo-**ah**-do a watered; abstemious

aguantar, ah-goo-**ahn**-tar v to suffer; to endure; to bear

aguante, ah-goo-**ahn**-tay s fortitude; firmness; patience

aguardar, ah-goo-**ar**-dar v to expect; to wait for

aguardiente, ah-goo-**ar**-de-en-tay s brandy

aguarrás, ah-goo-**ar**-rrahs s turpentine oil

aguazal, ah-goo-ah-**thahl** s marsh

agudeza, ah-doo-**day**-thah s acuteness; repartee; wit

agudo*, ah-**goo**-do a sharp; acute

agüero, ah-goo-**ay**-ro s augury; omen

aguerrir, ah-gair-**rreer** v to harden to war

águila, ah-**ghee**-lah s eagle

aguileño, ah-ghee-**lay**-n'yo a aquiline

aguinaldo, ah-ghee-**nahl**-do s Christmas bonus

aguja, ah-**goo**-Hah s needle

agujerear, ah-goo-Hay-ray-**ar** v to pierce; to bore

agujero, ah-goo-**Hay**-ro s hole

aguzar, ah-goo-thar v to sharpen; to whet

aherrojar, ah-air-rro-Har v to fetter; to chain

ahijado, ah-e-Hah-do s godchild

ahijar, ah-e-Har v to adopt

ahinco, ah-een-ko s exertion; eagerness

ahogar, ah-o-gar v to smother; to choke; to drown

ahogo, ah-o-go s oppression; anguish; suffocation

ahondar, ah-on-dar v to dig; to go deep

ahora, ah-o-rah adv now

ahorcar, ah-or-kar v to hang

ahorrar, ah-or-rrar v to save; to spare

ahorro, ah-or-rro s economy; saving

ahuchar, ah´oo-char v to hoard

ahuecar, ah´oo´ay-kar v to make hollow

ahumar, ah´oo-mar v to smoke; to cure (meat, etc)

ahuyentar, ah´oo´yen-tar v to put to flight; to frighten away

airado, ah´e-rah-do a irritated; angry

aire, ah´e-ray s air; gait; gracefulness

aislado*, ah´iss-lah-do a isolated

ajar, ah-Har v to ruffle; to wither; to spoil

ajedrez, ah-Hay-dreth s chess

ajeno, ah-Hay-no a another's; foreign

ajetrearse, ah-Hay-tray-ar-say v to tire; to fidget; to bustle about

ajo, ah-Ho s garlic

ajuar, ah-Hoo´ar s household furniture

ajuiciado, ah-Hoo´ee-the-ah-do a judicious

ajustado*, ah-Hoos-tah-do a exact; stingy

ajustamiento, ah-Hoos-tah-me-en-to s agreement; settling

ajusticiar, ah-Hoos-te-the-ar v to execute; to put to death

ala, ah-lah s wing; row; brim

alabanza, ah-lah-bahn-thah s praise

alabar, ah-lah-bar v to praise; s boast

alabastro, ah-lah-bahs-tro s alabaster

alacena, ah-lah-thay-nah s cupboard

alacrán, ah-lah-krahn s scorpion

alado, ah-lah-do a winged

alambicar, ah-lahm-be-kar v to distill; to scrutinize

alambique, ah-lahm-bee-kay s still

alambre, ah-lahm-bray s wire

alameda, ah-lah-may-dah s poplar; grove; public walk

álamo, ah-lah-mo s poplar

alarde, ah-lar-day s parade; ostentation

alardear, ah-lar-day-ar v to boast

alargamiento, ah-lar-gah-me-en-to s lengthening out

alargar, ah-lar-gar v to lengthen; to protract; to increase

alarido, ah-lah-ree-do s outcry; howl

alarma, ah-lar-mah s alarm

alba, ahl-bah s dawn; daybreak

albahaca, ahl-bah-ah-kah s basil

albañal, ahl-bahn-y´ahl s sewer

albañil, ahl-bahn-y´eel s

bricklayer; mason

albarda, ahl-**bar**-dah *s* saddle

albaricoque, ahl-bar-re-**co**-kay *s* apricot

albedrío, ahi-bay-**dree**-o *s* free will

alberca, ahl-**bair**-kah *s* reservoir; tank

albergar, ahl-bair-**gar** *v* to lodge; to harbor

albo, ahl-bo *a* very white

albor, ahl-**bor** *s* whiteness; daybreak

alborotado*, ahl-bo-ro-**tah**-do *a* turbulent; restless

alborotar, ahl-bo-ro-**tar** *v* to disturb; to agitate

alboroto, ahl-bo-**ro**-to *s* tumult; riot; fuss

alborozo, abl-bo-**ro**-tho *s* merriment; joy

albricias, ahl-**bree**-the-ahs *s* reward for good news

albufera, ahl-boo-**fay**-rah *s* pond; lagoon

albur, ahl-**boor** *s* risk; chance; hazard

alcachofa, ahl-kah-**cho**-fah *s* artichoke

alcalde, ahl-**kahl**-day *s* mayor; justice of the peace

alcance, ahl-**kahn**-thay *s* overtaking; balance;

arm's length; ability; reach

alcancía, ahl-kahn-**the**-ah *s* piggybank

alcanfor, ahl-kahn-**for** *s* camphor

alcantarilla, ahl-kahn-tah-**reel**-l´yah *s* small bridge; sewer; drain

alcanzar, ahl-kahn-**thar** *v* to catch up; to reach; to obtain; to comprehend; to suffice

alcaparra, ahl-kah-**par**-rrah *s* caper

alcaravea, ahl-kah-rah-**vay**-ah *s* caraway seed

alcarraza, ahl-kar-**rrah**-thath *s* watercooler

alcatraz, ahl-kah-**trath** *s* pelican

alcayata, ahl-kah-**yah**-tah *s* hook

alcázar, ahl-kah-**thar** *s* castle; fortress

alcoba, ahl-**ko**-bah *s* alcove

alcohol, ahl-ko-**ol** *s* alcohol; antimony

alcohólico, ahl-**ko**-ole-ko *a* alcoholic

alcornoque, ahl-kor-**no**-kay *s* cork tree

aldaba, ahl-**dah**-bah *s* door knocker

aldabada, ahl-dah-**bah**-

dah *s* knock at the door

aldabón, ahl-dah-**bon** *s* small knocker

aldea, ahl-**day**-ah *s* small village; hamlet

aldea global, ahl-day-ah glo-**bahl** *s* global village

aldeano, ahl-day-**ah**-no *s* villager

aldeorrio, ahl-day-or-**rre**-o *s* remote village

aleación, ah-lay-ah-the-**on** *s* alloy

alear, ah-lay-**ar** *v* to alloy; to flutter

alegación, ah-lay-gah-the-**on** *s* allegation

alegar, ah-lay-**gar** *v* to allege; to plead

alegoría, ah-lay-go-**ree**-ah *s* allegory

alegrar, ah-lay-**grar** *v* to cheer; to rejoice

alegre*, ah-**lay**-gray *a* merry; joyful; cheerful

alegría, ah-lay-**gree**-ah *s* merriment; mirth; joy

alejamiento, ah-lay-**Hah**-me-en-to *s* removal; strangeness; distance; remoteness

alejar, ah-lay-**Har** *v* to remove to a distance

alelarse, ah-lay-**lar**-say *v* to become stupid

alelí, ah-lay-**lee** *s*

wallflower

alentado, ah-len-**tah**-do *a* courageous

alentar, ah-len-**tar** *v* to breathe; to encourage; to cheer

alergia, ah-**layr**-He-ah *s* allergy

alérgico, ah-**layr**-He-ko *a* allergic (to)

alero, ah-**lay**-ro *s* eaves

alertar, ah-lair-**tahr** *v* to alert

aleta, ah-**lay**-tah *s* small wing; fish fin

aleve, ah-**lay**-vay *a* treacherous

alfabeto, ahl-fah-**bay**-to *s* alphabet

alfalfa, ahl-**fahl**-fah *s* alfalfa

alfarería, ah-fah-ray-**ree**-ah *s* pottery

alféizar, ahl-**fay**´e-thar *s* windowsill

alférez, ahl-**fay**-reth *s* ensign

alfiler, ahl-fe-**lair** *s* pin

alfombra, ahl-**fom**-brah *s* carpet

alforja, ahl-**for**-Hah *s* knapsack; saddlebag

algarabía, ahl-gah-rah-**bee**-ah *s* Arabic language; gibberish; din

algazara, ahl-gah-**thah**-rah

s clamor

álgebra, ahl-**Hay**-brah *s* algebra

algo, ahl-go *adv & pron* somewhat; something; ought

algodón, ahl-go-**don** *s* cotton

alguacil, ahl-goo´ah-**thill** *s* sheriff

alguien, ahlg-e-en *pron* someone; anyone

algún, ahl-**goon** *pron* see **alguno**

alguno, ahl-**goo**-no *a* some; any; somebody

alhaja, ahl-ah-Hah *s* jewel

alharaca, ahl-ah-**rah**-kah *s* clamor; fuss

alhóndiga, ahl-**on**-de-gah *s* public granary; wheat exchange

alhucema, ahl-oo-**thay**-mah *s* lavender

aliado, ah-le-**ah**-do *a* allied

alianza, ah-le-**ahn**-thah *s* alliance

alias, ah-le-ahs *adv* otherwise; alias

alicates, ah-le-**kah**-tess *s* pliers; pincers; nippers

aliciente, ah-le-the-**en**-tay *s* attraction; inducement

alienar, ah-le-ay-**nar**, (see **enajenar**)

aliento, ah-le-**en**-to *s* breath; strength; courage

aligerar, ah-le-**Hay**-rar *v* to lighten; to alleviate

alijar, ah-le-**Har** *v* to lighten; s wasteland

alijo, ah-lee-Ho *s* lightening of a ship

alimento, ah-le-**men**-to *s* nourishment; food

alinear, ah-le-nay-**ar** *v* to level; to line up

aliñar, ah-lee-n´**yar** *v* to adorn; to dress; to season

aliño, ah-lee-n´yo *s* ornament; dress; seasoning

alisar, ah-le-**sar** *v* to plane; to polish; to smooth

aliso, ah-lee-so *s* alder tree

alistar, ah-liss-**tar** *v* to enlist; to enroll

aliviar, ah-le-ve-**ar** *v* to ease; to soothe

alivio, ah-lee-ve-o *s* alleviation; relief

aljaba, ahl-**Hah**-bah *s* quiver

aljibe, ahl-**Hee**-bay *s* cistern

aljofaina, ahl-Ho-fah´e-nah *s* basin

alma, ahl-mah *s* soul;

mind; human being; substance

almacén, ahl-mah-**then** s warehouse; storehouse

almacenaje, ahl-mah-thay-**nah**-Hay s warehouse charge; storage charge

almacenar, ahl-mah-thay-**nar** v to warehouse; to store

almacenista, ahl-mah-thay-**niss**-tah s warehouse owner

almáciga, ahi-**mah**-the-gah s seedbed; nursery (trees)

almadreñas, ahl-mah-**dray**-n´yahs s wooden shoes

almagre, ahl-**mah**-gray s ocher

almanaque, ahl-mah-**nah**-kay s almanac

almeja, ahl-**may**-Hah s mussel

almenara, ahl-may-**nah**-rah s beacon; channel

almendra, ahl-**men**-drah s almond

almendro, ahl-**men**-dro s almond tree

almendrado, ahl-men-**drah**-do s macaroon; almond-shaped

almete, ahl-**may**-tay s helmet

almiar, ahl-me-**ar** s haystack

almíbar, ahl-**mee**-bar s syrup

almidón, ahl-me-**don** s starch

almirante, ahl-me-**rahn**-tay s admiral

almirez, ahl-me-**rayth** s brass mortar

almizcle, ahl-**mith**-clay s musk

almohada, ahl-mo-ah-dah s pillow; bolster; cushion

almohadilla, ahl-mo-ah-dee-l´yah s small pillow; pincushion

almohadón, ahl-mo-ah-don s large cushion

almoneda, ahl-mo-nay-dah s public auction

almorranas, ahl-mor-**rrah**-nahs s hemorroids

almorzar, ahl-mor-**thar** v to have lunch

almuerzo, ahl-moo´air-tho s lunch

alocado*, ahl-lo-**kah**-do a foolish; wild

alocución, ah-lo-koo-the-**on** s allocution

alojamiento, ah-lo-Hah-me-**en**-to s lodging

alojar, ah-lo-**Har** v to lodge

alón, ahl-**lon** s wing

alondra, ah-**lon**-drah s lark

alongamiento, ah-lon-gah-me-**en**-to s delay; lengthening

alpaca, ahl-**pah**-kah s alpaca

alpargata, ahl-par-gah-tah s rope-soled sandal

alquería, ahl-kay-**ree**-ah s farmhouse

alquilamiento, ahl-ke-lah-me-**en**-to s renting; leasing

alquilar, ahl-ke-**lar** v to rent; to lease; to hire

alquiler, ahl-ke-**lair** s hire; fare

alquitrán, ahl-ke-**trahn** s tar

alrededor, ahl-ray-**day**-dor adv around; about; s pl environs

alta tegnología, ahl-tah tek-no-lo-**Hee**´ah s high-tech

altanero, ahl-tah-**nay**-ro a haughty

altar, ahl-**tar** s altar

alterable, ahl-tay-**rah**-blay a changeable

alterar, ahl-tay-**rar** v to alter; to change; to stir up

altercado, ahl-tair-**kah**-do

s quarrel; contest

alternar, ahl-tair-nar v to alternate

alteza, ahl-tay-thah s height; highness

altilocuente, ahl-te-koo´en-tay a bombastic

altivez, ahl-te-veth s haughtiness; arrogance

altivo*, ahl-tee-vo a haughty; proud

alto, ahl-to a* tall, lofty; high; arduous; exalted

alto el fuego, ahl-to ell foo´ay-go s ceasefire

altura, ahl-too-rah s height; altitude; summit

alubia, ah-loo-be-ah s kidney bean

alucinación, ah-loo-the-nah-the-on s hallucination

alud, ah-lood s avalanche

aludir, ah-loo-deer v to allude

alumbrar, ah-loom-brar v to light; to enlighten; to illuminate

alumbre, ah-loom-bray s alum

aluminio, ah-loo-mee-ne-o s aluminum

alumno, ah-loom-no s pupil; student

alusión, ah-loo-se-on s allusion

alza, ahl-thah s increase in price; rise

alzada, ahl-thah-dah s height; stature

alzamiento, ahl-thah-me-en-to s raising up; uprising; revolt

alzar, ahl-thar v to raise; to erect

allá, ah-l´yah adv there; back in

allanar, ah-l´yah-nar v to level; to remove difficulties; to pacify; to flatten

allegado, ah-l´yay-gah-do a near; related

allegar, ah-l´yay-gar v to gather; to collect

allí, ah-l´yee adv there

ama, ah-mah s lady of the house

amable*, ah-mah-blay a kind

amaestrar, ah-mah-ess-trar v to instruct; to break in

amagar, ah-mah-gar v to threaten; to hint

amainar, ah-mah-ee-nar v to subside; to relax; to lessen

amamantar, ah-mah-mahn-tar v to suckle; to nurse

amancebamiento, ah-mahn-thay-bah-me-en-to s cohabitation

amancebarse, ah-mahn-thay-bar-say v to live together

amancillar, ah-mahn-se-l´yar v to stain; to defame

amanecer, ah-mah-nay-thair v to dawn; to arrive at break of day

amanerado, ah-may-may-nay-rah-do a affected

amansamiento, ah-mahn-sah-me-en-to s taming

amansar, ah-mahn-sar v to tame; to domesticate

amante, ah-mahn-tay s lover; mistress

amaño, ah-mah-n´yo s skill; dexterity

amapola, ah-mah-po-lah s poppy

amar, ah-mar v to love

amargar, ah-mar-gar v to embitter

amargo*, ah-mar-go a bitter

amargura, ah-mar-goo-rah s pain; grief; bitterness

amarillez, ah-mah-re-l´yeth s yellowness

amarillo, ah-mah-ree-l´yo a yellow

amarra, ah-mar-rrah s

mooring line

amarradero, ah-mar-rrah-**day**-ro s hitching post

amarrar, ah-mar-**rrar**, v to tie; to fasten

amartelar, áh-mar-tay-**lar** v to court; to woo

amasar, ah-mah-**sar** v to knead

amatista, ah-mah-**tiss**-tah s amethyst

ambicionar, ahm-be-the-o-**nar** v to covet; to aspire

ambicioso, ahm-be-the-o-so a ambitious; covetous

ambigüedad, ahm-be-goo´ay-**dahd** s ambiguity

ambos, ahm-bos a both

amedrentar, ah-may-dren-**tar** v to intimidate

amenazar, ah-man-nah-**thar** v to threaten

amenidad, ah-may-ne-**dahd** s amenity

ameno, ah-**may**-no a pleasant; agreeable

amianto, ah-me-**ahn**-to s asbestos

amiga, ah-**mee**-gah s friend; mistress; governess

amigable*, ah-me-**gah**-blay a friendly

amigo, ah-**mee**-go s friend

amilanar, ah-me-lah-**nar** v

to frighten

amistad, ah-mis-**tahd** s friendship; amity

amistar, ah-miss-**tar** v to reconcile

amo, ah-mo s master; owner

amohinar, ah-mo-e-**nar** v to vex; to annoy

amojonar, ah-mo-Ho-**nar** v to mark with boundaries

amoldar, ah-mol-**dar** v to mold

amonedar, ah-mo-nay-**dar** v to coin

amonestar, ah-mo-ness-**tar** v to admonish; to warn

amontonar, ah-mon-to-**nar** v to heap up

amor, ah-**mor** s love

amoratado, ah-mo-rah-**tah**-do a livid; purple

amoroso*, ah-mo-ro-so a loving

amortajar, ah-mor-tah-**Har** v to shroud

amortecer, ah-mor-tay-**thair** v to deaden; to swoon

amortiguar, ah-mor-te-goo´**ar** v to temper; to lessen

amortizar, ah-mor-te-**thar** v to amortize

amparar, ahm-pah-**rar** v to protect; to shelter

amparo, ahm-**pah**-ro s protection; aid; shelter

ampliación, ahm-ple-ah-the-**on** s amplification; enlargement

ampliar, ahm-ple-**ar** v to amplify; to enlarge

amplificador, ahm-ple-fe-kah-**dor** s amplifier

amplio*, ahm-ple-o a ample; large

ampolla, ahm-po-l´yah s blister; cruet

amputar, ahm-poo-**tar** v to amputate

amueblar, ah-moo´ay-**blar** v to furnish

amujerado, ah-moo-Hay-**rah**-do a effeminate

amuleto, ah-moo-**lay**-to s charm; talisman; amulet

ánade, **ah**-nah-day s duck

análisis, ah-**nah**-le-siss s analysis

analogía, ah-nah-lo-**Hee**-ah s analogy

anaquel, ah-nah-**kel** s shelf

anaranjado, ah-nah-rahn-**Hah**-do a orange-colored

anarquía, ah-nar-**kee**-ah s anarchy

anca, ahn-kah s haunch

anciano, ahn-the-**ah**-no *a* aged; old (man or woman)

ancla, **ahn**-klah *s* anchor

ancho*, **ahn**-cho *a* broad; wide

anchoa, ahn-**cho**-ah *s* anchovy

anchura, ahn-**choo**-rah *s* breadth; width

andamio, ahn-**dah**-me-o *s* scaffold; platform

andar, ahn-**dar** *v* to go; to walk

andén, ahn-**den** *s* sidewalk; railroad platform

andrajo, ahn-**drah**-Ho *s* rag; despicable person

anegar, ah-nay-**gar** *v* to flood

anejo, ah-**nay**-Ho *a* annexed; attached

anémico, ah-**nay**-me-ko *a* anemic

anexo, ah-**nek**-so *a* annexed; joined

angarillas, ahn-gah-ree-**l´**yahs *s* wheelbarrow

ángel, **ahn**-Hayl *s* angel

angina, ahn-**Hee**-nah *s* angina

angostar, ahn-gos-**tar** *v* to narrow; to contract

angosto*, ahn-**gos**-to *a* narrow

anguila, ahn-**ghee**-lah *s* eel

ángulo, **ahn**-goo-lo *s* angle; nook

anhelar, ahn-ay-**lar,** *v* to long for

anhelo, ahn-**ay**-lo *s* eagerness; longing

anillo, ah-**nee**-´yo *s* ring

animado, ah-ne-**mah**-do *a* lively; enthusiastic

animal, ah-ne-**mahl** *s* animal

animar, ah-ne-**mar** *v* to animate; to incite; to cheer up

ánimo, **ah**-ne-mo *s* courage; will; mind

animoso*, ah-ne-**mo**-so *a* brave; spirited

aniñado, ah-ne-**n´yah**-do *a* childish

aniquilar, ah-ne-ke-**lar** *v* to annihilate

anís, ah-**nees** *s* aniseed

anoche, ah-**no**-chay *adv* last night

anochecer, ah-no-chay-**thair** *v* to grow dark. al–, ahl–, at nightfall

anomalía, ah-no-mah-lee-ah *s* anomaly

anonadar, ah-no-nah-**dar** *v* to stun; to overwhelm

anónimo, ah-**no**-ne-mo *a* anonymous

anotar, ah-no-**tar** *v* to write notes; to annotate

ansia, **ahn**-se-ah *s* anxiety; longing

ansioso*, ahn-se-o-so *a* anxious; eager

antaño, ahn-**tah**-n´yo *adv* last year; long ago

ante, **ahn**-tay *prep* before; *s* buckskin; suede

anteanoche, ahn-tay-ah-**no**-chay *adv* the night before last

anteayer, ahn-tay-ah-**yair** *adv* the day before yesterday

antebrazo, ahn-tay-**brah**-tho *s* forearm

antecámara, ahn-tay-**kah**-mah-rah *s* antechamber; hall

antecedente, ahn-tay-thay-**den**-tay *a* antecedent; preceding

antecesores, ahn-tay-thay-**sso**-ress *s* predecessors

antedatar, ahn-tay-dah-**tar** *v* to back date

antelación, ahn-tay-lah-the-**on** *s* precedence (time)

antemano, ahn-tay-**mah**-no *adv* beforehand

anteojos, ahn-tay-o-Hos *s* spectacles

antepasados, ahn-tay-pah-**sah**-dos s forefathers; ancestors

anteponer, ahn-tay-po-**nair** v to prefer; to place

anterior, ahn-tay-re-or a anterior; previous; former

antes, ahn-tess adv before; rather; prep before; prior to

antibiótico, ahn-te-be′o-te-ko s antibiotic

anticipar, ahn-te-the-**par** v to anticipate

anticipo, ahn-te-thee-po s advance payment

anticonceptivo, ahn-te-kon-thep-**tee**-vo s & a contraceptive

anticongelante, ahn-te-kon-Hay-**lahn**-tay s antifreeze

antihistamínico, ahn-te-iss-tah-**me**-ne-ko s & a antihistamine

antorcha, ahn-**tor**-chah s torch

anual, ah-noo′**ahl** a yearly

anublar, ah-noo-**blar** v to cloud; to darken

anuencia, ah-noo-en-the-ah s compliance; consent

anular, ah-noo-**lar** v to annul; a annular

anunciar, ah-noon-the-**ar** v to announce

anuncios, ah-**noon**-the-os s advertising

anzuelo, ah-thoo′**ay**-lo s fishhook; allurement

añadir, ah-n′yah-**deer** v to add

añejar, ah-n′yay-**Har** v to make old

añejo, ah-n′**yay**-Ho a old; stale

añicos, ah-n′**yee**-kos s small pieces; smithereens

añil, ah-n′**yeel** s indigo

año, ah-n′yos s year

añoso, ah-n′yo-so a aged; old

añoranza, ah-n′yo-**rahn**-thah s homesickness; nostalgia

apacentar, ah-pah-then-**tar** v to tend grazing cattle

apacible, ah-pah-**thee**-blay a gentle; placid; calm

apadrinar, ah-pah-dre-**nar** v to support; to patronize; to act as godfather

apagar, ah-pah-**gar** v to quench; to extinguish; to switch off

apalabrar, ah-pah-lah-**brar** v to agree verbally

apalear, ah-pah-lah-**ar** v to beat; to cane

apañar, ah-pah-n′**yar** v to seize; to pilfer

aparador, ah-pah-rah-**dor** s sideboard

aparato, ah-pah-**rah**-to s apparatus; pomp

aparear, ah-pah-ray-**ar** v to match

aparecer, ah-pah-ray-**thair** v to appear; to turn up

aparejo, ah-pah-**ray**-Ho s harness; gear; equipment

aparente*, ah-pah-**ren**-tay a apparent

apariencia, ah-pah-re-en-the-ah s appearance

apartadero, ah-par-tah-**day**-ro s crossways; siding

apartar, ah-par-**tar** v to separate; to remove; to dislodge

apasionado, ah-pah-se-o-**nah**-do a passionate

apatía, ah-pah-**tee**-ah s apathy

apear, ah-pay-**ar,** v to alight; to measure land; to solve

apedrear, ah-pay-dray-**ar** v to stone

apegarse, ah-pay-**gar**-say v to attach oneself to

apelación, ah-pay-lah-the-on *s* appeal

apelar, ah-pay-lar *v* to appeal

apellido, ah-pay-l´yee-do *s* surname

apenas, ah-**pay**-nas *adv* scarcely

apercibir, ah-pair-the-beer *v* to provide; to warn

aperitivo, ah-pay-re-tee-vo *a* appetizing

apero, ah-**pay**-ro *s* implement; tools

apesadumbrar, ah-pay-sah-doom-**brar** *v* to vex; to afflict

apestar, ah-pess-tar *v* to infect; to nauseate; to stink

apetecer, ah-pah-tay-**thair** *v* to crave

apetecible, ah-pah-tay-thee-blay *a* desirable

apetito, ah-pah-tee-to *s* appetite

apiadarse, ah-pe-ah-dar-say *v* to pity

ápice, ah-pe-thay *s* apex

apilar, ah-pe-lar *v* to heap up

apio, ah-pe-o *s* celery

aplacar, ah-plah-kar *v* to appease; to pacify

aplanar, ah-plah-nar *v* to level

aplastar, ah-plahs-tar *v* to flatten; to crush; to smash

aplaudir, ah-plah´oo-**deer** *v* to applaud

aplauso, ah-**plah**´oo-so *s* applause

aplazar, ah-plah-thar *v* to defer; to adjourn; to postpone

aplicación, ah-ple-kah-the-on *s* application

aplicar, ah-ple-kar *v* to impute; to apply

aplomar, ah-plo-mar *v* to overload; to plumb

apocado, ah-po-kah-do *a* pusillanimous

apoderado, ah-po-day-**rah**-do *s* proxy; attorney

apoderar, ah-po-day-rar *v* to empower; to take possession

apodo, ah-**po**-do *s* nickname

apolillarse, ah-po-le-l´**yar**-say *v* to be moth-eaten

aportadero, ah-por-tah-**day**-ro *s* landing place

aposentar, ah-po-sen-tar *v* to lodge

aposento, ah-po-**sen**-to *s* room; apartment; inn

apostar, ah-poss-tar *v* to bet

apostilla, ah-poss-tee-l´yah *s* marginal note

·apóstrofe, ah-**poss**-tro-fay *s* apostrophe

apoyar, ah-po-yar *v* to support; to favor; to lean upon

apoyo, ah-po-yo *s* support; protection; prop;

apreciar, ah-pray-the-ar *v* to appreciate

aprehender, ah-pray-en-dair *v* to apprehend

apremiar, ah-pray-me-ar *v* to compel; to urge; to press

aprender, ah-pren-**dair** *v* to learn

aprendizaje, ah-pren-de-**than**-Hay *s* apprenticeship

aprensar, ah-pren-sar *v* to dress; to press

aprensión, ah-pren-se-on *s* apprehension

apresar, ah-pray-sar *v* to seize

aprestar, ah-press-sar *v* to make ready; to prepare

apresurarse, ah-pray-soo-rar-say *v* to make haste; to hurry; to hasten

apretar, ah-pray-tar *v* to compress; to tighten

aprieto, ah-pre-ay-to *s* difficulty; conflict

aprisa, ah-pre-**ay**-sah, ah-pre-**sah** *adv* in haste; fast

aprisionar, ah-pre-se-o-**nar** *v* to imprison

aprobar, ah-pro-**bar** *v* to approve; to pass

aprontar, ah-pron-**tar** *v* to prepare hastily

apropiar, ah-pro-pe-**ar** *v* to appropriate

aprovechable, ah-pro-vaych-**ah**-blay *a* profitable

aprovechar, ah-pro-vay-**char** *v* to profit by

aproximar, ah-prok-se-**mar** *v* to approach; to approximate

aptitud, ahp-te-**tood** *s* aptitude

apto*, ahp-to *a* apt; fit; convenient

apuesta, ah-poo´**ess**-tah *s* bet; wager

apuesto, ah-poo´**ess**-to *a* genteel; elegant; spruce

apuntamiento, ah-poon-tah-me-**en**-to *s* aiming; note

apuntar, ah-poon-**tar** *v* to aim; to mark; to note

apunte, ah-**poon**-tay *s* annotation; rough sketch

apurado, ah-poo-**rah**-do *a* needy; hard-up

apurar, ah-poo-**rar** *v* to

---

worry; to fret; to exhaust

apuro, ah-**poo**-ro *s* want; afflicition; difficulty

aquejar, ah-kay-**Har** *v* to afflict

aquel, aquella, aquello, ah-**kel,** ah-**kell**-yah, ah-**kell**-yo *pron* he; she; that; that one

aquí, ah-**kee** *adv* here

aquietar, ah-ke-ay-**tar** *v* to quiet; to appease

arado, ah-**rah**-do *s* plow

arancel, ah-rahn-**thel** *s* tariff duty

araña, ah-**rah**-n´yah *s* spider; chandelier

arañar, ah-rah-n´**yar** *v* to scratch

arar, ah-**rar** *v* to plow

arbitrar, ar-be-**trar** *v* to arbitrate

arbitrio, ar-bee-**tre**-o *s* free will; compromise

árbitro, ar-**be**-tro *s* arbitrator

árbol, ar-**bol** *s* tree

arbusto, ar-**booss**-to *s* shrub

arca, ar-kah *s* chest; safe

arcada, ar-**kah**-dah *s* arcade; nausea

arce, ar-**thay** *s* maple tree

arcilla, ar-**thee**-l´yah *s* clay

arco, ar-ko *s* arc; arch;

---

bow

archiduque, ar-che-**doo**-kay *s* archduke

archivar, ar-che-**var** *v* to file

archivo, ar-**chee**-vo *s* archives

arder, ar-**dair** *v* to burn; to glow

ardid, ar-**deed** *s* stratagem; artifice

ardiente, ar-de-en-tay *a* ardent; burning

ardilla, ar-**dee**-l´yah *s* squirrel

ardor, ar-**dor** *s* great heat; fervor; valor

arduo, ar-**doo´o** *a* arduous; difficult

área, ah-**ray**-ah *s* area

arena, ah-**ray**-nah *s* sand; grit; arena

arenga, ah-**ren**-gah *s* harangue

arenque, ah-**ren**-kay *s* herring

argénteo, ar-**Hen**-tay-o *a* silvery

argolla, ar-go-l´yah *s* large ring; pillory

argucia, ar-goo-**the**-ah *s* subtlety; sophistry; trick

argüir, ar-goo-**eer** *s* to argue

argumento, ar-goo-**men**-to *s* argument; plot

aria, ah-re-ah *s* aria

aridez, ah-re-**deth** *s* drought; barrenness

árido, ah-re-do *a* dry; arid

arisco, ah-**riss**-ko *a* fierce; untractable

aristocracia, ah-riss-to-**krah**-the-ah *s* aristocracy

aritmética, ah-ritt-**may**-te-kah *s* arithmetic

armada, ar-**mah**-dah *s* fleet; navy

armar, ar-**mar** *v* to arm; to mount; to adjust

armario, ar-**mah**-re-o *s* cupboard; wardrobe

armazón, ar-mah-**thon** *s* framework; skeleton

armería, ar-may-**ree**-ah *s* armory; arsenal

armónico, ar-mo-ne-ko *a* harmonic

armonio, ar-mo-ne-o *s* harmonium

arnés, ar-**ness** *s* harness

árnica, ar-ne-kah *s* arnica

aroma, ah-ro-mah *s* perfume; fragrance

arpa, ar-pah *s* harp

arpillera, ar-pe-l´**yay**-rah *s* burlap

arpón, ar-**pon** *s* harpoon

arqueología, ar-kay-o-lo-Hee-ah *s* archeology

arqueta, ar-**kay**-tah *s* small chest

arquitecto, ar-ke-**tek**-to *s* architect

arrabal, ar-rrah-**bahl** *s* suburb

arraigar, ar-rrah-e-gar *v* to root; to settle down

arraigo, ar-**rrah**-e-go *s* real estate

arrancar, ar-rrahn-**kar** *v* to eradicate; to pull out; to snatch away

arrapo, ar-**rrah**-po *s* tatter; rag; wretch

arrasar, ar-rrah-**sar** *v* to level; to raze; to demolish

arrastrar, ar-rrahs-**trar** *v* tó drag along

arrastre, ar-**rrahs**-tray *s* dragging; haulage

arre, ar-**rray** *interj* giddyap! get up!

arrebañar, ar-rray-bahn´**yar** *v* to gather; to scrape together

arrebatado, ar-rray-bah-**tah**-do *a* precipitate; hasty; sudden

arrebatar, ar-rray-bah-**tar** *v* to carry off; to snatch

arrebato, ar-rray-**bah**-to *s* sudden attack; fit

arreciar, ar-rray-the-**ar** *v* to increase in strength; to get more severe

arrecife, ar-rray-**thee**-fay *s* reef

arredrar, ar-rray-**drar** *v* to terrify

arreglado, ar-rray-**glah**-do *a* regular; moderate; neat

arreglar, ar-rray-**glar** *v* to arrange; to settle; to adjust

arreglo, ar-**rray**-glo *s* rule; order; arrangement

arremeter, ar-rray-may-tair *v* to assail; to attack

arrendar, ar-rren-**dar,** *v* to rent; to hire

arrendatario, ar-rren-dah-**tah**-re-o *s* renter; lessee

arrepentirse, ar-rray-pen-teer-say *v* to repent; to regret

arrestado, ar-ess-**tah**-do *a* intrepid; daring

arrestar, ar-rress-**tar** *v* to arrest; to imprison

arresto, ar-**rress**-to *s* boldness; arrest

arriba, ar-**rree**-bah *adv* above; on high; upstairs

arribar, ar-rre-**bar** *v* to arrive; to land

arriesgar, ar-rre-ess-**gar** *v* to risk

arrimar, ar-rre-**mar** *v* to bring near; to stow; to lean against

arrinconar, ar-rrin-ko-**nar** *v* to put away

arroba, ar-**rro**-bah *s* Spanish dry or liquid measure

arrodillarse, ar-rro-de-l´yar-say *v* to kneel down

arrogancia, ar-rro-**gahn**-the-ah *s* arrogance; haughtiness

arrojado*, ar-rro-**H**ah-do *a* rash; dashing

arrojar, ar-rro-**Har** *v* to dart; to fling

arrollar, ar-rro-l´yar *v* to roll up; to defeat

arropar, ar-rro-**par** *v* to cover; to wrap up with clothes; to tuck up in bed

arrostrar, ar-rros-trar *v* to fight face to face

arroyo, ar-**rro**-yo *s* rivulet; stream

arroz, ar-**rroth** *s* rice

arruga, ar-**rroo**-gah *s* wrinkle

arruinado, ar-rroo´e-**na**-do *a* broken

arruinar, ar-rroo´e-**nar** *v* to ruin; to demolish

arrullo, ar-rroo-l´yo *s* lullaby; cooing

arrumar, ar-rroo-**mar** *v* to stow cargo

arrumbar, ar-rroom-**bar** *v* to put away

arte, ar-**tay** *s* art

arteria, ar-tay-**ree**-ah *s* artery; artifice; cunning

artero, ar-**tay**-ro *a* artful; cunning

artesano, ar-tay-**sah**-no *s* artisan

ártico, ar-te-ko *a* arctic

artículo, ar-tee-koo-lo *s* article

artificio, ar-te-fe-the-o *s* art; craft; artifice

artillería, ar-te-l´yay-ree-ah *s* artillery

artimaña, ar-te-mah-n´yah *s* trap; snare

arzobispo, ar-tho-**biss**-po *s* archbishop

as, ahs *s* ace

asa, **ah**-sah *s* handle

asalto, ah-**sahl**-to *s* assault

asar, ah-**sar** *v* to roast

ascender, ahs-then-**dair** *v* to ascend; to be promoted

ascenso, ahs-**then**-so *s* promotion

ascensor, ahs-then-**sor** *s* lift; hoist

asco, **ahs**-ko *s* disgust; loathing

asear, ah-say-**ar** *v* to adorn; to clean

asechar, ah-say-**char** *v* to waylay

asegurar, ah-say-goo-**rar** *v* to secure; to insure; to assert; to verify

asemejar, ah-say-may-**Har** *v* to compare; to resemble

asenso, ah-**sen**-so *s* assent

asentada, ah-sen-**tah**-dah *s* sitting; **de una –**, day-oo-nah–, at once

asentar, ah-sen-**tar** *v* to seat; to secure; to affirm; to settle; to note; to assess

asentir, ah-sen-**teer** *v* to acquiesce

aseo, ah-**say**-o *s* cleanliness

asequible, ah-say-**kee**-blay *a* attainable; obtainable

aserción, ah-sair-the-**on** *s* assertion

aserrar, ah-sair-**rrar** *v* to saw

aserto, ah-**sair**-to, (see **aserción**)

asesinar, ah-say-se-**nar** *v* to assassinate

asestar, ah-**sess**-tar *v* to aim at; to strike

así, ah-**see** *adv* so; thus;. **–que–**, –kay, as soon as; so that

asidero, ah-se-**day**-ro *s* handle; pretext

asiduo, ah-se-doo´o *a* assiduous; *s* regular customer

asiento, ah-se-en-to *s* chair; seat; stability; contract; entry

asignar, ah-sig-nar *v* to assign

asilo, ah-see-lo *s* asylum; refuge

asimétrico, ah-se-may-tre-ko *a* lopsided

asimiento, ah-se-me-en-to *s* grasp; attachment

asimilar, ah-se-me-lar, *v* to assimilate

asimismo, ah-se-miss-mo *adv* just so; likewise

asistencia, ah-siss-ten-the-ah *s* attendance; presence; help; aid

asistenta, ah-siss-ten-tah *s* cleaning lady

asistir, ah-siss-teer *v* to be present; to help

asno, ahss-no *s* dunce

asociar, ah-so-the-ar *v* to associate

asolar, ah-so-lar *v* to devastate; to level

asomar, ah-so-mar *v* to show; to begin to appear

asombrar, ah-som-brar *v* to astonish; to amaze

asomo, ah-so-mo *s* indication; conjecture; hint

asordar, ah-sor-dar *v* to deafen

aspa, ahs-pah *s* sails of a windmill

aspaviento, ahs-pah-ve-en-to *s* exaggerated dread; wonder

aspecto, ash-pek-to *s* appearance; aspect

aspereza, ahs-pay-ray-thah *s* asperity; roughness

áspero*, ahs-pay-ro *a* rough; harsh

aspiradora, ahs-pe-rah-do-rah *s* vacuum cleaner

aspirar, ahs-pe-rar *v* to breathe in; to inhale

asqueroso*, ahs-kay-ro-so *a* filthy; loathsome

asta, ahs-tah *s* horn; staff; pole

astillar, ahs-te-l´yar *v* to chip; to splinter

astillero, ahs-te-l´yay-ro *s* shipyard

astro, ahs-tro *s* heavenly body; star

astrología, ahs-tro-lo-Hee-ah *s* astrology

astronauta, ahs-tro-nah´oo-tah *s* astronaut

astronomía, ahs-tro-no-mee-ah *s* astronomy

astucia, ahs-too-the-ah *s* crafty; cunning

astuto*, ahs-too-to *a* astute

asumir, ah-soo-meer *v* to assume

asunto, ah-soon-to *s* subject; business; affair

asustado, ah-sooss-tah-do *a* frightened

asustar, ah-sooss-tar *v* to frighten

atacar, ah-tah-kar *v* to fit tight; to attack

atadero, ah-tah-day-ro *s* cord; rope; place for tying

atado, ah-tah-do *s* bundle; parcel

atajar, ah-tah-Har *v* to go the shortest way; to intercept

atajo, ah-tah-Ho *s* shortcut

atañer, ah-tah-n'yair, *v* to concern; to have; to do with

atar, ah-tar, *v* to tie; to fasten; to knot

atareado, ah-tah-ray-ah-do *a* very busy

atasco, ah-tahs-ko *s* obstruction; traffic jam

ataúd, ah-tah-ood *s* coffin

atavío, ah-tah-vee-o *s* dress; finery

atemorizar, ah-tay-mo-re-

thar *v* to frighten; to daunt

atención, ah-ten-the-**on** *s* attention

atentar, ah-ten-**tar** *v* to attempt a crime

atento, ah-**ten**-to *a* attentive

atenuar, ah-tay-noo-**ar** *v* to attenuate

ateo, ah-**tay**-o *s* atheist

aterido, ah-tay-**ree**-do *a* stiff with cold

aterrador, ah-tair-rra-**dor** *a* frightening

aterrar, ah-tair-**rrar** *v* to terrify

aterrorizar, ah-tair-rro-re-**thar** *v* to terrorize

atestación, ah-tess-tah-the-**on** *s* attestation; affidavit

atestado, ah-tess-**tah**-do *a* attested; witnessed

atestados, ah-tess-**tah**-dos *s* testimonials

atiesar, ah-te-ay-**sar** *v* to stiffen

atisbar, ah-tiss-**bar** *v* to scrutinize; to pry

atizar, ah-te-**thar** *v* to poke the fire; to incite; to hit

atlas, aht-lahs *s* atlas

atlético, aht-**lay**-te-ko *a* athletic

atmósfera, aht-**mos**-fay-rah *s* atmosphere

atolondrado, ah-to-lon-**drah**-do *a* scatterbrained

atolondrar, ah-to-lon-**drar** *v* to confound; to amaze; to be thoughtless

atómico, ah-**to**-me-ko *a* atomic

atónito, ah-**to**-ne-to *a* astonished

atontar, ah-ton-**tar** *v* to stun; to stupefy

atormentar, ah-tor-men-**tar** *v* to torment

atornillar, ah-tor-ne-**l'yar** *v* to screw

atosigar, ah-to-se-**gar** *v* to poison; to harass; to put the pressure on

atraer, ah-trah-**air** *v* to attract

atragantarse, ah-trah-gahn-**tar**-say *v* to choke

atrancar, ah-trahn-**kar** *v* to bolt a door

atrapar, ah-trah-**par** *v* to catch

atrás, ah-**trahs** *adv* backwards; behind

atraso, ah-**trah**-so *s* backwardness; pl., arrears

atravesado, ah-trah-vay-**sah**-do *a* cross-eyed

atravesar, ah-trah-vay-**sar** *v* to place across; to cross over; to go over

atreverse, ah-tray-**vair**-say *v* to dare

atrevido, ah-tray-**vee**-do *a* bold; daring

atribuir, ah-tre-boo´**eer** *v* to attribute

atril, ah-**treel** *s* lectern; music stand

atrio, **ah**-tre-o *s* porch; portico

atropellar, ah-tro-pay-**l'yar** *v* to trample; to knock down

atroz, ah-**troth** *a* atrocious

atún, ah-**toon** *s* tuna fish

aturdido, ah-toor-**dee**-do *a* bewildered; giddy; rattled

aturdir, ah-toor-**deer** *v* to bewilder; to stun

aturrullar, ah-toor-rroo-**l'yar** *v* to confound; to bewilder; to be perplexed

atusar, ah-too-**sar** *v* to smooth the hair

audacia, ah´oo-**dah**-the-ah *s* audacity

audaz, ah´oo-**dath** *a* bold; audacious

auge, ah´oo-Hay *s* highest point; peak

augusto, ah´oo-**gooss**-to *a* august

aullar, ah-ool´**yar** *v* to howl; to yell

aullido, ah´oo-l´**yee**-do *s* howl

aumentar, ah´oo-men-**tar** *v* to increase

aún, ah´**oon** *adv* yet; still; nevertheless; even

aunque, ah´oon-**kay** *conj* though; although

auricular, ah´oo-re-koo-**lahr** *s* earpiece (telephone)

ausencia, ah´oo-**sen**-the-ah *s* absence

ausentarse, ah´oo-sen-**tar**-say *v* to absent oneself

ausente, ah´oo-**sen**-tay *a* absent

austeridad, ah´oo-tay-re-**dahd** *s* austerity

auto, ah´oo-to *s* judicial decree; writ; warrant

autobús, ah´oo-to-**booss** *s* bus

autógrafo, ah´oo-to-**grah**-fo *s* autograph

autor, ah´oo-**tor** *s* author

autorizar, ah´oo-to-re-**thar** *v* to authorize

autoservicio, ah´oo-to-sayr-**vee**-the-o *s* self-service

auxiliar, ah´ook-se-le-**ar** *v* to aid; *a* assistant

auxilio, ah´ook-**see**-le-o *s* assistance; help

avalorar, ah-vah-lo-**rar** *v* to value; to estimate

avanzar, ah-vahn-**thar** *v* to advance

avaricia, ah-vah-ree-**the**-ah *a* miserliness; greed; greediness

ave, ah-vay *s* bird

avejentar, ah-vay-Hen-**tar** *v* to become old

avellana, ah-vay-l´**yah**-nah *s* hazelnut

avena, ah-**vay**-nah *s* oats

avenencia, ah-vay-**nen**-the-ah *s* agreement

avenida, ah-vay-**nee**-dah *s* avenue; flood

aventajar, ah-ven-tah-**Har** *v* to surpass; to excel

aventurar, ah-ven-too-**rar** *v* to venture

avergonzado, ah-vair-gon-**thah**-do *a* ashamed

avergonzar, ah-vair-gon-**thar** *v* to shame; to put to shame

avería, ah-vay-**ree**-ah *s* damage; breakdown

averiguar, ah-vay-re-goo´**ar** *v* to inquire; to investigate

aversión, ah-vair-se-**on** *s* aversion

aviación, ah-ve-ah-the-**on** *s* aviation

avidez, ah-ve-**deth** *s* avidity; greed

ávido*, ah-**ve**-do *a* covetous; greedy

avieso, ah-ve-**ay**-so *a* perverse; crooked

avío, ah-**vee**-o *s* preparation; provision

avión, ah-ve-**on** *s* airplane

avisado, ah-ve-**sah**-do *a* prudent; wise

aviso, ah-**vee**-so *s* notice; warning; advice

avispa, ah-**viss**-pah *s* wasp

avistar, ah-viss-**tar** *v* to behold from a distance

avivar, ah-ve-**var** *v* to enliven; to revive

¡ay! ah´e *interj* alas! ow! ouch! oh dear!

ayer, ah-**yair** *adv* yesterday

ayuda, ah-**yoo**-dah *s* help

ayudante, ah-yoo-dahn-tay *s* assistant

ayunar, ah-yoo-**nar** *v* to fast

ayuntamiento, ah-yoon-tah-me-**en**-to *s* municipal council; city hall

azabache, ah-thah-**bah**-chay *s* jet black

azada, ah-**thah**-dah *s* hoe

azafata, ah-thah-**fah**-tah *s* stewardess; flight attendant

azafrán, ah-thah-**frahn** *s*
saffron

azar, ah-**thar** *s* chance;
hazard; fate

azogue, ah-**tho**-gay *s*
mercury

azorar, ah-tho-**rar** *v* to
alarm; to embarrass

azotar, ah-tho-**tar** *v* to
whip; to lash; to spank

azúcar, ah-**thoo**-kar *s*
sugar

azucarado, ah-thoo-kah-
rah-do *a* sugared; sweet

azucena, ah-thoo-**say**-nah
s white lily

azufre, ah-**thoo**-fray *s*
sulfur

azul, ah-**thool** *a* blue

azulejo, ah-thoo-**lay**-*Ho s*
glazed tile

azuzar, ah-thoo-**thar** *v* to
set the dogs on; to
incite

baba, bah-bah s drivel; spittle

babear, bah-bay-ar v to slaver; to drivel; to drool

babia, bah-be-ah s estar en–, es-tar en–, to be absent-minded; to be daydreaming

babieca, bah-be-ay-kah s ignorant; stupid fellow

babor, bah-bor s port (side)

babosa, bah-bo-sah s slug

bacalao, bah-kah-l'yah-o, bah-kah- lah-o s codfish

bacía, bah-thee-ah s basin

bacín, bah-theen s chamber-pot

bache, bah-chay s hole in the road

bachiller, bah-chil-l'yair s bachelor (degree); a garrulous

badajo, bah-dah-Ho s bell-clapper; idle talker

bádminton, bahd-meen-ton s badminton

bagatela, bah-gah-tay-lah s trifle

bahía, bah-ee-ah s bay; harbor

bailar, bah´e-lar v to dance

bailarín, bah´e-lah-reen s dancer

baile, bah´e-lay s dance; ball

baja, bah-Hah s drop; fall; casualty; vacancy

bajada, bah-Hah-dah s descent; slope

bajamar, bah-Hah-mar s low tide

bajar, bah-Har v to descend; to fall; to lessen; to go down

bajel, bah-Hel s ship; boat; vessel

bajo, bah-Ho adv under; below; s sandbank; bass; a low; abject; humble

bajón, bah-Hon s bassoon; decline; fall; drop

bala, bah-lah s bullet; bale

balada, bah-lah-dah s ballad

baladí, bah-lah-dee a trivial; worthless

baladrón, bah-lah-dron s boaster; bully

balance, bah-lahn-thay s balancing; balance sheet

balancear, bah-lahn-thay-ar v to balance; to weigh; to waver

balanza, bah-lahn-thah s scale; balance

balar, bah-lar v to bleat

balaustrada, bah-lah´oos-trah-dah s bannister; balustrade

balaustre, bah-lah´oos-tray s baluster

balazo, bah-lah-tho s gunshot; bullet wound

balbucear, bahl-boo-thay-ar v to stutter; to babble

balcón, bahl-kon s balcony

baldaquino, bahl-dah-

40

kee-no s canopy; dais

baldar, bahl-**dar** v to cripple

balde, bahl-day s bucket; a de–, gratis; **en–,** in vain

baldío, -bahl-**dee**-o a untilled; s wasteland

baldón, bahl-**don** s reproach; insult.

baldosa, bahl-**do**-sah s floor tile

balido, bah-**lee**-do s bleating; bleat

baliza, bah-lee-than s buoy

balneario, bahl-nay-**ah**-re-o s resort; beach; spa

bal-o, bah-**lon** s large football; large ball

balota, bah-lo-tah s ballot

balsa, bahl-sah s pool; pond; lake; raft

bálsamo, bahl-sah-mos s balsam; balm

baluarte, bah-loo-**ar**-tay s bulwark

balumba, bah-**loom**-bah s bulk

ballena, bah-l´**yay**-nah s whale

ballesta, bah-l´**yess**-tah s crossbow

bamba, bahm-bah s chance; fluke

bambolear, bahm-bo-lay-ar v to stagger; to swing;

to sway

bambolla, bahm-bo-l´**yah** s ostentation

bambú, bahm-**boo** s bamboo

banasta, bah-**nahs**-tah s large basket

banca, bahn-kah s banking

bancarrota, bahn-kahr-rro-tah s bankruptcy

banco, bahn-ko s bench; bank

banda, bahn-dah s sash; band; gang; covey

bandada, bahn-**dah**-dah s covey

bandeja, bahn-**day**-Hah s tray; salver

banderilla, bahn-day-**ree**-l´yah s dart with a flag, used in bullfighting

bandido, bahn-**dee**-do s bandit

bando, bahn-do s edict; faction

banquero, bahn-**kay**-ro s banker

banquete, bahn-**kay**-tay s banquet

banquillo, bahn-**kee**-l´yo s small stool

bañador, bahn-n´yah-**dor** s bathing suit

bañar, bah-n´**yar** v to bathe

baño, bah-n´yo s bath

baquetear, bah-kay-tay-ar v to vex; to beat

barahúnda, bah-rah-**oon**-dah s noise; confusion

baraja, bah-**rah**-Hah s complete pack of cards

baratear, bah-rah-tay-ar v to undersell

baratijas, bah-rah-**tee**-Hahs s inexpensive goods

baratillero, bah-rah-te-l´**yay**-ros s peddler

barato, bah-**rah**-to a cheap

barba, bar-bah s chin; beard

barbacoa, bar-bah-ko-ah s barbecue

barbarie, bar-bah-re-ay s barbarity; rusticity

bárbaro*, bar-bah-ro a barbarous

barbería, bar-bay-**ree**-ah s barber's shop or trade

barbero, bar-**bay**-ros s barber

barbiespeso, barbee-ess-**pay**-so a thick-bearded

barbihecho, bar-be-ay-cho a fresh-shaved

barbilindo, bar-be-**leen**-do a well-shaved and trimmed

barbilucio, bar-be-**loo**-

the-o *a* smooth-faced

barbilla, bar-bee-l´yah *s* point of the chin

barbón, bar-bon *s* long-bearded man

barbotar, bar-bo-tar *v* to mumble

barca, bar-kah *s* boat; barge

barco, bar-ko *s* boat; ship

barlovento, bar-lo-ven-to *s* windward

barman, bar-mahn *s* barman

barniz, bar-neeth *s* varnish

barómetro, bah-ro-may-tro *s* barometer

barón, bah-ron *s* baron

barquero, bar-kay-ro *s* boatman; ferryman

barquillo, bar-kee-l´yo *s* wafer; small boat

barra, bar-rrah *s* bar; rod

barraca, bar-**rrah-**kah *s* hut

barranca, bar-rrahn-kah *s* ravine; difficulty

barredura, bar-rray-doo-rah *s* sweeping

barrena, bar-rray-nah *s* drill; gimlet

barrenar, bar-rray-nar *v* to pierce; to bore

barreño, bar-rray-n´yo *s* washbasin; tub

barrer, bar-rrair *v* to sweep

barriada, bar-rree-ah-dah *s* district; suburb

barrica, bar-rree-kah *s* cask; barrel

barriga, bar-rree-gah *s* abdomen; belly

barril, bar-rreel *s* barrel

barrio, bar-rre-o *s* ward; suburb; district

barrio chino, bar-rre-o che-no *s* Chinatown

barro, bar-rro *s* clay; mud; earthenware

barrote, bar-rro-tay *s* iron bar

barruntar, bar-rroon-tar *v* to foresee

barrunto, bar-rroon-to *s* conjecture

bártulos, bar-too-los *s* tools; belongings

basar, bah-sar *v* to establish upon a base

báscula, bahs-koo-lah *s* platform scale

base, bah-say *s* base; basis

básico, bah-se-ko *a* basic

basta, bahs-tah *s* basting (needlework); *interj* enough!

bastante, bahs-**tahn-**tay *adv* enough

bastardo, bahs-tar-do *a* spurious; illegitimate

bastidor, bahs-te-dor *s* frame; stretcher; chassis

bastilla, bahs-tee-l´yah *s* hem

bastón, bahs-**ton** *s* cane; staff; stick

basura, bah-soo-rah *s* sweepings; refuse; rubbish

basurero, bah-soo-ray-ro *s* garbage can

bata, bah-tah *s* robe; housecoat

batacazo, bah-tah-**kah-**tho *s* heavy fall

batahola, bah-tah-o-lah *s* hurly-burly

batalla, bah-tah-l´yah *s* battle

batea, bah-tay-ah *s* painted tray; punt

batería, bah-tay-ree-ah *s* battery

batida, bah-tee-dah *s* battue; hunting party

batiente, bah-te-en-tay *s* jamb (door); leaf (door)

batir, bah-teer *v* to beat; to clout; to demolish; to stir

batista, bah-tiss-tah *s* batiste; cambric

baúl, bah´ool *s* trunk; chest

bautismo, bah´oo-tiss-mo *s* baptism

baya, bah-yah s berry

bayeta, bah-yay-tah s baize; rough cloth

bayoneta, bah-yo-nay-tah s bayonet

bazo, bah-tho a yellowish brown

bazofia, bah-tho-fe-ah s filth; hogwash

beata, bay-ah-tah s devout woman; bigot

beatitud, bay-ah-te-tood s blessedness; holiness

beato, bay-ah-to s pious person; a blessed

beber, bay-bair v to drink

bebida, bay-bee-dah s drink; beverage

beca, bay-kah s college sash; scholarship; grant

becada, bay-kah-dah s woodcock

becerro, bay-thair-rro s yearling calf; calfskin

bedel, bay-del s janitor; head porter

béisbol, bay´ees-bol s baseball

beldad, bel-dahd s beauty; belle

bélico, belicoso, bay-le-ko-, bay-le-**ko**-so a warlike

bellaco, bay-l´yah-ko s rogue; wickedness; a artful; sly; cunning

bellaquería, bay-l´yah-kay-ree-ah s knavery

belleza, bay-l´yay-thah s beauty; handsomeness

bello*, bay-l´yo a beautiful; handsome

bellota, bay-l´yo-tah s acorn

bencina, ben-thee-nah s benzine

bendecir, ben-day-theer v to bless; to consecrate

bendición, ben-de-the-on s benediction; blessing

bendito, ben-dee-to a blessed; simple

beneficiar, bay-nay-fe-the-ar v to benefit; to improve; to cultivate

beneficio, bay-nay-fe-the-o s benefit; benefaction; profit

beneficios adicionales, bay-nay-fe-the-os ah-de-the´o-nah-lays s perk

beneficioso, bay-nay-fe-the-o-so a beneficial

benemérito, bay-nay-may-re-to a meritorious; deserving

beneplácito, bay-nay-plah-the-to s approbation

benévolo, bay-nay-vo-lo a benevolent

benigno*, bay-nig-no a

benign

beodo, bay-o-do a drunk

berbiquí, bair-be-kee s carpenter's brace

berenjena, bay-ren-Hay-nah s aubergine; eggplant

bergante, bair-gahn-tay s ruffian

bergantín, bair-gahn-teen s brig; brigantine

bermejo, bair-may-Ho a bright red

bermellón, bair-mel-l´yon s vermilion

berrear, bair-rray-ar v to bellow; to howl

berrinche, bair-rreen-chay s rage; tantrum

berro, bair-rro s watercress

berza, bair-thah s cabbage

besar, bay-sar v to kiss

beso, bay-so s kiss

bestia, bess-te-ah s beast; idiot; ill-bred fellow

besugo, bay-soo-go s sea bream

besuquear, bay-soo-kay-ar v to kiss repeatedly

betún, bay-toon s bitumen; shoe polish

biberón, be-bay-ron s baby bottle

biblia, bee-ble-ah s Bible

biblioteca, be-ble-o-tay-

kah s library

bicicleta, be-the-**klay**-tah s bicycle

bicho, bee-cho s bug; insect

biela, be-**ay**-lah s (mech.) connecting rod

bien, be-**en** adv well; happily; very; s good; property; possession

bienandanza, be-en-ahn-**dahn**-thah s prosperity

bienaventurado, be-en-ah-ven-too-**rah**-do a blessed; fortunate

bienes, be-en-**ess** s property; riches

bienestar, be-en-es-**tar** s well-being

bienhablado, be-en-ah-**blah**-do a well-spoken

bienhechor, be-en-ay-**chor** s benefactor

bienio, be-en-**e**-o s space of two years

bienmandado, be-en-mahn-**dah**-do a obedient

bienquerer, be-en-kay-**rair** v to wish another well; to esteem

bienvenida, be-en-vay-**nee**-dah s welcome

bifurcación, be-foor-kah-the-**on** s branch (railroad); junction

bigamia, be-**gah**-me-ah s bigamy

bigarro, be-**gar**-rro s periwinkle

bigote, be-**go**-tay s moustache

bikini, be-**kee**-ne s bikini

bilingüe, bi-**leen**-goo´ay a bilingual

bilis, bee-liss s bile

billar, be-l´**yar** s billiards; billiards table

billete, be-l´**yay**-tay s bank note; ticket

billón, be-l´**yon** s billion

bimestre, be-**mess**-tray a of two months' duration

binóculo, be-**no**-koo-lo s binocle

biografia, be-o-grah-**fee**-ah s biography

biología, be-o-lo-**Hee**-ah s biology

biombo, be-**om**-bo s screen

biplano, be-**plah**-no s biplane

birlar, beer-**lar** v to kill with one shot; to snatch away

birlocha, beer-**lo**-chah s kite

birreta, beer-**rray**-tah s cardinal's cap

bisabuela, be-sah-boo´ay-lah s great-grandmother

bisabuelo, be-sah-boo´**ay**-lo s great-grandfather

bisagra, be-**sah**-grah s hinge

bisecar, be-say-**kar** v to bisect

bisel, be-**sel** s bevel edge

bisojo, be-so-Ho a squint-eyed

bisonte, be-**son**-tay s buffalo; bison

bisoño, s be-so-n´yo a inexperienced recruit; novice

bitácora, be-**tah**-ko-rah s binnacle

bizarría, be-thar-**rree**-ah s gallantry; generosity

bizarro*, be-**thar**-rro a gallant; generous

bizco, beeth-ko a cross-eyed

bizcocho, bith-**ko**-cho s sponge cake

bizma, beeth-mah s poultice

blanca, blahn-kah s copper coin

blanco, blahn-ko a white; blank; target

blandear, blahn-day-**ar** v to soften; to yield

blandir, blahn-**deer** v to brandish

blando, blahn-do a soft; mild

blandujo, blahn-**doo**-Ho *a*
flabby; softish

blanquear, blahn-kay-**ar** *v*
to bleach; to whitewash

blasfemar, blahs-fay-**mar** *v*
to blaspheme; to swear

blasón, blah-**son** *s*
heraldry; blazon

blasonar, blah-so-**nar** *v* to
boast; to praise oneself

blonda, blon-dah *s* blond;
lace

bloque, blo-kay *s* block;
block of stone

blusa, bloo-sah *s* blouse

boato, bo-**ah**-to *s*
ostentation

bobalicón, bo-bah-le-**kon**
s fool; nitwit

bobería, bo-bay-**ree**-ah *s*
foolish speech or action

bobo, bo-bo *s* simpleton;
fool

boca, bo-kah *s* mouth

bocacalle, bo-kah-**kah**-
l´yay *s* intersection

bocadillo, bo-kah-dee-l´yo
s sandwhich

bocado, bo-**kah**-do *s*
morsel; mouthful

bocal, bo-kahl *s* pitcher;
mouthpiece

bocanada, bo-kah-**nah**-
dah *s* whiff; puff of
smoke

boceto, bo-**thay**-to *s*
sketch

bocina, bo-**thee**-nahr *s*
horn

bochorno, bo-**chor**-no *s*
hot, sultry weather;
shame

boda, bo-dah *s* marriage;
wedding

bodega, bo-**day**-gah *s*
grocer

bodeguero, bo-day-**gay**-ro
s tavern keeper

bodoque, bo-**do**-kay *s*
pellet; dunce

bodrio, bo-**dre**-o *s*
hodgepodge

bofetada, bo-fay-**tah**-dah *s*
slap

boga, bo-gah *s* rowing

bogar, bo-**gar** *v* to row

bogavante, bo-gah-**vahn**-
tay *s* big lobster

bohardilla, bo-ar-dee-
l´yah (see **buhardilla**)

boj, boH *s* box tree;
boxwood

bola, bo-lah *s* ball; knob;
fib

bolero, bo-**lay**-ro *s* dance

boleta, bo-**lay**-tah *s* ballot;
health certificate

boletín, bo-lay-**teen** *s*
bulletin; official gazette

boliche, bo-lee-**chay** *s*
jack; small ball for
bowling

bólido, bo-le-do *s*
meteorite

bolígrafo, bo-lee-**grah**-fo *s*
ballpoint pen

bolillo, bo-lee-l´yo *s* jack;
bobbin

bolsa, bol-sah *s* bag;
pocket; exchange

bolsillo, bol-see-l´yo *s*
pocket

bollería, bo-l´yay-**ree**-ah *s*
bakery

bollero, bo-l´**yay**-ro *s*
pastry cook

bollo, bo-l´yo *s* roll; bun

bomba, bom-bah *s* pump;
bomb

bombero, bom-**bay**-ro *s*
fireman

bombilla, bom-bee-l´yah *s*
bulb (*elec*), – **de flas,** –
day flash flashbulb

bombo, bom-bo *s* large
drum

bombón, bom-**bon** *s*
bonbon; chocolate

bonanza, bo-**nahn**-thah *s*
fair weather at sea;
prosperity

bondad, bon-**dahd** *s*
goodness; kindness

bonete, bo-**nay**-tay *s* cap

bonificar, bo-ne-fe-**kar** *v*
to improve; to credit

bonito, bo-**nee**-to *a*
graceful; pretty

bono, bo-no s bond

boñiga, bo-n´yee-gah s cowdung

boqueada, bo-kay-ah-dah s gasp; gasping

boquear, bo-kay-ar v to gape; to gasp

boquete, bo-kay-tay s gap; narrow entrance

boquiabierto, bo-ke-ah-be-air-to a gaping

boquiancho, bo-ke-ahn-cho a wide-mouthed

boquilla, bo-kee-l´yah s mouthpiece; cigarette-holder; nozzle

boquín, bo-keen s coarse sort of baize

boquirroto, bo-keer-rro-to a loquacious

bórax, bo-rax s borax

borbollón, bor-bo-l´yon s bubbling

borbotar, bor-bo-tar v to gush out; to boil up

borceguí, bor-thay-ghee s ankle boot; laced shoe

borda, bor-dah s hut; cottage; gunwale

bordar, bor-dar v to embroider

borde, bor-day s border; rim; hem; a wild; bastard

bordillo, bor-dee-l´yo s curb

bordo, bor-do a on board

bordón, bor-don s staff; bass; refrain (music)

borla, bor-lah s tassel

bornear, bor-nay-ar v to blend; to twist

borona, bo-ro-nah s millet

borrachera, bor-rrah-chay-rah s booze

borrachez, bor-rrah-cheth s intoxication

borracho, bor-rrah-cho a intoxicated; drunk

borrador, bor-rrah-dor s rough draft; blotter; eraser

borrajear, bor-rrah-Hay-ar v to scribble

borrar, bor-rrar v to cross out; to blot; to erase

borrasca, bor-rrahs-kah s storm; squall; danger

borrego, bor-rray-go s lamb

borrico, bor-rree-ko s fool

borrón, bor-rron s ink blot; first sketch; blemish

borronear, bor-rro-nay-ar v to sketch; to scribble

bosque, bos-kay s wood; forest

bosquejar, bos-kay-Har v to sketch; to plan

bosquejo, bos-kay-Ho s sketch of a painting

bosquete, bos-kay-tay s small woods

bostezar, bos-tay-thar v to yawn

bota, bo-tah s small leather wine bag; boot

botana, bo-tah-nah s plug; plaster; scar

botar, bo-tar v to launch; to bounce

botarate, bo-tah-rah-tay s thoughtless person

botarga, bo-tar-gah s motley dress; harlequin; large sausage

bote, bo-tay s thrust; rebound; pot; boat

botella, bo-tay-l´yah s bottle

botica, bo-tee-kah s pharmacy; drugstore

boticario, bo-te-kah-re-o s pharmacist; druggist

botija, bo-tee-Hah s jar

botillería, bo-te-l´yay-ree-ah s ice shop

botín, bo-teen s ankle boot; spoils

botina, bo-tee-nah s lady's boot

botiquin, bo-te-keen s medicine chest

boto, bo-to a obtuse (person)

botón, bo-ton s bud; button

bóveda, bo-vay-dah s

4 6

arch; vault

boya, bo-yah s buoy

boyante, bo-**yahn**-tay a buoyant; prosperous

boyera, bo-**yay**-rah s ox pen

bozal, bo-**thahl** s muzzle

bozo, bo-tho s down (on upper lip)

bracear, brah-thay-ar v to swing the arms

bracero, brah-**thay**-ro s abuser

braguero, brah-**gay**-ro truss; bandage

bragueta, brah-**gay**-tah s fly (of pants)

brama, brah-mah s mating season

bramante, brah-**mahn**-tay s hemp; string

bramar, brah-**mar** v to roar; to bluster; to rage

bramido, brah-**mee**-do s cry uttered by wild animals; roaring

branquia, brahn-ke-ah s fish gill

brasa, brah-sah s live coal; ember

bravata, brah-**vah**-tah s bravado

braveador, brah-vay-ah-dor s bully

bravear, brah-vay-ar v to bully

braveza, brah-**vay**-thah s bravery; fury of the elements

bravío, brah-**vee**-o a ferocious; wild

bravo*, brah-vo a brave; excellent; hectoring

bravura, brah-**voo**-rah s ferocity of wild animals; courage; boast

braza, brah-thah s fathom; brace

brazalete, brah-thah-**lay**-tay s bracelet

brazo, brah-tho s arm; branch

brazuelo, brah-thoo-**ay**-lo s small arm; shoulder of animals

brea, bray-ah s pitch; tar; tarpaulin

brebaje, bray-bah-**Hay** s beverage; potion; concoction

brécol, bray-kol s broccoli

brecha, bray-chah s breach; wound

brega, bray-gah s strife; fray; jest

breve*, bray-yay a brief

breviario, bray-ve-ah-re-o s breviary

brezal, bray-**thahl** s land covered with heather

brezo, bray-tho s heather

briba, bree-bah s truancy; idleness

bribón, bre-bon s vagrant; scoundrel; rascal

brida, bree-dah s bridle

brigada, bre-**gah**-dah s brigade

brillante*, bre-l´yahn-tay a brilliant; sparkling; s diamond

brillar, bre-l´yar v to shine

brincar, brin-kar v to leap; to jump

brindis, breen-diss s toast

brío, bree-o s strength; vigor; mettle

brioso*, bre-o-so a courageous; spirited

brisa, bree-sah s breeze

brizna, breeth, -nah s fragment; splinter; chip

broca, bro-kah s reel; drill; shoemaker's tack

brocado, bro-kah-do s brocade

brocha, bro-chah s paintbrush

broche, bro-chay s clasp; brooch

broma, bro-mah s gaiety; merriment; joke

bromear, bro-may-ar v to make fun; to jest

bromista, bro-miss-tah s practical joker

bromo, bro-mo s bromine

bronca, bron-kah s

practical joke; quarrel

bronce, bron-thay s bronze; brass

bronceado, bron-thay-ah-dor s suntan

bronceador, bron-thay-ah-dor s suntan lotion

bronco, bron-ko a rough; rude; hard; harsh

bronquedad, bron-kay-dahd s harshness; rudeness

bronquio, bron-ke-o s bronchial tube

bronquitis, bron-kee-tiss s bronchitis

broquel, bro-kel s shield

brotar, bro-tar v to bud; to gush

broza, bro-thah s brushwood

bruces, (a or de), ah, day **broo-**thess adv face downwards

bruja, broo-Hah s witch

brujería, broo-Hay-**ree-**ah s witchcraft

brújula, broo-Hoo-lah s compass

bruma, broo-mah s fog; haziness

bruñido, broo-n´yee-do a polished

bruñir, broo-n´yeer v to polish

brusco, brooss-ko a rude; rough; abrupt

brusquedad, brooss-kay-dahd s abruptness

brutal, broo-tahl a brutal

brutalidad, broo-tah-le-dahd s roughness; brutality

bruto, broo-to s brute; a coarse; rough

bruza, broo-thah s brush

bubón, boo-bon s malignant tumor

bucarán, boo-kah-rahn s buckram

bucear, boo-thay-ar v to dive

bucle, boo-klay s curl; ringlet

buche, boo-chay s crop; craw; maw; stomach; mouthful

buen, bueno*, boo´en, boo´ay-no a good

buenaventura, boo´ay-nah-ven-too-rah s good luck

buey, boo-ay´e s ox

búfalo, boo-fah-lo s buffalo

bufanda, boo-fahn-dah s muffler; scarf

bufar, boo-far v to puff with anger; to snort

bufete, boo-fay-tay s desk; writing table; lawyer's practice

bufido, boo-fee-do s snorting

bufo, boo-fo s buffoon; mimic; jester

bufonada, boo-fo-nah-dah s buffoonery

buhardilla, boo´ar-dee-l´yah s dormer; attic

buho, boo´o s owl

buhonería, boo´o-nay-ree-ah s peddler's wares

buhonero, boo´o-nay-ro s peddler; hawker

buitre, boo´ee-tray s vulture

bujería, boo-Hay-ree-ah s bauble; knickknack

bujía, boo-Hee-ah s spark plug; wax candle

bula, boo-lah s papal bull

bulbo, bool-bo s bulb

bulto, bool-to s bulk; bundle; package

bulla, boo-l´yah s noise; bustle; crowd

bullanga, boo-l´yahn-gah s tumult; riot

bullicio, boo-l´yee-the-o s bustle; noise

bullir, boo-l´yeer v to boil; to bustle; to fluster

buñuelo, boo-n´yoo-ay-lo s fritter

buque, boo-kay s vessel; ship

burbuja, boor-boo-Hah s

bubble

burdel, boor-**del** s brothel

burdo, boor-do a coarse; common

buril, boo-**reel** s engraving tool

burilar, boo-re-**lar** v to engrave

burla, boor-lah s scoff; mockery; jest; jeer

burlar, boor-**lar** v to ridicule; to mock; to hoax

burlería, boor-lay-**ree**-ah s fun; artifice; drollery; illusion

burlesco, boor-**less**-ko a burlesque

burlón, boor-**lon** s jester; scoffer

burrada, boor-**rrah**-dah s stupid action

burro, boor-rro s donkey

burujón, boo-roo-**H** on s bump

busca, booss-kah s search; research

buscar, booss-**kar** v to seek; to search

buscón, booss-**kon** s searcher; pilferer

busto, booss-to s bust

butaca, boo-**tah**-kah s large armchair

buzo, boo-tho s diver

buzon, boo-**thon,** s mailbox; conduit

C

cabal, kah-**bahl** *a* exact; perfect; full

cabalgada, kah-bahl-**gah**-dah *s* cavalry raid

caballar, kah-bah-l'**yar** *a* equine

caballeresco, kah-bah-l'**yay**-**ress**-ko *a* chivalrous

caballería, kah-bah-l'**yay**-**ree**-ah *s* mount; cavalry

caballeriza, kah-bah-l'**yay**-**ree**-thah *s* stable; stud

caballero, kah-bah-l'**yay**-ro *s* gentleman; knight; horseman

caballete, kah-bah-l'**yay**-tay *s* ridge; trestle; easel

caballo, kah-**bah**-l'yo *s* horse; knight (chess)

cabaña, kah-**bah**-n'yah *s* hut; cottage

cabecear, kah-bay-thay-**ar** *v* to nod; to shake the head in disapproval

cabeceo, kah-bay-**thay**-o *s* nod; shake of the head

cabecera, kah-bay-**thay**-rah *s* head of a table, bed, etc; upper end

cabellera, kah-bay-l'**yay**-rah *s* long hair

cabello, kah-**bay**-l'yo *s* hair

cabelludo, kah-bay-l'**yoo**-do *a* hairy

caber, kah-**bair** *v* to contain; to be contained; to fit

cabestrillo, kah-bess-**tree**-l'yo *s* sling

cabeza, kah-**bay**-thah *s* head; chief; top; beginning

cabezada, kah-bay-**thah**-dah *s* stroke with the head; nod; halter

cabezal, kah-bay-**thahl** *s* bolster

cabezo, kah-bay-tho *s* summit of a hill

cabezudo, kah-bay-**thoo**-do *a* obstinate; stubborn

cabezuela, kah-bay-thoo'**ay**-lah *s* dolt; bran; rosebud

cabida, kah-**bee**-dah *s* content; capacity

cabildo, kah-**beel**-do *s* town hall; town council

cabizbajo, kah-bith-**bah**-Ho *a* crestfallen; thoughtful

cable, kah-blay *s* cable

cabo, kah-bo *s* extremity; cape; chief; rope

cabotaje, kah-bo-**tah**-Hay *s* coastal trading

cabra, kah-brah *s* female goat

cabrerizo, kah-bray-**ree**-tho *s* goatherd

cabrestante, kah-bress-**tahn**-tay *s* capstan

cabria, kah-bre-ah *s* crane; derrick

cabriola, kah-bre-o-lah *s* caper; gambol; jump

cabrito, kah-**bree**-to *s* kid (goat)

caca, **kah**-kah s
excrement

cacahuete, kah-kah-oo´ay-tay s peanut

cacao, kah-**kah**-o s cocoa tree; cocoa

cacarear, kah-kah-ray-**ar** v to cackle; to brag

cacera, kay-**thay**-rah s canal; channel

cacería, kah-thay-**ree**-ah s hunting party

cacerola, kah-thay-ro-lah s casserole; saucepan

cacto, **kahk**-to s cactus

cacha, **kah**-chah s knife handle

cachar, kah-**char** v to break in pieces

cacharro, kah-**char**-rro s earthen pot; useless object

cachete, kah-**chay**-tay s cheek; slap in the face

cachetero, kah-chay-**tay**-ro s dagger

cachetudo, kah-chay-**too**-do a chubby

cachipolla, kah-che-**po**-l´yah s dayfly

cachiporra, kah-che-**por**-rrah s club; cudgel

cachivache, kah-che-**vah**-chay s junk; pots; utensils

cacho, **kah**-cho s small piece

cachorrillo, kah-chor-**rree**-l´yo s small pistol

cachorro, kah-**chor**-rro s puppy; cub

cachupín, kah-choo-**peen** s Spanish colonist in Mexico and Central America

cada, **kah**-dah a every; each

cadalso, kah-**dahl**-so s scaffold

cadáver, kah-**dah**-vair s corpse

cadejo, kah-**day**-Ho s entangled hair; skein

cadena, kah-**day**-nah s chain; series

cadencia, kah-**den**-the-ah s cadence

cadeneta, kah-day-**nay**-tah s lace; chain stich

cadenilla, kah-day-**nee**-l´yah s small chain

cadente, kah-**den**-tay a rhythmical

cadera, kah-**day**-rah s hip

cadete, kah-**day**-tay s cadet

caducar, kah-doo-kar v to expire; to become out of date

caduco*, kah-**doo**-ko a worn out; decrepit

caedizo, kah-ay-dee-tho a tottering

caer, kah-**air** v to fall; to fall due; to happen to; to decline; to die

café, kah-**fay** s coffee; coffee-house

cafetera, kah-fay-**tay**-rah s coffeepot

cafetería, kah-fay-tay-**ree**-ah s café

cafetero, kah-fay-**tay**-ro s coffeeshop owner

caída, kah-ee-dah s fall; downfall; declivity

caído, kah-ee-do a languid; downfallen

caimiento, kah´e-me-**en**-to s languidness; dejection

cairel, kah´e-**rel** s fringe; trimmings

caja, **kah**-Hah s box; chest; cash; desk; coffin

cajero, kah-**Hay**-ro s cashier

cajero automático, kah-Hay-ro ah´oo-to-**mah**-te-ko s ATM automatic teller machine

cajetilla, kah-Hay-tee-l´yah s package (of cigarettes)

cajón, kah-**Hon** s box; chest; drawer; till

cal, kahl s lime

cala, kah-lah s creek; cove

calabaza, kah-lah-**bah**-thah s pumpkin

calabazada, kah-lah-bah-**thah**-dah s knock with the head

calabobos, kah-lah-**bo**-bos s drizzle

calabozo, kah-lah-**bo**-tho s dungeon

calafatear, kah-lah-fah-tay-**ar** v to calk

calamar, kah-lah-**mar** s squid

calambre, kah-**lahm**-bray s cramp

calamidad, kah-lah-me-**dahd** s calamity

calamitoso, kah-lah-me-**to**-so s calamitous

cálamo, **kah**-lah-mo s pen; flute

calamorra, kah-lah-**mor**-rrah s *(fam)* head

calandria, kah-**lahn**-dre-ah s calender; mangle

calaña, kah-**lah**-n´yah s pattern; character

calar, kah-**lar** v to penetrate; to permeate; to discover; to pierce; to put; to sink

calavera, kah-lah-**vay**-rah s skull; madcap

calcañal, kahl-kah-n'**yahl** s heel

calcar, kahl-**kar** v to trace; to copy

calce, **kahl**-thay s tire of a wheel

calceta, kahl-**thay**-tah s stocking; fetters

calcetería, kahl-thay-tay-**ree**-ah s hosiery shop or maker

calcetín, kahl-thay-**teen** s sock

calcina, kahl-**thee**-nah s mortar

calcinar, kahl-the-**nar** v to calcine

calcio, **kahl**-the-o s calcium

calco, **kahl**-ko s tracing

calculador, kahl-koo-lah-**dor** a calculating

calculadora, kahl-koo-lah-**dor** ah s calculator

cálculo, **kahl**-koo-lo s calculation; calculus

calda, **kahl**-dah s warming; heating

caldear, kahl-day-**ar** v to heat; to weld iron

caldera, kahl-**day**-rah s boiler; caldron

calderilla, kahl-day-**ree**-l´yah s copper coin; small change

caldillo, kahl-**dee**-l´yo s sauce; gravy

caldo, **kahl**-do s broth; bouillon

calefacción, kah-lay-fahk-the-**on** s heating

calendario, kah-len-**dah**-re-o s calendar

calentador, kah-len-tah-**dor** s warming pan; heater

calentar, kah-len-**tar** v to heat

calentura, kah-len-**too**-rah s fever; temperature

calenturiento, kah-len-too-re-**en**-to a feverish

calesa, kah-**lay**-sah s gig; chaise

caleta, kah-**lay**-tah s cove; creek

caletre, kah-**lay**-tray s understanding; discernment; acumen

calibrar, kah-le-**brar** v to gauge; to calibrate

calibre, kah-**lee**-bray s caliber

calicó, kah-le-**ko** s calico

calidad, kah-le-**dahd** s quality; rank; condition

cálido, **kah**-le-do a hot

caliente, kah-le-**en**-tay a warm; feverish; en -, en -, immediately

calificar, kah-le-fe-**kar** v to qualify; to rate; to classify; to attest

calígine, kah-lee-**He**-nay s mist; obscurity; dimness

cáliz, kah-lith *s* chalice; calyx

calizo, kah-lee-tho *a* calcareous

calma, kahl-mah *s* calm

calmante, kahl-**mahn**-tay *a* soothing; sedative; anodyne

calmar, kahl-**mar** *v* to calm; to allay; to soothe

calmo, kahl-mo *a* treeless; barren

calmoso, kahl-mo-so *a* tranquil; slow

caló, kah-lo *s* slang

calor, kah-**lor** *s* heat; warmth; glow; excitement

caloría, kah-lo-ree-ah *s* calorie

calumnia, kah-**loom**-ne-ah *s* slander; calumny

calumniador, kah-loom-ne-ah-**dor** *s* slanderer

calumniar, kah-loom-ne-**ar** *v* to slander

caluroso, kah-loo-ro-so *a* warm; hot; vehement

calva, kahl-vah *s* bald head

calvicie, kahl-**vee**-the-ay *s* baldness

calvo, kahl-vo *a* bald

calza, kahl-thah *s* trousers; hose

calzada, kahl-**thah**-dah *s* causeway; drive

calzado, kahl-**thah**-do *s* footwear

calzador, kahl-thah-**dor** *s* shoehorn

calzar, kahl-**thar** *v* to put on shoes

calzoncillos, kahl-thon-**thee**-l'yoss *s* drawers

calzones, kahl-tho-ness *s* trousers

callado*, kah-l'**yah**-do *a* silent; discreet; reserved

callar, kah-l'**yar** *v* to keep silence; to hush up

calle, kah-l'yay *s* street; road

calleja, kah-l'yay-**Hah**, (see **callejuela**)

callejuela, kah-l'yay-**Hoo´ay**-lah *s* narrow passage

callo, kah-l'yo *s* corn (on the feet)

cama, kah-mah *s* bed; couch; bestead; litter

camafeo, kah-mah-**fay**-o *s* cameo

cámara, kah-mah-rah *s* hall; cabin; camere –de aire, –day ah´e-ray *s* inner tube (tire)

camarada, kah-mah-**rah**-dah *s* comrade

camarera, kah-mah-**ray**-rah *s* waitress

camarilla, kah-mah-**ree**-l'yah *s* small room; clique

camarón, kah-mah-**ron** *s* shrimp; prawn

camarote, kah-mah-ro-tay *s* berth

cambalachear, kahm-bah-lah-chay-**ar** *v* to barter to change

cambiar, kahm-be-**ar** *v* to barter; to exchange; to change

cambio, kahm-be-o *s* barter; rate of exchange

cambista, kahm-**biss**-tah *s* broker; money-changer

camelar, kah-may-**lar** *v* to flirt; to woo; to seduce

camello, kah-**may**-l'yo *s* camel

camilla, kah-mee-l'yah *s* small bed; dressing room; stretcher

caminante, kah-me-**nahn**-tay *s* traveler; walker

caminar, kah-me-**nar** *v* to travel; to walk; to move along

caminata, kah-me-**nah**-tah *s* long walk; excursion

camino, kah-**mee**-no *s* road; way; journey; calling

camión, kah-me-**on** *s*

truck

camisa, kah-**mee**-sah s
shirt; chemise

camisero, kah-me-**say**-ro s
shirtmaker; haberdasher

camiseta, kah-me-**say**-tah
s undershirt; vest

camisola, kah-me-**so**-lah s
ruffled shirt

camomila, kah-moh-**mee**-
lah s camomile

camorra, kah-**mor**-rrah s
quarrel; row

camorrista, kah-mor-
rriss-tah s quarrelsome
person

campamento, kahm-pah-
mayn-to s campsite

campana, kahm-**pah**-nah s
bell

campanada, kahm-pah-
nah-dah s stroke of a
bell

campanario, kahm-pah-
nah-re-o s belfry

campanear, kahm-pah-
nay-**ar** v to ring the bell
frequently

campaña, kahm-**pah**-
n´yah s campaign; open
country

campar, kahm-**par** v to
excel; to camp

campeón, kahm-pay-**on** s
champion

campesino, kah-pay-**see**-

no a rural; rustic s
peasant; countryman

campiña, kahm-**pee**-n´yah
s campaign; field

campo, kahm-po s
country; field; **–santo,**
–sahn-to, cemetery

camuflaje, kah-moo-**flah**-
Hay s camouflage

can, kahn s dog

canal, kah-**nahl** s channel;
canal; drinking-trough

canalón, kah-nah-**lon** s
large gutter; spout

canalla, kah-**nah**-l´yah s
mob; rabble; scoundrel

canapé, kah-nah-**pay** s
couch; settee

canario, kah-**nah**-re-o s
canary

canasta, kah-**nahs**-tah s
basket; hamper; crate

cancela, kah-**thay**-lah s
front-door grating

cancelar, kahn-thay-**lar** v
to cancel; to annul

cancelaría, kahn-thay-
lah-**ree**-ah s papal
chancery

cáncer, kahn-thair s
cancer

cancilla, kahn-**thee**-l´yah
s wrought iron gate

canciller, kahn-thee-l´**yair**
s chancellor

canción, kahn-the-**on** s

song; ballad

candado, kahn-**dah**-do s
padlock

candar, kahn-**dar** v to
lock; to shut

candela, kahn-**day**-lah s
candle

candelabro, kahn-day-**lah**-
bro s chandelier;
candelabrum

candente, kahn-**den**-tay a
red-hot

candidato, kahn-de-**dah**-
to s candidate

candidez, kahn-de-**deth** s
candor; simplicity

cándido, kahn-de-do a
candid; simple; white

candonga, kahn-**don**-gah s
artful flattery; playful
trick

candonguear, kahn-don-
gay-**ar** v to jeer; to play
practical jokes

candor, kahn-**dor** s
candor; ingenuousness

candoroso, kahn-do-ro-so
a candid; sincere

canela, kah-**nay**-lah s
cinnamon

canelón, kah-nay-**lon** s
icicle; drainpipe

cangrejo, kahn-**gray**-Ho s
crab; crawfish

canguro, kahn-**goo**-ro s
kangaroo; baby-sitter

canicie, kah-**nee**-the-ay s whiteness of the hair

canijo, kah-**nee**-Ho a weak; sickly; infirm

canilla, kah-**nee**-l'yah s shinbone

canino, kah-**nee**-no a canine

canje, kahn-Hay s exchange

cano, kah-no a hoary; gray-haired

canoa, kah-**no**-ah s canoe

canon, kah-non s canon; rule

canónigo, kah-**no**-ne-go s canon; prebendary

cansado*, kahn-**sah**-do a tired; tedious; worn-out

cantante, kahn-**tahn**-tay s singer; lead singer

cansar, kahn-**sar** v to weary; to tire; to bore; to molest

cantar, kahn-**tar** v to sing; s song

cántara, **kahn**-tah-rah s pitcher; liquid measure

cantarillo, kahn-tah-**ree**-l'yo s small pitcher

cantera, kahn-**tay**-rah s stone quarry; talent

cantidad, kahn-te-**dahd** s quantity; measure; portion; number; sum of money

cantilena, kahn-te-**lay**-nah s ballad; irksome repetition of a subject

cantimplora, kahn-tim-**plo**-rah s water bottle

cantina, kahn-**tee**-nah s cellar; canteen

cantinero, kahn-te-**nay**-ro s butler

canto, kahn-to s singing; edge; point; stone

cant s. kahn-**ton** s corner; region

cantor, kahn-**tot** s singer; minstrel

cantueso, kahn-too´**ay**-so s French lavender

canuto, kah-**noo**-to s small tube

caña, kah-n'yah s cane; reed; stalk

cañada, kah-n´**yah**-dah s glen; dale; glade

cañamazo, kah-n´yah-**man**-tho s coarse canvas

cáñamo, kah-n´**yah**-mo s hemp

cañería, kah-n´**yay-ree**-ah s pipe; water main

caño, kah-n´yo s tube; pipe; sewer; conduit

cañón, kah-n´**yon** s tube; down; quill; cannon; gallery; gorge

cañonazo, kah-n´yo-**nay**-tho s cannon shot

cañonero, kah-n´yo-**nay**-ro s gunboat

caoba, kah-o-bah s mahogany

caolín, kah-o-**leen** s china clay

caos, kah-oss s chaos

caótico, kah-o-te-ko, a chaotic

capa, kah-pah s cloak; mantle; layer; cover; pretense; hinder; wrapper; coat of paint

capacidad, kah-pah-the-**dahd** s capacity; extent

capacha, kah-**pah**-chah s frail; hamper

capar, kah-**par** v to geld

caparazón, kah-pah-rah-**thon** s caparison; carcass of a fowl; feed-bag

caparrosa, kah-par-**rro**-sah s copperas

capataz, kah-pah-**tahth** s overseer; superintendent; foreman

capaz, kah-**path** a capable; competent; spacious

capazo, kah-**pah**-tho s large frail; hamper

capcioso, kahp-the-o-so a captious

capear, kah-pay-**ar** v to challenge a bull with a cloak; to deceive

capellán, kah-pay-l´**yahn** s

chaplain

capilla, kah-pee-l´yah s
hood; cowl; chapel;
choir; chapter; proofs

capirote, kah-pe-ro-tay s
hood

capital, kah-pe-**tahl** s
capital (money, town); a
capital; essential

capitán, kah-pe-**tahn** s
captain

capitanía, kah-pe-tah-nee-
ah s captainship;
captaincy

capitel, kah-pe-**tel** s
capital of a column

capitulación, kah-pe-too-
lah-the-**on** s
capitulation; p pl.,
articles of a
marriage
contract

capitular, kah-pe-too-**lar** v
to conclude an
agreement; to capitulate

capítulo, kah-**pee**-too-lo s
chapter of a cathedral;
chapter of a book

capón, kah-**pon** s capon;
gelding

caponera, kah-po-**nay**-rah
s coop

capote, kah-po-tay s
cloak; topcoat

capricho, kah-**pree**-cho s
caprice; whim; mood

caprichoso*, kah-pre-**cho**-

so a capricious

cápsula, **kahp**-soo-lah s
capsule; percussion cap

captar, kahp-tar v to
captivate

capturar, kahp-too-**rar** v
to apprehend; to arrest

capucha, kah-poo-chah s
hood

capuchina, kah-poo-**chee**-
nah s nasturtium

capucho, kah-**poo**-cho s
cowl; hood

capullo, kah-poo-l´yo s
cocoon; bud of flowers

cara, kah-rah s face; mien;
front; surface

carabela, kah-rah-**bay**-lah
s caravel

carabina, kah-rah-**bee**-
nah s carbine; caravan

caracol, kah-rah-**kol** s
snail; prancing of a
horse

caracolear, kah-rah-ko-
lay-**ar** v to twist

carácter, kah-**rahk**-tair s
character; handwriting;
type

carado, kah-**rah**-do a
faced; **bien –,** be-**en** –,
pleasant-looking; **mal –,**
mahl –, ugly-looking

¡caramba! kah-**rahm**-bah
interj hah ! strange !

carambola, kah-rahm-bo-

lah s cannon (billiards);
trick to deceive

caramelo, kah-rah-**may**-lo
s caramel; candy

caramillo, kah-rah-**mee**-
l´yo s flageolet; flute

carantoña, kah-rahn-to-
n´yay-ro s cajoler;
flatterer

carátula, kah-**rah**-too-lah
s mask

caravana, kah-rah-**vah**-
nah s caravan

carbón, kar-bon s
charcoal; coal; cinder

carbonato, kar-bo-**nah**-to
s carbonate

carboncillo, kar-bon-
thee-l´yo s small coal;
black crayon

carbonera, kar-bo-**nay**-
rah s coal celler; coal-pit

carbonero, kar-bo-**nay**-ro
s charcoal maker; coal
merchant

carbono, kar-**bo**-no s
carbon

carbunco, carbunclo,
carbúnculo, kar-**boon**-
ko, kar-**boon**-klo, kar-
boon-koo-lo s carbuncle

carcajada, kar-kah-**Hah**-
dah s loud laughter

cárcel, **kar**-thel s prison;
jail

carcelería, kar-thay-lay-ree-ah s imprisonment

carcelero, kar-thay-lay-ro s jailer

carcoma, kar-ko-mah s wood louse; anxious concern; dry rot

carcomer, kar-ko-mair v to gnaw; to consume by degrees

carda, kar-dah s carding; card

cardar, kar-dar v to card wool

cardenal, kar-day-nahl s cardinal

cardencha, kar-den-chah s teasel

cardenillo, kar-day-nee-l´yo s verdigris

cárdeno, kar-day-no a livid

cárdigan, kahr-de-gahn s cardigan

cardinal, kar-de-nahl a principal; fundamental

cardo, kar-do s thistle

carear, kah-ray-ar v to confront (criminals)

carecer, kah-ray-thair v to need; to lack

carena, kah-ray-nah s careening

carencia, kah-ren-the-ah s want; need; lack

careo, kah-ray-o s confrontation

carestía, kah-ress-tee-ah s scarcity; famine

careta, kah-ray-tah s mask

carga, kar-gah s load; freight; burden; weight; cargo; charge; tax

cargadero, kar-gah-day-ro s place where goods are loaded

cargador, kar-gah-dor s charger; freighter

cargamento, kar-gah-men-to s cargo

cargar, kar-gar v to load; to freight; to charge; to book

cargazón, kar-gah-thon s cargo

cargo, kar-go s burden; loading; office; charge; obligation

cariancho, kah-re-ahn-cho a broad-faced

caricia, kah-ree-the-ah s caress

caridad, kah-re-dahd s charity

caridoliente, kah-re-do-le-en-tay a sad-looking

caries, kah-re-ess s caries; cavities

carigordo, kah-re-gor-do a plump-faced

carilargo, kah-re-lar-go a long-faced

carilucio, kah-re-loo-

thee-o a bright-faced

carinegro, kah-re-nay-gro a of a swarthy complexion

cariño, kah-ree-n´yo s love; tenderness; affection

cariñoso, kah-re-n´yo-so a affectionate; loving

carirredondo, kah-re-rray-don-do a round-faced

caritativo, kah-re-tah-tee-vo a charitable

cariz, kah-reeth s aspect; prospect

carmen, kar-men s country house and garden

carmesí, kar-may-see a crimson

carmín, kar-meen s carmine

carnada, kar-nah-dah s bait

carnaval, kar-nah-vahl s carnival

carne, kar-nay s flesh; meat; pap; kin

carnero, kar-nay-ro s sheep; mutton

carnet de conducir, kar-nayt day kon-doo-theer s driver's license

carnicería, kar-ne-thay-ree-ah s shambles; slaughter; butcher's shop

carnicero, kar-ne-**thay**-ro s butcher; a carnivorous

carnoso, kar-**no**-so a fleshy

caro, kah-ro adv dearly; a dear; costly

carpa, kar-pah s carp (fish); tent

carpeta, kar-**pay**-tah s table cover; portfolio; docket

carpintero, kar-pin-**tay**-ro s carpenter

carpo, kar-po s carpus (wrist)

carraco, kar-**rrah**-ko a old; withered; decrepit

carral, kar-**rrahl** s barrel

carralero, kar-rrah-**lay**-ro s cooper

carraspera, kar-rrahs-**pay**-rah s hoarseness

carrera, kar-**rray**-rah s race; course; highway

carreta, kar-**rray**-tah s long narrow cart

carretada, kar-rray-**tah**-dah s cartload

carretaje, kar-rray-**tah**-Hay s cartage

carrete, kar-**rray**-tay s reel; film

carretear, kar-rray-tay-ar v to cart

carretera, kar-rray-**tay**-rah s highway

carretero, kar-rray-**tay**-ro s cartwright; cart maker; carter

carretilla, kar-rray-tee-l´yah s wheelbarrow

carril, kar-**rreel** s rut; rail (railroad)

carrillo, kar-**rree**-l´yo s cheek

carro, kar-rro s cart

carrocero, kar-rro-**thay**-ro s carriage-builder

carroña, kar-**rro**-n´yah s carrion

carroza, kar-**rro**-thah s large carriage

carruaje, kar-rroo´**ah**-Hay s vehicle of any kind

carta, kar-tah s letter; map; ordinance; card (playing)

cartabón, kar-tah-**bon** s square; rule

cartapacio, kar-tah-**pah**-the-o s satchel; portfolio

cartearse, kar-tay-ar-say v to correspond by letter

cartel, kar-**tel** s placard; poster; cartel

cartera, kar-**tay**-rah s portfolio; briefcase; wallet; pocketbook

cartero, kar-**tay**-ro s postman

cartilla, kar-tee-l´yah s primer; certificate

cartón, kar-ton s pasteboard; cartoon; cardboard

cartuchera, kar-too-**chay**-rah s cartridge box

cartucho, kar-**too**-cho s cartridge

cartulina, kar-too-lee-nah s pasteboard

casa, kah-sah s house; home; household

casaca, kah-**sah**-kah s coat

casación, kah-sah-the-on s annulment

casadero, kah-sah-**day**-ro a marriageable

casado, kah-**sah**-do a married

casamiento, kah-sah-me-en-to s marriage

casar, kah-**sar** v to marry

casarse, kah-**sar**-say v to get married

cascabel, kahs-kah-**bel** s small bell; jingle

cascada, kahs-**kah**-dah s cascade; waterfall

cascadura, kahs-kah-**doo**-rah s crack

cascajo, kahs-**kah**-Ho s gravel

cascanueces, kahs-kah-noo´**ay**-thess s nutcracker

cascar, kahs-**kar** v to crack; to burst; to break

cáscara, kahs-kah-rah s rind; peel; husk; bark

¡cáscaras!, kahs-kah-rahs interj (expressing surprise or admiration) wonderful!

cascarón, kahs-kah-**ron** s eggshell

cascarrón, kahs-kar-**rron** a rough; rude; harsh

casco, kahs-ko s helmet; cask; hull (of a ship); hoof

cascote, kahs-**ko**-tay s rubbish; débris

caserío, kah-say-**ree**-o s country house; hamlet

casero, kah-**say**-ro s landlord; house agent; a domestic; homey

caseta, kah-**say**-tah s small house; cottage

casete or **cassette, kah**-se-no s cassette; cassette player

casi, kah-se adv almost

casilla, kah-**see**-l´yah s cabin; box office; compartment; lodge

casimir, kah-se-**meer** s cashmere

casino, kah-se-no s casino

caso, kah-so s event; case; occurrence; accident; opportunity

caspa, kahs-pah s dandruff

¡cáspita!, kahs-pe-tah interj gracious!

casquete, kahs-**kay**-tay s helmet; skullcap

casquijo, kahs-kee-Ho s gravel

casquillo, kahs-kee-l´yo s tip; ferrule; socket; iron arrowhead

casta, kahs-tah s race; breed; kindred; kind; caste

castaña, kahs-**tah**-n´yah s chestnut

castañeta, kahs-tah-n´**yay**-tah s snapping of the fingers; castenet

castaño, kahs-**tah**-n´yo s chestnut tree; a hazel

castidad, kahs-te-**dahd** s chastity

castigar, kahs-te-**gar** v to chastise; to punish

castigo, kahs-tee-go s chastisement; punishment

castillejo, kahs-te-l´**yay**-Ho s small castle; go-cart; scaffolding

castillo, kahs-tee-l´yo s castle

castizo, kahs-tee-tho a pure-blooded; pure (language)

casto*, kahs-to a chaste

castor, kah-**tor** s beaver

castrar, kahs-**trar** v to geld; to castrate

casual*, kah-soo-**ahl** a casual; accidental

casualidad, kah-soo-´ah-le-**dahd** s chance; accident

casuca, casucha, kah-soo-kah, kah-**soo**-chah s hovel; hut

cata, kah-tah s trying by tasting; sampling

catador, kah-tah-**dor** s taster; sampler

catalejo, kah-tah-**lay**-Ho s telescope

catalogar, kah-tah-lo-**gar** v to catalog

catálogo, kah-tah-lo-go s catalog

cataplasma, kah tah-**plahs**-mah s poultice

catar, kah-**tar** v to taste; to sample

catarata, kah-tah-**rah**-tah s waterfall; cataract

catarro, kah-**tar**-rro s catarrh

catastro, kah-**tahs**-tro s land register

catástrofe, kah-**tahs**-tro-fay s catastrophe

cataviento, kah-tah-ve-en-to s weather-cock

cátedra, kah-tay-drah s professorial chair; professorship

catedral, kah-tay-**drahl** s cathedral

catedrático, kah-tay-**drah**-te-ko s professor

categórico kah-tay-**go**-re-ko a categorical

catequismo, kah-tay-**kiss**-mo s catechism

caterva, kah-**tair**-vah s multitude; throng; swarm

católico, kah-**to**-le-ko a Catholic

catorce, kah-**tor**-thay, s & a fourteen

catre, kah-**tray** s small bedstead; cot

cauce, kah´oo-thay s riverbed; ditch

caucihay kah´oo-the-**on** s caution; security; surety

caucionar, kah´oo-the-o-**nar** v to guard against; to bail

caucho, kah´oo-cho s rubber; rubber plant

caudal, kah´oo-**dahl** s fortune; health; volume of water

caudaloso, kah´oo-dah-lo-so a carrying much water; abundant; rich

caudillo, kah´oo-**dee**-l´yo s chief; leader

causa, kah´oo-sah s cause; motive; lawsuit

causante, kah´oo-**sahn**-tay s originator; constituent

causar, kah´oo-**sar** v to cause; to originate; to sue

cáustico, kah´ooss-te-ko a caustic

cautela, kah´oo-**tay**-lah s caution; prudence; heed

cauteloso, kah´oo-tay-lo-so a cautious

cauterio, kah´oo-**tay**-re-o s cauterization

cautivar, kah´oo-te-**var** v to imprison; to captivate

cautiverio, kah´oo-te-**vay**-re-o s captivity

cautivo, kah´oo-**te**-vo a captive

cauto, kah´oo-to a cautious; wary

cava, kah-vah s digging; wine cellar; sparkling wine

cavador, kah-vah-**dor** s digger

cavar, kah-**var** v to dig

cavidad, kah-ve-**dahd** s cavity

cavilación, kah-ve-lah-the-**on** s pondering

cavilar, kah-ve-**lar** v to cavil; to consider closely

caviloso*, kah-ve-lo-so a captious

caz, kath s canal for irrigation; flume

caza, kah-thah s hunt; game

cazador, kah-thah-**dor** s hunter

cazar, kah-**thar** v to chase; to hunt

cazo, kah-tho s saucepan; ladle; glue pot

cazón, kah-**thon** s dogfish

cazuela, kah-thoo´ay-lah s casserole; saucepan

cazurro, kah-**thoor**-rro a taciturn; sullen; sulky

CD, thay-day s abbr CD

CD ROM, a abbr CD ROM

ceba, thay-bah s fattening of animals

cebada, thay-**bah**-dah s barley

cebar, thay-**bar** v to fatten

cebo, thay-bo s food; fodder; bait

cebolla, thay-**bo**-l´yah s onion

cebón, thay-**bon** s fattened pig or hog

cebra, thay-brah s zebra

cecear, thay-thay-**ar** v to lisp

cecina, thay-**the**-nah s dried beef

cedazo, thay-**dah**-tho s sieve; strainer

ceder, thay-**dair** v to grant; to transfer; to submit; to abate

cedro, thay-dro s cedar

cédula, thay-doo-lah s slip of paper; order; bill; decree; warrant; identity card

céfiro, thay-fe-ro s zephyr

cegar, thay-**gar** v to blind

cegato, thay-**gah**-to a (fam) shortsighted

ceguedad, thay-gay-**dahd** s blindness

ceguera, thay-**gay**-rah s blindness

ceja, thay-Ha s eyebrow

cejar, thay-H ar v to relax; to slacken; to give up

celada, thay-**lah**-dah s helmet; ambush

celador, thay-lah-**dor** s curator; warden

celar, thay-**lar** v to fulfill duties carefully; to watch; to conceal; to engrave

celda, thel-dah s cell

celebérrimo, thay-lay-**bair**-rre-mo a most celebrated

celebrar, thay-lay-**brar** v to celebrate; to praise

celebración, thay-lay-bra-the-**on** s celebration

célebre,* thay-lay-bray a celebrated; famous

celeridad, thay-lay-re-**dahd** s rapidity

celeste, thay-**less**-tay a celestial; heavenly; perfect

celibato, thay-le-**bah**-to s celibacy

célibe, thay-le-bay s bachelor

celo, thay-lo s zeal; rut; pl jealousy

celosía, thay-lo-**see**-ah s Venetian blind; lattice; jealousy

celoso, thay-**lo**-so a zealous; jealous

célula, thay-loo-lah s cell

cementar, thay-men-**tar** v to cement

cementerio, thay-men-**tay**-re-o s cemetery

cemento, thay-**men**-to s cement

cena, thay-nah s supper

cenador, thay-nah-**dor** s arbor; bower

cenegal, thay-nah-**gahl** s quagmire; slough; bog

cenar, thay-**nar** v to dine

cencerro, then-**thair**-rro s cowbell

cendal, then-**dahl** s silk or linen; gauze

cenefa, thay-**nay**-fah s border; fringe

cenicero, thay-ne-**thay**-ro s ashtray; ashpit

cenit, thay-**neet** s zenith

ceniza, thay-**nee**-thah s ashes

cenizo, thay-**nee**-tho a ash-colored

censo, then-so s census; poll tax; annuity

censurar, then-soo-**rar** v to criticize; to censure; to blame

centavo, then-**tah**-vo s hundredth part; cent

centella, then-**tay**-l´yah s lightning; spark

centena, then-**tay**-nah s hundred

centenar, then-tay-**nar** s hundred; centenary; rye field

centeno, then-**tay**-no s rye; a hundredth

centésimo, then-**tay**-se-mo a hundredth

centígrado, then-te-**grah**-do s centigrade

centímetro, then-**tee**-may-tro s centimeter

céntimo, then-te-mo s centime

centinela, then-te-**nay**-lah s sentinel

central, then-**trahl** a central

centro, then-tro s center;

headquarters; club

céntuplo, then-too-plo *a*
hundredfold

ceñido, thay-n´**yee**-do *a*
close-fitting

ceñir, thay-n´**yeer** *v* to
gird; to hem in; to
abbreviate

ceño, thay-n´yo *s* frown;
ferrule

cepa, thay-pah *s* stump;
stock; grapevine

cepillo, thay-**pee**-l´yo *s*
brush; plane; alms

cepo, thay-po *s* anvil
(base); stocks; snare

cera, thay-rah *s* wax

cerafolio, thay-rah-**fo**-le-o
s chervil

cerato, thay-**rah**-to *s*
cerate

cerca, thair-kah *adv* close
by; near; *s* fence

cercado, thair-**kah**-do *s*
enclosure; fenced

cercanía, thair-kah-nee-
ah *s* proximity;
neighborhood

cercano, thair-**kah**-no *a*
near; close by

cercar, thair-**kar** *v* to
enclose; to hedge; to
hem

cercenar, thair-thay-**nar** *v*
to pare; to clip; to
curtail

cerciorar, thair-the-o-**rar**
v to assure; to affirm; to
ascertain

cerco, thair-ko *s* hoop;
ring; circle; blockade

cerda, thair-dah *s*
horsehair; bristle

cerdo, thair-do *s* hog; pig

cerdoso, thair-**do**-so *a*
bristly

cereal, they-ray-**ahl** *s*
cereal

cerebro, thay-**ray**-bro *s*
cerebrum; brain

cerero, thay-**ray**-ro *s*
candle-maker

cereza, thay-**ray**-thah *s*
cherry

cerilla, thay-ree-l´**yah** *s*
wax taper; earwax

cerner, thair-**nair** *v* to sift;
to blossom; to hover

cernidillo, thair-ne-dee-
l´yo *s* drizzle

cernidura, thair-ne-**doo**-
rah *s* sifting

cero, thay-ro *s* zero;
cipher

cerote, thay-ro-tay *s*
shoemaker's wax

cerquita, thair-kee-tah, *a*
very near; *s* small
enclosure

cerradero, thair-rrah-**day**-
ro *s* bolt staple

cerrado, thair-**rrah**-do *a*

closed; shut; reserved;
obscure; obstinate

cerrador, thair-rrah-**dor** *s*
shutter; fastener

cerradura, thair-rrah-**doo**-
rah *s* lock; closure;
locking-up

cerrajero, thair-rrah-*H*
ay-ro *s* locksmith

cerramiento, thair-rrah-
me-en-to *s* closure;
shutting up

cerrar, thair-**rrar** *v* to
close; to shut; to lock; to
fasten; to stop up

cerril, thair-**rreel** *a*
mountainous; rough;
wild

cerro, thair-rro *s* hill;
neck; backbone

cerrojo, thair-rro-*H*o *s*
bolt; latch

certamen, thair-**tah**-men *s*
competition; contest

certeza, certidumbre,
thair-**tay**-thah, thair-te-
doom-bray *s* certainty

certificado, thair-te-fe-
kah-do *s* certificate

certificar, thair-te-fe-**kar**
v to certify; – **una carta,**
– oo-nah-**kar**-tah, to
register a letter

cervato, thair-**vah**-to *s*
fawn

cervecería, thair-vay-thay-**ree**-ah s brewery; bar

cerveza, thair-**vay**-thah s beer

cerviz, thair- **veeth** s nape; cervix

cesación, thay-sah-the-**on** s cessation; stopping

cesar, thay-**sar** v to cease; to leave off; to stop

cese de hostilidades, thay-say day os-te-le-dah-days s ceasefire

cesible, thay-**see**-blay a transferable

cesión, thay-se-**on** s cession; transfer; assignment

cesionario, thay-se-o-**na**-re-o s transferee

cesionista, thay-se-o-**niss**-tah s transfer

césped, **thess**-payd s turf; sod; lawn

cesta, **thess**-tah s basket

cesto, **thess**-to s basket

cestón, thess-**ton** s large basket; gabion

cetrería, thay-tray-**ree**-ah s falconry

cetrino, thay-**tree**-no a citrine; jaundiced; melancholy

cetro, **thay**-tro s scepter; reign

cheque, **chay**-kay s check;

– **de viaje** traveler's check

chicle, **chi**-klay s chewing gum

ciática, the-ah-te-kah s sciatica

cicatería, the-kah-tay-**ree**-ah s stinginess

cicatero, the-kah-**ta**-ro a stingy

cicatriz, the-kah-**treeth** s scar

ciclo, **thee**-klo s cycle

ciclón, the-**klon** s cyclone

cidra, **thee**-drah s citron

ciego*, the-**ay**-go a blind; blocked (pipes)

cielo, the-**ay**-lo s heaven; sky; climate

cien, the-**en** a (used before nouns), one hundred

ciénaga, the-**en**-ah-gah s marsh

ciencia, the-**en**-the-ah s science; knowledge

cieno, the-**en**-o s mud; slough

ciento, the-**en**-to s & a one hundred

cierne, the-**air**-nay, **estar en** –, es-**tar** en –, to blossom

cierro, the-**air**-rro s closing; shutting

cierto, the-**air**-to a certain

cierva, the-**air**-vah s hind

ciervo, the-**air**-vo s deer

cierzo, the-**air**-tho s cold northerly wind

cifra, **thee**-frah s cipher; abbreviation; sum total

cigarra, the-**gar**-rrah s cicada

cigarrera, the-gar-**rray**-rah s cigar box

cigarrillo, the-gar-**rree**-l´yo s cigarette

cigarro, the-**gar**-rro s cigar

cigüeña, the-goo´**ay**-n´yah s stork

cilindro, the-**leen**-dro s cylinder

cima, **thee**-mah s summit; crest; top

cimarrón, the-mar-**rron** a wild; unruly

címbalo, **theem**-bah-lo s cymbal

cimborio, thim-**bo**-re-o s cupola; dome

cimbrar, thim-**brar** v to brandish; to vibrate; to shake

cimbreño, thim-**bray**-n´yo a pliant; flexible

cimentar, the-men-**tar** v to establish

cimiento, the-me-**en**-to s foundation; basis; origin

cinc, think s zinc

cincel, thin-**thel** s chisel

cincelar, thin-thay-**lar** v

to chisel; to engrave

cinco, thin-ko s & a five

cincuenta, thin-kov'en-tah s & a fifty

cincha, thin-chah s girth; belt

cine, thee-nay s movies

cíngaro, thin-gah-ro s gypsy

cinta, thin-tah s ribbon; tape; sash

cinteado, thin-tay-ah-do a adorned with ribbons

cinto, thin-to s belt

cintura, thin-too-rah s waist

cinturón, thin-too-ron s broad belt

ciprés, the-press s cypress tree

circo, theer-ko s circus

circuir, theer-koo´eer v to surround

circuito, theer-koo´ee-to s circuit

circular, theer-koo-lar v to circulate

círculo, theer-koo-lo s circle

circuncidar, theer-koon-the-dar v to circumcise

circundar, theer-koon-dar v to surround

circunflejo, theer-koon-flay-Ho a circumflex

circunloquio, theer-koon-lo-ke-o s circumlocution

circunspecto, theer-koons-pek-to a circumspect; cautious

circunstancia, theer-koons-tahn-the-ah s circumstance

circunstante, theer-koons-tahn-tay a surrounding; pl bystanders

circunvecino, theer-koon-vay-the-no a neighboring

cirio, theer-e-o s wax candle

ciruela, the-roo´ay-lah s plum

cirugía, the-roo-H ee-ah s surgery

cirujano, the-roo-H ah-no s surgeon

cisco, thiss-ko s coal dust; quarrel

cisma, thiss-mah s schism; discord

cisne, thiss-nay s swan

cita, thee-tah s quotation; summons; rendezvous

citación, the-tah-the-on s citation; quotation; summons

citar, the-tar v to convoke; to summon; to quote

cítara, thee-tah-ra s zither

citerior, the-tay-re-or a hither; toward this side

ciudad, the´oo-dahd s city; town

ciudadano, the´oo-dah-dah-no s citizen

ciudadela, the´oo-dah-day-lah s citadel

civilidad, the-ve-le-dahd s civility; urbanity

civismo, the-viss-mo s good citizenship

cizalla, the-thah-l´yah s shears; filings

cizaña, the-thah-n´yah s darnel (grasses); tare; discord

clamar, klah-mar v to cry out; to clamor; to want; to demand

clamor, klah-mor s clamor; outcry

clamorear, klah-mo-ray-ar v to clamor; to beg for assistance; to toll

clandestino, klahn-dess-tee-no a clandestine

clara, klah-rah s egg white

claraboya, klah-rah-bo-yah s skylight

clarear, klah-ray-ar v to lighten

clarete, klah-ray-tay s claret

claridad, klah-re-dahd s clearness; brightness;

distinctness

clarificar, klah-re-fe-**kar** v to clarify

clarín, klah-**reen** s bugle

clarinete, klah-re-**nay**-tay s clarinet

clarividencia, klah-re-ve-**den**-the-ah s clairvoyance

claro*, **klah**-ro a clear; transparent; lucid; thin; light; manifest; open

claroscuro, klah-ros-**koo**-ro s chiaroscuro; light and shade

clase, **klah**-say s class; rank; order; kind; description

clásico, **klah**-se-ko a classical; classic

claudicar, klah´oo-de-**kar** v to halt; to limp; to shirk

claustro, klah´**ooss**-tro s cloister

cláusula, klah´oo-soo-lah s clause; article; stipulation

clausular, klah´oo-soo-**lar** v to close (sentence, speech, etc)

clausura, klah´oo-**soo**-rah s closure; confinement

clava, **klah**-vah s club; cudgel

clavado, klah-**vah**-do a

nailed; exact; precise

clavar, klah-**var** v to nail; to fasten with nails

clave, **klah**-vay s key; code; clue

clavel, klah-**vel** s carnation

clavicordio, klah-ve-**kor**-de-o s clavichord

clavícula, klah-**vee**-koo-lah s clavicle; collarbone

clavija, klah-**vee**-Hah s pin; peg

clavillo, klah-**vee**-l´yos small nail; tack

clavo, **klah**-vo s nail; corn (on the feet); clove

clemencia, klay-**men**-the-ah s clemency

clemente*, klay-**men**-tay a clement; merciful

clerecía, klay-ray-**thee**-ah s clergy

clérigo, **klay**-re-go s priest; clergyman

clero, **klay**-ro s clergy

cliente, kle-**en**-tay s client

clientela, kle-en-**tay**-lah s clientele

clima, **klee**-mah s climate

clínica, **klee**-ne-kah s clinic

clisado, kle-**sah**-do s stereotyping

clisé, kle-**say** s stereotype

plate (printing); cliché

clistel, kliss-**tel** s enema

cloaca, klo-ah-kah s sewer

cloquear, klo-kay-**ar** v to cluck; to cackle

cloral, klo-**rahl** s chloral

cloro, **klo**-ro s chlorine

cloruro, klo-**roo**-ro s chloride

club, kloob s club; association

coacci, s ko-ahk-the-**on** s compulsion; coercion

coadyuvar, ko-ahd-yoo-**var** v to help; to assist

coagular, ko-ah-goo-**lar** v to coagulate

coalición, ko-ah-le-the-**on** s coalition

coartada, ko-ar-**tah**-dah s alibi

coartar, ko-ar-**tar** v to limit; to restrain

coba, ko-bah, s tall tale

cobarde, ko-**bar**-day a coward; fainthearted

cobardía, ko-bar-dee-ah s cowardice

cobertera, ko-bair-**tay**-rah s lid (pot); cover

cobertizo, ko-bair-**tee**-tho s shed

cobijar, ko-be-**Har** v to cover; to shelter

cobijo, ko-bee-**Ho** s shelter; lodge

cobrador, ko-brah-dor s
bill collector; railroad or
bus conductor

cobranza, ko-brahn-thah s
collection or recovery of
money

cobrar, ko-brar v to
recover; to collect; to
recuperate

cobre, ko-bray s copper

cobrizo, ko-bree-tho a
coppery

cobro, ko-bro, (see
cobranza)

cocción, kok-the-on s
cooking; boiling

cocear, ko-thay-ar v to
kick

cocer, ko-thair v to cook;
to boil

cocido, ko-thee-do s
boiled meat and
vegetables; a boiled;
baked; cooked

cocina, ko-thee-nah s
kitchen

cocinero, ko-thee-nay-ro s
cook

coco, ko-ko s coconut

cocodrilo, ko-ko-dree-lo s
crocodile

cocora, ko-ko-rah s bore;
nuisance

cochambre, ko-chahm-
bray, s (fam.) greasy,
dirty object

coche, ko-chay s car

cochero, ko-chay-ro s
coachman

cochina, ko-chee-nah s
sow

cochinamente, ko-che-
nah-men-tay adv dirtily;
filthily; basely

cochinería, ko-che-nay-
ree-ah s filthiness;
foulness

codazo, ko-dah-tho s push
with the elbow; nudge

codear, ko-day-ar v to
elbow

codeso, ko-day-so s
labernum

códice, ko-de-thay s
codex; old manuscript

codicia, ko-dee-the-ah s
covetousness; cupidity

codiciar, ko-de-the-ar v to
covet

codicioso, ko-de-the-o-so
a covetous

código, co-de-go s code
(of laws)

codillo, ko-dee-l'yo s
knee; angle; bend;
stirrup

codo, ko-do s elbow

codorniz, ko-dor-neeth s
quail

coercer, ko-air-thair v to
coerce

coerción, ko-air-the-on s

coercion

coetáneo, ko-ay-tah-nay-o
s contemporary

coexistir, ko-ek-siss-teer v
to coexist

cofia, ko-fe-ah s head
gear; hairnet

cofre, ko-fray s trunk (of
car)

cogedor, ko-Hay-dor s
dustpan; small shovel

coger, ko-H air v to catch;
to gather; to grasp; to
contain

cogote, ko-go-tay s nape

cohabitar, ko-ha-be-tar v
to cohabit

cohechar, ko-ay-char v to
bribe

cohecho, ko-ay-cho s
bribery

coherente, ko-ay-ren-tay
a coherent

cohesivo, ko-ay-see-vo a
cohesive

cohete, ko-ay-tay s rocket

cohibición, ko-e-be-the-
on s inhibition; restraint

cohibir, ko-e-beer v to
inhibit; to restrain

cohonestar, ko-o-ness-tar
v to gloss over

cohorte, ko-or-tay s
cohort

coincidir, ko-in-the-deer v
to coincide

cojear, ko-**Hay-ar** v to limp; to act immorally

cojera, ko-**H ay-**rah s lameness; limping

cojinete, ko-**He-nay-**tay s small cushion; pad

cojo, ko-**Ho** s & a lame; cripple

col, kol s cabbage

cola, ko-lah s tail; train; trail; glue

colaborar, ko-lah-bo-**rar** v to collaborate

colación, ko-lah-the-**on** s critical comparison; collation

colada, ko-lah-dah s wash

colador, ko-lah-**dor** s colander; strainer

coladura, ko-lah-doo-rah s straining

colapso, ko-**lahp-**so s collapse

colar, ko-lar v to strain; to collate; to enter stealthily

colcha, kol-chah s quilt; bedspread

colchón, kol-**chon** s mattress

colear, ko-lay-ar v to wag (tail)

colección, ko-lek-the-on s collection

colectar, ko-lek-**tar** v to collect (taxes)

colector, ko-lek-**tor** s collector; gatherer

colega, ko-**lay-**gah s colleague

colegatario, ko-lay-gah-tah-re-o s co-legatee

colegial, ko-lay-**He-ahl** s student; collegiate

colegiatura, ko-lay-He-ah-**too-**rah s scholarship

colegio, ko-**lay-He-o** s school

colegir, ko-lay-**Heer** v to collect; to infer

cólera, ko-lay-rah s cholera; fury; rage

colérico, ko-lay-re-ko a bad-tempered; irascible

colesterol, ko-lays-tay-**rol** s cholesterol

coleta, ko-**lay-**tah s ponytail; postscript

colgadero, kol-gah-**day-**ro s hanger; peg

colgadizo, kol-gah-dee-tho s shed; a hanging

colgadura, kol-gah-doo-rah s tapestry; hangings

colgar, kol-**gar** v to hang up; to adorn with hangings

cólico, ko-le-ko s colic

coliflor, ko-le-**flor** s cauliflower

coligarse, ko-le-**gar-**say v to unite; to associate

(with)

colina, ko-lee-nah s hill

colindante, ko-lin-**dahn**tay a contiguous

coliseo, ko-le-**say-**o s coliseum

colmar, kol-**mar** v to heap up; to make up

colmena, kol-**may-**nah s beehive

colmillo, kol-mee-l'yo s eye tooth; fang; tusk

colmo, kol-mo s heap; completion; height

colocación, ko-lo-kah-the-**on** s situation; employment

colocar, ko-lo-**kar** v to arrange; to place; to locate

colonia, ko-lo-ne-ah s colony; cologne

colonizar, ko-lo-ne-**thar** v to colonize

colono, ko-lo-no s colonist; settler

coloquio, ko-lo-ke-o s colloquy; talk

color, ko-**lor** s color; dye; dialogue

coloración, ko-lo-rah-the-**on** s coloring

colorado, ko-lo-**rah-**do a ruddy; red

colorar, ko-lo-**rar** v to color; to blush

colorear, ko-lo-ray-**ar** *v* to gloss over; to excuse; to redden

colorete, ko-lo-**ray**-tay *s* rouge

colorín, ko-lo-**reen** *s* linnet; vivid color

colorír, ko-lo-**reer** *v* to color

coloso, ko-**lo**-so *s* giant

columbrar, ko-loom-**brar** *v* to discern at a distance; to guess

columna, ko-**loom**-nah *s* column; pillar

columnata, ko-loom-**nah**-tah *s* colonnade

columpiar, ko-loom-pe-**ar** *v* to swing

colusorio, ko-loo-**so**-re-o *a* collusive

collado, ko-l'**yah**-do *s* hill; hillock; fell

collar, ko-l'**yar** *s* necklace; collar

coma, **ko**-mah *s* comma

comadre, ko-**mah**-dray *s* midwife; gossip

comadrear, ko-mah-dray-**ar** *v* to gossip

comadrona, ko-mah-**dro**-nah *s* midwife

comandar, ko-mahn-**dar** *v* to command

comandita, ko-mahn-dee-tah *s* partnership

comarca, ko-**mar**-kah *s* territory; district; boundary

comarcano, ko-mar-**kah**-no *a* neighboring

comba, **kom**-bah *s* curvature; bend; convexity

combadura, kom-bah-**doo**-rah *s* curvature; warping

combar, kom-**bar** *v* to curve; to bend; to warp

combate, kom-**bah**-tay *s* combat; fight; battle

combatir, kom-bah-**teer** *v* to fight; to combat; to contradict

combinar, kom-be-**nar** *v* to combine

comedero, ko-may-**day**-ro *s* dining room; *a* edible

comediante, ko-may-de-**ahn**-tay *s* actor; comedian

comedido, ko-may-**dee**-do *a* polite; courteous; gentle

comedirse, ko-may-**deer**-say *v* to control oneself; to be restrained

comedor, ko-may-**dor** *s* eater; dining room

comendador, ko-men-dah-**dor** *s* commander (of a military order)

comentar, ko-men-**tar** *v* to comment

comentario, ko-men-**tah**-re-o *s* commentary

comento, ko-**men**-to *s* comment; explanation

comenzar, ko-men-**thar** *v* to begin

comer, ko-**mair** *v* to eat; to dine

comerciante, ko-mair-the-**ahn**-tay *s* storeowner; businessman

comercio, ko-**mair**-the-o *s* trade; commerce

cometa, ko-**may**-tah *s* comet; kite

cometer, ko-may-**tair** *v* to commit; to entrust; to perpetrate

cometido, ko-may-**tee**-do *s* commission; trust

comezón, ko-may-**thon** *s* itching; longing

cómico, **ko**-me-ko *s* comedian; *a* comical

comida, ko-**mee**-dah *s* food; lunch; fare

comidilla, ko-me-dee-l'**yah** *s* to be the talk of a town; hobby

comido, ko-**mee**-do *a* fed; satiate

comienzo, ko-me-en-tho *s* beginning; origin

comilón, ko-me-**lon** s gourmand; glutton

comillas, ko-mee-l'yahs s quotation marks

comisar, ko-me-**sar** v to confiscate; to attach

comisario, ko-me-**sah**-re-o s commissary

comisión, ko-me-se-**on** s commission; trust; mandate

comisionar, ko-me-se-o-**nar** v to commission

comisionista, ko-me-se-o-**niss**-tah s agent; representative

comiso, ko-**mee**-so s confiscation

comitiva, ko-me-**tee**-vah s suite; retinue

commutador, kom-moo-tah-**dor** s commuter

como, ko-mo adv how; in what manner; like; as; why

cómoda, ko-mo-dah s chest of drawers; bureau

comodidad, ko-mo-de-**dahd** s comfort; convenience; ease; profit

cómodo, **ko**-mo-do a convenient; handy; suitable; comfortable

compacto, kom-**pak**-to a compact

compadecer, kom-pah-day-**thair** v to pity

compadre, kom-**pah**-dray s godfather; friend

compaginar, kom-pah-He-**nar** v to arrange; to compare

compañero, kom-pahn´yay-ro s companion; friend; associate

compañía, kom-pahn´yee-ah s company

comparación, kom-pah-rah-the-on s comparison

comparar, kom-pah-**rar** v to compare; to confront

comparecencia, kom-pah-ray-**then**-the-ah s appearance (law)

comparecer, kom-pah-ray-**thair** v to appear (court)

comparición, kom-pah-re-the-**on** s appearance (court)

comparsa, kom-**par**-sah s extras (theater)

compartimiento, kom-par-te-me-**en**-to s compartment

compartir, kom-par-**teer** v to divide into equal parts; to share

compás, kom-**pahs** s compass

compasar, kom-pah-**sar** v to measure; to regulate

compasivo, kom-pah-see-vo a compassionate

compatible, kom-pah-te-blay a compatible

compeler, kom-pay-**lair** v to compel; to force

compendiar, kom-pen-de-ar v to epitomize; to summarize

compendio, kom-**pen**-de-o s compendium

compendioso, kom-pen-de-o-so a abridged; concise

compensar, kom-pen-**sar** v to compensate; to balance

competencia, kom-pay-ten-the-ah s competition; competence; aptitude

competente, kom-pay-ten-tay a competent; apt; adequate

competir, kom-pay-**teer** v to compete; to contest

competitivo, kon-pay-te-**tee**-vo a competitive

compinche, kom-peen-chay s friend; buddy; pal

complacencia, kom-plah-then-the-ah s pleasure; complacency

complacer, kom-plah-thair v to please; to be pleased

complaciente, kom-plah-the-**en**-tay *a* pleasing; agreeable

completar, kom-play-**tar** *v* to complete

completo*, kom-**play**-to *a* complete; finished

complicar, kom-ple-**kar** *v* to complicate

cómplice, kon-**ple**-thay *s* accomplice

complot, kom-**plot** *s* plot; conspiracy

componedor, kom-po-nay-**dor** *s* referee; compositor; arbitrator

componer, kom-po-**nair** *v* to compose; to construct; to advise; to restore; to reconcile

componible, kom-po-**nee**-blay *a* arrangeable; reconcilable

comportable, kom-por-**tah**-blay *a* tolerable

comportar, kom-por-**tar** *v* to suffer; to tolerate

comportarse, kom-por-**tar**-say *v* to behave oneself

comporte, kom-**por**-tay *s* conduct; manner

composición, kom-po-se-the-**on** *s* composition; settlement; cleanliness; compact; modesty

compota, kom-**po**-tah *s* compote; jam

compra, kom-**prah** *s* purchase; shopping

comprador, kom-prah-**dor** *s* purchaser; buyer

comprar, kom-**prar** *v* to buy; to purchase

comprender, kom-**pren**-**dair** *v* to understand; to comprise

comprensible, kom-pren-**see**-blay *a* comprehensible

comprensión, kom-pren-se-**on** *s* comprehension; understanding

comprimir, kom-pre-**meer** *v* to compress; to restrain

comprobar, kom-pro-**bar** *v* to verify; to prove

comprometer, kom-pro-may-**tair** *v* to compromise; to jeopardize; to bind

compromisario, kom-pro-me-**sah**-re-o *s* arbitrator

compuerta, kom-poo´**air**-tah *s* lock; sluice

compuesto, kom-poo´**ess**-to, *s & a* compound; composed

compulsivo, kon-pool-**see**-vo *a* compulsive

compunción, kom-poon-the-**on** *s* compunction; repentance; remorse

compungirse, kom-poon-H **eer**-say *v* to feel compunction; to feel remorseful

compungivo, kom-poon-H **ee**-vo *a* remorseful

computar, kom-poo-**tar** *v* to compute; to reckon

comulgar, ko-mool-**gar** *v* to administer or receive the sacrament

común, ko-**moon** *a* common; customary; vulgar

comunal, ko-moo-**nahl** *s* communal

comunero, ko-moo-**nay**-ro *s* commoner; *a* popular

comunicado, ko-moo-ne-**kah**-do *s* statement

comunicar, ko-moo-ne-**kar** *v* to communicate; to impart

comunidad, ko-moo-ne-**dahd** *s* community

comunismo, ko-moo-**niss**-mo *s* communism

comunista, ko-moo-**niss**-tah *a* communist

comúnmente, ko-**moon**-men-tay *adv* commonly

con, kon *prep* with; by; for; in; among

conato, ko-**nah**-to s effort; endeavor; attempt

concadenar, kon-kah-day-**nar** v to link together

cóncabo, kon-**kah**-vo a concave

concebir, kon-thay-**beer** v to conceive; to understand

conceder, kon-thay-**dair** v to give; to grant; to concede

concejal, kon-thay-H **ahl** s councilman; alderman

concejo, kon-**thay**-Ho s town council

concentrar, kon-then-**trar** v to concentrate

concepto, kon-**thep**-to s thought; opinion; concept

conceptuar, kon-thep-too-**ar** v to conceive; to judge

concernir, kon-thair-**neer** v to concern; to relate to

concertar, kon-thair-**tar** v to arrange; to regulate; to agree

concesionario, kon-thess-e-o-**nah**-re-o s licensee

conciencia, kon-the-**en**-the-ah s conscience

concienzudo, kon-the-en-**thoo**-do a conscientious

concierto, kon-the-**air**-to s agreement; accommodation; concert

conciliar, kon-the-le-**ar** v to conciliate; to reconcile

concilio, kon-**thee**-le-o s council

concisión, kon-the-se-**on** s conciseness

conciso*, kon-**thee**-so a concise

concitar, kon-the-**tar** v to stir up; to agitate

conciudadano, kon-the-oo-dah-**dah**-no s fellow citizen

concluir, kon-kloo'**eer** v to conclude; to infer; to end

concluyente*, kon-kloo-**yen**-tay a conclusive

concordar, kon-kor-**dar** v to conciliate; to agree

concorde, kon-**kor**-day a in agreement

concretar, kon-kray-**tar** v to sum up; to realize

concurrir, kon-koor-**rreer** v to concur; to assist; to contribute

concursar, kon-koor-**sar** v to declare insolvent; to compete

concurso, kon-**koor**-so s assembly; aid; competition

concha, kon-chah s shell

conchabar, kon-chah-**bar** v to join; to conspire

conchado, kon-**chah**-do a scaly

conchudo, kon-**choo**-do a shell-bearing; cunning

condado, kon-**dah**-do s county; earldom

conde, kon-day s count; earl

condecorar, kon-day-ko-**rar** v to decorate; to honor; to reward

condena, kon-**day**-nah s sentence

condenación, kon-day-nah-the-**on** s condemnation; conviction (of a criminal)

condenar, kon-day-**nar** v to condemn; to sentence

condensar, kon-den-**sar** v to condense

condesa, kon-**day**-sah s countess

condescender, kon-dess-then-**dair** v to condescend

condestable, kon-dess-**tah**-blay s constable

condicionar, kon-de-the-

o-**nar** v to agree; to
prepare

condigno*, kon-**dig**-no a
fitting; deserved

condimentar, kon-de-
men-tar v to flavor; to
season; to spice

condiscípulo, kon-diss-
thee-poo-lo s fellow
student

condolerse, kon-do-**lair**-
say v to sympathize; to
be sorry for

condominio, kon-do-**mee**-
ne-o s joint ownership

condón, kon-**don** s
condom

condonación, kon-do-
nah-the-**on** s forgiving

condonar, kon-do-**nar** v to
pardon; to remit

conducción, kon-**dook**-
the-**on** s driving;
transportation

conducir, kon-doo-**theer** v
to drive; to conduct; to
guide

conducta, kon-**dook**-tah s
behavior; convoy

conducto, kon-**dook**-to s
conduit

conductor, kon-**dook**-tor s
conductor

conectar, ko-nek-**tar** v to
connect

conejo, ko-**nay**-Ho s

rabbit

conexionar, ko-nek-se-o-
nar v to connect

conexo, ko-**nek**-so a
connected

confección, kon-fek-the-
on s confection;
clothing; making

confeccionar, kon-fek-
the-o-**nar** v to make; to
compound

conferencia, kon-fay-**ren**-
the-ah s conference;
lecture

conferir, kon-fay-**reer** v to
confer; to compare; to
bestow

confesado, kon-fay-**sah**-do
a confessed; penitent

confesar, kon-fay-**sar** v to
confess

confesionario, kon-fay-se-
o-**nah**-re-o s
confessional

confiado, kon-fe-**ah**-do a
trusting

confianza, kon-fe-**ahn**-
thah s confidence

confiar, kon-fe-**ar** v to
confide; to hope; to
trust in

confidencia, kon-fe-**den**-
the-ah s confidence;
confidential information

confidente, kon-fe-**den**-
tay s confidant; a*

trustworthy

confín, kon-**feen** s limit;
boundary; confine

confinar, kon-fe-**nar** v to
banish; to border upon

confirmar, kon-feer-**mar** v
to confirm

confite, kon-fe-tay s
candy; sweet

confitera, kon-fe-**tay**-rah s
candy box or dish

confitería, kon-fe-tay-**ree**-
ah s candy store

confitero, kon-fe-**tay**-ro s
confectioner

confitura, kon-fe-**too**-rah
s jam; confection

conflicto, kon-**fleek**-to s
conflict

confluir, kon-floo´eer v to
meet (of rivers)

conformar, kon-for-**mar** v
to conform; to suit; to
fit; to comply

conforme, kon-**for**-may
adv agreeably; similar;
alike

confortar, kon-for-**tar** v to
comfort

confraternidad, kon-frah-
tair-ne-**dahd** s fraternity

confrontar, kon-fron-**tar** v
to compare; to confront

confundir, kon-foon-**deer**
v to confound; to
confuse; to embarrass

confuso, kon-**foo**-so *a*
confused; obscure;
perplexed

confutar, kon-foo-**tar** *v* to
disprove

congelador, kon-**Hay**-la-
dor *s* freezer

congelar, kon-**Hay**-lar *v* to
congeal; to freeze

congénito, kon-**H** ay-ne-
to *a* congenital

conglomerarse, kon-glo-
may-**rar**-say *v* to
conglomerate

congoja, kon-**go**-Hah *s*
anguish; sorrow

congojoso, kon-go-**H** o-so
a painful; distressing

congraciamiento, kon-
grah-the-ah-**men**-to *s*
obsequiousness; flattery

congraciarse, kon-grah-
the-**ar**-say *v* to ingratiate
oneself

congratular, kon-grah-
too-**lar** *v* to
congratulate; to
compliment

congregar, kon-gray-**gar** *v*
to assemble; to gather

congreso, kon-**gray**-so *s*
congress; convention

congrio, kon-**gre**-o *s*
conger-eel

congruencia, kon-groo-
en-the-ah *s* congruence;

consistency

conjetura, kon-Hay-**too**-
rah *s* conjecture; guess

conjunción, kon-Hoon-
the-**on** *s* conjunction

conjunto*, kon-**H** oon-to
a united; connected

conjurado, kon-Hoo-**rah**-
do *s* conspirator

conjurador, kon-Hoo-rah-
dor *s* plotter

conjurar, kon-Hoo-**rar** *v*
to conspire; to exercise;
to entreat

conjuro, kon-Hoo-ro *s*
incantation; exorcism

conmemorar, kon-may-
mo-**rar** *v* to
commemorate

conmigo, kon-**mee**-go
pron with me

conminación, kon-me-
nah-the-**on** *s* threat;
menace

conmutar, kon-moo-**tar** *v*
to commute

connatural, kon-nah-too-
rahl *a* innate

connaturalizarse, kon-
nah-too-rah-le-**thar**-say
v to acclimatize oneself

connotar, kon-no-**tar** *v* to
connote; to imply

cono, **ko**-no *s* cone

conocedor, ko-no-thay-
dor *s* connoisseur;

expert

conocer, ko-no-**thair** *v* to
know; to be acquainted
with; to understand

conocible, ko-no-**thee**-
blay *a* knowable

conocido, ko-no-**thee**-do *s*
acquaintance; *a* well-
known

conocimiento, ko-no-the-
me-**en**-to *s* knowledge;
acquaintance; voucher

conquista, kon-**kiss**-tah *s*
conquest

conquistador, kon-kiss-
tah-**dor** *s* conqueror

conquistar, kon-kiss-**tar** *v*
to conquer

consabido, kon-sah-**bee**-
do *a* said; in question

consagrar, kon-sah-**grar** *v*
to consecrate

consciente, kons-the-**en**-
tay *a* conscious

consecución, kon-say-
koo-the-**on** *s* attainment

consecuencia, kon-say-
koo'en-the-ah *s*
consequence

consecuente, kon-say-
koo'en-tay *a* consequent

conseguir, kon-say-**gheer**
v to attain; to get

conseja, kon-say-Hah *s*
fable; tale

consejero, kon-say-**H** ay-ro s adviser; counselor

consejo, kon-**say**-Ho s counsel; advice; council

consenso, kon-**sen**-so s consensus

consentimiento, kon-sen-te-me-**en**-to s consent

consentir, kon-sen-**teer** v to consent

conserje, kon-**sair**-Hay s concierge

conserva, kon-**sair**-vah s preserve

conservar, kon-**sair**-var v to preserve; to pickle; to keep

considerado*, kon-se-day-**rah**-do a prudent; considerate

considerar, kon-se-day-**rar** v to consider; to meditate; to think over

consigna, kon-**sig**-nah s slogan; baggage check

consignación, kon-sig-nah-the-**on** s deposit (money); consignment

consignador, kon-sig-nah-**dor** s depositer

consignar, kon-sig-**nar** v to consign; to make over; to deposit in trust; to assign

consignatario, kon-sig-nah-**tah**-re-o s consignee; trustee

consigo, kon-**see**-go pron with oneself

consiguiente, kon-se-ghee-**en**-tay a consequent

consistencia, kon-siss-**ten**-the-ah s consistence; consistency; stability

consistir, kon-siss-**teer** v to consist

consola, kon-**so**-lah s console

consolar, kon-so-**lar** v to console; to cheer

consonante, kon-so-**nahn**-tay a concordant; consonant

consonar, kon-so-**nar** v to harmonize; to rhyme; to agree

consorcio, kon-**sor**-the-o s partnership; fellowship

consorte, kon-**sor**-tay s consort; spouse; accomplice

conspirar, kons-pe-**rar** v to conspire; to plot

constancia, kons-**tahn**-the-ah s constancy; steadiness; written evidence

constar, kons-**tar** v to be evident; to consist of

consternar, kons-tair-**nar** v to terrify; to shock

constipado, kons-te-**pah**-do a to have a cold; s a cold

constiparse, kons-te-par-**say** v to catch a cold

constituir, kons-te-too´**eer** v to constitute

construir, kons-troo´**eer** v to construct; to build

consuelo, kon-soo´**ay**-lo s consolation; joy

cónsul, kon-**sool** s consul

consulado, kon-soo-**lah**-do s consulate

consulta, kon-**sool**-tah s consultation; question

consultar, kon-sool-**tar** v to consult

consultivo, kon-sool-**tee**-vo a advisory

consultor, kon-sool-**tor** s adviser

consumación, kon-soo-mah-the-**on** s consummation

consumado, kon-soo-mah-**do** a consummate; complete

consumir, kon-soo-**meer** v to consume

consumo, kon-**soo**-mo s consumption (of food and merchandise); excise tax

consunción, kon-soon-the-**on** s consumption

contabilidad, kon-tah-be-le-**dahd** s bookkeeping

contacto, kon-**tak**-to s contact

contado, kon-**tah**-do *a* scarce; rare; **de**–, day –, instantly; **al** –, ahl –, for cash

contador, kon-tah-**dor** s accountant; counter

contagiar, kon-tah-**He**-ar *v* to infect

contaminar, kon-tah-me-**nar** *v* to contaminate

contante, kon-**tahn**-tay s ready money; cash

contar, kon-**tar** *v* to count; to look upon; to rely

contemplar, kon-tem-**plar** *v* to contemplate

contemporáneo, kon-tem-po-**rah**-nay-o *a* contemporary

contemporizar, kon-tem-po-re-**thar** *v* to comply

contención, kon-ten-the-**on** s contention; emulation

contendiente, kon-ten-de-**en**-tay s litigant

contener, kon-tay-**nair** *v* to contain; to hold

contenido, kon-tay-**nee**-do s content; *a* moderate

contentar, kon-ten-**tar** *v* to content; to please

contestación, kon-tess-tah-the-**on** s reply; answer

contestador automático, kon-tays-tah-**dor** ah´oo-to-**mah**-te-ko s answering machine

contestar, kon-tess-**tar** *v* to reply; to attest; to agree

contienda, kon-te-**en**-dah s contest; conflict

contigo, kon-**tee**-go *pron* with you

contiguo, kon-**tee**-goo´o *a* contiguous; adjacent

continente, kon-te-**nen**-tay s continent; countenance; *a* containing

contingencia, kon-tin-**Hen**-the-ah s contingency; emergency

continuar, kon-te-noo´**ar** *v* to continue

continuo*, kon-**tee**-noo´o *a* continuous

contonearse, kon-to-nay-**ar**-say *v* to strut

contorno, kon-**tor**-no s surroundings; outline

contra, kon-trah *prep* against; opposite to

contrabando, kon-trah-**bahn**-do s contraband; smuggling

contradanza, kon-trah-**dahn**-thah s quardrille; cotillon

contradecir, kon-trah-day-**theer** *v* to contradict; to oppose

contraer, kon-trah-**air** *v* to contract

contrahacer, kon-trah-ah-**thair** *v* to counterfeit; to forge

contralor, kon-trah-**lor** s comptroller

contraluz, kon-trah-**looth** s backlight

contramandar, kon-trah-mahn-**dar** *v* to countermand

contraorden, kon-trah-**or**-den s countermand

contrapelo, kon-trah-**pay**-lo *adv* against the grain; the wrong way

contraponer, kon-trah-po-**nair**, *v* to compare; to oppose

contraprueba, kon-trah-proo´**ay**-bah s counter evidence

contrariar, kon-trah-re-**ar** *v* to contradict; to thwart; to disappoint

contrariedad, kon-trah-re-ay-**dahd** s obstacle

contrario*, kon-trah-re-o *a* contrary; adverse

contrarrestar, kon-trah-rress-tar *v* to check; to counteract

contraseña, kon-trah-say-n´yah *s* countersign; password

contrastar, kon-trahs-tar *v* to contrast; to oppose

contraste, kon-**trahs**-tay *s* opposition; contrast

contrata, kon-**trah**-tah *s* contract

contratante, kon-trah-**tahn**-tay *s* contractor

contratar, kon-trah-**tar** *v* to contract; to trade

contratista, kon-trah-**tiss**-tah *s* contractor

contrato, kon-**trah**-to *s* contract; agreement

contraveneno, kon-trah-vay-**nay**-no *s* antidote

contravenir, kon-trah-vay-**neer** *v* to contravene

contraventana, kon-trah-ven-**tah**-nah *s* storm window

contribución, kon-tre-boo-the-**on** *s* tax; duty; contribution

contribuir, kon-tre-boo´**eer** *v* to contribute

contrincante, kon-trin-**kahn**-tay *s* rival

contristar, kon-triss-**tar** *v*

to sadden; to grieve

contrito, kon-**tree**-to *a* penitent

controvertir, kon-tro-vair-**teer** *v* to controvert; to argue

contundente, kon-toon-**den**-tay *a* convincing; powerful; conclusive

conturbar, kon-toor-**bar** *v* to disturb; to perturb

convalecer, kon-vah-lay-**thair** *v* to regain health

convecino, kon-vay-**thee**-no *a* neighboring

convencer, kon-ven-**thair** *v* to convince

convencimiento, kon-ven-the-me-**en**-to *s* conviction

convenible, kon-vay-**nee**-blay *a* compliant; docile; suitable

conveniencia, kon-vay-ne-en-the-ah *s* utility; convenience

conveniente, kon-vay-ne-**en**-tay *a* useful; convenient

convenio, kon-vay-ne-o *s* agreement; pact

convenir, kon-vay-**neer** *v* to agree; to correspond; to convene

convento, kon-**ven**-to *s* convent

convergir, kon-vair-**Heer** *v* to converge

conversable, kon-vair-**sah**-blay *a* sociable

conversar, kon-vair-**sar** *v* to converse; to talk; to chat

converso, kon-vair-so *s* convert

convertir, kon-vair-**teer** *v* to convert

convexo, kon-vek-so *a* convex

convicto, kon-veek-to *a* convicted; guilty

convidada, kon-ve-dah-dah *s* invitation to drink; treat

convidar, kon-ve-**dar** *v* to invite; to treat

convincente, kon-vin-**then**-tay *a* convincing

convite, kon-vee-tay *s* invitation

convocar, kon-vo-**kar** *v* to convoke; to summon; to convene

conyugal, kon-yoo-**gahl** *a* conjugal

cónyuges, kon-yoo-Hess *s* husband and wife

cooperar, ko-o-pay-**rar** *v* to cooperate

cooperario, ko-o-pay-**rah**-re-o *s* cooperator

coopositor, ko-o-po-se-**tor**

s competitor; rival

coordenado, ko-or-day-nah-do *a* coordinate

coordinar, ko-or-de-nar *v* to coordinate

copa, ko-pah *s* cup; goblet; *pl* hearts (at cards)

copete, ko-pay-tay *s* toupee; tuft

copia, ko-pe-ah *s* abundance; copy

copiar, ko-pe-ar *v* to copy; to mimic

copioso, ko-pe-o-so *a* copious; plentiful

copla, ko-plah *s* couplet; lampoon; ballad

copo, ko-po *s* snowflake

copón, ko-pon *s* large goblet

cópula, ko-poo-lah *s* coupling; sexual union

coqueta, ko-kay-tah *s* coquette; flirt

coquetería, ko-kay-tay-ree-ah *s* coquetry; flirtation

coracero, ko-rah-thay-ro *s* cuirassier

coraje, ko-rah-Hay *s* courage; bravery; anger; passion

coraza, ko-rah-thah *s* cuirass; shell

corazón, ko-rah-thon *s* heart; core

corbata, kor-bah-tah *s* cravat; tie

corcovado, kor-ko-vah-do *a* hunchbacked; crooked

corcovar, kor-ko-var *v* to curve

corchete, kor-chay-tay *s* clasp; crotch

corcho, kor-cho *s* cork

cordaje, kor-dah-Hay *s* rigging

cordel, kor-del *s* cord; rope

cordero, kor-day-ro *s* lamb

cordillera, kor-de-l´yay-rah *s* mountain range

cordón, kor-don *s* cord; twisted lace; military cordon

cordonero, kor-do-nay-ro *s* lace-maker; rope-maker

cordura, kor-doo-rah *s* prudence; judgment

corea, ko-ray-ah *s* dance accompanied with singing; St Vitus's dance

cornada, kor-nah-dah *s* thrust with a horn

corneja, kor-nay-Hah *s* crow; fetlock

corneta, kor-nay-tah *s* cornet; horn

cornijal, kor-ne-H ahl *s*

corner; angle

cornudo, kor-noo-do *a* horned

coro, ko-ro *s* choir; chorus

corona, ko-ro-nah *s* crown; coronet; tonsure; halo; regal power

coronar, ko-ro-nar *v* to crown; to complete

coronario, ko-ro-nah-re-o *a* coronary

coronel, ko-ro-nel *s* colonel

coronilla, ko-ro-nee-l´yah *s* small crown; top of the head

corpanchón, kor-pahn-chon *s* very big body or carcass (fowl)

corpiño, kor-pee-n´yo *s* waist; corset

corporal, kor-po-rahl *a* corporal; bodily

corpóreo, kor-por-ray-o *a* corporeal

corral, kor-rrahl *s* yard; pen; fold

correa, kor-rray-ah *s* leather strap; leash; leather belt

correcto*, kor-rrek-to *a* correct

corredera, kor-rray-day-rah *s* slide; cockroach

corredor, kor-rray-dor *s* runner; broker; corridor

corregidor, kor-rray-He-dor s corregidor (mayor of a town); corrector

corregir, kor-rray-Heer v to correct; to temper; to mitigate

correntío, kor-rren-tee-o a current; running

correo, kor-rray-o s post; postman; post office

correo electrónico, kor-rray-o ay-lek-tro-ne-ko s e-mail

correr, kor-rrair v to run; to flow; to expand; to be current; to flourish

correspondencia, kor-rres-pon-den-the-ah s correspondence

corresponder, kor-rress-pon-dair v to return a favor; to correspond; to regard

corresponsal, kor-rress-pon-sahl s correspondent; agent

corretaje, kor-rray-tah-Hay s brokerage

corretear, kor-rray-tay-ar v to run about

corrida, kor-rree-dah s bullfight; race

corrido, kor-rree-do a experienced; abashed

corriente, kor-rre-en-tay s current; flow; course; a running; ordinary; normal

corrillo, kor-rree-l´yo s small group

corrimiento, kor-rre-me-en-to s landslide; embarrassment

corro, kor-rro, (see corrillo)

corroborar, kor-rro-bo-rar v to strengthen

corroer, kor-rro-air v to corrode

corromper, kor-rrom-pair v to corrupt

corruptela, kor-rrop-tay-lah s corruption

corruptor, kor-rrop-tor s corrupter

corsario, kor-sah-re-o s privateer

corsé, kor-say s corset

corta, kor-tah s felling of wood; cutting

cortabolsas, kor-tah-bol-sahs s pickpocket

cortado, kor-tah-do a clipped; cut; sour; abrupt; shy

cortafrío, kor-tah-free-o s cold chisel

cortar, kor-tar v to cut; to curtail; to chop

corte, kor-tay s cutting edge; cut; s f. court; retinue; levee; yard

cortedad, kor-tay-dahd s shortness; dullness; timidity

cortejar, kor-tay-H ar v to court; to woo; to escort

cortejo, kor-tay-Ho s courtship; homage

cortés, kor-tess a courteous; polite

cortesanía, kor-tay-sah-nee-ah s courtesy

cortesano, kor-tay-sah-no a courtlike; courteous; s courtier

cortesía, kor-tay-see-ah s courtesy; compliment

corteza, kor-tay-thah s bark; rind; crust; rusticity

corto*, kor-to a short; small

cortocircuito, korr-to-theer-koo´ee-to s short-circuit

corvadura, kor-vah-doo-rah s curvature

corvo, kor-vo a bent; crooked

cosa, koh-sah s thing; substance; object

cosecha, ko-say-chah s harvest; crop

cosechar, ko-say-char v to reap; to gather; to harvest

coselete, ko-say-lay-tay s

corselet (armor)

coser, ko-**sair** v to sew

cosido, ko-**see**-do s sewing; needlework

cosquilloso, kos-ke-l´yo-so a ticklish

costa, **kos**-tah s cost; charge; coast

costado, kos-**tah**-do s side

costal, kos-**tahl** s sack

costanero, kos-tah-**nay**-ro a sloping

costar, kos-**tar** v to cost; to be difficult

coste, **kos**-tay s cost; expense

costear, kos-tay-**ar** v to pay the cost; to sail along the coast

costilla, kos-tee-l´yah s rib; cutlet

costo, **kos**-to s cost; price; charge

costoso*, kos-**to**-so a costly; difficult

costra, **kos**-trah s crust; scab

costumbre, kos-**toom**-bray s custom

costura, kos-**too**-rah s seam; needlework

costurera, kos-too-**ray**-rah s seamstress

costurero, kos-too-**ray**-ro s sewing basket

costur., kos-too-**ron** s

large scar

cota, **ko**-tah s coat of armor

cotejar, ko-tay-**H ar** v to compare; to confront

cotejo, ko-**tay**-Ho s comparison; collation

cotidiano, ko-te-de-**ah**-no a daily

cotilla, ko-tee-l´yah s busybody

cotización, ko-te-thah-the-**on** s quotation; current price

cotizar, ko-te-**thar** v to quote prices

coto, **ko**-to s enclosure; district; landmark

cotón, ko-**ton** s printed cotton

cotorra, ko-**tor**-rrah s parakeet; loquacious woman

covacha, ko-**vah**-chah s small cave

coyuntura, ko-yoon-**too**-rah s articulation; opportunity; moment

coz, koth s kick; drawback; recoil

cráneo, **krah**-nay-o s skull

crápula, **krah**-poo-lah s intoxication; debauchery

crasitud, krah-se-**tood** s body fat; stupidity

craso*, **krah**-so a fat; greasy; thick

creador, kray-ah-**dor** s the Creator; creator; originator

crear, kray-**ar** v to create; to establish

crecer, kray-**thair** v to grow; to increase

creces, kray-**thess** s increase; excess

crecida, kray-**thee**-dah s swelling of rivers

crecido, kray-**thee**-do a increased; large; grown

creciente, kray-the-**en**-tay s swell; leaven; crescent; flood tide; a growing

crecimiento, kray-the-me-**en**-to s increase; growth

crédito, **kray**-de-to s credit

credulidad, kray-doo-le-**dahd** s credulity

crédulo, **kray**-doo-lo a credulous

creedero, kray-ay-**day**-ro a credible

creedor, kray-ay-**dor**, (see **crédulo**)

creencia, kray-en-the-ah s belief; creed

creer, kray-**air** v to believe

creíble, kray-ee-blay a credible

crema, kray-mah s cream

cremallera, kray-mah-l´yay-rah s zipper

crematorio, kray-mah-**tor**-ree-o s crematorium

crepúsculo, kray-**pooss**-koo-lo s twilight

crespo, kress-po a crisp; curled

crespón, kress-**pon** s crepe

cresta, kress-tah s coxscomb; top; crest

creta, kray-tah s chalk

creyente, kray-**yen**-tay s believer

cría, kree-ah s brood of animals; breeding

criada, kre-**ah**-dah s maid

criadero, kre-ah-**day**-ro s nursery; breeding place

criado, kre-**ah**-do s servant

criador, kre-ah-**dor** s breeder; creator; a fecund

crianza, kre-**ahn**-thah s breeding; education

criar, kre-**ar** v to breed; to rear

criatura, kre-ah-**too**-rah s creature

criba, kree-bah s sieve

cribar, kre-**bar** v to sift

crimen, kree-men s crime

criminar, kre-me-**nar** v to incriminate

criminoso, kre-me-**no**-so a criminal

crín, kreen s mane; horsehair

cripta, kreep-tah s crypt

crisis, kree-sis s crisis

crisol, kre-**sol** s crucible

crispar, kriss-**par** v to convulse

crispatura, kriss-pah-**too**-rah s spasmodic contraction

cristal, kriss-**tahl** s crystal; mirror

Cristiandad, kriss-te-ahn-**dahd** s Christianity; Christendom

Cristo, kriss-to s Christ

criterio, kre-**tay**-re-o s criterion

crítica, kree-te-kah s criticism; critique; censure

criticar, kre-te-**kar** v to criticize; to find fault

crítico, kree-te-ko s critic

criticón, kre-te-**kon** s would-be critic

croar, kro-**ar** v to croak

crónico, cro-ne-ko a chronic

cronicón, kro-ne-**kon** s brief chronicle

cronómetro, kro-no-**may**-tro s chronometer

croqueta, kro-**kay**-tah s croquette; fritter

cruce, kroo-thay s crossroads

crucero, kroo-**thay**-ro s transept; crossbearer; cruise

cruceta, kroo-**thay**-tah s intersection

crucial, kroo-the-**ahl** a crucial

crucificar, kroo-the-fe-**kar** v to crucify

crucifijo, kroo-the-**fee**-Ho s crucifix

crudeza, kroo-**day**-thah s crudeness; rudeness

crudo*, kroo-do a raw; crude

cruel*, kroo´el a cruel

crueldad, kroo´el-**dahd** s cruelty

cruento, kroo´en-to a bloody; cruel

crujía, kroo-H ee-ah s passage; corridor

crujido, kroo-H ee-do s crack; creak; clash; crackling; rustle

crujir, kroo-H eer v to crackle; to rustle

cruz, krooth s cross

cruzado, kroo-**thah**-do s crusader; a crosswise; crossed

cruzar, kroo-**thar** v to cross; to cruise

cuaderno, koo´ah-**dair**-no

s notebook

cuadra, koo´ah-drah s stable; hall; block (of houses)

cuadrado, koo´ah-**drah**-do a square

cuadragésimo, koo´ah-drah-H **ay**-se-mo a fortieth

cuadrante, koo´ah-**drahn**-tay s quadrant; sundial; clock face

cuadrar, koo´ah-**drar** v to square; to fit; to adjust; to accomodate

cuadrilongo, koo´ah-dre-**lon**-go a oblong

cuadrilla, koo´ah-**dree**-l´yah s gang; crew; band

cuadro, koo´ah-**dro** s painting; picture; square; diagram

cuádruplo, koo´ah-**droo**-plo a quadruple

cuajar, koo´ah-H **ar** v to coagulate; to curdle

cual, koo´ahl adv as pron which

caulidad, koo´ah-le-**dahd** s quality

cualificado, koo´ah-le-fe-**kah**-do a qualified

cualquiera, koo´ahl-ke-ay-rah pron anyone; whoever

cuan, koo´ahn adv how; as

cuando, koo´ahn-do adv when; if; although; even

cuantía, koo´ahn-**tee**-ah s amount; quality

cuantioso, koo´ahn-te-o-so a numerous; copious; rich

cuanto, koo´ahn-to adv respecting; while; a how much; how many; as much as; the more; –antes, –ahn-tess, immediately; –más, –mahs, moreover

cuarenta, koo´ah-**ren**-tah s & a forty

cuarentena, koo´ah-ren-tay-nah s forty days, months or years; Lent; quarantine

cuaresma, koo´ah-**ress**-mah s Lent

cuarta, koo´ar-tah s fourth; quarter

cuartear, koo´ar-tay-ar v to divide into four parts

cuartel, koo´ar-**tel** s quarter; district; ward; barracks

cuarterón, koo´ar-tay-ron s quarter of a pound

cuarteto, koo´ar-tay-to s quartet

cuartilla, koo´ar-tee-l´yah s fourth part; sheet of paper

cuarto, koo´ar-to s fourth; quarter; room; apartment

cuartos, koo´ar-tos s cash; money

cuatro, koo´ah-tro, s & a four

cuba, koo-bah s cask; tub; (fam) drunkard

cubeta, koo-bay-tah s small cask

cúbico, koo-be-ko a cubic; cubical

cubierto, koo-be-air-to s place setting (table); shelter; dinner course; cutlery

cubilete, koo-be-lay-tay s basin; bowl; goblet

cubo, koo-bo s cube; pail

cubrir, koo-breer v to cover; to screen

cucaracha, koo-kah-rah-chah s cockroach

cuclillas, koo-clee-l´yahs adv en -, en -, in a cowering manner

cuclillo, koo-klee-l´yo s cuckoo

cuco, koo-ko s cuckoo a dainty; cunning; crafty

cuchara, koo-chah-rah s spoon

cucharón, koo-chah-ron s large spoon; ladle

cuchichear, koo-che-chay-**ar** v to whisper

cuchilla, koo-**chee**-l'yah s large kitchen knife

cuchillero, koo-che-l'**yay**-ro s knifemaker

cuchillo, koo-**chee**-l'yo s knife

cuchitril, koo-che-**treel** s very small room; den

cuchufleta, koo-choo-**flay**-tah s joke; jest; fun

cuelga, koo´**el**-gah s cluster of dried fruit

cuello, koo´ay-l'yo s neck; collar (of clothing)

cuenca, koo´**en**-kah s wooden bowl; river basin

cuenta, koo´**en**-tah s reckoning; account; bill; reason; report

cuentista, koo´**en**-tiss-tah s storyteller; gossiper

cuento, koo´**en**-to s relation; tale; fairy tale; fable

cuerda, koo´air-dah s cord; rope; string; chain

cuerdo, koo´**air**-do a prudent; discreet; wise

cuerna, koo´**air**-nah s drinking horn

cuerno, koo´air-no s horn; feeler

cuero, koo´**ay**-ro s pelt; hide; leather

cuerpo, koo´air-po s body; the trunk

cuervo, koo´**air**-vo s raven; crow

cuesco, koo´ess-ko s stone

cuesta, koo´ess-tah s hill; slope

cuestión, koo´ess-te-**on** s question; dispute; problem

cuestionar, koo´ess-te-o-**nar** v to question; to dispute

cueva, koo´ay-vah s cave; cellar

cuévano, koo´**ay**-vah-no s basket; hamper

cuidado, koo´e-**dah**-do s care; custody; anxiety

cuidadoso, koo´e-dah-**do**-so a careful; mindful

cuidar, koo´e-**dar** v to heed; to care

cuita, koo´**ee**-tah s grief; affliction

cuitado, koo´e-**tah**-do a anxious; wretched; timid

culata, koo-lah-tah s butt of a gun; rear end

culebra, koo-lay-brah s snake

culebrear, koo-lay-bray-**ar** v to move along like a snake

culminar, kool-me-**nar** v

to culminate

culo, koo-lo s rump; bottom; socket

culpa, kool-pah s fault; sin; guilt

culpable, kool-**pah**-blay a guilty

culpado, kool-**pah**-do a accused

culpar, kool-**par** v to impeach; to reproach; to accuse

cultivar, kool-te-**var** v to cultivate

culto, kool-to s worship; religion; cult; a* elegant; affected; polished

cultura, kool-**too**-rah s culture

cumbre, **koom**-bray s top; summit

cumpleaños, koom-play-ah-n´yos s birthday

cumplido, koom-**plee**-do s compliment; a* large; plentiful

cumplimiento, koom-ple-me-**en**-to s fulfillment; completion

cumplir, koom-**pleer** v to discharge; to perform; to fulfill

cúmulo, **koo**-moo-lo s heap; pile

cuna, koo-nah s cradle;

source; origin

cundir, koon-**deer** v to spread (liquids or news)

cunear, koo-nay-**ar** v to rock a cradle

cuneta, koo-**nay**-tah s gutter

cuña, koo-n´yah s wedge; useful person

cuñada, koo-n´**yah**-dah s sister-in-law

cuñado, koo-n´**yah**-do s brother-in-law

cuño, koo-n´yo s die; stamp

cuota, koo´o-tah s quota; share

cupón, koo-**pon** s coupon

cúpula, koo-poo-lah s cupola; dome; vault

cura, koo-rah s parish priest; care; treatment

curación, koo-rah-the-**on** s cure; healing

curador, koo-rah-**dor** s curator

curar, koo-**rar** v to cure; to preserve; to heal

curia, koo-re-ah s ecclesiastical court

curiosear, koo-re-o-say-**ar** v to pry into others affairs

curiosidad, koo-re-o-se-**dahd** s curiosity; neatness; rarity

cursado, koor-**sah**-do a skilled; accustomed

cursar, koor-**sar** v to frequent a place; to do a thing frequently; to study

curso, koor-so s course; series; route

curtido, koor-**tee**-do a expert; weather-beaten; tanned

curtidos, koor-**tee**-dos s tanned leather

curtir, koor-**teer** v to tan; to harden

curva, koor-vah s curve; bend

curvo, koor-vo a curved; crooked

cúspide, kooss-pe-**day** s summit; apex; top

custodia, kooss-**to**-de-ah s custody; guardianship; guard

custodio, kooss-**to**-de-o s custodian

cutis, koo-tiss s skin

cuyo, cuya, koo-yo, koo-yah pron poss of which; of whom; whose

chabacanería, chah-bah-kah-nay-**ree**-ah s vulgarity; coarseness

chabacano, chah-bah-**kah**-no a coarse; vulgar

chacota, cha-ko-tah s

banter

chacotear, chah-ko-tay-**ar** v to joke

cháchara, chah-chah-rah s chatter; chit-chat

chafallar, cha-fah-l´**yar** v to botch

chafallón, chah-fah-l´**yon** s shoddy workman

chaflán, chah-**flahn** s bevel

chal, chahl s shawl

chalán, chah-**lahn** s hawker; horse-dealer

chalanear, chah-lah-nay-**ar** v to break horses; to deal in horses

chalanería, chah-lah-nay-**ree**-ah s tricks

chaleco, chah-**lay**-ko s vest

chalina, chah-lee-nah s necktie; scarf

chalote, chah-lo-tay s shallot

chalupa, chah-**loo**-pah s sloop

chamarillero, chah-mah-re-l´**yay**-ro s dealer in secondhand furniture

chambelán, chahm-bay-**lan** s chamberlain

chambón, cham-**bon** a awkward

chamorro, chah-**mor**-rro a shorn

chamuscar, chah-moos-**kar** v to singe; to scorch

chanciller, chahn-the-l´**yair** s chancellor

chancla, chahn-klah s old shoe

chancleta, chahn-**klay**-tah s slipper

chanclo, chahn-klo s galosh

chanflón, chahn-**flon** a awkward; clumsy

chanza, chahn-thah s joke; jest; fun

chapa, chah-pah s thin metal sheet

chaparrón, chah-par-**rron** s violent rain shower

chapear, cha-pay-**ar** v to cover with metal sheets

chápiro, chah-pe-ro, word used only in: **ivoto al chápiro! ipor vida del chápiro!** good gracious!

chapitel, chah-pe-**tel** s capital of a pillar; spire

chapodar, chah-po-**dar** v to prune; to trim

chapón, chah-**pon** s ink blot

chapotear, chah-po-tay-ar v to wet with a sponge; to dabble

chapucear, chah-poo-thay-**ar** v to botch; to bungle

chapucero, chah-poo-thay-ro s careless worker a clumsy; bungling

chapurrar, chah-poor-**rrar** v to talk gibberish

chapuz, chah-**pooth** s ducking

chapuzar, chah-poo-**thar** v to duck; to dive

chaqueta, chah-**kay**-tah s jacket

charanga, chah-**rahn**-gah s fanfare

charca, charco, char-kah, char-ko s pool; puddle

charla, char-lah s chat; talk

charlar, char-**lar** v to chatter; to chat; to talk

charlatán, char-lah-**tahn** s charlatan; quack

charolar, chah-ro-**lar** v to varnish

charrada, char-**rrah**-dah s coarse speech or action

charretera, char-rray-**tay**-rah s epaulet

charro, char-rro a tawdry; gaudy

chasco, chahs-ko s fun; jest; trick

chasquear, chahs-kay-**ar** v to crack with a whip; to fool

chato, chah-to a flat; flat-nosed

chico, chee-ko s little boy; a little; small

chicolear, che-ko-lay-**ar** v to pay compliments (to a woman)

chicote, che-ko-tay s fine boy

chicuelo, che-koo´**ay**-lo s youngster

chichón, che-**chon** s bump on the head

chifla, chee-**flah** s whistle; paring knife

chiflar, che-**flar** v to whistle; to become insane

chillar, che-l´**yar** v to scream; to shriek

chillido, c´he-l´**yee**-do s shriek; scream

chillón, che-l´**yon** a shrill; showy

chimenea, che-may-**nay**-ah s chimney

chimpancé, chim-pahn-**thay** s chimpanzee

china, chee-nah s pebble; porcelain

chinche, cheen-chay s bug

chincheta, cheen-**chay**-ta s thumbtack

chinchoso, chin-**cho**-so a tiresome

chinela, che-**nay**-lah s slipper

chinero, che-**nay**-ro s

china cabinet

chiquirritín, che-keer-rre-teen s tiny baby; tot

chirigota, che-re-go-tah s jest; joke

chiripa, che-ree-pah s fluke (billiards); lucky hit

chirivía, che-re-vee-ah s parsnip

chirle, cheer-lay a (fam.) insipid; tasteless

chirlo, cheer-lo s large scar on the face

chirriar, cheer-rre-ar v to hiss; to creak; to chirp

chirrido, cheer-rree-do s chirping; chattering; shrill sound

chirrión, cheer-rre-on s leather whip

¡chis! chiss *interj* hush!

chisme, chiss-may s gadget; thing; piece of gossip; tale

chismear, chiss-may-ar v to tattle; to tell tales; to gossip

chispa, chiss-pah s spark; very small diamond; acumen

chisporrotear, chiss-por-rro-tay-ar v to throw off sparks; to hiss

chistar, chiss-tar v to mutter; to mumble

chiste, chiss-tay s witticism; joke

chistoso, chiss-to-so a gay; facetious; amusing

chiticalla, che-te-kah-l'yah s discreet person

¡chiton! chee-to, che-ton *interj* hush!

chivo, chee-vo s kid (goat)

chocar, cho-kar v to collide; to clash; to fight

chocarrería, cho-kar-rray-ree-ah s dirty joke

chocolate, cho-co-lah-tay s chocolate

chochear, cho-chay-ar v to be senile; to grow feeble

choque, cho-kay s shock; collison; skirmish; dispute

choricería, cho-re-thay-ree-ah s sausage store

chorrera, chor-rray-rah s spout; shirt frill

chorro, chor-rro s jet; spurt; **a chorros,** ah chor-rros abundantly

choza, cho-thah s hut; hovel; shanty

chubasco, choo-bahs-ko s squall; shower

chuchería, choo-chay-ree-ah s bauble; trinket; knick-knack; sweet

chufar, choo-far v to mock

chufletear, choo-flay-tay-ar v to sneer; to taunt

chulada, choo-lah-dah s droll speech or action; breach of manners

chulear, choo-lay-ar v to sneer; to boast

chulería, choo-lay-ree-ah s pleasing manner; flashiness

chuleta, choo-lay-tah s chop; cutlet

chulo, choo-lo s lighthearted; flashy; insolent

chunga, choon-gah s jest; joke

chunguearse, choon-gay-ar-say v to make fun of

chupa, choo-pah s vest

chupar, choo-par v to suck; to sponge upon; to fool

chupón, choo-pon s parasite

churro, choor-rro s fritter; a coarse (wool)

chuscada, choos-kah-dah s joke; witticism

chusco, choos-ko a pleasant; droll

chusma, choos-mah s rabble; mob

chuzo, choo-tho s pike;

llover a chuzos, l´yo-
vair ah **choo**-thos, to
rain heavily

dable, dah-blay *a* practical; feasible

dactilógrafo, dahk-te-lo-grah-fo *s* typist; typewriter

dádiva, dah-de-vah *s* gift

dadivoso, dah-de-vo-so *a* genérous

dado, dah-do *s* dice; die; *a* given, **-que,** - kay, provided; assuming that

dador, dah-dor *s* giver; bearer of a letter

daga, dah-gah *s* dagger

¡dale! dah! -lay *interj* expressing displeasure at obstinacy

dama, dah-mah *s* lady; queen (checkers)

damasco, dah-**mahs**-ko *s* damask; damson (plum)

damería, dah-may-ree-ah *s* prudishness

damisela, dah-me-**say**-lah *s* young lady

damnificar, dahm-ne-fe-**kar** *v* to hurt; to damage

danzar, dahn-**thar** *v* to dance

dañar, dah-n'**yar** *v* to hurt; to damage

daño, dah-n´yo *s* damage; harm; prejudice; loss

dañoso*, dah-n'yo-so *a* hurtful; injurious

dar, dar *v* to give; to bestow; to supply; to impart; to yield; **–a, –ah,** to be situated; **–con, –kon,** to find; **–de, –day,** to fall down; **–en, –en,** to fall into; to find; **–que, –kay,** to cause

dársena, dar-say-nah *s* dock; basin

data, dah-tah *s* date; item

datar, dah-**tar** *v* to date

dátil, dah-til *s* date (fruit)

dato, dah-to *s* datum

de, day *prep* of; from; for; by

deán, day-**ahn** *s* dean

debajo, day-bah-**Ho** *adv* under; beneath; **-de,-**day *prep* under

debate, day-bah-tay *s* debate

debatir, day-bah-**teer** *v* to debate

debe, day-bay *s* debtor side of an account; debit

deber, day-**bair** *v* to owe; to be obliged to; *s* duty; obligation; debt

debido*, day-bee-do *a* due; proper

débil, day-bil *a* feeble; weak; frail; pusillanimous

debilidad, day-be-le-**dahd** *s* debility; weakness

debilitar, day-be-le-**tar** *v* to debilitate; to weaken

débito, day-be-to *s* debt; duty

década, day-kah-dah *s* decade

decadencia, day-kah-**den**-the-ah *s* decay; decline

decaer, day-kah-**air** *v* to

decline; to decay; to fade

decano, day-**kah**-no s senior; dean

decantación, day-kahn-tah-the-**on** s decanting

decantar, day-kahn-**tar** v to exaggerate; to decant

decapitar, day-kah-pe-**tar** v to behead

decenal, day-thay-**nahl** a decennial

decencia, day-**then**-the-ah s decency; modesty

decenio, day-**thay**-ne-o s decade; ten-year period

deceno, day-**thay**-no a tenth

decente, day-**then**-tay a decent; honest; decorous

decidido*, day-the-**dee**-do a determined; resolute

decidir, day-the-**deer** v to decide

decidor, day-the-**dor** s fluent speaker

décimo, **day**-the-mo a tenth

decir, day-**theer** v to say; to tell; to speak; to state; to name; to denote

decisión, day-the-se-**on** s decision; judgment; verdict

decisivo, day-the-**se**-vo a

decisive

declamar, day-klah-**mar** v to declaim; to recite

declarar, day-klah-**rar** v to declare; to expound

declinar, day-kle-**nar** v to decline; to decay; to sink

declive, day-**klee**-vay s declivity; slope

decorar, day-ko-**rar** v to decorate

decoro, day-**ko**-ro s honor; circumspection; integrity; decorum

decoroso, day-ko-**ro**-so a decorous; decent

decrecer, day-kray-**thair** v to decrease

decrépito, day-**kray**-pe-to a decrepit

decretar, day-kray-**tar** v to decree; to resolve

decreto, day-**kray**-to s decree; decision

décuplo, **day**-koo-plo a tenfold

decurso, day-**koor**-so s course; lapse (of time)

dechado, day-**chah**-do s sample; pattern; model

dedal, day-**dahl** s thimble

dedicar, day-de-**kar** v to dedicate

dedicatoria, day-de-kah-to-re-ah s dedication

dedillo, day-dee-**l´yo** s little finger

dedo, **day**-do s finger; toe

deducir, day-doo-**theer** v to deduce; to infer; to deduct

defecto, day-**fek**-to s defect; fault

defectuoso*, day-fek-too-**o**-so a defective

defender, day-fen-**dair** v to defend; to protect

defendible, day-fen-**dee**-blay a defensible

defensa, day-**fen**-sah s defense; vindication

defensor, day-fen-**sor** s defender; supporter

deferente, day-fay-**ren**-tay a deferential; deferring

deferir, day-fay-**reer** v to defer; to submit; to yield

deficiente, day-fe-the-**en**-tay a deficient; defective

definible, day-fe-nee-**blay** a definable

definir, day-fe-**neer** v to define; to determine

deformar, day-for-**mar** v to deform

deforme, day-**for**-may a disfigured; ugly

defraudación, day-frah´oo-dah-the-**on** s fraud; deceit

defraudar, day-frah´oo-

dar v to defraud; to cheat

defunción, day-foon-the-on s decease

degeneración, day-Hay-nay-rah-the-on s degeneracy

degenerar, day-Hay-nay-rar v to degenerate

degollar, day-go-l´yar v to behead; to ruin; to annihilate

degradar, day-grah-dar v to degrade

dehesa, day-ay-sah s pasture

deidad, day-e-dahd s deity; divinity

dejación, day-Hah-the-on s abandonment; relinquishment

dejadez, day-Hah-deth s slovenliness; neglect

dejado, day-Hah-do a indolent; dejected

dejar, day-Har v to leave; to omit; to forsake; to yield; to allow

delación, day-lah-the-on s denunciation

delantal, day-lahn-tahl s apron

delante, day-lahn-tay adv before; prep in front of; facing

delantera, day-lahn-tay-rah s front; forefront; advantage

delantero, day-lahn-tay-ro s leader; a foremost

delatar, day-lah-tar v to denounce

delator, day-lah-tor s informer; denouncer

delegado, day-lay-gah-do s & a delegate; deputy

delegar, day-lay-gar v to delegate

deleitable, day-lay´e-tah-blay a delectable

deleite, day-lay´e-tay s delight

deletéreo, day-lay-tay-ray-o a deleterious

deletrear, day-lay-tray-ar v to spell

deleznable, day-leth-nah-blay a brittle; fragile; frail; perishable

delfín, del-feen s dolphin

delgadez, del-gah-deth s thinness; slenderness

delgado, del-gah-do a thin; slim

deliberación, day-le-bay-rah-the-on s deliberation; reflection

deliberar, day-le-bay-rar v to deliberate; to discuss

delicadez, day-le-kah-deth s delicacy; weakness

delicadeza, day-le-kah-day-thah s delicateness; fineness; subtlety

delicado*, day-le-kah-do a delicate; weak; exquisite; thin

delicia, day-lee-the-ah s delight

delicioso*, day-le-the-o-so a delicious

delincuente, day-lin-koo´en-tay a delinquent; offender

delinear, day-le-nay-ar v to sketch

delinquir, day-lin-keer v to break the law

deliquio, day-lee-ke´o s faint; ecstasy

delirar, day-le-rar v to rave; to talk wildly

delirio, day-lee-re-o s delirium

delito, day-lee-to s transgression; delinquency; crime; offense

delusorio*, day-loo-so-re-o a deceitful

demacrado, day-mah-krah-do a emaciated; wasted away

demanda, day-mahn-dah s demand; claim; request

demandador, day-mahn-dah-dor s plaintiff (law)

demandar, day-mahn-dar

v to demand

demarcar, day-mar-**kar** *v* to demarcate

demás, day-**mahs** *adv* besides; moreover; **lo, la, los, las–,** lo, lah, los, lahs–, the rest

demasía, day-mah-**see**-ah *s* excess; surplus

demasiado, day-mah-se-ah-do *adv* excessively; *a* excessive

demencia, day-**men**-the-ah *s* dementia; insanity

dementar, day-men-**tar** *v* to drive mad

demente, day-**men**-tay *a* demented; mad; insane

demérito, day-**may**-re-to *s* demerit

democracia, day-mo-**krah**-the-ah *s* democracy

demócrata, day-**mo**-krah-tah *s* democrat

democrático, day-mo-**krah**-te-ko *a* democratic

demoler, day-mo-**lair** *v* to demolish

demonio, day-**mo**-ne-o *s* demon

demora, day-**mo**-rah *s* delay

demorar, day-mo-**rar** *v* to delay; to remain; to tarry

demostrar, day-mos-**trar** *v* to demonstrate; to prove

denegar, day-nay-**gar** *v* to deny

dengue, den-**gay** *s* affectedness; affection; short veil; dengue

denigración, day-ne-grah-the-**on** *s* denigration; defamation

denigrar, day-ne-**grar** *v* to revile; to defame

denodado, day-no-**dah**-do *a* intrepid; daring

denominar, day-no-me-**nar** *v* to designate; to name

denotar, day-no-**tar** *v* to denote; to signify

densidad, den-se-**dahd** *s* density

denso, den-so *a* dense; thick; compact

dentado, den-**tah**-do *a* indented; serrated

dentadura, den-tah-**doo**-rah *s* denture

dentellear, den-tel-l'yay-**ar** *v* to bite

dentista, den-**tiss**-tah *s* dentist

dentro, den-tro *adv* inside; within

denuedo, day-noo´**ay**-do *s* boldness; intrepidity

denuesto, day-noo´**ess**-to *s* affront; insult

denunciador, day-noon-the´ah-**dorr** *s* informant; accuser

denunciar, day-noon-the-**ar** *v* to denounce; to betray; to accuse

deparar, day-pah-**rar** *v* to offer; to furnish

departamento, day-par-tah-**men**-to *s* department

departir, day-par-**teer** *v* to converse

dependencia, day-pen-**den**-the-ah *s* dependence; business; staff

depender, day-pen-**dair** *v* to depend

dependiente, day-pen-de-en-tay *s* dependent; employee

deplorar, day-plo-**rar** *v* to deplore

deponer, day-po-**nair** *v* to depose; to attest

deportar, day-por-**tar** *v* to banish; to exile; to deport

deporte, day-**por**-tay *s* amusement; diversion; sport

deposición, day-po-se-the-**on** *s* deposition; declaration; degradation

depositador, day-po-se-tah-**dor** s depositor

depositar, day-po-se-**tar** v to deposit

depositario, day-po-se-tah-re-o s depositary; trustee; receiver

depósito, day-**po**-se-to s deposit; warehouse; sediment

depravar, day-prah-**var** v to harm

deprecación, day-pray-kah-the-**on** s petition; prayer

deprecar, day-pray-**kar** v to implore; to pray

depreciar, day-pray-the-**ar** v to depreciate; to undervalue

depredar, day-pray-**dar** v to rob; to pillage

deprimir, day-pre-**meer** v to depress; to humble

depurar, day-poo-**rar** v to purify; to cleanse

derecha, day-**ray**-chah s right hand; right side

derecho, day-**ray**-cho s right; justice; law; tax; duty; a right; straight

derechura, day-ray-**choo**-rah s right way; straightness

derivar, day-re-**var** v to derive; to deflect

derogatorio, day-ro-gah-**tor**-re-o a derogatory

derogar, day-ro-**gar** v to derogate; to annul; to reform

derramamiento, dair-rrah-mah-me-**en**-to s overflow; shedding; effusion; scattering

derramar, dair-rrah-**mar** v to pour; to spill; to spread; to waste

derrame, dair-**rrah**-may s leakage; overflow

derredor, dair-rray-**dor** s circumference; en–, en–, about

derrengado, dair-rren-**gah**-do a crooked; sprained

derrengar, dair-rren-**gar** v to sprain; to wrench

derretir, dair-rray-**teer** v to dissolve; to consume; to melt; to fuse

derribar, dair-rre-**bar** v to demolish; to ruin; to throw down

derribo, dair-**rree**-bo s demolition

derrocar, dair-rro-**kar** v to pull down

derrochar, dair-roo-**char** v to waste; to squander

derrota, dair-**rro**-tah s ship's course; road; defeat of an army

derrotar, dair-rro-**tar** v to destroy; to rout; to defeat

derruir, dair-rroo´**eer** v to demolish

derrumbar, dair-rroom-**bar** v to collapse; to knock down; to hurl down

desabonarse, day-sah-bo-**nar**-say v to cancel a subscription

desabotonar, day-sah-bo-to-**nar** v to unbutton; to blossom

desabrido, day-sah-**bree**-do a tasteless; peevish

desabrigar, day-sah-bre-**gar** v to uncover

desabrigo, day-sah-**bree**-go s nudity; destitution

desabrir, day-sah-**breer** v to make insipid; to harass

desabrochar, day-sah-bro-**char** v to unclasp; to unfasten

desacalorarse, dess-ah-kah-lo-**rar**-say v to cool off; to calm down

desacato, day-sah-**kah**-to s disrespect

desacertar, day-sah-thair-**tar** v to commit a mistake; to err

desacierto, day-sah-the-**air**-to *s* mistake; blunder

desacomodado, day-sah-ko-mo-**dah**-do *a* destitute; unemployed

desacomodar, day-sah-ko-mo-**dar** *v* to inconvenience; to dismiss

desaconsejar, day-sah-kon-say-**Har** *v* to dissuade

desacordar, day-sah-kor-**dar** *v* to get out of tune

desacorde, day-sah-**kor**-day *a* discordant

desacostumbrado, day-sah-kos-toom-**brah**-do *a* unusual; unaccustomed

desacreditar, day-sah-kray-de-**tar** *v* to discredit

desacuerdo, day-sah-koo´**air**-do *s* disagreement; mistake

desafecto, day-sah-**fek**-to *s* ill-will; *a* disaffected

desafiar, day-sah-fe-**ar** *v* to challenge

desafición, day-sah-fe-the-on *s* dislike

desafío, day-sah-**fee**-o *s* challenge; contest

desaforado, day-sah-fo-**rah**-do *a* lawless; huge

desafortunado, day-sah-for-too-**nah**-do *a* unfortunate; unlucky

desafuero, day-sah-foo´**ay**-ro *s* act of injustice; outrage

desagradable, day-sah-grah-**dah**-blay *a* disagreeable; unpleasant

desagradar, day-sah-grah-**dar** *v* to displease

desagradecer, day-sah-grah-day-**thair** *v* to be ungrateful

desagrado, day-sah-**grah**-do *s* displeasure

desagraviar, day-sah-grah-ve-**ar** *v* to make amends

desaguadero, day-sah-goo´**ah**-day-ro *s* drain

desaguar, day-sah-goo´**ar** *v* to drain

desahogado, day-sah-o-**gah**-do *a* impudent; unencumbered; well-to-do; roomy; large

desahogar, day-sah-o-**gar** *v* to ease pain; to recover

desahogo, day-sah-o-go *s* alleviation; easing; release

desahuciar, day-sah-oo-the-**ar** *v* to evict; to deprive of hope

desairado, day-sah´e-**rah**-do *a* disregarded; slighted; rejected

desairar, day-sah´e-**rar** *v* to disregard; to rebuff

desaire, day-**sah**´e-ray *s* rebuff; disdain

desalentar, day sah-len-**tar** *v* to discourage

desaliento, day-sah-le-**en**-to *s* dismay; dejection

desaliño, day-sah-**lee**-n´yo *s* slovenliness; dirtiness

desalmado, day-sahl-**mah**-do *a* heartless; inhuman; cruel

desalojar, day-sah-lo-**Har** *v* to dislodge; to move

desalterar, day-sahl-tay-**rar** *v* to allay; to calm

desamoldar, day-sah-mol-**dar** *v* to disfigure

desamparar, day-sahm-pah-**rar** *v* to forsake; to abandon

desamueblar, day-sah-moo´ay-**blar** *v* to strip of furniture

desandrajado, day-sahn-drah-**Ha**-do *a* ragged

desangrar, day-sahn-**grar** *v* to bleed profusely

desanimar, day-sah-ne-**mar** *v* to dishearten; to discourage

desánimo, day-**sah**-ne-mo *s* discouragement

desanudar, day-sah-noo-**dar** *v* to untie; to disentangle

desapacible, day-sah-pah-**thee**-blay *a* disagreeable

desaparecer, day-sah-pah-ray-**thair** *v* to disappear

desapego, day-sah-**pay**-go *s* alienation of affection

desapercibido, day-sah-pair-the-**bee**-do *a* unnoticed

desapiadado, day-sah-pe-ah-**dah**-do *a* merciless

desapoderado, day-sah-po-day-**rah**-do *a* impetuous

desapreciar, day-sah-pray-the-**ar** *v* to depreciate

desaprender, day-sah-pren-**dair** *v* to unlearn

desapretar, day-sah-pray-**tar** *v* to slacken; to loosen

desaprisionar, day-sah-pre-se-o-**nar** *v* to set free

desaprobar, day-sah-pro-**bar** *v* to disapprove

desaprovechar, day-sah-pro-vay-**char** *v* to not use; to waste

desarmar, day-sar-**mar** *v* to disarm

desarraigar, day-sar-rrah´e-**gar** *v* to root out; to eradicate

desarrapado, day-sar-rrah-**pah**-do *a* ragged

desarreglo, day-sar-**rray**-glo *s* disorder; confusion

desarrimar, day-sar-rre-**mar** *v* to remove

desarrollar, day-sar-rro-l´**yar** *v* to develop; to promote; to expand

desaseado, day-sah-say-ah-do *a* slovenly; untidy

desaseo, day-sah-**say**-o *s* slovenliness; untidiness

desasir, day-sah-**seer** *v* to loosen

desasosiego, day-sah-so-se-**ay**-go *s* restlessness

desastrado, day-sahs-**trah**-doo *a* ragged; slovenly

desatar, day-sah-**tar** *v* to untie; to undo; to unfasten; to loose

desatavío, day-sah-tah-vee-o *s* disarray; untidiness

desatención, day-sah-ten-the-**on** *s* inattention; incivility

desatender, day-sah-ten-**dair** *v* to disregard

desatentar, day-sah-ten-**tar** *v* to confuse

desatento, day-sah-ten-to *a* inattentive; discourteous

desatinado, day-sah-te-**nah**-do *a* extravagant; foolish; wild

desatino, day-sah-**tee**-no *s*

extravagance; nonsense; folly

desatracar, day-sah-trah-**kar** *v* to sheer off

desatrancar, day-sah-trahn-**kar** *v* to unbar; to clear; to unblock

desautorizado, day-sah´oo-to-re-**thah**-do *a* unauthorized

desautorizar, day-sah´oo-to-re-**thar** *v* to repudiate; to disown

desavenencia, day-sah-vay-**nen**-the-ah *s* discord

desaventajado, day-sah-ven-tah-**Hah**-do *a* unprofitable; inferior

desayunarse, day-sah-yoo-nar-say *v* to breakfast

desayuno, day-sah-**yoo**-no *s* breakfast

desazón, day-sah-**thon** *s* insipidity; disgust; restlessness

desbandarse, dess-bahn-dar-say *v* to disband

desbarajuste, dess-bah-rah-**Hooss**-tay *s* disorder; confusion

desbaratar, dess-bah-rah-**tar** *v* to destroy; to smash

desbarrar, dess-bar-**rrar** *v* to slip; to talk nonsense

desbastar, dess-bahs-tar *v* to smooth; to waste

desbocado, dess-bo-kah-do *a* bolting (horse)

desbordar, dess-bor-dar *v* to overflow

desbravar, dess-brah-var *v* to tame; to break in (horse); to abate

desbroce, dess-bro-thay *s* clearing

descabellado, dess-kah-bay-l'yah-do *a* disheveled; preposterous; absurd

descabezar, dess-kah-bay-thar *v* to behead

descaecer, dess-kah-ay-thair *v* to decline

descafeinado, dess-kah-fay-ee-nah-do *a* decaffeinated

descalabro, dess-kah-lah-bro *s* misfortune; considerable loss

descalificar, dess-kah-le-fe-kar *v* to disqualify

descalzar, dess-kahl-thar *v* to take off shoes and socks

descaminar, dess-kah-me-nar *v* to lead astray; to misguide

descampado, dess-kahm-pah-do *a* open space; empty ground

descansar, dess-kahn-sar *v* to rest; to pause

descanso, dess-kahn-so *s* rest; repose

descarado, dess-kah-rah-do *a* impudent

descararse, dess-kah-rar-say *v* to behave insolently

descarbonizar, dess-kahr-bo-ne-thar *v* to decarbonize

descarga, dess-kar-gah *s* unloading

descargadero, dess-kar-gah-day-ro *s* wharf

descargar, dess-kar-gar *v* to unload; to discharge

descargo, dess-kar-go *s* unloading; acquittal

descaro, dess-kah-ro *s* shamelessness

descarriar, dess-kar-rre-ar *v* to misguide; to mislead

descarrío, dess-kar-rree-o *s* losing one's way

descartar, dess-kar-tar *v* to discard; to dismiss

descasar, dess-kah-sar *v* to divorce

descascarar, dess-kahs-kah-rar *v* to shell; to peel

descastado, dess-kahs-tah-do *a* unaffectionate

descender, dess-then-dair *v* to descend; to get down

descenso, dess-then-so *s* descent

descifrar, dess-the-frar *v* to decipher; to figure out

desclavar, dess-klah-var *v* to unnail

descocarse, dess-ko-kar-say *v* to be impudent

descoco, dess-ko-ko *s* impudence

descoger, dess-ko-Hair *v* to unfold; to expand

descolgar, dess-kol-gar *v* to take down

descollar, dess-ko-l'yar *v* to surpass; to stand out

descombrar, dess-kom-brar *v* to extricate

descomedido, dess-ko-may-dee-do *a* insolent; excessive; rude

descompasado, dess-kom-pah-sah-do *a* disproportionate

descomponer, dess-kom-po-nair *v* to discompose; to decompose; to disturb; to upset

descompuesto, dess-kom-poo´ess-to *a* out of order; insolent

descomunal, dess-ko-moo-nahl *a* uncommon;

huge; colossal

desconcertar, dess-kon-thair-**tar** v to disturb; to baffle

desconfiar, dess-kon-fe-**ar** v to distrust

desconocer, dess-ko-no-**thair** v to disregard; to ignore; to disown

desconocido, dess-ko-no-**thee**-do a unknown

desconsiderado, dess-kon-se-day-**rah**-do a inconsiderate

desconsolado, dess-kon-so-**lah**-do a disconsolate; dejected

desconsuelo, dess-kon-soo-**ay**-lo s affliction

descontar, dess-kon-**tar** v to discount; to take for granted

descontento, dess-kon-**ten**-to s discontent

desconvenir, dess-kon-vay-**neer** v to disagree

descorazonar, dess-ko-rah-tho-**nar** v to dishearten

descorrer, dess-kor-**rrair** v to draw (a curtain)

descortés, dess-kor-**tess** a impolite; discouteous

descortesía, dess-kor-tay-see-ah s incivility

descoser, dess-ko-**sair** v to unstitch; to rip

descosido, dess-ko-see-do s tear; rip; idle talker

descoyuntar, dess-ko-yoon-**tar** v to dislocate; to annoy

descrédito, dess-**kray**-de-to s discredit

descreer, dess-kray-**air** v to disbelieve; to discredit

describir, dess-kre-**beer** v to describe

descripción, dess-krip-the-**on** s description

descuartizar, dess-koo´ar-te-**thar** v to quarter; to carve

descubierto, dess-koo-be-**air**-to a bareheaded; uncovered; discovered

descubrir, dess-koo-**breer** v to discover

descuento, dess-koo´**en**-to s discount

descuidar, dess-koo´e-**dar** v to neglect

descuido, dess-koo´ee-do s carelessness; negligence

desde, dess-day prep from; since

desdén, des-**den** s disdain; contempt

desdentado, dess-den-**tah**-do a toothless

desdeñar, dess-day-n´**yar** v to disdain

desdeñoso, dess-day-n´**yo**-so a disdainful

desdicha, dess-dee-chah s misfortune

desdoblar, dess-do-**blar** v to unfold

deseable, day-say-**ah**-blay a desirable

desear, day-say-**ar** v to desire; to wish

desecar, day-say-**kar** v to dry; to desiccate

desechable, day-say-cha-blay a disposable

desechar, day-say-**char** v to depreciate; to reject; to cast off

desecho, day-**say**-cho s residue; refuse; disregard

desembalar, day-sem-bah-**lar** v to unpack

desembarazar, day-sem-bah-rah-**thar** v to clear; to free; to ease

desembarcar, day-sem-bar-**kar** v to land; to disembark

desembarco, day-sem-**bar**-ko s landing

desembolsar, day-sem-bol-**sar** v to disburse

desembragar, dess-em-brah-**garr** v to disengage; to disconnect

desembrollar, day-sem-bro-l´**yar** v to

disentangle

desemejante, day-say-may-**H**ahn-tay *a* dissimilar

desemejanza, day-say-may-**H**ahn-thah *s* dissimilarity

desempapelar, day-sem-pah-pay-lar *v* to unwrap

desempaquetar, day-sem-pah-kay-tar *v* to unpack

desempeñar, day-sem-payn'yar *v* to redeem; to clear from debt; to fulfill

desempeño, day-sem-**payn**'yo *s* redeeming a pledge; fulfillment

desencajar, day-sen-kah-**H**ar *v* to disjoint; to disconnect

desencantar, day-sen-kahn-**tar** *v* to disenchant

desenconar, day-sen-ko-**nar** *v* to relieve the inflammation of; to calm; to soothe; to pacify

desenfadar, day-sen-fah-dar *v* to appease

desenfado, day-sen-**fah**-do *s* freedom; ease; relaxation

desenfreno, day-sen-**fray**-no *s* looseness; licentiousness

desenganchar, day-sen-gahn-**char** *v* to unhook; to unfasten

desengañar, day-sen-gahn'yar *v* to make one realize the truth; to disappoint

desenlace, day-sen-lah-thay *s* denouement

desenmarañar, day-sen-mah-rah-n'yar *v* to disentangle

desenmascarar, day-sen-mahs-kah-**rar** *v* to unmask

desenojar, day-say-no-**H**ar *v* to pacify

desenredar, day-sen-ray-dar *v* to disentangle; to extricate

desenrollar, day-sen-ro-l'yar *v* to unroll

desensortijado, day-sen-sor-te-**H**ah-do *a* displaced

desentenderse, day-sen-ten-**dair**-say *v* to pretend ignorance; to take no notice

desenterrar, day-sen-tair-rrar *v* to unearth; to dig up

desentono, day-sen-to-no *s* discord

desentrañar, day-sen-trah-n'yar *v* to disembowel;

to get to the bottom of

desenvainar, day-sen-vah'e-nar *v* to unsheathe

desenvoltura, day-sen-vol-**too**-rah *s* effrontery; sprightliness

desenvolver, day-sen-vol-vair *v* to unroll

desenvuelto, day-sen-voo'el-to *a* free; easy; sprightly

deseo, day-**say**-o *s* desire

deseoso, day-say-o-so *a* desirous

desertar, day-sair-tar *v* to desert

desesperación, day-sess-pay-rah-the-on *s* despair

desesperado, day-sess-pay-rah-do *a* desperate

desesperanzar, day-sess-pay-rahn-thar *v* to deprive of hope; to discourage

desfachatado, dess-fah-chah-tah-do *a* shameless

desfalcar, dess-tahl-kar *v* to cut off; to embezzle

desfallecer, dess-fah-l'yay-thair *v* to weaken; to faint

desfavorable, dess-fah-vo-rah-blay *a* unfavorable

desfavorecer, dess-fah-vo-ray-**thair** *v* to disfavor

desfigurar, dess-fe-goo-**rar** v to disfigure

desfiladero, dess-fe-lah-**day**-ro s defile; gorge

desflorar, dess-flo-**rar** v to tarnish

desgajar, dess-gah-**Har** v to rip; to break in pieces

desgana, dess-**gah**-nah s reluctance; lack of appetite

desgarbado, dess-gar-**bah**-do a uncouth; gawky

desgarrado, dess-gar-**rrah**-do a torn; tattered

desgarrar, dess-gar-**rrar** v to rend; to tear

desgastar, dess-gahs-**tar** v to consume; to wear away

desgobierno, dess-go-be-**air**-no s misrule; mismanagement

desgracia, dess-**grah**-the-ah s misfortune; disgrace

desgraciadamente, dess-grah-the-ah-dah-**men**-tay adv unfortunately

desgraciar, dess-grah-the-**ar** v to displease; to ruin

desgranar, dess-grah-**nar** v to thrash grain; to shell (as peas)

desgrasar, dess-grah-**sar** v to remove the grease

desguarnecer, dess-goo´ar-nay-**thair** v to strip of ornaments; to dismantle

deshabitado, day-sah-be-**tah**-do a uninhabited

deshabituar, day-sah-be-too´ar v to disaccustom

deshacer, day-sah-**thair** v to undo; to destroy; to liquefy; to cancel

deshacerse, day-sah-**thair**-say v to get rid of; to part with

desharrapado, day-sar-rrah-**pah**-do a shabby

deshelar, day-say-**lar** v to thaw

desheredar, day-say-ray-**dar** v to disinherit

deshidratado, dess-e-drah-**tah**-do a dehydrated

deshielo, day-se-**ay**-lo s thaw

deshilar, day-se-**lar** v to unravel

deshincar, day-sin-**kar** v to draw out; to remove

deshoje, day-so-**Hay** s falling of leaves

deshollinador, day-so-l´yee-nah-**dor** s chimney sweep

deshonestidad, day-so-ness-te-**dahd** s dishonesty

deshonesto*, day-so-ness-to a dishonest

deshonorar, day-so-no-**rar** v to dishonor; to deprive of office

deshonra, day-**sonn**-rah s dishonor; disgrace; affront

deshonrar, day-sonn-**rar** v to defame; to disgrace; to insult

deshora, day-**so**-rah s inconvenient time

deshuesar, day-soo´ay-**sar** v to take out the bones

desidia, day-**see**-de-ah s idleness; laziness

desierto, day-se-**air**-to s desert; a deserted

designar, day-sig-**nar** v to plan; to appoint; to designate

designio, day-**seeg**-ne-o s design; intention

desigual, day-se-goo´**ahl** a unequal; uneven

desinterés, day-sin-tay-**ress** s disinterestedness

desistir, day-siss-**teer** v to desist; to give up

desjuntar, dess-Hoon-**tar** v to disjoint; to separate

deslavado, dess-lah-**vah**-do a barefaced

desleal, dess-lay-**ahl** a disloyal

desleír, dess-lay-**eer** v to

dilute

deslenguado, dess-len-goo´**ah**-do *a* foul-mouthed

desliar, dess-le-**ar** *v* to untie

desligar, dess-le-**gar** *v* to loosen; to untie; to disentangle

deslindar, dess-lin-**dar** *v* to delimit

deslinde, dess-**leen**-day *s* demarcation

desliz, dess-**leeth** *s* false step; slip; fault

deslizadizo, dess-le-thah-**dee**-tho *a* slippery

deslucir, dess-loo-**theer** *v* to tarnish

deslumbrar, dess-loom-**brar** *v* to dazzle

deslustrar, dess-looss-**trar** *v* to tarnish; to dim

desmadejar, dess-mah-day-**Har** *v* to enervate

desmán, dess-**mahn** *s* misbehavior

desmandar, dess-mahn-**dar** *v* to countermand; to transgress

desmanotado, dess-mah-no-**tah**-do *a* awkward

desmaña, dess-**mah**-n´yah *s* clumsiness

desmayar, dess-mah-**yar** *v* to dismay; to be

dispirited; to faint

desmayo, dess-**mah**-yo *s* faint; dismay

desmedido, dess-may-**dee**-do *a* out of proportion

desmejora, dess-may-**Ho**-rah *s* deterioration

desmejorar, dess-may-**Ho**-rar *v* to debase; to impair

desmembrar, dess-mem-**brar** *v* to dismember

desmentir, dess-men-**teer** *v* to prove false; to contradict; to deny

desmenuzar, dess-may-noo-**thar** *v* to crumble; to break in bits

desmerecer, dess-may-ray-**thair** *v* to become unworthy of; to deteriorate

desmesurado, dess-may-soo-**rah**-do *a* immeasurable; excessive

desmigar, dess-me-**gar** *v* to crumble bread

desmochar, dess-mo-**char** *v* to lop; to mutilate

desmontar, dess-mon-**tar** *v* to fell wood; to dismount; to take apart

desmoralizar, dess-mo-rah-le-**thar** *v* to demoralize

desnatada, dess-nah-**tah**-

dah *a* skimmed

desnatar, dess-nah-**tar** *v* to skim milk

desnivel, dess-ne-**vel** *s* unevenness

desnudar, dess-noo-**dar** *v* to denude; to undress

desnudo, dess-**noo**-do *a* naked; bare

desnutrición, dess-noo-tre-the-**on** *s* malnutrition

desobedecer, day-so-bay-day-**thair** *v* to disobey

desobediencia, day-so-bay-de-en-the-**ah** *s* disobedience

desobligar, day-so-ble-**gar** *v* to relieve from an obligation; to disoblige

desocupado, day-so-koo-**pah**-do *a* disengaged; empty

desodorante, day-so-do-**rahn**-tay *s* deodorant

desoír, day-so-**eer** *v* to ignore; to disregard

desolado, day-so-**lah**-do *a* desolate

desollado, day-so-l´**yah**-do *a* impudent

desollar, day-so-l´**yar** *v* to flay; to skin

desorden, day-**sor**-den *s* disorder; confusion; disturbance

desordenar, day-sor-day-**nar** *v* to disturb; to disarrange

desorejado, day-so-ray-Hah-do *a* degraded

desorganizar, day-sor-gah-ne-**thar** *v* to disorganize

desorientado, day-so-re-´en-**tah**-do *a* disorientated

desorientar, day-so-re-en-**tar** *v* to bewilder; to disconcert

despabilar, dess-pah-be-**lar** *v* to snuff a candle

despacio, dess-**pah**-the-o *adv* slowly; gently

despacito, dess-pah-**thee**-to *adv* very gently

despachar, dess-pah-**char** *v* to forward; to expedite

despacho, dess-**pah**-cho *s* dispatch; expedient; custom; warrant; office

desparejar, dess-pah-ray-Har *v* to make uneven

despavorido, dess-pah-vo-**ree**-do *a* terrified

despechar, dess-pay-**char** *v* to enrage; to make indignant; to fret

despectivo, dess-**payk-tee**-vo *a* derogatory

despedida, dess-pay-**dee**-dah *s* leave-taking; farewell; dismissal

despedir, dess-pay-**deer** *v* to discharge; to dismiss

despedirse, dess-pay-**deer**-say *v* to take leave

despegado, dess-pay-**gah**-do *a* unglued; harsh; unaffectionate

despego, dess-**pay**-go *s* asperity; indifference

despejado, dess-pay-Hah-do *a* clear; unobstructed

despejar, dess-pay-**Har** *v* to clear away obstructions; to become bright

despejo, dess-**pay**-Ho *s* clearing; sprightliness

despenar, dess-pay-**nar** *v* to relieve from pain

despensa, dess-**pen**-sah *s* pantry

despensero, dess-pen-**say**-ro *s* butler; caterer

despeñadero, dess-pay-n´yah-**day**-ro *s* precipice

despeñar, dess-pay-n´**yar** *v* to precipitate; to fling down; to hurl from a height

desperdiciar, dess-pair-de-the-**ar** *v* to squander; to waste

desperdigar, dess-pair-de-**gar** *v* to separate; to scatter

desperezarse, dess-pay-

ray-**thar**-say *v* to stretch one's limbs

desperfecto, dess-pair-**fek**-to *s* blemish; imperfection

despernado, dess-pair-**nah**-do *a* weary

despertar, dess-pair-**tar** *v* to awake

despiadado, dess-ah-**dah**-do *a* unmerciful

despierto, dess-pe-**air**-to *a* awake

despilfarrar, dess-pil-far-**rrar** *v* to squander

despintar, dess-pin-**tar** *v* to efface; to blot; to fade

desplacer, dess-plah-**thair** *v* to displease; *s* displeasure

desplegar, dess-play-**gar** *v* to unfold; to display

desplomarse, dess-plo-mar-say *v* to fall to the ground; to collapse

desplumar, dess-ploo-**mar** *v* to fleece; to pluck

despoblar, dess-po-**blar** *v* to depopulate

despojar, dess-po-Har *v* to strip off; to dispossess

despojo, dess-po-Ho *s* spoliation; *pl* leftovers; scraps; remains; giblets

desposado, dess-po-**sah**-do *a* newly married

desposar, dess-po-**sar** v to marry; to betroth

desposeer, dess-po-say-**air** v to dispossess

desposorios, dess-po-so-re-os s betrothal

déspota, dess-po-tah s despot

despreciable, dess-pray-the-**ah-blay** a despicable; contemptible

despreciar, dess-pray-the-ar v to despise

desprecio, dess-**pray**-the-o s scorn; contempt

desprender, dess-pren-**dair** v to unfasten; to separate

desprendimiento, dess-pren-de-me-**en**-to s detachment; release; disinterestedness; landslide

desprevención, dess-pray-ven-the-**on** s improvidence; unpreparedness

desprevenido, dess-pray-vay-**nee**-do a unprovided; unprepared

desproporción, dess-pro-por-the-**on** s disproportion

despropósito, dess-pro-po-se-to s absurdity

desprovisto, dess-pro-**viss**-to a unprovided

después, dess-poo´**ess** adv after; afterwards, next

despuntar, dess-poon-**tar** v to blunt; to bud

desquitar, dess-ke-**tar** v to retrieve a loss; to retaliate

desquite, dess-**kee**-tay s recovery of a loss; revenge

destacamento, dess-tah-kah-**men**-to s detachment

destacar, dess-tah-**kar** v to detach

destajo, dess-**tah**-Ho s piecework

destapar, dess-tah-**par** v to uncover

destello, dess-**tay**-l´yo s sparkle; flash

desteñir, dess-tay-n´**yeer** v to discolor

desterrar, dess-tair-**rrar**, to exile; to banish

destiempo, dess-te-**em**-po adv a –, ah –, at the wrong time

destierro, dess-te-**air**-rro s exile; banishment

destilar, dess-te-**lar** v to distill

destinar, dess-te-**nar** v to intend

destino, dess-**tee**-no s destiny; fate; profession

destituir, dess-te-too´**eer** v to deprive; to dismiss

destorcer, dess-tor-**thair** v to untwist

destornillado, dess-tor-ne-l´**yah**-do a crazy

destornillador, dess-tor-ne-l´**vah-dor** s screwdriver

destornillar, dess-tor-ne-l´**yar** v to unscrew; to act or speak* rashly

destrabar, dess-trah-**bar** v to unfasten; to separate

destramar, dess-trah-**mar** v to unweave

destreza, dess-**tray**-thah s dexterity; skill

destripar, dess-tre-**par** v to eviscerate; to crush; to gut; to rip open

destrozar, dess-tro-**thar** v to destroy; to break into pieces

destrucción, dess-trook-the-**on** s destruction

destruir, dess-troo´**eer** v to destroy; to waste

desunir, day-soo-**neer** v to separate

desusar, day-soo-**sar** v to disuse

desvaído, dess-vah´**ee**-do a pallid

desválido, dess-vah-**lee**-do *a* helpless; destitute

desván, dess-**vahn** *s* attic; loft

desvanecer, dess-vah-nay-**thair** *v* to disintegrate; to evaporate; to vanish

desvanecimiento, dess-vah-nay-the-me-en-to *s* giddiness; dizziness

desvariar, dess-vah-re-**ar** *v* to rave; to be delirious

desvarío, dess-vah-**ree**-o *s* delirium; caprice

desvelar, dess-vay-**lar** *v* to keep awake; to reveal; to solve

desvencijado, dess-ven-the-**Hah**-do *a* rickety; shaky

desventaja, dess-ven-**tah**-Hah *s* disadvantage

desventajoso, dess-ven-tah-**Ho**-so *a* disadvantageous

desventura, dess-ven-**too**-rah *s* misfortune

desventurado, dess-ven-too-**rah**-do *a* unfortunate

desvergonzado, dess-vair-gon-**thah**-do *a* impudent; shameless

desvergüenza, dess-vair-goo´**en**-thah *s* shamelessness;

effrontery

desvío, dess-**vee**-o *s* deviation; aversion; sidetrack

detallar, day-tah-l´**yar** *v* to detail; to itemize

detalle, day-**tah**-l´yay *s* detail

detallista, day-tah-l´**yiss**-tah *s* retailer; *a* thoughtful

detener, day-tay-**nair** *v* to detain; to stop; to hold up

detenido, day-tay-**nee**-do *a* arrested; detailed; thorough

detentar, day-ten-**tar** *v* to keep unlawfully

detergente, day-tair-**Hen**-tay *s* detergent

deteriorar, day-tay-re-o-**rar** *v* to deteriorate

determinar, day-tair-me-**nar** *v* to determine

detersión, day-tair-se-**on** *s* cleansing a sore

detestar, day-tess-**tar** *v* to detest

detractar, day-trak-**tar** *v* to detract

detraer, day-trah-**air** *v* to take away; to defame

detrás, day-**trahs** *adv* behind; after

detrimento, day-tre-**men**-

to *s* detriment

deuda, day´oo-dah *s* debt

deudo, day´oo-do *s* relative

deudor, day´oo-dor *s* debtor

devanar, dav-vah-**nar** *v* to reel; to wind

devanear, day-vah-nay-**ar** *v* to rave

devastar, day-vahs-**tar** *v* to devastate; to ravage

devengar, dav-ven-**gar** *v* to earn

devoción, day-vo-the-**on** *s* devotion; piety

devolver, day-vol-**vair** *v* to return; to restore

devorar, day-vo-**rar** *v* to devour

devoto, day-**vo**-to *a* devout; devoted

devuelto, day-voo´**el**-to *a* returned

día, dee-ah *s* day; –**útil,** –oo-til, working day

diablo, de-ah-blo *s* devil

diáfano, de-ah-**fah**-no *a* transparent

dialéctica, de-ah-**lek**-te-kah *s* dialectics

diálogo, de-ah-lo-go *s* dialogue

diamante, de-ah-**mahn**-tay *s* diamond

diario, de-ah-re-o *s* daily

paper; diary; *a* daily

diarrea, de-**ar-rray**-ah *s* diarrhea

dibujar, de-boo-**Har** *v* to draw; to design; to sketch

diccionario, dik-the-o-**nah**-re-o *s* dictionary

diciembre, de-the-**em**-bray *s* December

dictado, dik-**tah**-do *s* dictation

dictador, dik-tah-**dor** *s* dictator

dictamen, dik-**tah**-men *s* opinion; judgment

dictar, dik-**tar** *v* to dictate

dicho, dee-cho *s* saying; sentence; *a* said

dichoso, de-**cho**-so *a* happy

diecinueve, de-eth-e-noo´ay-vay *s & a* nineteen

diente, de-**en**-tay *s* tooth; fang

diesel, de´ay-sayl *s* diesel

diestra, de-**ess**-trah *s* right hand

diestro*, de-**ess**-tro *a* right; dexterous; skillful

dieta, de-ay-tah *s* diet

dietario, de-ay-**tah**-re-o *s* memo book

diez, de-**eth** *s & a* ten

diezmo, de-**eth**-mo *s* tithe; tenth part

difamar, de-fah-**mar** *v* to defame

diferente*, de-fay-**ren**-tay *a* different

diferir, de-fav-**reer** *v* to delay; to differ

difícil, de-**fee**-thil *a* difficult; hard

dificultad, de-fe-kool-**tahd** *s* difficulty

dificultoso, de-fe-kool-to-so *a* difficult

difundir, de-foon-**deer** *v* to diffuse; to divulge

difunto, de-**foon**-to *a* deceased; late

difuso, de-**foo**-so *a* diffuse

digerible, de-**Hay**-ree-blay *a* digestible

digerir, de-**Hay-reer** *v* to digest

digital, de-**He**-tahl *s* foxglove; *a* digital

dígito, dee-**He**-to *s* digit

dignarse, dig-nar-say *v* to deign

dignidad, dig-ne-**dahd** *s* dignity

dignificar, dig-ne-fe-**kar** *v* to dignify

digno, dig-no *a* worthy; deserving

dije, dee-**Hay** *s* relic; child's trinkets; *pl* toys

dilacerar, de-lah-thay-**rar**

v to harm

dilación, de-lah-the-**on** *s* delay

dilapidar, de-lah-pe-**dar** *v* to waste; to squander

dilatar, de-lah-**tar** *v* to dilate; to protract

dilección, de-lek-the-**on** *s* affection; love

dilecto, de-**lek**-to *a* loved; beloved

diligente*, de-le-**Hen**-tay *a* diligent

diluir, de-loo´eer *v* to dilute

diluviar, de-loo-ve-**ar** *v* to rain like a deluge

diluvio, de-**loo**-ve-o *s* deluge; flood

dimanación, de-mah-nah-the-**on** *s* issuing from

dimanar, de-mah-**nar** *v* to emanate; to spring from

diminuir, de-me-noo´eer *v* to diminish

diminuto*, de-me-**noo**-to *a* very small

dimisión, de-me-se-**on** *s* resignation

dimitir, de-me-**teer** *v* to resign

dinero, de-**nay**-ro *s* coin; money; coinage

dintel, din-**tel** *s* lintel

diócesis, de-o-thay-siss *s* diocese

Dios, de-**os** s God

diosa, de-**o**-sah s goddess

diplomático, de-plo-**mah**-te-ko a diplomatic

diputado, de-poo-**tah**-do s congressman; congresswoman

diputar, de-poo-**tar** v to deputize; to delegate

dique, dee-**kay** s dike

dirección, de-rek-the-**on** s direction; guidance; address

directo, de-**rek**-to a straight; direct

dirigir, de-re-**Heer** v to direct; to guide; to manage

dirimir, de-re-**meer** v to dissolve; to annul

discernimiento, diss-thair-ne-me-en-to s discernment; judgment

discernir, diss-thair-**neer** v to discern; to discriminate

disciplina, diss-the-plee-nah s discipline; instruction

discípulo, diss-**thee**-poo-lo s disciple

disco, diss-ko s disk; record

discordar, diss-kor-**dar** v to disagree; to discard

discorde, diss-kor-day a discordant

discoteca, diss-ko-**tay**-kah s disco; discotheque

discrecional, diss-kray-the-o-**nahl** a optional

discrepar, diss-kray-**par** v to differ

disculpa, diss-**kool**-pah s excuse; apology

disculpar, diss-**kool**-par v to exculpate; to forgive; to apologize

discurrir, diss-koor-**rreer** v to ramble about; to discuss; to contrive

discursar, diss-koor-**sar** v to lecture

discurso, diss-**koor**-so s speech; discourse; course of time

discutible, diss-koo-tee-blay a controvertible; disputable

discutir, diss-koo-**teer** v to discuss

disecar, de-say-**kar** v to dissect

diseminar, de-say-me-**nar** v to disseminate

disensión, de-sen-se-**on** s dissension

disentería, de-sen-tay-ree-ah s dysentery

disentimiento, de-sen-te-me-**en**-to s dissent

diseñar, de-say-n´**yar** v to

sketch; to outline; to design

diseño, de-say-n´**yo** s drawing; design; sketch

disertar, de-sair-**tar** v to lecture; to debate; to argue

diserto, de-**sair**-to a eloquent; fluent

disforme, diss-**for**-may a hideous; huge; deformed

disfraz, diss-**frath** s mask; disguise

disfrute, diss-**froo**-tay s use; enjoyment

disgustar, diss-gooss-**tar** v to disgust; to displease; to dislike

disgusto, diss-**goos**-to s disgust; displeasure

disidente, de-se-**den**-tay s & a dissident; dissenter

disimular, de-se-moo-**lar** v to to hide; to disguise; to dissemble; to overlook

disipar, de-se-**par** v to dissipate; to drive away

dislocar, diss-lo-**kar** v to dislocate

disoluto, de-so-**loo**-to a dissolute

disolver, de-sol-**vair** v to dissolve; to melt

disparar, diss-pah-**rar** v to shoot; to fire

disparatado, diss-pah-rah-

tah-do a absurd; foolish

disparatar, diss-pah-**rah**-**tar** v to act or talk absurdly; to blunder

disparate, diss-pah-**rah**-**tay** s nonsense; absurdity; blunder

disparidad, diss-pah-re-**dahd** s disparity

disparo, diss-**pah**-ro s shot; nonsense

dispendioso, diss-pen-de-o-so a expensive

dispensa, diss-**pen**-sah s exemption; dispensation

dispensar, diss-pen-**sar** v to dispense; to dispense with; to deal out

dispersar, diss-pair-**sar** v to scatter; to rout

disperso, diss-**pair**-so a dispersed; scattered

displicencia, diss-ple-**then**-the-ah s displeasure

displicente, diss-ple-**then**-tay a displeasing; peevish; fretful

disponer, diss-po-**nair** v to dispose; to arrange; to prepare; to distribute; to regulate

disponible, diss-po-**nee**-blay a disposable

dispuesto, diss-poo´**ess**-to a disposed; ready;

comely

disputa, diss-**poo**-tah s dispute; controversy

disputar, diss-poo-**tar** v to dispute; to argue

disquete, diss-**kay**-tay s floppy disk

distancia, diss-**tahn**-the-ah s distance

distar, diss-**tar** v to be distant; to be different

distinción, diss-tin-the-**on** s distinction

distinguir, diss-tin-**gheer** v to distinguish

distinto***, diss-**teen**-to a distinct; different; pl several

distraer, diss-trah-**air** v to distract; to amuse

distraído, diss-trah´**ee**-do a absentminded; heedless

distribuir, diss-tre-boo´**eer** v to distribute; to sort

distrito, diss-**tree**-to s district

disturbio, diss-**toor**-be-o s disturbance

disuadir, de-soo´ah-**deer** v to dissuade

diurno, dee´**oor**-no a diurnal

divagar, de-vah-**gar** v to ramble; to digress

divergente, de-vair-**Hen**-

tay a divergent

divergir, de-vair-**Heer** v to diverge

diversidad, de-vair-se-**dahd** s diversity

diversión, de-vair-se-**on** s diversion; recreation

diverso, de-**vair**-so a diverse; different

diversos, de-**vair**-sos a several; sundry

divertido, de-vair-**tee**-do a hilarious

divertir, de-vair-**teer** v to divert; to amuse

dividendo, de-ve-**den**-do s dividend

dividir, de-ve-**deer** v to divide; to separate

divieso, de-ve-**ay**-so s boil

divino, de-**vee**-no a divine

divisa, de-**vee**-sah s badge; motto; mark; pl foreign exchange; hard currency

divisar, de-ve-**sar** v to perceive indistinctly

divorciar, de-vor-the-**ar** v to divorce

divorcio, de-**vor**-the-o s divorce; disunion

divulgar, de-vool-**gar** v to divulge; to spread; to circulate

dobladillo, do-blah-dee-l´yo s hem

doblado, do-**blah**-do a

thickset; deceitful; doubled; folded

dobladura, do-blah-**doo**-rah s fold; crease

doblar*, do-**blar** v to double

doble*, do-blay a double; thickset; artful

doblez, do-**bleth** s fold; crease; duplicity

doblón, do-**blon** s doubloon (ancient Spanish gold coin)

doce, do-**thay** s & a twelve

docena, do-**thay**-nah s dozen

doceno, do-**thay**-no a twelfth

dócil, do-thil a docile

docto, dok-to a learned

doctor, dok-**tor** s doctor; physician

doctrina, dok-**tree**-nah s doctrine

doctrinar, dok-tre-**nar** v to teach; to instruct

doctrinero, dok-tre-**nay**-ro s catechist

documento, do-koo-**men**-to s document

dogo, do-**go** s terrier; bulldog

dolar, do-**lar** v to plane; to smooth

dólar, do-lar m dollar

dolencia, do-**len**-the-ah s affliction; ailment

doler, do-**lair** v to ache; to hurt

dolerse, do-**lair**-say v to repent; to feel for; to complain

doliente, do-le-**en**-tay a suffering; sorrowful

dolor, do-**lor** s pain; aching; grief

dolorido, do-lo-**ree**-do a sore; distressed; pained

doloroso, do-lo-**ro**-so a sorrowful; painful

doloso, do-**lo**-so a deceitful

domador, do-mah-**dor** s tamer; horsebreaker

domar, do-**mar** v to tame; to subdue

domesticar, do-mess-te-**kar** v to domesticate

doméstico, do-**mess**-te-ko a domestic

domiciliarse, do-me-the-le-**ar**-say v to take up residence

domicilio, do-me-**thee**-le-o s domicile

dominar, do-me-**nar** v to dominate; to sway

domingo, do-**meen**-go s Sunday

dominio, do-**mee**-ne-o s dominion; territory;

estate

dominó, do-me-**no** s domino

don, don s title for a gentleman; equivalent to Mr., but used only before Christian names; gift; present; talent

donador, do-nah-**dor** s donation; giver

donaire, do-nah´e-ray s grace; elegance

donar, do-**nahr** v donate

donatario, do-nah-tee-re-o s recipient (of gift, etc)

donativo, do-nah-tee-vo s donation; gift

doncella, don-thel-l´yah s maid; virgin; girl

doncellez, don-thel-l´yeth s virginity

donde, don-day adv where; **de**–, day–, from what place? – **quiera,** – ke-ay-rah, anywhere

donoso, do-**no**-so a graceful; pleasant; witty

doña, do-n´yah s lady; Mrs. (used only before a Christian name)

dorado, do-**rah**-do a golden; gilt; gilded

dorar, do-**rar** v to gild; to palliate

dormir, dor-**meer** v to

sleep

dormitar, dor-me-**tar** *v* to doze

dormitorio, dor-me-to-re-o s dormitory; bedroom

dorso, dor-so s back part

dos, doss s & *a* two

dosel, do-sel s canopy

dosis, do-siss s dose

dotar, do-**tar** *v* to endow; to provide

dote, do-tay s dowry; *pl* talents

draga, drah-gah s dredge

dragón, drah-**gon** s dragon

dramático, drah-mah-te-ko *a* dramatical

drástico, drahs-te-ko *a* drastic

drenaje, dray-nah-Hay s draining; drainage

droga, dro-gah s drug

droguería, dro-gay-ree-ah s drugstore or drug manufacturer

droguero, dro-gay-ro s druggist

dual, doo-**ahl** *a* dual

dualidad, doo-ah-le-**dahd** s duality

dubitativo, doo-be-tah-**tee**-vo *a* doubtful

ducado, doo-kah-do s duchy; dukedom; ducat

ducéntesimo, doo-**then**-tay-se-mo *a* two

hundredth

dúctil, dook-til *a* ductile

ducha, doo-chah s shower

duda, doo-dah s doubt; suspense

dudable, doo-**dah**-blay *a* dubious; doubtful

dudar, doo-**dar** *v* to doubt

dudoso, doo-do-so *a* doubtful; uncertain

duelo, doo´ay-lo s duel; sorrow; mourning

duende, doo´enn-day s elf; hobgoblin; ghost

dueña, doo´ay-n´yah s chaperone; married lady; landlady

dueño, doo´ay-n´yo s owner; master

dueto, doo´ay-to s duet

dulce*, dool-thay *a* sweet; mild; gentle

dulcedumbre, doo-thay-**doom**-bray s sweetness

dulzura, dool-**thoo**-rah s sweetness; gentleness; graciousness

duna, doo-nah s dune

dúo, doo´o s duet

duodécimo, doo´o-**day**-the-mo *a* twelfth

duplicado, doo-ple-kah-do s duplicate

duplicar, doo-ple-**kar** *v* to double; to duplicate; to repeat

duplicidad, doo-ple-the-**dahd** s duplicity

duplo, doo-plo s double; duplicate

duque, doo-kay s duke

duquesa, doo-kay-sah s duchess

durable, doo-rah-blay *a* lasting; durable

duración, doo-rah-the-**on** s duration

duradero, doo-rah-day-ro *a* lasting

durante, doo-**rahn**-tay *adv* while; during

durar, doo-**rar** *v* to last; to endure

durazno, doo-**rath**-no s peach

dureza, doo-**ray**-thah s hardness; obstinacy; callosity

durmiente, door-me-en-tay *a* dormant; s sleeper (railroad)

duro, doo-ro s 5 pesetas; *a** hard; harsh

ebanista, ay-bah-**niss**-tah s cabinetmaker; carpenter

ébano, ay-bah-no s ebony

ebrio, ay-bre-o a intoxicated

eccema, ayk-ce-mah s eczema

eclipse, ay-**kleep**-say s eclipse

eco, ay-ko s echo

economía, ay-ko-no-**mee**-ah s economy

económico, ay-ko-no-me-ko a economic

ecónomo, ay-**ko**-no-mo s curator; trustee

ecuador, ay-koo´ah-**dor** s equator

ecuanimidad, ay-koo´ah-ne-me-**dahd** s equanimity

ecuestre, ay-koo-ess-tray a equestrian

echada, ay-**chah**-dah s cast; throw

echar, ay-**char** v to cast; to throw; to cast away

edad, ay-**dahd** s age

edición, ay-de-the-**on** s edition; issue

edicto, ay-**deek**-to s edict

edificar, ay-de-fe-**kar** v to build; to edify

edificio, ay-de-**fee**-the-o s edifice; building

editor, ay-de-**tor** s publisher; editor

educación, ay-doo-kah-the-**on** s education

educar, ay-doo-**kar** v to educate

educir, ay-doo-**theer** v to educe; to bring out

efectivo, ay-fek-**tee**-vo a effective

efecto, ay-**fek**-to s effect; result

efectos, ay-**fek**-tos s effects; goods; assets

efectuar, ay-fek-too´**ar** v to execute; to effect

efemérides, ay-fay-**may**-re-dess s ephemeris

efervescente, ay-fer-vess-**then**-tay a fizzy

eficacia, ay-fe-kah-the-ah s efficacy; efficiency

eficaz, ay-fe-**kath** a efficacious; efficient

eficiencia, ay-fe-the-**en**-the-ah s efficiency

eficiente*, ay-fe-the-**en**-tay a efficient

egoísmo, ay-go-**iss**-mo s selfishness

egregio, ay-**gray**-He-o a egregious; eminent; distinguished

eje, ay-Hay s axis

ejecución, ay-Hay-koo-the-**on** s execution; performance

ejecutar, ay-Hay-koo-**tar** v to execute; to perform

ejecutor, ay-Hay-koo-**tor** s executor; executioner

ejemplar, ay-Hem-**plar** s example; copy; pattern; a exemplary

ejemplificar, ay-Hem-ple-fi-**kahr** *v* to illustrate

ejemplo, ay-Hem-plo *s* example; pattern

ejercer, ay-Hair-thair *v* to exercise; to practice

ejercicio, ay-Hair-**thee**-the-o *s* exercise; office

ejercitar, ay-Hair-the-**tar** *v* to exercise

ejército, ay-Hair-the-to *s* army

ejido, ay-H ee-do *s* common; public land

el, ell *masculine article* the

elaborar, ay-lah-bo-**rar** *v* to elaborate

elación, ay-lah-the-**on** *s* elation

elástico, ay-**lahs**-te-ko *a* elastic

elección, ay-lek-the-**on** *s* election; choice

electo, ay-**lek**-to *s* elect; *a* chosen; elect

electricidad, ay-lek-tre-the-**dahd** *s* electricity

eléctrico, ay-**lek**-tre-ko *a* electric

electrónico, ay-lek-**tro**-ne-ko *a* electronic

elefante, ay-lay-**fahn**-tay *s* elephant

elegancia, ay-lay-**gahn**-the-ah *s* elegance; neatness

elegante, ay-lay-**gahn**-tay *a* elegant; graceful

elegible, ay-lay-H ee-blay *a* eligible

elegir, ay-lay-H eer *v* to choose; to elect; to select

elemento, ay-lay-**men**-to *s* element

elenco, ay-**len**-ko *s* catalog; index; list

elevación, ay-lay-vah-the-**on** *s* elevation; height; rise

elevado, ay-lay-**vah**-do *a* elevated; exalted

elevar, ay-lay-**var** *v* to raise; to lift; to exalt

elocución, ay-lo-koo-the-**on** *s* elocution

elocuente, ay-lo-koo´**en**-tay *a* eloquent

elogiar, ay-lo-He-ar *v* to praise

elogio, ay-lo-He-o *s* eulogy; praise

elucidar, ay-loo-the-**dar** *v* to elucidate

eludir, ay-loo-**deer** *v* to elude

ella, ell-yah *pron* she

ello, ell-yo *pron* it

emanar, ay-mah-**nar** *v* to emanate

embadurnar, em-bah-door-**nar** *v* to daub; to smear

embaimiento, em-bah´e-me-**en**-to *s* delusion; imposture

embajada, em-bah-**Hah**-dah *s* embassy

embajador, em-bah-**Hah**-dor *s* ambassador

embalaje, em-bah-lah-Hay *s* packing; package

embalar, em-bah-**lar** *v* to pack

embalsamar, em-bahl-sah-**mar** *v* to embalm; to perfume

embarazada, em-bah-rah-**thah**-dah *a* pregnant

embarazar, em-bah-rah-**thar** *v* to embarrass

embarazo, em-bah-**rah**-tho *s* embarrassment; pregnancy

embarazoso, em-bah-rah-**tho**-so *a* difficult; entangled; embarrassing

embarcación, em-bar-kah-the-**on** *s* embarkation; craft; ship

embarcadero, em-bar-kah-**day**-ro *s* quay; wharf

embarcar, em-bar-**kar** *v* to embark

embargar, em-bar-**gar** *v* to seize; to restrain

embargo, em-**bar**-go *s* embargo; sequestration

embarnizar, em-bar-ne-thar *v* to varnish

embarque, em-**bar**-kay *s* shipment

embarrancarse, em-bar-rrahn-**kar**-say *v* to run aground

embarrar, em-bar-**rrar** *v* to plaster; to smear

embastar, em-bahs-**tar** *v* to baste; to stitch

embate, em-**bah**-tay *s* pounding of the waves

embaucar, em-bah´oo-**kar** *v* to deceive; to trick

embaular, em-bah´oo-**lar** *v* to cram

embeber, em-bay-**bair** *v* to absorb; to contain; to soak

embelecar, em-bay-lay-**kar** *v* to deceive

embeleco, em-bay-lay-ko *s* fraud

embelesar, em-bay-ay-**sar** *v* to charm; to fascinate

embellecer, em-bay-l'yay-**thair** *v* to embellish

embellecimiento, em-bay-l'yay-the-me-**en**-to *s* adornment; embellishment

embestida, em-bess-**tee**-dah *s* assault, charge

embestir, em-bess-**teer** *v* to assail; to attack

embobado, em-bo-**bah**-do *a* spellbound

embobar, em-bo-**bar** *v* to amuse; to fascinate

embobarse, em-bo-bar-say *v* to stand gaping

embocadura, em-bo-kah-doo-rah *s* mouthpiece

embolsar, em-bol-**sar** *v* to put money in a purse; to reimburse

emborrachar, em-bor-rrah-**char** *v* to intoxicate

emboscada, em-boss-**kah** dah *s* trap; ambush

embotado, em-bo-**tah**-do *a* blunt; dull

embotar, em-bo-**tar** *v* to blunt

embotellamiento, em-bo-tay-l'yah-me-**en**-to *s* traffic jam

embotellar, em-bo-tay-l'yar *v* to bottle

embozo, em-bo-tho *s* muffler

embragar, em-brah-**gar** *v* to clutch; to connect

embravecer, em-brah-vay-**thair** *v* to enrage; to infuriate

embriagar, em-bre-ah-**gar** *v* to intoxicate; to enrapture

embridar, em-bre-**dar** *v* to bridle

embrocar, em-bro-**kar** *v* to decant

embrollar, em-bro-l'yar *v* to embroil

embrollo, em-bro-l'yo *s* trickery; tangle

embromado, em-bro-**mah**-do *a* misty; hazy; vexed

embromar, em-bro-**mar** *v* to tease; to make fun of; to chaff

embrujar, em-broo-Har *v* to bewitch

embrutecer, em-broo-tay-**thair** *v* to brutalize; to coarsen

embuchado, em-boo-**chah**-do *s* large pork sausage

embudo, em-**boo**-do *s* funnel

embuste, em-**booss**-tay *s* tale; lie

embustero, em-booss-**tay**-ro *s* liar; cheat

embutido, em-boo-**tee**-do *s* sausage

emergencia, ay-mair-H en-the-ah *s* emergency

emigrar, ay-me-**grar** *v* to emigrate

eminencia, ay-me-**nen**-the-ah *s* eminence

eminente*, ay-me-**nen**-tay *a* eminent

emisario, ay-me-**sah**-re-o *s*

emissary

emisión, ay-me-se-**on** *s* emission; issue; broadcasting

emisora, ay-me-**so**-rah *s* radio station

emitir, ay-me-**teer** *v* to emit; to issue; to broadcast

emoción, ay-mo-the-**on** *s* emotion

empacho, em-**pah**-cho *s* indigestion; bashfulness; embarrassment

empadronar, em-pah-dro-**nar** *v* to take a census

empalagar, em-pah-lah-**gar** *v* to cloy; to surfeit

empalagoso, em-pah-lah-go-so *a* cloying; annoying

empalar, em-pah-**lar** *v* to impale

empalizada, em-pah-le-**thah**-dah *s* palisade

empalmar, em-pahl-**mar** *v* to join; to put together

empalme, em-**pahl**-may *s* branch (railroad); junction

empanada, em-pah-**nah**-dah *s* meat-pie; empanada

empañar, em-pah-n'**yar** *v* to blur

empapar, em-pah-**par** *v* to

imbibe; to soak

empapelar, em-pah-pay-**lar** *v* to wrap in paper

empaque, em-pah-**kay** *s* packing; appearance

empaquetar, em-pah-kay-**tar** *v* to pack

emparedar, em-pah-ray-**dar** *v* to confine; to immure

emparejar, em-pah-ray-**Har** *v* to level; to match; to equal

emparrado, em-par-**rrah**-do *s* bower

empastar, em-pahs-**tar** *v* to paste

empatar, em-pah-**tar** *v* to equal; to tie; to draw

empate, em-**pah**-tay *s* equality of votes; draw; tie

empedernir, em-pay-dair-**neer** *v* to harden

empedrado, em-pay-**drah**-do *s* stone pavement

empedrar, em-pay-**drar** *v* to pave

empegado, em-pay-**gah**-do *s* tarpaulin

empegar, em-pay-**gar** *v* to pitch

empeine, em-**pay**'e-nay *s* groin; instep; hoof

empellón, em-pay-l'**yon** *s* push; heavy blow

empeñado, em-pay-n'**yah**-do *a* in debt; determined

empeñar, em-pay-n'**yar** *v* to pawn; to oblige

empeño, em-pay-n'yo *s* pledge; engagement; determination

empeorar, em-pay-o-**rar** *v* to impair; to worsen

emperador, em-pay-rah-**dor** *s* emperor

emperatriz, em-pay-rah-**treeth** *s* empress

empero, em-pay-ro *conj* yet; however

emperrarse, em-pair-**rrar**-say *v* to persist obstinately in

empezar, em-pay-**thar** *v* to begin

empinar, em-pe-**nar** *v* to raise; to drink heavily

emplastar, em-plahs-**tar** *v* to plaster; to obstruct

emplazar, em-plah-**thar** *v* to summon; to locate

empleado, em-play-**ah**-do *s* employee

emplear, em-play-**ar** *v* to employ; to invest

empleo, em-**play**-o *s* employment; investment

emplomar, em-plo-**mar** *v* to cover with lead

empobrecer, em-po-bray-

thair v to impoverish

empolvar, em-pol-**var** v to powder

emponzoñamiento, em-pom-tho-n´yah-me-en-to s poisoning

emponzoñar, em-pon-thon´yar v to poison

emporcar, em-por-kar v to soil; to foul

emporio, em-po-re-o s emporium

emprender, em-pren-**dair** v to undertake

empresa, em-**pray**-sah s undertaking; firm; company

empresario, em-pray-**sah**-re-o s businessman; employer

empréstito, em-**press**-te-to s loan

empujar, em-poo-**Har** v to push; to impel

empuje, em-poo-**Hay** s push; pressure

empujón, em-poo-**Hon** s violent shove; push

empuñar, em-poo-n´yar v to grasp; to grip with the fist

emular, ay-moo-**lar** v to emulate

émulo, ay-moo-lo s competitor; rival

emulsión, ay-mool-se-on s

emulsion

en, en prep in; for; on; upon; at; into

enaguas, ay-**nah**-goo´ahs s slip

enajenación, ay-nah-Hay-nah-the-on s alienation; distraction; insanity

enajenar, ay-nah-Hay-nar v to alienate

enamorado*, ay-nah-mo-rah-do a in love

enamorar, ay-nah-mo-rar v to inspire love; to win the love of

enano, ay-**nah**-no s dwarf; a dwarfish

enarbolar, ay-nar-bo-lar v to hoist

enardecer, ay-nar-day-thair v to inflame

encabezamiento, en-kah-bay-thah-me-en-to s heading; title; census-taking

encabezar, en-kah-bay-thar v to put on a heading or title; to lead

encadenar, en-kah-day-nar v to chain; to link; to shackle

encajar, en-kah-Har v to encase; to insert; to fit together

encaje, en-kah-Hay s insertion; lace; inlaid

work

encajonar, en-kah-Ho-nar v to pack in a box

encandilar, en-kahn-de-lar v to dazzle

encantador, en-kahn-tah-dor s enchanter; a charming

encantar, en-kahn-tar v to enchant; to delight

encanto, en-**kahn**-to s enchantment; delight

encañonar, en-kah-n´yo-nar v to put in a tube; to plait

encapotar, en-kah-po-tar v to cloak; to become cloudy

encapricharse, en-kah-pre-**char**-say v to be infatuated

encapuchar, en-kah-poo-char v to cover with a hood

encarado, en-kah-rah-do a faced; **bien, mal**–, be-en, mahl–, good-looking; sick-looking

encaramar, en-kah-rah-mar v to climb; to raise

encarar, en-kah-rar v to face

encarcelación, en-kar-thay-lah-the-on s imprisonment

encarcelar, en-kar-thay-lar *v* to imprison

encarecer, en-kah-ray-**thair** *v* to raise the price; to extol

encarecimiento, en-kah-ray-the-me-en-to *s* enhancement

encargado, de negocios, en-kar-**gah**-do day nay-go-the-os *s* chargé d'affaires; agent

encargar, en-kar-**gar** *v* to commission; to order

encargo, en-**kar**-go *s* assignment; order; charge; commission

encariñarse, en-kah-ren'**yar**-say *v* to become fond of

encarnado, en-kar-**nah**-do *a* incarnate; flesh-colored

encarnecer, en-kar-nay-**thair** *v* to grow fat

encarnizar, en-kar-ne-**thar** *v* to enrage; to infuriate

encarrilar, en-kar-rre-**lar** *v* to direct; to set right

encartar, en-kar-**tar** *v* to proscribe; to summon

encenagarse, en-thay-nah-**gar**-say *v* to wallow in mud

encender, en-then-**dair** *v* to kindle; to light

encendido, en-then-**dee**-do *a* inflamed; red; *s* ignition

encendimiento, en-then-de-me-**en**-to *s* burning; ardor

encerado, en-thay-**rah**-do *s* oilcloth; blackboard; *a* wax-colored

encerrar, en-thair-**rrar** *v* to lock or shut up; to contain

enchufar, en-choo-**far** *v* to plug in

encía, en-**thee**-ah *s* gum (of the teeth)

encierro, en-the-**air**-rro *s* confinement; prison

encima, en-**thee**-mah *adv* above; over

encina, en-**thee**-nah *s* evergreen; oak

enclavar, en-klah-**var** *v* to nail; to embed

enclavijar, en-klah-ve-**Har** *v* to peg

encoger, en-ko-**Hair** *v* to contract; to shrink

encogido*, en-ko-**Hee**-do *a* pusillanimous; shrunken; timid; shy

encojar, en-ko-**Har** *v* to cripple

encolar, en-ko-**lar** *v* to glue

encolerizar, en-ko-lay-re-

thar *v* to anger

encomendar, en-ko-men-**dar** *v* to commend; to entrust

encomiar, en-ko-me-**ar** *v* to praise

encomienda, en-ko-me-**en**-dah *s* command; commission; patronage

enconar, en-ko-**nar** *v* to inflame; to irritate

encontrar, en-kon-**trar** *v* to meet; to encounter; to find

encopetado, en-ko-pay-**tah**-do *a* boastful

encorvar, en-kor-**var** *v* to bend; to curve

encrespar, en-kress-**par** *v* to curl; to ruffle; to anger; to irritate

encrucijada, en-kroo-the-**Hah**-´ah *s* crossway

encrudecer, en-kroo-day-**thair** *v* to exasperate

encuadernar, en-koo´ah-dair-**nar** *v* to bind books

encubierto*, en-koo-be-**air**-to *a* hidden

encubrir, en-koo-**breer** *v* to hide; to cloak

encuentro, en-koo´**en**-tro *s* encounter; collision; meeting

encumbrado, en-ko-m-**brah**-do *a* elevated;

lofty; eminent

encurtidos, en-koor-tee-dos s pickles

endeble, en-day-blay a feeble; weak

endemoniado, en-day-mo-ne-**ah**-do a devilish

enderezado,* en-day-ray-**thah**-do a fit; appropriate

enderezar, en-day-ray-**thar** v to straighten

endiablado, en-de-ah-**blah**-do a devilish

endibia, en-dee-be-ah s endive

endiosamiento, en-de-o-sah-me-**en**-to s haughtiness; vanity; conceit

endosante, en-do-**sahn**-tay s endorser

endoso, en-**do**-so s endorsement

endulzar, en-dool-**thar** v to sweeten

endurecer, en-doo-ray-**thair** v to toughen; to harden

enebro, ay-**nay**-bro s juniper

enemiga, ay-nay-mee-gah s enmity; ill will

enemigo, ay-nay-mee-go s enemy; a inimical

enemistad, ay-nay-miss-tahd s enmity

energía, ay-nair-H ee-ah s energy

enérgico, ay-**nair**-He-ko a energetic

enero, ay-**nay**-ro s January

enervar, ay-nair-**var** v to enervate

enfadar, eh-fah-**dar** v to annoy; to anger; to irritate

enfado, en-**fah**-do s annoyance; irritation

énfasis, **en**-fah-siss s emphasis

enfermar, en-fair-**mar** v to get sick

enfermedad, en-fair-may-**dahd** s illness

enfermo, en-**fair**-mo a ill; sick

enfilar, en-fe-**lar** v to place in a line

enflaquecer, en-flah-kay-**thair** v to weaken; to become thin

enfrenar, en-fray-**nar** v to bridle; to curb

enfrente, en-**fren**-tay adv opposite

enfriar, en-fre-**ar** v to cool

enfurecer, en-foo-ray-**thair** v to make furious

engalanar, en-gah-lah-**nar** v to adorn

engallado, en-gah-l´**yah**-do a arrogant; haughty

enganchar, en-gahn-**char** v to hook; to ensnare; to enlist

engañabobos, en-gah-n´yah-**bo**-bos s trickster; fooltrap

engañador, en-gah-n´yah-**dor** a deceiving; cheating

engañar, en-gah-n´**yar** v to cheat; to fool

engaño, en-gah-n´yo s deceit; hoax

engaste, en-**gahs**-tay s enchasing; setting

engendrar, en-Hen-**drar** v to engender

engolfado, en-gol-**fah**-do a engrossed; absorbed

engolosinar, en-go-lo-se-**nar** v to inspire a longing for; to allure

engomar, en-go-**mar** v to glue; to stick

engordar, en-gor-**dar** v to fatten

engorro, en-**gor**-rro s bother; nuisance

engranaje, en-grah-nah-Hay s gear; gearing

engranar, en-grah-**nar** v to gear

engrandecer, en-grahn-day-**thair** v to enlarge

engrasar, en-grah-**sar** v to

grease; to lubricate

engreimiento, en-gray´e-me-**en**-to s conceit

engullir, en-goo-l´**yeer** v to swallow; to devour

enharinar, en-ah-re-**nar** v to flour

enhestar, en-ess-**tar** v to set upright

enhilar, en-e-**lar** v to thread; to bind

enhorabuena; en-o-rah-boo´ay-nah adv well and good; s congratulation

enhoramala, en-o-rah-**mah**-lah adv in an evil hour

enigmático, ay-nig-**mah**-te-ko a enigmatic; mysterious

enjabonar, en-Hah-bo-**nar** v to soap

enjambrar, en-Ham-**brar** v to hive bees; to swarm

enjaular, en-Hah´oo-lar v to cage; to imprison

enjoyar, en-Ho-**yar** v to adorn with jewels

enjuagar, en-Hoo´ah-gar v to rinse

enlace, en-**lah**-thay s connection; coherence; link; affinity

enladrillado, en-lah-dre-l´**yah**-do s brick pavement

enlazar, en-lah-**thar** v to unite; to bind; to lace

enlodar, en-lo-**dar** v to bemire; to stain

enloquecer, en-lo-kay-**thair** v to madden

enlucido, en-loo-**thee**-do s plastered; whitewashed

enlutar, en-loo-**tar** v to cast into mourning

enmarañar, en-mah-rahn´**yar** v to entangle; to complicate

enmascarar, en-mahs-kah-**rar** v to mask

enmendación, en-men-dah-the-**on** s emendation

enmendar, en-men-**dar** v to amend; to correct; to improve

enmienda, en-me-**en**-dah s amendment; reward

enmohecer, en-mo-ay-**thair** v to mold

enmudecer, en-moo-day-**thair** v to be silent

ennegrecer, en-nay-gray-**thair** v to blacken

enojadizo, ay-no-Hah-**dee**-tho a fretful; peevish

enojar, ay-no-**Har** v to anger; to annoy

enojoso, ay-no-Ho-so a vexatious; annoying

enorme,* ay-**nor**-may a enormous

enormidad, ay-nor-me-**dahd** s enormity

enranciarse, en-rahn-the-**ar**-say v to grow rancid; to get stale

enrarecer, en-rah-ray-**thair** v to rarefy

enredar, en-ray-**dar** v to entangle; to complicate; to involve

enredo, en-**ray**-do s entanglement; intricacy

enrejado, en-ray-Hah-do s trellis; railing; grating

enriquecer, en-re-kay-**thair** v to enrich

enriscado, en-riss-**kah**-do a craggy

enrizar, en-re-**thar** v to curl

enrojecer, en-ro-Hay-**thair** v to make red-hot; to redden; to blush

enrollar, en-ro-l´**yar** v to roll; to wind; to coil

enronquecer, en-ron-kay-**thair** v to make hoarse

enroscar, en-ros-**kar** v to twist; to coil

ensalada, en-sah-lah-dah s salad; hodgepodge

ensaladera, en-sah-lah-**day**-rah s salad bowl

ensalmar, en-sahl-**mar** v

to set bones

ensamblador, en-sahm-blah-**dor** s joiner

ensanche, en-**sahn**-chay s dilatation; widening; gore

ensañar, en-sah-n´yar v to irritate; to enrage

ensartar, en-sar-**tar** v to string; to thread

ensayar, en-sah-**yar** v to assay; to test; to rehearse

ensenada, en-say-**nah**-dah s creek

enseña, en-say-n´yah s standard

enseñanza, en-say-n´**yahn**-thah s teaching

enseñar, en-say-n´**yar** v to teach

enseñorearse, en-say-n´yo-ray-**ar**-say v to possess oneself of

enseres, en-**say**-ress s chattels; implements; furniture

ensillar, en-se-l´**yar** v to saddle

ensogar, en-so-**gar** v to fasten with a rope

ensopar, en-so-**par** v to dunk

ensordecer, en-sor-day-**thair** v to deafen

ensuciar, en-soo-the-**ar** v to dirty; to mess up; to

defile; to pollute

entablar, en-tah-**blar** v to cover with boards; to start a negotiation; to initiate

entallador, en-tah-l´**yah**-dor s sculptor; engraver

entallar, en-tah-l´**yar** v to engrave

entallecer, en-tah-l´**yay**-thair v to shoot; to sprout

entapizar, en-tah-pe-**thar** v to hang with tapestry

ente, en-tay s being; entity

entendederas, en-ten-day-**day**-rahs s (fam) understanding

entender, en-ten-**dair** v to understand; to judge

entendido, en-ten-**dee**-do a wise; learned

entendimiento, en-ten-de-me-**en**-to s understanding; knowledge

enterar, en-tay-**rar** v to inform; to instruct

entereza, en-tay-**ray**-thah s integrity; strength; rectitude

enternecer, en-tair-nay-**thair** v to move to compassion

entero, en-**tay**-ro a entire;

sound; complete; whole

enterramiento, en-tair-rrah-me-**en**-to s interment; burial

enterrar, en-tair-**rrar** v to inter; to bury

entibiar, en-te-be-**ar** v to make lukewarm

entidad, en-te-**dahd** s entity

entierro, en-te-**air**-rro s funeral; burial

entoldar, en-tol-**dar** v to cover with awnings

entonación, en-to-nah-the-**on** s intonation

entonar, en-to-**nar** v to intone; to intonate

entonces, en-**ton**-thess adv then

entono, en-**to**-no s intonation; arrogance

entontecer, en-ton-tay-**thair** v to make foolish

entornar, en-tor-**nar** v to set ajar

entorpecer, en-tor-pay-**thair** v to obstruct; to slow down; to benumb

entrada, en-**trah**-dah s entrance; admission

entrambos, en-**trahm**-bos pron both

entrampar, en-trahm-**par** v to trap; to ensnare

entrañable, en-trahn-yahblay *a* intimate; affectionate

entrañas, en-trah-n´yahs *s* bowels; entrails

entrar, en-trar *v* to enter

entre, en-tray *prep* between; among; amongst

entreabierto, en-tray-ah-be-air-to *a* ajar

entrecejo, en-tray-thay-Ho *s* space between the eyebrows; frown

entreclaro, en-tray-klah-ro *a* dim

entrecoger, en-tray-ko-Hair *v* to catch; to intercept

entrecortar, en-tray-kor-tar *v* to cut without dividing

entrecubiertas, en-tray-koo-be-air-tahs *s* between decks

entredicho, en-tray-dee-cho *s* interdiction

entrefino, en-tray-fee-no *a* medium quality

entrega, en-tray-gah *s* delivery

entregar, en-tray-gar *v* to deliver; to pay

entrelazar, en-tray-lah-thar *v* to interlace

entremedias, en-tray-may-de-ahs *adv* in the meantime

entremés, en-tray-mess *s* interlude; side dish

entremeter, en-tray-may-tair *v* to insert; – **se**, – say, to intrude; to meddle; to interfere

entremetido, en-tray-may-tee-do *s* meddler

entrepaño, en-tray-pah-n´yo *s* panel

entresacar, en-tray-sah-kar *v* to choose; to sift

entresuelo, en-tray-soo´ay-lo *s* mezzanine

entretanto, en-tray-tahn-to *adv* meanwhile

entretela, en-tray-tay-lah *s* interlining

entretener, en-tray-tay-nair *v* to amuse

entretenido, en-tray-tay-nee-do *a* amusing

entretenimiento, en-tray-tay-ne-me-en-to *s* entertainment

entretiempo, en-tray-te-em-po *s* spring or autumn

entrever, en-tray-vair *v* to have a glimpse of

entrevista, en-tray-viss-tah *s* interview

entristecer, en-triss-tay-thair *v* to sadden

entronque, en-tron-kay *s* relationship; connection; railroad junction

entumecer, en-too-may-thair *v* to be numb

enturbiar, en-toor-be-ar *v* to disturb; to cloud; to muddle

entusiasmar, en-too-se-ahs-mar *v* to enrapture; to fill with enthusiasm

entusiasta, en-too-se-ahs-tah *s* addict

enumerar, ay-noo-may-rar *v* to enumerate

enunciar, ay-noon-the-ar *v* to enunciate; to declare

envanecer, en-vah-nay-thair *v* to make vain

envase, en-vah-say *s* cask; container

envejecer, en-vay-Hay-thair *v* to make or grow old

envenenar, en-vay-nay-nar *v* to poison

envés, en-vess *s* wrong side

enviado, en-ve-ah-do *s* envoy; messenger

enviar, en-ve-ar *v* to send; to remit

envidia, en-vee-de-ah *s* envy; spite

envidiar, en-ve-de-ar *v* to

envy; to grudge

envilecer, en-ve-lay-**thair** v to degrade

envío, en-**vee**-o s remittance; shipment

envoltura, en-vol-**too**-rah s wrapper; covering

envolver, en-vol-**vair** v to involve; to wrap up

enyesar, en-yay-**sar** v to plaster

épico, **ay**-pe-ko a epic

epidemia, ay-pe-**day**-me-ah s epidemic

epidémico, ay-pe-**day**-me-ko a epidemic

epilogar, ay-pe-lo-**gar** v to sum up

episódico, ay-pe-so-de-ko a episodical

episodio, ay-pe-so-**de**-o s episode

epístola, ay-**piss**-to-lah s epistle; letter

epíteto, ay-**pee**-tay-to s epithet

epitomar, ay-pe-to-**mar** v to epitomize; to summarize

época, **ay**-po-kah s epoch; period; time

equilibrio, ay-ke-lee-bre-o s equilibrium

equipaje, ay-ke-pah-**Hay** s baggage; equipment; crew

equipo, ay-**kee**-po s outfit; equipment; team

equivaler, ay-ke-vah-**lair** v to be equivalent

equivocación, ay-ke-vo-kah-the-**on** s mistake

equivocado, ay-ke-vo-kah-do a mistaken

equivocar, ay-ke-vo-**kar** v to mistake

equívoco, ay-**kee**-vo-ko s equivocal; a ambiguous

era, **ay**-rah s era; age

erario, ay-**rah**-re-o s funds

erección, ay-rek-the-**on** s erection; foundation

erguir, air-**gheer** v to raise up straight

erigir, ay-re-**H** eer v to erect

erizado, ay-re-**thah**-do a bristly

erizo, ay-**ree**-tho s hedgehog

erosionar, ay-ro-se´-o-**nahr** v erode

erótico, ay-ro-te-ko a erotic

erradizo, air-rrah-dee-tho a wandering

errar, air-**rrar** v to err; to mistake; to roam

error, air-**rror** s error; mistake; fault

esbelto, ess-**bel**-to a slender; slim; well-

shaped

esbozo, ess-**bo**-tho s sketch; outline

escabeche, ess-kah-**bay**-chay s souse; pickle; pickled fish

escabroso, ess-kah-**bro**-so a rough; rugged

escabullirse. ess-kah-boo-l´**yeer**-say v to slip away

escala, ess-**kah**-lah s ladder; scale

escalada, ess-kah-**lah**-dah s rock climbing

escaldar, ess-kahl-**dar** v to scald

escalera, ess-kah-**lay**-rah s staircase

escalfador, ess-kahl-fah-**dor** s chafing-dish

escalfar, ess-kahl-**far** v to poach eggs

escalón, ess-kah-**lon** s step; grade

escama, ess-**kah**-mah s scale (of fishes)

escándalo, ess-**kahn**-dah-lo s scandal

escaño, ess-kah-n´yo s bench with a back; seat in Congress

escapada, ess-kah-**pah**-dah s flight; escapade; escape

escapar, ess-kah-**par** v to escape; to flee

escaparate, ess-kah-pah-rah-tay s glass case; store-window

escape, ess-kah-pay s escape; leak; leakage

escaramuza, ess-kah-rah-moo-thah s skirmish

escarapela, ess-kah-rah-pay-lah s badge

escarcha, ess-kar-chah s frost

escardar, ess-kar-dar v to weed

escarlata, ess-kar-lah-tah s scarlet color

escarlatina, ess-kar-lah-tee-nah s scarlet fever

escarmentar, ess-kar-men-tar v to be warned by experience

escarnecer, ess-kar-nay-thair v to scoff; to ridicule

escarola, ess-kah-ro-lah s endive

escarpado, ess-kar-pah-do a steep; craggy

escaso*, ess-kah-so a short; scarce; scanty

escatimar, ess-kah-te-mah v to curtail

escena, ess-thay-nah s stage; scene; sight

escéptico, ess-thep-te-ko a skeptical

esclarecer, ess-klah-ray-thair v to lighten; to illustrate

esclarecido, ess-klah-ray-thee-do a illustrious

esclavina, ess-klah-vee-nah s cloak

esclavitud, ess-klah-ve-tood s slavery

esclavo, ess-klah-vo s slave

esclusa, ess-kloo-sah s lock; sluice

escoba, ess-ko-bah s broom

escobilla, ess-ko-bee-l'yah s brush

escocer, ess-ko-thair v to sting or feel a sharp pain; to smart

escoger, ess-ko-Hair v to select; to pick out; to choose

escogimiento, ess-ko-He-me-en-to s selection

escolar, ess-ko-lar s scholar; student

escolta, ess-kol-tah s escort; guard

escollera, ess-ko-l'yay-rah s breakwater; jetty

escombro, ess-kom-bro s debris

esconder, ess-kon-dair v to conceal; to hide

escondite, ess-kon-dee-tay s concealment; hiding place

escopeta, ess-ko-pay-tah s shotgun

escopeteo, ess-ko-pay-tay-o s discharge of guns

escoplear, ess-ko-play-ar v to chisel

escoplo, ess-ko-plo s chisel

escorbuto, ess-kor-boo-to s scurvy

escoria, ess-ko-re-ah s scum; worthless thing

escoriar, ess-ko-re-ar v (see excoriar)

escorpión, ess-kor-pe-on s scorpion

escotar, ess-ko-tar v to cut out; to contribute

escote, ess-ko-tay s low-necked dress; share; quota

escotilla, ess-ko-tee-l'yah s hatchway

escozor, ess-ko-thor s pungent pain

escribanía, ess-kre-bih-nee-ah s notary's office; writing desk

escribano, ess-kre-bah-no s clerk

escribiente, ess-kre-be-en-tay s clerk

escribir, ess-kre-beer v to write

escrito, ess-kree-to s writing; literary

composition

escritor, ess-kre-**tor** s
writer; author

escritorio, ess-kre-to-re-o s writing desk; office

escritura, ess-kre-too-rah s writing; deed

escrúpulo, ess-**kroo**-poo-lo s doubt; scruple

escrutar, ess-kroo-**tar** v to scrutinize

escuchar, ess-koo-**char** v to listen; to heed

escudar, ess-koo-**dar** v to shield

escudo, ess-**koo**-do s shield; coat of arms; coin

escuela, ess-koo´ay-lah s school

escueto, ess-koo´**ay**-to a bare; clean; short

esculpir, ess-kool-**peer** v to sculpt

escultura, ess-kool-**too**-rah s sculpture

escupidera, ess-koo-pe-**day**-rah s spittoon

escupir, ess-koo-**peer**, to spit

escurrir, ess-koor-**rreer** v to drain; to wring

ese, esa, ay-say, ay-sah, demonstr. adj., that

ése, ésa, ay-say, ay-sah pron that

esencia, ay-**sen**-the-ah s essence

esfera, ess-**fay**-rah s sphere

esfinge, ess-**fin**-Hay s sphinx

esforzado, ess-for-**thah**-do a strong; valiant

esforzar, ess-for-**thar** v to strengthen; **–se, –say**, to make efforts

esfuerzo, ess-foo´**air**-tho s courage; effort

esgrima, ess-**gree**-mah s fencing

esgrimir, ess-gre-**meer** v to brandish; to fence

eslabón, ess-lah-**bon** s link of a chain; steel for striking fire

esmalte, ess-**mahl**-tay s enamel

esmerado, ess-may-**rah**-do a highly finished; carefully done

esmeril, ess-may-**reel** s emery

esmero, ess-**may**-ro s careful attention

eso, ay-so pron that

espaciar, ess-pah-the-**ar** v to extend; to spread; to space

espacio, ess-**pah**-the-o s space; distance; slowness

espada, ess-**pah**-dah s sword

espalda, ess-**pahl**-dah s back

espaldilla, ess-pahl-**dee**-l´yah s shoulder-blade

espantadizo, ess-pahn-tah-dee-tho a timid; shy

espantapájaros, ess-pahn-tah-pa-Har-ho s scarecrow

espantar, ess-pahn-**tar** v to frighten; to terrify

espantoso, ess-pahn-to-so a frightful

esparadrapo, ess-pah-rah-**drah**-po s fabric tape

esparcido, ess-par-**thee**-do a scattered

esparcir, ess-par-**theer** v to scatter; to spread

espárrago, ess-**par**-rrah-go s asparagus

esparto, ess-**par**-to s esparto grass

espasmo, ess-**pahs**-mo s spasm

espátula, ess-**pah**-too-lah s spatula

especia, ess-**pay**-the-ah s spice

especial, ess-pay-the-**ahl** a special

especie, ess-**pay**-the-ay s kind; sort

especificar, ess-pay-the-fe-**kar** v to specify

específico, ess-pay-**the**-fe-ko s specific

espectáculo, ess-pek-**tah**-koo-lo s spectacle; show

espectador, ess-pek-tah-**dor** s spectator

espectro, ess-**pek**-tro s specter; spectrum

especular, ess-pay-koo-**lar** v to speculate

espéculo, ess-**pay**-koo-lo s speculum

espejo, ess-**pay**-Ho s mirror

espera, ess-**pay**-rah s expectation; wait; respite

esperanza, ess-pay-**rahn**-thah s hope

esperar, ess-pay-**rar** v to hope; to wait for

espesar, ess-pay-**sar** v to thicken

espeso, ess-**pay**-so a thick; dense

espía, ess-**pee**-ah s spy

espiga, ess-**pee**-gah s ear of corn

espigar, ess-pe-**gar** v to glean

espina, ess-**pee**-nah s thorn; fish bone; spine

espinaca, ess-pe-**nah**-kah s spinach

espinazo, ess-pe-**nah**-tho s backbone

espino, ess-**pee**-no s hawthorne

espinoso, ess-pe-**no**-so a thorny; arduous

espionaje, ess-pe´o-**nah**-Hay s espionage

espiral, ess-pe-**rahl** a spiral

espirar, ess-pe-**rar** v to expire; to exhale

espíritu, ess-**pee**-re-too s spirit; soul; ardor; courage; life; alcohol

espiritual, ess-pe-re-too-**ahl** a spiritual; ghostly

esplendidez, ess-plen-de-**deth** s splendor

espléndido, ess-**plen**-de-do a splendid

esplendor, ess-plen-**dor** s splendor

espliego, ess-ple-**ay**-go s lavender

espolada, ess-po-**lah**-dah s prick with a spur

espolón, ess-po-**lon** s spur

esponja, ess-**pon**-Hah s sponge

esponjar, ess-pon-**Har** v to sponge

esponsales, ess-pon-**sah**-less s betrothal

espontáneo*, ess-pon-**tah**-nay-o a spontaneous

esposa, ess-**po**-sah s wife; pl handcuffs

esposo, ess-**po**-so s husband

espuela, ess-poo´**ay**-lah s spur; stimulus

espuerta, ess-poo´**air**-tah s basket; frail

espuma, ess-**poo**-mah s froth; lather; foam; scum

espumajear, ess-poo-mah-**Hay**-ar v to foam at the mouth

espumar, ess-poo-**mar** v to skim; to foam

espumoso, ess-poo-**mo**-so a frothy; foamy

esquela, ess-**kay**-lah s note; invitation; death announcement

esqueleto, ess-kay-**lay**-to s skeleton

esquema, ess-**kay**-mah s scheme; plan

esquí, ess-**kee** s ski; skiing

esquiar, ess-kee´**ahr** v ski

esquilar, ess-ke-**lar** v to shear; to clip; to fleece

esquilmar, ess-kil-**mar** v to harvest; to impoverish

esquina, ess-**kee**-nah s corner; angle

esquivar, ess-ke-**var** v to shun; to avoid; to elude

esquivo, ess-**kee**-vo a elusive; shy; reserved

estabilidad, ess-tah-be-le-**dahd** s stability

estable*, ess-**tah**-blay a stable

establecer, ess-tah-blay-**thair** v to establish

establecido, ess-tah-blay-**thee**-do a established in business

establo, ess-tah-blo s stable

estaca, ess-**tah**-kah s stake; stick; cudgel

estacada, ess-tah-**kah**-dah s palisade; fence

estacazo, ess-tah-**kah**-tho s blow with a stake

estación, ess-tah-the-**on** s condition; season; time; station

estacionarse, ess-tah-the-o-**nar**-say v to remain stationary

estadio, ess-tah-de-o s stadium

estadista, ess-tah-**diss**-tah s statesman

estadístico, ess-tah-**diss**-te-ko a statistical

estadizo, ess-tah-**dee**-tho a stagnant

estado, ess-**tah**-do s state; condition; rank

estafa, ess-**tah**-fah s swindle; theft

estafador, ess-tah-fah-**dor** s swindler

estafar, ess-tah-**far** v to swindle

estafeta, ess-tah-**fay**-tah s post-office branch

estallar, ess-tah-l´**yar** v to burst; to explode

estallido, ess-tah-l´**yee**-do s´ crack; explosion

estambre, ess-**tahm**-bray s worsted (fabric); stamen

estameña, ess-tah-**may**-n´yah s serge

estampa, ess-**tahm**-pah s print; stamp; pattern

estampar, ess-tahm-**par** v to print; to stamp

estampido, ess-tahm-**pee**-do s report of a gun; crash

estampilla, ess-tahm-**pee**-l´yah s rubber stamp; signet

estancamiento, ess-tahn-kah-mee-en-to s stagnation

estancar, ess-tahn-**kar** v to stem a current; to be stagnant; to hold up

estancia, ess-tahn-the-**ah** s stay; dwelling

estanco, ess-**tahn**-ko s tobacco shop

estandarte, ess-tahn-**dar**-tay s banner; standard

estanque, ess-**tahn**-kay s pond; reservoir

estante, ess-**tahn**-tay s stand; shelf

estaño, ess-**tah**-n´yo s tin

estar, ess-**tar** v to be; to be in a place, state, or condition

estatua, ess-tah-**too**´ah s statue

estatuto, ess-tah-**too**-to s statute; law

este, ess-tay s east

este, esta, estos, estas, ess-tay, ess-tah, ess- tos, ess-tahs *demonstr adj* this; these

éste, ésta, ess-tay, ess-tah *pron* this

estela, ess-**tay**-lah s wake of a ship

estera, ess-**tay**-rah s mat

estercolar, ess-tair-ko-**lar** v to fertilize

estereofónico, ess-tair-re´o-fo-ne-ko a stereophonic

estéril, ess-**tay**-ril a barren; fruitless

esternón, ess-tair-**non** s sternum

estero, ess-**tay**-ro s estuary

estética, ess-**tay**-te-kah s esthetics

estiaje, ess-te-**ah**-Hay s low-water mark

estibador, ess-te-bah-**dor** s stevedore

estiércol, ess-te-**air**-kol s manure

estigma, ess-**tig**-mah s

stigma

estilar, ess-te-**lar** v to use; to be accustomed

estilo, ess-**tee**-lo s style; custom

estilográfica, ess-te-lo-**grah**-fe-kah s fountain pen

estimar, ess-te-**mar** v to estimate; to esteem; to judge

estímulo, ess-**tee**-moo-lo s stimulus

estío, ess-**tee**-o s summer

estipendio, ess-te-**pen**-de-o s stipend; salary

estipular, ess-te-poo-**lar** v to stipulate

estirar, ess-te-**rar** v to stretch; to pull

estirón, ess-te-**ron** s pulling; stretching

estirpe, ess-**teer**-pay s race; origin

esto, ess-to *pron* this

estocada, ess-to-**kah**-dah s stab; thrust

estofa, ess-to-**fah** s quilted stuff; quality

estofado, ess-to-**fah**-do s stew; *a* decorated; stewed

estofar, ess-to-**far** v to quilt; to stew

estoico, ess-to-e-ko *a* stoic

estólido, ess-to-le-do *a* stupid

estómago, ess-to-**mah**-go s stomach

estoque, ess-to-**kay** s rapier

estorbo, ess-**tor**-bo s impediment; obstruction

estornino, ess-tor-**nee**-no s starling

estornudar, ess-tor-noo-**dar** v to sneeze

estrada, ess-**trah**-dah s road

estrado, ess-**trah**-do s living room; dais

estrambótico, ess-trahm-**bo**-te-ko *a* eccentric; queer

estrangular, ess-trahn-goo-**lar** v to strangle

estraperlo, ess-trah-**payr**-lo s black market

estrategia, ess-trah-**tay**-He-ah s strategy

estratégico, ess-trah-**tay**-He-ko *a* strategical

estrato, ess-**trah**-to s stratum; layer

estraza, ess-**trah**-thah s rag

estrechar, ess-tray-**char** v to tighten; to contract; to compress

estrecho*, ess-**tray**-cho s straight; *a* narrow; close; tight; intimate;

penurious

estregar, ess-tray-**gar** v to rub; to scratch

estrella, ess-tray-**l'yah** s star

estrellado, ess-tray-**l'yah**-do *a* starry; smashed; shattered

estrellar, ess-tray-**l'yar** v to shatter

estremecer, ess-tray-may-**thair** v to shake; to tremble; to shudder

estrenar, ess-tray-**nar** v to use for the first time; to inaugurate

estreñido, ess-tray-n'**yee**-do *a* constipated

estreno, ess-**tray**-no s first use; first performance

estreñir, ess-tray-n'**yeer** v to tie close; to constipate

estrépito, ess-**tray**-pe-to s din; clamor; crash

estribar, ess-tre-**bar** v to rest upon; to be based on

estribillo, ess-tre-bee-**l'yo** s chorus

estribo, ess-**tree**-bo s stirrup; buttress

estricto*, ess-**treek**-to *a* strict; accurate; severe

estropear, ess-tro-pay-**ar** v to maim; to damage; to

spoil

estructura, ess-trook-**too**-rah s structure

estruendo, ess-troo´en-do s clamor; turmoil

estrujar, ess-troo-Har v to press; to squeeze

estuario, ess-too-**ah**-re-o s estuary; inlet

estuco, ess-**too**-ko s stucco

estuche, ess-**too**-chay s case (for jewelry, scissors, etc.)

estudiante, ess-too-de-**ahn**-tay s student

estudiar, ess-too-de-ar v to study

estudio, ess-**too**-de-o s study; library; studio

estudioso, ess-too-de-o-so a studious

estufa, ess-**too**-fah s stove; heater

estupefacto, ess-too-pay-**fahk**-to a stupefied

estupendo, ess-too-**pen**-do a stupendous

estupidez, ess-too-pe-**deth** s stupidity

estúpido, ess-**too**-pe-do a stupid

estupor, ess-too-por s stupor; amazement

esturión, ess-toore-**on** s sturgeon

etapa, ay-**tah**-pah s stage;

phase

éter, ay-**tair** s ether

eternizar, ay-tair-ne-**thar** v to perpetuate

eterno, ay-**tair**-no a eternal

ética, ay-te-kah s ethics

ético, ay-te-ko a ethical

etiqueta, ay-te-**kay**-tah s etiquette; label

étnico, **ayt**-ne-ko a ethnic

etnólogo, et-no-lo-go s ethnologist

eucalipto, ay´oo-kah-**leep**-to s eucalyptus

eucaristía, ay´oo-kah-riss-**tee**-ah s Eucharist

eufónico, ay´oo-fo-ne-ko a euphonic

Europa, ay´oo-ro-pah s Europe

evacuar, ay-vah-koo´**ar** v to evacuate

evadir, ay-vah-**deer** v to evade

evaluación, ay-vah-loo´ah-the-**on** s evaluation; assessment

evaluar, ay-vah-loo´**ar** v to evaluate; to assess

evaporar, ay-vah-po-rar v to evaporate

evasión, ay-vah-se-**on** s evasion; escape

evento, ay-**ven**-to s event

evidente, ay-ve-**den**-tay a

evident

evitable, ay-ve-tah-blay a avoidable

evitar, ay-ve-tar v to avoid

evocar, ay-vo-**kar** v to evoke

evolución, ay-vo-loo-the-on s evolution

exacción, ek-sahk-the-**on** s exaction; extortion

exacerbar, ek-sah-thair-bar v to exasperate

exactitud, ek-sahk-te-**tood** s exactness; accuracy

exacto*, ek-**sahk**-to a exact; punctual

exagerar, ek-sah-**Hay**-rar v to exaggerate

exaltar, ek-sahl-**tar** v to exalt; to extol

examen, ek-sah-men s examination

examinador, ek-sah-me-nah-**dor** s examiner

examinar, ek-sah-me-**nar** v to examine; to test

exangüe, ek-**sahn**-goo´ay a bloodless; anemic

exánime, ek-**sah**-ne-may a spiritless; weak; lifeless

exasperar, ek-sahs-pay-**rar** v to exasperate

excavar, eks-kah-var v to excavate

excedente, eks-thay-**den**-tay s excess; a excessive;

exceeding

exceder, eks-thay-**dair** v to exceed; to excel

excelente*, eks-thay-**len**-tay a excellent

excelsitud, eks-thel-se-**tood** s loftiness

excelso, eks-**thel**-so a sublime; elevated; lofty

excéntrico, eks-**then**-tre-ko a eccentric

excepción, eks-thep-the-**on** s exception

excepto, eks-**thep**-to adv except that; excepting

exceptuar, eks-thep-too´**ar** v to exclude; to except; to exempt

excesivo, eks-thay-**see**-vo a excessive

exceso, eks-**thay**-so s excess

excitar, eks-the-**tar** v to excite

exclamar, eks-klah-**mar** v to exclaim

excluir, eks-kloo´**eer** v to exclude

excomulgar, eks-ko-mool´**gar** v to excommunicate

excoriar, eks-ko-re-**ar** v to excoriate

excreción, eks-kray-the-**on** s excretion

excremento, eks-kray-**men**-to s excrement

excursión, eks-koor-se-**on** s excursion

excusa, eks-**koo**-sah s excuse

excusar, eks-koo-**sar** v to excuse

exento, ek-**sen**-to a exempt; free

exequias, ek-**say**-ke-ahs s obsequies

exhalar, ek-sah-**lar** v to exhale

exhausto, ek-sah´**ooss**-to a exhausted

exhibir, ek-se-**beer** v to exhibit

exhortar, ek-sor-**tar** v to exhort

exhumar, ek-soo-**mar** v to disinter

exigente, ek-se-H **en**-tay a exacting; demanding

exigible, ek-se-H **ee**-blay a demandable

exigir, ek-se-H **eer** v to demand; to exact

exigüidad, ek-se-goo´**e-dahd** s smallness; exiguity

exiguo, ek-**see**-goo´o a exiguous

eximio, ek-**see**-me-o a very eminent

eximir, ek-se-**meer** v to exempt

existencia, ek-siss-**ten**-the-ah s existence; pl stock in hand

existente, ek-siss-**ten**-tay a existing

existir, ek-siss-**teer** v to exist

éxito, **ek**-se-to s issue; result; end; success

exonerar, ek-so-nay-**rar** v to exonerate

exorbitante, ek-sor-be-**tahn**-tay a exorbitant

exótico, ek-so-te-ko a exotic

expansión, iks-pahn-se-**on** s expansion

expatriarse, eks-pah-tre-**ar**-say v to emigrate

expectativa, eks-pek-tah-**tee**-vah s expectancy; hope

expectorar, eks-pek-to-**rar** v to expectorate

expedición, eks-pay-de-the-**on** s expedition; dispatch

expedidor, eks-pay-de-**dor** s sender; shipper; agent

expediente, eks-pay-de-**en**-tay s proceedings (law); expedient; resource; provision; pretext; file of papers

expedir, eks-pay-**deer** v to expedite; to send; to

draw up; to issue

expedito, eks-pay-**dee**-to *a* expeditious; prompt

expeler, eks-pay-**lair** *v* to expel

expendeduría, eks-pen-day-doo-**ree**-ah *s* tobacco shop

expensas, eks-**pen**-sahs *s* expenses; costs

experiencia, eks-pay-re-en-the-ah *s* experience; trial

experimento, eks-pay-re-**men**-to *s* experiment

experto, eks-**pair**-to *a* expert

expiación, eks-pe-ah-the-**on** *s* expiation

expirar, eks-pe-**rar** *v* to expire; to die

explanación, eks-plah-nah-the-**on** *s* explanation

explanar, eks-plah-**nar** *v* to explain; to level

explayar, eks-plah-**yar** *v* to extend; to dilate

explicacion, eks-ple-kah-the-**on** *s* explanation; reason

explicar, eks-ple-**kar** *v* to explain

explícito*, eks-**plee**-the-to *a* explicit

explorar, eks-plo-**rar** *v* to explore

explosión, eks-plo-se-**on** *s* explosion

explosivo, eks-plo-se-**vo** *s* & *a* explosive

explotar, eks-plo-**tar** *v* to work mines, lands, etc.; to exploit; to explode; to risk

expoliar, eks-po-le-**ar** *v* to despoil

exponer, eks-po-**nair** *v* to expose; to expound; to hazard

exportar, eks-por-**tar** *v* to export

expósito, eks-**po**-se-to *s* foundling

expresar, eks-pray-**sar** *v* to express

expresion, eks-**pray**-see-on *s* expression

expreso, eks-**pray**-so *s* express train; *a* express

exprimir, eks-pre-**meer** *v* to squeeze out

ex-profeso, eks-pro-**fay**-so *adv* on purpose

expulsar, eks-pool-**sar** *v* to expel

exquisito, eks-ke-**see**-to *a* exquisite

éxtasis, eks-**tah**-siss *s* ecstasy

extender, eks-ten-**dair** *v* to extend; to expand; to

enlarge

extenso, eks-**ten**-so *a* extensive

extenuar, eks-tay-noo-´ar *v* to extenuate; to debilitate

exterior, eks-tay-re-**or** *s* & *a* exterior; external

exterminio, eks-tair-**mee**-ne-o *s* extermination

externo, eks-**tair**-no *a* external; outward; foreign

extinguir, eks-tin-**gheer** *v* to extinguish

extintor, eks-tin-**tor** *s* extinguisher

extirpar, eks-teer-**par** *v* to remove (surgically)

extra, eks-trah *a* extra; high quality

extracción, eks-trahk-the-**on** *s* extraction

extractar, eks-trahk-**tar** *v* to extract

extracto, eks-**trahk**-to *s* extract

extraer, eks-trah-**air** *v* to extract; to remove

extranjero, eks-trahn-**Hay**-ro *s* foreigner; stranger; *a* foreign

extrañar, eks-trah-n´**yar** *v* to wonder; to find odd

extrañeza, eks-trah-n´**yay**-thah *s* oddity;

wonderment;
estrangement

extraño, eks-**trah**-n´yo *a*
strange; foreign; rare

extraviado, eks-trah-ve-
ah-do *a* mislaid; missing

extraviar, eks-trah-ve-**ar** *v*
to mislead; to misplace

extremado, eks-tray-**mah**-
do *a* extreme

extremar, eks-tray-**mar** *v*
to carry to an extreme;
to complete

extremaunción, eks-tray-
mah´oon-the-**on** *s*
extreme unction; last
rites

extremo, eks-**tray**-mo *a*
extreme; last

extremoso, eks-tray-**mo**-so
a extreme; excessive

extrínseco, eks-**treen**-say-
ko *a* extrinsic

extrovertido, eks-tro-vayr-
te-do *s* & *a* extrovert

fábrica, fah-bre-kah *s*
factory

fabricante, fah-bre-**kahn-**
tay *s* manufacturer

fabriquero, fah-bre-**kay-**ro
s manufacturer; church
warden; artisan

fábula, fah-boo-lah *s*
fable; story

fabuloso, fah-boo-**lo-**so *a*
fabulous

facción, fahk-the-on *s*
faction; feature

fácil, fah-thil *a* easy; facile

facilidades, fah-the-le-
thah-dess *s* facilities

facilitar, fah-the-le-**tar** *v*
to facilitate

facineroso, fah-the-nay-
ro-so *a* extremely
wicked

factible, fahk-tee-blay *a*
feasible

factor, fahk-tor *s* factor

factura, fahk-too-rah *s*
invoice

facturar, fahk-too-**rar** *v* to
invoice

facultad, fah-kool-**tahd** *s*
faculty

facultar, fah-kool-**tar** *v* to
empower; to authorize

facultativo, fah-kool-tah-
tee-vo *s* practitioner; *a*
optional

facundo, fah-koon-do *a*
eloquent; fluent

facha, fah-chah *s*
appearance; look

fachada, fah-chah-dah *s*
façade; frontage

fachenda, fah-chen-dah *s*
conceit

faena, fah-ay-na *s* work;
chore; task

faisán, fah´e-sahn *s*
pheasant

faja, fah-Hah *s* band; sash;
girdle

fajo, fah-Ho *s* bundle

falacia, fah-lah-the-ah *s*
fallacy

falaz, fah-lahth *a* deceitful

falda, fahl-dah *s* skirt; lap;
slope

faldellín, fahl-day-l´yeen *s*
slip

faldón, fahl-don *s* long
flowing skirt

falible, fah-lee-blay *a*
fallible

falsario, fahl-sah-re-o *s*
forger

falsear, fahl-say-**ar** *v* to
falsify; to forge

falsedad, fahl-say-**dahd** *s*
falsehood; untruth

falsete, fahl-say-tay *s*
falsetto voice

falso*, fahl-so *a* false;
counterfeit

falta, fahl-tah *s* fault;
offense; want; flaw

faltar, fahl-tar *v* to be
wanting; to fail; to need;
to be absent

faltriquera, fahl-tre-**kay-**
rah *s* pocket

fallar, fah-l´yar *v* to pass
judgment; to miss; to

fail

fallecer, fahl-´yay-**thair** v
to die

fallecimiento, fah-l´yay-
the-me-**en**-to s death

fallido, fah-l´**yee**-do a
unsuccessful; bankrupt

fallo, fah-l´yo s sentence;
verdict

fama, fah-mah s fame;
reputation

familia, fah-**mee**-le-ah s
family

familiar, fah-me-le-**ar** a
familiar; domestic;
frequent

famoso, fah-**mo**-so a
famous

fanal, fah-**nahl** s
lighthouse; lantern

fanatismo, fah-nah-**tiss**-
mo s fanaticism

fandango, fahn-**dahn**-go s
fandango; Spanish
dance

fanfarrón, fahn-far-**rron** s
blusterer; show-off

fangal, fahn-**gahl** s slough;
quagmire

fango, fahn-go s mire;
mud

fantasía, fahn-tah-**see**-ah s
fantasy; fancy; caprice

fardel, far-del s bag;
knapsack

fardo, far-do s bale of

goods; parcel

farfante, far-**fahn**-tay s
boaster

farfullar, far-foo-l´**yar** v to
jabber

faringe, fah-**reen**-Hay s
pharynx

farmacéutico, far-mah-
thay´oo-te-ko s chemist;
druggist

farmacia, far-mah-**the**-ah
s pharmacy

faro, fah-ro s lighthouse

farol, fah-**rol** s lantern

farolear, fah-ro-lay-**ar** v to
strut

farsa, far-sah s farce

farsante, far-**sahn**-tay s
comic actor; fraud

fas (por –o por nefas),
fahs (por – o por **nay**-
fahs) adv justly or
unjustly

fascinar, fahs-the-**nar** v to
fascinate

fase, fah-say s phase

fastidiar, fahs-te-de-**ar** v to
annoy; to bother

fastidio, fahs-**tee**-de-o s
disgust; loathing

fastidioso, fahs-te-de-o-so
a annoying; bothersome

fastuoso, fahs-too-o´-so a
ostentatious

fatalidad, fah-tah-le-**dahd**
s fatality; misfortune

fatídico, fah-**tee**-de-ko a
ominous; fateful

fatiga, fah-**tee**-gah s
fatigue; weariness

fatigar, fah-te-**gar** v to tire

fatigoso, fah-te-**go**-so a
tiresome

fatuidad, fah-too´e-**dahd** s
foolishness

fatuo, fah-too´o a fatuous

fauces, fah´oo-thess s
fauces; gullet

fausto, fah´**ooss**-to s
splendor; pomp; a
happy; fortunate

fautor, fah´oo-**tor** s
accomplice; helper

favor, fah-**vor** s favor

favorable*, fah-vo-**rah**-
blay s favorable

favorecer, fah-vo-ray-
thair v to favor; to
protect

favorito, fah-vo-**ree**-to s
& a favorite

fax, fahks s fax

faz, fath s face

fe, fay s faith; certificate

fealdad, fay-ahl-**dahd** s
ugliness

febrero, fay-**bray**-ro s
February

febril, fay-**breel** a feverish

fecal, fay-**kahl** a feculent;
fecal

fecundar, fay-koon-**dar** v

to fecundate; to fertilize

fecundo, fay-**koon**-do *a* fruitful; prolific

fecha, fay-chah *s* date (of a letter, etc)

fechar, fay-char *v* to date

fechoría, fay-cho-ree-ah *s* misdeed

felicidad, fay-le-the-**dahd** *s* happiness

felicitar, fay-le-the-tar *v* to congratulate

feligrés, fay-le-**gress** *s* parishioner

feliz, fay-**leeth** *a* happy; fortunate

felonía, fay-lo-nee-ah *s* felony; treachery

felpudo, fel-**poo**-do *s* doormat; *a* shaggy

femenino, fay-may-nee-no *a* feminine

fementido, fay-men-tee-do *a* false; unfaithful

fenecer, fay-nay-thair *v* to finish; to die

fenecimiento, fay-nay-the-me-en-to *s* termination; death

fenómeno, fay-**no**-may-no *s* phenomenon

feo*, fay-o *a* ugly; deformed

feracidad, fay-rah-the-**dahd** *s* fertility

feraz, fay-**rath** *a* fertile

féretro, fay-ray-tro *s* bier; coffin

feria, fay-re-ah *s* fair

feriar, fay-re-ar *v* to buy; to sell; to barter

fermento, fair-men-to *s* leaven

ferocidad, fay-ro-the-**dahd** *s* ferocity

feroz, fay-**roth** *a* ferocious

ferrería, fair-rray-**ree**-ah *s* foundry

ferretería, fair-rray-tay-**ree**-ah *s* hardware store

ferrocarril, fair-rro-kar-**rreel** *s* railroad

fértil, fair-til *a* fertile

férula, fay-roo-lah *s* ferrule; authority

ferviente, fair-ve-en-tay *a* fervent

fervor, fair-vor *s* fervor; ardor

festejar, fess-tay-Har *v* to feast; to woo

festejo, fess-tay-Ho *s* feast; courtship

festín, fess-teen *s* feast; banquet

festivo*, fess-tee-vo *a* festive; merry

festón, fess-ton *s* festoon; wreath

fetidez, fay-te-deth *s* stench

fétido, fay-te-do *a* foul

smelling

feudo, fay-**oo**-do *s* fief; feud

fiado, (al), ahl fe-**ah**-do *adv* on credit

fiador, fe-ah-dor *s* surety; guarantor

fiambre, fe-**ahm**-bray *a* cold (meat or food)

fianza, fe-**ahn**-thah *s* security; bail

fiar, fe-ar *v* to guarantee; to set bail; to give credit; to entrust

fibra, fee-brah *s* fiber

ficción, fik-the-on *s* fiction; tale

ficticio, fik-tee-the-o *a* fictitious

ficha, fee-chah *s* marker; index card

fidedigno, fe-day-**dig**-no *a* trustworthy

fideicomisario, fe-day´e-ko-me-sah-re-o *s* trustee

fideicomiso, fe-day´e-ko-mee-so *s* trust

fidelidad, fe-day-le-**dahd** *s* fidelity

fideos, fe-day-os *s* vermicelli

fiebre, fe-´ay-bray *s* fever

fiel, fe-´ell *a* faithful

fieltro, fe-´ell-tro *s* felt

fiera, fe-´ay-rah *s* wild animal

fiereza, fe´ay-ray-thah s
fierceness; cruelty

fiero, fe´ay-ro a fierce;
ferocious; cruel

fiesta, fe´ess-tah s feast;
holiday

figón, fe-gon s cheap
restaurant

figonero, fe-go-nay-ro s
restaurant owner

figura, fe-goo-rah s figure;
shape; face; picture

figurar, fe-goo-rar v to
shape; to figure; to
sketch

figurilla, fe-goo-ree-l´yah
s figurine

figurón, fe-goo-ron s
pretentious nobody

fija, fee-Hah s door hinge

fijar, fe-Har v to fix; to
fasten; to settle (on); to
decide

fijeza, fe-Hay-thah s
firmness; stability

fijo*, fee-Ho a firm; fixed;
secure; settled

fila, fee-lah s row; line;
tier; rank

filamento, fe-lah-men-to s
filament; fiber

filete, fe-lay-tay s fillet;
hem; steak

filetear, fe-lay-tay-ar v to
fillet; to crease

filiación, fe-le´ah-the-on s
connection; relationship

filigrana, fe-le-grah-nah s
filigree

filo, fee-lo s cutting edge

filón, fe-lon s vein; lode

filosofía, fe-lo-so-fee-ah s
philosophy

filtrador, fil-trah-dor s
filter

filtro, feel-tro s filter; love
potion

fin, feen s end; conclusion

finado, fe-nah-do a
defunct; deceased

final*, fe-nahl a final

finalmente, fe-nahl-men-
tay adv finally

finca, feen-kah s real
estate

fineza, fe-nay-thah s
fineness; delicacy

fingimiento, fin-He-me-
en-to s simulation

fingir, fin-Heer v to feign;
to fake; to simulate

finiquito, fe-ne-kee-to s
closing of an account;
settlement

finito, fe-nee-to a finite

fino*, fee-no a fine; pure;
delicate; acute;
sagacious

finura, fe-noo-rah s
fineness; purity; delicacy

firma, feer-mah s
signature; firm;

company

firmar, feer-mar v to sign

firme*, feer-may a firm;
stable; secure; constant;
resolute

fiscal, fiss-kahl s district
attorney; a fiscal

fisco, fiss-ko s national
treasury

fisga, fiss-gah s banter;
chaff

fisgar, fiss-gar v to pry; to
peep

física, fee-se-kah s physics

físico, fee-se-ko s
naturalist; physician;
face; a physical

fisonomía, fe-so-no-mee-
ah s physiognomy

fístula, fiss-too-lah s
water-pipe; fistula

fisura, fe-soo-rah s fissure;
crack

flaco, flah-ko a lean; thin;
skinny

flacura, flah-koo-rah s
skinniness; meagerness;
weakness

flagrante, flah-grahn-tay a
flagrant; en –, en –, in
the act

flamante, flah-mahn-tay a
flaming; brand-new

flanco, flahn-ko s flank;
side

flaquear, flah-kay-ar v to

flag; to slacken; to dismay

flaqueza, flah-**kay**-thah *s* leanness; feebleness; weakness

flato, flah-to *s* flatulence; wind

flatulento, flah-too-**len**-to *a* flatulent

flauta, flah´oo-tah *s* flute

flautín, flah´oo-**teen** *s* piccolo

flautista, flah´oo-**tiss**-tah *s* flute player

fleco, flay-ko *s* fringe

flecha, flay-chah *s* arrow

flechero, flay-**chay**-ro *s* archer

fleje, flay-Hay *s* iron strap or hoop

flema, flay-mah *s* phlegm

flemático, flay-**mah-**te-ko *a* impassive

flemudo, flay-**moo-**do *a* sluggish; slow

fletador, flay-tah-**dor** *s* freighter; shipper

fletamento, flay-tah-**men**-to *s* freight; chartering

fletar, flay-tar *v* to hire; to charter

flete, flay-tay *s* freight; cargo

flexión, flek-se-**on** *s* flexion

flojedad, flo-Hay-**dahd** *s* slackness; looseness; weakness; laxity; laziness

flojo, flo-Ho *a* lazy; slack; feeble; flexible

flor, flor *s* flower

florear, flo-ray-**ar** *v* to adorn with flowers

florecer, flo-ray-**thair** *v* to blossom

florera, flo-**ray**-rah *s* flower girl

florero, flo-**ray**-ro *s* flower-pot

floresta, flo-**ress**-tah *s* forest; thicket

florete, flo-**ray**-tay *s* fencing foil

florido, flo-**ree**-do *a* florid; flowery

florón, flo-**ron** *s* large flower

flota, flo-tah *s* fleet

flotante, flo-**tahn**-tay *a* floating

flotar, flo-**tar** *v* to float

flote, flo-tay *s* floating; a –, ah –, afloat

flotilla, flo-tee-**l´yah** *s* small fleet

fluctuar, flook-too´**ar** *v* to fluctuate

fluidez, floo´e-**deth** *s* fluidity; fluency

flúido, floo´e-do *a* fluid; fluent

fluir, floo´**eer** *v* to flow; to run

flujo, floo-Ho *s* flux; flow

foca, fo-kah *s* seal

foco, foh-ko *s* focus; source; spotlight; floodlight

fofo, fo-fo *a* spongy; soft; flabby

fogata, fo-**gah**-tah *s* blaze; bonfire

fogón, fo-**gon** *s* hearth; cooking place; stove

fogoso, fo-**go**-so *a* impetuous; vehement

foliar, fo-le-**ar** *v* to foliate

folio, fo-le-o *s* folio; leaf

follaje, fo-l´**yah**-Hay *s* foliage

folletín, fo-l´yay-**teen** *s* serial story in a newspaper

folletista, fo-l´yay-**tiss**-tah *s* pamphleteer

folleto, fo-l´**yay**-to *s* pamphlet; tract

follón, fo-l´**yon** *&* a lazy; mess; chaos

fomentar, fo-men-**tar** *v* to foment; to promote

fomento, fo-**men**-to *s* promotion; fomentation

fonda, fon-dah *s* inn; hotel

fondista, fon-**diss**-tah *s* innkeeper

fondo, fon-do *s* bottom; depth; stock

fondos, fon-dos *s* funds; stocks

fonética, fo-nay-te-kah *s* phonetics

fónico, fo-ne-ko *a* acoustic; phonic

fonógrafo, fo-no-grah-fo *s* phonograph

fontanal, fon-tah-nahl *s* spring of water

forajido, fo-rah-Hee-do *s* outlaw

foráneo, fo-rah-nay-o *a* foreign; strange

forastero, fo-rahs-tay-ro *a* strange; exotic; *s* stranger; visitor

forcejear, for-thay-Hay-ar *v* to struggle; to strive

forcejeo, for-thay-Ho *s* struggle

forense, fo-ren-say *a* forensic

forja, for-Hah *s* forge; iron foundry

forjador, for-Hah-dor *s* forger; blacksmith

forma, for-mah *s* form; shape; manner

formar, for-mar *v* to form; to shape; to educate; to line up

formalidad, for-mah-le-dahd *s* formality; requisite; requirement

formalizar, for-mah-le-thar *v* to make complete; to legalize

formón, for-mon *s* chisel

fórmula, for-moo-lah *s* formula; recipe

fornicario, for-ne-kah-re-o *s* fornicator

fornido, for-nee-do *a* robust; stout

foro, fo-ro *s* court of justice; bar

forraje, for-rrah-Hay *s* fodder

forrar, for-rrar *v* to line; to cover

fortachón, for-tah-chon *a* very strong

fortalecer, for-tah-lay-thair *v* to strengthen; to encourage

fortaleza, for-tah-lay-thah *s* fortitude; courage; vigor; fortress

fortificar, for-te-fe-kar *v* to fortify

fortín, for-teen *s* small fort

fortuito*, for-too´e-to *a* fortuitous

fortuna, for-too-nah *s* fortune; chance; fate

forzadamente, for-thah-dah-men-tay *adv* forcefully

forzamiento, for-thah-me-en-to *s* forcing

forzoso, for-tho-so *a* unavoidable; compulsory

forzudo, for-thoo-do *a* strong

fosa, fo-sah *s* grave; pit

fosco, fos-ko *a* frowning; cross

fosforera, fos-fo-ray-rah *s* matchbox

fósforo, fos-fo-ro *s* phosphorus; match

fósil, fo-sil *s* & *a* fossil

foso, fo-so *s* pit; moat; ditch

fotografía, fo-to-grah-fee-ah *s* photography

fotógrafo, fo-to-grah-fo *s* photographer

frac, frahk *s* tails (clothing)

fracasar, frah-kah-sar *v* to fail

fracaso, frah-kah-so *s* downfall; ruin; failure

fracturar, frahk-too-rar *v* to fracture; to break

fragancia, frah-gahn-the-ah *s* fragrance; scent

fragata, frah-gah-tah *s* frigate

frágil, frah-Hil *a* fragile; brittle; frail

fragmento, frag-men-to *s*

fragment

fragoso, frah-**go**-so *a* craggy; rough; eneven

fragua, frah-goo´ah *s* forge

fraguar, frah-goo´ar *v* to forge; to contrive

fraile, frah´e-lay *s* friar

frambuesa, frahm-boo´ay-sah *s* raspberry

francachela, frahn-kah-chay-lah *s* luxurious feast

franco, frahn-ko *s* franc; *a* frank; open; free

franela, frah-**nay**-lah *s* flannel

franja, frahn-Hah *s* fringe

franquear, franh-kay-**ar** *v* to exempt; to prepay; to disengage

franqueo, frahn-**kay**-o *s* postage

franqueza, frahn-**kay**-thah *s* freedom; frankness

franquicia, frahn-**kee**-the-ah *s* exemption

frasco, frahs-ko *s* flask

frase, frah-say *s* phrase

frasquera, frahs-**kay**-rah *s* case (for bottles)

fraude, frah´oo-day *s* fraud

fraudulento, frah´oo-doo-len-to *a* fraudulent

fray, frah´e *s* friar

frecuentar, fray-koo´en-tar *v* to frequent

frecuente*, fray-koo´en-tay *a* frequent

fregadero, fray-gah-**day**-ro *s* kitchen sink

fregar, fray-**gar** *v* to rub; to scour; to scrub

fregona, fray-**go**-nah *s* mop

freir, fray-eer *v* to fry

frenesí, fray´nay-**see** *s* frenzy

frenético, fray-nay-te-ko *a* mad; frantic

freno, fray-no *s* bridle; brake

frente, fren-tay *s* front; face; **en–,** en–, opposite

fresa, fray-sah *s* strawberry

frescachón, fress-kah-chon *a* stout; good-looking

fresco, fress-ko *a* fresh; cool; recent

frescura, fress-koo-rah *s* freshness; frankness; tranquillity; boldness

fresno fress-no *s* ash tree

frialdad, fre-ahl-**dahd** *s* coldness

fricción, frik-the-on *s* friction

friegaplatos, fre´ay-gah-plah-tos *s* dishwasher

frigidez, fre-**He**-deth *s* frigidity

frígido, free-**He**-do *a* frigid

frigo, free-go *s* fridge

frigorífico, fre-go-**ree**-fe-ko *s* refrigerator

frío, free-o *a* cold; indifferent

friolento, fre-o-len-to *a* very sensitive to cold

frisar, fre-**sar** *v* to frizzle; to resemble; to approach

fritada, fritura, fre-**tah**-dah, fre-**too**-rah *s* dish of fried fish

frito, free-to *a* fried

frívolo, free-vo-lo *a* frivolous

frondoso, fron-**do**-so *a* leafy

frontal, fron-**tahl** *a* frontal

frontera, fron-**tay**-rah *s* frontier

fronterizo, fron-tay-**ree**-tho *a* bordering upon; opposite

frotación, fro-tah-the-**on** *s* rubbing; friction

frotar, fro-**tar** *v* to rub

fructuoso, frook-too´**o**-so *a* fruitful; profitable

frugal, froo-**gahl** *a* frugal; sparing

fruición, froo´e-the-**on** *s*

fruition; enjoyment

fruncir, froon-**theer** v to pucker; to frown

fruslería, frooss-lay-**ree**-ah s trifle; futility

frustrar, frooss-**trar** v to frustrate

fruta, froo-tah s fruit

frutero, froo-**tay**-ro s fruit seller; fruit dish

fruto, froo-to s fruit; profit

¡fu! foo interj phew! **ni – ni fa,** ne – ne fah, (fam) neither the one nor the other

fuego, foo´ay-go s fire

fuente, foo´en-tay s fountain; source; dish

fuera, foo´ay-rah adv from outward; interj out of the way!

fuero, foo´ay-ro s statute; jurisdiction

fuerte, foo´air-tay adv strongly; a vigorous; strong

fuerza, foo´air-thah s strength; force

fuga, foo-gah s flight; escape

fugarse, foo-**gar**-say v to escape; to fly

fugaz, foo-**gath** a fugacious; fleeting

fugitivo, foo-He-**tee**-vo a

fugitive; runaway

fulano, foo-**lah**-no s such a one; –, sutano y mengano, –, soo-**tah**-no e men-**gah**-no, Tom, Dick and Harry

fulgente, fool-**Hen**-tay a dazzling; bright

fulgor, fool-**gor** s resplendence; radiance

fuliginoso, foo-le-He-**no**-so a dark; obscure

fulminante, fool-me-**nahn**-tay s cap; a fulminating; explosive

fullería, fool-l´yay-**ree**-ah s cheating at play

fullero, fool-l´**yay**-ro s card shark; cheat

fumadero, foo-mah-**day**-ro s smoking-room

fumador, foo-mah-**dor** s smoker

fumar, foo-**mar** v to smoke

función, foon-the-**on** s function; festival; performance

funcionar, foon-the-o-**nar** v to work; to operate

funcionario, foon-the-o-**nah**-re-o s official; functionary

funda, foon-dah s case; sheath; cover; envelope

fundador, foon-dah-**dor** s founder

fundamental, foon-dah-men-**tahl** a basic

fundamento, foon-dah-**men**-to s foundation; basis

fundar, foon-**dar** v to found; to ground

fundible, foon-dee-**blay** a fusible

fundición, foon-de-the-on s fusion; foundry; melting

fundir, foon-**deer** v to melt metals; to fuse

fúnebre, foo-nay-bray a mournful; sad

funesto, foo-**ness**-to a fatal; disastrous

furgón, foor-gon s van; wagon

furia, foo-re-ah s fury

furibundo, foo-re-**boon**-do a furious; frantic

furioso, foo-re-o-so a furious; raging

furor, foo-ror s fury

furtivo, foor-tee-vo a furtive

fuselaje, foo-say-lah-Hay s fuselage

fusil, foo-**seel** s rifle; gun; musket

fusilero, foo-se-lay-ro s rifleman

fusión, foo-se-on s fusion; alliance; amalgamation

fusta, fooss-tah *s*
  whiplash
fustán, fooss-**tahn** *s*
  fustian (fabric)
fustigar, fooss-te-**gar** *v* to
  cudgel; to fustigate
fútil, foo-til *a* futile
futilidad, foo-te-le-**dahd** *s*
  futility
futuro, foo-**too**-ro *a* future

gabán, gah-**bahn** s
overcoat

gabardina, gah-bar-**dee**-nah s gabardine;
raincoat

gabarra, gah-**bar**-rrah s
lighter; barge

gabarro, gah-**bar**-rro s
defect in cloth; error in
accounts

gabela, gah-**bay**-lah s
burden; duty; excise

gabinete, gah-be-**nay**-tay s
cabinet; study

gaceta, gah-**thay**-tah s
gazette

gachas, gah-**chahs** s
porridge; gruel

gacho, gah-cho a curved;
bent downwards

gafa, gah-fah s hook; pl
glasses

gafetes, gah-**fay**-tess s
hooks and eyes; clasp

gaita, gah´e-tah s bagpipe;
flageolet

gajo, gah-Ho s branch;
bunch

gala, gah-lah s gala; full
dress

galán, gah-**lahn** s gallant;
a handsome man

galano, gah-**lah**-no a
genteel; elegant

galante*, gah-**lahn**-tay a
gallant; courtly

galantear, gah-lahn-tay-ar
v to court; to flirt

galanteo, gah-lahn-**tay**-o s
courtship; flirting

galantería, gah-lahn-tay-**ree**-ah s gallantry

galanura, gah-lah-**noo**-rah
s showiness; gracefulness

galápago, gah-lah-pah-go s
fresh-water tortoise

galardón, gah-lar-**don** s
reward

galardonar, gah-lar-do-**nar** v to reward; to
recompense

galbana, gahl-**bah**-nah s
laziness

galeote, gah-lay-o-tay s
galley-slave

galera, gah-**lay**-rah s
galley; wagon

galería, gah-lay-**ree**-ah s
gallery

galgo, **gahl**-go s greyhound

gálico, **gah**-le-ko s syphilis

galimatías, gah-le-mah-**tee**-ahs s gibberish

galocha, gah-lo-chah s
galosh; clog

galón, gah-**lon** s lace;
braid; trimming

galonear, gah-lo-nay-ar v
to trim with lace

galopar, gah-lo-par v to
gallop

galope, gah-**lo**-pay s gallop

galopín, gah-lo-**peen** s
scoundrel; smart aleck

gallarda, gah-l´**yar**-dah s
Spanish dance

gallardear, gah-l´yar-day-ar v to act with grace

gallardía, gah-l´yar-dee-ah
s gracefulness

gallardo*, gah-l´yar-do *a* gay; graceful; gallant

gallear, gah-l´yay-ar *v* to shout; to assume an air of importance

galleta, gah-l´yay-tah *s* biscuit; cookie

gallina, gah-l´yee-nah *s* hen

gallinero, gah-l´yee-nay-ro *s* chicken-coop

gallito, gah-l´yee-to *s* beau; coxcomb

gallo, gah-l´yo *s* cock

gama, gah-mah *s* range; gamut

gamberro, gahm-bay-rro *s* hooligan

gamberro, gahm-bay-rro *s* hooligan

gambeta, gahm-bay-tah *s* prance; caper

gamella, gah-may-l´yah *s* wooden trough

gamo, gah-mo *s* buck

gamuza, gah-moo-thah *s* chamois; chamois leather

gana, gah-nah *s* appetite; inclination; desire

ganadero, gah-nah-day-ro *s* cattle owner, cattle dealer

ganado, gah-nah-do *s* cattle; herd; drove

ganancia, gah-nahn-the-ah *s* gain; profit

ganar, gah-nar *v* to gain; to win

gancho, gahn-cho *s* hook

ganga, gahn-gah *s* bargain

gangoso, gahn-go-so *a* nasal; twangy

ganoso, gah-no-so *a* desirous

gansada, gahn-sah-dah *s* stupidity

ganso, gansa, gahn-so, gahn-sah *s* gander; goose; silly person

ganzúa, gahn-thoo-ah *s* picklock

gañán, gah-n´yahn *s* laborer

garabatear, gah-rah-bah-tay-ar *v* to hook; to scrawl; to scribble

garabato, gah-rah-bah-to *s* hook; scribble

garante, gah-rahn-tay *s* guarantor

garantía, gah-rahn-tee-ah *s* guarantee; security

garantizar, gah-rahn-te-thar *v* to guarantee

garañón, gah-rah-n´yon *s* stallion

garbanzo, gar-bahn-tho *s* chick pea

garbear, gar-bay-ar *v* to affect an air of dignity

garbillar, gar-be-l´yar *v* to sift

garbillo, gar-bee-l´yo *s* sieve

garbo, gar-bo *s* gracefulness; elegance

garboso, gar-bo-so *a* graceful; gallant

garfio, garfe-o *s* hook; gaff

gargajear, gar-gah-Hay-ar *v* to spit; to expectorate

garganta, gar-gahn-tah *s* throat; ravine

gargantilla, gar-gahn-tee-l´yah *s* necklace

gárgara, gar-gah-rah *s* gargle

gargarismo, gar-gah-riss-mo *s* gargle

gárgola, gar-go-lah *s* gargoyle

garguero, gar-gay-ro *s* windpipe

garita, gah-ree-tah *s* cabin; lavatory

garito, gah-ree-to *s* gambling casino

garlar, gar-lar *v* to chatter

garlito, gar-lee-to *s* snare; trap

garra, gar-rrah *s* claw; talon

garrafa, gar-rrah-fah *s* decanter; carafe

garrafal, gar-rrah-fahl *s* great; huge

garrafón, gar-rrah-**fon** s large carafe

garrapata, gar-rrah-**pah**-tah s tick (insect)

garrapatear, gar-rrah-pah-tay-**ar** v to scribble

garrocha, gar-**rro**-chah s dart; pole (vaulting)

garrote, gar-**rro**-tay s club; truncheon; garrote (strangulation)

garrotillo, gar-rro-tee-l´yo s croup

garrucha, gar-**rroo**-chah s pulley

gárrulo, gar-rroo-lo a chirping; prattling; garrulous

garulla, gah-roo-l´yah s (fam) rabble

garza, gar-thah s heron

garzo, gar-tho a blue-eyed

gas, gahs s gas

gasa, gah-sah s gauze

gasolina, gah-so-lee-nah s gas

gasolinera, gah-so-lee-nay-rah s gas station

gastador, gahs-tah-**dor** s spendthrift; wasteful; pioneer

gastar, gahs-**tar** v to expend; to spend; to waste; to use

gasto, gahs-**to** s expense; amount; spent

gata, gah-tah s female cat

gatear, gah-tay-**ar** v to climb up; to clamber

gato, gah-to s cat

gatuno, gah-**too**-no a feline; catlike

gaveta, gah-**vay**-tah s drawer; till; locker

gavilán, gah-ve-**lahn** s sparrow-hawk

gavilla, gah-vee-l´yah s sheaf; stalk

gavión, gah-ve-**on** s gabion

gaviota, gah-ve-o-tah s seagull

gavota, gah-vo-tah s gavotte

gayo, gah-yo a gay; merry

gazapo, gah-**thah**-po s young rabbit; error; blunder

gazmoñería, gath-mo-n´yay-**ree**-ah s prudishness; hypocrisy

gaznate, gath-**nah**-tay s windpipe

gazuza, gah-**thoo**-thah s violent hunger

gema, Hay-mah s gem

gemelo, Hay-**may**-lo s twin; m pl binocular; cufflinks

gemido, Hay-mee-do s groan; moan

gemir, Hay-**meer** v to moan

genciana, Hen-the-**ah**-nah s gentian

generador, Hay-nay-rah-**dor** s generator

general, Hay-nay-**rahl** s general; a general

genérico, Hay-**nay**-re-ko a generic

género, Hay-nay-ro s genus; class; kind; genre; **– humano,** – oo-**mah**-no, mankind

generoso*, Hay-nay-**ro**-so a generous

génesis, Hay-nay-siss s genesis; origin; beginning

genio, Hay-ne-o s genius; disposition; temper

gente, Hen-tay s people; folk; nation; family

gentecilla, Hen-tay-thee-l´yah s riffraff

gentil, Hen-**teel** s heathen; a genteel; elegant

gentileza, Hen-te-lay-thah s gentility; refinement

gentilhombre, Hen-til-om-bray s aristocrat

gentilidad, Hen-te-le-**dahd** s paganism

gentío, Hen-**tee**-o s crowd

genuino, Hay-noo´ee-no a

genuine

geografía, Hay-o-grah-**fee**-ah s geography

geométrico, Hay-o-**may**-tre-ko a geometrical; geometric

gerencia, Hay-**ren**-the-ah s management

gerente, Hay-**ren**-tay s manager

germen, Hair-men s germ; origin

germinar, Hair-me-**nar** v to germinate; to sprout

gestear, Hess-tay-**ar** v to make grimaces; to gesture

gesticular, Hess-te-koo-**lar** v to gesticulate

gestión, Hess-te-**on** s management; negotiation; measure; step

gestionar, Hess-te-o-**nar** v to negotiate; to procure; to deal; to manage

gesto, Hess-to s face; gesture

gestor, Hess-**tor** s manager; promoter

giba, Hee-bah s hump; hunch

gibado, He-**bah**-do a hunchbacked

gigante, He-**gahn**-tay s giant; a gigantic

gimnasio, Hem-**nah**-se´o s gym

gimotear, He-mo-tay-**ar** v to whine

ginebra, He-**nay**-brah s gin

gira, Hee-rah s tour; excursion

girado, He-**rah**-do s drawee

girador, He-rah-**dor** s drawer (of checks)

girar, He-**rar** v to rotate; to revolve; to turn round; to draw (checks)

girasol, He-rah-**sol** s sunflower

giro, Hee-ro s turning round; expression; draft; circulation (of checks)

gitanear, He-tah-nay-**ar** v to flatter; to wheedle

gitano, He-**tah**-no s gypsy

glacial, glah-the-**al** a icy

glándula, **glahn**-doo-lah s gland

glaseado, glah-**say**-ah-do a glazed; glossy

globo, **glo**-bo s globe; sphere; balloon

gloria, **glo**-re-ah s glory

gloriarse, glo-re-**ar**-say v to glory; to boast in

glorieta, glo-re-**ay**-tah s arbor; bower; roundabout

glorificar, glo-re-fe-**kar** v to glorify

glorioso, glo-re-**o**-so a glorious

glosa, **glo**-sah s gloss; commentary

glosario, glo-**sah**-re-o s glossary

glotón, glo-**ton** s glutton

glotonería, glo-to-nay-**ree**-ah s gluttony

glutinoso, gloo-te-**no**-so a glutinous; viscous

gobernación, go-bair-nah-the-**on** s government

gobernador, go-bair-nah-**dor** s governor; ruler

gobernar, go-bair-**nar** v to govern

gobierno, go-be-**air**-no s government

gobio, **go**-be-o s gudgeon

goce, **go**-thay s enjoyment

gola, **go**-lah s gullet; throat; gorge

goleta, go-**lay**-tah s schooner

golfo, **gol**-fo s gulf; bay; ragamuffin

golondrina, go-lon-**dree**-nah s swallow

golosina, go-lo-**see**-nah s titbit; delicacy

golpe, **gol**-pay s blow; stroke; hit; knock; dent

golpeador, gol-pay-ah-**dor**

s striker; knocker

golpear, gol-pay-**ar** *v* to beat; to strike; to knock; to bruise

golpeo, gol-**pay**-o *s* beating; striking

goma, go-**mah** *s* gum

gondolero, gon-do-**lay**-ro *s* gondolier

gordal, gor-**dahl** *a* fat; fleshy; big

gordo, **gor**-do *a* fat; corpulent

gordura, gor-**doo**-rah *s* grease; plumpness; corpulence

gorgorito, gor-go-**ree**-to *s* quiver of the voice; warble

gorila, go-**ree**-lah *s* gorilla

gorjeo, gor-**Hay**-o *s* trill; quaver

gorra, **gor**-rrah *s* cap; bonnet

gorrión, gor-rre-**on** *s* sparrow

gorrista, gor-**rriss**-tah *s* parasite; sponger

gorro, **gor**-rro *s* night cap

gorrón, gor-**rron** *s* parasite; sponge

gorronear, gor-rro-nay-**ahr** *v* scrounge

gota, go-**tah** *s* drop; gout

gotear, go-tay-**ar** *v* to drop; to dribble; to drip

gotera, go-**tay**-rah *s* gutter; leakage; leak

gotoso, go-**to**-so *a* gouty

gozar, go-**thar** *v* to enjoy

gozo, **go**-tho *s* joy; pleasure

gozoso, go-**tho**-so *a* joyful

grabador, grah-bah-**dor** *s* engraver

grabar, grah-**bar** *v* to engrave

gracia, **grah**-the-ah *s* grace; favor

grácil, **grah**-thil *a* slender; fine

gracioso, grah-the-**o**-so *a* graceful; funny; amusing

grada, **grah**-dah *s* step of a staircase; bleachers

gradar, grah-**dar** *v* to harrow

gradería, grah-day-**ree**-ah *s* series of seats or steps

grado, **grah**-do *s* step; degree; will; pleasure

graduado, grah-doo-´**ah**-do *s* graduate; *a* graduated

graduar, grah-doo-´**ar** *v* to grade; to divide into degrees; to graduate

gráfica, **grah**-fe-kah *s* graph

gráfico, **grah**-fe-ko *a* graphic; graphical

grafito, grah-**fee**-to *s* graphite

grajo, **grah**-Ho *s* rook

gramática, grah-**mah**-te-kah *s* grammar

gramo, **grah**-mo *s* gram

gramófono, grah-**mo**-fo-no *s* phonograph

gran, grahn *a* used only before substantives in the singular (see **grande**)

grana, **grah**-nah *s* grain; cochineal

granada, grah-**nah**-dah *s* pomegranate; shell; grenade

granado, grah-**nah**-do *a* notable; select; pomegranate tree

granar, grah-**nar** *v* to seed

grande, **grahn**-day *s* grandee; *a* great; large; big; grand

grandeza, grahn-**day**-thah *s* greatness; grandeur; grandeeship

grandioso, grahn-de-o-so *a* grand; splendid

grandor, grahn-**dor** *s* size; tallness

granel, grah-**nel** *s* heap of grain; a –, ah –, in bulk

granero, grah-**nay**-ro *s* granary; barn

granito, grah-**nee**-to *s* granite

granizada, grah-ne-**thah**-

dah *s* hailstorm

granizar, grah-ne-**thar** *v* to hail

granja, grahn-Hah *s* farm

granjear, grahn-Hay-ar *v* to gain; to earn; to profit

granjería, grahn-Hay-ree-ah *s* gain; profit

grano, grah-no *s* grain

granuja, grah-**noo**-Hah *s* rogue; ragamuffin

grapa, grah-pah *s* staple

grasa, grah-sah *s* grease; drippings; fat

grasera, grah-say-rah *s* dripping pan

grasiento, grah-se-**en**-to *a* greasy; filthy; oily

graso, grah-so *a* fat; oily

gratificar, grah-te-fe-**kar** *v* to reward; to tip; to gratify

gratitud, grah-te-**tood** *s* gratitude

grato*, grah-to *a* pleasant; acceptable; grateful

gratuito, grah-too´ee-to *a* gratuitous; free of charge

gravamen, grah-**vah**-men *s* charge; obligation; mortgage

gravar, grah-**var** *v* to burden

grave, grah-vay *a* weighty; grave; important; serious

gravedad, grah-vay-**dahd** *s*

gravity; heaviness; seriousness

gravoso, grah-**vo**-so *a* onerous; unbearable

graznar, grath-**nar** *v* to croak; to cackle

greda, gray-dah *s* chalk; loam; clay

greguería, gray-gay-ree-ah *s* outcry; uproar

gremio, gray-me-o *s* society; corporation; union

greña, gray-n´yah *s* long, entangled hair

greñudo, gray-n´yoo-do *a* disheveled

gresca, gress-kah *s* clatter; tumult; wrangle; confusion

grey, gray´e *s* flock; herd; congregation

grieta, gre-ay-tah *s* crevice; crack; flaw

grietarse, gray-ay-tar-say *v* to crack; to split

grifo, gree-fo *s* griffin (myth); tap

grifón, gre-**fon** *s* large faucet

grillete, gre-l´yay-tay *s* shackles; fetters

grillo, gree-l´yo *s* cricket (insect); *pl* fetters

grima, gree-mah *s* uneasiness; aversion;

disgust

gripe, gree-pay *s* influenza; flu

gris, griss *a* dull; gray

grita, gree-tah *s* uproar; clamor

gritar, gre-tar *v* to shout; to scream; to cry out; to shriek

griterío, gre-tay-ree-oh *s* outcry; shouting

grito, gree-to *s* cry; scream; shout

grosella, gro-say-´lyah *s* red currant

grosería, gro-say-ree-ah *s* rudeness; ill-breeding

grosero, gro-**say**-ro *a* coarse; rude

grosura, gro-soo-rah *s* grease; fat

grúa, groo´ah *s* crane (machine)

gruesa, groo´ay-sah *s* gross (twelve dozen)

grueso, groo´ay-so *s* corpulence; *a* bulky; gross; large; coarse

grulla, groo-l´yah *s* crane (bird)

grumete, groo-**may**-tay *s* cabin-boy

grumo, groo-mo *s* lump; curd; cluster; clot

gruñido, groo-n´yee-do *s* grunt; growl

gruñir, groo-n´**yeer** v to grunt; to creak

grupa, **groo**-pah s croup

grupo, **groo**-po s group

gruta, **groo**-tah s grotto; cavern

guadaña, goo´ah-**dah**-n´yah s scythe

guadañar, goo´ah-dah-n´**yar** v to mow

guantada, goo´ahn-**tah**-dah s slap with the open hand

guante, goo´**ahn**-tay s glove

guantería, goo´ahn-tay-ree-ah s glove shop

guantero, goo´ahn-**tay**-ro s glover

guapeza, goo´ah-**pay**-thah s courage; good looks; prettiness

guapo, goo´ah-po a good looking; handsome; valiant

guarda, goo´**ar**-dah s guard; keeper; custody

guardabosque, goo´ar-dah-**bos**-kay s forester; gamekeeper

guardabrisa, goo´ar-dah-**bree**-sah s shade

guardacantón, goo´ar-dah-kahn-ton s cornerstone

guardacostas, goo´ar-dah-

kos-tahs s coastguard

guardameta, goo-ar-dah-**may**-tah s goalkeeper

guardar, goo´**ar**-dar v to keep; to guard

guardarropa, goo´ar-dar-**rro**-pah s wardrobe

guardería infantil, goo´ar-day-**ree**-ah in-fahn-**teel** s creche

guardia, goo´**ar**-de-ah s guard; watch

guardián, goo´**ar**-de-ahn s keeper; guardian

guardilla, goo´ar-dee-l´yah s attic

guardoso, goo´ar-**do**-so a stingy

guarecer, goo´ah-ray-**thair** v to shelter; to assist; to aid; to cure

guarida, goo´ah-**ree**-dah s den; haunt; hideout; shelter

guarismo, goo´ah-**riss**-mo s number; cipher; figure

guarnecer, goo´ar-nay-**thair** v to garnish; to set; to adorn

guarnición, goo´ar-ne-the-on s equipment; adornment; garnish

guarro, goo´**ar**-rro s pig

guasa, goo´ah-sah s jest; irony

guason, goo´ah-**son** a

joking; humoress; dull

gubia, goo-be-ah s gouge

guedeja, gay-**day**-Hah s lion's mane; lock of hair

guerra, gair-rrah s war; warfare; hostility

guerrero, gair-**rray**-ro s warrior; a warlike

guerrilla, gair-**rree**-l´yah s guerrilla warfare

guerrillero, gair-rree-l´**yay**-ro s partisan; guerrilla fighter

guía, **ghee**-ah s guidebook; guide

guiar, ghee-**ar** v to guide

guija, ghee-Hah s pebble

guijarro, ghee-**Har**-rro s pebble; stone; cobblestone

guinda, **gheen**-dah s cherry

guindilla, gheen-dee-l´yah s red pepper

guiñada, ghee-n´**yah**-dah s wink

guiñapo, ghee-n´**yah**-po s tatter; rag

guiñar, ghee-n´**yar** v to wink

guión, ghee-**on** s script; outline; standard; hyphen

guirnalda, gheer-**nahl**-dah s garland

guisado, ghee-**sah**-do s

stew

guisante, ghee-**sahn**-tay s
pea

guisar, ghee-**sar** v to cook

guiso, ghee-**so** s seasoning;
cooked dish

guitarra, ghee-**tar**-rrah s
guitar

gula, goo-lah s gluttony

gusano, goo-**sah**-no s
worm

gustar, gooss-**tar** v to taste;
to like; to enjoy

gusto, gooss-to s taste;
pleasure

gustoso*, gooss-**to**-so a
tasty; pleasing

gutural, goo-too-**rahl** a
guttural

haba, ah-bah *s* bean

habanera, ah-bah-**nay-rah** *s* Cuban dance

habano, ah-**bah**-no *s* Havana cigar

haber, ah-**bair** *v* to have, – **de,** – day, to have to... *s* property; assets

habichuela, ah-be-choo´ay-lah *s* French bean

hábil*, **ah-bil** *a* capable; skillful

habilidad, ah-be-le-**dahd** *s* ability; skill

habilitado, ah-be-le-**tah**-do *s* paymaster; *a* qualified

habitante, ah-be-**tahn-tay** *s* inhabitant

hábito, ah-**be**-to *s* dress; habit; custom

habituar, ah-be-too´ar *v* to accustom

habla, **ah**-blah *s* speech; language

hablador, ah-blah-**dor** *s* chatterbox; gossip; gossipy

habladuría, ah-blah-doo-**ree**-ah *s* gossip; slanderous talk

hablar, ah-**blar** *v* to speak; to talk

hacedero, ah-thay-**day**-ro *a* feasible

hacendado, ah-then-**dah**-do *s* landholder

hacendista, ah-then-**diss**-tah *s* financier; economist

hacer, ah-**thair** *v* to make; to do; to perform; to produce

hacer autostop, *v* hitchhike

hacia, **ah**-the-ah *adv* towards; about; near

hacienda, ah-the-**en**-dah *s* large farm; landed property; wealth; public treasury

hacinar, ah-the-**nar** *v* to pile up

hacha, **ah**-chah *s* ax; hatchet

hachear, ah-chay-**ar** *v* to hew; to cut

halagar, ah-lah-**gar** *v* to cajole; to flatter

halagos, ah-**lah**-gos *s* cajolery; flattery

halagüeño, ah-lah-goo´ay-n´yo *a* flattering; alluring

halar, ah-**lar** *v* to haul; to pull on

halcón, ahl-**kon** *s* falcon

hálito, **ah**-le-to *s* breath; vapor

hallar, ah-l´yar *v* to find; to meet with

hallazgo, ah-l´yath-go *s* find; discovery

hamaca, ah-**mah**-kah *s* hammock

hambre, **ahm**-bray *s* hunger; famine; longing

hambrear, ahm-bray-**ar** *v* to starve; to be hungry

hambriento, ahm-bre-en-to *a* hungry; eager

hamburguesa, ahm-boor-gay-sah *s* hamburger

haragán, ah-rah-gahn *s* idler; loiterer

harapo, ah-rah-po *s* rag; tatter

harina, ah-ree-nah *s* flour; meal

harinoso, ah-re-no-so *a* floury; mealy

hartar, ar-tar *v* to exasperate; to tire; to cloy; to satiate

harto, ar-to *adv* enough; *a* satiated; sufficient

hartura, ar-too-rah *s* satiety

hasta, ahs-tah *prep* until; up to; down to; as far as

hastío, ahs-tee-o *s* loathing; weariness; tedium

hato, ah-to *s* flock; herd

haya, ah-yah *s* beech tree

haz, ath *s* bunch; bundle; sheaf

hazaña, ah-thah-n´yah *s* feat; exploit; heroic deed

hazañería, ah-thah-n´yay-ree-ah *s* affectation

hazañero, ah-thah-n´yay-ro *a* affected

hazañoso, ah-thah-n´yo-so *a* valiant; heroic

hazmerreir, ath-mair-rray-eer *s* laughingstock

hebilla, ay-bee-l´yah *s* buckle; clasp

hebra, ay-brah *s* needful; thread; fiber

hechicero, ay-che-thay-ro *s* charmer; wizard; sorcerer; *a* bewitching

hechizar, ay-che-thar *v* to enchant; to bewitch

hechizo, ay-chee-tho *s* enchantment

hecho, ay-cho *s* action; feat; point in litigation; *a* made; ready-made; done

hechura, ay-choo-rah *s* form; shape; make; workmanship

heder, ay-dair *v* to stink

hedor, ay-dor *s* stench; stink

helada, ay-lah-dah *s* frost; nip

helado, ay-lah-do *s* ice cream; *a* frozen

helar, ay-lar *v* to freeze; to congeal

hélice, ay-le-thay *s* helix; propeller

helicóptero, ay-le-kop-tay-ro *s* helicopter

hembra, em-brah *s* female

hemorragia, ay-mor-rrah-Hee-ah *s* hemorrhage

hemorroide, ay-mor-rroe-day *s* hemorrhoids; piles

henchir, en-cheer *v* to fill up; to stuff

hendedura, en-day-doo-rah *s* crack; chink; cranny

hender, en-dair *v* to crack; to cleave; to split

heno, ay-no *s* hay

heraldo, ay-rahl-do *s* herald

herbaje, air-bah-Hay *s* herbage; pastureland

herborizar, air-bo-re-thar *v* to gather herbs

heredad, ay-ray-dahd *s* farm; property

heredar, ay-ray-dar *v* to inherit

heredero, ay-ray-day-ro *s* heir

hereje, ay-ray-Hay *s* heretic

herejía, ay-ray-Hee-ah *s* heresy

herencia, ay-ren-the-ah *s* inheritance

herida, ay-ree-dah *s* wound

herir, ay-reer *v* to wound; to strike; to offend

hermana, air-mah-nah *s* sister

hermanar, air-mah-**nar** v to match; to suit; to fraternize

hermanastra, air-mah-**nahs**-trah s stepsister

hermanastro, air-mah-**nahs**-tro s stepbrother

hermandad, air-mahn-**dahd** s fraternity; conformity; brotherhood

hermano, air-**mah**-no s brother

hermoso, air-**mo**-so a beautiful; handsome

hermosura, air-mo-**soo**-rah s beauty

héroe, **ay**-ro-ay s hero

heroína, ay-ro-ee-nah s heroine

herrador, air-rrah-**dor** s blacksmith

herradura, air-rrah-**doo**-rah s horseshoe

herramental, air-rrah-men-**tahl** s tool kit

herrar, air-**rrar** v to shoe horses

herrero, air-**rray**-ro s blacksmith

herrumbre, air-**rroom**-bray s rust

hervir, air-**veer** v to boil

hervor, air-**vor** s boil

hético, **ay**-te-ko a consumptive

hez, eth s lee; scum; dregs; pl **heces**, **ay**-thess, excrement

hidalgo, e-**dahl**-go s nobleman

hidalguía, e-dahl-**ghee**-ah s nobility

hiedra, e-ay-drah s ivy

hiel, e-**ell** s gall; bile

hielo, e-**ay**-lo s frost; ice

hiena, e-ay-nah s hyena

hierba, e-**air**-bah s grass; weed; herb

hierro, e-**air**-rro s iron tool

hígado, **ee**-gah-do s liver

higiene, e-He'**ay**-nay s hygiene

higo, **ee**-go s fig

higuera, e-**gay**-rah s fig tree

hijo, **ee**-Ho s son

hija, **ee**-Hah s daughter

hijuela, e-Hoo'**ay**-lah s patch; mattress; little daughter

hila, **ee**-lah s row; line

hilacha, e-**lah**-chah s loose thread; filament

hilado, e-**lah**-do s spun material; yarn; a spun

hilador, e-lah-**dor** s spinner

hilar, e-**lar** v to spin

hilaridad, e-lah-re-**dahd** s hilarity

hilera, e-**lay**-rah s row; line; file

hilo, **ee**-lo s thread

hilván, il-**vahn** s basting

hilvanar, il-vah-**nar** v to tack; to baste; to stitch

himeneo, e-may-**nay**-o s marriage

himno, **eem**-no s hymn

hincapié, in-kah-pe-**ay** s insistence; strong effort

hincar, in-**kar** v to thrust in

hinchado, in-**chah**-do a swollen; arrogant; vain

hinchar, in-**char** v to inflate; to swell

hinchazón, in-chah-**thon** s swelling; inflammation

hinojo, in-o-**Ho** s fennel

hipar, e-**par** v to hiccup; to pant

hipo, **ee**-po s hiccup; desire; anger

hipocresía, e-po-cray-**see**-ah s hypocrisy

hipoteca, e-po-**tay**-kah s mortgage

hipótesis, e-po-**tay**-siss s hypothesis

histerismo, iss-tay-**riss**-mo s hysterics

historia, iss-**to**-re-ah s history

histórico, iss-**to**-re-ko a historical

historieta, iss-to-re-ay-tah *s* short story

hita, ee-tah *s* brad; wire-nail

hito, ee-to *s* landmark; post; milestone

hocicar, o-the-kar *v* to fall face down

hocico, o-thee-ko *s* snout. (*fam*) face

hogaño, o-gah-n´yo *adv* this year

hogar, o-gar *s* hearth; home

hoguera, o-gay-rah *s* bonfire

hoja, o-Hah *s* leaf; sheet; blade

hojalata, o-Hah-lah-tah *s* tinplate

hojalatero, o-Hah-lah-tay-ro *s* tinsmith

hojaldre, o-Hahl-dray *s* puff pastry

hojear, o-Hay-ar *v* to turn the leaves of a book; to skim through

hola, o-lah *interj* hello

holgado, ol-gah-do *a* loose; large; at leisure; well-off

holgar, ol-gar *v* to rest; to be at ease; to take pleasure in

holgazán, ol-gah-**than** *s* idler; loiterer

holgura, ol-**goo**-rah *s* ease; looseness; comfort

hollar, o-l´yar *v* to trample; to tread

hollejo, o-l´yay-Ho *s* peel; rind; pellicle

hollín, o-l´yeen *s* soot

holocausto, o-lo-kah´ooss-to *s* holocaust

hombrada, om-**brah**-dah *s* manly action

hombre, om-bray *s* man

hombro, om-bro *s* shoulder

hombruno, om-**broo**-no *a* virile; manly

homenaje, o-may-nah-Hay *s* homage

homicidio, o-me-thee-de-o *s* manslaughter; murder

homónimo, o-mo-ne-mo *a* namesake; homonymous

homosexual, o-mo-sek-soo´ahl *s* & *a* gay

honda, on-dah *s* sling

hondo*, on-do *a* profound; deep

hondón, on-don *s* bottom

hondura, on-doo-rah *s* depth; profundity

honesto*, o-ness-to *a* honest

hongo, on-go *s* fungus; mushroom

honor, o-nor *s* honor

honra, on-rah *s* honor; reputation; chastity (in women)

honrado, on-rah-do *a* honest; honorable

honrar, on-rar *v* to honor; to praise; to credit

honroso, on-ro-so *a* honorable

hopo, o-po *s* bushy tail

hora, o-rah *s* hour

horadar, o-rah-dar *v* to bore; to pierce

horca, or-kah *s* pitchfork; gallows

horcajadas (a), ah-or-kah-Hah-dahs; *adv* astride

horchata, or-chah-tah *s* orgeat (almond syrup)

horda, or-dah *s* horde; clan; tribe

horizonte, o-re-thon-tay *s* horizon

horma, or-mah *s* mold

hormiga, or-mee-gah *s* ant

hormigón, or-me-gon *s* concrete

hormiguero, or-me-gay-ro *s* anthill

hormona, or-mo-nah *s* hormone

hornero, or-nay-ro *s* baker

hornillo, or-nee-l´yo *s* small stove

horno, or-no *s* oven

horquilla, or-kee-l´yah *s* forked stick; hairpin

horrendo, or-**ren**-do *a* dreadful; awful

horro, or-rro *a* enfranchised; free

horror, or-**rror** *s* horror; consternation

horrorizar, or-rro-re-**thar** *v* to cause horror

horroroso, or-rro-ro-so *a* horrid; hideous

hortaliza, or-tah-lee-thah *s* vegetable; garden produce

hortelano, or-tay-**lah**-no *s* gardener

hortera, or-**tay**-rah *s* wooden bowl; *a* tasteless

hosco, os-ko *a* dark-colored; sullen

hospedaje, os-pay-**dah**-Hay *s* hospitality; lodging

hospedar, os-pay-**dar** *v* to lodge

hospedería, os-pay-day-ree-ah *s* hospice; hostelry

hospedero, os-pay-**day**-ro *s* host; innkeeper

hospicio, os-pee-the-o *s* hospice; orphanage

hospital, os-pe-**tahl** *s* hospital

hospitalidad, os-pe-tah-le-

dahd *s* hospitality

hostelero, os-tay-**lay**-ro *s* innkeeper

hostería, os-tay-**ree**-ah *s* inn; tavern; hostelry

hostia, os-te-ah *s* host

hostigar, os-te-**gar** *v* to harass; to scourge

hostil, os-**teel** *a* hostile

hoy, o´e *adv* today

hoya, hoyo, o-yah, o-yo *s* hole; pit; grave

hoyoso, o-yo-so *a* full of holes

hoz, oth *s* sickle

hucha, oo-chah *s* piggybank

hueco, oo´ay-ko *a* hollow; empty

huelga, oo´ell-gah *s* rest; recreation; strike

huelgo, oo´ell-go *s* breath

huella, oo´ay-l´yah *s* track; footprint; mark; sign

huérfano, oo´air-fah-no *s* orphan

huero, oo´ay-ro *a* empty; addle

huerta, oo´air-tah *s* vegetable garden

huerto, oo´air-to *s* orchard

hueso, oo´ay-so *s* bone; stone; core

huésped, oo´ess-ped *s*

guest; innkeeper; host

hueste, oo´ess-tay *s* army in campaign

hueva, oo´ay-vah *s* spawn; roe

huevo, oo´ay-vo *s* egg

huida, oo´ee-dah *s* flight; escape

huir, oo´eer *v* to fly; to escape

hulla, oo-l´yah *s* coal

humanidad, oo-mah-ne-dahd *s* mankind

humano*, oo-mah-no *a* human; humane

humazo, oo-mah-tho *s* dense smoke

humear, oo-may-ar *v* to smoke

humedad, oo-may-**dahd** *s* humidity; moisture

humedecer, oo-may-day-**thair** *v* to moisten; to wet; to soak

húmedo, oo-may-do *a* humid; wet

humero, oo-**may**-ro *s* smokestack

humildad, oo-mil-**dahd** *s* humility

humilde, oo-**meel**-day *a* humble; meek

humillar, oo-me-l´yar *v* to humiliate; to subdue

humo, oo-mo *s* smoke; fume

humor, oo-**mor** *s* humor; disposition; temper

humorada, oo-mo-**rah**-dah *s* joke

humorista, oo-mo-**rrees**-tah *s* humorist

humoso, oo-**mo**-so *a* smoky

hundimiento, oon-de-me-**en**-to *s* sinking; collapse

hundir, oon-**deer** *v* to submerge; to sink; to crush

huracán, oo-rah-**kahn** *s* hurricane

hurgar, oor-**gar** *v* to stir; to excite; to poke

hurgón, oor-**gon** *s* poker

hurón, oo-**ron** *s* ferret

hurtadillas (a), ah-oor-tah-**dee**-l´yahs; *adv* stealthily

hurtar, oor-**tar** *v* to steal; to rob

hurto, oor-**to** *s* theft; robbery

húsar, oo-sar *s* hussar

husma, (andar a la), ahn-**dar** ah lah **ooss**-mah *v* to pry

husmear, ooss-may-**ar** *v* to smell out; to pry; to peep

husmo, **ooss**-mo *s* smell of tainted meat

huso, **oo**-so *s* spindle

I

ictericia, ik-tay-ree-the-ah *s* jaundice

ida, ee-dah *s* departure; sally (fencing)

idea, e-day-ah *s* idea; scheme

ideal, e-day-ahl *s* & *a* ideal

idear, e-day-ar *v* to form an idea; to plan

idéntico, e-den-te-ko *a* identical

idilio, e-dee-le-o *s* idyll

idioma, e-de-o-mah *s* language; idiom

idiota, e-de-o-tah *s* idiot; *a* idiotic

ídolo, ee-do-lo *s* idol

idoneidad, e-do-nay-e-dahd *s* fitness; capacity

idóneo, e-do-nay-o *a* suitable; qualified; competent

iglesia, e-glay-se-ah *s* church

ígneo, ig-nay-o *a* igneous

ignífugo, ig-nee-foo-go *a* fireproof

ignorancia, ig-no-rahn-the-ah *s* ignorance

ignorante, ig-no-rahn-tay *a* ignorant

ignoto, ig-no-to *a* unknown

igual, e-goo´ahl *a* equal

igualar, e-goo´ah-lar *v* to equalize

igualdad, e-goo´ahl-dahd *s* equality

ilación, e-lah-the-on *s* inference; connection

ilegal, e-lay-gahl *a* illegal; unlawful

ilegible, e-lay-Hee-blay *a* illegible

ileso, e-lay-so *a* unhurt

ilimitado, e-le-me-tah-do *a* unlimited

iluminar, e-loo-me-nar *v* to illuminate; to enlighten

ilusión, e-loo-se-on *s* illusion

iluso, e-loo-so *a* easily deceived; deluded

ilustrar, e-looss-trar *v* to illustrate

ilustración, e-looss-trah-the´on *s* illustration

ilustre, e-looss-tray *a* illustrious

imagen, e-mah-Hen *s* image

imaginar, e-mah-He-nar *v* to imagine

imaginario, e-mah-He-na-re´o *a* imaginary

imaginativa, e-mah-He-nah-tee-vah *s* imaginativeness

imaginería, e-mah-He-nay-ree-ah *s* fancy embroidery in colors

imán, e-mahn *s* magnet

imantar, e-mahn-tar *v* to magnetize

imbécil, im-bay-thil *a* imbecile

imberbe, im-bair-bay *s* beardless youth

imbuir, im-boo´eer *v* to

imbue; to inculcate

imitado, e-me-**tah**-do *a* imitated; similar

imitar, e-me-**tar** *v* to imitate

impaciencia, im-pah-the-en-**the**-ah *s* impatience

impacientar, im-pah-the-en-**tar** *v* to make impatient; to irritate

impaciente, im-pah-the-en-**tay** *a* impatient

impacto, im-**pahk**-to *a* impact

impar, im-**par** *a* odd; uneven

imparcial, im-par-the-**ahl** *a* impartial

impartible, im-par-tee-blay *a* indivisible

impartir, im-par-**teer** *v* to impart

impávido, im-**pah**-ve-do *a* intrepid; fearless; bold; calm

impecable, im-pay-**kah**-blay *a* impeccable; faultless

impedir, im-pay-**deer** *v* to impede; to obstruct

impeler, im-pay-**lair** *v* to impel; to drive

impensable, im-pen-**sah**-blay *a* unthinkable

impensado, im-pen-**sah**-do *a* unexpected;

unforeseen

imperar, im-pay-**rar** *v* to rule

imperdible, im-payr-**de**-blay *s* safety pin

imperdonable, im-pair-do-**nah**-blay *a* unpardonable

imperecedero, im-pay-ray-thay-**day**-ro *a* imperishable

imperfecto, im-pair-**fek**-to *a* imperfect

impericia, im-pay-ree-the-ah *s* unskillfulness

imperio, im-**pay**-re-o *s* empire

imperioso, im-pay-re-o-so *a* imperious

imperito, im-pay-**ree**-to *a* unskilled; inexperienced

impertérrito, im-pair-**tair**-rre-to *a* dauntless; unafraid; fearless

imperturbable, im-pair-**toor**-bah-blay *a* unmoved

ímpetu, **eem**-pay-too *s* impetus; impulse

impío, im-**pee**-o *a* impious

implicar, im-ple-**kar** *v* to implicate

implorar, im-plo-**rar** *v* to implore; to entreat

impolítica, im-po-lee-te-kah *s* discourtesy

impolítico, im-po-**lee**-te-ko *a* impolitic; impolite

imponer, im-po-**nair** *v* to impose; to impute .falsely; to instruct

importancia, im-por-**tan**-the-ah *s* importance; significance

importante, im-por-**tan**-tay *a* important; considerable

importar, im-por-**tar** *v* to import; to concern

importe, im-**por**-tay *s* amount; value

importunar, im-por-too-**nar** *v* to importune

imposibilitar, im-po-se-be-le-**tar** *v* to render impossible; to disable

imposible, im-po-**see**-blay *a* impossible

impostura, im-pos-**too**-rah *s* false imputation; imposture

imprenta, im-**pren**-tah *s* printing; printing office

impresión, im-pray-se-**on** *s* impression; stamp; edition

impresionar, im-pray-se-o-**nar** *v* to imprint; to impress

impreso, im-**pray**-so *s* printed matter

impresor, im-pray-**sor** *s*

printer

imprevisión, im-pray-ve-se-on s improvidence

imprevisto, im-pray-viss-to a unforeseen

imprimir, im-pre-**meer** v to print; to stamp

ímprobo, **eem**-pro-bo a dishonest; laborious; strenuous

improperio, im-pro-**payr**e-o s reproach; insult

impropiedad, im-pro-pe-ay-**dahd** s impropriety; unsuitability

impropio, im-**pro**-pe-o a improper; unfit

improvisar, im-pro-ve-**sar** v to improvise; to extemporize

improviso, im-pro-**vee**-so a unforeseen; unexpected

impúdico, im-**poo**-de-ko a unchaste; impudent

impuesto, im-poo´**ess**-to s tax; duty; a informed

impugnación, im-poog-nah-the-**on** s opposition

impugnar, im-poog-**nar** v to impugn; to oppose; to contest; to challenge

impulsar, im-pool-**sar** v to impel; to prompt

impulsor, im-pool-**sor** s propellant; driver

impune, im-**poo**-nay a unpunished

impureza, im-poo-**ray**-thah s impurity

imputar, im-poo-**tar** v to impute; to accuse

inacabable, in-ah-kah-**bah**-blay a interminable

inacción, in-ahk-the-**on** s inaction

inaceptable, in-ah-thep-**tah**-blay a unacceptable

inadecuado, in-ah-day-koo´**ah**-do a inadequate

inadmisible, in-ad-me-**see**-blay-do a inadmissable

inadvertido, in-ahd-vair-**tee**-do a unnoticed; unobserved

inagotable, in-ah-goh-**tah**-blay a inexhaustible

inaguantable, in-ah-goo´ahn-**tah**-blay a intolerable; unbearable

inajenable, in-ah-**Hay**-nah-blay a inalienable

inalterado, in-ahl-tay-**rah**-do a unchanged

inamovible, in-ah-mo-**vee**-blay a immovable

inapagable, in-ah-pah-**gah**-blay a unquenchable

inapetente, in-ah-pay-**ten**-tay a without appetite

inasequible, in-ah-say-**kee**-blay a unattainable

inaudito, in-ah´oo-**dee**-to a unheard of

inaugurar, in-ah´oo-goo-**rar** v to inaugurate

incalificable, in-kah-le-fe-**kah**-blay a unqualifiable

incansable, in-kahn-**sah**-blay a indefatigable; tireless

incapacitar, in-kah-pah-the-**tar** v to incapacitate; to disable

incapaz, in-kah-**path** a unable; incapable

incauto, in-**kah**´oo-to a incautious

incendio, in-**then**-de-o s conflagration; fire

incertidumbre, in-thair-te-**doom**-bray s uncertainty

incesante*, in-thay-**sahn**-tay a unceasing

incidencia, in-the-**den**-the-ah s incidence; incident

incidente, in-the-**den**-tay s & a incident

incidir, in-the-**deer** v to fall into or upon

incienso, in-the-**en**-so s incense

incierto, in-the-**air**-to a uncertain

incinerar, in-the-nay-**rar** v to cremate

inciso, in-**thee**-so s clause (in a long sentence)

incitación, in-the-tah-the-**on** s incitement

incitar, in-the-**tar** v to incite; to instigate

incivilidad, in-the-ve-le-**dahd** s incivility

inclemencia, in-klay-**men**-the-ah s inclemency

inclinado, in-kle-**nah**-do a slanting; sloping

inclinar, in-kle-**nar** v to incline; to slope

incluir, in-kloo´**eer** v to include

incluso, in-**kloo**-so a enclosed

incoar, in-ko-**ar** v to begin; to initiate

incobrable, in-ko-**brah**-blay a irrecoverable; irretrievable

incógnito, in-**kog**-ne-to a unknown

incoherencia, in-ko-ay-**ren**-the-ah s incoherence

incoloro, in-ko-**lo**-ro a colorless

incólume, in-**ko**-loo-may a sound; safe

incomodar, in-ko-mo-**dar** v to inconvenience; to disturb

incómodo, in-ko-mo-do a inconvenient; uncomfortable

incompasivo, in-kom-pah-**see**-vo a pitiless

incompleto, in-kom-**ple**-toe a incomplete; unfinished

incomprensible, in-kom-pren-**see**-blay a incomprehensible

incomprimible, in-kom-pre-**mee**-blay a incompressible

incomunicar, in-ko-moo-ne-**kar** v to isolate

inconcebible, in-kon-thay-**bee**-blay a inconceivable

inconexo, in-ko-**nek**-so a unconnected

inconfeso, in-kon-**fay**-so a who has not admitted his guilt

inconquistable, in-kon-kiss-**tah**-blay a unconquerable

inconsciente, in-kons-the-**en**-tay a unconscious

incontable, in-kon-**tah**-blay a uncountable

incontrastable, in-kon-trahs-**tah**-blay a insurmountable; indisputable

inconvenible, in-kon-vay-nee-blay a inconvenient

incorrección, in-kor-rrek-the-**on** s inaccuracy; impropriety

incorregible, in-kor-rray-Hee-blay a incorrigible

incrédulo, in-kray-doo-lo a incredulous

increíble, in-kray-ee-blay a incredible

incremento, in-kray-men-toe s increase; growth; rise

increpación, in-kray-pah-the-**on** s reprehension

increpar, in-kray-**par** v to reprehend; to rebuke

incriminar, in-kre-me-**nar** v to incriminate

incubar, in-koo-**bar** v to incubate; to hatch

inculpar, in-kool-**par** v to inculpate; to blame

inculto, in-**kool**-to a uncultivated; uncultured

incultura, in-kool-**too**-rah s lack of culture

incumplir, in-**koom**-pleer v to break; to disobey; to fail to observe

incuria, in-**koo**-re-ah s carelessness; neglect

incurrir, in-koor-**rreer** v

to incur

indagación, in dah-gah-the-on *s* investigation

indagar, in-dah-**gar** *v* to investigate

indebido, in-day-bee-do *a* undue; unlawful

indecente, in-day-**then**-tay *a* indecent

indecible*, in-day-**thee**-blay *a* inexpressible

indeciso*, in-day-**thee**-so *a* irresolute; undecided

indecoroso*, in-day-ko-**ro**-so *a* indecorous

indefectible*, in-day-fek-**tee**-blay *a* unfailing

indefenso, in-day-**fen**-so *a* defenseless

indeleble, in-day-**lay**-blay *a* indelible

indemne, in-**dem**-nay *a* unhurt

indemnizar, in-dem-ne-**thar** *v* to indemnify

independiente, in-day-pen-de-**en**-tay *a* independent

indescifrable, in-dess-the-**frah**-blay *a* undecipherable

indescriptible, in-dess-krip-**tee**-blay *a* indescribable

indeterminado, in-day-tair-me-**nah**-do *a*

indeterminate; indefinite; irresolute

indicación, in-de-kah-the-on *s* indication

indicar, in-de-**kar** *v* to indicate; to suggest

indicción, in-dik-the-on *s* convocation

índice, in-de-thay *s* index; forefinger

indiciar, in-de-the-**ar** *v* to give reasons to suspect; to indicate

indicio, in-dee-the-o *s* indication; sign

indígena, in-dee-Hay-nah *s & a* indigenous; native

indigesto, in-de-**Hess**-to *a* indigestible

indignar, in-dig-**nar** *v* to irritate; to make indignant

indigno, in-**dig**-no *a* unworthy

indirecta, in-de-rek-tah *s* innuendo; insinuation

indirecto*, in-de-**rek**-to *a* indirect

indisculpable, in-diss-kool-**pah**-blay *a* inexcusable

indisponer, in-diss-po-**nair** *v* to disable; to indispose

indispuesto, in-diss-poo´**ess**-to *a* indisposed

indistinguible, in-diss-tin-**ghee**-blay *a* undistinguishable

individuo, in-de-vee-doo´o *s* individual

indiviso, in-de-vee-so *a* undivided

indocto, in-**dok**-to *a* ignorant

índole, een-do-lay *s* disposition; temper; nature; character

indomable, in-do-**mah**-blay *a* untamable

inducción, in-dook-the-on *s* induction; inducement

inducir, in-doo-**theer** *v* to induce; to persuade

indudable, in-doo-**dah**-blay *a* unquestionable; indubitable

indulgente, in-dool-**Hen**-tay *a* indulgent

indulto, in-**dool**-to *s* pardon; reprieve

industria, in-**dooss**-tre-ah *s* industry

inédito, in-ay-de-to *a* unpublished; unknown; unheard of

ineficaz, in-ay-fe-**kahth** *a* inefficacious; ineffective; inefficient

ineludible, in-ay-loo-dee-blay *a* unavoidable

ineptitud, in-ep-te-**tood** s
ineptitude

inerme, in-**air**-may a
unarmed; defenseless

inerte, in-**air**-tay a inert;
lifeless

inesperado, in-ess-pay-**rah**-do a unexpected

inexhausto, in-ek-**sah**´ooss-to a
inexhaustible

inexperto, in-eks-**pair**-to a
inexperienced

inextinguible, in-eks-tin-**ghee**-blay a
inextinguishable

infamación, in-fah-mah-the-**on** s defamation

infamar, in-fah-**mar** v to
defame

infame, in-**fah**-may a
infamous

infanta, in-**fahn**-tah s
infanta; female infant

infantil, in-fahn-**teel** a
childlike

infatigable, in-fah-te-**gah**-blay a tireless;
indefatigable

infausto, in-**fah**´ooss-to a
unlucky; unhappy

infectar, in-fek-**tar** v to
infect; to contaminate;
to corrupt

infecto, in-**fek**-to a
infected

infecundo, in-fay-**koon**-do a barren; sterile

infelicidad, in-fay-le-the-**dahd** s unhappiness;
misfortune

infeliz, in-fay-**lith** a
unhappy

inferioridad, in-fay-re-o-re-**dahd** s inferiority

inferir, in-fay-**reer** v to
infer; to deduce

infiel, in-fe-**ell** a
unfaithful; disloyal

infierno, in-fe-**air**-no s
hell

infiltrar, in-fil-**trar** v to
infiltrate

ínfimo, een-fe-mo a
lowest; vilest

inflamar, in-flah-**mar** v to
inflame

inflar, in-**flar** v to inflate;
to swell

inflexible, in-flek-see-blay
a inflexible; unbending

infligir, in-fle-**Heer** v to
inflict

influir, in-floo´**eer** v to
influence

influjo, in-**floo**-Ho s
influx; influence

influyente, in-floo-**yen**-tay a influential

informante, in-for-**man**-tay s informant

informar, in-for-**mar** v to
inform

informatica, in-for-ma-te-ka s computer science;
data processing

informe, in-**for**-may s
information; report; a
shapeless

infortunio, in-for-**too**-nee-o s misfortune

infractor, in-frahk-**tor** s
infringer; transgressor

infrascrito, in-frah-**skree**-to a undersigned

infringir, in-frin-**Heer** v to
infringe

infructuoso, in-frook-too´o-so a fruitless

ínfulas, een-foo-lahs s
presumption; conceit

infundado, in-foon-**dah**-do a groundless

infundir, in-foon-**deer** v
to infuse; to instill

ingeniar, in-Hay-ne-**ar** v
to conceive; to devise

ingeniero, in-Hay-ne-**ay**-ro s engineer

ingeniería, in-Hay-ne-ay-**ree**-ah s engineering

ingenio, in-Hay-**ne**-o s
genius; cleverness

ingénito, in-Hay-ne-to a
inborn; innate

ingenuidad, n-Hay-noo´e-**dahd** s ingenuousness;
candor

ingerir, in-Hay-reer *v* to swallow

Inglaterra, een-glah-**tay**-rrah *s* England

ingle, een-**glay** *s* groin

inglés, een-**glays** *s* & *a* English

inglete, in-**glay**-tay's diagonal

ingrato, in-**grah**-to *a* ungrateful; unpleasant

ingresar, in-gray-**sar** *v* to enter

ingreso, in-**gray**-so *s* ingress; entry

inhábil, in-**ah**-bil *a* incapable; unqualified

inhabitado, in-ah-be-tah-do *a* uninhabited

inhalar, in-ha-**lar** *v* to inhale

inhibición, in-e-be-the-**on** *s* inhibition

inhibir, in-e-**beer** *v* to inhibit; to prohibit

inhumación, in-oo-mah-the-**on** *s* burial

inhumano, in-oo-**mah**-no *a* inhuman

inicial, in-e-the-**al** *a* initial

iniciar, in-e-the-**ar** *v* to initiate

iniciativa, in-e-the-a-**te**-vah *s* initiative

inicuo, in-ee-**koo**'o *a* iniquitous

injertar, in-Hair-**tar** *v* to graft

injuriar, in-Hoo-re-**ar** *v* to injure; to insult; to wrong

inmaculado, in-mah-koo-**lah**-do *a* pure; spotless

inmanejable, in-mah-nay-**Hah**-blay *a* unruly

inmediato*, in-may-de-**ah**-to *a* immediate

inmenso, in-**men**-so *a* immense; boundless

inmerecido, in-may-ray-**thee**-do *a* undeserved

inmergir, in-mair-**Heer** *v* to immerse

inmigración, in-mee-grah-the´**on** *s* immigration

inmiscuir, in-miss-koo´**eer** *v* to meddle with; to interfere

inmoral, in-mo-**rahl** *a* immoral; licentious

inmortal, in-mor-**tahl** *a* immortal; everlasting

inmóvil, in-**mo**-vil *a* motionless

inmovilizar, in-mo-vil-e-**thar** *v* to immobilize

inmueble, in-moo´**ay**-blay *s* real estate

inmundo, in-**moon**-do *a* filthy; obscene

inmune, in-**moo**-nay *a*

immune

inmutar, in-moo-**tar** *v* to change; to alter

innato, in-**nah**-to *a* inborn

innegable, in-nay-**gah**-blay *a* undeniable

innoble, in-**no**-blay *a* ignoble; of obscure birth

inobediente, in-o-bay-de-**en**-tay *a* disobedient

inobservancia, in-ob-sair-vahn-**the**-ah *s* nonobservance; disregard

inodoro, in-o-**do**-ro *a* odorless

inquietar, in-ke-ay-**tar** *v* to worry; to disturb; to upset

inquietud, in-ke-ay-**tood** *s* worry; uneasiness; restlessness

inquilino, in-ke-**lee**-no *s* tenant; lodger

inquina, in-**kee**-nah *s* aversion; hatred

inquirir, in-ke-**reer** *v* to inquire; to search

insaciable, in-sah-the-**ah**-blay *a* insatiable

insalubre, in-sah-**loo**-bray *a* unhealthy

insano, in-**sah**-no *a* insane; mad

inscribir, ins-kre-**beer** *v* to inscribe; to register; to enroll

insecto, in-**sek**-to s insect

inseguro, in-say-**goo**-ro a insecure; unsafe; uncertain

insensatez, in-sen-sah-**teth** s stupidity

insensible, in-sen-see-blay a senseless; insensitive

insepulto, in-say-**pool**-to a unburied

inservible, in-sair-vee-blay a unserviceable; useless

insidioso, in-se-de-**oh**-so a insidious

insigne, in-**sig**-nay a notable; noted

insignia, in-**sig**-ne-ah s decoration; badge

insinuar, in-se-noo´**ar** v to insinuate; to suggest

insipidez, in-se-pe-**deth** s insipidness

insistir, in-sis-**teer** v to insist; to dwell upon

insociable, in-so-the-**ah**-blay a unsociable

insolación, in-so-lah-the-**on** s sunstroke

insolente, in-so-**len**-tay a insolent

insólito, in-**so**-le-to a uncommon; unusual

insomnio, in-**som**-ne-o s sleeplessness; insomnia

insoportable, in-so-por-**tah**-blay a intolerable; unbearable

insostenible, in-sos-tay-**nee**-blay a indefensible; unsustainable

inspeccionar, ins-pek-the-o-**nar** v to inspect; to oversee; to examine

inspirar, ins-pe-**rar** v to inspire; to induce

instancia, ins-**tahn**-the-ah s request; application; petition

instante, ins-**tahn**-tay s instant; moment

instar, ins-**tar** v to press; to urge

instaurar, ins-tah´oo-**rar** v to restore; to reestablish

instituir, ins-te-too´**eer** v to institute

institutriz, ins-te-too-**treeth** s governess

instruir, ins-troo´**eer** v to instruct; to inform; to drill

insubordinar, in-soo-bor-de-**nar** v to rebel

insufrible, in-soo-**free**-blay a insufferable

insulso, in-**sool**-so a tasteless; dull

insulto, in-**sool**-to s insult

insustancial, in-sooss-tahn-the-**al** a unsubstantial

intacto, in-**tahk**-to a untouched; intact

integración, in-te-grah-the-**on** s integration

integral, in-te-**grahl** a whole-wheat

integrar, in-te-**grar** v to integrate

íntegro, **in**-te-gro a intact

inteligencia, in-tey-le-hen-the-ah s intelligence; mind; understanding

intemperie, in-tem-**pay**-re-ay s bad weather; **a la –**, ah lah –, outdoors

intempestivo, in-tem-pes-tee-do a unseasonable; ill-timed

intencion, in-ten-the-on s intention; purpose; plan

intencionado, in-ten-the-o-**nah**-do a deliberate; intentional

intentar, in-ten-**tar** v to try; to attempt

intento, in-**ten**-to s intent

interceder, in-tair-thay-**dair** v to intercede

interdecir, in-tair-day-**theer** v to prohibit

interés, in-tay-**ress** s interest; profit; share; concern

ínterin, **een**-tay-rin adv meanwhile

interino, in-tay-**ree**-no *a* provisional; interim

interior, in-tay-re-**or** *a* interior

internar, in-tair-**nar** *v* to intern; to penetrate inland

interpelar, in-tair-pay-**lar** *v* to appeal to; to summon

interponer, in-tair-po-**nair** *v* to interpose

intérprete, in-**tair**-pray-tay *s* interpreter

interrogar, in-tair-rro-**gar** *v* to interrogate; to question

interrumpir, in-tair-room-**peer** *v* to interrupt

intervalo, in-tair-**vah**-lo *s* interval

intervenir, in-tair-vay-**neer** *v* to intervene

interventor, in-tair-ven-**tor** *s* comptroller; inspector; supervisor

intestino, in-tess-**tee**-no *s* intestine

intimidar, in-te-me-**dar** *v* to intimidate

íntimo, **een**-te-mo *a* innermost; intimate

intraducible, in-trah-doo-**thee**-blay *a* untranslatable

intransigente, in-trahn-se-**Hen**-tay *a* uncompromising; intransigent

intransitable, in-trahn-se-**tah**-blay *a* impassable

intratable, in-trah-**tah**-blay *a* intractable

intrépido, in-**tray**-pe-do *a* fearless; dauntless

intrigar, in-tre-**gar** *v* to intrigue; to plot

intrincar, in-trin-**kar** *v* to entangle; to involve

introducir, in-tro-doo-**theer** *v* to introduce

intruso, in-**troo**-so *s* intruder; *a* intrusive

inundar, in-oon-**dar** *v* to inundate; to flood

inusitado, in-oo-se-**tah**-do *a* unusual

inútil, in-**oo**-til *a* useless

inutilizar, in-oo-te-le-**thar** *v* to render useless

invadir, in-vah-**deer** *v* to invade

inválido, in-**vah**-le-do *a* weak; invalid; null

invasor, in-vah-**sor** *s* invader

invencible, in-ven-**thee**-blay *a* unconquerable

invendible, in-ven-**dee**-blay *a* unsalable; unmarketable

inventario, in-ven-**tah**-re-o *s* inventory

inventiva, in-ven-**tee**-vah *s* inventiveness

invernada, in-vair-**nah**-dah *s* winter season

invernadero, in-vair-nah-**day**-ro *s* hothouse; greenhouse

invernal, in-vair-**nahl** *a* wintry

inverosímil, in-vay-ro-see-**mil** *a* unlikely

invertir, in-vair-**teer** *v* to invert; to invest

investigación, in-vess-te-ga-the-**on** *s* investigation

investigar, in-vess-te-**gar** *v* to investigate

inveterado, in-vay-tay-**rah**-do *a* old; chronic; obstinate

invicto, in-**veek**-to *a* unconquerable; invincible

invierno, in-ve-**air**-no *s* winter

invitación, in-ve-tah-the-**on** *s* invitation

invitar, in-ve-**tar** *v* to invite; to treat

invocar, in-vo-**kar** *v* to invoke

involuntario, in-vo-loon-**tah**-re-o *a* involuntary

inyectar, in-yek-**tar** v to inject

ir, eer v to go

ira, ee-rah s anger; wrath

iracundo, e-rah-**koon**-do a enraged; furious

iris, ee-riss s rainbow; iris

ironía, e-ro-**nee**-ah s irony

irrazonable, ir-rrah-tho-**nah**-blay a unreasonable

irrecuperable, ir-rray-koo-pay-**rah**-blay a irrecoverable

irrecusable, ir-rray-koo-**sah**-blay a unimpeachable

irredimible, ir-rray-de-**mee**-blay a irredeemable

irreflexión, ir-rray-flek-the-**on** s rashness

irrefragable, ir-rray-frah-**gah**-blay a irrefutable

irregular, ir-rray-goo-**lar** a abnormal; irregular

irremediable, ir-rray-may-de-**ah**-blay a incurable; helpless

irreprensible, ir-rray-pren-**see**-blay a irreproachable

irresoluble, ir-rray-so-**loo**-blay a irresolute

irresponsable, ir-rress-pon-**sah**-blay a irresponsible

irrigar, ir-rre-**gar** v to irrigate

irrisible, ir-rre-**see**-blay a laughable; absurd

irritar, ir-rre-**tar** v to irritate

isla, eess-lah s isle; island

isleño, iss-**lay**-n´yo s islander

islote, iss-lo-**tay** s small barren island

istmo, eest-mo s isthmus

Italia, e-ta-le´ah s Italy

itinerario, e-te-nay-**rah**-re-o s itinerary; timetable

izar, e-**thar** v to hoist

izquierdo, ith-ke-**air**-do a left-handed; left

J

jabalí, Hah-bah-**lee** s wild boar

jabalina, Hah-bah-**lee**-nah s wild sow; javelin

jabón, Hah-**bon** s soap

jabonado, Hah-bo-**nah**-do s washing

jabonar, Hah-bo-**nar** v to soap

jabonería, Hah-bo-nay-**ree**-ah s soap factory

jaca, Hah-**kah** s small horse; pony

jacinto, Hah-**theen**-to s hyacinth

jaco, Hah-**ko** s nag; pony

jactancia, Hahk-**tahn**-the-ah s boasting

jactarse, Hahk-**tar**-say v to boast

jadear, Hah-day-**ar** v to pant; to gasp

jaez, Hah-**eth** s harness; kind; quality

jalea, Hah-**lay**-ah s jelly

jalear, Hah-lay-**ar** v to shout; to urge on

jalón, Hah-**lon** s pole; stake

jamás, Hah-**mahs** s adv never

jamba, Hahm-bah s doorjamb

jamón, Hah-**mon** s ham

jaque, Hah-**kay** s check at chess

jaqueca, Hah-**kay**-kah s migraine; headache

jarabe, Hah-**rah**-bay s syrup

jardín, Har-**deen** s garden

jardinería, Har-de-nay-**ree**-ah s gardening

jardinero, Har-de-**nay**-ro s gardener

jarra, **Har**-rrah s jug; jar; pitcher

jarrete, Har-**rray**-tay s hock

jarretera, Har-rray-**tay**-rah s garter

jarro, **Har**-rro s jug

jaula, Hah´oo-lah s cage; coop; cell

jayán, Hah-**yahn** s tall, robust person

jazmín, Hath-**meen** s jasmine

jefe, Hay-**fay** s chief; head; leader

jengibre, Hen-hee-**bray** s ginger

jerarquía, Hay-rar-**kee**-ah s hierarchy

jerez, Hay-**reth** s sherry

jerga, **Hair**-gah s coarse cloth; jargon

jergón, Hair-**gon** s straw mattress

jerigonza, Hay-re-**gon**-thah s gibberish

jeringa, Hay-**reen**-gah s

syringe

jersey, Hayr-**say**-e *s* pullover

jibia, Hee-be-ah *s* cuttlefish

jilguero, Hil-**gay**-ro *s* goldfinch

jinete, He-**nay**-tay *s* horseman

jira, Hee-rah *s* tour; picnic; strip of cloth

jirafa, He-**rah**-fah *s* giraffe

jirón, He-**ron** *s* rag

jocoso*, Do-ko-so *a* humorous; comic; jocular

jornada, Hor-**nah**-dah *s* journey; expedition; day's work; stages

jornal, Hor-**nahl** *s* day's work; day's wages

joroba, Ho-ro-bah *s* hump; importunity

jorobado, Ho-ro-**bah**-do *s* hunchback

jorobar, Ho-ro-**bar** *v* to bother; to tease

jota, Ho-tah *s* iota; jot; Spanish dance

joven, Ho-ven *s* youth; young man or woman; *a* young

jovial, Ho-ve-**ahl** *a* jovial

joya, Ho-yah *s* jewel; present

joyería, Ho-yay-**ree**-ah *s*

jewelry; jeweler's shop

joyero, Ho-**yay**-ro *s* jeweler

juanete, Hoo-**ah-nay**-tay *s* bunion

jubilación, Hoo-be-lah-the-**on** *s* retirement

jubilar, Hoo-be-**lar** *v* to pension off

júbilo, Hoo-be-lo *s* merriment; rejoicing

jubón, Hoo-**bon** *s* doublet; jacket

judas, Hoo-dahs *s* traitor

judía, Hoo-**dee**-ah *s* French bean

judicial, Doo-de-the-**ahl** *a* judicial; juridical

judío, Hoo-**dee**-o *s* & *a* Jew; Jewish

juego, H´ay-go *s* play; game; set

jueves, Hoo´ay-vess *s* Thursday

juez, Hoo-**eth** *s* judge

jugada, Hoo-**gah**-dah *s* play; move

jugar, Hoo-**gar** *v* to play; to gamble; to risk

jugo, Hoo-go *s* sap; juice

jugoso, Hoo-**go**-so *a* juicy; succulent

juguete, Hoo-**gay**-tay *s* toy; trinket

juguetear, Hoo-gay-tay-**ar** *v* to play; to toy

juguetón, Hoo-gay-**ton** *a* playful

juicio, Hoo´ee-the-o *s* judgment

juicioso, Hoo´e-the-o-so *a* judicious

julio, Hoo-le-o *s* July

jumento, Hoo-**men**-to *s* donkey; stupid person

juncal, Hoon-**kahl** *s* clump of rushes

junco, Hoon-ko *s* rush

junio, Hoo-ne-o *s* June

junta, Hoon-tah *s* assembly; council

juntar, Hoon-**tar** *v* to join; to assemble; put together

junto, Hoon-to *adv* near; close to; at hand

juntura, Hoon-**too**-rah *s* juncture; joint

jurado, Hoo-**rah**-do *s* jury; juryman; *a* sworn

juramento, Hoo-rah-**men**-to *s* oath

jurar, Hoo-**rar** *v* to swear; to declare upon oath

jurista, Hoo-**riss**-tah *s* jurist; lawyer

justa, Hooss-tah *s* joust; tournament

justicia, Hooss-tee-the-ah *s* justice; equity

justificado, Hooss-te-fe-**kah**-do *a* justified

justificar, Hooss-te-fe-**kar**
 v to justify

justipreciar, Hooss-te-
 pray-the-**ar** v to
 estimate; to appraise

justo*, Hooss-to adv
 justly; tightly; a just;
 lawful; correct

juvenil, Hoo-vay-**neel** a
 juvenile

juventud, Hoo-ven-**tood** s
 youthfulness; youth

juzgado, Hooth-**gah**-do s
 court; tribunal;
 judicature

juzgar, Hooth-**gar** v to
 judge

K

kilo, ke-lo *s* kilo

kilogramo, ke-lo-**grah**-mo *s* kilogram

kilómetro, ke-lo-may-tro *s* kilometer

kiosco, ke-os-ko *s* kiosk

la, lah *feminine article* the; *pron* her; it

laberinto, lah-bay-**reen**-to s maze

labio, lah-**be**-o s lip

labor, lah-**bor** s labor; task; work; toil; tillage

laborioso*, lah-bo-re-o-so *a* hardworking; industrious

labrado, lah-**brah**-do s cultivated land; *a* worked

labrador, lah-brah-**dor** s laborer; farmer; peasant

labrar, lah-**brar** *v* to plow; to till; to carve

labriego, lah-bre-**ay**-go s peasant

laca, lah-**kah** s hairspray; lacquer

lacayo, lah-**kah**-yo s lackey; groom

lacerar, lah-thay-**rar** *v* to tear in pieces; to hurt

lacio, lah-**the**-o *a* languid; straight (hair)

lacra, lah-**krah** s scar; fault

lacrar, lah-**krar** *v* to seal with sealing wax; to infect; to harm

lacre, lah-**kray** s sealing wax

lácteo, lahk-tay-o *a* milky

ladear, lah-day-**ar** *v* to tilt; to incline on one side

ladera, lah-**day**-rah s slope; hillside

ladilla, lah-dee-l'yah s barley

ladino, lah-dee-no *a* sagacious; cunning

lado, lah-do s side

ladrar, lah-**drar** *v* to bark

ladrillo, lah-**dree**-l'yo s brick

ladrón, lah-**dron** s thief

ladronera, lah-dro-**nay**-rah s den of thieves

lagarto, lah-**gar**-to s lizard; artful person

lago, lah-go s lake

lágrima, lah-**gre**-mah s tear; drop

laguna, lah-**goo**-nah s lagoon; pond; gap

lagunoso, lah-goo-no-so *a* marshy

lama, lah-mah s mud; slime; ooze

lamentar, lah-men-**tar** *v* to lament

lamento, lah-**men**-to s lament; lamentation

lamer, lah-**mair** *v* to lick; to lap up

lámina, lah-me-nah s plate; sheet

laminar, lah-me-**nar** *v* to roll metal into sheets

lámpara, lahm-pah-rah s lamp

lamparero, lahm-pah-**ray**-ro s lamplighter

lamparilla, lahm-pah-**ree**-l'yah s small lamp

lampiño, lahm-pee-n'yo *a* beardless

lana, lah-nah s wool

lanar, lah-**nar** *a* wool-bearing

lance, lahn-thay s cast;
occurrence

lancear, lahn-thay-**ar** v to
lance

lancero, lahn-**thay**-ro s
lancer

lancha, lahn-chah s barge;
lighter; launch

lanero, lah-**nay**-ro s dealer
in wool; a woolen

langosta, lahn-**gos**-tah s
lobster

langostín, lahn-gos-**teen** s
crawfish

languidecer, lahn-ghe-
day-**thair** v to languish

lanilla, lah-nee-l´yah s
fine flannel

lanoso, lah-**no**-so a woolly

lanza, lahn-thah s lance;
spear

lanzadera, lahn-thah-**day**-
rah s shuttle

lanzar, lahn-**thar** v to
throw; to dart; to fling

lapa, lah-pah´ s limpet;
nuisance

lápida, lah-pe-dah s grave
stone

lápiz, lah-pith s pencil

lardar, lar-**dar** v to baste
with lard

lardo, lar-do s lard

largamente, lar-gah-**men**-
tay; adv largely; for a

long time

largar, lar-**gar** v to loosen;
to release; to let go; to
give

largo, lar-go a long;
lengthy; good

largor, lar-**gor** s length;
longitude

largura, lar-**goo**-rah s
length; stretch

laringe, lah-**reen**-Hay s
larynx

lascivia, lahs-**thee**-ve-ah s
lasciviousness; lust

láser, lah-sayr s laser

laso, lah-so a weary; tired

lástima, lahs-te-mah s
sympathy; compassion;
pitiful object

lastimar, lahs-te-**mar** v to
wound; to offend

lastimero, lahs-te-**may**-ro
a harmful; doleful

lastrar, lahs-**trar** v to
ballast a ship

lastre, lahs-tray s ballast

lata, lah-tah s tin-plate;
can; nuisance

latente, lah-**ten**-tay a
latent

latido, lah-**tee**-do s
panting; throbbing

látigo, lah-te-go s whip

latir, lah-**teer** v to
palpitate; to beat

lato, lah-to a large;

extensive

latón, lah-**ton** s brass

latrocinio, lah-tro-**thee**-
ne-o s robbery; theft

laúd, lah´ood s lute

laudo, lah´oo-do s award;
finding (of a tribunal,
etc)

laurel, lah´oo-rel s laurel

lauro, lah´oo-ro s glory;
honor; triumph

lavabo, lah-**vah**-bo s wash
basin; washstand;
lavatory

lavadero, lah-vah-**day**-ro s
laundry

lavadora, lah-vah-**do**-rah s
washing machine

lavandería, lah-vahn-day-
ree-ah s laundry

lavandería automática,
lah-vahn-day-**ree**-ah ah-
oo-to-**mah**-te-ka s
launderette

lavaplatos, lah-vah-**plah**-
tos s dishwasher

lavar, lah-**var** v to wash

laxante, lahk-**sahn**-tay s
laxative

laxar, lahk-**sar** v to loosen;
to relax

laxitud, lahk-se-**tood** s
laxity

laxo, lahk-so a lax; slack

laya, lah-yah s quality;
kind; class; spade

lazada, lah-**thah**-dah s bowknot

lazo, lah-**tho** s slipknot; bow; ribbon; snare

le, lay *pers pron* to him; to her; him; her

leal, lay-**ahl** *a* loyal

lealtad, lay-ahl-**tahd** s loyalty

lebrato, lay-**brah**-to s young hare

lebrel, lay-**brel** s greyhound

lección, lek-the-**on** s lesson; reading; reprimand

lectura, lek-**too**-rah s reading; lecture

lecha, lay-**chah** s roe

leche, lay-**chay** s milk

lechería, lay-chay-**ree**-ah s dairy

lecho, lay-**cho** s bed; litter; layer

lechón, lay-**chon** s sucking pig

lechuga, lay-**choo**-gah s lettuce

lechuza, lay-**choo**-thah s owl

leer, lay-**air** *v* to read; to lecture

legado, lay-**gah**-do s deputy; legacy

legajo, lay-**gah**-*Ho* s file; bundle of papers

légamo, **lay**-gah-mo s slime; mud

legaña, lay-**gah**-n´yah s sleep

legar, lay-**gar** *v* to leave; to bequeath

legatario, lay-gah-**tah**-re-o s legatee

legislar, lay-*Hiss*-**lar** *v* to legislate

legítimo*, lay-*Hee*-te-mo *a* legitimate; lawful; genuine

lego, **lay**-go s layman; *a* lay; ignorant

legua, **lay**-goo´ah s league

legumbre, lay-**goom**-bray s vegetables; legume

leido, lay-**ee**-do *a* well-read

lejano, lay-*Hah*-no *a* distant; remote

lejos, lay-*Hos* *adv* far-off; s far, far away

lelo, **lay**-lo *a* stupid

lema, **lay**-mah s theme; text; motto

lencería, len-thay-**ree**-ah s linens; lingerie

lengua, **len**-goo´ah s tongue; language; idiom

lenguado, len-goo´**ah**-do s sole (fish)

lenguaje, len-goo´**ah**-*Hay* s language; speech

lenguaz, len-goo´**ath** *a*

talkative

lengüeta, len-goo´**ay**-tah s tab; small tongue; epiglottis; needle of a balance

lenidad, lay-ne-**dahd** s lenience

lente, **len**-tay s lens

lenteja, len-**tay**-*Hah* s lentil

lentitud, len-te-**tood** s slowness

lento, **len**-to *a* slow

leña, **lay**-n´yah s firewood

leñador, lay-n´yah-**dor** s woodman; woodcutter

leñero, lay-n´**yay**-ro s timber merchant

leño, **lay**-n´yo s block; log; dull person

león, lay-**on** s lion

leona, lay-o-**nah** s lioness

lepra, **lay**-prah s leprosy

lerdo, **lair**-do *a* slow; dull; obtuse

lesbiana, lays-be´**ah**-nah s lesbian

lesión, lay-se-**on** s wound; injury

letanía, lay-tah-**nee**-ah s litany

letargo, lay-**tar**-go s lethargy

letra, **lay**-trah s letter; type; inscription

letrado, lay-**trah**-do s

lawyer. *a* learned

letrero, lay-**tray**-ro s label; lettering; inscription; notice; poster

letrina, lay-**tree**-nah s lavatory

leva, lay-vah s act of weighing anchor; levy; lever

levadizo, lay-vah-**dee**-tho *a* that can be lifted

levadura, lay-vah-**doo**-rah s leaven; yeast

levantamiento, lay-vahn-tah-me-**en**-to s elevation; uprising; lifting

levantar, lay-vahn-**tar** *v* to raise; to lift

levante, lay-**vahn**-tay s east; east wind

levar, lay-**var** *v* to weigh anchor

leve, lay-vay *a* light; trifling

levedad, lay-vay-**dahd** s levity

ley, lay´e s law

leyenda, lay-**yen**-dah s legend; story

liar, le-**ar** *v* to tie; to bind

libar, le-**bar** *v* to sip; to suck

libelo, le-**bay**-lo s lampoon; libel; petition

libertad, le-bair-**tahd** s

liberty; freedom

libertar, le-bair-**tar** *v* to free; to release; to deliver

libertinaje, le-bair-te-nah-**Hay** s licentiousness

libidinoso*, le-be-de-**no**-so *a* lustful

libra, lee-brah s pound

librado, le-**brah**-do s drawee

librador, le-**brah**-dor s liberator; deliverer; drawer

libramiento, le-brah-me-**en**-to s liberation; warrant; order of payment

librancista, le-brahn-**thiss**-tah s holder of a payment

libranza, le-**brahn**-thah s bill; check

librar, le-**brar** *v* to free; to deliver; to exempt; to draw

libre, lee-bray *a* free; clear; licentious

librea, le-**bray**-ah s livery

librejo, le-**bray**-Ho s booklet; worthless book

librería, le-bray-**ree**-ah s bookshop; bookcase

librero, le-**bray**-ro s bookseller

libreta, le-**bray**-tah s

notebook

librete, le-**bray**-tay s booklet

libro, lee-bro s book

licencia, le-then-the-ah s license; permit; discharge

licenciar, le-then-the-**ar** *v* to permit; to allow; to license; to discharge

licitar, le-the-**tar** *v* to bid at auction

lícito, lee-the-to *a* lawful; licit

licor, le-**kor** s liquor

licorista, le-ko-**riss**-tah s liquor dealer

licuación, le-koo´ah-the-on s liquefaction

licuar, le-koo´**ar** *v* to liquefy

lidiar, le-de-**ar** *v* to fight; to oppose; to contend

liebre, le-**ay**-bray s hare

lienzo, le-**en**-tho s linen; canvas

liga, lee-gah s garter; birdlime; league; alloy

ligadura, le-gah-**doo**-rah s ligature; bond; tie

ligar, le-**gar** *v* to bind; to alloy

ligazón, le-gah-**thon** s tie; fastening

ligereza, le-**Hay**-ray-thah s lightness; levity

ligero, le-Hay-ro *a* light; swift; trifling

lijar, le-Har *v* to sand

lila, lee-lah *s* lilac tree or flower

lima, lee-mah *s* lime tree; file

limadura, le-mah-**doo**-rah *s* filings

limar, le-**mar** *v* to file; to polish

limbo, leem-bo *s* limbo; limb

limitar, le-me-**tar** *v* to limit; to bound; to restrain

límite, lee-me-tay *s* limit; boundary

limítrofe, le-mee-tro-fay *a* bordering; neighboring

limo, lee-mo *s* slime; mud

limón, li-**mon** *s* lemon

limosna, le-mos-nah *s* alms; charity

limosnero, le-mos-**nay**-ro *s* beggar; *a* charitable

limoso, le-**mo**-so *a* slimy; muddy

limpia, limpiadura, leem-pe-ah lim-pe-ah-**doo**-rah *s* cleaning

limpiaparabrisas, leem-pe-ah-pah-rah-**bre**-sahs *s* windshield wiper

limpiar, lim-pe-**ar** *v* to clean; to cleanse; to scour

limpieza, lim-pe-**ay**-thah *s* cleanliness; purity

limpio, leem-pe-o *a* clean; pure; clear

linaje, le-nah-Hay *s* lineage

linaza, le-nah-thah *s* linseed

lince, leen-thay *s* lynx

lindante, lin-**dahn**-tay *a* bordering

lindar, lin-**dar** *v* to be contiguous; to adjoin

lindero, lin-**day**-ro *a* bordering

lindeza, lin-**day**-thah *s* elegance; prettiness

lindo, leen-do *a* pretty; fine

línea, lee-nay-ah *s* line; boundary

lingote, lin-**go**-tay *s* ingot

lino, lee-no *s* flax; linen; canvas

linterna, lin-**tair**-nah *s* lantern

lío, lee-o *s* bundle; parcel

liquen, lee-ken *s* lichen

liquidar, le-ke-**dar** *v* to liquefy; to liquidate

líquido, lee-ke-do *s* cash; balance; *a* liquid; clear

lira, lee-ra *s* lyre

lirio, lee-re-o *s* lily

lirón, le-**ron** *s* dormouse

lis, leess *s* iris; fleur-de-lis

lisiar, le-se-**ar** *v* to injure; to cripple; to hurt

liso, lee-so *a* plain; even; flat; straight

lisonja, le-son-Hah *s* adulation; flattery

lisonjear, le-son-Hay-**ar** *v* to flatter; to wheedle

lisonjero, le-son-Hay-ro *s* flatterer

lista, liss-tah *s* list; strip; catalog

listar, liss-**tar** *v* to list

listo, liss-to *a* ready; active; prompt; clever

listón, liss-**ton** *s* ribbon; tape; strip; lath

lisura, le-soo-rah *s* smoothness; evenness; sincerity

litera, le-tay-rah *s* litter; berth; bunkbed

literato, le-tay-**rah**-to *s* writer. *a* literary

literatura, le-tay-rah-**too**-rah *s* literature

litigar, le-te-**gar** *v* to litigate; to dispute

litigio, te-tee-He-o *s* litigation; contest

litografía, le-to-grah-**fe**-ah *s* lithography

litoral, le-to-**rahl** *s* littoral; coast; shore

litro, lee-tro *s* liter

liviano, le-ve-**ah**-no *a* light; fickle; lewd

lividez, le-ve-**deth** *s* lividity

lluvia ácida, l'yoo-ve-ah **ah**-the-dah *s* acid rain

lo, lo *neuter art* the; *pers pron* him; it

loa, lo-ah *s* praise

loable, lo-ah-blay *a* praiseworthy

loar, lo-**ar** *v* to praise

loba, lo-bah *s* female wolf

lobato, lo-**bah**-to *s* wolf cub

lobo, lo-bo *s* wolf

lóbrego, lo-bray-go *a* murky; gloomy

lóbulo, lo-boo-lo *s* lobe

local, lo-**kahl** *s* premises. *a* local

localidad, lo-kah-le-**dahd** *s* locality; location; town

localización, lo-kah-le-thah-the**'on** *s* location

loco, lo-ko *a* mad; crazy

locuaz, lo-koo**'ahth** *a* loquacious

locura, lo-**koo**-rah *s* madness; folly

locutorio, lo-koo-**to**-re-o *s* telephone booth; visiting room

lodo, lo-do *a* mud; mire

lógica, lo-**He**-kah *s* logic

lograr, lo-**grar** *v* to gain; to get

logro, lo-gro *s* gain; profit; interest

loma, lo-mah *s* hillock

lomo, lo-mo *s* back; loin

lona, lo-nah *s* canvas

Londres, lon-drays *s* London

longevo, lon-H ay-vo *a* long-lived

longitud, lon-He-**tood** *s* length; longitude

lonja, lon-Hah *s* exchange; warehouse; slice of meat

lonjista, lon-H iss-tah *s* grocer

lontananza, lon-tah-**nahn**-thah *s* distance

loquear, lo-kay-**ar** *v* to play the fool

loro, lo-ro *s* parrot

los, los *plur art* the; *pron* them

losa, lo-sah *s* flagstone; slab

lote, lo-tay *s* lot; share; part

lotería, lo-tay-ree-ah *s* lottery

loza, lo-thah *s* chinaware; crockery

lozanía, lo-thah-nee-ah *s* luxuriance; freshness

lozano, lo-**than**-no *a* luxuriant; sprightly

lúbrico, loo-**bre**-ko *a* slippery; lewd

lucerna, loo-**thair**-nah *s* glowworm

lúcido*, loo-the-do *a* lucid; brilliant

lucir, loo-**theer** *v* to shine; to exceed; to display; to dress well

lucrativo, loo-krah-**tee**-vo *a* lucrative

lucro, loo-kro *s* gain; profit

luctuoso, look-too**'o**-so *a* sad; mournful

lucha, loo-chah *s* struggle; strife; fight

luchar, loo-**char** *v* to fight; to wrestle; to struggle; to debate

luego, loo**'ay**-go *adv* then; afterwards; later

lugar, loo-**gar** *s* place; spot; town; village; space; occasion; motive

lugareño, loo-gah-**ray**-n´yos villager

lugarteniente, loo-**gar**-tay-ne-**en**-tay *s* deputy; lieutenant

lúgubre, loo-goo-bray *a* sad; lugubrious

lujo, loo-Ho *s* luxury

lujuria, loo-H oo-re-ah *s* lewdness; lust

lujurioso*, loo-Hoo-re-o-so *a* lustful

lumbre, loom-bray *s* fire; spark; brightness

luminar, loo-me-**nar** *s* luminary

luminaria, loo-me-nah-re-ah *s* illumination

luna, loo-nah *s* moon; plate glass; mirror

lunar, loo-**nar** *s* mole; blemish; beauty spot; *a* lunar

lunes, loo-ness *s* Monday

luneta, loo-**nay**-tah *s* orchestra seat

lustrar, looss-**trar** *v* to purify; to shine; to polish

lustro, looss-tro *s* luster; gloss; period of five years

luto, loo-to *s* mourning; sorrow

luz, looth *s* light

llaga, l´**yah**-gah *s* sore; wound; crack

llagar, l´yah-**gar** *v* to wound; to hurt

llama, l´**yah**-mah *s* flame; blaze

llamada, l´yah-**mah**-dah *s* call; reference mark

llamar, l´yah-**mar** *v* to call; to name; to invoke

llamarada, l´yah-mah-**rah**-dah *s* blaze

llana, l´**yah**-nah *s* trowel; plain

llaneza, l´yah-**nay**-thah *s* plainness; simplicity

llano*, l´**yah**-no *a* plain; level; even; simple

llanta, l´**yahn**-tah *s* tire

llanto, l´**yahn**-to *s* flood of tears

llanura, l´yah-**noo**-rah *s* evenness; prairie

llave, l´**yah**-vay *s* key; lock (of a gun)

llavero, l´yah-**vay**-ro *s* keyring

llavín, l´yah-**veen** *s* latchkey

llegada, l´yah-**gah**-dah *s* arrival

llegar, l´yay-**gar** *v* to arrive; to amount to

llenar, l´yay-**nar** *v* to fill; to occupy; to satisfy

lleno, l´**yay**-no *a* full

llevadero, l´yay-vah-**day**-ro *a* tolerable

llevar, l´yay-**var** *v* to carry; to convey; to bear; to lead; to endure

llorar, l´yo-**rar** *v* to weep; to mourn

lloro, l´**yo**-ro *s* weeping

lloroso, l´yo-**ro**-so *a* mournful; tearful

llovediza, l´yo-vay-**dee**-thah *s* rainwater

llover, l´yo-**vair** *v* to rain;

to shower

lloviznar, l´yo-vith-**nar** *v* to drizzle

lluvia, l´**yoo**-ve-ah *s* rain

lluvioso, l´yoo-ve-**o**-so *a* rainy; showery

maca, **mah**-kah s bruise (in fruit); stain

macarrones, mah-kar-**rro**-ness s macaroni

macarse, mah-**kar**-say v to rot (fruit)

maceta, mah-**thay**-tah s flowerpot

macizo, mah-**thee**-tho a solid; massive

machacar, mah-chah-**kar** v to crush; to pound; to harp (on a subject)

machacón, mah-chah-**kon** a tiresome; insistent

machete, mah-**chay**-tay s large knife; machete

machista, mah-**chiss**-tah s & a chauvinist

macho, **mah**-cho s male animal

machorra, mah-**chor**-rrah s barren woman

madeja, mah-**day**-Hah s skein; lock of hair

madera, mah-**day**-rah s timber; wood

maderaje, mah-day-**rah**-Hay s timber; woodwork

madero, mah-**day**-ro s beam; log

madrastra, mah-**drahs**-trah s stepmother

madre, **mah**-dray s mother; riverbed

madreselva, mah-dray-**sel**-vah s honeysuckle

madriguera, mah-dre-**gay**-rah s burrow; den

madrina, mah-**dree**-nah s godmother

madrugada, mah-droo-**gah**-dah s dawn

madrugar, mah-droo-**gar** v to rise early

madurar, mah-doo-**rar** v to ripen

madurez, mah-doo-**reth** s maturity

maduro, mah-**doo**-ro a mature; ripe

maestra, mah-**ess**-trah s schoolteacher

maestre, mah-**ess**-tray s grand master of a military order

maestría, mah-ess-**tree**-ah s expertise; mastery; master's degree

maestro, mah-**ess**-tro s master

mágico, **mah**-He-ko a magical

magistrado, mah-Hiss-**trah**-do s magistrate

magnánimo, mahg-**nah**-ne-mo a magnanimous

magnesia, mahg-**nay**-se-ah s magnesia

magnético, mahg-**nay**-te-ko a magnetic

magnífico, mahg-**nee**-fe-ko a magnificent

magno, **mahg**-no a great

mago, **mah**-go s magician

magra, **mah**-grah s slice of bacon; rasher

magro, **mah**-gro a lean; meager

magullar, mah-goo-l´**yar** v

to bruise; to mangle

maíz, mah-**eeth** s maize; corn

majada, mah-**Hah**-dah s sheepfold

majadería, mah-Hah-day-ree-ah s foolishness

majador, mah-Hah-**dor** s pounder; pestle

majestad, mah-Hess-**tahd** s majesty

majo, mah-Ho a gallant; nice

majuelo, mah-Hoo´ay-lo s hawthorn

mal, mahl adv badly; s evil; illness; a ill; bad

malbaratar, mahl-bah-rah-**tar** v to squander

malcontento, mahl-con-ten-to a discontented

malcriado, mahl-kre-ah-do a ill-bred

maldad, mahl-**dahd** s wickedness

maldecir, mahl-day-**theer** v to curse; to defame

maldición, mahl-de-the-**on** s curse; damnation

maldito, mahl-**dee**-to a cursed; wicked; perverse

malecón, mah-lay-**kon** s embankment; mole; dike

maledicencia, mah-lay-de-**then**-the-ah s slander

maleficio, mah-lay-**fee**-the-o s witchcraft; charm

maléfico, mah-**lay**-fe-ko a mischievous

malestar, mah-less-**tar** s uneasiness

maleta, mah-**lay**-tah s suitcase; valise

malévolo, mah-**lay**-vo-lo a malevolent

maleza, mah-**lay**-thah s underbrush; weeds

malgastar, mahl-gahs-**tar** v to squander; to waste

malhablado, mahl-ah-**blah**-do a foul-mouthed

malhecho, mahl-**ay**-cho s evil deed; a ill-shaped

malhechor, mahl-ay-**chor** s malefactor; wicked

malicia, mah-le-the-**ah** s wickedness

maligno, mah-**leeg**-no a malignant; evil

malintencionado, mahl-in-ten-the-o-**nah**-do a ill-disposed

malmandado, mahl-mahn-**dah**-do a disobedient

malo, mah-lo a bad; evil

malograr, mah-lo-**grar** v to lose (an opportunity); to miss; to spoil

malogro, mah-lo-gro s failure

malparado, mahl-pah-**rah**-do a impaired

malparto, mahl-**par**-to s miscarriage

malquerer, mahl-kay-**rair** v to bear ill will

malsano, mahl-**sah**-no a unwholesome; unhealthy

maltratar, mahl-trah-**tar** v to treat ill; to abuse

malva, mahl-vah s mallow; mauve

malvado, mahl-**vah**-do a wicked

malversar, mahl-vair-**sar** v to embezzle; to distort

malla, mah-l´yah s mesh of netting; tights

mamar, mah-**mar** v to suck

mampara, mahm-**pah**-rah s screen

mamparo, mahm-**pah**-ro s bulkhead; partition

manada, mah-**nah**-dah s herd; flock

manadero, mah-nah-**day**-ro s spring; source; shepherd

manantial, mah-nahn-te-**ahl** s source; spring

manar, mah-**nar** v to spring from

mancar, mahn-**kar** v to

MANCEBA MANSIÓN

maim

manceba, mahn-**thay**-bah s mistress

mancebo, mahn-**thay**-bo s youth; apprentice

mancillar, mahn-the-l´**yar** v to stain

manco, mahn-ko s handless; armless

mancomún, mahn-ko-**moon** adv jointly

mancha, mahn-chah s stain; blot

manchar, mahn-**char** v to stain; to soil; to defile

manda, mahn-dah s legacy

mandadero, mahn-dah-**day**-ro s porter; messenger

mandado, mahn-**dah**-do s mandate; message; errand

mandamiento, mahn-dah-me-**en**-to s command; order; commandment

mandar, mahn-**dar** v to command; to order; to transmit

mandatario, mahn-dah-**tah**-re-o s agent

mandato, mahn-**dah**-to s mandate

mandil, mahn-**deel** s apron

mando, mahn-do s order; authority

mandón, mahn-**don** a bossy; domineering

mandril, mahn-**dreel** s mandrel

manear, mah-nay-**ar** v to hobble

manecilla, mah-nay-**thee**-l´yah s small hand; handle

manejar, mah-nay-**Har** v to manage

manejo, mah-**nay**-Ho s management; intrigue

manera, mah-**nay**-rah s manner; way; fashion

manga, mahn-gah s sleeve; hose (water)

mango, mahn-go s handle; haft; mango

manguera, mahn-**gay**-rah s hose

manguito, mahn-**ghee**-to s muff

manía, mah-**nee**-ah s mania; peculiarity; dislike

maniatar, mah-ne-ah-**tar** v to handcuff

manicomio, mah-ne-**ko**-me-o s mental hospital

manifestar, mah-ne-fess-**tar** v to manifest; to declare

manifiesto, mah-ne-fe-**ess**-to s manifesto; a plain; obvious

manija, mah-nee-**Hah** s handle

manilargo, mah-ne-**lat**-go a long-handed; liberal

manilla, mah-**nee**-l´yah s bracelet; manacle

maniobra, mah-ne-o-**brah** s maneuver

maniobrar, mah-ne-o-**brar** v to maneuver

manipular, mah-ne-poo-**lar** v to manipulate

maniquí, mah-ne-**kee** s mannequin

manir, mah-**neer** v to tenderize meat

manirroto, mah-neer-**rro**-to a extravagant; spendthrift

manivela, mah-ne-**vay**-lah s crank

manjar, mahn-**Har** s food; victuals

mano, man-no s hand; quire of paper

manojo, mah-**no**-Ho s bunch; bundle

manosear, mah-no-say-**ar** v to handle

manotear, mah-no-tay-**ar** v to slap; to gesticulate

mansedumbre, mahn-say-**doom**-bray s meekness; gentleness

mansión, mahn-se-**on** s mansion

manso, mahn-so *a* meek; gentle; tame

manta, mahn-tah *s* blanket; traveling rug

manteca, mahn-tay-kah *s* butter; lard; fat

mantecada, mahn-tay-kah-dah *s* buttered toast

mantel, mahn-tel *s* tablecloth

mantelería, mahn-tay-lay-ree-ah *s* table linen

mantequera, mahn-tay-kay-rah *s* churn; butter-dish

mantequilla, mahn-tay-kee-lyah *s* butter

mantilla, mahn-tee-l´yah *s* mantilla; head-shawl

mantillo, mahn-tee-l´yo *s* mold; humus

manto, mahn-to *s* cloak; mantle

manubrio, mah-noo-bre-o *s* handle; crank

manufactura, mah-noo-fahk-too-rah *s* manufacture

manutención, mah-noo-ten-te-on *s* maintenance

manzana, mahn-thah-nah *s* apple; block of houses

manzanilla, mahn-thah-nee-l´yah *s* camomile

maña, mah-n´yah *s* skill;

dexterity; knack

mañana, mah-n´yah-nah *adv* tomorrow; *s* morning; morrow; – **por la –, – por lah –,** tomorrow morning

mañear, mah-n´yay-ar *v* to manage with cleverness

mañoso, mah-n´yo-so *a* dexterous; handy; crafty

mapa, mah-pah *s* map

máquina, mah-ke-nah *s* machine

maquinaria, mah-ke-nah-re-ah *s* machinery

maquinismo, mah-ke-niss-mo *s* mechanization

maquinista, mah-ke-niss-tah *s* engineer; mechanic

mar, mar *s* sea

maraña, mah-rah-n´yah *s* tangle

maratón, mah-rah-ton *s* marathon

maravilla, mah-rah-vee-l´yah *s* wonder; marigold

maravillar, mah-rah-ve-l´yar *v* to admire; to marvel

maravilloso, mah-rah-ve-l´yo-so *a* wonderful

marca, mar-kah *s* mark; stamp; sign; label; brand

marcar, mar-kar *v* to mark; to stamp; to label; to note

marco, mar-ko *s* frame; frame; mark

marcha, mar-chah *s* march; speed

marchamo, mar-chah-mo *s* customs' mark on goods

marchante, mar-chahn-tay *s* dealer; customer

marchar, mar-che-ar *v* to leave; to go; to function

marchitable, mar-che-tah-blay *a* perishable

marchitar, mar-che-tar *v* to wither

marea, mah-ray-ah *s* tide

mareo, mah-ray-o *s* seasickness

marfil, mar-feel *s* ivory

marga, mar-gah *s* loam; ticking

margarita, mar-gah-ree-tah *s* periwinkle; daisy

margen, mar-Hen *s* margin; edge; fringe

marginar, mar-He-nar *v* to make marginal notes; to exclude; to leave out

marica, mah-ree-kah *s* magpie

marido, mah-ree-do *s* husband

marihuana, mah-re-

oo**´ah**-nah s cannabis

marimacho, mah-re-**mah**-cho s mannish woman

marimorena, mah-re-mo-**ray**-nah s (*fam*) quarrel

marina, mah-**ree**-nah s shore; navy; seamanship

marinar, mah-re-**nar** v to marinate

marinero, mah-re-**nay**-ro s mariner; sailor; a seaworthy

marino, mah-**ree**-no s mariner; a marine

mariposa, mah-re-po-sah s butterfly

mariquita, mah-re-**kee**-tah s lady-bird

mariscal, mah-**riss**-kahl s marshal; farrier

marisma, mah-**riss**-mah s marsh

marmita, mar-**mee**-tah s kettle; pot

maroma, mah-**ro**-mah s rope; cable

marqués, mar-**kess** s marquis

marquesa, mar-**kay**-sah s marchioness

marquesina, mar-kay-**see**-nah s canopy

marquetería, mar-kay-tay-**ree**-ah s marquetry; inlaid work

marrana, mar-**rrah**-nah s sow

marrar, mar-**rrar** v to deviate; to err

marras, mar-**rrahs** adv long ago

marroquí, mar-rro-**kee** s morocco (leather)

marrullero, mah-rroo-**l´yay**-ro a cunning; deceitful

marsopla, mar-so-**plah** s porpoise

martes, mar-**tess** s Tuesday

martillo, mar-tee-**l´yo** s hammer

martinete, mar-te-**nay**-tay s drop hammer

mártir, mar-**teer** s martyr

martirio, mar-tee-re-o s martyrdom

marzo, mar-tho s March

mas, mahs conj but; yet; more

más, mahs adv more; moreover; besides

masa, **mah**-sah s dough; mortar; mass; crowd

masada, mah-**sah**-dah s farm

mascar, mahs-**kar** v to masticate; to chew

máscara, **mahs**-kah-rah s mask

mascarada, mahs-kah-**rah**-dah s masquerade

mascarón, mahs-kah-**ron** s grotesque face; figurehead

mascullar, mahs-koo-l´**yar** v to mumble

masilla, mah-see-**l´yah** s putty

masón, mah-**son** s Freemason

masonería, mah-so-nay-**ree**-ah s freemasonry

masticar, mahs-te-**kar** v to masticate

mástil, **mahs**-til s mast

mastín, mahs-**teen** s mastiff

mastuerzo, mahs-too´**air**-tho s watercress

mata, **mah**-tah s shrub; sprig; head of hair

matadero, **mah**-tah-**day**-ro s slaughterhouse

matador, mah-tah-**dor** s killer

matanza, mah-**tahn**-thah s slaughter

matar, mah-**tar** v to kill; to murder; to worry

matasanos, mah-tah-**sah**-nos s quack

mate, **mah**-tay s checkmate

matemáticas, mah-tay-**mah**-te-kahs s mathematics

materia, mah-**tay**-re-ah s material; substance; stuff

maternidad, mah-tair-ne-**dahd** s maternity

matiz, mah-**teeth** s shade of colors; touch

matón, mah-**ton** s bully

matorral, mah-tor-**rrahl** s thicket; underbrush

matoso, mah-**to**-so a bushy

matricular, mah-tre-koo-**lar** v to register; to enroll; to matriculate

matrimonio, mah-tre-mo-ne-o s marriage

matriz, mah-**treeth** s womb; nut screw; mold; a principal

matrona, mah-**tro**-nah s matron; midwife

matutino, mah-too-**tee**-no a matutinal; early

maullar, mah´oo-l´**yar** v to mew

máxime, mahk-se-may adv principally; especially

máximo, mahk-se-mo a maximum; chief; principal; very great

maya, mah-yah s daisy

mayo, mah-yo s May

mayonesa, mah-yo-**nay**-sah s mayonnaise

mayor, mah-**yor** s superior; chief; a greater; bigger; elder; **por –,** por

–, by wholesale

mayordomo, mah-yor-**do**-mo s steward; butler

mayoría, mah-yo-**ree**-ah s majority; greater part; legal age

maza, mah-thah s club

mazapán, mah-thah-**pahn** s marzipan

mazo, mah-tho s mallet; bundle

me, may pers pron me; to me

mecánico, may-**kah**-ne-ko s mechanic; a mechanical

mecanización, may-kah-ne-thah-the-**on** s mechanization

mecedora, may-thay-**dor**-rah s rocking chair

mecer, may-**thair** v to rock

mecha, may-chah s wick; fuse

mechero, may-**chay**-ro s cigarette lighter

medalla, may-**dah**-l´yah s medal

media, may-de-ah s stocking; hose

medianero, may-de-ah-**nay**-ro s mediator; a mediatory

medianía, may-de-ah-**nee**-ah s mediocrity; average

mediante, may-de-**ahn**-tay

adv by means of

mediar, may-de-**ar** v to mediate; to be in the middle

medicación, may-de-ka-the-**on** s medication

medicina, may-de-**thee**-nah s medicine

medición, may-de-the-**on** s measurement

médico, may-de-ko s physician; doctor; a medical

medida, may-**dee**-dah s measure

medio, may-de-o s middle; midway; a half

medio ambiente, may-de-o ahm-bi´**ayn**-te s environment

mediocre, may-de-o-**kray** a mediocre

mediodía, may-de-o-**dee**-ah s noon

medios de comunicación, may-de-os day ko-moo-ne-kah-the-**on** s media

medir, may-**deer** v to measure

meditar, may-de-**tar** v to meditate

Mediterráneo, may-de-tay-**rrah**-nay-o a Mediterránean Sea

medrar, may-**drar** v to thrive; to improve

medro, may-dro *s*
progress; improvement

medroso, may-**dro**-so *a*
timorous; fearful

médula, may-doo-lah *s*
marrow; pith

mejor, may-Hor *adv* & *a*
better

mejora, may-Ho-rah *s*
improvement; increase

mejorar, may-Ho-rar *v* to
improve; to enhance; to
recover from illness or
calamity

mejunje, may-Hoon-Hay *s*
mixed beverage

melado, may-lah-do *a*
honey-colored

melancólico, may-lahn-
ko-le-ko *a* sad; gloomy

melena, may-lay-nah *s*
long hair; mane

melocotón, may-lo-ko-ton
s peach

melodioso, may-lo-de-o-so
a melodious

melón, may-lon *s* melon

meloso, may-lo-so *a*
honeyed; mellow

mellado, may-l´yah-do *a*
notched; toothless

mellar, may-l´yar *v* to
notch; to injure

mellizo, may-l´yee-tho *a*
twin

membrete, mem-bray-tay
s note; address; heading

membrillo, mem-**bree**-l´yo
s quince; quince tree

memo, may-mo *a* silly

memorandum, may-mo-
rahn-doom *s*
memorandum; memo

memoria, may-mo-re-ah *s*
memory; memorial;
reminder

memorial, may-mo-re-**ahl**
s notebook

menaje, may-nah-Hay *s*
household furniture

mención, men-the-on *s*
mention

mendigar, men-de-gar *v* to
beg

mendigo, men-dee-go *s*
beggar

menear, may-nay-ar *v* to
move; to stir

meneo, may-nay-o *s*
movement; shake;
waddling motion of the
body

menester, may-ness-tair *s*
necessity; want; need; *pl*
bodily needs

menestra, may-ness-trah *s*
mixed vegetables

menestral, may-ness-trahl
s artisan; mechanic

mengano, men-gah-no *s*
(used after **fulano**) so
and so

mengua, men-goo´ah *s*
diminution; disgrace

menguado, men-goo´ah-
do *s* poltroon; wretch;
decrease; *a* decreased;
diminished; cowardly;
impaired

menguante, men-
goo´ahn-tay *s* ebb-tide;
decline; decreasing;
diminishing

menguar, men-goo´ar *v* to
diminish; to decay; to
wane

menor, may-nor *s*
underage; *a* less; smaller

menoría, may-no-ree-ah *s*
inferiority

menos, may-nos *adv* less

menoscabar, may-nos-
kah-bar *v* to impair; to
lessen; to discredit

menospreciar, may-nos-
pray-the-ar *v* to
underrate; to despise

mensaje, men-sah-Hay *s*
message; errand

mensajería, men-sah-Hay-
ree-ah *s* steamship line;
forwarding agency

mensajero, men-sah-Hay-
ro *s* messenger

menstruación, mens-
troo´ah-the-on *s*
menstruation

menstruo, mens-troo´o *s*

menses

mensual, men-soo-´ahl *a*
monthly

mensualidad, men-
soo´ah-le-**dahd** *s*
monthly salary

menta, men-tah *s* mint;
peppermint

mentar, men-**tar** *v* to
mention

mente, men-tay *s* mind;
understanding; will

mentecato, men-tay-**kah**-
to *a* silly; simpleton

mentir, men-**teer** *v* to lie;
to deceive; to feign

mentira, men-tee-rah *s*
lie; fib

menudear, may-noo-day-
ar *v* to repeat

menudillos, may-noo-dee-
l´yos *s* giblets

menudo*, may-**noo**-do *a*
minute; small. **a** –, ah –,
repeatedly; frequently

meñique, may-n´yee-kay *s*
little finger

meollo, may-o-l´yo *s*
marrow; essence; core;
substance

mequetrefe, may-kay-
tray-fay *s* busybody

meramente, may-rah-
men-tay *adv* merely

mercachifle, mair-kah-
chee-flay *s* peddler;

hawker

mercadería, mair-kah-
day-**ree**-ah *s*
merchandise;
commodity

mercado, mair-**kah**-do *s*
market

mercancía, mair-kahn-
thee-ah *s* goods; wares;
merchandise

mercante, mair-**kahn**-tay
s & a dealer

mercar, mair-**kar** *v* to buy

merced, mair-**thed** *s* gift;
grace; mercy

mercería, mair-thay-**ree**-
ah *s* haberdashery

mercero, mair-**thay**-ro *s*
haberdasher; salesman

merecedor, may-ray-**thay**-
dor *a* deserving

merecer, may-ray-**thair** *v*
to deserve

merecimiento, may-ray-
the-me-**en**-to *s* merit

merendar, may-ren-**dar** *v*
to have a snack

meridiano, may-re-de-**ah**-
no *s* meridian; *a*
meridional

merienda, may-re-**en**-dah
s snack

merino, may-**ree**-no *s*
merino wool

mérito, **may**-re-to *s* merit;
desert

merluza, mair-**loo**-thah *s*
hake

merma, **mair**-mah *s*
diminution; decrease

merodear, may-ro-day-**ar** *v*
to pillage

mes, mess *s* month

mesa, **may**-sah *s* table

mesar, may-**sar** *v* to pull
one's hair

meseta, may-**say**-tah *s*
landing of a staircase;
plateau

mesilla, may-**see**-l´yah *s*
small table

mesón, may-**son** *s* inn;
hostelry

mesonero, may-so-**nay**-ro
s innkeeper

mestizo, mess-tee-tho *a* of
mixed parentage

mesura, may-**soo**-rah *s*
moderation; gravity

mesurado, may-soo-**rah**-
do *a* moderate;
restrained; calm;
circumspect

meta, **may**-tah *s*
boundary; goal

metáfora, may-**tah**-fo-rah
s metaphor

metal, may-**tahl** *s* metal

metálico, may-**tah**-le-ko *a*
metallic

meteoro, may-tay-o-ro *s*
meteor

meter, may-**tair** *v* to put; to insert

método, may-to-do *s* method

metralla, may-**trah**-l´yah *s* grapeshot; shrapnel

metro, may-tro *s* meter (measure and verse)

mezcla, meth-klah *s* mixture

mezclador, meth-klah-dorr *s* mixer

mezclar, meth-**klar** *v* to mix; to blend

mezquino, meth-**kee**-no *a* mean; petty

mezquita, meth-**kee**-tah *s* mosque

mi, me *poss a* my; *s* (music, E)

mí, me *pers pron* me

miaja, me-**ah**-Hah *s* crumb; bit

mico, mee-ko *s* monkey

microbio, me-**kro**-be-o *s* microbe

micrófono, me-**kro**-fo-no *s* microphone

microonda, me-kro-**on**-dah *s* microwave

miedo, me-**ay**-do *s* fear

miel, me-**ell** *s* honey

miembro, me-**em**-bro *s* member; limb; penis

mientras, me-**en**-trahs *adv* meanwhile

miera, me-**ay**-rah *s* juniper oil; resin

miércoles, me-**air**-ko-less *s* Wednesday

mies, me-**ess** *s* ripe wheat; harvest; harvest-time

miga, mee-gah *s* crumb; bit

mijo, mee-Ho *s* millet

mil, meel *s* one thousand

milagro, me-**lah**-gro *s* miracle; wonder

milano, me-**lah**-no *s* kite

milésimo, me-**lay**-se-mo *a* thousandth

milímetro, me-**les**-may-tro *s* millimeter (0.039 inch)

militante, me-le-**tahn**-tay *a* militant

militar, me-le-**tar** *v* to serve in the army; *s* soldier; *a* military

milla, mee-l´yah *s* mile

millar, me-l´yar *s* thousand; a great number

millón, mel-´yon *s* million

millonésimo, me-l´yo-nay-se-mo *a* millionth

mimar, me-**mar** *v* to spoil; to pet

mimbre, meem-bray *s* wicker

mímica, mee-me-kah *s* mimicry

mimo, mee-mo *s* caress; petting

mimoso, me-**mo**-so *a* delicate; soft

mina, mee-nah *s* mine; conduit; source

minar, me-**nar** *v* to mine; to sap; to ruin

minería, me-nay-**ree**-ah *s* mine work; mining

minero, me-**nay**-ro *s* miner

mingo, meen-go *s* red ball (billiards)

mínimo, mee-ne-mo *s* minimum; *a* the smallest

ministerio, me-niss-**tay**-re-o *s* ministry; office

ministro, me-**niss**-tro *s* minister

minorar, me-no-**rar** *v* to lessen; to reduce

minoría, me-no-**ree**-ah *s* minority

minucia, me-**noo**-the-ah *s* minuteness; trifle

minucioso, me-noo-the-**o**-so *a* meticulous; minutely precise

minué, me-noo-**ay** *s* minuet

minusválido, me-noos-**vah**-le-do *a* disabled; *s* handicapped

minutario, me-noo-**tah**-re-o *s* ledger

minuto, me-noo-to s minute

mío, mee-o poss pron my; mine

miope, mee-o-pay a shortsighted; myopic

mira, mee-rah s aim of a gun; care; vigilance; purpose

mirada, me-rah-dah s glance; gaze; look

mirado, me-rah-do a considerate; prudent

mirador, me-rah-dor s observatory; balcony

mirar, me-rar v to look; to observe

mirilla, me-ree-l´yah s peephole

mirlo, meer-lo s blackbird

mirón, me-ron s onlooker

mirto, meer-to s myrtle

misa, mee-sah s mass

misántropo, me-sahn-tro-po s misanthrope

miscelánea, miss-thay-lah-nay-ah s medley

miscelaneo, miss-thay-lah-nay-oh s miscellaneous

miseria, me-say-re-ah s misery; meanness

misericordia, me-say-re-kor-de-ah s pity; compassion

misionero, me-se-o-nay-ro s missionary

misiva, me-see-vah s missive

mismo, miss-mo a same; similar; equal

misterio, miss-tay-re-o s mystery

mitad, me-tahd s half

mitigar, me-te-gar v to mitigate

mito, mee-to s myth

mitón, me-ton s mitten

mixto, meeks-to a mixed; composite; cross-breed

mixturar, miks-too-rar v to mix

mobiliario, mo-be-le-a-re-o s furniture

moblar, mo-blar v to furnish

mocedad, mo-thay-dahd s youth

mocetón, mo-thay-ton s robust youth

mochila, mo-chee-lah s backpack; rucksack

mochuelo, mo-choo´ay-lo s red owl

moda, mo-dah s fashion; mode

modelo, mo-day-lo s model; pattern; standard; exemplar

moderar, mo-day-rar v to moderate

modesto, mo-dess-to a modest

módico, mo-de-ko a moderate in price

modificar, mo-de-fe-kar v to modify

modismo, mo-diss-mo s idiom

modista, mo-diss-tah s dressmaker; milliner

modo, mo-do s way; mode; method

modorra, mo-dor-rrah s drowsiness

modoso, mo-do-so a quiet; temperate; well-behaved

módulo, mo-doo-lo s modulation; module

mofa, mo-fah s mockery; jeer

mofarse, mo-far-say v to mock

mofeta, mo-fay-tah s gas spring; skunk

mogollón, mo-go-l´yon s parasite

mogote, mo-go-tay s hillock

mohina, mo-ee-nah s annoyance; sadness; mournfulness

mohíno, mo-ee-no a gloomy; depressed; fretful; peevish

moho, mo-o s moss; mold; rust

mohoso, mo-o-so a moldy;

rusty

mojada, mo-*H*ah-dah *s* wetting; sop

mojama, mo-*H*ah-mah *s* salted tunafish

mojar, mo-*H*ar *v* to wet; to dampen

mojicón, mo-*H*e-kon *s* punch; blow with clenched fist

mojiganga, mo-*H*e-**gahn**-gah *s* masquerade

mojigato, mo-*H*e-**gah**-to *a* hypocritical; prudish

mojón, mo-*H*on *s* landmark; milestone

molde, mol-day *s* mold; pattern

moldear, mol-day-ar *v* to mold; to cast

moldura, mol-doo-rah *s* molding

mole, mo-lay *s* mass; bulk

molecula, mo-lay-koo-lah *s* molecule

moledor, mo-lay-dor *s* miller; grinder; bore

moler, mo-lair *v* to grind; to mill

molestar, mo-less-tar *v* to molest; to annoy

molestia, mo-**less**-te-ah *s* molestation; annoyance; bother; inconvenience

molicie, mo-lee-the-ay *s* softness; effeminacy

molienda, mo-le-**en**-dah *s* grinding; weariness

molinero, mo-le-**nay**-ro *s* miller; grinder

molino, mo-lee-no *s* windmill

mollar, mo-l´yar *a* soft; lean; boneless; credulous

molleja, mo-l´yay-*H*ah *s* gizzard; sweetbread

mollera, mo-l´yay-rah *s* crown of the head

mollete, mo-l´yay-tay *s* plump cheek; small roll (bread)

momento, mo-**men**-to *s* moment

momia, mo-me-ah *s* mummy

monada, mo-**nah**-dah *s* charming thing

monaguillo, mo-nah-**ghee**-l´yo *s* acolyte

monarca, mo-**nar**-kah *s* monarch

monarquía, mo-nar-kee-ah *s* monarchy; kingdom

monasterio, mo-nahs-**tay**-re-o *s* monastery

monda, mon-dah *s* pruning

mondadientes, mon-dah-de-**en**-tess *s* toothpick

mondadura, mon-dah-**doo**-rah *s* cleaning; peel

mondar, mon-dar *v* to

trim; to peel

mondongo, mon-**don**-go *s* tripe

monear, mo-nay-ar *v* to monkey around

moneda, mo-**nay**-dah *s* money; coin; currency

monería, mo-nay-ree-ah *s* mimicry; prank

monigote, mo-ne-go-tay *a* rag doll; puppet; humorous sketch

monja, mon-*H*ah *s* nun

monje, mon-*H*ay *s* monk

mono, mo-no *s* monkey; *a* neat; pretty

monóculo, mo-no-koo-lo *s* monocle

monótono, mo-no-to-no *a* monotonous

monopatín, mo-no-pah-teen *s* skateboard

monseñor, mon-say-n´**yor** *s* monseigneur

monstruo, mons-troo´o *s* monster

monta, mon-tah *s* amount; sum

montante, mon-**tahn**-tay *s* upright; standard; amount

montaña, mon-**tah**-n´yah *s* mountain

montañero, mon-tah-n´**yay**-ro *s* mountaineer

montañismo, mon-tah-

n´yees-mo s
mountaineering

montar, mon-**tar** v to ride;
to mount; to amount to

montaraz, mon-tah-**rahth**
a mountainous; wild

montear, mon-tay-**ar** v to
hunt

montera, mon-**tay**-rah s
cloth cap; hunting cap

montero, mon-**tay**-ro s
hunter

montés, mon-**tess** a wild

montículo, mon-**tee**-koo-
lo s mound

monto, mon-to s amount;
sum

montón, mon-**ton** s heap;
pile

montuoso, mon-too´o-so
a mountainous

montura, mon-**too**-rah s
saddle; mount; setting
(jewelry)

monzón, mon-**thon** s
monsoon

moña, mo-n´yah s
ornament of ribbons;
badge on a bull's neck in
the ring; drunkenness

moño, mo-n´yo s bun;
chignon; tuft

moñudo, mo-n´yoo-do a
crested

moquear, mo-kay-**ar** v to
have a runny nose

mora, mo-rah s blackberry

morada, mo-**rah**-dah s
residence; home

morado, mo-**rah**-do a
violet; mulberry-colored

morador, mo-rah-**dor** s
inhabitant; lodger

moral*, mo-**rahl** s
morality; a moral

moraleja, mo-rah-**lay**-Hah
s moral

morar, mo-**rar** v to
inhabit; to lodge; to live

morbidez, mor-be-**deth** s
softness; mellowness;
morbidity

mórbido, mor-be-do a
morbid; mellow

morbo, mor-bo s disease;
illness; unhealthy
curiosity

morcilla, mor-thee-l´yah s
blood pudding

mordaz, mor-**dath** a
sarcastic; biting

mordedura, mor-day-**doo**-
rah s bite

morder, mor-**dair** v to
bite; to gnaw

mordiente, mor-de-en-tay
s mordant

mordiscar, mor-diss-**kar** v
to nibble at; to gnaw

morena, mo-**ray**-nah s
brunette

moreno, mo-**ray**-no a

brown; dark; tanned

morera, mo-**ray**-rah s
mulberry tree

moribundo, mo-re-**boon**-
do a dying

morigerar, mo-re-Hay-**rar**
v to moderate

morir, mo-**reer** v to die

moro, mo-ro a moorish

moroso, mo-ro-so a slow;
tardy; lazy

morral, mor-**rrahl** s
knapsack

morralla, mor-rrah-l´yah s
small fry; rubbish

morriña, mor-rree-n´yah s
melancholy;
homesickness

morsa, mor-sah s walrus

mortaja, mor-tah-Hah s
shroud; cigarette paper

mortal*, mor-**tahl** s & a
mortal

mortecino, mor-tay-**thee**-
no a dying; pale; weak

mortero, mor-**tay**-ro s
mortar; cement

mortífero, mor-tee-fay-ro
a deadly

mortificar, mor-te-fe-**kar**
v to mortify; to torment

mortuorio, mor-too-o-re-
o s burial; a mortuary

mosaico, mo-sah´e-ko s
mosaic; marquetry

mosca, moss-kah s fly

moscatel, moss-kah-**tel** s muscatel

moscón, moss-**kon** s large fly

mosquete, moss-kay-tay s musket

mosquitero, moss-ke-**tay**-ro s mosquito net

mosquito, moss-**kee**-to s mosquito

mostacera, moss-tah-**thay**-rah s mustard pot

mostaza, moss-**tah**-thah s mustard

mosto, moss-to s must; new wine

mostrador, moss-trah-door s counter

mostrar, moss-**trar** v to show; to prove

mostrenco, moss-**tren**-ko a stray; vagabond

mota, mo-tah s mote; speck; burl in cloth

mote, mo-tay s motto; nickname

motín, mo-**teen** s mutiny

motivar, mo-te-**var** v to motivate

motivo, mo-**tee**-vo s motive; cause; reason

motocicleta, mo-to-the-**klay**-tah s motorcycle

motón, mo-**ton** s pulley

motor, mo-**tor** s motor

mousse, moos s mousse

movedizo, mo-vay-**dee**-tho a movable; shifting

mover, mo-**vair** v to move; to drive

móvil, mo-vil a movable

movilizar, mo-ve-le-**thar** v to mobilize

movimiento, mo-ve-me-**en**-to s movement; motion; activity

moza, mo-thah s girl; lass; maid; servant

mozalbete, mo-thahl-**bay**-tay s lad; youth

mozo, mo-tho s youth; man-servant; a young

muchacha, moo-**chah**-chah s girl; lass

muchacho, moo-**chah**-cho s boy; lad

muchedumbre, moo-chay-**doom**-bray s multitude; abundance

mucho, moo-cho adv much; a much; plenty

muda, moo-dah s change; alteration; molting

mudable, moo-dah-blay a changeable; fickle

mudanza, moo-**dahn**-thah s removal; move; change

mudar, moo-**dar** v to change; to molt; to change one's residence

mudez, moo-**deth** s dumbness

mudo, moo-do a dumb

mueblaje, moo´ay-**blah**-Hay s household furniture

mueble, moo´ay-blay s piece of furniture; a movable

mueca, moo´ay-kah s grimace

muela, moo´ay-lah s millstone; grindstone; molar teeth

muelle, moo´ay-l´yay s spring; wharf; dock; a tender; soft

muellaje, moo´ay-l´yah-Hay s wharfage

muérdago, moo´air-dah-go s mistletoe

muerte, moo´air-tay s death

muerto, moo´air-to s corpse; a dead

muesca, moo´ess-kah s notch; groove

muestra, moo´ess-trah s pattern; sample

muestrario, moo´ess-trah-re-o s set of samples

mugido, moo-Hee-do s moo; bellow

mugir, moo-Heer v to bellow

mugre, moo-gray s dirt; grime

mujer, moo-Hair s

woman; wife

mujeril, mo-Hay-reel *a* womanish; womanly

mula, moo-lay *s* female mule

muladar, moo-lah-**dar** *s* dunghill

mulato, moo-**lah**-to *s* mulatto

muleta, moo-**lay**-tah *s* crutch; prop

multa, mool-tah *s* fine; penalty; forfeit

multar, mool-**tar** *v* to fine; to swindle

múltiple, mool-té-play *a* multiple

multiplicar, mool-te-ple-**kar** *v* to increase; to multiply

multitud, mool-te-**tood** *s* multitude

mullir, moo-l´**yeer** *v* to make soft; to mollify

mundo, moon-do *s* world

munición, moo-ne-the-**on** *s* ammunition

municionar, moo-ne-the-o-**nar** *v* to store; to supply with ammunition

municipio, moo-ne-**thee**-pe-o *s* municipality

munífico, moo-nee-fe-ko *a* munificent

muñeca, moo-n´**yay**-kah *s* wrist; doll

muñeco, moo-n´**yay**-ko *s* puppet

muñón, moo-n´**yon** *s* stump of an amputated limb

muralla, moo-rah-l´yah *s* rampart; wall

murciélago, moor-the-**ay**-lah-go; *s* bat (animal)

murga, moor-gah *s* band of street musicians

murmurar, moor-moo-Hay-**ar** *v* to murmur

murmurio, moor-**moo**-re-o *s* murmur

muro, moo-ro *s* wall; rampart

murrio, moor-rre-o *a* sad; melancholy

musaraña, moo-sah-**rah**-n´yah *s* mouse

músculo, mooss-koo-lo *s* muscle

muselina, moo-say-**lee**-nah *s* muslin

museo, moo-**say**-o *s* museum

musgo, mooss-go *s* moss

música, moo-se-kah *s* music

músico, moo-se-ko *s* musician; *a* musical

musitar, moo-se-**tar** *v* to mumble; to mutter

muslo, mooss-lo *s* thigh

mustio, mooss-te-o *a*

withered; sad

musulmán, moo-sool-**mahn** *s* & *a* muslim

mutilar, moo-te-**lar** *v* to mutilate; to maim

mutuamente, moo-too´ah-**men**-tay *adv* mutually

mutuo, moo-too´o *a* mutual

muy, moo´e *adv* greatly; very

nabo, nah-bo s turnip

nácar, nah-kar s mother-of-pearl

nacer, nah-**thair** v to be born

nacido, nah-**thee**-do a proper; apt; fit; pp to be born

nacimiento, nah-the-me-**en**-to s birth; origin

nación, nah-the-**on** s nation

nada, nah-dah s nothing

nadadero, nah-dah-**day**-ro s swimming place

nadador, nah-dah-**dor** s swimmer

nadar, nah-**dar** v to swim

nadie, nah-de-ay pron nobody

nado, (a), ah nah-**do** adv afloat

naipe, nah´e-pay s playing card

nalga, nahl-gah s buttock; rump

nao, na-o s ship

naranja, nah-**rahn**-Hah s orange

naranjado, nah-rahn-Hah-do a orange-colored

narciso, nar-**thee**-so s daffodil; narcissus

nardo, nar-do s spikenard; tuberose

narigón, nah-re-gon a large-nosed

nariz, nah-**reeth** s nose; nostril

narrar, nar-**rrar** v to narrate; to relate

nasa, nah-sah s fish-trap

nata, nah-tah s cream

natación, nah-tah-the-**on** s swimming

natalicio, nah-tah-lee-the-o s birthday

natátil, nah-**tah**-til a able to swim

natillas, nah-**tee**-l´yahs s custard

nato, nah-to a born

natural, nah-too-**rahl** a natural; native

naturaleza, nah-too-rah-lay-thah s nature; characteristic

naufragar, nah´oo-frah-**gar** v to be shipwrecked

naufragio, nah´oo-**frah**-He-o s shipwreck

náufrago, nah´oo-frah-go a shipwrecked

nauseabundo, nah´oo-say-ah-**boon**-do a nauseous

náusea, nah´**oo**-say-ah s nausea

nausear, nah´oo-say-**ar** v to nauseate

náutica, nah´oo-te-kah s navigation

navaja, nah-**vah**-Hah s razor; clasp-knife

navajada, navajazo, nah-vah-Hah-dah, nah-vah-Hah-tho s gash with a razor or knife

nave, nah-vays s ship; nave

navegar, nah-vay-**gar** v to

navigate

navidad, nah-ve-**dahd** s Christmas day

naviero, nah-ve-**ay**-ro s shipowner

navío, nah-**vee**-o s ship

neblina, nay-**blee**-nah s mist; fog

nebuloso, nay-boo-**lo**-so a misty; foggy; cloudy

necedad, nay-thay-**dahd** s gross ignorance; stupidity; stubbornness

necesaria, nay-thay-**sah**-re-ah s water closet

necesario*, nay-thay-**sah**-re-o a necessary; needful

neceser, nay-thay-**sair** s toilet-case

necesidad, nay-thay-se-**dahd** s necessity

necesitado, nay-thay-se-**tah**-do a necessitous; needy

necesitar, nay-thay-se-**tar** v to necessitate; to need

necio*, nay-**the**-o a ignorant; foolish; imprudent

nefasto, nay-**fahs**-to a ominous; unlucky

negable, nay-**gah**-blay a deniable

negado, nay-**gah**-do a incapable; inapt

negar, nay-**gar** v to deny; to refuse; to forbid

negligente, nay-gle-**Hen**-tay a negligent; heedless

negociado, nay-go-the-**ah**-do s department; bureau; business

negociante, nay-go-the-**ahn**-tay s merchant; dealer

negociar, nay-go-the-**ar** v to trade; to negotiate

negocio, nay-**go**-the-o s occupation; business; transaction

negrear, nay-gray-**ar** v to grow or appear black

negro, nay-gro a black; dark

negrura, nay-**groo**-rah s blackness

neón, nay-**on** s neon

nervio, nair-**ve**-o s nerve

nervioso, nair-ve-o-so a nervous

nervudo, nair-**voo**-do a vigorous

neto, nay-to a neat; pure

neumático, nay´oo-**mah**-te-ko a pneumatic

neurótico, nay-oo-ro-te-ko s & a neurotic

neutral, neutro, nay´oo-trahl, nay´oo-tro a neutral; neuter

nevada, nay-**vah**-dah s snowfall

nevar, nay-**var** v to snow

nevería, nay-vay-**ree**-ah s ice cream parlor

ni, ne conj neither; nor

nicho, nee-cho s niche; recess in a wall

nido, nee-do s nest

niebla, nay-**blah** s fog; mist; haze

nieto, ne-ay-to s grandson

nieve, ne-**ay**-vay s snow

nimio*, nee-me-o a excessively careful; prolix; scrupulous; minute

ningún, ninguno, nin-**goon,** nin-**goo**-no a none; not one

niña, nee-n´yah s young girl; (fig)the apple of somebody's eye

niñera, ne-n´**yay**-rah s nanny

niñería, ne-n´yay-**ree**-ah s puerility; childish action

niñez, ne-n´**yeth** s childhood

niño, nee-n´yo s child; infant; a childish

níquel, nee-kel s nickel

níspero, niss-pay-ro s medlar tree

nítido, nee-te-do a bright; shining; clean; smooth

nitrato, ne-**trah**-to s nitrate

nitro, nee-tro s saltpeter

nivel, ne-vel s level

no, no adv no; not

nobiliario, no-be-le-ah-re-o a nobiliary

noble, no-blay s nobleman; a* noble

nobleza, no-blay-thah s nobleness; nobility

noción, no-the-on s notion

nocivo, no-thee-vo a noxious

nocturno, nok-toor-no a nocturnal

noche, no-chay s night

nochebuena, no-chay-boo´ay-nah s Christmas eve

nodriza, no-dree-thah s wet nurse

nogal, no-gahl s walnut tree

nombradía, nom-brah-dee-ah s fame; reputation

nombrar, nom-brar v to name; to appoint

nombre, nom-bray s name; title; reputation; noun

nómina, no-me-nah s list; catalog; payroll

non, non a odd; uneven

nonada, no-nah-dah s trifle

nonagésimo, no-nah-Hay-se-mo a ninetieth

nono, no-no a ninth

no obstante, no-obs-tahn-tay adv nevertheless

nordeste, nor-dess-tay s northeast

noria, no-re-ah s ferris wheel

norte, nor-tay s north

nos, nos pron us

nosotros, nos-o-tros pron we; us; ourselves

nota, no-tah s note; mark; remark; censure; renown; bill

notar, no-tar v to note; to heed; to censure

notario, no-tah-re-o s notary

noticia, no-tee-the-ah s news; notice; knowledge; advice

noticiar, no-te-the-ar v to give notice

noticiero, no-te-the-ay-ro s reporter

noticioso, no-te-the-o-so a informed; learned

notificar, no-te-fe-kar v to notify

notorio, no-to-re-o a notorious

novedad, no-vay-dahd s novelty; newness

novela, no-vay-lah s novel; tale

noveno, no-vay-no a ninth

noventa, no-ven-tah s & a ninety

novia, no-ve-ah s bride; girlfriend

novicio, no-vee-the-o s novice

noviembre, no-ve-em-bray s November

novilla, no-vee-l´yah s young cow

novillo, no-vee-l´yo s young bull; steer

novio, no-ve-o s bridegroom; boyfriend

novísimo, no-vee-se-mo a newest; latest

nubada, noo-bah-dah s rain shower; abundance

nubarrón, noo-bar-rron s large cloud

nube, noo-bay s cloud

nublado, noo-blah-do a cloudy

nuca, noo-kah s nape of the neck

nuclear, noo-klay-ahr a nuclear

núcleo, noo-klay-o s nucleus

nudillo, noo-dee-l´yo s knuckle

nuera, noo´ay-rah s daughter-in-law

nuestro, noo´ess-tro, *poss pron* our

nueve, noo´ay-vay s & a nine

nuevo*, noo´ay-vo a new; novel; fresh

nuez, noo´eth s nut

nulidad, noo-le-dahd s nullity; insignificance; nobody

nulo, noo-lo a null; void

numerar, noo-may-rar v to number; to enumerate; to count; to page

número, noo-may-ro s number; figure

nunca, noon-kah adv never

nuncio, noon-the-o s messenger

nupcias, noop-the-ahs s nuptials; wedding

nutria, noo-tre-ah s otter

nutricio, noo-tree-the-o a nutritious

nutrición, noo-tre-the-on s nutrition

nutrimento, noo-tre-men-to s food; nourishment; nutrition

nutrir, noo-treer, v to nourish

ñagaza, n´yah-gah-thah s bird call; decoy

ñame, n´yah-may s yam

ñaque, n´yah-kay s group of useless things

ñocio, n´yo-klo s macaroon

ñoñería, n´yo-n´yay-ree-ah s dotage; senility

ñoño, n´yo-n´yo a decrepit; plain; simple

o, o *conj* or; either

obcecar, ob-thay-**kar** *v* to blind; to obscure; to obfuscate

obedecer, o-bay-day-**thair** *v* to obey

obediente, o-bay-de-**en**-tay *a* obedient

obertura, o-bair-**too**-rah *s* (music) overture

obesidad, o-bay-se-**dahd** *s* obesity

óbice, o-be-thay *s* obstacle

obispo, o-**biss**-po *s* bishop

óbito, o-be-to *s* decease; death

objeción, ob-Hay-the-**on** *s* objection

objetar, ob-Hay-**tar** *v* to object

objeto, ob-**Hay**-to *s* object

oblea, o-**blay**-ah *s* wafer

oblicuo, -oblee-koo´o *a* oblique; slanting; inclined

obligación, o-ble-gah-the-**on** *s* obligation; duty; bond; debenture

obligar, o-ble-**gar** *v* to compel; to bind; to constrain

obligatorio, o-ble-gah-**to**-re-o *a* binding; obligatory

obra, o-**brah** *s* work; book; writings; power; toil

obrador, o-brah-**dor** *s* workshop

obraje, o-**brah**-Hay *s* manufacture

obrar, o-**brar** *v* to work; to operate; to perform

obrero, o-**bray**-ro *s* workman; laborer

obscurecer, obs-koo-ray-**thair** *v* to obscure; to darken

obscuridad, obs-koo-re-**dahd** *s* obscurity; darkness

obscuro*, obs-**koo**-ro *a* obscure; dark; gloomy

obsequiar, ob-say-ke-**ar** *v* to court; to pay attentions; to serve

obsequioso, ob-say-ke-o-**so** *a* obsequious

observar, ob-sair-**var** *v* to observe

obsesión, ob-say-se-**on** *s* obsession

obstáculo, obs-**tah**-koo-lo *s* obstacle

obstinarse, obs-te-**nar**-say *v* to be obstinate

obstruir, obs-troo´**eer** *v* to obstruct

obtención, ob-ten-the-**on** *s* attainment

obtener, ob-tay-**nair** *v* to obtain; to attain

obturador, ob-too-rrah-**dorr** *s* gasket (*mech*)

obtuso, ob-**too**-so *a* obtuse; blunt

obviar, ob-ve-**ar** *v* to obviate

obvio, ob-ve-o *a* obvious

oca, o-**kah** *s* goose

ocasionar, o-kah-se-o-**nar**

v to cause; to occasion

ocaso, o-**kah**-so, *s* sunset

océano, o-**thay**-ah-no *s* ocean

ocio, o-the-o *s* leisure; pastime

ociosidad, o-the-o-se-**dahd** *s* idleness; leisure

ocioso, o-the-o-so *a* idle; fruitless

octavo, ok-**tah**-vo *a* eighth

octogésimo, ok-to-**Hay**-se-mo *a* eightieth

octubre, ok-**too**-bray *s* October

oculista, o-koo-**liss**-tah *s* oculist

ocultación, o-kool-tah-the-**on** *s* concealment

ocultar, o-kool-**tar** *v* to hide; to mask; to keep secret

oculto, o-**kool**-to *a* hidden; secret

ocupante, o-koo-**pahn**-tay *s* occupier

ocupar, o-koo-**par** *v* to occupy; to fill; to employ

ocurrir, o-koor-**rreer** *v* to happen; to occur; to take place

ochavado, o-chah-**vah**-do *a* octagonal

ochavo, o-chah-vo *s* small brass coin

ochenta, o-**chen**-tah *s* & *a* eighty

ocho, o-cho *s* & *a* eight

odio, o-de-o *s* hatred

odioso, o-de-o-so *a* odious; hateful

odorífero, o-do-ree-**fay**-ro *a* odoriferous; fragrant

odre, o-dray *s* leather bag for wine

oeste, o'**ess**-tay *s* west; west wind

ofender, o-fen-**dair** *v* to offend

ofensa, o-fen-sah *s* offense

ofensor, o-fen-**sor** *s* offender

oferta, o-**fair**-tah *s* offer; tender

oficial, o-fe-the-**ahl** *s* workman; workmaster; clerk; *a* official

oficiar, o-fe-the-**ar** *v* to officiate

oficina, o-fe-**thee**-nah *s* workshop; office

oficio, o-**fee**-the-o *s* office; occupation

oficioso, o-fe-the-o-so *a* officious; meddling

ofrecer, o-fray-**thair** *v* to offer; to present; to bid

ofrecimiento, o-fray-the-me-en-to *s* offer; promise

ofuscación, o-fooss-kah-the-**on** *s* dimness of sight; obfuscation

ofuscar, o-fooss-**kar** *v* to darken; to dazzle; to obfuscate

oible, o'**ee**-blay *a* audible

oido, o'ee-do *s* hearing; ear; *pp* heard

oidor, o'**e**-dor *s* hearer; judge of the Supreme Court

oir, o'eer *v* to hear; to listen

¡ojalá! o-**Hah**-lah *interj* it would be great

ojeada, o-**Hay**-ah-dah *s* glance; glimpse

ojear, o-**Hay**-ar *v* to eye; to glance

ojeriza, o-**Hay**-ree-thah *s* spite; grudge; ill will

ojete, o-**Hay**-tay *s* eyelet

ojinegro, o-**He**-nay-gro *a* black-eyed

ojiva, o-**Hee**-vah *s* Gothic or painted window

ojo, o-Ho *s* eye

ola, o-lah *s* wave; billow

oleada, o-lay-**ah**-dah *s* surge

óleo, o-lay-o *s* oil

oleoso, o-lay-o-so *a* oily

oler, o-**lair** *v* to smell; to scent

olfato, ol-**fah**-to *s* sense of smell

oliscar, o-liss-**kar** *v* to smell persistently; to

scent

oliva, o-**lee**-vah *s* olive

olmo, ol-mo *s* elm tree

olor, o-**lor** *s* smell; odor

oloroso, o-lo-ro-so, see **odorífero**

olvidadizo, ol-ve-dah-**dee**-tho *a* forgetful

olvidar, ol-ve-**dar** *v* to forget

olvido, ol-**vee**-do *s* forgetfulness; oblivion

olla, o-l´yah *s* stewpot; – **podrida**, – po-**dree**- dah stew

ollería, o-l´yay-**ree**-ah *s* pottery; crockery shop

ombligo, om-**blee**-go *s* navel

ominoso, o-me-**no**-so *a* ominous

omisión, o-me-se-**on** *s* omission; negligence

omiso, o-**mee**-so *a* neglectful; remiss

omitir, o-me-**teer** *v* to omit; to leave out

omnipotente, om-ne-po-**ten**-tay *a* omnipotent; almighty

omnisciente, om-niss-thee-**en**-tay *a* omniscient

once, **on**-thay *s* & *a* eleven

onda, **on**-dah *s* wave

ondear, on-day-**ar** *v* to

undulate

on-line, on-lain *a, adv comput* on-line; en línea

opaco, o-**pah**-ko *a* opaque; dark

opción, op-the-**on** *s* option

operar, o-pay-**rar** *v* to operate

operarío, o-pay-**rah**-re-o *s* working man

ópimo, o-pe-mo *a* rich; fruitful

opinar, o-pe-**nar** *v* to opine; to consider

opíparo, o-pe-pah-ro *a* sumptuous

oponer, o-po-**nair** *v* to oppose

oportuno*, o-por-**too**-no *a* opportune; seasonable

opositor, o-po-se-**tor** *s* opponent

opresor, o-pray-**sor** *s* oppressor

oprimir, o-pre-**meer** *v* to oppress

oprobio, o-**pro**-be-o *s* opprobrium; ignominy

optar, op-**tar** *v* to choose; to select

óptico, op-te-ko *a* optical; visual

óptimo, op-te-mo *a* best; optimal

opuesto, o-poo´**ess**-to *a*

opposite; contrary; adverse

opugnar, o-poog-**nar** *v* to impugn; to resist

opulento, o-poo-**len**-to *a* opulent

opúsculo, o-**pooss**-koo-lo *s* booklet; tract; short treatise

oquedad, o-kay-**dahd** *s* cavity

ora, o-ra *conj* now; then; either; whether

orador, o-rah-**dor** *s* orator; public speaker

orar, o-**rar** *v* to harangue; to pray

orbe, or-**bay** *s* sphere; orb

órbita, orr-be-tah *s* orbit

orden, or-den *s* order (in all its meanings)

ordenación, or-day-nah-the-**on** *s* arrangement; ordination

ordenador, or-day-nah-**dor** *a* computer

ordenador personal, or-day-nah-**dor** payr-so-**nal** *s* personal computer

ordenanza, or-day-**nahn**-thah *s* order; ordinance; orderly

ordenar, or-day-**nar** *v* to put in order; to order; to command; to confer holy orders

ordeñar, or-day-n´yar *v* to
milk

ordinario, or-de-nah-re-o
s ordinary fare; *a*
ordinary; customary

orear, o-ray-ar *v* to air; to
ventilate

oreja, o-ray-Hah *s* auricle;
ear

orejudo, o-ray-Hoo-do *a*
long-eared

orfandad, or-fahn-dahd *s*
orphanage

orfebrería, or-fay-bray-
ree-ah *s* gold and silver
work

organizar, or-gah-ne-thar
v to organize

órgano, or-gah-no *s* organ

orgasmo, or-gahs-mo *s*
orgasm

orgía, or-Hee-ah *s* orgy;
frantic revel

orgullo, or-goo-l´yo *s*
pride; haughtiness

orgulloso, or-goo-l´yo-so *a*
proud; haughty

oriente, o-re-en-tay *s*
Orient; east

orífice, o-ree-fe-thay *s*
goldsmith

orificio, o-re-fee-the-o *s*
orifice; aperture

origen, o-ree-Hen *s* origin;
source; lineage

originar, o-re-He-nar *v* to
originate

orilla, o-ree-l´yah *s* limit;
border; margin; edge;
shore

orillar, o-re-l´yar *v* to
arrange; to conclude; to
border

orillo, o-ree-l´yo *s* selvage

orín, o-reen *s* iron rust; *pl*
urine

orina, o-ree-nah *s* urine

orinal, o-re-nahl *s* urinal

orinar, o-ree-nahr *v*
urinate

orla, or-lah *s* list; selvage;
border; fringe

orlar, or-lar *v* to border

ornar, or-nar *v* to adorn

oro, o-ro *s* gold

orondo, o-ron-do *a*
pompous; hollow

oropel, o-ro-pel *s* tinsel

orquesta, or-kess-tah *s*
orchestra

ortiga, or-tee-gah *s* nettle

orto, or-to *s* rising of the
sun or a star

oruga, o-roo-gah *s*
caterpillar

orujo, o-roo-Ho *s* peel of
pressed grapes or olives

orzuelo, or-thoo-ay-lo *s*
sty (tumor on the
eyelids); snare; trap

os, os *pron* you; ye

osa, o-sah *s* female bear

osadía, o-sah-dee-ah *s*
daring; intrepidity

osado*, o-sah-do *a* bold;
audacious

osar, o-sar *v* to dare; to
venture

oscilar, os-the-lar *v* to
oscillate

ósculo, os-koo-lo *s* kiss

oscurecer, os-koo-ray-
thair, (see **obscurecer**)

oscuro, os-koo-ro, (see
obscuro)

óseo, o-say-o *a* bony

oso, o-so *s* bear

ostentar, os-ten-tar *v* to
show; to exhibit; to
boast

ostra, os-trah *s* oyster

osudo, o-soo-do *a* bony

otear, o-tay-ar *v* to watch
from a high point; to
examine

otoñada, o-to-n´yah-dah *s*
autumn season

otoñal, o-to-n´yahl *a*
autumnal

otoño, o-to-n´yo *s* autumn

otorgamiento, o-tor-gah-
me-en-to *s* grant; licence

otorgar, o-tor-gar *v* to
consent; to agree; to
covenant; to execute

otro, o-tro *a* other;
another

otrosí, o-tro-see *adv*

moreover; besides

ovación, o-vah-the-**on** s
ovation

óvalo, o-vah-lo s oval

ovar, o-**var** v to lay eggs

ovario, o-**vah**-re-o s ovary

oveja, o-**vay**-*H*ah s female
sheep

ovillo, o-**vee**-l´yo s clew;
ball

óvulo, o-**voo**-lo s ovule

óxido, **ok**-se-do s oxide

oxidado, ok-se-**dah**-do a
rusty

oyente, o-**yen**-tay s
auditor; hearer

ozono, o-**tho**-no s ozone

pabellón, pah-bay-l'yon s
pavilion; arbor; flag

pábilo, pah-be-lo s wick;
snuff of a candle

paca, pah-kah s package

pacato, pah-kah-to a
pacific; gentle

pacer, pah-thair v to
pasture; to feed

paciencia, pah-the-en-
the-ah s patience

pacífico*, pah-thee-fe-ko
a peaceful

pacotilla, pah-ko-tee-l´yah
s venture goods

pactar, pahk-tar v to
convenant; to contract

pacto, pahk-to s contract;
agreement; pact

pachón, pah-chon s
phlegmatic man; pointer
(dog)

pachorra, pah-chor-rrah s
slowness; sluggishness

padecer, pah-day-thair v
to suffer; to bear

padecimiento, pah-day-
the-me-en-to s suffering

padrastro, pah-drahs-tro s
stepfather

padre, pah-dray s father

padrino, pah-dree-no s
godfather

padrón, pah-dron s poll;
note of infamy

paga, pah-gah s payment;
fee; wages

pagadero, pah-gah-day-ro
a payable

pagaduría, pah-gah-doo-
ree-ah s paymaster's
office

pagamento, pah-gah-men-
to s payment

pagano, pah-gah-no s & a
heathen; pagan

pagar, pah-gar v to pay

pagaré, pah-gah-ray s
promissory note

página, pah-He-nah s
page (of a book)

pago, pah-go s payment

país, pah-iss s country;
region; landscape

paisaje, pah´e-sah-Hay s
landscape

paisano, pah´e-sah-no s
countryman

paja, pah-Hah s straw

pájaro, pah-Hah-ro s bird;
sly fellow (fam)

pajarota, pah-Hah-ro-tah
s false report

paje, pah-Hay s page
(boy)

pala, pah-lah s shovel;
blade; spade

palabra, pah-lah-brah s
word

palabrero, pah-lah-bray-
ro a loquacious

palabrita, pah-lah-bree-
tah s short word; word
full of meaning

palaciego, pah-lah-the-ay-
go s courtier; a
pertaining to a palace

palacio, pah-lah-the-o s
palace

paladar, pah-lah-dar s

palate; taste; relish

paladear, pah-lah-day-**ar** v to relish

paladino, pah-lah-dee-no a manifest; evident; public

palafrenero, pah-lah-fray-nay-ro s groom

palanca, pah-**lahn**-kah s lever; crowbar

palanquín, pah-lahn-**keen** s public porter; covered litter

palco, **pahl**-ko s box (theater)

paleto, pah-**lay**-to s fallow deer; rustic

paliar, pah-le-**ar** v to palliate

palidecer, pah-le-day-**thair** v to grow pale

palidez, pah-le-**deth** s paleness; wanness

pálido, **pah**-le-do a pallid; pale

palio, **pah**-le-o s cloak; pall

palique, pah-**lee**-kay s small talk

palizada, pah-le-**thah**-dah s palisade

palma, **pahl**-mah s palm tree; palm leaf; palm of the hand

palmada, pahl-**mah**-dah s slap; applause

palmear, pahl-may-**ar** v to clap hands

palmera, pahl-**may**-rah s palm tree

palmo, **pahl**-mo s an 8-inch span

palo, **pah**-lo s stick; cudgel; mast; blow with a stick

paloma, pah-**lo**-mah s pigeon; dove

palomar, pah-lo-**mar** s dovecote

palomera, pah-lo-**may**-rah s dovecote

palpar, pahl-**par** v to feel; to touch; to grope

palurdo, pah-**loor**-do s & a rustic

pamplina, pahm-**plee**-nah s duckweed; futility

pan, pan s bread; loaf; food

panadería, pah-nah-day-**ree**-ah s bakery

panal, pah-**nahl** s honeycomb

pandear, pahn-day-**ar** v to bend; to bulge out

pandereta, pahn-day-**ray**-tah s tambourine

pandilla, pahn-dee-l'yah s party; gang

panecillo, pah-nay-**thee**-l'yo s small loaf; French roll

panela, pah-**nay**-lah s small biscuit

pánfilo, **pahn**-fe-lo a slow; sluggish

paniaguado, pah-ne-ah-goo-**ah**-do s servant; protégé

pánico, **pah**-ne-ko s & a panic

pantalón, pahn-tah-**lon** s pants; slacks

pantalla, pahn-**tah**-l'yah s screen; lampshade

pantano, pahn-**tah**-no s swamp; marsh; bog; reservoir; dam

panteón, pahn-tay-**on** s pantheon; mausoleum

pantera, pahn-**tay**-rah s panther

pantomina, pahn-to-**mee**-mah s pantomime; dumb show

pantorrilla, pahn-tor-**rree**-l'yah s calf of the leg

pantuflo, pahn-**too**-flo s slipper

panza, **pahn**-thah s paunch; belly

pañal, pah-n'**yahl** s diaper

pañería, pah-n'**yay**-ree-ah s draper's shop

pañero, pah-n'**yay**-ro s draper

paño, pah-n'yo s cloth;

drapery

pañol, pah-n-´yol s storeroom (in a ship)

pañuelo, pah-n´yoo-ay-lo s handkerchief

papa, pah-pah s Pope

papada, pah-**pah-**dah s double chin

papagayo, pah-pah-**gah-**yo s parrot

papanatas, pah-pah-**nah-**tahs s simpleton

páparo, **pah-**pah-ro s rustic; ignorant peasant

papel, pah-**pel** s paper; writing; part; role; document

papel higiénico, pah-**pel** ee-*He´ay*-ne-ko s toilet paper

papelera, pah-pay-**lay-**rah s wastepaper basket; writing desk

papelería, pah-pay-lay-**ree-**ah s stationery

papelero, pah-pay-**lay-**ro s stationer

papeleta, pah-pay-**lay-**tah s slip of paper; card; paper bag

papilla, pah-**pee-**l´yah s pap; guile; deceit

paquebote, pah-kay-bo-tay s packet-boat

paquete, pah-**kay-**tay s parcel; package

par, par s pair; peer; a equal; even

para, pah-rah *prep* for; to; in order to; toward

parabién, pah-rah-be-en s congratulation

parabrisas, pah-rah-**bree-**sahs s windshield

parábola, pah-**rah-**bo-lah s parable; parabola

paracaídas, pah-rah-kah-ee-dahs s parachute

parada, pah-**rah-**dah s halt; pause; stall

parada de autobús, pah-rah-dah day ah´oo-to-booss s bus stop

paradera, pah-rah-**day-**rah s sluice

paradero, pah-rah-**day-**ro s halting place; end

parado, pah-**rah-**do a remiss; inactive; indolent

paraguas, pah-**rah-**goo´ahs s umbrella

paragüero, pah-rah-goo´**ay-**ro s umbrella stand

paraíso, pah-rah-ee-so s paradise

paraje, pah-**rah-***Hay* s place

paralelo, pah-rah-**lay-**lo s comparison; a parallel

parálisis, pah-**rah-**le-siss s paralysis

paramento, pah-rah-**men-**to s ornament

páramo, pah-rah-mo s wilderness

parangón, pah-rahn-gon s paragon; model; comparison

parar, pah-**rar** v to stop; to halt; to detain

pararrayos, pah-rar-**rrah-**yos s lightning rod or conductor

parcela, par-**thay-**lah s plot of land

parcial*, par-the-ahl a partial

parco*, par-ko a sober; sparing; moderate

parche, par-chay s plaster; sticking plaster

pardal, par-**dahl** s sparrow; leopard a rustic

pardear, par-day-ar v to become gray

¡pardiez! par de-eth *interj* by God! upon my word!

pardo, par-do a brown; dark gray

parear, pah-ray-**ar** v to match; to couple

parecer, pah-ray-**thair** v to appear; to seem; s opinion; look

parecido, pah-ray-**thee-**do a like; similar; looking

pared, pah-**red** s wall

paredón, pah-ray-**don** s thick wall

pareja, pah-**ray**-Hah s pair; match; coupling

parejo, pah-**ray**-Ho a equal; similar; even

parentela, pah-ren-**tay**-lah s parentage

pareo, pah-**ray**-o s coupling; matching

paridad, pah-re-**dahd** s parity

pariente, parienta, pah-re-**en**-tay, pah-re-en-**tah** s & a relative

parihuela, pah-re-oo´ay-lah s barrow; stretcher

parir, pah-**reer** v to give birth

parla, **par**-lah s loquacity; talk

parlamentar, par-lah-men-**tar** v to parley

parlamento, par-lah-**men**-to s parliament; speech

parlar, par-**lar** v to speak with case; to chatter

parlón a talkative

parodia, pah-**ro**-de-ah s parody

parpadear, par-pah-day-**ar** v to wink

párpado, **par**-pah-do s eyelid

parque, par-**kay** s park; paddock

parra, **par**-rrah s vine on stakes or on a wall

párrafo, **pah**-rrahf-o s paragraph

parrilla, par-**rree**-l´yah s gridiron; grate

párroco, **pah**-rro-ko s parson; rector

parroquia, par-**rro**-ke-ah s parish

parte, **par**-tay s part; share; place; interest; party

partera, par-**tay**-rah s midwife

partible, par-tee-**blay** a divisible

partición, par-te-the-**on** s partition; division; distribution

participar, par-te-the-**par** v to inform; to participate

partícipe, par-tee-the-**pay** s partner; a sharing

partícula, par-tee-koo-lah s particle

partida, par-tee-dah s departure; item; entry; parcel; stakes; game; pl talents

partidario, par-te-dah-re-o s partisan

partido, par-tee-do s party; district; utility; game; a divided

partir, par-**teer** v to part; to divide; to depart

parto, **par**-to s childbirth

párvulo, **par**-voo-lo s child; a innocent; humble

pasa, **pah**-sah s raisin

pasada, pah-sah-dah s passage; previous

pasadero, pah-sah-**day**-ro a supportable; passable

pasadizo, pah-sah-**dee**-tho s passage

pasador, pah-sah-**dor** s bolt; pin; peg

pasaje, pah-**sah**-Hay s passage

pasajero, pah-sah-**Hay**-ro s passenger; a transitory

pasamano, pah-sah-**mah**-no s handrail

pasaporte, pah-sah-**por**-tay s passport

pasar, pah-**sar** v to pass; to convey; to exceed –a, –ah, to proceed on

pasatiempo, pah-sah-te-**em**-po s pastime

pascua, **pahs**-koo´ah s Easter

pase, **pah**-say s pass; permit

pasear, pah-say-**ar** v to walk; to take a walk

paseo, pah-**say**-o s walk;

to perpetrate

perpetuo*, pair-**pay**-too´o *a* perpetual

perplejo*, pair-**play**-Ho *a* perplexed

perramente, pair-rrah-**men**-tay *adv* very badly

perrería, pair-rray-ree-ah *s* pack of dogs; vexation

perro, **pair**-rro *s* dog

perruno, pair-**rroo**-no *a* canine

perseguir, pair-say-**gheer** *v* to pursue; to harrass

perseverar, pair-say-vay-**rar** *v* to persevere

persiana, pair-se-**ah**-nah *s* window-blind; shutter

persignarse, pair-sig-**nar**-say *v* to make the sign of the cross

persistir, pair-siss-**teer** *v* to persist

persona, pair-**so**-nah *s* person

personaje, pair-so-nah-Hay *s* personage

perspectiva, pair-spek-**tee**-vah *s* perspective; view; prospect

perspicacia, pair-spe-kah-the-ah *s* perspicacity

perspicaz, pair-spe-**kath** *a* perspicacious

perspicuo*, pair-spee-koo´o *a* clear

persuadir, pair-soo´ah-**deer** *v* to persuade

pertenecer, pair-tay-nay-**thair** *v* to belong to; to appertain

pértiga, **pair**-te-gah *s* pole; rod

pertiguero, pair-te-**gay**-ro *s* verger

pertinaz*, pair-te-**nath** *a* pertinacious

pertrechos, pair-**tray**-chos *s* stores; ammunition; tools

perturbar, pair-toor-**bar** *v* to perturb

perverso, pair-**vair**-so *a* perverse; wicked

pesa, **pay**-sah *s* weight

pesada, pay-**sah**-dah *s* weighing; quantity weighed

pesadez, pay-sah-**deth** *s* heaviness; gravity; slowness; drowsiness

pesado*, **pay**-**sah**-do *a* heavy; cumbrous; sluggish; vexatious

pesadumbre, pay-sah-**doom**-bray *s* grief; sorrow

pésame, **pay**-sah-may *s* expression of condolence

pesantez, pay-sahn-**teth** *s* gravity; heaviness

pesar, pay-**sar** *v* to weigh; to cause regret; to ponder; *s* sorrow; regret; **a —de**, ah — day, in spite of

pesaroso, pay-sah-**ro**-so *a* sorrowful; repentant

pesca, **pess**-kah *s* fishing; catch

pescado, pess-**kah**-do *s* fish

pescador, pess-kah-**dor** *s* fisherman

pescante, pess-**kahn**-tay *s* wire; jib

pescar, pess-**kar** *v* to fish

pescuezo, pess-koo´ay-tho *s* neck

pesebre, pay-**say**-bray *s* crib; manger

peseta, pay-**say**-tah *s* Spanish monetary unit

pésimo*, **pay**-se-mo *a* very bad

peso, **pay**-so *s* weight; load

pesquería, pess-kay-ree-ah *s* fishing; fishery

pesquisa, pess-**kee**-sah *s* enquiry; search

pestaña, pess-**tah**-n´yah *s* eyelash; flange

pestañear, pess-tah-n´yay-ar *v* to blink; to wink

peste, **pess**-tay *s* pest; pestilence

pestillo, pess-**tee**-l´yo s bolt

petaca, pay-**tah**-kah s tobacco pouch

petardear, pay-tar-day-**ar** v to cheat

petardista, pay-tar-**diss**-tah s cheat; swindler

petardo, pay-**tar**-do s petard; firework

peto, pay-to s bodice; bib

pez, peth s fish

pezón, pay-**thon** s nipple

pezuña, pay-**thoo**-n´yah s hoof

piadoso, pe-ah-**do**-so a pious; merciful

pian, piano, pe-**ahn,** pe-**ah**-no adv gently; softly; slowly

piano, pe-**ah**-no s pianoforte

piar, pe-**ar** v to cheep

piara, pe-**ah**-rah s herd of swine

pica, pee-kah s pike; spear

picada, pe-kah-dah s puncture

picadero, pe-kah-**day**-ro s riding-school

picador, pe-kah-**dor** s riding-master; (bull-fights) pricker

picadura, pe-kah-**doo**-rah s (insect) bite, sting

picante, pe-**kahn**-tay s hot

tast; chilli sauce; a hot; spicy

picaporte, pe-kah-**por**-tay s spring-latch; latch-key; door-knocker

picar, pe-**kar** v to prick; to sting; to nibble; to peck; to itch

picardía, pe-kar-dee-ah s mischief

picaresco, pe-kah-**ress**-ko a roguish

pícaro, pee-kah-ro a knavish; mischievous

picatoste, pe-kah-**tos**-tay s buttered toast

picazón, pe-kah-**thon** s itching; displeasure

pico, pee-ko s beak; bill; nib; peak; garrulity

picota, pe-**ko**-tah s pillory; top

picotear, pe-ko-tay-**ar** v to peck; to nibble

pictórico, pik-**to**-re-ko a pictorial; picturesque

pichón, pe-**chon** s young pigeon

pie, pe-**ay** s foot; basis; trunk; foundation; motive; **a —firme,** ah **— feer**-may, steadfastly

piedad, pe-ay-**dahd** s piety; mercy; pity

piedra, pe-ay-drah s stone; hail

piel, pe-**ell** s skin; hide; peel

pierna, pe-**air**-nah s leg; leg of mutton; limb

pieza, pe-**ay**-thah s piece; coin

pifia, pee-fe-ah s (billiards) miss

pila, pee-lah s pile; heap; font; trough for cattle

pila, pee-lah s battery

pilar, pe-**lar** s basin of a fountain; column; pillar

píldora, peel-do-rah s pill

pilón, pe-**lon** s basin of a fountain; cattle trough

piloto, pe-lo-to s pilot

pillada, pe-l´yah-dah s knavish trick

pillar, pe-l´yar v to plunder

pillo, pee-l´yo s rogue; thief; a roguish

pimentón, pe-men-**ton** s red pepper; paprika

pimienta, pe-me-en-tah s pepper

pimpollo, pim-po-l´yo s sprout; shoot; lively youth

pina, pee-nah s conical mound; jaunt

pinar, pe-**nar** s pine-grove

pincel, pin-**thell** s painter's brush

pincelar, pin-thay-**lar** v to

shop

peliagudo, pay-le-ah-**goo**-do *a* difficult; skillful

pelicano, pay-le-**kah**-no *a* gray-haired

pelícano, pay-**lee**-kah-no *s* pelican

película, pay-**lee**-koo-lah *s* film

peligrar, pay-le-**grar** *v* to be in danger

peligro, pay-**lee**-gro *s* peril; danger

peligroso*, pay-le-**gro**-so *a* dangerous

pelillo, pay-lee-**l´yo** *s* short hair; trifle

pelo, pay-lo *s* hair; down; flaw

peloso, pay-lo-so *a* hairy

pelota, pay-lo-tah *s* ball; Spanish ball game

pelote, pay-lo-tay *s* goat's hair

pelotear, pay-lo-tay-**ar** *v* to play ball; to argue

pelotera, pay-lo-**tay**-rah *s* quarrel

peltre, pell-tray *s* pewter

peluca, pay-**loo**-kah *s* wig

peludo, pay-**loo**-do *a* hairy; shaggy

peluquero, pay-loo-**kay**-ro *s* hairdresser

pelusa, pay-**loo**-sah *s* fuzz of plants or fruit

pella, pay-**l´yah** *s* pellet; fleece; lump of molten metal; lard; heron

pellejo, pay-**l´yay**-*H*o *s* skin; hide; peel; wine-skin; tippler

pelliza, pay-**l´yee**-thah *s* pelisse

pellizcar, pay-**l´yeeth-kar** *v* to pinch

pena, pay-nah *s* punishment; pain

penado, pay-**nah**-do *a* punished; painful

penar, pen-**nar** *v* to chastise; to suffer pain; to grieve

pendencia, pen-**den**-the-ah *s* dispute; quarrel

pendenciero, pen-den-the-**ay**-ro *a* quarrelsome

pender, pen-**dair** *v* to hang; to depend

pendiente, pen-de-**en**-tay *s* earring; slope; *a* hanging

pendón, pen-**don** *s* banner; pennant

péndulo, pen-**doo**-lo *s* pendulum; *a* hanging

penetrar, pay-nay-**trar** *v* to penetrate

penicilina, pay-nee-the-**lee**-nah *s* penicillin

penique, pay-**nee**-kay *s* penny

penitenciar, pay-ne-ten-the-**ar** *v* to impose penance

penoso*, pay-**no**-so *a* painful

pensado, pen-sah-do *pp* pensar; **de** –, day –, purposely

pensamiento, pen-sah-me-**en**-to *s* thought

pensar, pen-**sar** *v* to think

pensativo, pen-sah-**tee**-vo *a* pensive; thoughtful

pensión, pen-se-**on** *s* pension; boardinghouse

pensionista, pen-se-o-**niss**-tah *s* boarder

penúltimo, pay-**nool**-te-mo *a* penultimate; next to last

penuria, pay-**noo**-re-ah *s* extreme poverty

peña, pay-**n´yah** *s* rock; large stone

peñasco, pay-**n´yahs**-ko *a* large rock

peón, pay-**on** *s* unskilled worker; foot soldier; spinning top

peonada, pay-o-**nah**-dah *s* day's work

peor, pay-**or** *adv* & *a* worse

pepino, pay-**pee**-no *s* cucumber

pepita, pay-**pee**-tah *s*

kernel; pip

pequeñez, pay-kay-n´yeth s smallness

pequeño, pay-kay-n´yo a little; small; young

pera, pay-rah s pear

percance, pair-kahn-thay s mishap

percibir, pair-the-**beer** v to receive; to collect; to perceive

percutir, pair-koo-**teer** v to strike

percha, pair-chah s pole; perch (fish)

perder, pair-**dair** v to lose

pérdida, pair-de-dah s loss; waste

perdiz, pair-**deeth** s partridge

perdón, pair-**don** s pardon

perdonar, pair-do-**nar** v to forgive; to remit; to excuse

perdurable, pair-doo-rah-blay a lasting

perecedero, pay-ray-thay-day-ro a perishable

perecer, pay-ray-**thair** v to perish

peregrino, pay-ray-gree-no s pilgrim; a strange

perejil, pay-ray-**Heel** s parsley

perendengue, pay-ren-den-gay s earring; cheap

ornament

perentorio, pay-ren-**to**-re-o a peremptory

pereza, pay-**ray**-thah s laziness; slowness

perezoso, pay-ray-**tho**-so a lazy; idle; indolent

perfeccionamiento, pair-fek-the-o-nah-me-**en**-to s perfection; improvement

perfecto*, pair-**fek**-to a perfect; complete

pérfido, pair-fe-do a perfidious

perfil, pair-**feel** s profile; side view

perfilar, pair-fe-**lar** v to outline

perforar, pair-fo-**rar** v to perforate

perfume, pair-foo-may s perfume

pergamino, pair-gah-mee-no s parchment

pericia, pay-**ree**-the-ah s skill; expertness

perifollo, pay-re-fo-l´yo s chervil; pl women's ornaments

perímetro, pay-**ree**-may-tro s perimeter; contour

periódico, pay-re-o-de-ko s newspaper; a periodical

peripuesto, pay-re-

poo´ess-to a dressy

periquito, pay-re-**kee**-to s parakeet

perito, pay-**ree**-to a skillful; experienced

perjudicar, pair-Hoo-de-**kar** v to prejudice; to injure

perjuicio, pair-Hoo-ee-the-o s prejudice

perjurio, pair-Hoo-re-o s perjury

perjuro, pair-Hoo-ro s perjurer; a forsworn

perla, pair-lah s pearl

permanecer, pair-mah-nay-**thair** v to remain; to stay

permanente*, pair-mah-nen-tay a permanent

permeable, pair-may-ah-blay a permeable

permiso, pair-mee-so s permission; leave; license

permitir, pair-me-**teer** v to permit; to allow

permutar, pair-moo-**tar** v to exchange; to permute

pernear, pair-nay-**ar** v to kick; to shake the legs

pernetas (en), en pair-nay-tahs adv bare-legged

pernicioso, pair-ne-the-o-so a pernicious

pernil, pair-**neel** s hock;

ham

pernio, pair-ne-o *s* door or window hinge

pernoctar, pair-nok-tar *v* to spend the night

pero, pay-ro *conj* but; yet

perogrullada, pay-ro-grool´yah-dah *s* obvious and commonplace truth

perol, pay-rol *s* boiler; kettle

peroné, pay-ro-nay *s* fibula

peroración, pay-ro-rah-the-on *s* peroration

perorata, pay-ro-rah-tah *s* harangue; speech

perpetrar, pair-pay-trar *v* to perpetrate

perpetuo*, pair-pay-too´o *a* perpetual

perplejo*, pair-play-Ho *a* perplexed

perra, pair-rrah *s* bitch (dog); – gorda, – gordah,10 céntimos piece; – chica, – chee-kah, 5 céntimos piece

perramente, pair-rrah-men-tay *adv* very badly

perrería, pair-rray-ree-ah *s* pack of dogs; vexation

perro, pair-rro *s* dog

perruno, pair-rroo-no *a* canine

perseguir, pair-say-gheer *v* to pursue; to harass

perseverar, pair-say-vay-rar *v* to persevere

persiana, pair-se-ah-nah *s* venetian blind

persignarse, pair-sig-nar-say *v* to make the sign of the cross

persistir, pair-siss-teer *v* to persist

persona, pair-so-nah *s* person

personaje, pair-so-nah-Hay *s* personage

perspectiva, pair-spek-tee-vah *s* perspective; view; prospect

perspicacia, pair-spe-kah-the-ah *s* perspicacity

perspicaz, pair-spe-kath *a* perspicacious

perspicuo*, pair-spee-koo´o *a* clear; transparent; smooth

persuadir, pair-soo´ah-deer *v* to persuade

pertenecer, pair-tay-nay-thair *v* to belong to; to appertain

pértiga, pair-te-gah *s* pole; rod

pertinaz*, pair-te-nath *a* obstinate; headstrong; pertinacious

pertrechos, pair-tray-chos *s* stores; ammunition;

tools

perturbar, pair-toor-bar *v* to perturb

perverso, pair-vair-so *a* perverse

pesa, pay-sah *s* weight

pesada, pay-sah-dah *s* weighing; quantity weighed

pesadez, pay-sah-deth *s* heaviness; gravity; slowness; drowsiness

pesado*, pay-sah-do *a* heavy; sluggish; vexatious

pesadumbre, pay-sah-doom-bray *s* grief; sorrow

pésame, pay-sah-may *s* expression of condolence

pesantez, pay-sahn-teth *s* gravity; heaviness

pesar, pay-sar *v* to weigh; to cause regret; to ponder; *s* sorrow; regret; a – de, ah – day, in spite of

pesaroso, pay-sah-ro-so *a* sorrowful; repentant

pesca, pess-kah *s* fishing; catch

pescado, pess-kah-do *s* fish

pescador, pess-kah-dor *s* fisherman

pescante, pess-**kahn**-tay *s* jib of a crane or derrick (*naut*)

pescar, pess-**kar** *v* to fish

pescuezo, pess-koo´ay-tho *s* neck

pesebre, pay-**say**-bray *s* crib; manger

peseta, pay-**say**-tah *s* Spanish monetary unit

pésimo*, pay-se-mo *a* very bad; worst

peso, **pay**-so, *s* weight; load

pesquería, pess-kay-ree-ah *s* fishing; fishery

pesquisa, pess-**kee**-sah *s* inquiry; search

pestaña, pess-**tah**-n´yah *s* eyelash; flange

pestañear, pess-tah-n´yay-ar *v* to blink; to wink

peste, **pess**-tay *s* pest; pestilence

pestillo, pess-tee-l´yo *s* bolt

petaca, pay-**tah**-kah *s* tobacco pouch

petardear, pay-tar-day-ar *v* to cheat

petardista, pay-tar-**diss**-tah *s* cheat; swindler

petimetre, pay-te-may-tray *s* conceited; ostentatious

peto, **pay**-to *s* breastplate (armor)

pez, peth *s* fish

pezón, pay-**thon** *s* nipple

pezuña, pay-**thoo**-n´yah *s* hoof

piadoso, pe-ah-**do**-so *a* pious; merciful

pian, piano, pe-ahn, pe-ah-no *adv* gently; softly; slowly

piano, pe-ah-no *s* piano

piar, pe-ar *v* to chirp

piara, pe-**ah**-rah *s* herd of swine

pica, **pee**-kah *s* pike; spear

picada, pe-**kah**-dah *s* puncture

picadero, pe-kah-**day**-ro *s* riding school

picador, pe-kah-**dor** *s* riding master; pricker (bullfights)

picadura, pe-kah-**doo**-rah *s* bite (insect), sting

picante, pe-**kahn**-tay *s* spicy; *a* piquant; stinging

picaporte, pe-kah-**por**-tay *s* latch; latch-key; door knocker

picar, pe-**kar** *v* to prick; to sting; to nibble; to peck; to itch

picardía, pe-kar-dee-ah *s* mischief

picaresco, pe-kah-**ress**-ko *a* roguish

pícaro, pee-kah-ro *a* mischievous

picatoste, pe-kah-**tos**-tay *s* buttered toast

picazón, pe-kah-**thon** *s* itching; displeasure

pico, pee-ko *s* beak; bill; nib; peak; garrulity

picón, pe-kon *s* lampoon

picota, pe-ko-tah *s* pillory; top

picotear, pe-ko-tay-ar *v* to peck; to wrangle

pictórico, pik-to-re-ko *a* pictorial

pichón, pe-chon *s* young pigeon

pie, pe-ay *s* foot; basis; trunk; foundation; motive; a – firme, ah – feer-may, steadfastly

piedad, pe-ay-**dahd** *s* piety; mercy; pity

piedra, pe-ay-drah *s* stone; hail

piel, pe-ell *s* skin; hide; peel

pierna, pe-**air**-nah *s* leg; leg of lamb; limb

pieza, pe-**ay**-thah *s* piece; coin

pifia, pee-fe-ah *s* miss (billiards); mistake

pila, pee-lah *s* battery

pila, pee-lah *s* pile; heap;

font; trough for cattle

pilar, pe-lar s basin of a fountain; column; pillar

píldora, peel-do-rah s pill

pilón, pe-lon s basin of a fountain

piloto, pe-lo-to s pilot

pillada, pe-l´yah-dah s knavish trick

pillar, pe-l´yar v to plunder

pillo, pee-l´yo s rogue; thief; a roguish

pimentón, pe-men-ton s red pepper; paprika

pimienta, pe-me-en-tah s pepper

pimpollar, pim-po-l´yar s nursery (plants)

pimpollo, pim-po-l´yo s sprout; shoot; lively youth; child (boy or girl)

pina, pee-nah s conical mound; jaunt

pinar, pe-nar s pine-grove

pincel, pin-**thell** s paintbrush

pincelar, pin-thel-lar v to paint

pinchadiscos, pin-cha-**diss**-kos s disk jockey

pinchar, pin-**char** v to prick; to puncture

pineda, pe-nay-dah s pine-grove

pingajo, pin-**gah**-Ho s rag; tatter

ping-pong, peeng-pong s table tennis

pingüe, peen-goo´ay a abundant; rich (profit); fertile

pino, pee-no s pine-tree; a steep

pinocha, pe-no-chah s pinecone

pinta, peen-tah s spot; stain; pint

pintado, pin-tah-do a painted; mottled; just; exact

pintar, pin-tar v to paint

pintiparado, pin-te-pah-rah-do a perfectly like

pintor, pin-tor s painter

pintoresco, pin-to-ress-ko a picturesque

pintorrear, pin-tor-rray-ar v to daub

pintura, pin-too-rah s painting; picture

pinzas, pin-thahs s nippers; tweezers; tongs

pinzón, pin-thon s chaffinch

piña, pee-n´yah s pinecone; pineapple

pío, pee-o s longing; puling of chickens; a pious; merciful

piojo, pe-o-Ho s louse

pipa, pee-pah s cask; tobacco pipe

pipote, pe-po-tay s keg

pique, pee-kay s a –, on the point of; echar a –, ay-char ah –, to sink (a ship); irse a –, eer-say ah –, to founder (ship)

piquete, pe-kay-tay s small wound; small hole; picket

pira, pee-rah s funeral pile

pirata, pe-rah-tah s pirate

piratería, pe-rah-tay-ree-ah s piracy

piropo, pe-ro-po s compliment; flattery

pirueta, pe-roo´ay-tah s pirouette

pisada, pe-sah-dah s footstep; footprint

pisar, pe-sar v to tread; to trample; to step on

pisaverde, pe-sah-**vair**-day s (fam.) fop

piscina, piss-**thee**-nah s fish pond; swimming pool

piso, pe-so s floor; story (building); apartment

pisotear, pe-so-tay-ar v to trample

pista, piss-tah s track; trail; scent; trace

pisto, piss-to s thick broth

pistola, piss-**to**-lah s pistol

pistolete, piss-to-**lay**-tay s small gun

pistón, piss-**ton** s piston; embolus; percussion cap

pitada, pe-**tah**-dah s blow of a whistle

pitanza, pe-**tahn**-thah s pittance; daily allowance; stipend

pitillo, pe-tee-l´yo s cigarette

pito, **pee**-to s whistle

pitón, pe-**ton** s lock of hair; sprig; nozzle; horn

pizarra, pe-**thar**-rrah s slate; blackboard

pizca, **pith**-kah s bit; jot

pizpireta, pith-pe-**ray**-tah s lively (woman)

placa, **plah**-kah s plate; insignia of an order of knighthood

pláceme, **plah**-thay-may s congratulation

placentero, plah-then-**tay**-ro a pleasant; joyful; mirthful

placer, plah-**thair** v to please; s pleasure; consent

placidez, plah-the-**deth** s placidity

plácido, **plah**-the-do a placid

plaga, **plah**-gah s plague

plagar, plah-**gar** v to plague; to infest

plagio, plah-**He**-o s plagiarism

plan, plahn s plan; design; scheme; plot

plana, **plah**-nah s trowel; page (book); plain

plancha, **plahn**-chah s plate; iron (clothes); –**de vapor,** day vah-**porr** s steam iron

planchar, plahn-**char** v to iron (clothes); to press

planicie, plah-**nee**-the-ay s plain; prairie

plano, **plah**-no s plan; map; chart; a plain; level; flat

planta, **plahn**-tah s sole of the foot; plant; building plan

plantar, plahn-**tar** v to plant; to fix upright; to jilt

plantear, plahn-tay-**ar** v to plan; to trace

plantel, plahn-**tell** s nursery-garden; training school

plantilla, plahn-tee-l´yah s young plant; pattern; inner shoe sole

plantón, plahn-**ton** s sprout; sentry

plañidero, plah-n´yee-

day-ro a mournful

plañido, plah-n´yee-do s moan; lamentation

plasmar, plahs-**mar** v to mold

plástico, **plahs**-te-ko a plastic

plata, **plah**-tah s silver; (fam) money

plátano, **plah**-tah-no s banana; plane tree

platea, plah-**tay**-ah s orchestra (theater); pit

platear, plah-tay-**ar** v to plate

platería, plah-tay-**ree**-ah s silversmith's shop or trade

platero, plah-**tay**-ro s silversmith

plática, **plah**-te-kah s conversation; chat

platillo, plah-tee-l´yo s small dish; saucer

platino, plah-**tee**-no s platinum

plato, **plah**-to s dish; plate; daily fare

playa, **plah**-yah s shore; beach

plaza, **plah**-thah s square; marketplace; fortified town; employment

plazo, **plah**-tho s term; date; installment; deadline

pleamar, play-ah-**mar** s high-water

plebe, play-bay s common people; lowest social class

plebeyo, play-**bay**-yo a plebian

plegable, play-**gah**-blay a pliable

plegar, play-**gar** v to fold; to plait; to double

plegaria, play-**gah**-re-ah s prayer

pleitear, play´e-tay-**ar** v to plead; to litigate

pleito, play´e-to s lawsuit proceedings

plenilunio, play-ne-**loo**-ne-o s full moon

plenitud, play-ne-**tood** s fullness

pliego, ple-**ay**-go s sheet of paper

pliegue, ple-**ay**-gay s fold; plait; crease

plomada, plo-**mah**-dah s plumbing line

plomero, plo-**may**-ro s plumber

plomizo, plo-**mee**-tho a leaden

plomo, plo-mo s lead

pluma, ploo-mah s feather; pen

plumero, ploo-**may**-ro s plume; feather-duster

plumón, ploo-**mon** s down; feather-bed

pluvial, ploo-ve-**ahl** a rainy; pluvial

población, po-blah-the-**on** s population

poblado, po-**blah**-do s town; village; inhabited place

poblar, po-**blar** v to people; to found; to occupy; to stock; to settle

pobre*, po-**bray** a poor

pobreza, po-**bray**-thah s poverty

pocilga, po-**theel**-gah s pigsty

pócima, po-the-mah s potion; brew

poco, po-ko adv a little; s small quantity; a little; scanty; few

poda, po-dah s pruning

poder, po-**dair** v to be able; s power; authority; force

poderdante, po-dair-**dahn**-tay s constituent

poderío, po-day-**ree**-o s power; might; dominion

poderoso, po-day-**ro**-so a powerful; eminent

podre, po-dray s pus; matter

podredumbre, po-dray-**doom**-bray s putrid matter; corruption

podrir, po-**dreer,** (see **pudrir**)

poesía, po-ay-see-ah s poetry

polaina, po-lah´ee-nah s legging; gaiter

polea, po-**lay**-ah s pulley

policía, po-le-**thee**-ah s police

poliéster, po-le-**ays**-tayr s polyester

polígloto, po-lee-**glo**-to s linguist

polígono, po-lee-**go**-no s polygon; a polygonal

polilla, po-lee-l´yah s moth

política, po-lee-te-**kah** s politics

póliza, po-le-thah s policy; scrip

polizonte, po-le-**thon**-tay s detective (fam)

polo, po-lo s pole

poltrón, pol-**tron** a idle; lazy

poltrona, pol-**tro**-nah s easy chair

polvareda, pol-vah-**ray**-dah s dust cloud

polvo, pol-vo s dust; powder

pólvora, pol-vo-rah s gunpowder

polvorear, pol-vo-ray-ar *v* to powder

polla, po-l´yah *s* pullet; young hen

pollada, po-l´yah-dah *s* hatch; covey

pollero, po-l´yay-ro *s* poulterer

pollino, po-l´yee-no *s* donkey; stupid fellow

pollo, po-l´yo *s* chicken; nestling; young man

polluelo, po-l´yoo´ay-lo *s* small chicken

polución, po-loo-the-on *s* pollution

pomada, po-mah-dah *s* pomade; salve

pomar, po-mar *s* orchard

pomez, po-meth *s* pumice

pomo, po-mo *s* fruit; apple; pommel; flask

pompa, pom-pah *s* pomp; pageant

pomponearse, pom-po-nay-ar-say *v* to strut

ponche, pon-chay *s* punch

ponderación, pon-day-rah-the-on *s* consideration; weighing (words)

ponderar, pon-day-rar *v* to ponder; to exaggerate

ponderoso*, pon-day-ro-so *a* ponderous; grave

ponedero, po-nay-day-ro *a* egg-laying

poner, po-nair *v* to put; to place; to lay eggs; to contribute

ponerse, po-nair-say *v* to set about; to wear

poniente, po-ne-en-tay *s* west; west wind

pontífice, pon-tee-fe-thay *s* Pope; pontiff

pontón, pon-ton *s* pontoon

pontonero, pon-to-nay-ro *s* pontooner

ponzoña, pon-tho-n´yah *s* poison

popa, po-pah *s* poop (ship); stern

populacho, po-poo-lah-cho *s* populace; mob

poquedad, po-kay-dahd *s* paucity; cowardice

poquito, po-kee-to *a* very little

por, por *prep* for; by; about; through; by means of; on account of

porcelana, por-thay-lah-nah *s* porcelain; chinaware

porcino, por-thee-no *a* hoggish; swinish

porción, por-the-on *s* part; portion; lot

porcuno, por-koo-no *a* porcine; hoggish

porche, por-chay *s* porch; covered walk

pordiosero, por-de-o-say-ro *s* beggar

porfía, por-fee-ah *s* obstinacy; stubborness; insistence

porfiado, por-fe-ah-do *a* obstinate; insistent

porfiar, por-fe-ar *v* to wrangle; to persist; to insist

pormenor, por-may-nor *s* detail

poro, po-ro *s* pore

porque, por-kay *conj* because

¿por qué? por kay *conj* why?

porquería, por-kay-ree-ah *s* nastiness; filth; foulness

porrillo (a), ah por-rree-l´yo *adv* copiously

porrón, por-rron *s* pitcher

portada, por-tah-dah *s* portal; frontispiece; title page; cover

portador, por-tah-dor *s* carrier; bearer; tray

portaequipajes, por-tah-ay-ke-pah-Hayss *s* luggage-rack

portal, por-tahl *s* porch; portico

portamonedas, por-tah-mo-**nay**-dahs s purse

portarse, por-**tar**-say v to behave

portátil, por-**tah**-til a portable

portazgo, por-**tahth**-go s toll; turnpike duty

porte, por-tay s porterage; postage; carriage; conduct

portear, por-tay-ar v to convey

portento, por-**ten**-to s portent

portero, por-**tay**-ro s janitor; doorkeeper; goalkeeper

portillo, por-tee-l´yo s aperture; gap; breach

portón, por-**ton** s inner door of a house

porvenir, por-vay-**neer** s future

pos (en), en pos adv after; behind; in pursuit of

posada, po-**sah**-dah s lodging house; inn

posadero, po-sah-**day**-ro s innkeeper; host

poseedor, po-say-ay-**dor** s possessor

poseer, po-say-**air** v to hold; to possess; to own

poseído, po-say-ee-do a possessed by the devil

posibilitar, po-se-be-le-**tar** v to render possible

posible*, po-**see**-blay a possible; s pl wealth; means

posición, po-se-the-**on** s position; posture; pose; attitude; situation

positivo, po-se-**tee**-vo a positive; true; certain

poso, po-so s sediment; dregs

posponer, pos-po-**nair** v to postpone

posta, pos-tah s post stage; relay

poste, pos-tay s post; pillar

postema, pos-tay-mah s abscess; tumor

postergar, pos-tair-**gar** v to leave behind; to delay

posterior*, pos-tay-re-or a posterior; hinder

postigo, pos-tee-go s wicket; postern; shutter

postilla, pos-tee-l´yah s scab on wounds; crust

postilloso, pos-te-l´yo-so a scabby

postizo, pos-tee-tho a artificial; false

postor, pos-**tor** s bidder

postrar, pos-**trar** v to prostrate

postre, pos-tray s dessert; a last in order

postremo, pos-**tray**-mo a

last; descendant

postrer, pos-**trair** a last; hindermost

postulado, pos-too-**lah**-do s postulate

póstumo, pos-too-mo a posthumous

postura, pos-too-rah s posture; bet; wager; agreement

potable, po-tah-blay a drinkable

potaje, po-tah-Hay s pottage; medley

potasa, po-tah-sah s potash

pote, po-tay s pot; jar; standard measure or weight

potencia, po-ten-the-ah s power; potency

potencial, po-ten-the-**ahl** a potential; virtual

potente, po-ten-tay a potent

potestad, po-tess-**tahd** s power

potra, po-trah s hernia; filly

potro, po-tro s colt; foal; rack

poyo, po-yo s stone bench

poza, po-thah s puddle

pozal, po-**thahl** s bucket; pail; coping of a well

pozo, po-tho s well

practicante, prahk-te-**kahn**-tay *s* practitioner; intern

practicar, prahk-te-**kar** *v* to practice; to exercise

pradera, pradería, prah-**day**-rah, prah-day-**ree**-ah *s* meadow

prado, prah-do *s* lawn; meadow

pre, pray *s* daily pay allowed to soldiers; prefix meaning before

preboste, pray-**bos**-tay *s* provost

precaver, pray-kah-**vair** *v* to provide against

precavido*, pray-kah-**vee**-do *a* cautious

preceder, pray-thay-**dair** *v* to precede

precepto, pray-**thep**-to *s* precept; order; mandate

preces, pray-**thess** *s* prayers

preciado, pray-the-**ah**-do *a* valued; prized

preciarse, pray-the-**ar**-say *v* to boast; to take a prize in

precio, pray-**the**-o *s* price; coat; value; reward

precipitar, pray-the-pe-**tar** *v* to precipitate; to rush

precisar, pray-the-**sar** *v* to fix with precision; to

compel; to need; to oblige

precisión, pray-the-se-**on** *s* necessity; compulsion; preciseness

preciso, pray-**thee**-so *a* necessary; precise; concise

preclaro, pray-**klah**-ro *a* illustrious; cleared

preconizar, pray-ko-ne-**thar** *v* to eulogize; to proclaim

preconocer, pray-ko-no-**thair** *v* to foreknow

precoz, pray-**koth** *a* precocious

precursor, pray-koor-**sor** *s* harbinger; forerunner

predecir, pray-day-**theer** *v* to foretell; to know in advance

prédica, pray-de-kah *s* sermon

predicador, pray-de-kah-**dor** *s* preacher

predicar, pray-de-**kar** *v* to publish; to preach

predilecto, pray-de-**lek**-to *a* preceding

predio, pray-**de**-o *s* landed property; farm

predisponer, pray-diss-po-**nair** *v* to predispose; to predict

predominio, pray-do-**mee**-

ne-o *s* predominance

preestreno, prays-**tray**-no *s* preview

prefacio, pray-**fah**-the-o *s* preface

preferible, pray-fay-**ree**-blay *a* preferable

preferir, pray-fay-**reer** *v* to prefer

prefijo, pray-**fee**-Ho *s* prefix

pregonar, pray-go-**nar** *v* to proclaim; to cry out

pregonero, pray-go-**nay**-ro *s* town crier; auctioneer; common crier

pregunta, pray-**goon**-tah *s* question; inquiry

preguntar, pray-goon-**tar** *v* to ask; to question; to inquire

preguntón, pray-goon-**ton** *a* inquisitive

prejuzgar, pray-Hooth-**gar** *v* to prejudge

prelado, pray-**lah**-do *s* prelate

premiar, pray-me-**ar** *v* to reward; to remunerate

premio, pray-**me**-o *s* reward; premium

premioso*, pray-me-o-so *a* tight; troublesome; rigid

premura, pray-**moo**-rah *s* urgency

prenda, pren-**dah** *s*

pledge; token; garment; pawn; person or object dearly loved; *pl* talents

prender, pren-**dair** *v* to seize; to imprison; to light (fire); to put on (*elec*)

prendería, pren-day-ree-ah *s* pawnbroker's shop

prensa, pren-sah *s* press; printing press

prensar, pren-**sar** *v* to press

preñada, pray-n´yah-da *s* pregnant

preñéz, pray-nee-ath *s* pregnancy

preparar, pray-pah-**rar** *v* to prepare

preponderar, pray-pon-day-**rar** *v* to prevail

prepotente, pray-po-**ten-**tay *a* very powerful; predominant

presa, pray-sah *s* capture; seizure; prey; dam

presagiar, pray-sah-*He*-**ar** *v* to presage; to forebode

presbiterio, press-be-**tay-**re-o *s* parsonage; chancel

presbítero, press-**bee-**tay-ro *s* priest

precindir, press-thin-**deer** *v* to prescind; to cut off; to do without

prescribir, press-kre-**beer** *v* to prescribe

presenciar, pray-sen-the-**ar** *v* to be present; to witness

presentar, pray-sen-**tar** *v* to present; to exhibit; to give

presente, pray-**sen-**tays present; gift; *a** present; actual

presentir, pray-sen-**teer** *v* to have a presentiment

preservar, pray-sair-**var** *v* to preserve

presidiario, pray-se-de-**ah-**re-o *s* convict

presidio, pray-**see-**de-o *s* garrison; fortress; penitentiary

presidir, pray-se-**deer** *v* to preside

presilla, pray-**see-**l´yah *s* noose; loop

presión, pray-se-**on** *s* pressure

preso, pray-so *s* prisoner

prestación, press-tah-the-**on** *s* lending

prestamista, press-tah-**miss-**tah *s* lender; pawnbroker

préstamo, press-tah-mo *s* loan

prestar, press-**tar** *v* to lend

presteza, press-**tay-**thah *s*

quickness; haste; speed

prestigio, press-**tee-**He-o *s* prestige; sleight of hand

presto, press-to *adv* quickly; *a* quick; prompt; ready

presumible, pray-soo-**mee-**blay *a* presumable

presumido, pray-soo-**mee-**do *a* presumptuous; arrogant; vain

presumir, pray-soo-**meer** *v* to presume; to conjecture

presunción, pray-soon-the-**on** *s* presumption; conjecture

presuntivo, pray-soon-**tee-**vo *a* presumptive

presentuoso,* pray-soon-too´o-so *a* presumptuous

presuponer, pray-soo-po-**nair** *v* to presuppose

presupuesto, pray-soo-poo´**ess-**to *s* estimate; budget

presuroso*, pray-soo-ro-so *a* hasty; prompt

pretender, pray-ten-**dair** *v* to pretend; to claim; to endeavor

pretenso, pray-**ten-**so *v pp* to pretend

pretericíon, pray-tay-re-the-**on** *s* omission

pretérito, pray-**tay-**re-to *a*

preterit; past

pretextar, pray-teks-**tar** v to use a pretext

pretil, pray-**teel** s railing; parapet

pretina, pray-tee-nah s girdle; waistband; belt

prevalecer, pray-vah-lay-**thair** v to prevail; to surpass

prevaricar, pray-vah-re-**kar** v to prevaricate; to lie

prevención, pray-ven-the-**on** s foresight; warning; prevention

prevenido, pray-vay-nee-do a prepared; provided; cautious; careful

prevenir, pray-vay-**neer** v to foresee; to prevent; to advise

prever, pray-**vair** v to foresee; to forecast

previo*, pray-**ve**-o, previous; former

prieto, pre-ay-to a very black; compressed; tight

prima, **pree**-mah s premium; female cousin; first

primavera, pre-mah-**vay**-rah s spring season; primrose

primero, pre-**may**-ro adv first; rather; sooner; a

first; principal; former

primo, **pree**-mo s male cousin; a first

primogénito, pre-mo-**Hay**-ne-to s & a firstborn

primor, pre-**mor** s beauty; dexterity; nicety

primoroso, pre-mo-ro-so a neat; elegant; exquisite

princesa, prin-**thay**-sah s princess

principal, prin-the-**pahl** s capital; a principal

príncipe, **prin**-the-pay s prince

principiar, prin-the-pe-**ar** v to begin

principio, prin-**thee**-pe-o s beginning; principle

pringar, prin-**gar** v to baste; to grease; to slander

pringue, **preen**-gay s grease; lard; greasiness

prior, pre-**or** s prior; a prior; precedent

prisa, **pree**-sah s hurry

prisión, pre-se-**on** s seizure; prison; fetters

prisionero, pre-se-o-**nay**-ro s prisoner

prisma, **priss**-mah s prism

privada, pre-**vah**-dah s private; secret

privado, pre-**vah**-do s

favorite; a private

privar, pre-**var** v to deprive; to prohibit

privilegio, pre-ve-lay-**He**-o s privilege

pro, pro s mf. profit; benefit; advantage; **en** –, en –, in favor of

probanza, pro-bahn-thah s proof; evidence

probar, pro-**bar** v to try; to prove; to taste

probatura, pro-bah-too-rah s trial; test; tasting

probeta, pro-**bay**-tah s test tube

probidad, pro-be-**dahd** s honesty; integrity

procacidad, pro-kah-the-**dahd** s petulance; sauciness; impudence

procaz, pro-**kahth** a bold; insolent

procedencia, pro-thay-**den**-the-ah s origin

proceder, pro-thay-**dair** v to proceed; to emanate

procedimiento, pro-thay-de-me-**en**-to s proceeding; procedure; process

proceloso, pro-thay-lo-so a tempestuous; stormy

prócer, pro-thair a lofty; eminent

procesar, pro-thay-**sar** v to

prosecute; to indict

proceso, pro-**thay**-so s
process; lawsuit

proclama, pro-**klah**-mah s
proclamation

proclividad, pro-kle-ve-
dahd s proclivity;
propensity; inclination

procura, pro-**koo**-rah s
power of attorney

procurador, pro-koo-rah-
dorr s solicitor; attorney

prodigar, pro-de-**gar** v to
lavish; to waste

prodigio, pro-dee-**He**-o s
prodigy

pródigo*, **pro**-de-go a
prodigal

producir, pro-doo-**theer** v
to produce

producto, pro-**dook**-to s
product

proeza, pro-**ay**-thah s
prowess; bravery

profano, pro-**fah**-no a
profane

proferir, pro-fay-**reer** v to
pronounce; to express;
to utter

profesar, pro-fay-**sar** v to
profess

profesor, pro-fay-**sor** s
professor; teacher

profeta, pro-**fay**-tah s
prophet

profético, pro-fay-te-ko a

prophetic

profetizar, pro-fay-te-**thar**
v to prophesy; to
predict; to foretell

prófugo, pro-**foo**-go a
fugitive

profundo*, pro-**foon**-do a
profound; deep

progenitura, pro-Hay-ne-
too-rah s progeny

programa, pro-**grah**-mah s
program

programador, pro-grah-
mah-**dorr** s programmer

progreso, pro-**gray**-so s
progress; advancement

prohibir, pro-e-**beer** v to
prohibit; to forbid

prohijar, pro-e-**Har** v to
adopt

prohombre, pro-om-**bray** s
leader

prójimo, pro-**He**-mo s
fellow-creature;
neighbor

prole, pro-**lay** s issue;
offspring; race; lineage;
long excessive

prolijo, pro-lee-**Ho** s
prolix

prólogo, pro-**lo**-go s
prologue; preface

prolongadamente, pro-
lon-gah-dah-**men**-tay
adv protractedly

prolongar, pro-lon-**gar** v

to prolong

promedio, pro-**may**-de-o s
middle; average

promesa, pro-**may**-sah s
promise; pious offering

prometer, pro-may-**tair** v
to promise

prometido, pro-may-tee-
do s betrothed;
fiancé(é); pp promised

prominencia, pro-me-
nen-the-ah s
prominence;
protuberance

promiscuo, pro-**miss**-
koo´o a promiscuous

promover, pro-mo-**vair** v
to promote; to forward;
to initiate

pronombre, pro-**nom**-bray
s pronoun

prontitud, pron-te-**tood** s
promptness

pronto*, **pron**-to adv
promptly; s sudden
impulse; a prompt

prontuario, pron-too´**ah**-
re-o s memorandum-
book

pronunciamiento, pro-
noon-the-ah-me-**en**-to s
insurrection

pronunciar, pro-noon-
the-**ar** v to pronounce;
to rebel

propalar, pro-pah-**lar** v to

divulge

propasar, pro-pah-**sar** *v* to go beyond; to transgress

propender, pro-pen-**dair** *v* to incline

propenso, pro-**pen**-so *a* inclined; prone

propicio*, pro-pee-the-o *a* propitious

propiedad, pro-pe-ay-**dahd** *s* ownership; property; dominion

propina, pro-pee-**nah** *s* fee; gratuity; tip

propincuo, pro-**peen**-koo´o *a* near; close

propio, pro-**pe**-o *s* messenger; *a** private; proper; fit; natural

proponer, pro-po-**nair** *v* to propose; to suggest

proporcionar, pro-por-the-o-**nar** *v* to proportion; to adjust; to afford

propósito, pro-po-**se**-to *s* purpose; purport; a propo of

propuesta, pro-poo´**ess**-tah *s* proposal; tender

propulsión, pro-pool-se-**on** *s* propulsion

propulsor, pro-pool-**sor** *s* propeller

prorrata, pror-**rrah**-tah *s* quota

prórroga, pror-**rro**-gah *s* prorogation; extension; renewal

prorrumpir, pror-rroom-**peer** *v* to break forth

prosa, pro-**sah** *s* prose

proscribir, pros-kre-**beer** *v* to proscribe

proseguir, pro-say-**gheer** *v* to pursue; to prosecute

prosélito, pro-**say**-le-to *s* proselyte; convert

prospecto, pros-**pek**-to *s* prospectus

próspero*, pros-**pay**-ro *a* prosperous

prosternarse, pros-tair-**nar**-say *v* to prostrate oneself; to kneel

prostituir, pros-te-too´**eer** *v* to prostitute

prostituta, pros-te-too-**tah** *s* prostitute

proteger, pro-tay-**Hair** *v* to protect

protervo, pro-**tair**-vo *a* perverse

protestar, pro-tess-**tar** *v* to protest

provecho, pro-**vay**-cho *s* profit; benefit; advantage

provechoso*, pro-vay-**cho**-so *a* profitable

proveeduría, pro-vay-ay-doo-**ree**-ah *s* store-

house; purveyor's office

proveer, pro-vay-**air** *v* to provide; to supply with

proveído, pro-vay´**ee**-do *s* judgment; sentence

proveimiento, pro-vay´**e**-me-**en**-to *s* supply

provenir, pro-vay-**neer** *v* to proceed from

próvido, pro-**ve**-do *a* provident; careful; diligent

provocar, pro-vo-**kar** *v* to provoke

provocativo, pro-vo-ka-**tee**-vo *a* sexy

próximo, pro-**k**-se-mo *a* next

proyecto, pro-**yek**-to *s* project; scheme; design

prudente*, proo-**den**-tay *a* prudent

prueba, proo´**ay**-bah *s* proof; test; experiment

prurito, proo-**ree**-to *s* itching; yearning

psicoanalista, psee-ko´ah-nah-**les**-ta *s* psychoanalyst

psicológico, psee-ko-lo-**He**-ko *a* psychological

psicópata, psee-ko-lo-**He**-ko *s* psychopath

psiquiatra, psee-kee-**ah**-trah *s* psychiatrist

psiquiatría, psee-kee-ah-

tree-ah s psychiatry

púa, poo´ah s prickle; prong; graft

pubertad, poo-bair-**tad** s adolescence

publicar, poo-ble-**kar** v to publish; to proclaim; to reveal

publicidad, poo-ble-the-**dahd** s advertising

público*, poo-ble-ko a public

puchero, poo-**chay**-ro s earthen pot; stew

púdico, poo-de-ko a chaste; modest

pudiente, poo-de-en-tay a rich; opulent

pudor, poo-**dor** s modesty; bashfulness

pudrir, poo-**dreer** v to rot

pueblo, poo´**ay**-blo s town; village; population

puente, poo´**en**-tay s bridge

puerca, poo´**air**-kah s sow; female pig

puerco, poo´**air**-ko s pig; a filthy; coarse

pueril, poo´ay-**reel** a puerile; childish

puerro, poo´**air**-rro s leek

puerta, poo´**air**-tah s door

puerto, poo´**air**-to s port; haven; harbor

pues, poo´**ess** conj then; therefore; since; interj well then!

puesta, poo´**ess**-tah s setting; sunset

puesto, poo´**ess**-to s place; spot; stand; employment; – **que**, – kay, although; inasmuch as

púgil, poo-Hil s boxer; pugilist

pugna, poog-nah s combat; conflict; struggle

pugnar, poog-**nar** v to fight; to struggle

puja, poo-Hah s outbidding at auction sale

pujante, poo-**Hahn**-tay a powerful; strong

pujanza, poo-**Hahn**-thah s might; strength

pujar, poo-**Har** v to outbid

pulcritud, pool-kre-**tood** s neatness; tidiness

pulcro, pool-kro a tidy; neat

pulga, pool-gah s flea

pulgada, pool-**gah**-dah s inch

pulgar, pool-g´ar s thumb

pulido, poo-lee-do a neat; clean; polished

pulimento, poo-le-**men**-to s polish

pulir, poo-**leer** v to polish; to burnish

pulmón, pool-**mon** s lung

pulmonía, pool-mo-nee-ah s pneumonia

pulpa, pool-pah s pulp

pulpo, pool-po s octopus

pulsar, pool-**sar** v to feel the pulse

pulso, pool-so s pulse

pulla, poo-l´yah s loose expression; repartee; sharp expression

pundonor, poon-do-**nor** s point of honor

punta, poon-tah s point

puntada, poon-**tah**-dah s stitch

puntal, poon-**tahl** s prop

puntapié, poon-tah-pe-ay s kick

puntear, poon-tay-ar v to play the guitar; to dot

puntería, poon-tay-ree-ah s aim

puntilla, poon-tee-l´yah s narrow lace edging; **de** –**s,** day –s, on tiptoe

punto, poon-to s point; dot; aim; stitch; spot; gist; period (in grammar)

puntual*, poon-too´ahl a punctual; prompt; exact

punzada, poon-**thah**-dah s

prick; sting;
compunction

punzar, poon-**thar** *v* to
prick; to sting

punzón, poon-**thon** *s*
punch; awl

puñado, poo-n´**yah**-do *s*
handful; a few

puñal, poo-n´**yahl** *s*
dagger

puño, **poo**-n´yo *s* fist; cuff

pupa, **poo**-pah *s* pimple

pupilaje, poo-pe-**lah**-Hay *s*
boarding school

pupilo, poo-**pee**-lo *s* pupil;
scholar

pupitre, poo-**pee**-tray *s*
school desk; writing
desk

pureza, poo-**ray**-thah *s*
purity; innocence

purga, **poor**-gah *s* purge

purificar, poo-re-fe-**kar** *v*
to purify

puro*, **poo**-ro *a* pure;
mere; genuine;
incorrupt; chaste

púrpura, **poor**-poo-rah *s*
purple

pusilánime*, poo-se-**lah**-
ne-may *a* pusillanimous

putrefacto, poo-tray-**fahk**-
to *a* rotten; putrid

pútrido, **poo**-tree-do *a*
putrid

puya, **poo**-yah *s* goad

que, kay *pron* that; who; which; what

quebrada, kay-**brah**-dah *s* broken ground; ravine

quebradizo, kay-brah-dee-tho *a* brittle; frail

quebradura, kay-brah-**doo**-rah *s* fracture; rupture

quebrantamiento, kay-brahn-tah-me-**en**-to *s* fracture; weariness; breaking out of a prison; violation of the law

quebrantar, kay-brahn-**tar** *v* to break; to grind; to violate; to tire

quebrar, kay-**brar** *v* to break

quedar, kay-**dar** *v* to stay; to remain; to resolve; to agree

quedo, kay-do *adv* gently; softly

quehacer, kay-ah-**thair** *s* business; occupation

queja, kay-*Hah s* complaint; grudge

quejarse, kay-*Har*-say *v* to complain

quejido, kay-*Hee*-do *s* complaint; moan

quejoso*, kay-*Ho*-so *a* querulous; complaining

quema, kay-mah *s* burning; combustion

quemadura, kay-mah-**doo**-rah *s* burn

quemar, kay-**mar** *v* to burn

quemazón, kay-mah-**thon** *s* burning; fire

querella, kay-ray-l´yah *s* complaint; plaint; quarrel; dispute

querellarse, kay-ray-l´yar-say *v* to lament; to complain

querencia, kay-**ren**-the-ah *s* affection

querer, kay-**rair** *v* to wish; to desire; to will; to love

quesera, kay-**say**-rah *s* dairy; cheese dish

queso, kay-so *s* cheese

quiebra, ke-ay-brah *s* crack; fracture; bankruptcy

quiebro, ke-ay-bro *s* trill; inclination of the body

quien, ke-en *pron* who; whom; which

quienquiera, ke-en-ke-ay-rah *pron* whoever

quieto*, ke-ay-to *a* quiet; still; peaceable

quietud, ke-ay-**tood** *s* quietude; peace

quijada, ke-*Hah*-dah *s* jaw; jawbone

quijotada, ke-*Ho*-**tah**-dah *s* quixotic action

quijote, ke-*Ho*-tay *s* quixotic person

quilate, ke-**lah**-tay *s* carat

quimera, ke-**may**-rah *s* chimera; illusion

química, kee-me-kah *s* chemistry

quincalla, kin-**kah**-l´yah *s* hardware

quince, keen-thay *s* & *a* fifteen

quinceañero, kin-thay-ah-n´**yay**-ro *s* teenager

quinceno, kin-**thay**-no *a* fifteenth

quincuagésimo, kin-koo´ah-**Hay**-se-mo *a* fiftieth

quinientos, ke-ne-**en**-tos *a* five hundred

quinqué, kin-**kay** *s* oil lamp

quinta, keen-tah *s* country house; cottage

quintañón, kin-tah-n´**yon** *s* centenarian

quintar, kin-**tar** *v* to draw one out of five

quinto, keen-to *s* one fifth; conscript

quiosco, ke´os-ko *s* kiosk

quisquilloso, kiss-ke-l´**yo**-so *a* fastidious; peevish

!quita!kee-tah *interj* God forbid!; away with you!

quitar, ke-**tar** *v* to remove; to rob; to take away

quito, kee-to *a* free; quit; exempt

quizá, quizás, ke-**thah**, ke-**thahs** *adv* perhaps

rabadilla, rrah-bah-dee-l´yah *s* rump; coccyx

rábano, rrah-bah-no *s* radish

rabia, rrah-be-ah *s* rabies; rage; fury

rabieta, rrah-be-ay-tah *s* fretting; impatience; temper tantrum

rabioso, rrah-be-o-so *a* rabid; furious

rabo, rrah-bo *s* tail

racha, rrah-chah *s* gust of wind; period of time

racimo, rrah-thee-mo *s* bunch of grapes

raciocinar, rrah-the-o-the-nar *v* to reason; to judge; to argue

ración, rrah-the-on *s* ration; share

racismo, rrah-thees-mo *s* racism

racista, rrah-thees-tah *s* & *a* racist

rada, rrah-dah *s* roadstead; bay; anchorage

radiación, rah-de-ah-the-on *s* radiation

radiador, rah-de-ah-dorr *s* radiator

radiar, rrah-de-ar *v* to radiate

radio, rrah-de-o *s* radius; ray; radio; –actividad, –ahk-te-ve-dahd *s* radioactivity; –difusión, –de-foo-se-on *s* broadcasting

radioactivo, rrah-dee-o´ahk-te-vo *a* radioactive; **residuo** – radioactive waste

raedura, rrah-ay-doo-rah *s* erasure; scrapings

raer, rrah-air *v* to scrape; to erase

ráfaga, rrah-fah-gah *s* violent squall of wind

raído, rrah´ee-do *a* scraped; worn out

raigón, rrah´e-gon *s* strong root; root of a tooth

raimiento, rrah´e-me-en-to *s* scraping; erasure

raíz, rrah´eeth *s* root; base; basin; origin

raja, rrah-Hah *s* crack; cranny; splinter; slice (of fruit)

rajadura, rrah-Hah-doo-rah *s* cleft; rent; split

rajar, rrah-Har *v* to split; to rend; to cleave

ralea, rrah-lay-ah *s* race; breed; species

rallar, rrah-l´yar *v* to grate

rama, rrah-mah *s* branch

ramaje, rrah-mah-Hay *s* mass of branches; foliage

rambla, rrahm-blah *s* sandy beach

ramilla, rrah-mee-l´yah *s* twig; sprig

ramillete, rrah-me-l´yay-tay *s* nosegay; bouquet

ramo, rrah-mo *s* branch; cluster; bunch; line of business

rampa, rrahm-pah *s* slope;

ramp

ramplón, rrahm-**plon** *a* rude; unpolished

rana, rrah-nah *s* frog

rancio, rrahn-the-o *a* rancid; rank; old

ranchería, rrahn-chay-ree-ah *s* mess; horde; camp

ranchero, rrahn-**chay**-ro *s* camp cook; ranch owner; small farmer

rancho, rrahn-cho *s* mess; food; ranch; cattle ranch

rango, rrahn-go *s* rank; quality

ranura, rrah-**noo**-rah *s* groove; slot

rapacejo, rrah-pah-**thay**-Ho *s* fringe; border; child; rascal

rapacería, rrah-pah-thay-ree-ah *s* childish action

rapadura, rrah-pah-**doo**-rah *s* shaving; haircut

rapar, rrah-**par** *v* to shave; to rob

rapaz, rrah-**path** *s* young boy; *a* rapacious

rapaza, rrah-**pah**-thah *s* young girl

rapidez, rrah-pe-**deth** *s* rapidity

rápido*, rrah-pe-do *a* rapid

rapiña, rrah-pee-n´yah *s* plunder

raposa, rrah-**po**-sah *s* female fox; vixen; cunning person; deceitful person

raposo, rrah-**po**-so *s* fox

rapto, rrahp-to *s* ecstasy; rapture; abduction

raptor, rrahp-**tor** *s* ravisher; abductor

raqueta, rrah-**kay**-tah *s* racket

raquítico, rrah-**kee**-te-ko *a* rickety; feeble

rareza, rrah-**ray**-thah *s* rarity; rareness

raro*, rrah-ro *adv* rarely; *a* rare; scarce; queer; odd

ras, rrahs *s* level; even surface

rasar, rrah-**sar** *v* to level with a strickle; to graze

rascacielos, rrah-kah-the´ay-lohs *s* skyscraper

rascadura, rrahs-kah-**doo**-rah *s* scratching; scraping

rascapiés, rrahs-kah-pe-**ess** *s* door-scraper

rascar, rrahs-**kar** *v* to scratch; to scrape

rascazón, rrahs-kah-**thon** *s* itching

rasero, rrah-**say**-ro *s* strickle

rasgar, rrahs-**gar** *v* to tear; to rend; to sliver

rasgón, rrahs-**gon** *s* rent; rag; tatter

rasguñar, rrahs-goo-n´**yar** *v* to scratch; to scrape

raso, rrah-so *a* plain; flat; clear

raspar, rrahs-**par** *v* to rub off; to scrape; to rasp

rastra, rrahs-trah *s* sledge; train; track

rastrear, rrahs-tray-**ar** *v* to trace; to track; to rake

rastrero, rrahs-**tray**-ro *a* creeping; groveling; low; cringing

rastro, rrahs-tro *s* track; trail; rake

rasurar, rrah-soo-**rar** *v* to shave

rata, rrah-tah *s* rat

ratear, rrah-tay-**ar** *v* to filch; to commit petty thefts

ratero, rrah-**tay**-ro *s* pickpocket; *a* creeping

rato, rrah-to *s* short time

ratón, rrah-**ton** *s* mouse

ratonera, rrah-to-**nay**-rah *s* mousetrap; mousehole

raudal, rrah´oo-**dahl** *s* torrent

raya, rrah-yah *s* stroke; line; boundary; skate (fish)

rayano, rrah-**yah**-no *a* neighboring; contiguous

raza, rrah-thah s race; lineage; breed

razón, rrah-**thon** s reason; motive; cause; account; firm

razonar, rrah-tho-**nar** v to reason; to discourse; to talk

reacio, rray-ah-the-o a stubborn; to go against

reagudo, rray-ah-goo-do a very acute

real, rray-ahl a real; true; royal

realce, rray-ahl-thay s embossment; highlight

realidad, ray-ah-le-dahd s reality

realzar, rray-ahl-thar v to elevate; to emboss

reasumir, rray-ah-soo-meer v to resume

rebaja, rray-bah-Hah s abatement; rebate

rebajar, rray-bah-Har v to abate; to lessen

rebalsar, rray-bahl-sar v to dam water

rebanar, rray-bah-nar v to slice

rebaño, rray-bah-n´yo s flock; herd

rebasar, rray-bah-sar v to sail past; to go beyond; to overflow; to exceed

rebatir, rray-bah-teer v to resist; to repel; to refute

rebato, rray-bah-to s alarm

rebeca, rray-be-kah s cardigan

rebelde, rray-bell-day s rebel; a rebellious

reblandecer, rray-blahn-day-thair v to soften

rebolludo, rray-bo-l´yoo-do a thickset; rough (diamond)

rebosar, rray-bo-sar v to run over; to overflow; to abound

rebotar, rray-bo-tar v to rebound; to clinch

rebozo, rray-bo-tho s muffler

rebullir, rray-boo-l´yeer v to begin to move

reburujar, rray-boo-roo-Har v to wrap up

rebusca, rray-booss-kah s research; gleaning; remains

rebuznar, rray-booth-nar v to bray

recabar, rray-kah-bar v to obtain by negotiating

recado, rray-kah-do s message; greetings; outfit

recaer, rray-kah-air v to fall back; to devolve; to relapse

recaída, rray-kah´ee-dah s relapse

recalar, rray-kah-lar v to soak; to reach land

recalcar, rray-kahl-kar v to squeeze in; to harp upon; to emphasize

recalcitrar, rray-kahl-the-trar v to wince; to resist

recalentar, rray-kah-len-tar v to heat again

recámara, rray-kah-mah-rah s dressing room; bedroom; breech of a gun

recambio, rray-kahm-be-o s spare part

recapacitar, rray-kah-pah-the-tar v to recall to mind

recargo, rray-kar-go s surcharge

recatado*, rray-kah-tah-do a circumspect; shy; modest

recatar, rray-kah-tar v to conceal; to take care

recaudar, rray-kah´oo-dar v to collect; to gather; to obtain

recaudo, rray-kah´oo-do s collection; surety

recelar, rray-thay-lar v to fear; to distrust

receloso, rray-thay-lo-so a distrustful; suspicious

receta, rray-thay-tah s recipe; prescription

recetar, rray-thay-**tar** v to prescribe medicines

recibimiento, rray-the-be-me-**en**-to s reception; receipt

recibir, rray-the-**beer** v to receive; to admit

recibo, rray-**thee**-bo s receipt; bill; voucher

recién, rray-the-**en** adv recently

reciente*, rray-the-en-tay a recent

recinto, rray-**theen**-to s enclosure; precinct

recio, rray-the-o adv stoutly; a strong; coarse

reclamar, rray-klah-**mar** v to claim; to demand

reclamo, rray-**klah**-mo s call; decoy (bird)

reclinar, rray-kle-**nar** v to lean on or upon

reclinatorio, rray-kle-nah-to-re-o s couch; kneeling stool

recluir, rray-kloo´**eer** v to shut up; to seclude

reclutar, rray-kloo-**tar** v to recruit

recobrar, rray-ko-**brar** v to recover

recodo, rray-**ko**-do s corner; turn

recoger, rray-ko-**Hair** v to collect; to gather; to

shelter

recogida, rray-ko-**Hee**-dah s gathering; harvesting

recogimiento, rray-ko-He-me-**en**-to s concentration; abstraction from worldly concerns

recomendar, rray-ko-men-**dar** v to recommend

recompensa, rray-kom-pen-sah s compensation; reward

recóndito, rray-**kon**-de-to a recondite; secret; concealed

reconocer, rray-ko-no-**thair** v to examine; to recognize; to acknowledge

reconocido, rray-ko-no-**thee**-do a grateful

reconocimiento, rray-ko-no-the-me-**en**-to s gratitude; inspection

recontar, rray-kon-**tar** v to recount

reconvención, rray-kon-ven-the-**on** s recrimination

reconvenir, rray-kon-vay-**neer** v to recriminate; to censor

recopilar, rray-ko-pe-**lar** v to compile

recordar, rray-kor-**dar** v to

remind; to remember

recorrer, rray-kor-**rrair** v to run over ; to peruse; to travel over

recortar, rray-kor-**tar** v to cut away

recorte, rray-**kor**-tay s outline; cutting

recoser, rray-ko-**sair** v to sew again

recostar, rray-kos-**tar** v to lean against

recrear, rray-kray-**ar** v to amuse

recreo, rray-**kray**-o s recreation; recess

rectificar, rrek-te-fe-**kar** v to rectify

recto*, rrek-to a straight; right; just; honest; direct

recuento, rray-koo´**en**-to s inventory; recount

recuerdo, rray-koo´**air**-do s remembrance; memory

recuesto, rray-koo´**ess**-to s declivity

recular, rray-koo-**lar** v to fall back; to recoil

recuperar, rray-koo-pay-**rar** v to regain

recurrir, rray-koor-**rreer** v to resort; to recur

recurso, rray-**koor**-so s recourse

rechazar, rray-chah-**thar** v to repel; to repulse; to

reject

rechazo, rray-**chah**-tho s rebound; rejection

rechiflar, rray-che-**flar** v to mock; to ridicule

rechinar, rray-che-**nar** v to creak; to squeak; to gnash the teeth

rechoncho, rray-**chon**-cho a chubby

red, rred s net; web

redacción, rray-dak-the-**on** s wording; editing; editorial staff

redactor, rray-dak-**tor** s editor

redada, rray-**dah**-dah s catch; haul

rededor, rray-day-**dor** s environs; more or less; **al** –, **ahl** –, round about

redentor, rray-den-**tor** s redeemer

redimir, rray-de-**meer** v to redeem; to ransom

rédito, **rray**-de-to s revenue; rent; interest; yield

redituar, rray-de-too´**ar** v to yield

redoblar, rray-do-**blar** v to redouble; to rivet

redoma, rray-**do**-mah s vial

redonda, rray-**don**-dah s district; pasture

redondel, rray-don-**dell** s

circle; round; roundabout

redondo, rray-**don**-do a round

redopelo, rray-do-**pay**-lo s rubbing against the grain; scuffle

reducir, rray-doo-**theer** v to reduce

reducto, rray-**dook**-to s redoubt

redundante, rray-doon-**dahn**-te a redundant

redundar, rray-doon-**dar** v to be redundant; to overflow; to redound

reelegir, rray-ay-lay-**Heer** v to reelect

reembolsar, rray-em-bol-**sar** v to reimburse

reemplazar, rray-em-plah-**thar** v to replace; to restore

reencuentro, rray-en-koo´**en**-tro s encounter; clash

refacción, rray-fahk-the-**on** s refection; repast

referéndum, rray-fay-**rayn**-doom s referendum

referir, rray-fay-**reer** v to relate; to refer; to report

refinado, rray-fe-**nah**-do a refined

refinar, rray-fe-**nar** v to refine

reflejo, rray-**flay**-Ho s reflex; glare; reflection; a reflected; reflex

reflexión, rray-flek-the-**on** s reflection

refluir, rray-floo´**eer** v to flow back

reforzar, rray-for-**thar** v to strengthen; to reinforce

refrán, rray-**frahn** s proverb; saying

refregar, rray-fray-**gar** v to rub one thing against another

refrenar, rray-fray-**nar** v to restrain; to curb

refrendar, rray-fren-**dar** v to countersign

refresco, rray-**fress**-ko s refreshment

refriega, rray-fre-**ay**-gah s fray; skirmish

refrigerio, rray-fre-**Hay**-re-o s refreshment

refuerzo, rray-foo´**air**-tho s reinforcement

refugiar, rray-foo-**He**-ar v to shelter; to take refuge

refundir, rray-foon-**deer** v to recast; to melt metal again; to rearrange

refunfuñar, rray-foon-fon-n´**yar** v to grumble; to growl

refutar, rray-foo-**tar** v to refute

regadera, rray-gah-**day**-rah
s watering can; sprinkler;
showerhead

regalado, rray-gah-**lah**-do
a delicate; dainty; given
as a present; extremely
cheap

regalo, rray-**gah**-lo s
present; gift; keepsake

regalón, rray-gah-**lon** a
pampered

regañar, rray-gah-n´**yar** v
to snarl; to growl; to
quarrel; to reprimand

regar, rray-**gar** v to water;
to irrigate

regata, rray-**gah**-tah s
small water channel;
regatta; boat race

regate, rray-**gah**-tay s
dodging

regatear, rray-gah-tay-**ar** v
to haggle; to bargain

regazo, rray-**gah**-tho s lap

regentar, rray-**Hen**-tar v to
rule; to govern

regidor, rray-**He**-dor s
councilman; a governing

régimen, rray-**He**-men s
rule; management;
regulations

regimiento, rray-**He**-me-
en-to s administration;
government; regiment

regio***, rray-**He**-o a royal

región, rray-**He**-on s
region; district

regir, rray-**Heer** v to rule;
to control

registrador, rray-**Hiss**-trah-
dor s registrar; recorder;
–**de cinta
magnetofónica**, day
thin-tah mag-nay-to-fo-
ne-kah s tape recorder

registrar, rray-**Hiss**-trar v
to search; to examine; to
register

registro, rray-**Hiss**-tro s
search; registry;
enrollment

regla, rray-glah s rule;
statute

reglado***, rray-**glah**-do a
regulated; temperate

reglamento, rray-glah-
men-to s regulation;
ordinance; bylaw

reglar, rray-**glar** v to
regulate; a regular

regocijar, rray-go-the-**Har**
v to rejoice

regocijo, rray-go-**thee**-Ho
s joy; merriment;
pleasure

regodeo, rray-go-**day**-o s
joy; mirth

regordete, rray-gor-**day**-
tay a chubby; plump

regresar, rray-gray-**sar** v to
return; to regress

regreso, rray-**gray**-so s
return; regression

regüeldo, rray-goo-**ell**-do s
belching

reguera, rray-**gay**-rah s
irrigation canal

reguero, rray-**gay**-ro s
rivulet; gutter; drain

regular, rray-goo-**lar** v to
regulate; a* regular

regurgitar, rray-goor-**He**-
tar v to overflow; to
regurgitate

rehacer, rray-ah-**thair** v to
make again; to mend; to
revive

rehecho, rray-**ay**-cho a
remade

rehén, rray-**en** s hostage

rehilete, rray´e-lay-tay s
shuttlecock

rehusar, rray´oo-**sar** v to
refuse; to decline

reidero, rray´e-**day**-ro a
laughable

reina, rray´ee-nah s queen

reinado, rray´e-**nah**-do s
reign

reinar, rray´e-**nar** v to
reign

reincidir, rray-in-the-**deer**
v to relapse

reintegrar, rray-in-tay-**grar**
v to restore; to refund

reír, rray´**eer** v to laugh

reja, rray´**Hah** s plowing;
grate; railing

rejón, rray-**Hon** s dagger; spear

rejuvenecer, rray-Hoo-vay-nay-**thair** v to make or grow young again

relacionar, rray-lah-the-o-**nar** v to relate; to connect

relajación, rray-lah-Hah-the-**on** s relaxation; laxity

relajar, rray-lah-**Har** v to relax; to slacken; to remit

relamido, rray-lah-**mee**-do a prim; affected

relámpago, rray-**lahm**-pah-go s flash of lightning

relance, rray-**lahn**-thay s fortuitous event

relapso, rray-**lahp**-so a relapsed

relatar, rray-lah-**tar** v to relate

relato, rray-**lah**-to s narrative

releer, rray-lay-**air** v to read over again

relente, rray-**len**-tay s night dew

relevación, rray-lay-vah-the-**on** s liberation; relief; remission

relevante, rray-lay-**vahn**-tay a excellent; great; eminent

relevar, rray-lay-**var** v to emboss; to exonerate; to relieve

relevo, rray-**lay**-vo s relief

relieve, rray-le-**ay**-vay s raised work; relief

religar, rray-le-**gar** v to bind more tightly

religión, rray-le-**He**-on s religion

relinchar, rray-lin-**char** v to neigh

relindo, rray-**leen**-do a very neat

reliquia, rray-lee-ke-ah s residue; remains; relics

reloj, rray-loH s clock; watch

relojero, rray-lo-**Hay**-ro s watchmaker

relucir, rray-loo-**theer** v to shine; to excel

relumbrar, rray-loom-**brar** v to sparkle; to glisten

rellano, rray-l´**yah**-no s landing place of a staircase

rellenar, rray-l´**yay**-nar v to refill; to stuff

relleno, rray-l´**yay**-no s stuffing; a satiated

remachar, rray-mah-**char** v to rivet; to clinch

remanente, rray-mah-**nen**-tay s remainder

remar, rray-**mar** v to row;

to paddle

rematar, rray-mah-**tar** v to finish; to auction

remate, rray-**mah**-tay s conclusion

remedio, rray-**may**-de-o s remedy

rememorar, rray-may-mo-**rar** v to recall to mind

remendar, rray-men-**dar** v to patch; to repair

remendón, rray-men-**don** s cobbler; patcher

remero, rray-**may**-ro s rower; oarsman

remesa, rray-**may**-sah s shipment

remiendo, rray-me-en-do s patch; clout; repair

remilgado, rray-mil-**gah**-do a affected; fastidious

remirado, rray-me-**rah**-do a prudent; cautious

remirar, rray-me-**rar** v to revise; to act with care

remisión, rray-me-se-on s pardon; forgiveness; remission

remiso*, rray-**mee**-so a remiss; slack

remitir, rray-me-**teer** v to remit; to forgive; to defer

remo, rray-mo s oar; hard work

remoción, rray-mo-the-on s removal

remojar, rray-mo-**Har** *v* to
steep; to soak

remolacha, rray-mo-**lah**-
chah *s* beet

remolcador, rray-mol-kah-
dor *s* tugboat

remolcar, rray-mol-**kar** *v*
to tow

remolinar, rray-mo-le-**nar**
v to whirl

remolino, rray-mo-lee-no *s*
whirl; whirlpool

remolque, rray-**mol**-kay *s*
towing

remontar, rray-mon-**tar** *v*
to soar; to go up (river)

remorder, rray-mor-**dair** *v*
to cause remorse; to fret

remordimiento, rray-mor-
de-me-**en**-to *s* remorse

remoto*, rray-**mo**-to *a*
remote

remover, rray-mo-**vair** *v* to
remove; to stir up

removimiento, rray-mo-
ve-me-**en**-to *s* removal

remozar, rray-mo-**thar** *v* to
make or look young; to
rejuvenate

remunerar, rray-moo-nay-
rar *v* to reward; to
remunerate

renacer, rray-nah-**thair** *v*
to be born again

renacimiento, rray-nah-
the-me-**en**-to *s* new
birth; renaissance

renacuajo, rray-nah-
koo´ah-Ho *s* tadpole

rencilla, rren-thee-l´yah *s*
grudge; discard; feud

rencor, rren-**kor** *s* rancor

rendición, rren-de-the-**on**
s surrender; yield

rendidamente, rren-de-
dah-**men**-tay *adv* humbly

rendija, rren-dee-**Hah** *s*
crevice; crack

rendimiento, rren-de-me-
en-to *s* income; yield

rendir, rren-**deer** *v* to
subdue; to surrender; to
yield

renegar, rray-nay-**gar** *v* to
disown; to swear

renglón, rren-**glon** *s* line

reniego, rray-ne-ay-go *s*
blasphemy

reno, **rray**-no *s* reindeer

renombre, rray-**nom**-bray *s*
renown

renovar, rray-no-**var** *v* to
renovate; to renew

renta, **rren**-tah *s* income;
rent

rentero, rren-**tay**-ro *s*
farmer; lessee

rentista, rren-**tiss**-tah *s*
person with
independent means

renuencia, rray-noo´en-
the-ah *s* reluctance

renuevo, rray-noo´**ay**-vo *s*
sprout; renewal

renunciar, rray-noon-the-
ar *v* to renounce

reñir, rray-n´**yeer** *v* to
quarrel; to scold

reo, **rray**-o *s* offender;
culprit; defendant

reojo, rray-o-Ho *adv* de –,
day –, askance

reparar, rray-pah-**rar** *v* to
notice; to repair

reparo, rray-**pah**-ro *s*
repair; consideration;
doubt; objection

repartir, rray-par-**teer** *v* to
distribute

repasar, rray-pah-**sar** *v* to
repass; to revise

repecho, rray-**pay**-cho *s*
declivity

repeler, rray-pay-**lair** *v* to
repel; to refute; to reject

repeloso, rray-pay-**lo**-so *a*
touchy; peevish

repente, rray-**pen**-tay *adv*
de –, day–, suddenly

repercutir, rray-pair-koo-
teer *v* to reflect; to
reverberate; to rebound

repetir, rray-pay-**teer** *v* to
repeat

repicar, rray-pe-**kar** *v* to
chime

repique, rray-**pee**-kay *s*
chime

repisa, rray-**pee**-sah *s* bracket; shelf

replegar, rray-play-**gar** *v* to refold

repleto, rray-**play**-to *a* replete; very full

réplica, rray-ple-kah *s* reply; retort

repliegue, rray-ple´**ay**-gay *s* doubling; fold

reponer, rray-po-**nair** *v* to replace; to restore

reponerse, rray-po-**nair**-say *v* to recover lost health

reportar, rray-por-**tar** *v* to refrain; to carry; to inform

reposo, rray-**po**-so *s* rest; repose

repostería, rray-pos-tay-**ree**-ah *s* confectionery; pantry; pastry shop

represa, rray-**pray**-sah *s* dam; sluice; lock

represar, rray-pray-**sar** *v* to recapture; to retain

representar, rray-pray-sen-**tar** *v* to represent; to perform; to act

reprimir, rray-pre-**meer** *v* to repress

reprobable, rray-pro-**bah**-blay *a* reprehensible

reprobar, rray-pro-**bar** *v* to reprove; to rebuke

réprobo, rray-**pro**-bo *s* & *a* reprobate

reprochar, rray-pro-**char** *v* to reproach; to blame

reproducir, rray-pro-doo-**theer** *v* to reproduce

reptil, rrep-**teel** *s* reptile

república, rray-**poo**-ble-kah *s* republic

repudiar, rray-poo-de-**ar** *v* to repudiate; to disclaim

repuestos, rray-poo´**ess**-tos *s pl* spare parts

repulsa, rray-**pool**-sah *s* refusal; repulse

repulsar, rray-pool-**sar** *v* to reject; to decline

reputar, rray-poo-**tar** *v* to repute; to estimate

requerir, rray-kay-**reer** *v* to request; to require

requesón, rray-kay-**son** *s* curd

requiebro, rray-ke-**ay**-bro *s* endearing expression

res, ress *s* head of cattle; beast

resabiar, rray-sah-be-**ar** *v* to become vicious

resabio, rray-**sah**-be-o *s* unpleasant; taste; viciousness

resaca, rray-**sah**-kah *s* surge; surf; redraft

resaltar, rray-sahl-**tar** *v* to jut out; to be evident

resarcimiento, rray-sar-the-me-**en**-to *s* compensation

resarcir, rray-sar-**theer** *v* to compensate

resbalar, ress-bah-**lar** *v* to slip; to slide

rescatar, ress-kah-**tar** *v* to redeem; to recover

rescate, ress-**kah**-tay *s* ransom

rescisión, ress-the-se-**on** *s* recision; cancellation

rescoldo, ress-**kol**-do *s* embers

resentirse, rray-sen-**teer**-say *v* to grow weak; to resent

reseña, rray-**say**-n´yah *s* review; brief description

reserva, rray-**sayr**-vah *s* reservation

reservar, rray-sair-**var** *v* to reserve; to save

resfriado, ress-fre-**ah**-do *s* cold

resguardar, ress-goo´ar-**dar** *v* to preserve; to defend; to be on one's guard

resguardo, ress-goo´**ar**-do *s* guard; security

residencia, rray-se-**den**-the-ah *s* home; domicile; residence

residenciar, rray-se-**den**-

the-**ar** v to impeach

residir, rray-se-**deer** v to reside

residuo, rray-**see**-doo´o s residue; remnant

resignar, rray-sig-**nar** v to resign; to give up

resistente, rray-siss-**ten**-tay a tough; resisting; strong

resma, rress-mah s ream of paper

resoluto, rray-so-**loo**-to a resolute; bold

resolver, rray-sol-**vair** v to resolve

resollar, rray-so-l´yar v to breath heavily

resonar, rray-so-**nar** v to resound; to echo

resoplar, rray-so-**plar** v to breath audibly; to snort

resorte, rray-**sor**-tay s spring; resiliency; elastic

respaldar, rress-pahl-**dar** v to endorse; to back up

respaldarse, rress-pahl-**dar**-say v to lean back

respaldo, rress-**pahl**-do s backof of seat; endorsement

respetar, rress-pay-**tar** v to respect; to honor

respeto, rress-**pay**-to s respect; regard

respigar, rress-pe-**gar** v to glean

respirador, rrss-pe-ra-**dor** s breathing tube; snorkel

respirar, rrss-pe-**rar** v to breathe; to live

respiro, rress-**pee**-ro s breathing; respite

resplandecer, rress-plahn-day-**thair** v to shine; to glitter

responder, rress-pon-**dair** v to answer; to be responsible for

respuesta, rress-poo´**ess**-tah s answer; reply

resquebrar, rress-kay-**brar** v to crack; to split; to burst

resquemar, rress-kay-**mar** v to burn or sting the tongue

resquicio, rress-**kee**-the-o s chink; crack; aperture between jamb and leaf of a door

resta, rress-tah s rest; remainder

restablecer, rress-tah-blay-**thair** v to reestablish; to reinstate

restante, rress-**tahn**-tay s remainder

restañar, rress-tah-n´yar v to stanch; to stop blood; to re-tin

restar, rrss-**tar** v to subtract

restaurar, rrss-tah-´oo-rar v to restore; to repair

restituir, rrss-te-too´**eer** v to give back; to refund

resto, rress-to s residue; balance; pl remains

restregar, rress-tray-**gar** v to scrub

restringir, rress-trin-*Heer* v to restrain; to restrict

resuelto, rray-soo´**ell**-to a resolute

resuello, rray-soo´**ay**-l´yo s breathing; panting

resulta, rray-**sool**-tah s consequence; result

resultado, rray-sool-**tah**-do s result

resumen, rray-**soo**-men s summary; recapitulation

resumir, rray-soo-**meer** v to abridge; to sum up

retal, rray-**tahl** s remnant; clipping

retallo, rray-tah-l´yo s new shoot

retama, rray-**tah**-mah s broom; gorse

retar, rray-**tar** v to challenge

retardar, rray-tar-**dar** v to retard; to delay

retazo, rray-**tah**-tho s remnant; piece; cutting

retemblar, rray-tem-**blar** v to tremble; to vibrate

retén, rray-**ten** s store; stock; reserve

retener, rray-tay-**nair** v to retain

retentiva, rray-ten-tee-**vah** s retentiveness

reticencia, rray-te-**then**-the-ah s reticence

retina, rray-**tee**-nah s retina

retintín, rray-tin-**teen** s tinkling; jingle

retinto, rray-**teen**-to a dark; obscure

retirada, rray-te-rah-**dah** s retreat; retirement; privy

retirar, rray-te-**rar** v to withdraw; to retire

retiro, rray-**tee**-ro s retreat; retirement

reto, **rray**-to s challenge

retocar, rray-to-**kar** v to retouch; to finish

retoñar, rray-to-n´yar v to sprout; to reappear

retoque, rray-**to**-kay s finishing stroke

retorcer, rray-tor-**thair** v to twist; to distort; to retort

retornar, rray-tor-**nar** v to come back; to give back

retorno, rray-**tor**-no s return; exchange

retorsión, rray-tor-se-**on** s retort; rejoinder

retozo, rray-**to**-tho s friskiness; gaiety

retractar, rray-**trahk**-tar v to retract; to recant

retraer, rray-trah-**air** v to dissuade; –se, to retire; to shun

retraído, rray-trah-ee-**do** s lover of solitude; v to take refuge

retraimiento, rray-trah-e-me-**en**-to s retreat; refuge; solitude

retrasar, rray-trah-**sar** v to defer

retraso, rray-trah-**so** s delay

retratar, rray-trah-**tar** v to portray; to photograph

retrato, rray-**trah**-to s portrait

retrechero, rray-tray-**chay**-ro a flattering; winsome; charming; cunning

retreta, rray-**tray**-tah s tattoo; bugle sound for retreat

retrete, rray-**tray**-tay s closet; toilet

retribuir, rray-tre-boo´eer v to retribute; to recompense; to reward

retroceso, rray-tro-**thay**-so s retrocession

retrógrado, rray-tro-grah-do a retrograde

retronar, rray-tro-**nar** v to thunder again

retumbar, rray-toom-**bar** v to resound

reuma, rray´oo-mah s rheumatism

reunir, rray´oo-**neer** v to reunite

revalidación, rray-vah-le-dah-the-**on** s confirmation

revalidar, rray-vah-le-**dar** v to ratify

revejecer, rray-vay-Hay-**thair** v to grow old prematurely

revender, rray-ven-**dair** v to retail; to resell

revenirse, rray-vay-neer-**say** v to grow sour; to shrink

reventar, rray-ven-**tar** v to burst; to crack; to molest

rever, rray-**vair** v to review; to revise

reverbero, rray-vair-**bay**-ro s reflector; street lamp

reverenciar, rray-vay-ren-the-**ar** v to revere; to venerate

reverendo, rray-vay-**ren**-do a reverend

reverente, rray-vay-**ren**-tay a respectful

reverso, rray-**vair**-so s reverse side

reverter, nay-vair-**tair** v to overflow

revés, rray-**vess** s back side; wrong side

revestir, rray-vess-**teer** v to dress; to clothe; to coat over

revisar, rray-ve-**sar** v to revise; to review

revisor, rray-ve-**sor** s revisor; ticket collector

revista, rray-**viss**-tah s review; magazine

revivir, rray-ve-**veer** v to revive

revocar, rray-vo-**kar** v to revoke

revolcarse, rray-vol-**kar**-say v to wallow; to drag

revoloteo, rray-vo-lo-**tay**-o s fluttering; hovering

revoltillo, rray-vol-**tee**-l'yo s medley; jumble; confusion

revoltoso, rray-vol-**to**-so a turbulent; s rioter

revolucionar, rray-vo-loo-the-o-**nar** v to revolutionize

revolvedor, rray-vol-vay-**dor** s disturber

revolver, rray-vol-**vair** v to revolve; to stir

revólver, rray-**vol**-vair s revolver (pistol)

revoque, rray-**vo**-kay s whitewashing; plastering

revuelta, rray-voo-**ell**-tah s revolt

revuelto, rray-voo-**ell**-to a restless; intricate; mixed up

rey, rray´e s king

reyerta, rray-**yair**-tah s dispute; wrangle

rezago, rray-**thah**-go s remainder; residue

rezar, rray-**thar** v to pray

rezongar, rray-thon-**gar** v to grumble

rezumarse, rray-thoo-**mar**-say v to ooze; to leak

ría, rree-ah s mouth of a river

riada, rre-**ah**-dah s overflow; inundation

ribazo, rre-**bah**-tho s sloping bank

ribera, rre-**bay**-rah s shore; beach

ribete, rre-**bay**-tay s trimming; seam; border

ricacho, rre-**kah**-cho a very rich

ricino, rre-**thee**-no s castor-oil plant

rico*, rree-ko a rich; wealthy

ridiculez, rre-de-koo-**leth** s ridiculous action

ridículo, rre-**dee**-koo-lo a ridiculous

riego, rre-**ay**-go s irrigation

rienda, rre-**en**-dah s rein; bridle; restraint

riesgo, rre-**ess**-go s risk; danger

rifa, rree-fah s raffle

rígido, rree-He-do a rigid; severe

rigor, rre-**gor** s rigor

rimbombar, rim-bom-**bar** v to resound

rimero, rre-**may**-ro s heap; pile

rincón, rrin-**kon** s corner; nook

ringlera, rrin-**glay**-rah s row; file

riña, rree-n´yah s dispute; quarrel

riñón, rre-n´**yon** s kidney

río, rree-o s river; stream

riqueza, rre-**kay**-thah s riches; wealth

risa, rree-sah s laugh; laughter; laughingstock

risada, rre-**sah**-dah s horse laugh

risco, rriss-ko s crag; cliff

risueño, rre-soo´ay-n´yo a smiling; pleasing

rival, rre-**vahl** s rival; competitor

rivalidad, rre-vah-le-**dahd** s rivalry; emulation

rizado, rree-**thah**-do a curly

rizo, rree-tho s ringlet; curl

robar, rro-bar v to rob; to plunder; to steal

roble, rro-blay s oak

roblón, rro-**blon** s rivet

robo, rro-bo s robbery; theft; spoilation

robusto*, rro-**booss**-to a robust

roca, rro-kah s rock; cliff; stone

rocalla, rro-kah-l´yah s stone chippings

rocanrol, rro-kahn-**rrol** s rock and roll

roce, rro-thay s friction; familiarity

rociar, rro-the-ar v to sprinkle

rocín, rocinante, rro-theen, rro-the-**nahn**-tay s hack; jade

rocío, rro-thee-o s dew; slight shower

rodada, rro-dah-dah s rut; wheel track

rodar, rro-dar v to roll; to wander about

rodear, rro-day-ar v to surround; to encompass

rodeo, rro-day-o s turning; winding; delay; evasion; rodeo

rodilla, rro-dee-l´yah s knee; clout

rodillo, rro-dee-l´yo s roller

roedor, rro-ay-dor s rodent

roer, rro-air v to gnaw

rogación, rro-gah-the-on s petition; supplication

rogar, rro-gar v to implore; to pray; to beg

rojear, rro-Hay-ar v to redden

rojo, rro-Ho a red

rol, rrol s list; roll; catalog

rollizo, rro-l´yee-tho a plump; round; robust

rollo, rro-l´yo s roll; roller

romana, rro-mah-nah s steelyard

romance, rro-**mahn**-thay s Spanish language

romántico, rro-**mahn**-te-ko s & a romantic

romería, rro-may-ree-ah s pilgrimage; picnic

romero, rro-may-ro s pilgrim; rosemary

rompecabezas, rrom-pay-kah-**bay**-thahs s jigsaw

rompedero, rrom-pay-**day**-ro a brittle; fragile

romper, rrom-pair v to break; to wear out

ron, rron s rum

ronca, rron-kah s threat; boast; bullying

roncar, rron-kar v to snore

roncería, rron-thay-**ree**-ah s sloth; cajolery

roncero, rron-**thay**-ro a slow; lazy

ronco, rron-ko a hoarse; husky; coarse

roncha, rron-chah s bump; welt; hive

ronda, rron-dah s night patrol; round

rondar, rron-dar v to patrol; to serenade

ronquera, rron-**kay**-rah s hoarseness

ronquido, rron-**kee**-do s snore; harsh sound

roña, rro-n´yah s scab; filth; mange

roñería, rro-n´yay-ree-ah s cunning; stinginess

roñoso, rro-n´yo-so a scabby; stingy; filthy

ropa, rro-pah s cloth; material; wearing apparel

ropa interior, rro-pah in-tay-re-or s lingerie

ropería, rro-pay-**ree**-ah s clothing store or business

ropón, rro-pon s loose gown worn over the clothes

roquete, rro-**kay**-tay s rochet; barbed spearhead

rosa, rro-sah s rose

rosca, rros-kah s screw;

pink; spiral

rosetón, rro-say-**ton** s rose-window (archit)

rostro, rros-tro s feature; human face; wreath

rota, rro-tah s rout; course; rattan

rotar, rro-**tar** v to rotate

roto, rro-to a broken; leaky; ragged; lewd

rotular, rro-too-**lar** v to label; to ticket; to endorse

rótulo, rro-too-lo s label; lettering; title

rotura, rro-**too**-rah s rupture; breakage; cleft

roya, rro-yah s rust; mildew; blight

rozadura, rro-thah-**doo**-rah s friction; gall; abrasion

rozamiento, rro-thah-me-**en**-to s friction; rubbing

rozar, rro-**thar** v to brush against

rozo, rro-tho s weeding

rubí, rroo-**bee** s ruby

rubia, rroo-be-ah s blond girl; madder

rubio, rroo-be-o a golden; fair (hair); blonde

rubor, rroo-bor s blush; flush; shamefulness

rubro, rroo-bro a red; reddish; s title

rucio, rroo-the-o a silver gray; gray-haired

ruda, rroo-dah s rue

rudeza, rroo-**day**-thah s roughness; rudeness

rudo*, rroo-do a rude; rough

rueda, rroo´ay-dah s wheel; turn; circle

ruedo, rroo´ay-do s rotation; border; mat; bullring

ruego, rroo´ay-go s request; entreaty; prayer

rugby, rroog-bee s rugby

rugido, rroo-Hee-do s roar

rugir, rroo-Heer v to roar; to bellow

rugoso, rroo-go-so a wrinkled

ruibarbo, rroo´e-**bar**-bo s rhubarb

ruido, rroo´ee-do s noise

ruidoso*, rroo´e-**do**-so a noisy

ruin, rroo´een a vile; mean; despicable

ruina, rroo ee-nah s ruin

ruindad, rroo´een-**dahd** s meanness

ruinoso*, rroo´e-**no**-so a ruinous

ruiseñor, rroo´e-say-n´**yor** s nightingale

ruleta, rroo-**lay**-tah s roulette

rumbo, rroom-bo s bearing; course; route

rumbón, rroom-**bon** a pompous; liberal

rumiar, rroo-me-**ar** v to ruminate; to harp on a subject

rumor, rroo-mor s rumor

runrún, rroon-**rroon** s rumor; report

rústico*, rrooss-te-ko a rustic

ruta, rroo-tah s route; itinerary

rutina, rroo-**ree**-nah s routine; custom

sábado, sah-bah-do s
Saturday

sábana, sah-bah-nah s
sheet

sabañón, sah-bah-n´yon s
chilblain

sabedor, sah-bay-dor s
well-informed person

saber, sah-bair v to know

sabido, sah-bee-do a
learned

sabiduría, sah-be-doo-ree-
ah s learning; wisdom;
knowledge

sabio*, sah-be-o a wise;
learned

sable, sah-blay s saber;
cutlass

sabor, sah-bor s relish;
taste; savor

saborear, sah-bo-ray-ar v
to relish; to taste; to
enjoy

sabroso*, sah-bro-so a
savory; tasty

sabueso, sah-boo´ay-so s
bloodhound

saca, sah-kah s
exportation; sack

sacacorchos, sah-kah-kor-
chos s corkscrew

sacadineros, sah-kah-de-
nay-ros s sideshow

sacamuelas, sah-kah-
moo´ay-lahs s dentist

sacar, sah-kar v to draw
out; to extort; to
remove; to take out

sacerdote, sah-thair-do-
tay s priest

saciar, sah-the-ar v to
satiate

saciedad, sah-the-ay-dahd
s satiety

saco, sah-ko s sack; bag

sacro, sah-kro a holy;
sacred

sacudida, sah-koo-dee-
dah s shake; jerk

sacudido*, sah-koo-dee-
do a harsh; intractable

sacudir, sah-koo-deer v to
shake; to jerk; to beat

saeta, sah-ay-tah s arrow;
dart

sagaz*, sah-gath a
sagacious

sagrado*, sah-grah-do a
sacred; consecrated

sagrario, sah-grah-re-o s
tabernacle; chapel

sagú, sah-goo s arrowroot

sahumar, sah-oo-mar v to
fumigate

saín, sah-een s grease; fat

sainete, sah´e-nay-tay s
one-act farce

sajar, sah-Har v to make
an incision

sal, sahl s salt

sala, sah-lah s hall;
saloon; living room

salado, sah-lah-do a
salted; witty; winsome

saladura, sah-lah-doo-rah
s salting; salted
provisions

salar, sah-lar v to salt

salazón, sah-lah-thon s
salted meat

salchicha, sahl-**chee**-chah s sausage

saldar, sahl-**dar** v to liquidate; to settle

salero, sah-**lay**-ro s saltshaker; (*fam*) wit

saleroso, sah-lay-**ro**-so a graceful; witty

saleta, sah-**lay**-tah s small hall

salida, sah-**lee**-dah s departure; outlet; exit

salina, sah-**lee**-nah s salt pit

salir, sah-**leer** v to go out; to appear

salitre, sah-**lee**-tray s saltpeter

saliva, sah-**lee**-vah s saliva; spittle

salmón, sahl-**mon** s salmon

salmuera, sahl-moo´**ay**-rah s brine

salobre, sah-lo-bray a brackish; briny

salón, sah-**lon** s saloon; hall

salpicar, sahl-pe-**kar** v to spatter; to splash

salpimentar, sahl-pe-men-**tar** v to season with pepper and salt

salsa, sahl-sah s sauce; gravy

salsera, sahl-**say**-rah s gravy boat

saltar, sahl-**tar** v to leap; to spring; to rebound; to jump

saltarín, sahl-tah-**reen** s dancer; restless young person

saltear, sahl-tay-**ar** v to rob on the highway

salteo, sahl-**tay**-o s assault on the highway

salterio, sahl-**tay**-re-o s psalter

salto, sahl-to s leap; jump

saltón, sahl-**ton** s grasshopper; *ojos saltones,* o-Hos sahl-**to**-ness, goggle-eyes

salubre, sah-**loo**-bray a healthful

salud, sah-**lood** s health

saludar, sah-loo-**dar** v to greet; to salute

saludo, sah-**loo**-do s salutation; bow; greeting

salva, sahl-vah s salvo; salver

salvado, sahl-**vah**-do s bran

salvador, sahl-vah-**dor** s savior

salvaguardia, sahl-vah-goo´**ar**-de-ah s safeguard

salvaje*, sahl-**vah**-Hay a savage

salvajería, sahl-vah-Hay-**ree**-ah s savageness; brutal action

salvamento, sahl-vah-**men**-to s salvage

salvar, sahl-**var** v to save

salvavidas, sahl-vah-**vee**-dahs s life preserver

¡ salve ! sahl-vay *interj* hail!

salvia, sahl-ve-ah s sage (plant)

salvilla, sahl-**vee**-l´yah s salver

salvo, sahl-vo *adv* excepting; a* safe

salvoconducto, sahl-vo-kon-**dook**-to s safe conduct

san, sahn a (abbrev. of **santo**) saint

sanar, sah-**nar** v to heal

sanativo, sah-nah-**tee**-vo a curative

sanción, sahn-the-**on** s sanction

sandez, sahn-**deth** s folly; stupidity

sandía, sahn-**dee**-ah s watermelon

sandio, sahn-de-o a foolish; nonsensical

saneamiento, sah-nay-ah-me-**en**-to s indemnification; drainage

sanear, sah-nay-**ar** v to

indemnify; to drain

sangrar, sahn-**grar** v to bleed

sangre, sahn-gray s blood; race

sangría, sahn-**gree**-ah s bleeding

sangriento*, sahn-gre-**en**-to a bloody; gory

sanguijuela, sahn-ghee-Hoo´**ay**-lah s leech

sanidad, sah-ne-**dahd** s soundness; health

sano*, sah-no a sound; sane

santiamén, sahn-te-ah-**men** s moment; twinkling of an eye

santidad, sahn-te-**dahd** s sanctity; holiness

santiguar, sahn-te-goo´**ar** v to make the sign of the Cross .

santo*, sahn-to a saint; holy; sacred

saña, sah-n´**yah** s anger; passion; rage

sañudo, sah-n´**yoo**-do a furious

sapo, sah-po s large toad

saquear, sah-kay-**ar** v to ransack; to plunder

saqueo, sah-**kay**-o s pillage

sarampión, sah-rahm-pe-**on** s measles

sarao, sah-**rah**-o s ball; dance

sardina, sar-dee-nah s sardine

sarga, sar-gah s serge

sargento, sar-**Hen**-to s sergeant

sarmiento, sar-me-**en**-to s vine shoot

sarna, sar-nah s itch; mange

sarracina, sar-rrah-**thee**-nah s tumultuous contest

sarro, sar-rro s tartar on teeth

sarta, sar-tah s string of beads; line; row; series

sartén, sar-ten s frying pan

sastre, sahs-tray s tailor

sastrería, sahs-tray-**ree**-ah s tailor's shop

satélite, sah-**tay**-le-tay s satellite

sátira, sah-te-rah s satire

satisfacer, sah-tiss-fah-**thair** v to satisfy; to atone

satisfecho, sah-tiss-**fay**-cho a satisfied; conceited

sauce, sah´oo-thay s willow

saúco, sah´oo-ko s elderberry

savia, sah-ve-ah s sap

saya, sah-yah s petticoat

sayo, sah-yo s smock

sayón, sah-**yon** s corpulent; ugly-looking fellow

sazón, sah-**thon** s maturity; season; flavor

sazonar, sah-tho-**nar** v to season; to mature

se, say pron himself; herself; itself; themselves; oneself; to him; to her

sebo, say-bo s fat; suet; candle grease

secador, say-kah-**dor** s dryer

secar, say-**kar** v to dry

seco*, say-ko a dry; parched; barren; bare

secreta, say-**kray**-tah s toilet

secretear, say-kray-tay-**ar** v to talk privately

secreto, say-**kray**-to s secrecy; **secreta,** say-**kray**-ta a* secret

secuela, say-koo´**ay**-lah s sequel; continuation

secuestro, say-koo´**ess**-tro s sequestration

secundar, say-koon-**dar** v to second; to aid

sed, sed thirst; eagerness

seda, say-dah s silk

sede, say-day s seat; headquarters

sedería, say-day-ree-ah s silk stuff

sedoso, say-do-so a silken; silky

seducir, say-doo-theer v to seduce; to entice

segadora, say-gah-do-rah s reaper; harvest

segar, say-gar v to reap; to mow

segregación racial, say-gray-gah-the-on rrah-the-ahl s apartheid

segregar, say-gray-gar v to segregate

seguida, say-ghee-dah s succession; followers

seguido*, say-ghee-do a continued; successive

seguir, say-gheer v to follow; to pursue

según, say-goon prep according to

segundo, say-goon-do s second (time); a second

seguro, say-goo-ro s assurance; insurance; a* secure; sure; certain

seis, say´iss s six

selva, sel-vah s forest

sellar, say-l´yar v to seal, to stamp; to conclude

sello, say-l´yo s seal; stamp

semana, say-mah-nah s week

semanal, say-mah-nahl a weekly

sembrar, sem-brar v to sow; to scatter; to seed; to plant

semejante, say-may-Hahn-tay a similar; like; fellow creature

semejanza, say-may-Hahn-thah s resemblance

semestre, say-mees-tray s semester; a half yearly

semi, say-me prefix semi; half

semidiós, say-me-de-os s demigod

semilla, say-mee-l´yah s seed; origin

seminario, say-me-nah-re-o s seminary (a school)

sémola, say-mo-lah s semolina

senado, say-nah-do s senate

sencillez, sen-the-l´yeth s simplicity; artlessness

sencillo*, sen-thee-l´yo a simple; guileless

senda, sen-dah s path; trail; footpath

senil, say-neel a sinus; senile

seno, say-no s breast; bosom

sensato, sen-sah-to a judicious; prudent; reasonable

sensible, sen-see-blay a sensible; perceptible; painful

sensual*, sen-soo´ahl a sensuous; sensual

sentado, sen-tah-do a sedate; judicious

sentar, sen-tar v to fit; to set up; to seat; to suit

sentenciar, sen-ten-the-ar v to sentence; to express an opinion; to pass judgment

sentido, sen-tee-do s sense; reason; meaning; a* sensible

sentimiento, sente-me-en-to s sentiment; grief; opinion

sentina, sen-tee-nah s sink; drain

sentir, sen-teer v to feel; to perceive; to suffer; to regret

seña, say-n´yah s sign; token; signal; password

señal, say-n´yahl s sign; signal; token; landmark

señalado*, say-n´yah-lah-do a famous

señalar, say-n´yah-lar v to stamp; to mark; to brand

señor, say-n´**yor** s sir; mister; lord

señora, say-n´**yo**-rah s lady; mistress; madam

señorear, say-n´yo-ray-**ar** v to domineer; to excel; to master

separado*, say-pah-**rah**-do a separated; separate

separar, say-pah-**rar** v to separate

sepelio, say-**pay**-le-o s burial

septiembre, sep-te-em-bray s September

séptimo, sep-te-mo a seventh

sepulcro, say-**pool**-kro s sepulchre; grave

sepultar, say-pool-**tar** v to bury

sequedad, say-kay-**dahd** s dryness; barrenness

sequía, say-**kee**-ah s dryness; drought

séquito, say-**ke**-to s retinue; train; suite

ser, sair v to be; to exist; to happen; to belong; to become

serenar, say-ray-**nar** v to clear up; to settle; to pacify

sereno, say-**ray**-no s night watchman; a* serene; cloudless

serie, say-re-ay s series

seriedad, say-re-ay-**dahd** s seriousness; sincerity

serio*, **say**-re-o a serious; severe

sermonear, sair-mo-nay-ar v to reprimand; to lecture

serpiente, sair-pe-en-tay s serpent

serranía, sair-rrah-nee-ah s ridge of mountains

serrano, sair-**rrah**-no s mountaineer

serrar, sair-**rrar** v to saw

serrín, sair-**rreen** s sawdust

servible, sair-vee-blay a serviceable

servicial, sair-ve-the-**ahl** a obsequious; obliging

servicio, sair-vee-the-o s service

servidero, sair-ve-day-ro a fit for service

servidumbre, sair-ve-doom-bray s servitude

servil, sair-veel a servile; groveling

servilleta, sair-ve-l´yay-tah s napkin

servir, sair-veer v to serve; to wait at table –se, to deign; to please

sesenta, say-sen-tah s & a sixty

sesentón, say-sen-ton s & a sexagenarian

sesgado*, sess-gah-do a slanting

sesgar, sess-gar v to slope; to bevel

sesgo, sess-go s bias; slope; a sloped; biased

seso, say-so s brain; intelligence

sesudo*, say-soo-do a judicious; discreet; wise

seta, say-tah s mushroom

setenta, say-ten-tah s & a seventy

setentón, say-ten-ton s & a septuagenarian

seto, say-to s fence; enclosure; hedge

seudónimo, say´oo-do-ne-mo s pseudonym

severidad, say-vay-re-dahd s severity

severo*, say-vay-ro a severe

sexagésimo, sek-sah-Hay-se-mo a sixtieth

sexista, sek-sees-tah s & a sexist

sexo, sek-so s sex

sexto, seks-to a sixth

sexy, sek-see a sexy

sí, see adv yes; pron himself; herself, etc.

si, see conj if

sibilante, se-be-lahn-tay a

hissing

SIDA see-dah s abbr acquired immune deficiency syndrome, AIDS

sidra, see-drah s cider

siega, se-ay-gah s reaping; harvest time

siempre, se-em-pray adv always; **–jamás, –Hah-mahs,** for ever and ever

sien, se-en s temple (of the head)

sierpe, se-air-pay s serpent; snake

sierra, se-air-rrah s saw; ridge of mountains

siervo, se-air-vo s serf; slave; servant

siesta, se-ess-tah s afternoon nap

siete, se-ay-tay s & a seven

sifón, se-fon s syphon

sigilar, se-He-lar v to seal; to conceal

sigilo, se-Hee-lo s secret; secrecy

sigiloso, se-He-lo-so a reserved; silent

siglo, see-glo s century

signar, sig-nar v to sign; **–se,** to make the sign of the Cross

significar, sig-ne-fe-kar v to signify; to mean

signo, seeg-no s sign; mark

siguiente, se-ghee-en-tay a following

silbar, sil-bar v to whistle

silbato, sil-bah-to s whistle

silbido, sil-bee-do s hiss; whistling

silencio, se-len-the-o s silence

silicio, se-lee-the´o s silicon

silueta, se-loo´ay-tah s silhouette

silvestre, sil-vess-tray a wild; rustic

silla, see-l´yah s chair; see; saddle; seat

sillar, se-l´yar s ashlar; horseback

sillero, se-l´yay-ro s saddler

sillón, se-l´yon s easy-chair; armchair

símbolo, seem-bo-lo s symbol; sign

simiente, se-me-en-tay s seed

símil, see-mil s simile; a similar

simio, see-me-o s male ape

simpatía, sim-pah-tee-ah s sympathy

simpleza, sim-play-thah s

silliness; rusticity

simplificar, sim-ple-fe-kar v to simplify

simulado, se-moo-lah-do a feigned

sin, sin prep without; **– embargo,** – em-bar-go, notwithstanding; nevertheless

sincerar, sin-thay-rar v to exculpate; to justify

sincero*, sin-thay-ro a sincere

sincopa, seen-ko-pah s fainting spell

sindicado, sin-de-kah-do s syndicate

síndico, seen-de-ko s trustee; receiver

singlar, sin-glar v to sail over a course

singularizar, sin-goo-lah-re-thar v to distinguish; to single out

siniestra, se-ne´ess-trah s left hand

siniestro, se-ne´ess-tro s disaster; a* sinister

sino, see-no conj if not; except; only; but

sinónimo, se-no-ne-mo a synonymous

sinrazón, sin-rah-thon s wrong; injustice

sinsabor, sib-sah-bor s displeasure; disgust

sintaxis, sin-**tahk**-siss *s* syntax

sintético, sin-**tay**-te-ko *a* synthetic

síntoma, **seen**-to-mah *s* symptom

sinuoso, se-noo´**o**-so *a* sinuous

siquiera, se-ke´**ay**-rah *conj* at least; **ni –,** ne **–,** not even

sirena, se-**ray**-nah *s* siren

sirgar, seer-**gar** *v* to tow a vessel

sirvienta, seer-ve-**en**-tah *s* maid; servant

sisa, **see**-sah *s* petty theft

sisar, se-**sar** *v* to pilfer; to size for gilding

sisón, se-**son** *s* a Spanish wading bird

sistema métrico, sees-**tay**-mah **may**-tre-ko *s* metric system

sitial, se-te-**ahl** *s* seat of honor; stool

sitiar, se-te-**ar** *v* to besiege

sitio, **see**-te-o *s* place; site; siege

sito, **see**-to *a* situated

situado, se-too´**ah**-do *a* placed; situate

situar, se-too´**ar** *v* to place

so, so *prep* under; below

soba, **so**-bah *s* softening; beating; rubbing

sobaco, so-**bah**-ko *s* armpit

sobar, so-**bar** *v* to handle; to soften; to pummel

soberanía, so-bay-rah-**nee**-ah *s* sovereignty; dominion

soberano, so-bay-**rah**-no *s* & *a* sovereign

soberbia, so-**bair**-be-ah *s* pride; haughtiness

soberbio*, so-**bair**-be-o *a* proud; superb

sobornar, so-bor-**nar** *v* to bribe

sobra, **so**-brah *s* surplus; excess; offense *pl* offals

sobradillo, so-brah-dee-l´yo *s* shelter over a balcony

sobrado, so-**brah**-do *s* attic; *a* wealthy; excessive; abundant

sobrante, so-**brahn**-tay *s* residue; surplus

sobrar, so-**brar** *v* to have more than necessary; to be left

sobre, **so**-bray *prep* above; over; *s* envelope

sobrecama, so-bray-**kah**-mah *s* bedcover

sobrecargar, so-bray-kar-**gar** *v* to overload; to overchange

sobrecargo, so-bray-**kar-**

go *s* supercargo; purser; airline attendant

sobrecejo, so-bray-**thay**-Ho *s* frown

sobrecito, so-bray-**the**-to *s* sachet

sobrecoger, so-bray-ko-**Hair** *v* to surprise

sobredicho, so-bray-**dee**-cho *a* aforesaid

sobredorar, so-bray-do-**rar** *v* to gild; to palliate

sobrehumano, so-bray´**oo**-mah-no *a* superhuman

sobrellevar, so-bray-l´yay-**var** *v* to endure; to undergo; to bear; to tolerate

sobremanera, so-bray-mah-**nay**-rah *adv* excessively

sobremesa, so-bray-**may**-sah *s* tablecloth; dessert; immediately after dinner

sobrenadar, so-bray-nah-**dar** *v* to float

sobrenatural*, so-bray-nah-too-**rahl** *a* supernatural

sobrenombre, so-bray-**nom**-bray *s* surname; nickname

sobrentender, so-bren-ten-**dair** *v* to understand

sobrepaga, so-bray-**pah-**

gah s extra pay

sobrepeso, so-bray-**pay**-so s overweight

sobreponer, so-bray-po-**nair** v to put over; to overcome

sobreprecio, so-bray-**pray**-the-o s extra price

sobrepujar, so-bray-poo-Har v to surpass; to excel; to exceed

sobresalir, so-bray-sah-leer v to surpass; to outvie

sobresaltar, so-bray-sahl-tar v to startle; to frighten

sobrescrito, so-bress-**kree**-to s address of a letter

sobreseer, so-bray-say-**air** v to desist

sobreseguro, so-bray-say-**goo**-ro adv without risk

sobreseimiento, so-bray-say´e-me-**en**-to s suspension; stay of proceedings (law)

sobrestante, so-bress-**tahn**-tay s overseer; foreman

sobretarde, so-bray-tar-day s close of the evening

sobretodo, so-bray-**to**-do s overcoat

sobreveedor, so-bray-vay-

ay-**dor** s supervisor

sobrevenir, so-bray-vay-neer v to supervene; to happen

sobrevivir, so-bray-ve-veer v to survive; to outlive

sobrina, so-**bree**-nah s niece

sobrino, so-**bree**-no s nephew

sobrio*, so-bre-o a sober; frugal

socaliñar, so-kah-le-n´yar v to extort by trickery

socapa, so-**kah**-pah s pretext; pretense

socarrar, so-kar-rrar v to singe

socarrón, so-kar-rron a cunning; crafty

socavar, so-kah-var v to undermine

sociedad, so-the´ay-**dahd** s society

socio, so-the-o s associate; partner

socolor, so-ko-**lor** s pretext; pretense

socorrido, so-kor-rree-do a supplied

socorro, so-**kor**-rro s help; aid; succor

sodio, so-de-o s sodium

soez, so-**eth** a mean; vile; coarse

sofá, so-**fah** s sofa

sofocar, so-fo-**kar** v to suffocate; to quench

software, soft-oo-ayr s software

soga, so-gah s rope; halter

sojuzgar, so-Hooth-**gar** v to subdue

sol, sol s sun

solana, so-lah-nah s sunny place

solano, so-lah-no s easterly wind

solapa, so-lah-pah s lapel; pretext

solapado, so-lah-**pah**-do a cunning; artful

solapar, so-lah-par v to button up; to conceal

solar, so-**lar** s ground-plot a solar

solaz, so-lath s solace; consolation

solazar, so-lah-**thar** v to console; to comfort; to cheer

solazo, so-lah-tho s scorching sun

soldada, sol-dah-dah s wages; soldier's pay

soldadesco, sol-dah-dess-ko a soldierlike

soldado, sol-**dah**-do s soldier; private

soldadura, sol-dah-doo-rah s soldering

soldar, sol-**dar** v to solder; to weld; to mend

soledad, so-lay-**dahd** s solitude; loneliness; desert

solemne*, so-**lem**-nay a solemn; grand

soler, so-**lair** v to use to; to be accustomed to

solera, so-**lay**-rah s beam

solería, so-lay-**ree**-ah s pavement; sole-leather

solicitar, so-le-the-**tar** v to solicit

solícito*, so-**lee**-the-to a solicitous

solicitud, so-le-the-**tood** s solicitude; application

solidaridad, so-le-dah-rre-**dahd** s solidarity

solidez, so-le-**deth** s solidity

sólido*, **so**-le-do a solid

solio, **so**-le-o s canopied throne

solitario, so-le-**tah**-re-o a solitary; lonely

sólito, **so**-le-to a accustomed

soliviar, so-le-ve-**ar** v to lift up

solo, **so**-lo a alone; lonely

sólo, **so**-lo adv only.

solomillo, solomo, so-lo-**mee**-l'yo, so-**lo**-mo s loin

soltar, sol-**tar** v to untie; to loosen

soltería, sol-tay-**ree**-ah s celibacy

soltero, sol-**tay**-ro s bachelor; a single; unmarried

soltura, sol-**too**-rah s agility; ease; skill

solución, so-loo-the-**on** s solution

solvencia, sol-**ven**-the-ah s solvency

sollozar, so-l'yo-**thar** v to sob

somanta, so-**mahn**-tah s beating

sombra, **som**-brah s shade; shadow

sombrerera, som-bray-ray-**rah** s hatbox

sombrero, som-**bray**-ro s hat

sombrío, som-**bree**-o a shady; somber; dark

sombrilla, som-**bree**-l'yah s parasol; sunshade

someter, so-may-**tair** v to subject; to subdue

sometimiento, so-may-te-me-**en**-to s submission

somnífero, som-**nee**-fay-ro s sleeping pill

son, son s sound; report

sonado, so-**nah**-do a celebrated

sonar, so-**nar** v to play (music); to sound; to blow the nose

sonda, **son**-dah s plummet; sounding; catheter

sondar, sondear, son-**dar**, son-day-**ar** v to sound; to gauge

soneto, so-**nay**-to s sonnet

sonido, so-**nee**-do s sound

sonreírse, son-ray-**eer**-say v to smile

sonrisa, son-**ree**-sah s smile

sonrojo, son-ro-**Ho** s blush

sonsacar, son-sah-**kar** v to draw one out

soñar, so-n´**yar** v to dream

soñoliento, so-n´yo-le-**en**-to a sleepy; drowsy; lazy

sopa, **so**-pah s soup

sopapo, so-**pah**-po s slap; blow

sopera, so-**pay**-rah s soup tureen

soplar, so-**plar** v to blow; to steal artfully; to prompt

soplete, so-**play**-tay s blowtorch

soplón, so-**plon** s informer

sopor, so-**por** s drowsiness; sleepiness

soportar, so-por-**tar** v to

suffer; to tolerate; to endure

soporte, so-por-tay s support; base

sor, sor s sister (nun)

sorber, sor-bair v to sip; to suck

sorbete, sor-bay-tay s sherbet

sordera, sordez, sor-day-rah, sor-deth s deafness

sordidez, sor-de-deth s sordidness; nastiness; covetousness

sórdido*, sor-dee-do a sordid; nasty; licentious

sordo, sor-do a deaf; noiseless; muffled

sorna, sor-nah s irony

sorprender, sor-pren-dair v to surprise

sorpresa, sor-pray-sah s surprise

sortija, sor-tee-Hah s ring (jewelry); hoop

sosa, so-sah s glasswort; soda

sosegado, so-say-gah-do a quiet; peaceful

sosegar, so-say-gar v to appease; to rest

sosería, so-say-ree-ah s insipidity

sosiego, so-se-ay-go s tranquility; calmness

soslayar, sos-lah-yar v to do or place obliquely

soso*, so-so a tasteless

sospecha, sos-pay-chah s suspicion

sospechar, sos-pay-char v to suspect

sospesar, sos-pay-sar v to suspend; to lift; to weigh

sostén, sos-ten s support; brassiere

sostener, sos-tay-nair v to sustain; to prop; to support

sota, so-tah s jack (cards)

sotabanco, so-tah-bahn-ko s attic

sotana, so-tah-nah s cassock

sótano, so-tah-no s underground cellar; basement

sotavento, so-tah-ven-to s leeward; lee

sotechado, so-tay-chah-do s shed; roofed place

soto, so-to s grove; thicket

su, soo pron his; her; its; their; one's

suave*, soo´ah-vay a smooth; soft; gentle

suavizar, soo´ah-ve-thar v to soften

subarrendar, soob-ar-rren-dar v to sublet; to sublease

subasta, soo-bahs-tah s auction

súbdito, soob-de-to s & a subject

subida, soo-bee-dah s mounting; ascent; increase

subir, soo-beer v to ascend; to mount; to increase; to go up; to climb

súbito, soo-be-to adv suddenly; unexpectedly; a* sudden; unforeseen

sublevar, soo-blay-var v to excite rebellion

sublime*, soo-blee-may a sublime

subrayar, soob-rrah-yar v to underline

subrepción, soob-rrep-the-on s hidden action

subrogar, soob-rro-gar v to surrogate

subsanar, soob-sah-nar v to excuse; to repair

subscribir, soobs-kre-beer v to subscribe

subsidiar, soob-se-de-ar v to subsidize

subsiguiente, soob-se-ghee-en-tay a subsequent

subsistencia, soob-siss-ten-the-ah s subsistence; livelihood

subsistir, soob-siss-teer v

to subsist

substancia, soobs-**tahn**-the-ah *s* substance; aliment; nature of things

substituir, soobs-te-too-eer *v* to substitute; to replace

substraer, soobs-trah-**air** *v* to subtract; –se, to withdraw

subteniente, soob-tay-ne-**en**-tay *s* second lieutenant

subtitular, soob-tee-too-lahr *v* subtitle

subtítulo, soob-**tee**-too-lo *s* subtitle

suburbio, soo-**boor**-be-o *s* suburb

subvenir, soob-vay-**neer** *v* to aid; to assist; to provide for

subversivo, soob-vair-see-vo *a* subversive

subyugar, soob-yoo-**gar** *v* to subdue

suceder, soo-thay-**dair** *v* to succeed; to inherit; to follow; to happen

suceso, soo-**thay**-so *s* success; occurrence; issue

sucio*, soo-**the**-o *a* dirty; nasty; filthy

suco, soo-ko *s* juice; sap

sucumbir, soo-koom-**beer** *v* to succumb

sucursal, soo-koor-**sahl** *s* branch office

sudar, soo-**dar** *v* to sweat; to perspire

sudeste, soo-**dess**-tay *s* southeast

sudoeste, soo-do-**ess**-tay *s* southwest

suegra, soo´**ay**-grah *s* mother-in-law

suegro, soo´**ay**-gro *s* father-in-law

suegros, soo´**ay**-gros *s* in-laws

suela, soo´**ay**-lah *s* sole of the shoe

sueldo, soo´**ell**-do *s* wages; pay; salary

suelo, soo´**ay**-lo *s* soil; ground; floor

suelto, soo´**ell**-to *a* loose; swift; free; easy

sueño, soo´**ay**-n´yo *s* sleep; dream; vision

suero, soo´**ay**-ro *s* whey; serum

suerte, soo´**air**-tay *s* chance; fortune; luck; fate; kind; manner

suficiente*, soo-fe-the-en-tay *a* sufficient; apt; fit

sufragar, soo-frah-**gar** *v* to defray; to aid; to assist

sufrible, soo-**free**-blay *a* bearable

sufridor, soo-fre-**dor** *s & a* long-suffering

sufrimiento, soo-fre-me-en-to *s* sufferance

sufrir, soo-**freer** *v* to suffer; to tolerate; to undergo

sugerir, soo-**Hay**-reer *v* to suggest

sujeción, soo-**Hay**-the-**on** *s* subjection

sujetador, soo-**Hay**-ta-**dor** *s* bra

sujetar, soo-**Hay**-tar *v* to subdue; to subject; to fasten

sujeto, soo-**Hay**-to *s* subject; matter; *a* subject; liable

suma, soo-mah *s* sum; amount; addition

sumar, soo-**mar** *v* to summarize; to add

sumario, soo-**mah**-re-o *s & a* summary

sumergir, soo-mair-**Heer** *v* to submerge; to immerse; to plunge

sumidero, soo-me-day-ro *s* sewer; drain

suministrar, soo-me-niss-**trar** *v* to supply; to provide

sumir, soo-**meer** *v* to sink;

to depress

sumiso, soo-**mee**-so *a* submissive

sumo*, soo-mo *a* highest; greatest

suntuoso*, soon-**too**'o-so *a* sumptuous

supeditar, soo-pay-de-**tar** *v* to subdue; to subject

superar, soo-pay-**rar** *v* to overcome; to surpass; to excel

superávit, soo-pay-**rah**-vit *s* surplus

superchería, soo-pair-chay-**ree**-ah *s* fraud; cheat

superficie, soo-pair-fee-the-ay *s* surface area

supermercado, soo-payr-mayr-**kah**-do *s* supermarket

supervivencia, soo-pair-ve-ven-the-ah *s* survival

superviviente, soo-pair-ve-ve-en-tay *s & a* survivor

suplantar, soo-plahn-**tar** *v* to supplant; to falsify a document

suplemento, soo-play-**men**-to *s* supplement

súplica, soo-ple-kah *s* petition; plea

suplicar, soo-p.e-**kar** *v* to implore; to entreat; to appeal

suplicio, soo-**plee**-the-o *s* torture

suplir, soo-**pleer** *v* to supply; to furnish; to fill up

suponer, soo-po-**nair** *v* to suppose; to assume

suprimir, soo-pre-**meer** *v* to suppress

supuesto, soo-poo'**ess**-to *s* supposition; *a* supposed

sur, soor *s* south

surco, **soor**-ko *s* furrow; line

surf, soorf *s* surfing

surgir, soor-**Heer** *v* to emerge

surtido, soor-**tee**-do *s* assortment; supply

surtidor, soor-te-**dor** *s* spurt

surtir, soor-**teer** *v* to provide; to supply

suscitar, sooss-the-**tar** *v* to excite; to promote; to rouse

suspender, sooss-pen-**dair** *v* to suspend

suspicaz*, sooss-pe-**kath** *a* suspicious; distrustful

suspirar, sooss-pe-**rar** *v* to sigh; to long for

sustancia, sooss-**tahn**-the-ah, (see **substancia**)

sustentable, sooss-ten-tah-blay *a* defensible; sustainable

sustentáculo, sooss-ten-tah-koo-lo *s* prop; support

sustentar, sooss-ten-**tar** *v* to sustain; to nourish

sustento, sooss-**ten**-to *s* food; sustenance

sustituir, sooss-te-too'**eer** *v* to substitute

susto, **sooss**-toh *s* scare; fright; shock

susurrar, soo-soor-**rrar** *v* to whisper; to murmur

sutil*, soo-**teel** *a* subtle; keen; flimsy; delicate

sutileza, soo-te-**lay**-thah *s* subtlety; acumen

suyo, soo-yo *pron* his; hers; theirs; *pl* family friends; servants

taba, tah-bah s small bone in the foot

tabaco, tah-bah-ko s tobacco

tábano, tah-bah-no s hornet

tabaquero, tah-bah-**kay**-ro s tobacconist

tabardillo, tah-bar-dee-l´yo s burning fever; typhus

taberna, tah-bair-nah s tavern

tabernero, tah-bair-**nay**-ro s tavern-keeper

tabicar, tah-be-**kar** v to wall up

tabique, tah-bee-kay s partition wall

tabla, tah-blah s board; table; index; list

tablado, tah-blah-do s scaffold; stage

tablazón, tah-blah-**thon** s platform; planks

tableta, tah-blay-tah s tablet

tablilla, tah-blee-l´yah s bulletin board; tablet

tablón, tah-blon s plank; thick board

taburete, tah-boo-**ray**-tay s stool

tacañería, tah-kah-n´yay-**ree**-ah s meanness

tacaño, tah-kah-n´yo a stingy; sordid

tácito*, tah-the-to a tacit; implied

taco, tah-ko s stopper; wad; billiard cue

tacón, tah-kon s heel

taconear, tah-ko-nay-ar v to walk arrogantly

tacha, tah-chah s fault; defect

tachar, tah-char v to find fault with; to efface

tacto, tahk-to s touch; tact

tafetán, tah-fay-**tahn** s taffeta

tafilete, tah-fe-lay-tay s morocco leather

tahona, tah-o-nah s bakery

tahonero, tah-o-**nay**-ro s baker

tahur, tah´oor s gambler; cheat

taimado, tah´e-**mah**-do a sly; crafty

taja, tah-Hah s cut; dissection; tally

tajadura, tah-Hah-**doo**-rah s cut; notch; section

tajamar, tah-Hah-**mar** s cutwater (on ship)

tajar, tah-Har v to cut; to chop; to hew

tajo, tah-Ho s cut; incision

tal, tahl a such; so; as; similar; equal

tala, tah-lah s felling of trees; devastation

taladrar, tah-lah-**drar** v to bore; to drill; to pierce

taladro, tah-lah-dro s bit; borer; drill

talar, tah-**lar** *v* to fell trees; to lay waste

talco, tahl-ko *s* talcum powder

talega, tah-lay-gah *s* bag; sack; bagful

talento, tah-**len**-to *s* talent

talión, tah-le-**on** *s* retaliation

talismán, tah-liss-**mahn** *s* talisman; amulet

talmente, tahl-**men**-tay *adv* in the same manner

talón, tah-**lon** *s* heel; counterfoil; receipt

talud, tah-**lood** *s* slope; ramp

talla, tah-l´yah *s* raised work; sculpture

tallar, tah-l´yar *v* to cut; to carve in wood

talle, tah-l´yay *s* shape; size; waist

taller, tah-l´yair *s* workshop; laboratory

tallista, tah-l´yeess-tah *s* woodcarver

tallo, tah-l´yo *s* shoot; sprout; stem

tamaño, tah-**mah**-n´yo *s* size; *a* as large; so large

tambalear, tahm-bah-lay-ar *v* to stagger; to waver

también, tahm-be-**en** *adv* & *conj* also; as well

tambor, tahm-bor *s* drum; drummer

tamboril, tahm-bo-**reel** *s* tabor; taboret

tamiz, tah-**meeth** *s* fine sieve

tamo, tah-mo *s* fluff; dust

tampoco, tahm-po-ko *adv* neither

tampón, tahm-pon *s* tampon

tan, tahn *adv* so; so much; *s* sound of the drum

tanda, tah-dah *s* turn; task; gang; batch

tanganillo, tahn-gah-nee-l´yo *s* small prop

tantear, tahn-tay-ar *v* to measure; to proportion; to examine

tanteo, tahn-tay-o *s* calculation; computation

tanto, tahn-to *adv* so; *s* quantity; *a* so much

tañedor, tah-n´yay-dor *s* player on a musical instrument

tañer, tah-n´yair, (see **tocar**)

tapa, tah-pah *s* lid; cover

tapar, tah-par *v* to cover; to conceal

tapete, tah-pay-tay *s* small carpet; rug; table cover

tapiar, tah-pe-ar *v* to wall up .

tapicería, tah-pe-thay-ree-ah *s* tapestry

tapiz, tah-**peeth** *s* tapestry

tapón, tah-pon *s* cork; plug

taquigrafía, tah-ke-grah-fee-ah *s* shorthand

taquígrafo, tah-kee-grah-fo *s* stenographer; shorthand-typist

taquilla, tah-kee-l´yah *s* box office; ticket office; filing cabinet

tara, tah-rah *s* defect

tardanza, tar-dahn-than *s* slowness; delay

tardar, tar-dar *v* to delay; to put off; to tarry

tarde, tar-day *adv* late; *s* afternoon; evening

tardiamente, tar-de-ah-men-tay *adv* too late

tardío, tar-dee-o *a* late; too late

tardo, tar-do *a* slow; sluggish; tardy

tarea, tah-ray-ah *s* task; day's work

tarifa, tah-ree-fah *s* tariff

tarima, tah-ree-mah *s* stand; daïs; platform

tarjeta, tar-Hay-tah *s* card; – **postal,** – pos-**tahl,** postcard

tarro, tar-rro *s* jar

tartajear, tartamudear,

tar-tah-Hay-ar, tar- tah-moo-day-ar v to stutter; to stammer

tartamudo, tar-tah-moo-do s stutterer; stammerer

tártaro, tar-tah-ro s tartar; hell

tarugo, tah-roo-go s wooden peg or pin

tasa, tah-sah s rate; price; valuation

tasación, tah-sah-the-on s appraisement

tasar, tah-sar v to appraise; to value

tatarabuelo, tah-tah-rah-boo´ay-lo s great-great-grandfather

¡tate! tah-tay interj beware!

taza, tah-thah s cup; bowl; basin of a fountain

té, tay s tea

te, tay pron thee

tea, tay-ah s torch

teatro, tay-ah-tro s theater; playhouse

tecla, tay-klah s key of a piano or organ

teclado, tay-klah-do s keyboard

técnica, tek-ne-kah s technique

tecnología, tek-no-lo-Hee´ah s technology

techo, tay-cho s roof; ceiling

techumbre, tay-choom-bray s upper roof

tedio, tay-de-o s loathing; tediousness

teja, tay-Hah s roof tile

tejedor, tay-Hay-dor s weaver

tejer, tay-Hair v to weave

tejido, tay-Hee-do s texture; fabric; web

tela, tay-lah s cloth

telar, tay-lar s loom

telaraña, tay-lah-rah-n´yah s cobweb

telefonear, tay-lay-fo-nay-ar v to telephone

teléfono, tay-lay-fo-no s telephone

telegrafiar, tay-lay-grah-fe-ar v to telegraph; to wire

telégrafo, tay-lay-grah-fo s telegraph

telegrama, tay-lay-grah-mah s telegram

telémetro, tay-lay-may-tro s range-finder camera

telescopio, tay-less-ko-pe-o s telescope

telesquí, tay-lays-kee s ski lift

televisión, tay-lay-ve-se-on s television

telón, tay-lon s curtain (theater)

tema, tay-mah s theme

temblar, tem-blar v to tremble; to shake; to quiver

temblón, tem-blon a tremulous

temblor, tem-blor s trembling; tremor; earthquake

temer, tay-mair v to fear; to doubt

temerario*, tay-may-rah-re-o a rash; imprudent; reckless

temeroso*, tay-may-ro-so a timid; timorous

temible, tay-mee-blay a terrible; frightful

temor, tay-mor s dread; fear

témpano, tem-pah-no s iceberg; big piece of ice

tempestad, tem-pess-tahd s tempest; storm

templado, tem-plah-do a temperate

templador, tem-plah-dor s tuner

templar, tem-plar v to temper; to tune

temple, tem-play s temper (metal)

templo, tem-plo s temple

temporada, tem-po-rah-dah s spell; season

temporal, tem-po-rahl s

tempest; season; *a* temporary; temporal

temprano, tem-**prah**-no *adv* early; *a* precocious

tenacillas, tay-nah-**thee**-l´yahs *s* tweezers

tenaz*, tay-**nath** *a* tenacious

tenazas, tay-**nah**-thahs *s* tongs; pincers

tenca, ten-kah *s* tench (fish)

tender, ten-**dair** *v* to stretch out; to expand

tendero, ten-**day**-ro *s* shopkeeper; haberdasher

tendido, ten-**dee**-do *s* row of seats in a circus

tenebroso*, tay-nay-**bro**-so *a* dark; obscure

tenedor, tay-nay-**dor** *s* holder; fork

tenencia, tay-**nen**-the-ah *s* possession; lieutenancy

tener, tay-**nair** *v* to have; to hold; to posses;; to contain; to retain

teniente, tay-ne-en-tay *s* deputy; lieutenant

tenor, tay-**nor** *s* tenor; purport; tenor (singer)

tensión arterial, ten-se-**on** ar-tay-ree-**ahl** *s* blood pressure

tentar, ten-**tar** *v* to touch; to try; to tempt

tentativa, ten-tah-**tee**-vah *s* attempt; trial

tenue*, tay-noo´ay *a* thin; slender

tenuidad, tay-noo´e-**dahd** *s* tenuity; weakness

teñir, tay-n´**yeer** *v* to tinge; to dye

teoría, tay-o-ree-ah *s* theory

terapia, tay-**rah**-pe-ah *s* therapy

tercer, tercero, tair-**thair**, tair-**thay**-ro *a* third

tercería, tair-thay-**ree**-ah *s* mediation

tercero, tair-**thay**-ro *s* third person

terciado, tair-the-**ah**-do *s* cutlass; *a* crosswise

terciar, tair-the-**ar** *v* to divide in three parts; to mediate

tercio, tair-the-o *s* third part

terciopelo, tair-the-o-**pay**-lo *s* velvet

terco, tair-ko *a* pertinacious; obstinate; stubborn

tergiversar, tair-He-vair-sar *v* to twist; to misrepresent

terminal, tayr-me-**nahl** *s* (air) terminal

término, tair-me-no *s* term; end; boundary; condition

termómetro, tair-mo-may-tro *s* thermometer

termos, tair-mos *s* vacuum flask; thermos bottle

termostato, tair-mo-**stah**-to *s* thermostat

ternero, tair-**nay**-ro *s* calf; bullock

terneza, tair-**nay**-thah *s* softness; tenderness

terno, tair-no *s* three-piece suit; ternary number

ternura, tair-**noo**-rah *s* tenderness

terquedad, tair-**kay**-dahd *s* stubbornness

terrado, tair-**rrah**-do *s* terrace

terraplén, tair-rrah-**plen** *s* embankment

terremoto, tair-rray-mo-to *s* earthquake

terrenal, terreno, tair-rray-nahl, tair-rray-no *a* terrestrial

terrible*, tair-**rree**-blay *a* terrible

terrón, tair-**rron** *s* cold; mound; lump

terror, tair-**rror** *s* terror; dread

terrorista, tay-rro-res-**tah** *s* terrorist

terso, tair-so *a* smooth; glossy

tersura, tair-soo-rah *s* smoothness

tertulia, tair-too-le-ah *s* evening party; circle; assembly; conversation

tesón, tay-son *s* tenacity

tesoro, tay-so-ro *s* treasure; treasury

testa, tess-tah *s* head

testador, tess-tah-dor *s* testator

testamento, tess-tah-men-to *s* will; testament

testar, tess-tar *v* to make a will

testarudo, tess-tah-roo-do *a* obstinate

testificación, tess-te-fe-kah-the-on *s* attestation

testigo, tess-tee-go *s* witness

testimoniar, tess-te-mo-ne-ar *v* to testify; to attest

testimonio, tess-te-mo-ne-o *s* testimony; attestation

tesura, tay-soo-rah *s* stiffness

teta, tay-tah *s* teat; udder; breast

tetera, tay-tay-rah *s* teapot

tétrico, tay-tre-ko *a* gloomy; sullen

tez, teth *s* complexion

ti, tee *pron* you; yourself; thee; thyself

tía, tee-ah *s* aunt

tibieza, te-be-ay-thah *s* lukewarmness

tibio, tee-be-o *a* lukewarm

tiburón, te-boo-ron *s* shark

tiempo, te-em-po *s* time; term; occasion; season; weather; once in a while

tienda, te-en-dah *s* tent; awning; tilt; shop

tiento, te-en-to *s* touch; tact; blow; a –, ah –, gropingly

tierno*, te-air-rr *a* tender

tierra, te-air-rrah *s* earth; land; ground; native country

tieso, te-ay-so *a* stiff; hard; rigid

tifus, tee-fooss *s* typhus

tigre, tee-gray *s* tiger

tijeras, te-Hay-rahs *s* scissors; shears

tildar, til-dar *v* to brand

tilde, teel-day *s* sign of the letter ñ; iota; very small thing

tilo, tee-lo *s* lime tree

timbrar, tim-brar *v* to stamp

timbre, teem-bray *s* stamp; doorbell; ring

timidez, te-me-deth *s* timidity

tímido,* tee-me-do *a* timid

timón, te-mon *s* helm; rudder

tina, tee-nah *s* vat; tub

tinaja, te-nah-Hah *s* large earthen jar

tinglado, tin-glah-do *s* shed; platform

tinieblas, te-ne´ayblahs *s* darkness

tino, tee-no *s* skill in touch; knack; judgment

tinta, teen-tah *s* ink; tint

tinte, teen-tay *s* tint; dye

tintero, tin-tay-ro *s* inkstand; inkwell

tinto, teen-to *a* dyed; red (wine)

tintura, tin-too-rah *s* tincture; dye; rouge

tiña, tee-n´yah *s* ringworm of the scalp

tío, tee-o *s* uncle

típico, tee-pe-ko *a* typical

tipo, tee-po *s* guy; type; pattern; standard

tira, tee-rah *s* strip; list; band

tirabuzón, te-rah-boo-thon *s* corkscrew

tirada, te-rah-dah *s* cast; throw; distance

tiranía, te-rah-nee-ah *s*

tyranny

tirano, te-**rah**-no s tyrant; despot

tirante, te-**rahn**-tay s joist; gear; trace; a drawn; tight

tirar v to throw; to cast; to pull; to draw; to shoot; to aim at

tiritar, te-re-**tar** v to shiver

tiro, **tee**-ro s cast; throw; shot; fling; prank

tirón, te-**ron** s pull; haul

tirria, **teer**-rre-ah s aversion; dislike

tisana, te-**sah**-nah s infusion; tisane

tisis, **tee**-siss s tuberculosis; consumption

tisú, te-**soo** s gold and silver tissue

títere, **tee**-tay-ray s puppet; marionette

titubear, te-too-bay-**ar** v to vacillate; to doubt; to hesitate

título, **tee**-too-lo s title

tiza, **tee**-thah s chalk; clay

tiznar, tith-**nar** v to stain (reputation); to tarnish

tizne, **teeth**-nay s soot

tizón, te-**thon** s half-burnt wood

toalla, to´**ah**-l´yah s towel

tobillo, to-**bee**-l´yo s ankle

toca, **to**-kah s headdress; thin fabric

tocadiscos, to-kah-**dess**-koss s record-player

tocador, to-kah-**dor** s player (music); dressing room; boudoir

tocante, to-**kahn**-tay prep relating to; a relative

tocar, to-**kar** v to touch; to play on; to concern; –se, to put one's hat on

tocayo, to-**kah**-yo s namesake

tocinero, to-the-**nay**-ro s seller of pork

tocino, to-**thee**-no s bacon; salt pork

tocón, to-**kon** s stump

tocho, **to**-cho a unpolished; uncultured (person)

todavía, to-dah-**vee**-ah adv yet; still; even

todo, **to**-do s whole; a all; entire

toldo, **tol**-do s awning

tolerancia, to-lay-**rahn**-the-ah s indulgence; tolerance

tolerar, to-lay-**rar** v to tolerate

toma, **to**-mah s taking; grasp; capture; dose

tomar, to-**mar** v to take; to seize; to gasp; to drink

tomate, to-**mah**-tay s tomato

tomillo, to-**mee**-l´yo s thyme

tomo, **to**-mo s bulk; tome; volume

ton, ton s tone; **sin –ni son,** sin – ne son, without rhyme or reason

tonada, to-**nah**-dah s tune; song

tonel, to-**nell** s cask; barrel

tonelada, to-nay-**lah**-dah s ton

tonelaje, to-nay-**lah**-Hay s tonnage; capacity

tono, **to**-no s tone; tune

tontada, ton-**tah**-dah s nonsense

tontear, ton-tay-**ar** v to fool about

tonto*, **ton**-to a foolish; silly

topar, to-**par** v to collide; to run against

tope, **to**-pay s butt; top

topera, to-**pay**-rah s mole hole

topetar, to-pay-**tar** v to bump against

tópico, **to**-pe-ko s topic; subject; a topical

top-less, **top**-lays a topless

topo, **to**-po s mole

toque, to-**kay** s touch; ringing of bells

torbellino, tor-bay-l´yee-no s whirlwind

torcer, tor-thair v to twist; to distort

torcido*, tor-thee-do a tortuous; twisted

tordo, tor-do s thrush; a speckled; gray horse

toreo, to-ray-o s bullfighting

torero, to-ray-ro s bullfighter

tormenta, tor-men-tah s storm

tormento, tor-men-to s torment; anguish; torture

torna, tor-nah s restitution; return

tornar, tor-nar v to return; to restore

tornasol, tor-nah-sol s sunflower

tornear, tor-nay-ar v to turn on a lathe

tornillo, tor-nee-l´yo s screw; clamp

torno, tor-no s lathe; gyration

toro, to-ro s bull

toronja, to-ron-Hah s grapefruit

torpe, tor-pay a slow; dull; obscene

torpeza, tor-pay-thah s heaviness; dullness;

lewdness

torre, tor-rray s tower

torrente, tor-rren-tay s torrent

torreón, tor-rray-on s fortified tower

torrero, tor-rray-roh s lighthouse-keeper

torrezno, tor-rreth-no s rasher of bacon

tórrido, tor-rre-do a torrid; parched; hot

torsión, tor-se-on s twist

torso, tor-so s trunk; human torso

torta, tor-tah s round cake; pie

tortilla, tor-tee-l´yah s omelet; tortilla

tórtola, tor-to-lah s turtledove

tortuga, tor-too-gah s turtle; tortoise

tortuoso, tor-too´o-soh a winding; sinuous

tortura, tor-too-rah s torsion; torture

torvo, tor-vo a stern; grim; severe

torzal, tor-thahl s cord; twist

tos, toss s cough

tosco*, toss-ko a coarse; uncouth; ill-bred; rough

toser, to-sair v to cough

tosquedad, toss-kay-dahd

s roughness; coarseness

tostada, toss-tah-dah s toast

tostar, toss-tar v to toast; to roast

total, to-tahl s & a whole; total

tozudo, to-thoo-do a obstinate

traba, trah-bah s tie; ligament; obstacle; trammel

trabajar, trah-bah-Har v to work

trabajo, trah-bah-Ho s work; difficulty; hardship

trabar, trah-bar v to join; to fasten; to fetter

trabilla, trah-bee-l´yah s stitch; strap; small clasp

tracción, trah-the-on s traction

tractor, trahk-tor s tractor

traducción, trah-dook-the-on s translation

traducir, trah-doo-theer v to translate

traductor, trah-dook-tor s translator

traer, trah-air v to bring; to carry; to wear; to attract

tráfago, trah-fah-go s traffic; business

traficar, trah-fe-kar v to

trade; to deal in illicit business

tráfico, trah-**fe**-ko s traffic; business; commerce

tragaluz, trah-gah-**looth** s skylight

tragantón, trah-gahn-**ton** a gluttonous

tragar, trah-**gar** v to swallow; to believe credulously

trago, trah-go s swig of liquor

tragón, trah-**gon** a gluttonous

traición, trah´e-the-on s treason

traido, trah´ee-do a worn-out

traidor, trah´e-**dor** s traitor; a treacherous

traílla, trah´ee-l´yah s leash; lash

traje, trah-**Hay** s costume; dress; suit

trajinar, trah-Hee-**nar** v to convey goods

trama, trah-mah s plot; conspiracy

tramar, trah-**mar** v to weave; to plot

trámite, trah-me-tay s business transaction

tramo, trah-mo s plot of ground; flight of stairs

tramoya, trah-**mo**-yah s trick (theater); wile

tramoyista, trah-mo-**yiss**-tah s stagehand

trampa, trahm-pah s trap; snare; trapdoor; fraud

trampear, trahm-pay-**ar** v to swindle; to deceive

trampista, trahm-**piss**-tah s swindler

tramposo, trahm-**po**-so a deceitful; swindling

trancar, trahn-**kar** v to barricade; to bar a door

trance, trahn-thay s danger; critical moment; hypnotic condition

tranco, trahn-ko s long step or stride

tranquilizante, trahn-kee-le-**thahn**-te s tranquilizer

tranquilo*, trahn-kee-lo a tranquil; calm; quiet

transacción, trahn-sahk-the-**on** s compromise; negotiation; transaction

transbordar, trahns-bor-**dar** v to transfer; to change vehicles

transcribir, trahns-kre-**beer** v to transcribe; to copy

transcurrir, trahns-koor-**rreer** v to elapse

transcurso, trahns-koor-so s lapse of time

transeúnte, trahn-say-**oon**-tay s passer-by; a transitory

transferir, trahns-fay-**reer** v to transfer

transfigurar, trahns-fe-goo-**rar** v to transfigure; to transform

transformar, trahns-for-**mar** v to transform

tránsfuga, trahns-**foo**-gah s deserter; runaway

transgredir, trahns-gray-**deer** v to transgress

transigir, trahn-se-**Heer** v to compound; to compromise

transitar, trahns-se-**tar** v to travel; to pass by

tránsito, trahn-se-to s transit

transmitir, trahns-me-**teer** v to transmit

transpirar, trahns-pe-**rar** v to transpire; to perspire

transportar, trahns-por-**tar** v to transport; to convey

tranvía, trahn-**vee**-ah s streetcar

trapacería, trah-pah-thay-**ree**-ah s fraud; cheat

trapacero, trah-pah-**thay**-ro s deceitful

trápala, trah-**pah**-lah s

stamping with the feet; uproar

trapecio, trah-**pay**-the-o *s* swing; trapeze

trapero, trah-**pay**-ro *s* dealer in rags

trapisonda, trah-pe-**son**-dah *s* noise; bustle

trapo, trah-po *s* rag; tatter

tras, trahs *prep* after; behind

trasbordador, trahs-bor-dah-**dor** *s* car ferry

trascender, trahs-then-**dair** *v* to transcend; to have a strong scent

trasegar, trah-say-**gar** *v* to upset; to decant

trasera, trah-**say**-rah *s* back part; rear

trasero, trah-**say**-ro *s* buttock; *a* hind

trasgo, trahs-go *s* hobgoblin; bogeyman

trasiego, trah-se-ay-go *s* decanting

traslación, trahs-lah-the-**on** *s* transfer; adjournment; translation

trasladar, trahs-lah-**dar** *v* to transport; to translate; to copy

traslado, trahs-**lah**-do *s* transcript; transfer; removal

traslúcido, trahs-**loo**-thee-do *a* transparent

traslumbrarse, trahs-loom-**brar**-say *v* to be dazzled; to vanish

trasluz, trahs-**looth** *s* light seen through a transparent body

trasnochar, trahs-no-**char** *v* to sit up all night

traspapelarse, trahs-pah-pay-**lar**-say *v* to be mislaid among other papers

traspasar, trahs-pah-**sar** *v* to go beyond; to pass over; to transfer; to trespass

traspaso, trahs-**pah**-so *s* conveyance; trespass

traspié, trahs-pe-**ay** *s* trip; slip; stumble

trasquilar, trahs-ke-**lar** *v* to shear; to lop; to clip

trastienda, trahs-te-**en**-dah *s* stockroom

trasto, trahs-to *s* old furniture; lumber; rubbish

trastornar, trahs-tor-**nar** *v* to overthrow; to disturb; to confuse

trastorno, trahs-**tor**-no *s* overthrow; disorder; confusion

trastrocar, trahs-tro-**kar** *v*

to invert the order of things

trasuntar, trah-soon-**tar** *v* to transcribe; to abridge

trasunto, trah-**soon**-to *s* copy; likeness

trata, trah-tah *s* trade

tratable, trah-tah-**blay** *a* tractable; compliant

tratado, trah-tah-do *s* treaty; treatise

tratamiento, trah-tah-me-en-to *s* treatment

tratante, trah-**tahn**-tay *s* dealer in provisions

tratar, trah-**tar** *v* to treat (a subject); to trade; to use

través, trah-**vess** *s* bias; misfortune; **al –**, ahl –, across

travesía, trah-vay-**see**-ah *s* passage; crossing

travesura, trah-vay-**soo**-rah *s* prank; frolic; mischief

travieso, trah-ve-ay-so *a* lively; frolicsome; mischievous

traza, trah-thah *s* first sketch; outline

trazado, trah-**thah**-do *s* layout

trazar, trah-**thar** *v* to plan out; to trace

trébol, tray-bol *s* clover

trece, tray-thay s & a
thirteen

trecho, tray-cho s space;
distance

tregua, tray-goo´ah s
truce

treinta, tray-in-tah s & a
thirty

tremendo, tray-men-do a
tremendous; formidable

trementina, tray-men-tee-
nah s turpentine

trémulo, tray-moo-lo a
trembling

tren, tren s train;
equipment; retinue

trencilla, tren-thee-l´yah s
braid

treno, tray-no s
lamentation

trenza, tren-thah s
braided hair

trepar, tray-par v to climb;
to crawl

trepidar, tray-pe-dar v to
shake; to quake

tres, tres s & a three

triaca, tre-ah-kah s
antidote

tribunal, tre-boo-nahl s
tribunal; court of justice

triciclo, tre-thee-klo s
tricycle

trigésimo, tre-Hay-se-mo
a thirtieth

trigo, tree-go s wheat

trigueño, tre-gay-n'yo a
swarthy; brunette

trillado, tre-l´yah-do a
thrashed; beaten; trite

trillar, tre-l´yar v to
thrash; to beat

trimestre, tre-mess-tray s
three months; quarterly

trincar, trin-kar v to break
into small pieces

trinchar, trin-char v to
carve

trino, tree-no s trill; a
containing three things

tripa, tree-pah s tripe

tripe, tree-pay s plush;
shag

tripudo, tre-poo-do a big-
bellied

**tripulación, tre-poo-lah-
the-on** s crew of a ship

tripular, tre-poo-lar v to
man a ship

triscar, triss-kar v to
stamp the feet; to frisk

triste*, triss-tay a sad

tristeza, triss-tay-thah s
sadness; sorrow

triturar, tre-too-rar v to
grind; to pound

triunfar, tre-oon-far v to
triumph

trocar, tro-kar v to barter;
to exchange

trofeo, tro-fay-o s trophy

tromba, trom-bah s

waterspout

trompa, trom-pah s horn;
wind instrument; trunk
of an elephant

trompeta, trom-pay-tah s
trumpet

tronada, tro-nah-dah s
thunderstorm

troncar, tron-kar v to
mutilate

tronco, tron-ko s trunk

troncho, tron-cho s sprig;
stem; stalk

trono, tro-no s throne

tropa, tro-pah s troop

tropel, tro-pell s rush;
bustle; crowd

tropezar, tro-pay-thar v to
stumble; to trip; to meet
by chance

troquel, tro-kell s die;
stamp

trotar, tro-tar v to trot

trozo, tro-tho s piece;
fragment

trucha, troo-chah s trout

trueno, troo´ay-no s
thunder

trueque, troo´ay-kay s
exchange; barter

trufa, troo-fah s truffle

truhán, troo´an s rascal;
scoundrel

truncar, troon-kar v to
truncate; to maim

tubérculo, too-bair-koo-lo

s tuber

tubo, too-bo s pipe; tube

tuerca, too´air-kah s nut (*mech*)

tuerto, too´air-to *a* squint-eyed; one-eyed

tuétano, too´ay-tah-no s marrow

tufo, too-fo s fume; strong and offensive smell

tul, tool s tulle

tulipán too-le-pahn s tulip

tullido, too-l´yee-do *a* crippled; maimed

tumbar, toom-bar *v* to throw down; to tumble

tumor, too-mor s tumor

túmulo, too-moo-lo s tomb; burial mound

tumulto, too-mool-to s tumult; uproar

tunante, too-nahn-tay s rake; *a* cunning

túnel, too-nel s tunnel

túnica, too-ne-kah s tunic

tuno, too-no s truant

tupir, too-peer *v* to press close; to make compact; **-se,** to gorge oneself

turba, toor-bah s crowd; rabble

turbación, toor-bah-the-on s disturbance

turbar, toor-bar *v* to disturb; to trouble

turbio*, toor-be-o *a* muddy; troubled; obscure

turbión, toor-be-on s heavy shower

turbulencia, toor-boo-layn-the-ah s turbulence

turbulento*, toor-boo-len-to *a* turbulent; disorderly

turnar, toor-nar *v* to alternate

turno, toor-no s turn; alternate order

turquesa, toor-kay-sah s turquoise

turquí, toor-kee s deep blue color

turrón, toor-rron s nougat

¡tús! tooss *interj* word used for calling dogs

tutela, too-tay-lah s guardianship; tutelage

tutor, too-tor s tutor; instructor

tuyo, tuya, too-yo, yoo-yah *a* yours; of yours; thy; of thine

U

ubre, oo-bray *s* teat; udder

ufanarse, oo-fah-**nar**-say *v* to boast

ufano*, oo-**fah**-no *a* arrogant; cheerful

ujier, oo-**He**-air *s* usher

úlcera, ool-**thay**-rah *s* ulcer

ultimar, ool-te-**mar** *v* to end; to finish

ultimo*, ool-te-mo *a* last; latest; final

ultrajar, ool-trah-**Har** *v* to outrage; to despise

ultraje, ool-trah-**Hay** *s* outrage

umbral, oom-**brahl** *s* threshold

un, oon *a* (for **uno**) one; a; an

unánime*, oo-**nah**-ne-may *a* unanimous

unción, oon-the-**on** *s* unction

ungüento, oon-goo´**en**-to *s* ointment

único*, oo-ne-ko *a* unique; sole; singular

unidad, oo-ne-**dahd** *s* unity

uniforme, oo-ne-**for**-may *s* & *a* uniform

unión, oo-ne-**on** *s* union; joint; fusion; consolidation

unir, oo-**neer** *v* to unite; to join; to blind; to blend; **–se,** to associate

universidad, oo-ne-vair-se-**dahd** *s* university

universo, oo-en-**vair**-so *s* universe

uno, oo-no *a* one; sole; only

untar, oon-**tar** *v* to anoint; to grease

untuoso, oon-too´**o**-so *a* unctuous

uña, oo-n´yah *s* nail; hoof; claw; talon

uñada, oo-n´**yah**-dah *s* scratch with the nail

urbano*, oor-**bah**-no *a* urban; urbane; polite

urdir, oor-**deer** *v* to warp; to contrive

urgente*, oor-**Hen**-tay *a* urgent

urgir, oor-**Heer** *v* to be urgent; to urge

urraca, oor-**rrah**-kah *s* magpie

usado, oo-**sah**-do *a* used; worn out; secondhand

usanza, oo-**sahn**-thah *s* usage; custom; use

usar, oo-**sar** *v* to use; to accustom

uso, oo-so *s* use; service; custom; fashion

usted, oos-ted *pron* you (contraction of Vuestra Merced, lit., "your Honor")

utensilio, oo-ten-**see**-le-o *s* utensil; tool; implement

útero, oo-**tay**-ro *s* uterus; womb

útil*, oo-til *a* useful

uva, oo-vah *s* grape

V

vaca, vah-**kah** s cow; beef

vacaciones, vah-kah-the-**o**-ness s holidays

vacada, vah-**kah**-dah s herd of cows

vacante, vah-**kahn**-tay s vacancy; a vacant

vacar, vah-**kar** v to vacate; to be vacant

vaciar, vah-the-**ar** v to empty; to hollow out

vacío, vah-**thee**-o s vacuum; a empty

vacunar, vah-koo-**nar** v to vaccinate

vadeable, vah-day-**ah**-blay a fordable

vagabundo, vah-gah-**boon**-do a vagabond

vagancia, vah-**gahn**-the-ah s vagrancy

vago, vah-**go** s vagabond; a vagrant; vague

vagón, vah-**gon** s wagon; van

vaguear, vah-gay-**ar** v to loiter; to rove

vaguedad, vah-gay-**dahd** s vagueness

vaina, vah**í**-e-nah s scabbard; pod; husk

vainilla, vah**í**-e-**nee**-l'yah s vanilla

vaivén, vah**í**-e-ven s swaying; oscillation

vajilla, vah-Hee-l'yah s dishes

vale, vah-lay s promissory note; voucher

valedero, vah-lay-**day**-ro a valid; available

valedor, vah-lay-**dor** s protector; defender

valentía, vah-len-**tee**-ah s valor; courage

valer, vah-**lair** v to protect; to be worth

valeroso*, vah-lay-ro-so a valiant; brave

valía, vah-**lee**-ah s valuation; credit; value

válido*, vah-le-do a valid; binding

valido, vah-**lee**-do s favorite; a favored; esteemed

valiente, vah-le-en-tay a valiant; brave

valija, vah-**lee** Hah s valise; mailbag; post

valijero, vah-le-H ay-ro s mailman

valimiento, vah-le-me-en-to s use; benefit; favor

valor, vah-**lor** s value; price; courage

valorar, vah-lo-**rar** v to value; to appraise

vals, vals s waltz

vallado, vah-l'yah-do s stockade; fence

valle, vah-l'yay s valley

vanagloria, vah-nah-glo-re-ah s vainglory; conceit

vanidad, vah-ne-**dahd** s vanity

vanidoso, vah-ne-do-so a vain; showy

vano*, vah-no a vain;

useless; conceited

vapor, vah-**por** s vapor; steam; steamboat

vapul (e) ar, vap-poo-**lar** (-lay-ar) v to flog; to beat

vaquería, vah-kay-ree-ah s herd of cattle; dairy

vaquero, vah-**kay**-ro s cowboy

vara, vah-rah s rod; pole; shaft; ell

varar, vah-**rar** v to launch a ship; to be stranded

variar, vah-re-**ar** v to vary; to change; to alter

varilla, vah-ree-l´yah s metal rod; spindle

vario*, vah-re-o a various; variable; pl some; several

varón, vah-**ron** s man (male human being)

varonil, vah-ro-**neel** a manly; vigorous

vasar, vah-**sar** s shelf in a kitchen

vasija, vah-**see** Hah s vessel for liquids; bowl

vaso, vah-so s vase; vessel; tumbler; glass (to drink)

vástago, vahs-tah-go s stem; bud; shoot; offspring

vasto, vahs-to a vast; huge

vaticinio, vah-te-thee-ne-o s prediction

vaya, vah-yah s scoff; jest

vecindad, vay-thin-**dahd** s neighborhood; vicinity

vecino, vay-**thee**-no s neighbor; a neighboring

veda, vay-dah s time when hunting or fishing is forbidden

vedar, vay-**dar** v to forbid; to impede

vega, vay-gah s open country; plain

vehículo, vay-ee-koo-lo s vehicle

veinte, vay-in-tay s & a twenty

vejación, vay-Hah-the-on s annoyance

vejar, vay-**Har** v to annoy

vejez, vay-**Heth** s old age; decay

vejiga, vay-**Hee**-gah s bladder

vela, vay-lah s vigil; watch; candle; sail; awning

velar, vay-**lar** v to watch; to be awake; to keep vigil; to work at night

veleidad, vay-lay´e-**dahd** s whim; faint desire; levity

veleta, vay-**lay**-tah s vane; pennant; fickle person

velo, vay-lo s veil

velocímetro, vay-lo-**thee-** may-tro s speedometer

veloz*, vay-**loth** a swift; fast

vello, vay-l´yo s down; nap

vellón, vay-l´**yon** s fleece; tuft of wool

velludo, vay-l´**yoo**-do s velvet; a woolly; downy; hairy

velocidad, vay-lo-thee-**dahd** s speed

vena, vay-nah s vein; seam (geol.)

venado, vay-**nah**-do s deer; stag

vencedor, ven-thay-**dor** s victor; winner

vencejo, ven-**thay**-Ho s string; band; swallow (bird)

vencer, ven-**thair** v to vanquish; to conquer; to win

vencido, ven-**thee**-do a conquered; matured; payable

vencimiento, ven-the-me-**en**-to s expiration (of note)

venda, ven-dah s bandage; fillet

vendar, ven-**dar** v to bandage

vendaval, ven-dah-**vahl** s strong south wind; gale

vendedor, ven-day-**dor** s
  vendor; seller
vender, ven-**dair** v to sell;
  to betray
vendimia, ven-dee-me-ah
  s vintage; grape harvest
veneno, vay-**nay**-no s
  venom; poison
venero, vay-**nay**-ro s vein
  of metal; source
venganza, ven-**gahn**-thah
  s vengeance
vengar, ven-**gar** v to
  revenge; –se, to be
  revenged on
venia, vay-ne-ah s
  pardon; leave; bow with
  the head
venida, vay-**nee**-dah s
  arrival
venidero, vay-ne-**day**-ro a
  future
venir, vay-**neer** v to come;
  to spring from
venta, **ven**-tah s sale;
  roadside inn
ventaja, ven-**tah**-Hah s
  advantage; commodity
ventajoso*, ven-tah-**Ho**-
  so a advantageous
ventana, ven-**tah**-nah s
  window
ventear, ven-tay-**ar** v to
  blow (wind); to sniff; to
  investigate; to look out
  the window often

ventisca, ven-**tiss**-kah s
  snow-storm
ventorillo, ven-to-**rree**-
  l´yo s small inn near a
  town
ventosa, ven-to-sah s
  vent; cupping; airhole
ventrudo, ven-**troo**-do a
  big-bellied
ventura, ven-**too**-rah s
  luck; venture; risk
venturoso*, ven-too-ro-so
  a fortunate
ver, vair v to see; to look;
  to observe
vera, **vay**-rah s edge
verano, vay-**rah**-no s
  summer season
veras, **vay**-rahs s truth; de
  –, day –, in truth
veraz, vay-**rath** a
  veracious
verbo, **vair**-bo s word;
  verb
verdad, vair-**dahd** s truth
verdadero, vair-dah-**day**-
  ro a true; real; genuine
verde, **vair**-day a green;
  immature
verdín, vair-**deen** s mold;
  v greening
verdugo, vair-**doo**-go s
  hangman; executioner
verdura, vair-**doo**-rah s
  verdure; greens
vereda, vay-**ray**-dah s

  path; footpath
vergel, vair-**Hell** s orchard
vergonzoso*, vair-gon-
  tho-so a bashful;
  shameful
vergüenza, vair-goo´**en**-
  thah s shame;
  bashfulness; disgrace
verídico, vay-**ree**-de-ko a
  truthful
verja, **vair**-Hah s grate;
  railing
vernáculo, vair-**nah**-koo-
  lo a native; vernacular
verosímil, vay-ro-**see**-mil
  a likely; credible
verruga, vair-**rroo**-gah s
  wart; pimple
versado, vair-**sah**-do a
  versed; conversant
versar, vair-**sar** v to be
  conversant
vertedor, vair-tay-**dor** s
  sewer
verter, vair-**tair** v to spill;
  to empty; to pour; to
  translate
vértice, **vair**-te-thay s top;
  apex; vertex
vertiente, vair-te-**en**-tay s
  watershed; slope
vespertino, vess-pair-**tee**-
  no a of the evening
vestíbulo, vess-**tee**-boo-lo
  s foyer
vestido, vess-**tee**-do s

dress; clothes; garment

vestir, vess-**teer** v to clothe; to dress; to adorn; to cloak

vestuario, vess-too´**ah**-re-o s clothes; wardrobe; uniform; vestry

veta, vay-tah s vein; lode

veterinario, vay-tay-re-**nah**-re-o s vet; veterinary surgeon

vez, veth s turn; time

vía, vee´ah s way; road; track (railroad)

viajar, ve´ah-**Har** v to travel

viaje, ve´**ah**-Hay s journey; travel; voyage

viajero, ve´ah-**Hay**-ro s traveler; passenger

víbora, vee-bo-rah s viper

vibrar, ve-brar v to vibrate

vicario, ve-kah-re-o s vicar; a vicarious

vice versa, ve-thay-**vayr**-sah adv vice versa

viciar, ve-the-ar v to vitiate; to adulterate

vicio, vee-the-o s vice

vid, vid s vine

vida, vee-dah s life

vídeo, vee-day-o s video

vídeojuego, vee-day´o-Hoo´ay-go s computer game

vidrio, vee-dre-o s glass

viejo, ve-ay-Ho a old; ancient

viento, ve-en-to s wind

vientre, ve-en-tray s stomach

viernes, ve-air-ness s Friday

viga, vee-gah s beam

vigente, ve-Hen-tay a in force; standing

vigésimo, ve-Hay-se-mo a twentieth

vigilar, ve-He-lar v to watch over; to invigilate

vigorar, ve-go-rar v to strengthen

vihuela, ve-oo´ay-lah s guitar

vil*, veel a vile; despicable

vileza, ve-lay-thah s vileness

vilipendiar, ve-le-pen-de-ar v to revile

villa, vee-l´yah s town; municipality

villanaje, ve-l´yah-**nah**-Hay s peasantry

villano, ve-l´yah-no s rustic; a* villainous

vinagre, ve-nah-gray s vinegar

vinatero, ve-nah-tay-ro s wine merchant

vinazo, ve-nah-tho s very

strong wine

vínculo, veen-koo-lo s tie; link

vindicar, vin-de-kar v to vindicate; to avenge

vindicta, vin-dik-tah s vengeance

vino, vee-no s wine

viña, vee-n´yah s vineyard

violado, ve-o-lah-do a violet; colored; violated

violar, ve-o-lar v to violate; to ravish; to profane; to rape

violento*, ve-o-len-to a violent; forced; strained

violín, ve-o-leen s violin; fiddle

violón, ve-o-lon s double bass

vírgen, veer-Hen s virgin

viril*, ve-reel a virile

virrey, veer-rray´e s viceroy

virtud, veer-tood s virtue; force; vigor

viruela, ve-roo´ay-lah s smallpox

virus, vee-roos s virus

viruta, ve-roo-tah s chip; pl woodshavings

visa, vee-sah s visa

visaje, ve-sah-Hay s grimace; grin

víscera, viss-thay-rah s vital organs; offal

visitar, ve-se-**tar** *v* to visit; to inspect

vislumbrar, viss-loom-**brar** *v* to have a glimpse of

viso, vee-so *s* prospect; outlook

visor, fotografía, ve-**sor** fo-to-grah-fee-ah *s* viewfinder (camera)

víspera, viss-**pay**-rah *s* eve; *pl* vespers

vista, viss-tah *s* sight; view; eye; appearance; landscape; purpose

vistazo, viss-**tah**-tho *s* glance

visto, viss-to *a* obvious; clear; – **que,** – kay, whereas

vistoso, viss-**to**-so *a* showy

vitalicio, ve-tah-lee-the-o *a* life

vitamina, vee-tah-**mee**-nah *s* vitamin

¡vítor! vee-tor *interj* long live!

vitualla, ve-too-**ah**-l'yah *s* victuals; food

vituperar, ve-too-pay-**rar** *v* to blame; to curse

viuda, ve-**oo**-dah *s* widow

viudo, ve-**oo**-do *s* widower

vivac, ve-**vahk** *s* bivouac; military camp

vívaracho, ve-vah-**rah**-cho *a* lively; frisky

vivaz, ve-**vath** *a* lively; active

víveres, vee-vay-res *s* provisions

viveza, ve-**vay**-thah *s* liveliness

vividero, ve-ve-**day**-ro *a* habitable

vivienda, ve-ve-en-dah *s* house

vivir, ve-**veer** *v* to live; to last; to reside

vivo*, vee-vo *a* living; lively; acute; vivid

vizconde, vith-**kon**-day *s* viscount

vocear, vo-thay-**ar** *v* to cry; to vociferate

vocinglería, vo-thin-glay-ree-ah *s* clamor; outcry

volandero, vo-lahn-**day**-ro *a* volatile; fortuitous; fleeting

volar, vo-**lar** *v* to fly; to blow up

volatería, vo-lah-tay-ree-ah *s* fowls; flock of birds

volátil, vo-lah-til *a* volatile

volatín, vo-lah-**teen** *s* tightrope walker

volcar, vol-**kar** *v* to overturn

voltear, vol-tay-**ar** *v* to turn over; to turn (one's

back, etc); to capsize

volteo, vol-**tay**-o *s* whirling; overturning

volumen, vo-loo-men *s* volume; size; bulk; tome

voluntad, vo-loon-**tahd** *s* will

volver, vol-**vair** *v* to return; to send back; to turn

vorágine, vo-rah-He-nay *s* vortex

voraz*, vo-**rath** *a* voracious

vos, vosotros, vos, vos-o-tros *pron* you

votar, vo-**tar** *v* to vow; to vote

voto, vo-to *s* vow; vote; opinion

voz, voth *s* voice; word; vote; opinion

vuelco, voo-**ell**-ko *s* overturning

vuelo, voo-**ay**-lo *s* flight; projection

vuelta, voo-**ell**-tah *s* turn; return; back side

vuestro, voo-**es**-tro *pron* your; yours

vulgo, vool-go *s* multitude; general public

vulnerar, vool-nay-**rar** *v* to injure the reputation

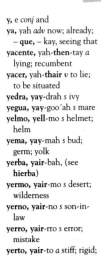

y, e *conj* and

ya, yah *adv* now; already;
– **que,** – kay, seeing that

yacente, yah-**then**-tay *a*
lying; recumbent

yacer, yah-**thair** *v* to lie;
to be situated

yedra, yay-drah *s* ivy

yegua, yay-goo´ah *s* mare

yelmo, yell-mo *s* helmet;
helm

yema, yay-mah *s* bud;
germ; yolk

yerba, yair-bah, (see
hierba)

yermo, yair-mo *s* desert;
wilderness

yerno, yair-no *s* son-in-
law

yerro, yair-rro *s* error;
mistake

yerto, yair-to *a* stiff; rigid;
motionless

yesca, yess-kah *s* tinder;
spunk

yeso, yay-so *s* gypsum;
plaster

yo, yo *pron* I

yogur, yo-**goor** *s* yogurt

yugo, yoo-go *s* yoke;
nuptial tie; oppressive
authority

yunta, yoon-tah *s* yoke
(of oxen)

yute, yoo-tay *s* jute

zaflo*, thah-fe-o *a* coarse; lacking manners

zaga, thah-gah *s* rear part; back of a carriage

zagal, thah-gahl *s* youth; shepherd

zaguán, thah-goo´ahn *s* porch; vestibule; entrance hall outside the house

zaherir, thah-ay-reer *v* to censure; to mortify

zahurda, thah´oor-dah *s* hovel; pigsty; ballast (*naut*)

zalamería, thah-lah-may-ree-ah *s* wheedling; flattery

zalear, thah-lay-ar *v* to shake something

zamarra, thah-mar-rrah *s* sheepskin jacket

zambo, thahm-bo *a* knock-kneed

zambra, thahm-brah *s* noisy mirth; feast

zambucar, thahm-boo-kar *v* to hide

zambullida, thahm-bool´yee-dah *s* ducking

zambullir, tham-bool´yeer *v* to plunge

zampar, thahm-par *v* to devour eagerly

zampuzar, thahm-poo-thar *v* to plunge; to dive

zanahoria, thah-nah-o-re-ah *s* carrot

zancada, thahn-kah-dah *s* stride

zancajo, thahn-kah-Ho *s* heel

zancarrón, thahn-kar-rron *s* fleshless bone

zanco, thahn-ko *s* stilt

zangandongo, thahn-gahn-don-go *s* idler; lazy person

zanganear, thahn-gah-nay-ar *v* to live in idleness

zángano, thahn-gah-no *s* drone; sluggard

zanja, thahn-Hah *s* ditch; trench

zanquear, thahn-kay-ar *v* to waddle

zaparrastrar, thah-par-rrahs-trar *v* to trail

zapata, thah-pah-tah *s* leather hinge

zapatero, thah-pah-tay-ro *s* shoemaker

zapato, thah-pah-to *s* shoe

zaque, thah-kay *s* leather flask; wineskin; tippler

zarabanda, thah-rah-bahn-dah *s* saraband (dance); bustle; noise

zaranda, thah-rahn-dah *s* screen; sieve

zarandajas, thah-rahn-dah-Hahs *s* trifles; odds; ends

zarandar, thah-rahn-dar *v* to winnow; to sift

zarapito, thah-rah-pee-to *s* curlew

zaraza, thah-rah-thah *s* chintz; printed cotton

zarceta, thar-**say**-tah *s*
moorhen

zarcillo, thar-**thee**-l´yo *s*
earring; tendril

zarpa, thar-pah *s* claw

zarrapastroso, thar-rrah-
pahs-**tro**-so *a* ragged;
shabby

zarria, thar-rre-ah *s*
leather thong; dirt on
clothes

zarzal, thar-**thahl** *s*
bramble patch

zarzamora, thar-thah-**mo**-
rah *s* blackberry

zarzuela, thar-thoo´**ay**-lah
s musical comedy;
vaudeville; light opera
or operetta

zascandil, thahs-kahn-**dil**
s busybody

zipizape, the-pe-**thah**-pay
s noisy scuffle

zócalo, tho-kah-lo *s* base;
footing

zoclo, tho-klo *s* wooden
shoe

zona, tho-nah *s* zone

zonzo*, thon-tho *a*
insipid; dull; stupid

zoquete, tho-**kay**-tay *s*
block; bit of bread;
blockhead

zorra, thor-rrah *s* female
fox; vixen; prostitute

zorro, thor-rro *s* male fox;

sly fellow

zorruno, thor-**rroo**-no *a*
foxy; foxlike

zorzal, thor-**thal** *s* thrush

zote, tho-tay *s* ignorant
lazy person; dunce

zozobra, tho-tho-brah *s*
uneasiness; anxiety

zueco, thoo´**ay**-ko *s* clog

zumba, thoom-bah *s* bell
worn by lead animal;
joke; jest

zumbido, thoom-**bee**-do *s*
buzzing sound

zumo, thoo-mo *s* sap;
juice

zurcir, thoor-**theer** *v* to
mend; to patch up

zurdo, thoor-do *a* left-
handed

zurrapa, thoor-**rrah**-pah *s*
lees; dregs; sediment

zurrar, thoor-**rrar** *v* to
curry; to dress; to tan; to
flog

zurriago, thoor-rre-**ah**-go
s leather whip

zurrido, thoor-**rree**-do *s*
humming; bustle

zurrón, thoor-**rron** *s*
leather pouch; husk

ENGLISH · SPANISH
INGLÉS · ESPAÑOL

a, ei *art* un; uno; una

aback, *a*-bAk´ *adv* detrás; atrás; **taken –,** sorprendido; desconcertado

abandon, *a*-bAn´-dñ *v* abandonar; **–ed** *a* abandonado; (morally) vicioso

abase, *a*-beis´ *v* humillar

abash, *a*-bAsh´ *v* avergonzar, consternar

abate, *a*-beit´ *v* disminuir; (price) rebajar

abbot, Ab´-ot *s* abad *m*.

abbreviate, *a*-brii´-vi-eit *v* abreviar

abbreviation *a*-brii´-vi-ei-shon *s* abreviatura *f*.; abreviación *f*.

abdicate, Ab´-di-keit *v* abdicar

abdomen, Ab´-do-men *s* abdomen *m*.

abduction, Ab-dŏk´-shon *s* abducción *f*.; rapto *m*.

abet, *a*-bet´ *v* apoyar; ayudar

abeyance, *a*-bei´-*a*ns *s* expectación *f*.; suspensión *f*.; **in –,** en suspenso

abhor, ab-joar´ *v* aborrecer

abhorrence, ab-jor´-ens *s* aborrecimiento *m*.

abide, *a*-baid´ *v* permanecer; **–by,** adherirse a

ability, *a*-bil´-i-ti *s* habilidad *f*.; aptitud f.

abject*, Ab´-CHekt *a* abyecto; vil

ablaze, *a*-bleis´ *a* en llamas; (emotion) ardiendo

able, ei-´bl *a* capaz, hábil; **to be –,** poder

ably, ei´-bli *adv* hábilmente

abnormal, Ab-noar´-mal *a* anormal; (misshapen) deforme

aboard, *a*-bó rd´ *a* a bordo

abode, *a*-boud´ *s* domicilio *m*.; residencia *f*.

abolish, *a*-bol´-ish *v* abolir; (cancel) anular

abominable, *a*-bom´-in-*a*-bl *a* abominable; pésimo

abominate, *a*-bom´-in-eit *v* abominar

aboriginal, Ab-o-riCH-in-al *a* aborigen

abortion, *a*-boar´-shon *s* aborto *m*.

abound, *a*-baund´ *v* abundar

about, *a*-baut´ *adv* casi; alrededor; *prep* alrededor de; cerca de; por; hacia

above, *a*-bŏv´ *adv* arriba; encima; *prep* encima de; sobre

abrasion, *a*-brei´-shon *s* raspadura *f*.; fricción

abreast, *a*-brest´ *adv* de frente

abridge, *a*-briCH´ *v*

abreviar

abroad, *a*-broad´ *adv* (to be –) estar en el extranjero; (to go –) ir al extranjero

abrupt*, *a*-rŏpt´ *a* abrupto; brusco

abscess, Ab´-ses *s* absceso *m.*

abscond, ab-skond´ *v* fugarse; huir

absence, *a*-sens *s* ausencia *f.*; (lack) falta *f.*

absent, Ab´-sent *a* ausente; –minded, - distraído

absentee, Ab-sen-tii´ *s* ausente *m.*

absolute*, Ab´-so-luut *a* absoluto; categórico

absolve, ab-solv´ *v* absolver; desligar

absorb, ab-soarb´ *v* absorber

abstain, ab-stein´ *v* abstenerse

abstainer, Ab-stein´-*a* *s* abstinente *m.*

abstemious, ab-stii´-mi-os *a* abstemio

abstinence, Ab´-sti-nens *s* abstinencia *f.*

abstract, Ab-strAkt´ *v* abstraer; extractar

abstract, Ab´-strAkt *s*

abstracto *m.*; *a* abstracto

abstruse*, Ab-struus´ *a* abstruso; recóndito

absurd*, ab-sĕrd´ *a* absurdo

abundant*, *a*-bŏn-dant *a* abundante

abuse, *a*-biuus´ *v* injuriar; abusar de

abuse, *a*-biuus´ *s* abuso *m.*; (insult) injuria *f.*

abusive*, *a*-biuus´-iv *a* abusivo; injurioso

abut, *a*-bŏt´ *v* lindar con

abyss, *a*-bis´ *s* abismo *m.*

academy, *a*-kAd´-i-mi *s* academia *f.*

accelerate, Ak-sel´-er-eit *v* acelerar

accent, Ak´-sent *s* acento *m.*; inflexión de voz *f.*

accentuate, Ak-sent´-tu-eit *v* acentuar

accept, ak-sept´ *v* aceptar; (opinion) acoger bien

acceptance, ak-sept´-ans *s* aceptación *f.*

accepter, ak-sept´-or *s* aceptante *m.*; (bill) aceptador *m.*

access, Ak´-ses *s* acceso *m.*; entrada *f.*

accession, Ak-se´-shon *s* (throne) ascenso m,; acceso *m.*

accessory, Ak´-ses-so-ri *s*

cómplice *m.*; *a* accesorio

accident, Ak´-si-dent *s* accidente *m.*

accidental*, Ak-si-den´-tl *a* accidental

acclaim, *a*-kleim´ *v* aclamar; aplaudir

acclimatize, *a*-klai´-met-ais *v* aclimatar

accommodate, *a*-kom´-o-deit *v* acomodar; adaptar; (lodge) alojar; (money) prestar dinero

accommodation, *a*-kom-o-dei´-shon *s* (lodging) alojamiento *m.*; (agreement) conveniencia *f.*

accompaniment, *a*-kŏm´-pa-ni-ment *s* acompañamiento *m.*

accompanist, *a*-kŏm´-pa-nist *s* acompañante *m.*

accompany, *a*-kŏm´-pa-ni *v* acompañar

accomplice, *a*-kom´-plis *s* cómplice *m.*

accomplish, *a*-kom´-plish *v* efectuar; concluir

accomplishment, *a*-kom´-plish-ment *s* cumplimiento *m.*; (completion) terminación *f.*; *pl* (talents) talentos *m. pl.*; prendas *f.*

accord, a-koard´ v
conceder; ajustar;
conciliar; s acuerdo m.

according to, a-koard´-ing
tu *prep* según, conforme

accordingly, a-koard´-ing-
li *adv* en conformidad

accordion, a-koard´-i-on s
acordeón m.

accost, a-kost´ v acercarse;
trabar conversación

account, a-kaunt´ s
cuenta f.; v dar cuenta;
(explain) explicar; **on
no –,** de ninguna
manera

accountable, a-kaunt´-a-bl
a responsable

accountant, a-kaunt´-ant
s contador m.; contable
mf.

accredit, a-kred´-it v
acreditar

accrue, a-kruu´ v crecer;
resultar

accumulate, a-kiuu´-miu-
leit v (gather)
amontonar; (hoard)
acumular

accumulator, a-kiuu´-
miu-lei-ta s acumulador
m.

accuracy, Ak´-iu-ra-si s
exactitud f.; precision

accurate*, Ak´-iu-reit a
exacto

accursed, a-kërst´ a
maldito; maldecido

accusation, a-kius -ei´-
shon s acusación f.

accuse, a-kiuus ´ v acusar

accustom, a-kös´-tm v
acostumbrar; soler

ace, eis s (cards) as m.

acetate, As´-si-teit s
acetato m.

ache, eik s dolor m.; mal
m.; v doler

achieve, a-chiiv´ v
ejecutar; (ambition)
lograr

achievement, a-chiiv´-
ment s ejecución f.;
(feat) hazaña f.

acid, As´-id, s & a ácido
m.

acid rain As´-id rein s
lluvia ácida f.

acidity, a-sid´-i-ti s acidez
f.

acknowledge, ak-nol´-eCH
v reconocer; confesar

acknowledgment, ak-
nol´-eCH-ment s
reconocimiento m.;
gratitud f.; confesión f.;
(receipt) acuse de recibo
m.

acme, Ak´-mi s colmo m.

acne Ak´-ni s acné m.

acorn, ei´-koarn s bellota
f.

acoustics, a-kus´-tiks s
acústica f.

acquaint, a-kueint´ v
familiarizar; informar;
(socially) conocer;
–ance, s conocimiento
m.; (person) conocido
m.

acquiesce, A-kui-es´ v
consentir, someterse;
–nce, s sumisión f.;
consentimiento m.

acquire, a-kuair´ v
adquirir; **–ment,** s
adquisición f.

acquisition, a-kui- s i´-
shon s adquisición f.

acquit, a-kuit´ v absolver;
liberar; exculpar

acquittal, a-kuit´-l s
absolución f.; descargo
m.

acre, ei´-kr s acre m.

acrid, Ak´-rid a acre;
mordaz

acrobat Ak´-ro-bAt s
acróbata mf.

across, a-kros´ adv a
través; prep a través de

act, Akt s (deed) hecho
m.; (of a play) acto m.;
(law) ley f. v operar; (in
theater) representar;
–or, s actor m.; **–ress,**
actriz f.

action, Ak´-shon s acción

f.; (law) proceso m.; (mil) batalla f.

active*, Ak´-tiv a activo

actual*, Ak´-tiu-al a actual; efectivo

actuate, Ak´-tiu-eit v impulsar; excitar

acumen, a-kiuu´-men s perspicacia f.

acute*, a-kiuut´ a agudo; (senses) penetrante

acuteness, a-kiuut´nes s (mind) perspicacia f.; (sharpness) agudeza f.

adage, Ad´-eiCH s adagio m.; refran m.

adamant, Ad´-a-mant a inexorable; firme

adapt, a-dApt´ v adaptar

adaptation, a-dAp-tei´-shon s adaptación f.

add, Ad v añadir; –up, sumar

adder, Ad´-a s (snake) víbora f.

addict, a-dikt´ v (oneself to) entregarse a; ta; s partidario/a mf.; entusiasta m.; med adicto/a mf.

addicted, a-dikt´-id a entregado; adicto; ta

addition, a-di´-shon s adición f.; in –, además

additional*, a-di´-sho-l a adicional

additive a-dikt´-iv s aditivo (alimenticio) m.

addle, Ad´-l a (egg) huero; (fig) inepto

address, a-dres´ v (letter, etc) dirigir; (a meeting) hablar; (a crowd) arengar; s (domicile) señas f. pl.; (speech) discurso m.; (to king, etc.) petición f.; dirección f.

addressee, A-dres´-ii s destinatario m.

adduce, a-diuus´ v aducir, alegar

adept, Ad´-ept s adepto m.; a hábil

adequacy, Ad´-i-kua-si s suficiencia f.

adequate*, Ad´-i-kuit a adecuado; proporcionado

adhere, Ad-jiir´ v adherir

adherence, Ad-jiir´-ens s adhesión f.; adherencia f.

adherent, Ad-jiir´-ent s (partisan) partidario m.; a adherente

adhesive, ad-jii´-siv s adhesivo m.; a adhesivo

adjacent, a-CHei´-sent a contiguo

adjective a-CHekt-iv s adjetivo m.

adjoin, a-CHoin´ v estar contiguo; (fields, etc) colindar; –ing a contiguo; colindante

adjourn, a-CHĕrn´ v aplazar; suspender

adjournment, a-CHĕrn´-ment s suspensión f.

adjudge, a-CHŏCH´ v adjudicar; (prize) conceder

adjudication, A-CHiu-di-kei´-shon s adjudicación f.

adjunct, A´-CHŏn-kt, s & a accesorio m., adjunto m.

adjust, a-CHŏst´ v arreglar; (mech) ajustar

adjustment, a-CHŏst´-ment s arreglo m.; (mech) ajuste m.

adjutant, A´-CHu-tant s ayudante m.

administer, ad-min´-is-ta v administrar

admirable, Ad´-mi-ra-bl a admirable

admiral, Ad´-mi-ral s almirante m.; –ty, ministerio de marina m.

admiration, ad-mi-rei´-shon s admiración f.

admire, ad-mair´ v admirar

admission, ad-mi´-shon s

entrada f.; acceso m.;
(confession) admisión f.
admit, ad-mit´ v (enter)
admitir; (acknowledge)
reconocer; (confess)
confesar
admittance, ad-mit´-ans s
entrada f.; admisión f.
admonish, ad-mon´-ish v
amonestar; reprender
admonition, ad-mo-ni´-
shon s amonestación f.
adolescence, Ad-o-les´-ens
s adolescencia f.;
pubertad f.
adolescent Ad-o-les´-ent s
& a adolescente mf.;
joven mf.
adopt, a-dopt´ v adoptar
adore, a-dór´ v adorar,
idolatrar
adorn, a-doarn´ v adornar
adornment, a-doarn´-
ment s adorno m.
adrift, a-drift´ adv (naut) a
la deriva, flotando
adroit, a-droit´ a diestro,
hábil
adulation, Ad-iu-lei´-shon
s adulación f.
adult, a-dŏlt´ s adulto m.;
a adulto
adulterate, a-dŏl´-te-reit v
adulterar
adultery, a-dŏl´-te-ri s
adulterio m.

advance, ad-vaans´ v
(ahead) adelantar; (push
forward) avanzar;
(price) encarecer; (lend)
anticipar; s (progress)
progreso m.; (money)
anticipo m.; (price) alza
f.; **in –,** (before)
anticipadamente;
(payment) por
adelantado; **–ment,** s
adelantamiento m.;
progreso m.
advantage, ad-vaan´-tiCH
s ventaja f.
advantageous*, ad-vaan-
tei´-CHos a ventajoso
advent, Ad´-vent s venida
f.; (eccl) adviento m.
adventitious, Ad-ven-
tish´-os a adventicio
adventure, ad-ven´-tiur s
aventura f.
adventurer, ad-ven´-tiur-a
s aventurero m.
adventurous*, ad-ven´-
tiur-os a aventurero;
(bold) valiente
adverb Ad´-věrb s
adverbio m.
adversary, Ad´-ver-sa-ri s
adversario m.
adverse*, Ad´-věrs a
adverso; contrario
advertise, Ad´-ver-tais v
anunciar; avisar;

publicar; notificar;**– er,** s
anunciante m.
advertisement, ad-věr´-tis
-ment s anuncio m.;
aviso m.
advertising, Ad-ver-tais´-
ing s publicidad f.;
propaganda f.; (adverts
collectively) anuncios
m. pl
advice, ad-vais´ s (opinion
offered) consejo m.;
(commerce) aviso m.
advisability, ad-vais´-a-
bil´-i-i s prudencia f.;
conveniencia f.
advisable, ad-vais´-a-bl a
aconsejabe; prudente
advise, ad-vais´ v
aconsejar; avisar;
notificar; **ill –d** mal
aconsejado; **well –d,**
bien aconsejado
adviser, ad-vais´-a s
consejero m.
advocate, ad-vo-kit´ s
abogado m.; v abogar
aerial, e-i´-ri-al s antena
f.; a aéreo
aerobics e´-er-o-biks s
aerobic m.
aerosol e´-er-o-sol s
aerosol m.
afar (from), a-faar´ adv
lejos
affable, Af´-a-bl a afable,

amable; cortés

affably, Af´-a-bli *adv*
afablemente

affair, a-fér´ *s* negocio *m.*;
(matter) asunto *m.*

affect, a-fekt´ *v* (act upon)
afectar; (pretend) fingir

affected*, a-fek´-id a
(moved) conmovido;
(assuming) afectado

affecting, a-fekt´-ing a
(pathetic) conmovedor

affection, a-fek´-shon *s*
afecto *m.*; cariño *m.*

affectionate*, a-fek´-shon-
eit a afectuoso; cariñoso

affidavit, A-fi-dei´-vit *s*
declaaración jurada *m.*

affiliate, a-fíl´-i-eit *v*
afiliar

affinity, a-fin´-i-ti *s*
afinidad *f.*

affirm, a-fèrm´ *v* afirmar

affirmation, A-fèr-mei´-
shon *s* afirmación *f.*

affirmative, a-fèrm´-at-iv
s afirmativa *f.*; a*
afirmativo

affix, a-fiks´ *v* pegar; (not
stick) fijar; sujetar; pegar

afflict, a-flikt´ *v* afligir

affliction, a-flik´-shon *s*
aflicción *f.*; desgracia *f.*;
(by death) duelo *m.*

affluence, Af´-lu-ens *s*
afluencia *f.*; opulencia

f.; riqueza *f.*

affluent, Af´-lu-ent *s*
afluente *m.*; a opulento;
copioso

afford, a-fórd´ *v* tener
medios para; permitirse

affray, a-frei´ *s* riña *f.*;
tumulto *m.*

affront, a-frònt´ *v*
afrentar; *s* afrenta *f.*

aflame, a-fleim´ *adv & a*
en llamas

afloat, a-flout´ *adv & a*
flotante; a flote

aforesaid, a-fór´-sed a
susodicho

afraid, a-fred´, **to be –** (of)
v tener miedo (de)

afresh, a-fresh´ *adv* de
nuevo

aft, aaft, *adv* (naut.) a
popa; en popa

after, aaft´-a *adv* después;
prep después de; según

aftermath, aft´-er-maaz *s*
consecuencias *f. pl.*

afternoon, aaft´-er-nuun *s*
la tarde *f.*

afterthought, aaft´-er-zoat
s reflexión tardía *f.*

afterwards, aaft´-er-uerds
adv después

again, a-guein´ *adv* otra
vez; de nuevo

against, a-gueinst´ *prep*
contra

age, eiCH *s* edad *f.*;
(period) siglo *m.*;
(ancient) antigüedad *f.*;
to be of –, ser mayor de
edad

aged, ei´-CHed a viejo;
anciano; *s* viejo *m.*

agency, ei´-CHen-si *s*
agencia *f.*; (fig.)
mediación *f.*

agenda A-CHen-da *s* orden
del día *m.*; asuntos *m. pl;*
a tratar

agent, ei´-CHent *s* agente
m.; comisionista *m.*

agglomerate, a-glom´-er-
eit *v* aglomerar

aggravate, Ag´-ra-veit *v*
agravar

aggregate, Ag´-ri-gueit *s*
agregado; totalidad *f.*; *v*
agregar

aggression, a-gre´-shon *s*
agresión *f.*

aggressive*, a-gres´-iv *a*
agresivo

aggrieve, a-griiv´ *v* apenar;
afligir; vejar

aghast, a-gaast´ *a*
estupefacto; horrorizado

agile, A´-CHil *a* ágil

agitate, A´-CHi-teit *v*
(shake) agitar; (mental)
perturbar; (stir up strife)
alborotar

agitation, A-CHi-tei´-shon

s agitación f.;
perturbación f.

ago, a- gou´ adv hace; **long
–,** hace mucho tiempo;
how long –? ¿ cuanto
tiempo hace ?

agog, a-gog´ adv & a
ansiosamente; con
curiosidad

agonize, Ag´-o-nais v
agonizar; torturar

agonizing*, Ag´-o-nais -
ing a atroz; angustioso

agony, ag´-o-ni s agonía f.;
(mental) angustia f.

agree, a-grii´ v concordar;
consentir; acceder;
convenir en; **–able** a
conveniente; agradable;
–ment s acuerdo m.;
convenio m.; (contract)
contrato m.

agricultural, a-gri-cŏl´-
tiu-ral a agrícola

agriculture, Ag-ri-cŏl-tiur
s agricultura f.

aground, a-graund´ adv
(naut) encallado

ahead, a-jed´ adv delante;
adelante

aid, eid s ayuda f.; socorro
m.; v ayudar; socorrer

AIDS eids s abbr of
acquired immune or
**immuno-deficiency
syndrome** síndrome m

de inmuno-deficiencia
adquirida, SIDA m.

ail, eil v estar enfermo;
estar malo; **–ing** a
enfermizo; **–ment** s
dolencia f.;
indisposición f.

aim, eim v (arms) apuntar;
(aspire) aspirar a; s
(arms) puntería f.;
(ambition) fin m.

aimless, eim´-les a sin
objeto; sin propósito

air, ér s aire m.; v (clothes,
etc) airear; **–
conditioning,** s
acondicionamiento de
aire m.; **–plane,** s avión
m.; aeroplano m.; **–gun,**
s escopeta de aire
comprimido f.; **–ily** adv
ligeramente; **–port** s
aeropuerto m.; **–ship** s
dirigible m.; **–tight** a
hermético; **–y** a aéreo;
(manners) airoso

aisle, ail s ala f.; nave
lateral f.; pasillo

ajar, a-CHaar´ a
entreabierto

akimbo, a-kim´-bou adv
en jarras

akin, a-kin´ a
emparentado; análogo

alabaster, Al´-a-baas-ta s
alabastro m.

alacrity, a-lAk´-ri-ti s
prontitud f.

alarm, a-laarm´ v alarmar;
s alarma f.; **–clock,**
despertador m.; **–ing*** a
alarmante; inquietante

alas! a-lass´ interj ¡ay!

albeit, oal-bii´-it conj
aunque; bien que

album, Al´-bom s álbum
m.

alcohol, Al´-ko-jol s
alcohol m.

alcoholic Al´-ko-jol-ik s &
a alcohólico/a mf.;
alcoholizado/a mf.

alderman, oal´-der-man s
concejal m.

alert, a-lërt´ a alerto;
activo; **on the –,** sobre
aviso; **–ness,** s viveza f.;
vigilancia f.

alias, ei´-li-as adv alias;
por otro nombre

alibi, Al´-i-bai s coartada f.

alien, eil´-yen s extranjero
m.; a ajeno

alienate, ei´-li-en-eit v
enajenar; (estrange)
alejar; apartar

alight, a-lait´ v bajar;
descender; apearse; a
encendido

alike, a-laik´ adv
igualmente; a semejante

alive, a-laiv´ a vivo;

activo

all, oal *a* todo; todos; *adv* enteramente, del todo; **–along,** todo el tiempo **;– but,** casi; **not at –,** de nada; de ningún modo; **–right,** bien

allay, a-lei´ *v* aliviar; calmar

allege, a-leCH´ *v* alegar; sostener

allegiance, a-lii´-CHi-ans *s* lealtad *f.*; fidelidad *f.*

allergic a-ler-CHik *a* alérgico/a *mf.* (to a)

allergy a-ler-CHik *s* alergia *f.* (to a)

alleviate, a-li´-vi-eit *v* aliviar; calmar

alley, Al´-i *s* callejuela *f.*; callejón *m.*

alliance, a-lai´-ans *s* alianza *f.*; unión *f.*

allied, a-laid´ *a* aliado; confederado

allocate, Al´-lou-keit *v* asignar; distribuir

allot, a-lot´ *v* asignar; (distribute) repartir; **–ment,** *s* (issue) reparto *m.*; (portion) lote *m.*

allow, a-lau´ *v* permitir; admitir; conceder

allowance, a-lau´-ans *s* (monetary) pensión *f.*; (food) ración *f.*;

(rebate) descuento *m.*

alloy, a-loi´ *s* aleación *f.*; mezcla; *v* alear

allude, a-liuud´ *v* aludir; referirse

allure, a-liur´ *v* atraer; fascinar; seducir

alluring, a-liur´-ing *a* atractivo; tentador; seductivo

allusion, a-liuu´-shon *s* alusión *f.*

ally, Al´-lai *s* aliado *m.*; *v* aliar; unir

almanac, oal´-ma-nak *s* almanaque *m.*

Almighty, oal-mai´-ti *s* El Omnipotente *m.*; *a* omnipotente

almond, aa´-mond *s* almendra *f.*

almost, oal´-moust *adv* casi; cerca de

aloft, a-loft´ *adv* arriba en alto

alone, a-loun´ *a* solo; solitario

along, a-long´ *adv* a lo largo; **–with,** *prep* con

alongside, a-long´-said *adv* al lado; (a ship) al costado

aloof, a-luuf´ *adv* lejos; lejos de; (reserved) apartado

aloud, a-laud´ *adv* alto; en

alta voz

alphabet Al´-fa-bet *s* alfabeto *m.*

already, oal-red´-i *adv* ya

also, oal´-sou *adv* también

altar, oal´-ta *s* altar *m.*

alter, oal´-ta *v* alterar; cambiar; reformar

alteration, oal-ter-ei´-shon *s* alteración *f.*; cambio *m.*; reforma *f.*

alternate, oal-těr´-neit *a* alternativo

alternating, oal-těr-nei´-ting *a* alternate

alternative, oal-těr´-na-tiv *s* alternativa *f.*; *a** alternativo

although, oal-Dou´ *conj* aunque; a pesar de que

altitude, Al´-ti-tiuud *s* altitud *f.*; altura *f.*

altogether, oal-tug-eD´-a *adv* en conjunto; completamente

alum, Al´-am *s* alumbre *m.*

aluminium, al-iu-min´-i-ŏm *s* aluminio *m.*

always, oal´-ues *adv* siempre

amass, a-mAs´ *v* acumular

amateur, Am´-a-tiur *s* aficionado *m.*

amaze, a-meis´ *v* asombrar; pasmar

amazement, a-meis´-ment

s asombro m.; pasmo m.

amazing*, a-meis´-ing a
asombroso; pasmoso

ambassador, Am-bAs´-a-dr
s embajador m.

amber, Am´-br s ámbar m.

ambiguous*, Am-bi´-guiu-
os a ambiguo; equívoco

ambiguousness, Am-bi´-
gui-os-nes s ambigüedad
f.

ambition, Am-bi´-shon s
ambición f.

ambitious*, ?m-bi´-shos a
ambicioso

ambulance, Am´-biu-lans
s ambulancia f.

ambush, Am´-bush s
emboscada f.; v asechar

ameliorate, a-mii´-lyor-eit
v mejorar

amenable, a-mii´-na-bl a
dócil; sumiso;
responsable

amend, a-mend´ v
enmendar; reformarse

amendment, a-mend´-
ment s enmienda f.

amends, a-mend´s´ s
compensación f.; make
– v compensar

amethyst, Am´-i-zist s
amatista f.

amiable, ei´-mi-a-bl a
amable; afable

amicable, Am´-i-ka-bl a

amigable; amistoso

amicably, Am´-i-ka-bli adv
amigablemente

amid, amidst, a-mid´, a-
midst´, prep entre; en
medio de; –ships, adv en
medio del buque

amiss, a-mis´ adv mal;
fuera de lugar; a malo;
irregular

amity, Am´-i-ti s amistad
f.; concordia f.

ammonia, a-mou´-ni-a s
amoníaco m.

ammunition, a-miu-ni´-
schon s munición f.

amnesty, Am´-nes-ti s
amnistía f.

among, amongst, a-
mŏng´, a-mŏngst´ prep
entre; en medio de; con;
en

amorous*, Am´-or-os a
enamorado

amount, a-maunt´ s
importe m.; suma f.; v
ascender a.; sumar

ample, Am´-pl a amplio;
abundante

amplifier, Am´-pli-fair s
amplificador m.

amplify, Am´-pli-fai v
ampliar

amputate, Am´-piu-teit v
amputar

amuck, a-mok´ adv

furiosamente

amuse, a-miuus´ v
entretener; divertir

amusement, a-miuus´-
ment s diversión f.;
entretenimiento m.

amusing*, a-miuus´-ing a
divertido

an, an art un; uno; una
(see a)

analogous*, a-nAl´-og-os a
análogo

analysis, a-nAl´-i-sis s
análisis f.

analyze, An´-a-lais v
analizar

anarchy, An´-aar-ki s
anarquismo m.

anathema, a-nAz´-i-ma s
anatema m.

ancestor, An´-ses-tr s
antepasado m.

ancestral, an-ses´-tral a
hereditario

ancestry, An´-ses-tri s
linaje m.

anchor, Añ´-ker s ancla m.
(in the plural, f.)

anchorage, Añ´-ker-eiCH s
anclaje m.

anchovy, An-chou´-vi s
anchoa f.

ancient*, ein´-shent a
antiguo

ancillary, An´-sil-a-ri a
auxiliar

and, And *conj* y ; e

anemic *a*-ni-mik *a med* anémico *m*.; (*fig*) débil; insípido *m*.

angel, ein´-CHel *s* ángel *m*.

anger, An´-guër *s* ira *f*.; cólera *f*.; *v* enfurecer; irritar; enfadar

angle, Añ´-gl *s* ángulo *m*.; (of a street) esquina *f*.; (opinion) punto de vista *m*.; opiniön *f*.; *v* (to fish) pescar con caña

angler, Añ´-gla *s* pescador de caña *m*.

angling, Añ´-gling *s* pesca con caña *m*.

angrily, Añ´-gri-li *adv* coléricamente

angry, Añ´-gri *a* enfadado; enojado

anguish, Añ´-guish *s* ansia *f*.; angustia *f*.

animal, An´-i-mal *s* animal *m*.; *a* animal

animate, An´-i-meit *v* animar; *a* animado

animated, An´-i-mei-tid *a* vivo; animado

animation, An-i-mei´-shon *s* animación *f*.; viveza *f*.

animosity, An-i-mou´- s i- ti *s* animosidad *f*.

aniseed, An´-i-siid *s* anís

m.

ankle, Añ´-kl *s* tobillo *m*.

annals, An´-*als* *s* anales *m*.

annex, An´-neks *s* anexo *m*.

annihilate, a-nai´-jil-eit *v* aniquilar

annihilation, a-nai-jil-ei´-shon *s* aniquilación *f*.

anniversary, An-i-vers´-a-ri *s* aniversario *m*.

annotate, An´-nou-teit *v* anotar; apuntar

announce, a-nauns´ *v* anunciar; publicar

announcement, a-nauns´-ment *s* anuncio *m*.

annoy, a-noi´ *v* molestar; dar la lata a…

annoying, a-noi´-ing *a* molesto; fastidioso

annual, An´-iu-al *a** anual; *s* anuario *m*.

annuity, a-niuu´-i-ti *s* anualidad *f*.; renta vitalicia *f*.

annul, a-nöl´ *v* anular; cancelar

annulment, a-nöl´-ment *s* anulación *f*.

anode, An´-oud *s* ánodo *m*.

anoint, a-noint´ *v* untar; ungir

anomalous*, a-nom´-a-los *a* anómalo

anonymous*, a-non´-i-mos *a* anónimo

another, a-nöD´-r *pron* & *a* otro; diferente

answer, aan´-sr *s* respuesta *f*.; contestación *f*.; solución *f*.; *v* responder; contestar

answerable, aan´-ser-a-bl *a* responsable; question que admite respuesta

answering machine aan´-sr-ing ma-shiin´ *s* contestador *m*.; automático

ant, Ant *s* hormiga *f*.

antagonist, An-tAg´-o-nist *s* antagonista *m*.

antecedent, An-ti-sii´-dent *s* & *a* antecedente *m*.

antechamber, An´-ti-CHeim´-br *s* antecámara *f*.

antedate, An´-ti-deit *v* antedatar

antediluvian, An´-ti-di-luu´-vi-an *a* antediluviano

antelope, An´-ti-loup *s* antílope *m*.

anterior, an-ti´-ri-or *a* anterior; precedente

anteroom, An´-ti-ruum *s* antesala *f*.; vestíbulo *m*.

anthem, An´-zem *s* antífona *f*.; (national

anthem) himno nacional m.

anthracite, An´-zra-sait s antracita f.

anthrax, An´-zraks s antrax m.

antibiotic An-ti-bai-o-tik s & a antibiótico m.

anticipate, An-tis´-i-peit v esperar; prever

anticipation, An-tis´-i-pei´-shon s anticipación f.; expectación f.

antics, An´-tiks s pl travesuras f.; payasadas f.

antidote, An´-ti-dout s antídoto m.

antifreeze, An´-ti-friis s anticogelante m.

antihistamine An-ti-jis-ta-miin s & a antihistamínico m.

antipathy, An-tip´-a-zi s antipatía f.

antiquarian, An´-ti-kua-rian s anticuario m.

antiquated, An´-ti-kueit-id a anticuado

antique, An-tiik´ s antigüedad f.; a antiguo

antiseptic, An-ti sep´ tik s & a antiséptico m.

antler, Ant´-la s asta del venado f.; cuerno m.

anvil, An´v-il s yunque m.

anxiety, Añk- s ai´-i-ti s ansiedad f.; inquietud f.

anxious*, Añk´-shos a ansioso; inquieto

any, en´-i a & adv cualquier; cualquiera; cualesquiera; alguno; algunos; alguna; algunas

anybody, en´-i-bo-di pron alguien; cualquiera

anyhow, en´-i-jau adv de cualquier manera

anyone, en´-i-uõn pron = **anybody** cualquier quiensea

anything, en´-i-zing pron algo; cualquier cosa

anyway, en´-i-ouei adv de cualquier modo

anywhere, en´-i-uè r adv en cualquier parte; donde quiera

apart, a-paart´ adv aparte; a un lado; separadamente

apartheid a-paar-tait s segregación racial f.; apartheid m.

apartment, a-paart´-ment s piso m.; apartamento m.

apathetic, Ap-a-zet´-ik a apático

apathy, Ap´-a-zi s apatía f.

ape, eip v imitar; s mono m.; mona f.

apéritif Ap´-e-re-tiif s aperitivo m.

aperture, Ap´-er-tiur s abertura f.

apex, ei´-peks s ápice m.

apiece, a-piis´ adv por persona; por cabeza; cada uno

apologize, a-pol´-o-CH ais v excusarse; excusar

apology, a-pol´-o-CHi s apología f.; justificación f.; disculpa f.

apostle, a-pos´-l s apóstol m.

apothecary, a-poz´-i-kari s boticario m.; farmacéutico m.

appall, a-poal´ v espantar; aterrar

appalling, a-poal´-ing a espantoso; aterrador

apparatus, Ap-a-rei´-tos s aparato m.; aparejo m.

apparel, a-pAr´-el s vestido m.; traje m.; indumentaria f.

apparent*, a-pei´-rent a aparente; manifesto; obvio

apparition, Ap-a-ri´-shon s aparición f.

appeal, a-piil´ s súplica f.; (legal) apelación f.; v apelar; suplicar

appear, a-pir´ v aparecer;

(in courts) comparecer

appearance, a-pir´-ans s apariencia f.; (in courts) comparecencia

appease, a-piis´ v calmar; apaciguar

appeasement, a-piis´-ment s apaciguamiento m.

appellant, a-pel´-ant s apelante m.; a apelante

append, a-pend´ v añadir; agregar; –age, s dependencia f.; accesorio m.

appendix, a-pen´-diks s apéndice m.

appetite, Ap´-i-tait s apetito m.; gana f.

appetizer, Ap´-i-tais -a s aperitivo m.

appetizing, Ap´-i-tais -ing a apetitoso; tentador

applaud, a-pload´ v aplaudir; alabar

applause, a-ploas´ s aplauso m.; aprobación f.

apple, Ap´-el s manzana f.; –tree, manzano m.

appliance, a-plai´-ans s utensilio m.; aparato m.

applicant, Ap´-li-kant s candidato m.; pretendiente m.; (petitioner) suplicante m.

application, Ap-li-kei´-shon s aplicación f.; uso m.

apply, a-plai´ v aplicar; (for employment, license, etc) solicitar; –to, dirigirse a; recurrir a

appoint, a-point´ v nombrar; (time) señalar; –ment, s (engagement) cita f.; (position) empleo m.; (official) nombramiento m.

apportion, a-pó r´-shon v distribuir; repartir; –ment, s repartición f.

apposite*, Ap´-o- s it a apropiado; oportuno

apposition, Ap-o- s i´-shon s aposición f.

appraise, a-pre s ´ v valuar; tasar; estimar; –ment, s valuación f.; tasación f.

appraiser, a-pre s ´-a s avaluador m.; tasador m.

appreciable, a-prii´-shi-a-bl a apreciable

appreciate, a-prii´-shi-eit v apreciar; valuar; tasar; (in value) subir en valor

appreciation, a-prii´-shi-ei´-shon s valuación f.; tasa f.; aprecio m.; (in value) alza f.

apprehend, Ap´-ri-jend v aprehender; arrestar; (understand) comprender; (fear) temer

apprehension, Ap-ri-jen´-shon s temor m.; comprensión f.; arresto m.

apprehensive*, Ap-ri-jen´-siv a aprensivo

apprentice, a-pren´-tis s aprendiz m.; v poner en aprendizaje

apprise, a-prais ´ v informar; avisar

approach, a-proach´ s acceso m.; v acercar; abordar

approbation, Ap-ro-bei´-shon s aprobación f.

approbatory, Ap´-ro-bat-ory a aprobativo

appropriate, a-prou´-pri-eit v apropiar; destinar; a* apropiado; conveniente

appropriateness, a-prou´-pri-eit´-nes s aptitud f.

approval, a-pruu´-val s aprobación f.

approve, a-pruuv´ v aprobar

approvingly, a-pruuv´-ing-li adv con aprobación

approximate, a-prox´-i-meit *a* aproximado; *v* aproximar; acercarse

appurtenance, *a-pĕr´-ten-ans* s pertenencia *f.*

apricot, *ei´-pri-kot* s albaricoque *m.*

April, *ei´-pril* s abril *m.*

apron, *ei´-pron* s delantal *m.*; (coarse) mandil *m.*

apt*, *Apt a* apto; (inclined) propenso

aptitude, aptness, *Ap´-ti-tiuud apt´-nes* s aptitud *f.*; (inclination) tendencia *f.*

aqueduct, *Ak´-ui-dŏkt* s acueducto *m.*

aqueous, *ei´kui-os a* ácueo

aquiline, *Ak´-uil-in a* aguileño

arable, *A r´-a-bl a* arable

arbitrary, *aar´-bi-tra-ri a* arbitrario

arbitrate, *aar´-bi-treit v* arbitrar

arbitration, *aar´-bi-trei´-chon* s arbitraje *m.*

arbitrator, *aar´-bi-treit-a* s árbitro *m.*

arbor, *aar´-ba* s emparrado *m.*; glorieta *f.*

arc, *aark* s arco *m.*; (shopping) galería comercial *f.*

arcade, *aar´-keid* s arcada *f.*

arch, *aarch* s arco *m.*; bóveda *f.*; *v* arquear; *a* principal

archaeology *aar´-ki-ol´-o-*CHi s arqueología *f.*

archbishop, *aarch-bish´-op* s arzobispo *m.*

archdeacon, *aarch-dii´-kn* s arcidecano *m.*

archer, *aarch´-a* s arquero *m.*

architect, *aar´-ki-tekt* s arquitecto *m.*

archive, *aar´-kaiv* s archivo *m.*

archway, *aarch´-uei* s arcada *f.*; bóveda *f.*

arctic, *aark´-tik a* ártico

ardent*, *aar´-dent a* ardiente

ardor, *aar´-da* s ardor *m.*; pasión *f.*

arduous*, *aar´-diu-os a* arduo

area, *é´-ri-a* s área *f.*; superficie *f.*

arena, *a-rii´-na* s arena *f.*; (bull ring) redondel *m.*; ruedo *m.*

argue, *aar´-guiuu v* discutir; disputar

argument, *aar´-guiu-ment* s argumento *m.*

aright, *a-rait´ adv* correctamente

arise, *a-rais´ v* elevarse; levantarse

aristocracy, *Ar-is-tok´-ra-ci* s aristocracia *f.*

aristocratic, *Ar-is-tok-rAt´-ik a* aristocrático

arithmetic, *a-riz´-met-ik* s aritmética *f.*

ark, *aark* s arca *f.*

arm, *aarm* s brazo *m.*; (gun) arma *f.*; *v* armar; armarse

armament, *aar´-ma-ment* s armamento *m.*; equipo *m.*

armchair, *aarm´-chér* s sillón *m.*

armful, *aarm´-ful* s brazada *f.*

armor, *aar´-ma* s armadura *f.*; coraza.*f*

armorer, *aar´-mo-a* s armero *m.*

armory, *aar´-mor-i* s armería *f.*; arsenal *m.*; museo de armas *m.*

armpit, *aarm´-pit* s sobaco *m.*; axila*f*

arms, *aarms* s armas *f.*; (crest) cota de armas *f.*

army, *aar´-mi* s ejército *m.*

aromatic, *Ar-o-mAt´-ik a* aromático

around, *a-raund´ adv* alrededor; *prep* cerca de

arouse, *a-raus´ v* despertar; excitar

arraign, *a*-rein´ *v* citar; acusar

arrange, *a*-reinCH´ *v* arreglar; colocar; convenir

array, *a*-rei´ *v* vestir; adornar; s formación *f.*; colección *f.*

arrear, *a*-rir´ s atraso *m.* –**s** s pl atrasos *m. pl.*

arrest, *a*-rest´ s detención *f.*; (goods) arresto *m.*; *v* prender; detener; arrestar

arrival, *a*-rai´-val s llegada *f.*

arrive, *a*-raiv´ *v* llegar

arrogant*, A´-ro-gant *a* arrogante

arrow, A´-rou s flecha *f.*; saeta *f.*

arsenal, aar´-sen-*al* s arsenal *m.*

arson, aar´-son s incendio premeditado *m.*

art, aart s arte *m.*

artery, aar´-ter-i s arteria *f.*

artful*, aart´-ful *a* artificioso; astuto

artichoke, aar´-ti-chouk s alcachofa *f.*

article, aar´-ti-kl s (news) artículo *m.*; (commodity) objeto *m.*; (clause) estipulación *f.*; *v* contratar; poner en aprendizaje

articulate, aar-tik´-iu-leit *v* articular

artificial*, aar-ti-fish´-*al* a artificial

artillery, aar-til´-*a*-ri s artillería *f.*

artisan, aar-ti- sAn´ s obrero *m.*; artesano *m.*

artist, aart´-ist s artista *m.*

artless*, aart´-les *a* natural; cándido; sin arte

artlessness, aart´-les-nes s candidez *f.*; naturalidad *f.*

as, A s conj como; tan; mientras; según; igualmente; pues que; –**for,** –**to,** en cuanto a; –**soon** –, tan pronto como; –**well,** también; –**yet,** hasta ahora

asbestos, as-bes´-tos s amianto *m.*; asbesto *m.*

ascend, *a*-send´ *v* ascender; subir

ascendancy, *a*-send´-en-si s ascendencia *f.*; poder *m.*

ascent, *a*-sent´ s subida *f.*; ascensión *f.*

ascertain, A-s*a*-tein´ *v* averiguar

ascribe, as-kraib´ *v* atribuir; asignar

ash, Ash s ceniza *f.*; (tree) fresno *m.*; –**tray,** cenicero *m.*

ashamed, *a*-sheimd´ *a* avergonzado

ashore, *a*-shór´ *adv* en tierra; *a* (aground) varado

ashtray Ash´-trei s cenicero *m.*

aside, *a*-said´ *adv* al lado; a un lado; aparte

ask, aask *v* preguntar; –**for,** pedir

askance, askew, aslant, *a*-skAns´, *a*-skiuu´, *a*-slaant´ *adv* al sesgo; oblícuamente

asleep, *a*-sliip´ *a* dormido

asp, asp s (snake) áspid *m.*

asparagus, as-pAr´-*a*-gos s espárrago *m.*

aspect, As´-pekt s aspecto *m.*

aspen, Asp´-n s álamo temblón *m.*

asperse, As-pěrs´ *v* calumniar

aspersion, As-pěr´-shon s difamación *f.*; calumnia

asphyxia, As-fik´-si-*a* s asfixia *f.*

aspirate, As´-pi-reit *v* aspirar; *a* aspirado

aspire, as-pair´ *v* aspirar

aspirin As-pi-rin s aspirina

f.

assail, *a*-seil´ *v* asaltar

assailant, *a*-sei-lant *s* agresor *m.*

assassinate, *a*-sAs´-si-neit *v* asesinar

assault, *a*-soalt´ *s* asalto *m.*; *v* asaltar; acometer

assay, *a*-sei´ *s* prueba *f.*; aquilatamiento *m.*; *v* aquilatar

assemble, *a*-sem´-bl *v* congregar; reunir

assembly, *a*-sem´-bli *s* asamblea *f.*; congreso *m.*; reunion *f.*

assent, *a*-sent´ *v* asentir; *s* asentimiento *m.*

assert, *a*-sĕrt´ *v* sostener; asegurar

assertion, *a*-sĕr´-shon *s* aserción *f.*; afirmación *f.*

assess, *a*-ses´ *v* (taxes) señalar; (damages) fijar; calcular; **–ment,** *s* tasación *f.*; valoración *f.*

assets, A´-sets *s pl* haber *m.*; capital *m.*; activo *m.*

assiduous*, *a*-sid´-iu-os *a* asiduo

assign, *a*-sain´ *v* asignar; (law) transferir; **–ee,** *s* apoderado *m.*; **–ment,** *s* asignación *f.*; cesión *f.*

assist, *a*-sist´ *v* ayudar; (charity) socorrer; (to be present) asistir; **–ant,** *s* ayudante *m.*; auxiliar *m.*; asistente *m.*

assistant *s* ayudante *mf*; auxiliar *mf*; (shop) dependiente/a *mf.*

associate, *a*-sou´-shi-eit *s* (partner) socio *m.* (companion) asociado *m.*; *v* asociar; asociarse

assort, *a*-soart´ *v* surtir; clasificar; ordenar; **–ment,** *s* surtido variado *m.*; clasificación *f.*

assuage, *a*-sueiCH´ *v* mitigar; apaciguar

assume, *a*-siuum´ *v* asumir; usurpar

assuming, *a*-siuum´-ing *a* presuntuoso; arrogante

assumption, *a*-sŏmp´-shon *s* suposición *f.*; postulado *m.*

assurance, *a*-shú r´-ans *s* seguridad *f.*; (insurance) seguro *m.*

assure, *a*-shúr´ *v* afirmar; (insure) asegurar

asterisk, *as*´-te-risk *s* asterisco *m.*

astern, *a*-stĕrn´ *adv* en popa

asthma, *az*´-ma *s* asma *f.*

astir, *a*-stĕr´ *a* activo; en movimiento

astonish, *as*-ton´-ish *v* asombrar; pasmar

astound, *as*-taund´ *v* aturdir; aterrar

astray, *a*-strei´ *adv* extraviado

astride, *a*-straid´ *adv* a horcajadas

astrology *a*-strol´-o-CHi *s* astrología *f.*

astronaut *as*´-tro-noat *s* astronauta *mf.*

astronomy *a*-stron-o-mi *s* astronomía *f.*

astute, *as*-tiut´ *a* astuto; sagaz

astuteness, *as*-tiut´-ness *s* astucia *f.*

asunder, *a*-sŏn´-da *adv* separar; romper en dos

asylum, *a*-sai´-lom *s* (mental) asilo *m.*; refugio *m.*

at, At *prep* a, en, sobre; **–all events,** en todo caso; **–home,** en casa; **–once,** enseguida; **–times,** de vez en cuando

atheist, ei-zi-ist *s* & *a* ateo/a *mf.*

athlete, Az´-liit *s* atleta *m.*

athletic, Az´-le-tik *a* atlético/a *mf.*

athwart, *a*-zuoart´ *adv* al través; *prep* a través de

atlas, At´-las *s* atlas *m.*

atmosphere, At-mos-fir s atmósfera f.; (fig) ambiente m.

atom, At´-om s átomo m.; **–ic** a atómico; **–ic energy** s energía atómica f.

atone, a-toun´ v expiar; reparar

atonement, a-toun´-ment s expiación f.

atrocious*, a-trou´-shos a atroz; espantoso

atrophy, At´-ro-fi s atrofía f.; v atrofiar

attach, a-tAch v (tie) atar; (stick) pegar; (annex) juntar; (law) embargar

attachment, a-tAch´-ment s adherencia f.; (liking) afecto m.; (law) embargo m.

attack, a-tak´ s ataque m.; agresión f.; v atacar

attain, a-tein´ v lograr; alcanzar

attainment, a-tein´-ment s logro m.; **–s,** (acquirements) conocimientos m. pl., alcances m. pl.

attempt, a-tempt´ v intentar; ensayar; (risk) emprender; (attack) atentar; s empresa f.; (attack) atentado m.

attend, a-tend´ v asistir a; **–to,** atender; (serve) servir; (nurse) cuidar

attendance, a-tend´-ans s servicio m.; asistencia

attendant, a-tend´-ant s sirviente m.; criado m.; compañero m.

attention, a-ten´-shon s atención f.

attest, a-test´ v atestiguar; atestar; certificar

attic, At´-ik s desván m.; guardilla f.

attire, a-tair´ s atavío m.; v vestir; adornar

attitude, A´-ti-tiuud s actitud f.; postura f.

attorney, a-tër´-ni s procurador m.; (commercial) apoderado m.

attract, a-trAkt´ v atraer

attraction, a-trAk´-shon s atracción f.

attractive*, a-trAkt´-iv a atractivo

attribute, a-trib´-iut v atribuir; imputar

attribute, At´-ri-biut s atributo m.; símbolo m.

attune, a-tiuun´ v acordar; armonizar

egg plant, oa´-ber-CHin s berenjena f.

auburn, oa´-ban a castaño

rojizo

auction, oak´-shon s subasta f.; almoneda f.

auctioneer, oak´-shon-ir s subastador m.

audacious*, oa-dei´-shos a audaz

audacity, oa-dAs´-i-ti s audacia f.

audible, oa´-di-bl a perceptible; audible

audience, oa´-di-ens s auditorio m.; publico m.; audiencia f.

audit, oa´-dit v intervenir; verificar una cuenta

auditor, oa´-dit-or s revisor de cuentas m.

augment, oag´-ment s aumento m.

augur, oa´-ga s presagio m.; v augurar; pronosticar

August, oa´-gost s agosto m.

august, oa-gŏst´ a augusto; majestuoso

aunt, aant s tía f.

auspicious*, oas-pi´-shos a propicio; favorable

austere*, oas-tir´ a austero

authentic, oa-zen´-tik a auténtico

author, oa´-za s autor m.; escritor m.

authoritative*, oa-zor´-i-ta-tiv *a* autoritativo; autoritario

authority, oa-zor´-i-ti *s* autoridad *f.*

authorize, oa´-zor-ais *v* autorizar

autograph, oa-to-graf *s, a* autógrafo *m.*; (signature) firma *f.*

automatic, oa-to-mAt´-ik *a* automático

automatic teller machine (ATM), kAsh dis-pen´- sa *s* cajero *m.*; automático

autumn, oa´-tom *s* otoño *m.*

auxiliary, oag-zil´-i-a-ri *a* auxiliar

au pair, oa´-pér *s* chica/o *fm.*; au pair

avail, a-veil´ *s* provecho *m.*; ventaja *f.*; *v* ser útil; –**oneself of,** valerse de

available, a-veil´-a-bl *a* disponible

avalanche, Av´-a-laanch *s* avalancha *f.*; alud *f.*

avarice, Av´-a-ris *s* avaricia *f.*

avaricious*, Av-a-ri´-shos *a* avaro; avaricioso

avenge, a-venCH´ *v* vengar

avenue, Av´-e-niuu *s* avenida *f.*; alameda *f.*

average, Av´-a-riCH *s*

término medio *m.*; *a* medio

averse, a-vêrs´ *a* adverso

aversely, a-vêrs´-li *adv* con repugnancia

aversion, a-vêr´-shon *s* aversión *f.*

avert, a-vêrt´ *v* prevenir

aviary, ei´-vi-a-ri *s* pajarera *f.*

aviation, ei-vi-ei´-shon *s* aviación *f.*

avidity, a-vid´-i-ti *s* avidez *f.*; voracidad *f.*

avocado, Av´-a-kaa-do˙ *s* aguacate *m.*

avoid, a-void´ *v* evitar

avow, a-vau´ *v* confesar; declarar

avowal, a-vau´-al *s* confesión *f.*; declaración *f.*

await, a-ueit´ *v* aguardar; esperar

awake, awaken, a-ueik´, a-ueik´-n *v* despertarse; (to call) despertar; *a* despierto

awakening, a-ueik´-ning *s* despertar *m.*

award, a-ouoard´ *s* sentencia *f.*; premio *m.*; *v* conceder

aware, a-ué´r´ *a* enterado; cauto

away, a-uei´ *adv* (absent)

ausente; **far–,** lejos

awe, oa *s* temor *m.*; (terror) pavor *m.*; *v* atemorizar; –**struck** *a* aterrado

awful*, oa´-ful *a* horroroso; terrible

awhile, a-uail´ *adv* poco tiempo; un rato

awkward*, oak´-uerd *a* (clumsy) desmañado; (inconvenient, embarrassing) embarazoso; (situation) violentô; difícil; –**ness,** *s* (clumsiness) torpeza *f.*

awl, oal *s* punzón *m.*

awning, oan´-ing *s* toldo *m.*

awry, oa-rai´ *adv* de través; *a* sesgado; torcido

ax, Aks *s* hacha *f.*

axle, Aks´-l *s* eje *m.*

azure, A´-sher *s* azul celeste *m.*

babble, bAb´-l s balbuceo m.; v balbucear

babe, baby, beib, bei´-bi s bebé m.; nene m.; infante m.

bacchanal, bAk´-a-nal s bacanal f.

bachelor, bACH´-el-or s soltero m.; (degree) licenciado m.

back, bAk s espalda f.; (animal) dorso m; v (support) apoyar; (bet) apostar; adv (behind) atrás; interj ¡atrás!
–bone, s espina dorsal f.;
–door, puerta trasera f.;
–ground, fondo m.;
–ing, apoyo m.; endoso m.; **–seat,** asiento de detrás m.; **–slide,** v reincidir; **–ward,** adv

atrás; a lento; atrasado;
–wards, adv atrás;
–water, s remanso m.

backer, bAk´-a s partidario m.; (sport) apostador m.

backpack, bAk´-pAk s mochila f.; v viajar con mochila

bacon, bei´-kn s tocino m.

bad*, bAd a malo; (health) enfermo

badge, bACH s divisa f.; símbolo m.; insignia f.

badger, bACH´-a s tejón m.; v molestar

badminton, bAd´-min-ton s bádminton m.

badness, bAd´-nes s maldad f.

baffle, bAf´-l, v frustrar; dejar perplejo

bag, bAg s saco m.; bolsa

f.; v ensacar

baggage, bAg´-iCH s equipaje m.

bagpipe, bAg´-paip s gaita f.

bail, beil s caución f.; fianza f.; v caucionar

bailer, beil´-a s fiador m.

bailiff, bei´-lif s alguacil m.

bait, beit s cebo m.; v azuzar; (molest) molestar

bake, beik, v cocer; (in oven) cocer en horno

baker, beik´-a s panadero m.

bakery, beik´-er-i s panadería f.

balance, bAl´-ans s (poise) balance m.; (accounts) saldo m.; (scale) balanza f.; v (poise) balancear; (accounts) saldar

balcony, bAl´-ko-ni s balcón m.

bald, boald a calvo; **–ness,** s calvicie f.

bale, beil s bala f.

baleful*, beil´-ful a triste; funesto

balk, boak, v frustrar; fracasar

ball, boal s bola f.; pelota f.; (dance) baile m.; **–point** (pen) s bolígrafo

m.

ballast, bAl´-*ast s* lastre *m.*

ballet, bAl´-ei *s* baile *m.*; ballet *m.*

balloon, ba-luun´ *s* balón *m.*, (toy) globo *m.*; globo dirigible *m.*

ballot, bal´-ot *s* votación *f.*; *v* votar; *s* cédula para votar *f.*

balm, baam *s* bálsamo *m.*; *v* embalsamar

balsam, boal´-sam *s* bálsamo *m.*

bamboo, bAm-buu´ *s* bambú *m.*

ban, bAn *v* proscribir; maldecir; *s* bando *m.*; (excommunication) pregón *m.*

banana, ba-naa´-na *s* plátano *m.*

band, bAnd *s* (brass) banda *f.*; (string) orquesta *f.*; (ligature) venda *f.*; *v* vendar

bandage, bAn´dicH *s* vendaje *m.*

bandleader, bAnd´-maas-tr *s* director de orquesta *m.*

bandy (legged), bAn´-di (legd) *a* estevado

bane, bein *s* veneno *m.*

baneful*, bein´-ful *a* venenoso; funesto

bang, bAñg *s* un golpe *m.*;

ruido *m.*; detonación *f.*; *v* (knock) golpear; (door) cerrar la puerta con estrépito

banish, bAn´-ish *v* desterrar

banister, bAn´-is-ta *s* baranda *f.*; barandilla *f.*

bank, bAñk *s* banco *m.*; (river) orilla *f.*; *v* (money, etc.) poner dinero en un banco; — **book,** *s* libreta de banco *f.*; **–er,** banquero *m.*; — **note,** billete de banco *m.*; **–rupt,** *a* insolvente; quebrado; **–ruptcy,** *s* bancarrota *f.*; quiebra *f.*

bank account, bAñk a-kaunt´ *s* cuenta bancaria *f.*

banner, bAn´-a *s* insignia *f.*; bandera *f.*

banquet, bAñ´-kuet *s* banquete *m.*; *v* banquetear

banter, bAn´-ta *s* zumba *f.*; burla *f.*; *v* burlarse

baptism, bAp´-tis m *s* bautismo *m.*

bar, baar *s* bar *m.*; (metal) barra *f.*; (courts) tribunal *m.*; *v* atrancar; (impede) impedir; **–maid,** *s* camarera de bar *f.*

barb, baarb *s* (implement) púa *f.*; lengüeta *f.*

barbarian, baar-be´-ri-an *s* bárbaro *m.*; *a* bárbaro

barbarity, baar-bAr´-i-ti *s* barbaridad *f.*

barbecue, baar-be-kiuu *s* barbacoa; *v* preparar en barbacoa

barbed, baarbd *a* armado de lengüetas

barber, baar´-ba *s* barbero *m.*

bard, baard *s* bardo *m.*; poeta *m.*

bare, bér, *v* desnudar; *a* desnudo; **–faced,** descarado; **–footed,** descalzo; **–headed,** descubierto; **–ness,** *s* desnudez *f.*; pobreza *f.*

barely, bér´-li *adv* apenas; escasamente

bargain, baar´-guin *s* ocasión *f.*; ganga *f.*; *v* regatear; **–ing,** *s* regateo *f.*

barge, baarCH *s* bote *m.*

bark, baark *s* (dog) ladrido *m.*; (tree) corteza *f.*; *v* ladrar; (tree) descortezar

barley, baar´-li *s* cebada *f.*

barman, baar-mAn *s* barman *m.*

barn, baarn *s* granero *m.*

barometer, ba-rom´-it-a *s*

barómetro m.

barracks, bAr´-aks s cuartel m.

barrel, bAr´-el s barril m.; (gun) cañón de escopeta m.

barren, bAr´-en a estéril; infructuoso

barrenness, bAr´-en-nes s esterilidad f.

barrier, bAr´-i-a s barrera f.

barring, baar´-ing prep salvo; excepto

barrow, bAr´-ou s carretón m.; carretilla f.

barter, baar´-ta v trocar; s trueque m.

base, beis v basar; fundar; s base f.; a* (vile) vil; bajo

baseball, beis-boal s béisbol m.

baseless, beis´-les a infundado

basement, beis´-ment s sótano m.

baseness, beis´-nes s bajeza f.; infamia f.

bashful*, bAsh´-ful a tímido; modesto; **–ness,** s timidez f.;,modestia f.

basic, bei´-sik a básico; fundamental; **-pay** sueldo m.; básico; **-rate** interés m.; base

basically, bei´-sik-ali adv esencialmente; fundamentalmente; en el fondo

basil, bAs-l s albahaca f.

basin, bei´-sn s palangana f.; (dish) tazón m.

basis, bei´-sis s base f.

bask, baask v ponerse al sol

basket, baas´-kit s cesta f.; canasta f.

basketful, baas´-kit-ful s cesta llena f.

bass, beis s (music) bajo; (fish) perca f.; róbalo

bassoon, ba-suun´ s fagot m.

baste, beist v pringar

bat, bAt s (mammal) murciélago m.; (games) bate m.

batch, bAch s (bakery) hornada f.; (things) cantidad f.; lote m.

bath, baaz s baño m.; **– room,** sala de baño f.

bathe, beiD, v bañar; bañarse

bather, beiD´-a s bañero m.

batter, bAt´-a s pasta f.; v apalear

battery, bAt´-a-ri s (car) batería f.; (of torch, radio) pila f.

battle, bAt´-l s batalla f.; v batallar

battleship, bAt´-l-ship s buque de guerra m.; acorazado m.

bauble, boa´-bl s baratija f.; chuchería f.

bawdy, boa´-di a impúdico; obsceno; indecente

bawl, boal v gritar

bay, bei s (geographical) bahía f.; (tree, leaf) laurel m.; a (color) bayo.; v (dog, etc) aullar

be, bi v ser; estar

beach, biich s playa f.

beacon, bii´-kon s fanal m.; faro m.

bead, biid s (adornment) cuenta f.; (drop) gota f.

beagle, bii´-gl s (hound) sabueso m.

beak, biik s pico m.; punta f.

beam, biim s (wood) viga f.; (light) rayo m.

beaming, biim´-ing a radiante

bean, biin s judía f.; haba f.; alubia f.

bear, bér s oso m.; (stock exchange) bajista m.; v (suffer) soportar; (burden) cargar; (produce) producir;

(birth) dar a luz

bearable, bér´-a-bl *a* soportable

beard, biird *s* barba *f.*

bearded, bird´-id *a* barbudo

beardless, bird´-les *a* imberbe

bearer, bér´-a *s* portador *m.*; (mech.) soporte *m.*

beast, biist *s* bestia *f.*; **wild –,** fiera *f.*

beastly, biist´-li *a** bestial; repugnante

beat, biit *v* (thrash) batir; golpear; (drum) tocar; (pulsate) palpitar; (vanquish) vencer; (time) marcar el compás; *s* (stroke) golpe *m.*; (pulse, etc) pulsación *f.*; (police) ronda *f.*

beating, biit´-ing *s* pulsación *f.*; (thrashing) paliza *f.*

beautiful*, biuu´-ti-ful *a* hermoso; bello

beautify, biuu´-ti-fai *v* embellecer

beauty, biuu´-ti *s* hermosura *f.*; **–spot,** lunar *m.*

beaver, bii´-va *s* castor *m.*

becalm, bi-kaam´ *v* calmar; (naut) encalmar

because, bi-koas´ *conj* porque; **–of,** a causa de

beckon, bek´-on *v* llamar por señas

become, bi-köm´ *v* hacerse; ponerse; llegar a ser; convenir a

becoming, bi-köm´-ing *a* decoroso; conveniente; favorecedor

bed, bed *s* cama *f.*; lecho *m.*; **–ding,** *s* ropa de cama *f.*; **–ridden,** *a* postrado en cama; **–room,** *s* alcoba *f.*; dormitorio *m.*

bedeck, bi-dek´ *v* adornar

bee, bii *s* abeja *f.*; **–hive,** *s* colmena *f.*

beech, biich *s* haya *f.*

beef, biif *s* carne de vaca *f.*

beer, bir *s* cerveza *f.*

beet, biit *s* biit-rut *f.*

beetle, bii´-tl *s* escarabajo *m.*

befall, bi-foal´ *v* suceder; acontecer

befitting, bi-fit´-ing *a* conveniente; propio

before, bi-fór´ *adv* antes; ya; *prep* delante de; enfrente de; ante; **–hand,** *adv* de antemano

befriend, bi-frend´ *v* amparar; ayudor

beg, beg *v* (charity) mendigar; (request) rogar; (implore) implorar

beget, bi-guet´ *v* engendrar

beggar, beg´-a *s* mendigo *m.*

beggarly, beg´-ar-li *adv* pobremente; *a* pobre

begin, bi-guin´ *v* empezar; comenzar

beginner, bi-guin´-a *s* novato *m.*; principiante *m.*

beginning, bi-guin-ing *s* principio *m.*; origen *m.*; comienzo *m.*

begone! bi-goon´ *interj* ¡fuera! ¡véte!

begrime, bi-graim´ *v* ensuciar

begrudge, bi-grŏcH´ *v* envidiar

beguile, bi-gail´ *v* engañar; seducir

behalf, bi-jaaf´, **on –of,** por; en nombre de; en favor de

behave, bi-jeiv´ *v* conducirse; comportarse bien

behavior, bi-jeiv´-ia *s* conducta *f.*; proceder *m.*

behead, bi-jed´ *v* decapitar

behest, bi-jest´ *s* mandato *m.*; orden *m.*

behind, bi-jaind´ *s*

posterior m.; adv atrás; por detrás; prep detrás

behindhand, bi-jaind´-jAnd adv con atraso; a atrasado

behold, bi-jould´ v mirar; observar; interj ¡he aquí! ¡mirad!

beholden, bi-joold´-n a obligado; deudor

being, bii´-ing s existencia f.; (human) ser m.; ente m.

belabor, bi-lei´-ba v apalear

belated, bi-lei´-tid a atrasado; tardío

belch, belch v (vulgar) eructar

belfry, bel´-fri s campanario m.

belie, bi-lai´ v desmentir; contradecir

belief, bi-liif´ s creencia f.; opinión f.

believable, bi-liiv´-a-bl a creíble

believe, bi-liiv´ v creer

believer, bi-liiv´-a s creyente m.; fiel m.

bell, bel s campana f.; (small size) campanilla f.; (sleigh) cascabel m.; (door, etc) timbre m.

belligerent, bel-li´-CHe-rent s beligerante m.

bellow, bel´-ou v vociferar; (bull, etc.) mugir

bellows, bel´-ous s fuelle m.

bellringer, bel-ring´-a s campanero m.

belly, bel´-i s vientre m.; panza f.

belong, bi-lŏng´ v pertenecer; atañer

belongings, bi-lŏng´-ings s pl posesiones f.; pl bienes m.

beloved, bi-lŏv´-id a querido; amado

below, bi-lou´ adv abajo; debajo; prep bajo

belt, belt, v ceñir s cinturón m.; (silk, etc); faja f.

bemoan, bi-moun´ v lamentar; deplorar

bench, bench s banco m.; tribunal de justicia m.

bend, bend v encorvar; plegar; curvar; s curva f.

bending, bend´-ing s recodo m.; a encorvado

beneath, bi-niiz´ adv & prep debajo; (unworthy) indigno de

benediction, ben-e-dik´-shon s bendición f.

benefactor, ben-i-fAk´-ta s bienhechor m.

beneficial*, ben-i-fi´-shal

a beneficioso; provechoso

beneficiary, ben-i-fi´-sha-ri s beneficiario m.

benefit, ben´-i-fit v beneficiar, aprovechar; s beneficio m.; provecho m.

benevolence, bi-nev´-o-lens s benevolencia f.

benevolent*, bi-nev´-o-lent a benévolo

benighted, bi-nait´-id a anochecido; ignorante

benign*, bi-nain´ a benigno

bent, bent a torcido; s (fig) inclinación f.

benumb, bi-nŏm´ v entorpecer; entumecer

benzine, ben´-s iin s bencina f.

bequeath, bi-kuiz´ v legar

bequest, bi-kuest´ s legado m.

bereave, bi-riiv´ v despojar; (death) desolar; privar; –ment, s aflicción f.; (death) duelo m.

berry, be´-ri s baya f.; (coffee) grano m.

berth, berz s (dock) anclaje m.; (on a train or ship, etc) camarote m.; (employment) empleo; *v* amarrar

beseech, bi-siich´ *v*
suplicar; implorar

beset, bi-set´ *v*
importunar; perseguir

beside, bi-said´ *prep* al
lado de

besides, bi-saids´ *adv*
además; *prep* adeás de

besiege, bi-sii CH´ *v* (*mil*)
sitiar; (*fig*) acosar

besmear, bi-smir´ *v*
embadurnar; untar

besotted*, bi-sot´-id *a*
tontb

best, best *adv* más bien; *a*
mejor; *s* lo mejor *n*.

bestial*, bes´-ti-al *a*
bestial; brutal

bestir (oneself), bi-stěr´
(uŏn-self´) *v* moverse

bestow, bi-stou´ *v* dar;
conferir

bestowal, bi-stou´-al *s*
donación *f*.; presente *m*.

bet, bet *v* apostar; *s*
apuesta *f*.; **–tor** *s*
apostador *m*.; **–ting,** *s*
apuesta *f*.

betide, bi-taid´ *v* suceder;
acontecer

betimes, bi-taims´ *adv*
temprano; al alba

betoken, bi-tou´-kn *v*
anunciar; indicar

betray, bi-trei´ *v* (*treason*)

traicionar; (*seduce*)
vender; (*secret*) revelar;
–al, *s* traición *f*.

betroth, bi-trouD´ *v*
desposar; **–al,** *s*
esponsales *m. pl*

better, bet´-a *s* superior
m.; *a* mejor; *adv* más,
mejor; *v* mejorar;
–ment, *s* (physically)
mejora *f*.; (materially)
mejoramiento *m*.

between, bi-tuiin´ *adv* en
medio; *prep* entre

bevel, bev´-l *v* sesgar; *s*
bisel *m*.; *a* sesgo

beverage, bev´-er-iCH *s*
bebida *f*.; brebaje *m*.

bevy, bev´-i *s* bandada *f*.

bewail, bi-ueíl´ *v* llorar;
lamentar

beware, bi-ué r´ *v*
guardarse de

bewilder, bi-uil´-da *v*
desconcertar; aturdir

bewilderment, bi-uil´-der-
ment *s* aturdimiento *m*.

bewitch, bi-uiCH´ *v*
embrujar; fascinar

beyond, bi-iond´ *adv* lejos;
prep tras; más allá; fuera
de

bias, bai´-as *v* influir; *s*
prejuico *m*.;
predisposicion

Bible, bai´-bl *s* Biblia *f*.

bibulous, bib-´-iu-los *a*
bebedor

bicker, bik´-a *v* reñir;
disputar

bickering, bik´-er-ing *s*
disputa *f*.; riña *f*.

bicycle, bai´-si-kl *s*
bicicleta *f*.

bid, bid *s* postura *f*.; pujar;
v licitar, ofrecer; **to
–good-bye,** *v* despedirse

bidder, bid-*a* postor *m*.

bidding, bid´-ing *s* postura
f.; subasta *f*.

bide, baid *v* esperar

bier, bir *s* féretro *m*.

big, big *a* grande; vasto

bigot, big´-ot *s* fanático *m*.

bigoted*, big´-ot-id *a*
fanático

bike, baik *s fam* bici *f*.; *v* ir
en bicicleta; ir en moto

bikini, bi-kii-ni *s* bikini
m.; biquini *m*.

bile, bail *s* bilis *f*.

bilingual, bai-ling´-ual *a*
bilingüe

bilious, bil´-i-os *a* bilioso

bill, bil *s* cuenta *f*.; (of
exchange) letra de
cambio *f*.; (poster)
cartel *m*.; (government)
proyecto de ley *m*.;
(bird) pico *m*.; **–of fare,**
lista de platos *f*.; **–of
lading,** conocimiento de

embarque *m*.

billet, bil´-et *s* (*mil*) alojamiento *f*.; *v* alojar

billiards, bil´-iards *s pl* billar *m*.

billion, bil´-yon *s* billón *m*.; (*mil*) millones *m*. *pl*

bimonthly, bai-mŏnz´-li *a* bimestral

bin, bin *s* cajón; ecipiente; hucha *f*.; (wine) portabotellas *m*.

bind, baind *v* atar; (-up) ligar; (books) encuadernar; **–over,** obligar a compareeer

binding, baind´-ing *s* (of books) encuadernación *f*.; *a* obligatorio

binocular(s), bai-nok´-iu-la(s) *s* binóculo *m*.; *s pl* gemelos *m*.

biography, bai-og´-ra-fi *s* biografía *f*.

biology, bai-ol´-o-CHi *s* biología *f*.

biped, bai´-ped *s* bípedo *m*.

birch, bĕrch *s* (tree) abedul *m*.; (punitive) férula *f*.

bird, bĕrd *s* ave *m*.; pájaro *m*.

bird's-eye view, bĕrds´-ai-viuu *adv* a vista de pájaro

birth, bĕrz *s* nacimiento *m*.

birthday, bĕrz´-dei *s* cumpleaños *m*.

birthplace, bĕrz´-pleis *s* lugar de nacimiento *m*.

birthrate, bĕrz´-reit *s* natalidad *f*.

biscuit, bis´-kit *s* bizcocho *m*.

bisect, bai-sekt´ *v* bisecar

bishop, bish´-op *s* obispo *m*.

bit, bit *s* pedazo *m*.; (horse) bocado del freno *m*.

bite, bait *v* morder; *s* mordedura *f*.; (insect) picadura *f*.

biting*, bai´-ting *a* (fig) cáustico

bitter*, bit´-a *a* amargo; **–ness,** *s* amargura *f*.

black, blAk *a* (color) negro *m*.; *a* negro; oscuro; *v* ennegrecer; (shoes) embetunar

blackberry, blAk´-be-ri *s* zarzamora *f*.

blackbird, blAk´-bĕrd *s* mirlo *m*.

blacken, blAk´-en *v* ennegrecer

blacking, blAk´-ing *s* betún *m*.

blackmail, blAk´-meil *s*

chantaje *m*.; *v* sacar dinero con amenazas

black market, blAk maar´-ket estraperlo *m*.; mercado *m*.; negro

blacksmith, blAk´-smiz *s* herrero *m*.; foriador *m*.

blackthorn, blAk´-zoarn *s* endrino *m*.

bladder, blAd´-a *s* vejiga *f*.

blade, bleid *s* (cutting part) hoja *f*.; (grass) brizna *f*.; (oar) pala de remo *f*.

blame, bleim *v* reprobar; censurar; *s* censura *f*.; culpa *f*.; **–less*,** *a* irreprochable

blanch, blaanch *v* blanquear

bland, blAnd *a* suave; blando

blandishment, blAn´-dish-ment *s* caricia *f*.

blank, blAñk *s* blanco *m*.; *a* (mental) desconcertado; (vacant) blanco

blanket, blAñ´-ket *s* manta *f*.

blare, blé r *v* vociferar; resonar

blaspheme, blAs-fiim´ *v* blasfemar

blasphemy, blAs´-fi-mi *s* blasfemia *f*.

blast, blaast v (explode) minar; (blight) marchitar; s (gust) ráfaga f.; (explosive) explosion

blatant, blei´-tant a ruidoso

blaze, bleis v flamear; s (flame) llama f.; (conflagration) hoguera f.; **–of light,** luz brillante f.

bleach, bliich v blanquear; s lejía

bleak*, bliik a (cold) frío; (desolate) desierto

bleat, bliit v balar; s balido m.

bleed, bliid v sangrar

bleeding, bliid´-ing s sangrante; sangriento

blemish, blem´-ish s imperfección f.; (character) deshonra f.; v infamar

blend, blend v mezclar; s mezcla f.

bless, bles v bendecir; **–ed,** a bendito

blight, blait s (disease) tizón m.

blind, blaind a (sight) ciego; v cegar; **–fold,** vendar los ojos; **–man,** s ciego m.; **–ness,** ceguera f.

blind, blaind s (window) persiana f.; (venetian) celosía f.

blink, bliňk v pestañear; **–er,** s (horse) anteojera f.

bliss, blis s felicidad f.; gloria f.

blissful*, blis´-ful a bienaventurado; dichoso

blister, blis´-ta s ampolla f.

blithe*, blaiD a alegre; contento

blizzard, blis ´-ard s ventisca f.

bloat, blout v hinchar; hincharse

bloater, blout´-a s arenque; ahumado m.

block, blok v bloquear; s bloque m.; v embotellar; bloquear

blockade, blok´-eid s bloqueo m.; v bloquear

blonde, blond s & a rubio/a mf.

blood, blŏd s sangre f.

bloodhound, blŏd´-jaund s sabueso m.

blood pressure, blŏd presh ¹er s presión f.; sanguinea; tensión f.; arterial; **high -** hipertensión

bloodshed, blŏd´-shed s matanza f.

bloodthirsty, blŏd´-zĕrs-ti a sanguinario

bloody, blŏd-i a sangriento

bloom, bluum s flor f.; v florecer

blossom, blos´-om s capullo m.; v florecer

blot, blot v emborronar; secar; s borrón m.; (character) mancha f.

blotch, bloch s roncha f.; mancha f.

blotting paper, blot´-ing-pei´-pa s papel secante m.

blouse, blaus s blusa f.

blow, blou v soplar; (wind) llevar; (nose, trumpet, etc) sonar; s (knock) golpe m.; soplo m.

blowpipe, blou´-paip s soplete m.

blubber, blŏb´-a s grasa de ballena f.; v gimotear

bludgeon, blŏ CH´-en s porra f.; garrote m.; garrotear

blue, bluu a azul; **--bell,** s campanilla f.; **--stocking,** s literata f.

bluff, blŏf s fanfarronada f.; v alardear

bluish, bluu´-ish a azulado; azulino

blunder, blŏn´-da v

cometer un error; s
disparate m.

blunt, blŏnt v embotar; a*
embotado; (brusque)
brusco; **–ness,** s
embotadura f.;
(manner) grosería f.

blur, blẽr v hacer borroso;
s borrón m.

blush, blŏsh v sonrojarse; s
rubor m.; sonrojo m.

bluster, blŏs´-ta v bravear;
s bravata f.; **–er,**
fanfarrón m.; **–ing*,** a
ruidoso; (gusty)
tempestuoso

boar, bó r s verraco m.;
wild –jabalí m.

board, bó rd s (wood)
tabla f.; (directors, etc)
consejo m.; (food)
pensión f.; v (carpentry)
entablar; **–er,** s huésped
m.; (school) interno m.;
–inghouse, casa de
huéspedes f.; pensión f.;
–ing school, internado
f.

boast, boust v jactarse; s
fanfarronada f.; alarde
m.

boaster, boust´-a s
fanfarrón m.; jaque m.

boat, bout s barco m.;
vapor m.; (row) bote de
remos m.; **motor–,**

lancha motora f.; **steam–**, buque de vapor m.

boathook, bout´-juk s
bichero m.

boating, bout´-ing s paseo
en bote m.

boatman, bout´-mAn s
barquero m.

boatswain, bou-s'n s
contramaestre m.

bob, bob v bambolearse

bobbin, bob´-in s bobina f.

bode, boud v presagiar

bodice, bod´-is s corpiño
m.

bodily, bod´-i-li adv
corporalmente; a
corpóreo

bodkin, bod´-kin s punzón
m.

body, bod´-i s cuerpo m.;
(vehicle) carrocería f.

bog, bog s pantano m.; v
atascar

bogeyman, bou´-gui s
(goblin) duende m.

boggy, bo´-gui a
pantanoso

boil, boil v (fluids) hervir;
(food in fluids) cocer; s
(tumor) furúnculo m.

boiler, boil´-a s olla f.;
caldera f.

boisterous*, boist´-er-os a
tempestuoso; borrascoso;
violento

bold*, bould a intrépido;
audaz

boldness, bould´-nes s
intrepidez f.; audacia f.

bolster, boul´-sta v apoyar;
s travesero m.

bolt, boult v cerrar con
cerrojo; (horse)
desbocarse; s cerrojo m.;
thunder–, rayo m.

bomb, bom s bomba f.

bombard, bom-baa rd´ v
bombardear

bombastic, bom-bAs´-tik a
rimbombante ampuloso

bond, bond s (link) lazo;
vínculo; (obligation,
stock) obligación f.;
bono m.; (customs) **in –,**
en depósito m.

bondage, bon´-diCH s
esclavitud f.;
servidumbre f.

bone, boun s hueso m.;
(fish) espina f.

bonfire, bon´-fair s
hoguera f.

bonnet, bon´-et s gorro
m.; gorra f.

bonus, bou´-nas s
bonificación f.

bony, bou´-ni a oseo;
huesudo

book, buk v registrar; s
libro m.; **–binder,** s
encuadernador m.;

–**case**, s librería m.; **–ing office**, s taquilla f.; –– **keeper**, s tenedor de libros m.; **–seller**, s librero m.; **–shop**, s librería f.; **–s**, puesto de libros m.; **–worm**, s ratón de biblioteca m.

boom, buum s (business) prosperidad f.; (noise) estampido m.; (ship) cadena de puerto f.; v (noise) dar bombo; (prices) estar en auge

boon, buun s beneficio m.; dicha f.

boor, bú r s patán m.; villano m.

boorish*, bú r´-ish a rústico

boot, buut s bota f.; –– **maker**, zapatero m.

booth, buuD s barraca f.; cabaña f.

booty, buu´-ti s botín m.; saqueo m.

booze, buus s bebida f.; alcohol m; borrachera f.; v beber; emborracharse

border, boar´-da s (ornamental edge) orilla f.; (frontier) frontera; v orillar

bordering, boar´-der-ing a contiguo; lindante

bore, bór v (pierce)

perforar; (drill) taladrar; s barreno m.; (caliber) calibre m.; (person) pesado m.

boring, bór´ing a aburrido

born, boarn a nacido

borough, bör´-o s distrito m.

borrow, bor´-ou v pedir prestado

bosom, bu´-s om s seno m.

botanist, bot´-a-nist s botánico m.

botany, bot´-a-ni s botánica f.

both, bouz a ambos; conj tanto como

bother, boD´-a v fastidiar, incomodarse; s molestia f.

bottle, bot´-el s botella f.; v embotellar

bottom, bot´-om s fondo m.; (seat) posterior m.

bottomless, bot´-om-les a sin fondo

boudoir, buu´-duaa r s tocador de (habitación) m.

bough, bau s rama de árbol f.

bounce, bauns v saltar; botar; s salto mf.

bound, baund v limitar; (jump) saltar; s (jump) salto m.; **–for**, a

destinado

boundary, baun´-da-ri s frontera f.; límite m.

bounteous*, **bountiful***, baun´-ti-os, baun´-ti-ful a generoso; liberal

bounty, baun´-ti s generosidad f.; (gift) prima f.

bouquet, bu´-kei s ramo m.; ramillete f.; (wine) olor m.

bout, baut s turno m.

bow, bau v saludar; inclinarse; (bend) doblarse; s inclinación f.; reverencia f.; (ship) proa f.

bow, bou s (archery) arco m.; (tie) corbata de lazo f.; (violin) arco de violín m.; (knot) nudo m.

bowels, bau´-els s pl intestinos m.

bower, bau´-a s cenador m.

bowl, baul, v bolear; s tazón m.; (ball) bola f.

box, boks s; (small) cajita f.; (medium size) caja f.; (large) cajón m.; (theater) palco m.; (on the ear) bofetada f.

boxing, bok´-sing s boxeo

m.

boy, boi s muchacho m.; niño m.; chico m.

boycott, boi´-kot s boicoteo m.; v excluir; boicotear

boyfriend, boi-frend s novio m.; amigo m.

boyhood, boi´-jud s niñez f.

boyish, boi´-ish a pueril; juvenil

bra, braa s sostén m.; sujetador m.

brace, breis v atar; (invigorate) bracear; s abrazadera f.; (two) par m.; –s, pl tirantes m.

bracelet, breis´-let s brazalete m.; pulsera f.

bracing, breis´-ing a fortificante

bracken, brAk´-n s helecho m.

bracket, brAk´-et s paréntesis m.; (wall) soporte m.; v poner en paréntesis

brackish, brAk´-ish a salobre

brag, brAg v jactarse; s jactancia f.

braggart, brAg´-aart s fanfarrón m.

braid, breid s trenza f.; galón m.; v trenzar

brain, brein s cerebro m.; sesos m. pl.

brainless, brein´-les a tonto

braise, breis v cocer en marmita

brake, breik s freno m.; v frenar

bramble, brAm´-bl s zarza f.

bran, brAn s salvado m.; afrecho m.

branch, braanch s rama f.; (business) sucursal f.; v ramificarse

brand, brAnd s (trademark) marca f.; (fire) tizón m.; (stigma) estigma f.; v marcar; estigmatizar; (cattle) herrar

brandish, brAn´-dish v blandir

brandy, brAn´-di s brandy m.

brass, braas s latón m.

brat, brAt s mocoso m.

bravado, brA-vaa´-dou s bravata f.

brave, breiv a* bravo; valiente.; v bravear

bravery, breiv´-er-i s valentía f.

brawl, broal v alborotar; s alboroto m.

brawn, broan s carne de cerdo f.; (muscle) fuerza muscular f.

brawny, broa´-ni a musculoso

bray, brei v rebuznar

brazen, brei´-s en a bronceado; (insolent) desvergonzado

brazier, brei´-s -a s latonero m.; (fire) brasero m.

Brazil nut, bres-il ill´-nöt s nuez del Brasíl f.

breach, briich s (aperture) brecha f.; (contract) rotura f.; (law) violación f.

bread, bred s pan m.

breadth, bredz s anchura f.

break, breik v romper; (tame) domar; (limb) fracturar; (law) violar; (contract, promise) romper; s rotura f.; (pause) pausa f.

breakage, breik´-iCH s fractura f.; rotura f.

breakdown, breik´-daun s derrumbamiento m.

breaker, breik´-a s rompedor m.; (law) infractor m.

breakers, breik´-a s, s pl (sea) olas grandes m.

breakfast, brek´-fast s desayuno m.; v

desayunarse

breakthrough, breik-zruu *v* salvar un obstáculo

breakwater, breik´-uo*a*-tr *s* rompeolas *m.*

bream, briim *s* (river) sargo *m.*; (sea) besugo *m.*

breast, brest *s* seno *m.*; (chest) pecho *m.*

breastbone, brest´-boun *s* esternón *m.*

breath, brez *s* respiración *f.*; (vapor) aliento *m.*

breathe, briiD, *v* respirar

breathless, brez´-les *a* falto de aliento

bred, bred *a* criado; educado

breech, briich *s* (arms) culata *f.*

breed, briid *v* criar; multiplicarse; *s* raza *f.*

breeder, briid´-*a s* criador *m.*, productor *m.*

breeding, briid´-ing *s* cría *f.*; educación *f.*

breeze, briis *s* brisa *f.*

breezy, brii´-si *a* fresco

brethren, breD´-ren *s pl* hermanos *m. pl.*

brevity, brev´-i-ti *s* brevedad *f.*; concisión *f.*

brew, bruu *v* hacer cerveza; *s* mezcla *f.*

brewer, bruu´-*a s*

cervecero *m.*

brewery, bruu´-ar-i *s* fábrica de cerveza *f.*

bribe, braib *v* sobornar; *s* soborno *m.*

bribery, brai-ber-i *s* soborno *m.*

brick, brik *s* ladrillo *m.*

bricklayer, brik´-lei-*a s* albañil *m.*

bridal, brai´-dl *s* boda *f.*; *a* nupcial

bride, braid *s* novia *f.*

bridegroom, braid´-gruum *s* novio *m.*

bridesmaid, braids ´-meid *s* dama de honor *f.*

bridge, briCH *s* puente *m.*; *v* levantar un puente

bridle, brai´-dl *s* brida *f.*; freno *m.*; *v* embridar; **-path,** *s* camino de herradura

brief, briif *s* informe *f.*; *a* breve; *v* instruir

brier, brai´-*a s* zarza *f.*

brigade, bri-guied´ *s* brigada *f.*

bright*, brait *a* claro; (lively) brillante

brighten, brait´-n *v* alegrar; (weather) aclarar; despejarse

brightness, brait´-nes *s* claridad *f.*; brillantez *f.*; (mental) viveza *f.*

brilliancy, bril´-yan-si *s* brillantez *f.*; fulgor *m.*

brilliant, bril´-yant *a** brillante; *s* brillante *m.*

brim, brim *s* borde *m.*; orilla *f.*; (glass) labio *m.*; borde *m.*; (hat) ala *f.*; **-over,** *v* desbordar

brimstone, brim´-stoun *s* azufre *m.*

brine, brain *s* salmuera *f.*

bring, bring *v* traer; llevar; **-forward,** (accounts) llevar una suma a otra cuenta; **-in-** (receipts) presentar; **-up,** (educate) educar; (rear) criar

brink, brink *s* borde *m.*; (river) orilla *f.*

briny, brai´-ni *a* salado

brisk*, brisk *a* (lively) vivo; (agile) activo

brisket, brisk´-et *s* pecho de buey *m.*

briskness, brisk´-nes *s* vivacidad *f.*; despejo *m.*

bristle, bris´-l *v* erizarse; *s* cerda *f.*

bristly, bris´-li *a* cerdoso

brittle, brit´-el *a* quebradizo; frágil

brittleness, brit´-el-nes *s* fragilidad *f.*

broad*, broad *a* ancho; (aĕcent) marcado

broadcast, broad´-kaast s emisión f.; difusión f.; v radiar; difundir; emitir; adv esparcidamente; **–ing,** s transmisión f.

brocade, bro-keid´ s brocado m.

broccoli, brok´-o-li s brécol m.

brochure, brou´-sher s folleto m.

brogue, broug s acento m.; (shoe) zapato de

broil, broil v asar; tostar; s (dispute) riña f.

broken, brou´-kn a roto; (ground) accidentado; quebrado; (machine) averiado; **-man** hombre m arruinado

broker, brou´-ka s corredor m.; **stock–,** agente de bolsa m.

bromide, brou´-maid s bromuro m.

bronchitis, bron-kai´-tis s bronquitis f.

bronze, bron s s bronce m.; v broncear

brooch, brouch s broche m.; prendedero m.

brood, bruud s oria f.; nidada f.; v empollar; meditar

brook, bruk s arroyo m.

broom, bruum s escoba f.;

(shrub) retama f.

broth, broaz s caldo m.

brother, brŏD´-a s hermano m.; **–in-law,** cuñado m.; **–hood,** s hermandad f.; **–ly,** a fraternal

brow, brau s frente f.

browbeat, brau´-biit v intimidar; amedrentar

brown, braun a moreno; marron m.; v poner tostado; tostar

brownish, braun´-ish a pardo

browse, braus, v pacer

bruise, bruus v magullar; s magulladura f.

brunette, bru-net´ s morena f.

brunt, brŏnt s choque m.; embate m.

brush, brŏsh s cepillo m.; (paint) pincel m.; (dynamo) cepillo m.; v acepillar

brushwood, brŏsh´-u´ud s broza f.; leña f.

brusque, brŏsk a brusco

brussels sprouts, brŏs´-els sprauts s pl coles de Bruselas m. pl

brutal*, bruu´-tl a brutal

brutality, bruu-tAl´-i-ti s brutalidad f.

brute, bruut s bruto m.;

bestia f.; a bruto; bestial

bubble, bŏb´-l s burbuja f.; v burbujear

buccaneer, bŏk-a-nir´ s bucanero m.

buck, bŏk s gamo m.

bucket, bŏk´-et s cubo m.; balde m.

buckle, bŏk´-l s hebilla f.; v hebillar; abrochar; (bend) doblarse

buckram, bŏk´-ram s bucarán m.; cinturilla f.

buckthorn, bŏk´-zórn s espino m.

bud, bŏd s yema f.; (rose) capullo m.; v brotar

budge, bŏ CH v moverse; menearse

budget, bŏ CH´-it s presupuesto m.

buff, bŏf s (color) color de ante m.

buffalo, bŏf´-a-lou s búfalo m.

buffer, bŏf´-a s (railway) tope m.

buffet, bŏf´-it s (refreshments) cantina f.; (blow) golpe m.; v (hit) abofetear

buffoon, bo-fuun´ s bufón m.

bug, bŏg s chinche m.; bicho m.

bugbear, bŏg´-bé r s

pesadilla f.

buggy, bŏg-i s calesa f.;
cochecito m. (de niño)

bugle, biuu´-gl s (military)
corneta f.

build, bild v edificar; s
estructura f.

builder, bil´-da s
constructor m.

building, bil´-ding s
edificio m.;
construcción f.

bulb, bŏlb s (plant) bulbo
m.; (lamp) bombilla f.

bulge, bŏlCH v hincharse;
sobresalir

bulk, bŏlk s volumen m.;
in –, a granel m.

bulky, bŏl´-ki a
voluminoso

bull, bul s toro m.; (papal)
bula f.; (stock
exchange) alcista m.;
–dog, s dogo m.; **–fight,**
s corrida de toros f.

bullet, bul´-et s bala f.

bulletin, bul´-i-tin s
boletín m.

bullion, bul´-yon s (gold)
oro en barras m.; (silver)
plata en barras f.

bullock, bul´-ok s buey m.;
cebón m.

bull's eye, buls´-ai s
(target) centro de
blanco m.

bully, bul´-i v maltratar; s
matón m.

bulrush, bul´-rŏsh s junco
m.

bulwark, bul´-uĕrk s
baluarte m.

bumblebee, bŏm´-bi-bii s
abejarrón m.

bump, bŏmp v chocar; s
topetazo m.; (bruise)
chinchón m.

bumper, bŏm´-pa s
(shock) tope m.

bumpkin, bŏmp´-kin s
(yokel) patán m.

bumptious, bŏm´-shos a
presumido

bun, bŏn s bollo m.

bunch, bŏnch s **–of
flowers,** manojo de
flores m.; **–of violets,**
ramillete de violetas m.;
–of grapes, racimo de
uvas m.; **–of keys,**
puñado de llaves m.

bundle, bŏn´-dl s paquete
m.; v empaquetar

bung, bŏng s tapón m.

bungalow, bŏñ´-ga-lou s
chálet m.; casa de un
piso f.

bungle, bŏñ´-gl v
chapucear; s chapucería
f.

bungler, bŏñ´-gla s
chapucero m.

bunion, bŏn´-yon s
juanete m.

bunk, bŏñk s litera f.

bunker, bŏñ´-ka s (ship's)
carbonera f.

bunkum, bŏñ´-kom s
patraña f.

bunting, bŏn´-ting s
estameña f.

buoy, boi v boyar; s boya f.

buoyancy, boi´-an-si s
ligereza f.; vivacidad f.

buoyant, boi´-ant a
flotante; vivo

burden, bĕr´-dn s carga f.;
(responsibility) fardo
m.; v cargar; gravar;
(oppress) agobiar

burdensome, bĕr´-den-
som a (expensive)
oneroso; (encumbrance)
molesto

bureau, biu´-rou s (office)
oficina f.; escritorio m.

bureaucracy, biu-ro´-kra-
si s burocracia f.

burglar, bĕr´-gla s ladrón
m.

burglary, bĕr´-gla-ri s
hurto m.; robo m.

burial, be´-ri-al s entierro
m.

burlesque, ber-lesk´ s
burlesco m.; a burlesco;
v parodiar

burly, bĕr´-li a corpulento;

297

robusto

burn, běrn *v* quemar; arder; *s* quemadura *f.*

burner, běrn´-*a* *s* mechero *m.*

burnish, běrn´-ish *v* bruñir

burrow, bŏr´-ou *v* minar; (by animals) horadar; *s* conejera *f.*

bursar, běr´-sa *s* tesorero *m.*

burst, běrst *v* reventar; (tears) brotar; *s* explosión *f.*; (crack) reventón *m.*

bury, ber´-i *v* enterrar

bus, bŏs *s* autobus *m.*

bush, bush *s* arbusto *m.*; mata *f.*

bushel, bush´-l *s* medida inglesa de áridos *f.*

bushy, bush´-i *a* matoso

busily, bis´-i-li *adv* activamente

business, bis´-nes *s* negocio *m.*; (or) negocios *pl.*

businesslike, bis´-nes-laik *a* serio; práctico

businessman, bis-nes-mAn *s* hombre *m.*; de negocios; empresario *m.*

businesswoman, bis-nes-uu´-man *s* mujer *f.*; de negocios; mujer *f.*;

empresaria

bus stop, bŏs stop *s* parada *f.*; de autobús

bust, bŏst *s* busto *m.*

bustle, bŏs´-l *v* bullir; menearse; *s* bullicio *m.*

bustling, bŏs´-ling *a* bullicioso; ruidoso

busy, bis´-i *a* ocupado

busybody, bis´-i-bod-i *s* entrometido *m.*

but, bŏt *conj* pero; mas; *sin embargo; prep* excepto; menos; *adv* solamente; no ... mas que; no ... sino

butcher, buch´-*a* *s* carnicero *m.*; *v* matar

butler, bŏt´-la *s* mayordomo *m.*

butt, bŏt *s* extremidad *f.*; (gun) culata *f.*; (cask) tonel *m.*; *v* topetar

butter, bŏt´-*a* *s* manteca *f.*; mantequilla *f.*; *v* untar con manteca; — **dish,** mantequera *f.*

buttercup, bŏt´-er-kŏp *s* botón de oro *m.*

butterfly, bŏt´-er-flai *s* mariposa *f.*

buttock, bŏt´-ok *s* nalga *f.*; anca *f.*

button, bŏt´-n *s* botón *m.*; *v* abotonar; (refl.) abotonarse; —**hole,** *s*

ojal *m.*

buttress, bŏt´-res *s* contrafuerte *m.*; estribo *m.*

buxom, bŏk´-som *a* (woman) rolliza

buy, bai *v* comprar

buyer, bai´-*a* *s* comprador *m.*

buzz, bŏ *s* *v* zumbar; *s* zumbido *m.*

buzzard, bŏ *s* ´-erd *s* aguila ratonera *f.*

buzzer, bŏsa *s* timbre *m.*

by, bai *adv* ahí; allí; *prep* por; a; en; de; cerca de; sobre; según

bylaw, bai´-loa *s* reglamento *m.*

bygone, bai´-goan *a* pasado

bypass, bai´-paas *s* carretera *f* de circunvalación; desviación; *v* evitar; prescindir; pasar de largo; **- operation** by-pass *m.*; operación de by-pass

bystander, bai´-stAn-dr *s* espectador *m.*

byway, bai´-uei *s* camino desviado *m.*

byword, bai´-uěrd *s* proverbio *m.*

cab, kAb s (motor) taxi m; (horse) coche m.

cabal, ka-bAl´ v maquinar; intrigar; s cábala f.

cabbage, kAb´-iCH s col f.

cabin, kAb´-in s camarote m.; (hut) choza f.

cabinet, kAb´-in-et s gabinete m.; ministerio m.

cabinetmaker, kAb´-in-et-meik´-a s ebanista m.

cable, kei´-bl s cable m.; v cablegrafiar

cablegram, kei´-bl-grAm s cablegrama m.

cable television, kei´-bl tel´-i-vish-on s televisión f.; por cable

cackle, kAk´-l v cacarear; s cacareo m.

cactus, kAk´-tus s cacto m.

cad, kAd s sinvergüenza m.

caddy, kAd s (tea) cajita para té f.

café, kAf´-ei s café m.; cafetería f.

cafeteria, kaf-tii´-ri-a s (restaurante m de) autoservicio

cage, keiCH s jaula f.; v enjaular

cajole, ka-CH oul´ v lisonjear; alabar

cake, keik s pastel m.; tarta f.; torta; (soap) pastilla de jabón f.; v coagularse

calamitous*, ka-lAm´-i-tos a calamitoso

calamity, ka-lAm´-i-ti s calamidad f.

calculate, kAl´-kiu-leit v calcular

calculator, kAl´-kiu-leit-or v calculadora f.

caldron, koal´-dron s caldero m.

calendar, kAl´-en-da s calendario m.

calender, kAl´-en-da s calandria f.

calf, kaaf s ternero m.; (leg) pantorrilla f.

calico, kAl´-i-kou s estampado m.; indiana f.; percal m.

call, koal s llamada f.; (visit) f.; v llamar; visitar; –ing, s profesión f.

callous*, kAl´-os a calloso; (unfeeling) endurecido

callow, kAl´-ou a inexperto

calm, kaam s calma f.; (weather) bonanza f.; a* tranquilo; quieto; v calmar

calmness, kaam´-nes s tranquilidad f.; sosiego m.

calorie, kAl´-o-ri s caloría f.

calumny, kAl´-om-ni s calumnia f.

cambric, keim´-brik s batista f.

camcorder, kAm´-koard-*a*
s cámara *f.*; de video
portátil

camel, kAm´-l s camello
m.

cameo, kAm´-i-ou s
camafeo *m.*

camera, kAm´-*er*-*a* s
cámera *f.*; cámara
fotográfica *f.*

camisole, kAm´-i-soul s
camiseta *f.*

camomile, kAm´-o-mail s
camomila *f.*

camouflage, kAm´-o-flaar
CH s camuflage *m.*; *v*
encubrir; camuflar

camp, kAmp *v* acampar; s
campo *m.*; campamento
m.

campaign, kAm-pein´ s
campaña *f.*; *v* servir en

camphor, kAm´-fa s
alcanfor *m.*

campsite, kAmp-sait s
cámping *m.*;
campamento *m.*

campus, kAm-pŏs s
campus *m.*

can, kAn s lata *f.*; *v*
(preserve) enlatar

can, kAn *v* (to be able)
poder; (to know how)
saber campaña

canal, ka-nal´ s canal *m.*

canary, ka-nei´-ri s

canario *m.*

cancel, kAn´-sl *v* cancelar;
anular

cancer, kAn´-sa s cáncer
m.

candid*, kAn´-did *a*
cándido; sincero

candidate, kAn´-di-deit s
candidato *m.*

candied, kAn´-did *a*
confitado

candle, kAn´-dl s vela *f.*;
candela *f.*

candlestick, kAn´-del-stik
s candelero *m.*

candor, kAn´-da s candor
m.; sinceridad *f.*

candy, kAn´-di s caramelo
m.; confite *m.*; *v*
confitar

cane, kein s caña *f.*;
(walking stick) bastón
m.

canine, kei´-nain *a* canino

canister, kAn´-is-ta s
canastillo *m.*; (tin) lata
f.

canker, kAñ´-ka s
gangrena *f.*

cannabis, kAn´-*a*-bis s
marihuana *f.*

canned, cAnd *a* en lata;
en conserva

cannibal, kAn´-i-bal s
caníbal *m.*

cannon, kAn´-on s cañón

m.

canoe, k *a*-nuu´ s canoa *f.*

canon, kAn´-on s (title)
canónigo *m.*; (law)
canon *m.*

can opener, kAn ou´-pn-*a*
s abrelatas *m.*

canopy, kAn´-o-pi s
baldaquín *m.*; (of bed)
pabellón *m.*

cant, kAnt s hipocresía *f.*;
v hablar en caló

cantankerous, kAn-tAñ´-
ker-*os* *a* pendenciero; s
arisco *m.*

canteen, kAn-tiin´ s
cantina *f.*

canter, kAn´-ta s medio
galope *m.*; *v* andar e
caballo a paso largo

canticle, kAn´-ti-kl s
cántico *m.*

canting, kAnt´-ing s falso
devoto *m.*; *a* hipócrita

canvas, kAn´-vas s (cloth)
lona *f.*; (sail) vela *f.*;
(painting) lienzo *m.*

canvass, kAn´-vas *v*
solicitar; s solicitación *f.*

cap, kAp s gorra *f.*;
(metal) cápsula *f.*

capable, kei´-pa-bl *a* capaz

capacity, ka-pass´-i-ti s
capacidad *f.*

cape, keip s
(geographical) cabo *m.*;

(cloak) capa f.

caper, kei´-pa v hacer cabriolas; s (pickle) alcaparra f.

capital, kAp´-i-tl s (city) capital f.; (money) capital m.; (letter) mayúscula f.

capitulate, ka-pit´-iu-leit v capitular

capon, kei´-pn s capón m.

capricious*, ka-prish´-os a caprichoso

capsize, kAp-sais ´ v volcar; (naut) zozobrar

capstan, kAp´-stan s cabrestante m.

capsule, kAp´-siul s cápsula f.

captain, kAp´-tin s capitán m.

captive, kAp´-tiv s & a cautivo m.; prisionero m.

captivity, kAp-tiv´-i-ti s cautiverio m.

capture, kAp´-tiur v capturar; s captura f.

car, kaar s coche m.; automóvil m.; (aero) barquilla f.

caramel, kAr´-a-mel s caramelo m.

carat, kAr´-at s quilate m.

caravan, kAr´-a-van s caravana f.

caraway, kAr´-a-uei s (seed) alcaravea f.

carbide, kaar´-baid s carburo m.

carbine, kaar´-bain s carabina f.

carbolic, kaar-bol´-ik s ácido fénico m.; a afenicado

carbon, kaar´-bon s carbón m.; carbono m.; – **paper,** papel carbón m.

carbuncle, kaar´-bön-kl s (med.) carbúnculo m.

carburetor, kaar´biu-ret-a s carburador m.

carcass, kaar´-kas s animal muerto m.

card, kaard s carta f.; (playing) naipe m.; (visiting) tarjeta f.; –**board,** s cartón m.

cardigan, kaar´-di-gan s chaqueta de punto sin solapas f.; rebeca f.; cárdigan m.

cardinal, kaar´-di-nal s cardenal m.; a cardinal

care, kér s cuidado m.; atención f.; (anxiety) inquietud f.; cuidar; –**for,** (persons) querer a; (things) gustar de; **take** –**of,** cuidar de; **c/o,** al cuidado de

career, ka-rir s carrera f.; profesión f.

careful*, kér´-ful a cuidadoso; atento

careless*, kér´-les a descuidado; indiferente

carelessness, kér´-les-nes s descuido m.

caress, ka-res´ v acariciar; s caricia f.

caretaker, ké r-tei´-ka s guardián m.; conserje m.

car ferry, kaar fer´-i s trasbordador m.; para coches; ferry m.

cargo, kaar´-gou s carga f.; cargamento m.

caricature, kAr´-i-ka-tiur s caricatura f.; v ridiculizar

carmine, kaar´-min s carmín m.

carnage, kaar´-niCH s matanza f.; carnicería f.

carnal*, kaar´-nl a carnal; sensual

carnation, kaar-nei´-shon s (flower) clavel m.

carnival, kaar´-ni-vl s carnaval m.

carol, kAr´-ol s (cantata) villancico m.

carousel, ka-rau-s l s francachela f.; juerga f.

carp, kaarp s carpa f.; v criticar

carpenter, kaar´-pen-*ta* s carpintero m.

carpet, kaar´-*pet* s alfombra f.

car phone, kaar-foun s teléfono móvil m.;

carping, kaarp´-ing a criticón

carriage, kAr´-iCH s (vehicle) coche m.; (freight) porte m.; (deportment) porte m.

carrier, kAr´-i-*a* s portador m.; (carter) carretero m.; (mule) arriero m.

carrion, kAr´-i-on s carroña f.

carrot, kAr´-ot s zanahoria f.; **-y,** a pelirrojo

carry, kAr´-i v llevar; transportar

cart, kaart s carro m.; (long and narrow) carreta f.; v carretear; **-age,** s acarreo m.; **-er,** s carretero m.; **-load,** s carretada f.

carton, kaar-tn s envase m; caja f.; cartón m.

cartoon, kaar-tuun´ s caricatura f.

cartridge, kaar´-triCH s cartucho m.

carve, kaarv v (wood) tallar; (meat, etc) trinchar

carving, kaarv´-ing s (wood) talla f.

cascade, kAs-keid´ s cascada f.

case, keis s caso m.; (box) caja f.; (cigarette, jewel, or eyeglass) estuche m.; **in –,** en caso

casement, keis´-ment s marca m.; ventana f.

cash, kAsh s dinero m.; (paying) dinero contante m.; v cobrar; **–book,** s libro de caja m.; **–ier,** s cajero m.

cashmere, kAsh´-mi r s cachemira f.

casino, kA-siin´-o s casino m. (de juego)

cask, kaask s barril m.; tonel m.; (for water) cuba f.

casket, kaas´-ket s estuche para joyas f.; (coffin) ataúd m.

casserole, kAs´-er-roul s cacerola f.; cazuela f.

cassock, kAs´-ok s sotana f.

cassette, kA-set s casete f.; cassette f.

cassette player, kA-set plei-*a* s casete m.

cast, kaast s (throw) tiro m.; (theater) reparto m.; (metal) molde m.; v tirar; fundir; modelar

castanet, kAs´-ta-net s castañuela f.

caste, kaast s casta f.

castigate, kAs´-ti-gueit v castigar

casting, kaas´-ting s moldura f.

castle, kaa´-sl s castillo m.; (fortress) fortaleza f.; (chess) torre f.; v enrocar

castor, kaas´-*tor* s (furniture bearings) ruedecilla f.; **–oil,** aceite de ricino m.

casual, kA sh´-iu-al a casual

casualties, kA sh´-iu-al-te s s pl pérdidas f. pl.; (war) bajas f. pl.

casualty, kA sh´-iu-al-ti s accidente m.

cat, kAt s gato m.

catalog, kAt´-a-log s catálogo m.

catarrh, ka-taar´ s catarro m.

catastrophe, ka-tAs´-tro-fi s catástrofe f.

catch, kACh v coger; (seize) asir; **–up,** alcanzar; s presa f.; (door, etc.) cerradera f.

catching, kACh´-ing a contagioso

catchword, kAch´-uĕrd s reclamo m.; slogan m.

category, kAt´-i-gor-i s categoría f.

cater, kei´-ta v abastecer; proveer

caterer, kei´-ter-a s abastecedor m.; proveedor m.

caterpillar, kAt´-er-pil-a s oruga f.

cathedral, ka-zii´-dral s catedral f.

catholic, kAz´-o-lik a católico

cattle, kAt´-l s ganado m.

caucus, koa´-kos s junta secreta f.

cauliflower, ko´-li-flau-er s coliflor f.

caulk, koak v calafatear

cause, koas s causa f.; origen m.; v causar

causeway, koas´-uei s calzada f.

caustic, koas´-tik s cáustico m.; a cóstico

cauterize, koa´-ter-ais v cauterizar

caution, koa´-shon s precaución f.; cuidado m.; (warning) aviso m.; v caucionar; prevenir

cautious*, koa´-shos a cauto, prudente

cavalier, kAv-a-li r´ s caballero m.

cavalry, kAv´-al-ri s caballería f.

cave, keiv s cueva f.; caverna f.

cavernous, kAv´-ern-os a cavernoso

cavil, kAv´-il v cavilar; criticar

cavity, kAv´-i-ti s hueco m.; cavidad f.; (tooth) caries f.

caw, koa v graznar

CD, sii-dii n abbr of **compact disc** disco m compacto

CD ROM, sii-dii rom s abbr of **compact disc read-only memory**

cease, sis v cesar; parar; –less*, a incesante

ceasefire, siis-fair s cese de hostilidades m.; alto el fuego m.

cedar, sii´-da s cedro m.

cede, siid v ceder

ceiling, siil´-ing s techo m.

celebrate, sel´-i-breit v celebrar; solemnizar

celebrated, sel´-i-breit-id a célebre

celebration, sel´-i-brei-shon s celebración f.; fiesta f.

celerity, si-ler´-i-ti s celeridad f.

celery, sel´-e-ri s apio m.

celestial*, si-les´-ti-al a celeste

celibacy, sel´-i-ba-si s celibato m.

cell, sel s calabozo m.; (anatomy) célula f.; (battery) par m.

cellar, sel´-a s sótano m.; (wine) bodega f.

celluloid, sel´-iu-loid s celuloide f.

cement, si-ment´ s cemento m.; v argamasar

cemetery, sem´-i-ta-ri s cementerio m.

cenotaph, sen´-o-taf s cenotafio m.

censer, sen´-sa s incensario m.

censor, sen´-sr s censor m.

censorship, sen´-sr-ship s censura f.

census, sen´-sos s censo m.

cent, sent s ciento m.; centavo m.; céntimo m.

centenary, sen´-ti-ner-i a centenario

center, sen´-tr s centro m.; v centralizar

centigrade, sent-i-greid a centígrado

centimeter, sent-i-mii´-ta s centímetro

central*, sen´-tral *a* central; **–heating**, *s* calefacción central *f.*; **–ize**, *v* centralizar

century, sen´-tiu-ri *s* siglo *m.*

ceramics, ser-Am´-iks *s* cerámica *f.*

cereal, si´-ri-al *s* & *a* cereal *m.*

cereals, sii´-rii-als *s pl* cereales *m. pl.*

ceremonious*, ser-i-mou´-ni-os *a* ceremonioso

ceremony, ser´-i-mou-ni *s* ceremonia *f.*

certain*, sĕr´-tin *a* cierto; **–ty**, *s* certeza *f.*

certificate, sĕr-tif´-i-keit *s* certificado *m.*; testimonio *m.*

certify, sĕr´-ti-fai *v* certificar

certitude, sĕr´-ti-tiuud *s* certidumbre *f.*

cessation, se-sei´-shon *s* cesación *f.*; suspensión *f.*

cesspool, ses´-puul *s* sumidero *m.*

chafe, cheif *v* (rub) calentar frotando; (fret) irritar

chaff, chaaf *s* paja *f.*; (tease) burla *f.*; *v* burlarse

chaffinch, chAf´-inch *s* pinzón *m.*

chafing dish, chei´-fing dish *s* calientaplatos *m.*

chain, chein *v* encadenar; *s* cadena *f.*; **–up**, *v* encadenar

chair, ché r *s* silla *f.*

chairman, ché r´-man *s* presidente *m.*

chalice, chAl´-is *s* cáliz *m.*

chalk, choak *s* greda *f.*; (crayon) tiza *f.*

chalky, choa´-ki *a* gredoso

challenge, chAl´-inch *s* desafío *m.*; (duel) provocación *f.*; *v* desafiar; provocar

chamber, cheim´-ba *s* (apartment) cúarto *m.*; (gun) cámara *f.*; **–s**, *pl* (lawyers', etc) estudio de abogado *m.*

chamberlain, cheim´-ber-lin *s* chambelán *m.*

chambermaid, cheim´-ber-meid *s* camarera *f.*; sirvienta *f.*

chamois, shAm´-uaa, shAm´-i *s* gamuza *f.*

champagne, shAm-pein´ *s* champaña *f.*

champion, chAm´-pi-on *s* campeón *m.*; *v* defender

chance, chaans *s* ventura *f.*; azar *m.*;

(opportunity) oportunidad *f.*; *a* casual; *v* acaecer

chancel, chaan´-sl *s* presbiterio *m.*

chancellor, chaan´-se-la *s* canciller *m.*

chandelier, shAn-di-lir´ *s* candelabro *m.*

chandler, shaand´-la *s* cerero *m.*; velero *m.*

change, cheinCH *s* (money, alteration, exchange) cambio *m.*; (residence) mudanza *f.*; *v* (money, opinion, habits, trains, gear, etc) cambiar; (clothing) mudar; **–able**, *a* variable

changeless, cheinCH´-les *a* inmutable

changing room, cheinCH-ing **ruum** *s* vestidor *m.*

channel, chAn´-l *s* canal *f.*; *v* acanalar

chant, chaant *v* cantar; *s* canto llano *m.*

chaos, kei´-os *s* caos *m.*

chap, chAp *v* agrietar; *s* grieta *f.*

chapel, chAp´-l *s* capilla *f.*

chaperon, shAp´-roun *s* acompañante *m/f.*; *v* escoltar

chaplain, chAp´-lin *s* capellán *m.*

chaplet, chAp´-let s
guirnalda f.; rosario m.

chapter, chAp´-ta s
capítulo m.

char, chaar v carbonizar

character, kAr´-ak-ta s
carácter m.

charcoal, chaar´-koul s
carbón m.

charge, chaar CH s coste
m.; ataque m.; acusación
f.; v acusar; atacar;
(price) cobrar; (battery)
cargar; **to be in –,** estar
encargado

chariot, chAr´-i-ot s
carroza f.

charitable, chAr´-it-a-bl a
caritativo

charity, chAr´-i-ti s
caridad f.

charm, chaarm v
encantar; s encanto m.;
–ing*, a ancantador;
(bewitching) hechicero

chart, chaart s carta de
navegar f.

charter, chaar´-ta v (ship)
fletar; s (grant) carta de
privilegio f.

chary, ché´-ri a cauteloso

chase, cheis v cazar;
perseguir; s caza f.

chasm, kA s m s abismo
m.

chaste*, cheist a casto;

virtuoso

chastise, chAs-tais´ v
castigar

chastisement, chAs´-tis -
ment s castigo m.

chastity, chAs´-ti-ti s
castidad f.

chat, chAt s charla f.; v
charlar

chattel, chAt´-l s bienes
muebles m. pl.

chatter, chA´-a v charlar;
(teeth) castañetear;
–box, s charlatán m.;
–ing, charla f.

chauffeur, shof´-a s chófer
m.

chauvinist, shou-vin-ist s
& a chauvinista mf.;
machista mf.;
patriotero/a mf.

cheap*, chiip a barato;
–en, v abaratar; **–er,** a
más barato; **–ness,** s
baratura f.

cheat, chiit v trampear; s
trampa f.

cheating, chiit´-ing s timo
m.; trampa f.

check, chek s cheque m.;
(restraint) rechazo m.;
(verification) revisión
f.; (chess) jaque m.;
(pattern) cuadrados m.
pl.; v refrenar; revisar;
(stop) parar; **–mate,** s

jaque mate m.; v dar
jaque mate; (book) s
libro de cheques m.

checkered, chek-erd a
variado

check in, chek in v
(baggage) facturar;
(hotel) registrarse; (fig)
llegar

check out, chek aut v
(luggage) recoger; (look
at) mirar; controlar;
(hotel) pagar y
marcharse

cheek, chiik s mejilla f.;
(fam) descaro m.

cheer, chi r s alegría f.;
(applause) vivas m. pl.;
v dar vivas; (brighten)
alegrar; **–ful*,** a alegre;
animado; **–less,** triste;
desanimado

cheese, chiis s queso m.

chef, shef s jefe de cocina;
cocinero

chemical*, kem´-i-kl a
químico (producto)

chemise, shi-miis´ s
camisa de señora f.

chemist, kem´-ist s
químico m.; (shop)
farmacéutico m.; **–ry,**
química f.

cherish, cher´-ish v querer

cherry, cher-i s cereza f.;
–tree, cerezo m.

cherub, cher´-ob s querubín m.

chess, ches s ajedrez m.

chest, chest s (human) pecho m.; (trunk) cofre m.; (box) cajón m.; **–of drawers,** cómoda f.

chestnut, ches´-nŏt s castaña f.; a castaño; **–tree,** s castaño m.; **horse–,** castaña de Indias f.

chew, chuu v masticar; (tobacco, etc) mascar; **–ing gum,** chuu-ing-gŏm s chicle m.; goma de mascar f.

chicken, chik´-n s gallina f.; pollo m.

chicken pox, chik´-n-poks s varicela f.

chide, chaid v regañar; reprender

chief, chiif s jefe m.; a* principal

chilblain, chil´-blein s sabañón m.

child, chaild s niño m.; **–ish*,** a infantil

chill, chil s escalofrío m.; v enfriar; (liquids) helar

chilly, chil´-i a frío

chime, chaim v repiquetear; s tañido de campanas m.; juego de campanas m.

chimney, chim´-ni s chimenea f.

chimneysweep, chim´-ni-suiip s deshollinador m.

chin, chin s barbilla f.

china, chai´-na s porcelana f.; loza f.

chink, chiñk s hendedura f.; v sonar

chintz, chints s zaraza f.

chip, chip v desmenuzar; s trozo m.; astilla f.

chiropodist, ki-rop´-o-dist s pedicuro m.; podólogo m.

chirp, chĕrp v chirriar; gorjear

chisel, chis ´-l s cincel m.; v cincelar

chivalrous, shiv´-al-ros a caballeresco

chive, chaiv s cebolleta f.

chloride, klo´-raid s cloruro m.

chlorine, klo´-rin s cloro m.

chloroform, klou´-rouform s cloroformo m.

chocolate, chok´-o-leit s chocolate m.

choice, chois s elección f.; a escogido; selecto

choir, kuair s coro m.

choke, chouk v (suffocate) sofocar; (strangle) ahogar; (block up) obstruir

cholera, kol´-er-a s cólera-morbo m.

cholesterol, kol-est-e-rol s colesterol m.

choose, chuu s v escoger; elegir

chop, chop s chuleta f.; costilla f.; v cortar; **–off,** tajar

chopper, chop´-a s cuchilla f.

choral, kó-ral a coral

chord, koard s cuerda f.; acorde m.

chorister, kor´-is-ta s corista f.

chorus, kó´-ros s coro m.

Christ, kraist s Cristo m.

christen, kris´-n v bautizar

christening, kris´-ning s bautismo m.

Christianity, kris-ti-An´-i-ti s cristianismo m.

Christmas, kris´-mas s Navidad f.; **– tree,** árbol de Navidad m.

chronic, kron´-ik a crónico

chronicle, kron´-ik-l s crónica f.; v contar

chrysanthemum, kri-san´-ze-mom s crisantemo m.

chubby, chŏb´-i a mofletudo; rechoncho

chuckle, chŏk´-l v reir entre dientes; s risa

ahogada f.

chum, chŏm s camarada m.

chunk, chŏnk s trozo m.; pedazo m.

church, chĕrch s iglesia f.

churchyard, chĕrch-yaar s cementerio m.

churl, chĕrl s rústico m.

churlish*, chĕr´-lish a rudo

churn, chern s mantequera f.; v batir la leche

cider, sai´-da s sidra f.

cigar, si-gaar´ s cigarro m.

cigarette, sig-a-ret´ s cigarrillo m.

cinder, sin´-da s escoria f.

cinema, sin´-i-ma s cinema m.

cinnamon, sin´-na-mon s canela f.

cipher, sai´-fa s cifra f.; v cifrar

circle, sĕr´-kl s círculo m.; v circundar

circlet, sĕr´-klet s (headband) corona f.

circuit, sĕr´-kit s circuito m.

circuitous*, sĕr-kiu´-it-os a tortuoso

circular, sĕr´-kiu-lar s circular f.; a* circular

circulate, sĕr´-kiu-leit v

circular; poner en circulación

circulating, sĕr´-kiu-leit-ing a circulante; –**library,** s biblioteca circulante f.

circumcise, sĕr-kŏm-sais v circuncisar

circumference, sĕr-kŏm´-fer-ens s circunferencia f.

circumflex, sĕr´-kom-fleks s circunflejo m.

circumscribe, sĕr´-kom-skraib v circunscribir

circumspect, sĕr´-kom-spect a circunspecto; prudente

circumstance, sĕr´-kom-stans, s circunstancia f.; –**s,** pl (financial) medios m. pl.

circumstancial*, sĕr-ko-stan´-shal a circunstancial; –**evidence,** s indicios vehementes m. pl.

circumvent, sĕr-kom-vent v engañar

circus, sĕr´-kos s circo m.

cistern, sis´-tern s cisterna f.

citadel, sit´-a-del s ciudadela f.

cite, sait v citar

citizen, sit´-i-sn s

ciudadano m.

citizenship, sit´-i-sn-ship s ciudadania f.

citron, sit´-ron s (fruit) cidra f.; (tree) cidro m.

city, sit´-i s ciudad f.

civil*, siv´-il a civil; (courteous) cortés

civilian, siv-il´-yan s paisano m.; burgués m.

civilization, siv´-il-ai-s ei´-sho s civilización f.

claim, kleim s demanda f.; (inheritance) título m.; (mine, etc) pertenencia f.; v reclamar

claimant, kleim´-ant s demandante m.; (throne) pretendiente m.

clamber, klAm´-ba v trepar; gatear

clamor, klAm´-er s clamor m.; v gritar; vociferar

clamorous*, klAm´-or-os a ruidoso; tumultuoso; clamoroso

clamp, klAmp s grapa f.; v amontonar; sujetar

clan, klAn s tribu f.; clan m.

clandestine, klAn-des-tin a clandestino

clang, klAñg s rechinamiento m.; v rechinar

clank, klAñk (see **clang**)

clap, klAp s aplauso m.; (thunder) trueno m.; v aplaudir

clapping, klAp´-ing s aplauso m.

claret, klAr´-et s clarete m.

clarify, klAr´-i-fai v clarificar

clarinet, klAr´-i-net s clarinete m.

clarion, klAr´-yon s clarín m.

clash, klAsh s (noise) choque m.; (differing) conflicto m.; v chocar; oponerse

clasp, klaasp s corchete m.; (embrace) abrazo m.; v abrochar; abrazar

class, klaas s clase f.; (quality) calidad f.; v clasificar

classify, klAs´-i-fai v clasificar

clatter, klAt´-a v resonar; s ruido m.

clause, kloas s cláusula f.; estipulación f.

claw, kloa s garra f.; uña f.; v arañar

clay, kiei s arcilla f.; barro m.

clayey, klei´-i a arcilloso

clean, kliin v limpiar; a* limplo

cleaning, kliin´-ing s limpieza f.

cleanliness, cleanness, klen´-li-nes, kliin´-nes s limpieza f.; aseo m.

cleanse, kien s v limpiar; purificar

clear*, kli r a despejado; evidente; claro; (profit) neto; v despejar; limpiar; (sky) aclarar; **–ness,** claridad f.

cleave, kliiv v hender

cleft, kleft s hendedura f.; grieta f.

clematis, kiem´-a-tis s clemátide f.

clemency, klem´-en-si s clemencia f.

clench, klench v remachar; (teeth, etc) cerrar

clergy, klĕr´-cHi s clero m.; **–man,** clérigo m.; eclesiástico m.

clerical, kier´-ik-l a clerical; **–error,** s error de escritura m.

clerk, klaark s dependiente m.; oficinista m.

clever*, klev´-a a inteligente; hábil; (manually) diestro

cleverness, klev´-er-nes s habilidad f.; (manual)

destreza f.

click, klik v hacer tictac; s golpe seco m.

client, klai´-ent s cliente m.

clientele, klai´-ent-il s clientela f.

cliff, klif s acantilado m.

climate, klai´-met s clima m.

climax, klai´-mAks s colmo m.;punto culminante m.

climb, klaim v trepar; escalar; **–er,** s trepador m.; (plant) enredadera f.

clinch, klinch (see **clench**)

cling, kling v pegarse; (fig) adherise

clinic, klin´-ik s clínica f.; centro médico (privado) m.

clinical, klin´-i-kal a clínico

clink, kliñk v hacer resonar; (metallic) retiñir s retintín m.

clip, klip s grapa f.; v engrapar–; (cut) cortar

cloak, klouk s capa f.; manto m.; v encapotar; (conceal) encubrir; **–room,** s (theater, restaurant) guardarropa

f.; (railroad) consigna f.
clock, klok s reloj m.;
alarm –, despertador m.;
–maker, relojero m.; **–**
work, mecanismo de
reloj m.
clod, klod s terrón m.
clog, klog s traba f.; (shoe)
zueco m.; v (mech)
trabar; (obstruct)
obstruir
cloister, klois´-ta s
claustro m.
close, klou s s fin m.;
conclusionf; v cerrar;
(terminate) terminar; a
(weather) pesado; adv
(near) cerca; prep cerca
de
closet, klo s ´-et s armario
m.; (public) retrete m.
closure, klou´-sh ur s
clausura f.; fin m.
clot, klot s cuajarón m.; v
cuajarse
cloth, kloz s tela f.; paño
m.; **table–,** mantel m.
clothe, klouD v vestir
clothes, klouD s s pl ropa
f.; vestidos m. pl.; **bed–,**
ropa de cama f.; **–**
brush, cepillo m.
clothier, klouD´-ya s
ropero m.
clothing, klouD´-ing s
vestidos m. pl.; ropa f.

cloud, klaud s nube f.; v
anublarse; **–burst,** s
chaparrón m.; **–less,** a
sin nubes; **–y,** nublado
clout, klaut s influncia f.;
(slap) bofetada f.; v
abofetear
clove, klouv s clavo m.
cloven, klouv´-n, **-footed**
a patihendido
clover, klou´-va s trébol
m.
clown, klaun s payaso m.
club, klöb s club m.;
(stick) porra f.; (cards)
bastos m. pl.; **–foot,**
oiezopo m.
cluck, klök v cloquear; s
cloqueo m.
clue, kluu, s pista f.;
indicio m.
clump, klömp s tarugo m.;
pisada fuerte f.; trozo m.
clumsiness, klöm´-s-nes s
torpeza f.
clumsy, klöm´-si a torpe;
desmañado
cluster, klös´-ta s grupo
m.; (fruit) racimo m.; v
agruparse; arracimarse
clutch, klöch s garra f.;
presa f.; (motor)
embrague m.; v agarrar
coach, kouch s coche m.;
(state) carroza f.; (tutor)
preceptor m.; v

(teaching) enseñar;
–man, s cochero m.
coagulate, kou-A´-giuu-
leit v coagular; (refl)
coagularse
coal, koul s carbón m.; **–**
mine, mina de carbón f.
coalition, kou-a-li´-shon s
coalición f.
coarse*, kours a tosco;
(manner) grosero
coarseness, kours´-nes s
grosería f.; tosquedad f.
coast, koust s costa f.;
litoral m.; v costear; **–**
guard, s guarda costas
m.
coat, kout s chaqueta f.;
abrigo m.; (animal)
pelaje m.; (paint) capa
de pintura f.; v vestir;
–ing, s revestimiento
m.; **–of arms,** escudo de
armas m.; **over–,** abrigo
m.
coax, kouks v engatusar
cob, kob s (horse) jaca f.;
mazorca f.
cobbler, kob´-la s
remendón m.
cobweb, kob´-ueb s
telaraña f.
cochineal, koch´-i-niil s
cochinilla f.
cock, kok s (bird) gallo
m.; (gun) gatillo m.;

–**ade,** escarapela *f.*; –**erel,** pollo *m.*

cockle, kok´-l *s* berberecho *m.*

cockroach, kok´-rouch *s* cucaracha *f.*

cocoa, kou´-kou *s* cacao *m.*; –**nut,** coco *m.*

cocoon, ko-kuun´ *s* capullo del gusano de seda *m.*

cod, kod *s* bacalao *m.*; –**liver oil,** aceite de hígado de bacalao *m.*

coddle, kod´-l *v* mimar; acariciar

code, koud *s* código *m.*

codicil, kod´-i-sil *s* codicilo *m.*

coerce, kou-ĕrs´ *v* forzar

coffee, kof´-i *s* café *m.*; –**house,** café *m.*

coffeepot, kof´-i-pot *s* cafetera *f.*

coffer, kof´-a *s* cofre *m.*; –**s,** *pl* tesoro *m.*

coffin, kof´-in *s* ataúd *m.*; féretro *m.*

cog, kog *s* diente de rueda *m.*; *v* dentar una rueda; –**wheel,** *s* rueda dentada *f.*

cogency, kou´-CHen-si *s* fuerza lógica *f.*; fuerza moral *f.*

cogitate, koCH´-i-teit *v*

pensar; meditar

cogitation, koCH-i-tei´-shon *s* meditación *f.*

cognac, ko-ñak´ *s* coñac *m.*

cognate, kog´-neit *a* consanguíneo; análogo

cognizance, kog´-ni-*s* ans *s* conocimiento *m.*

cognizant, kog´-ni-*s* ant *a* informado; enterado

coherence, kou-ji´-rens *s* coherencia *f.*

coherent*, kou-ji´-rent *a* coherente

cohesion, kou-jii´-s hon *s* cohesión *f.*

cohesive*, kou-jii´-siv *a* cohesivo

coil, koil *s* rollo *m.*; bobina *f.*; *v* enrollar

coin, koin *s* moneda *f.*; *v* acuñar

coincide, kou-in-said´ *v* coincidir

coke, kouk *s* coque *m.*

cold, kould *s* frío *m.*; (head) resfriado *m.*; *a* * frío

colic, kol´-ik *s* cólico *m.*

collaborate, ko-lAb´-o-reit *v* colaborar

collapse, ko-lAps´ *v* hundirse; *s* hundimiento *m.*

collar, kol´-r *s* cuello *m.*;

(dog) collar *m.*; –**bone,** clavícula *f.*

collate, ko-leit´ *v* comparar; cotejar; ordenar

collateral*, ko-lAt´-er-al *a* colateral

collation, ko-lei´-shon *s* cotejo *m.*

colleague, kol´-iig *s* colega *m.*

collect, ko-lekt´ *v* (stamps, art) coleccionar; (money) cobrar; –**ed,** *a* reunido; –**ion,** *s* colección *f.*; (money) cobro *m.*; –**ive,** *a* colectivo; –**or,** *s* (tax, etc) cobrador *m.*; (stamps, art, etc) coleccionador *m.*

college, kol´-ich *s* colegio *m.*; universidad *f.*

collide, ko-laid´ *v* chocar

collier, kol´-ya *s* minero *m.*; carbonero *m.*

colliery, kol´-yer-i *s* mina de carbón *f.*

collision, ko-li´-sh on *s* choque *m.*

collop, kol´-op *s* tajada *f.*; filete *m.*

colloquial*, ko-lou´-küi-al *a* familiar; coloquial

collusion, ko-luu´-shon *s* colusión *f.*

colon, kou´-lon *s* dos puntos *m. pl.*

colonel, kĕr´-nel *s* coronel *m.*

colonist, kol´-on-ist *s* colono *m.*

colonnade, ko-lon-eid´ *s* columnata *f.*

colony, kol´-o-ni *s* colonia *f.*

color, kŏl´-a *s* color *m.; v* colorar; **–ing,** *s* colorido *m.; color m.*

colossal, ko-los´-l *a* colosal

colt, koult *s* potro *m.*

column, kol´-om *s* columna *f.*

coma, kou´-ma *s* coma *f.;* letargo *m.*

comb, koum *s* (hair) peine *m.;* (bird) cresta *f.;* (honey) panal *m.; v* peinar

combat, kom´-bat *s* combate *m.; v* combatir; **–ant,** *s* combatiente *m.;* **–ive,** *a* belicoso

combination (s), kom-bi-nei´-shon(s) *s* combinación *f.;* combinaciones *f. pl.*

combine, kŏm-bain´ *s* asociación *f.; v* combinar

combustion, kom-bŏst´-yon *s* combustión *f.*

come, kŏm *v* venir; **–back,** volver; **–down,** bajar; **–in,** entrar; **–off,** (unfasten, disjoin, loose) separarse; **–out,** salir; **–up,** subir

comedian, ko-mii´-di-an *s* comediante *m.;* cómico *m.*

comedy, kom´-i-di *s* comedia *f.*

comeliness, kŏm´-li-nes *s* (grace) gracia *f.;* (beauty) belleza *f.*

comet, kom´-et *s* cometa *m.*

comfit, kŏm´-fit *s* confite *m.*

comfort, kŏm´-fort *s* (physical) comodidad *f.;* (solace) consuelo *m.;* (relief) alivio *m.; v* consolar; aliviar; **–able,** *a* cómodo; agradable

comic, kom´-ic *a* cómico

comma, kom´-a *s* coma *f.*

command, ko-maand´ *v* mandar; dominar; *s* orden *f.;* (knowledge) dominio *m.;* (mil) mando *m.;* **–er,** comandante *m.*

commandment (s), ko-maand´-ment(s) *s* mandamiento(s) de la ley de Dios *m. pl.*

commence, ko-mens´ *v* comenzar; principiar; **–ment,** *s* comienzo *m.;* principio *m.*

commend, ko-mend´ *v* recomendar; (praise) alabar; elogiar

commendation, ko-men-dei´-shon *s* elogio *m.*

comment, ko-ment´ *v* comentar; *s* comentario *m.*

commerce, kom´-ĕrs *s* comercio *m.*

commercial, kom-mer´-shal *a* comercial

commiserate, ko-mis´-er-eit *v* compadecer

commission, ko-mish´-on *v* comisionar; *s* comisión *f.;* (rank) patente *f.*

commit, ko-mit´ *v* (bind) comprometerse; (fault) cometer; (sentence) encarcelar

committal, ko-mit´-l *s* encarcelamiento *m.*

committee, ko-mit´-i *s* comité *m.*

commodious*, ko-moud´-i-os *a* cómodo

commodity, ko-mod´-i-ti *s* productos *m. pl.*

commodore, kom´-o-dór *s* jefe de escuadra *m.*

common, kom´-on *a**
común; ordinario;
vulgar; *s* (public land)
ejido *m.*

commoner, kom´-on-a *s*
plebeyo *m.*

commonplace, kom´-n-
pleis *a* común; trivial

commonwealth, kom´-on-
uelz *s* el estado *m.*; la
nación *f.*

commotion, ko-mou´-
shon *s* conmoción *f.*

commune, ko-miuun´ *v*
comulgar; conversar

communicate, ko-miuu´-
ni-keit *v* comunicar;
(eccl) comulgar

communication, ko-miuu-
ni-kei´-shon *s*
comunicación *f.*

communion, ko-miuu´-ni-
on *s* (eccl) comunión *f.*

communism, ko-miuu-
ni-sm *s* comunismo *m.*

communist, ko-miuu-
ni-st *a* comunista; *s*
comunista *mf.*

community, ko-miuu´-ni-
ti *s* comunidad *f.*

commute, ko-miuut´ *v*
viajar a diario; *leg*
conmutar; –er, *s* viajero
de cercanía

compact, kom-pAkt´ *s*
pacto *m.*; *a** compacto

companion, kom-pAn´-
yon *s* compañero *m.*;
–ship, compañerismo *m.*

company, kŏm´-pa-ni *s*
compañía *f.*

comparative*, kom-pAr´-
a-tiv *a* comparativo

compare, kom-pé r´ *v*
comparar; compararse

comparison, kom-pAr´-is-
n *s* comparación *f.*

compartment, kom-paart´-
ment *s* compartimiento
m.

compass, kŏm´-pAs *s*
(magnetic) brújula *f.*;
(range) alcance *m.*; (a
pair of)– es, *pl* compás
m.

compassionate*, kom-
pA´-shon-eit *a*
compasivo

compatible, kom-pat-i-bl
a compatible

compel, kom-pel´ *v* forzar;
constreñir

compensate, kom´-pen-
seit *v* compensar;
indemnizar

compensation, kom-pen-
sei´-shon *s*
compensación *f.*

compete, kom-piit´ *v*
concurrir; competir

competence, kom´-pi-tens
s competencia *f.*

competent, kom-pet-ant *a*
competente; capaz;
adecuado; suficiente

competition, kom-pi-ti´-
shon *s* (commercial)
competencia *f.*; (games)
concurso *m.*

competitive, kom-pet-it-
iv *a* (price) competitivo;
(spirit) competidor

competitor, kom-pet´-i-ta
s competidor *m.*; rival
m.

compile, kom-pail´ *v*
compilar

complacent*, kom-plei´-
sent *a* complaciente

complain, kom-plein´ *v*
quejarse

complaint, kom-pleint´ *s*
queja *f.*; (malady) mal
m.

complement, kom´-plii-
ment *s* complemento *m.*

complete, kom-pliit´ *v*
completar; terminar *a**
completo; –ly, *adv*
completamente; –ness, *s*
integridad

completion, kom-plii´-
shon *s* conclusión *f.*;
terminación *f.*

complex, kom´-plex *s*
complejo *m.*; *a* complejo

complexion, kom-plek´-
shon *s* (face) cutis *m.*

compliance, kom-plai´-*ans* s consentimiento *m.*

compliant*, kom-plai´-*ant a* complaciente

complicate, kom´-pli-keit *v* complicar

compliment, kom´-pliment s cumplido *m.; v* cumplementar; **–s,** s pl saludos *m. pl.*

comply, kom-plai´ *v* conformarse

component, kom-pou´-nent s & *a* componente *m.*

comport, kom-port´ *v* comportarse

compose, kom-pous´ *v* componer; calmar

composer, kom-pou´-sa s compositor *m.*

composite, kom´-po-sit *a* compuesto

composition, kom-pou-si´shon s (essay, music) composición *f.*

compositor, kom-pos´-i-tr s cajista *m.*

composure, kom-pou´-sher s calma *f.;* compostura *f.*

compound, kom-paund´ *v* componer; *a* compuesto; **–fracture,** s fractura múltiple *f.;* **–interest,** interés compuesto *m.*

comprehend, kom-prijend´ *v* comprender

comprehension, kom-prijen´-shon s comprensión *f.*

compress, kom-pres´ *v* comprimir; s compresa *f.*

comprise, kom-prais´ *v* contener

compromise, kom´-promais s compromiso *m.; v* comprometer

compulsion, kom-pŏl-shon s compulsión *f.*

compulsive, kom-pŏl-siv *a* compulsivo

compulsory, kom-pŏl´-sori *a* obligatorio

compunction, kom-pŏñk´-shon; s compunción *f.*

compute, kom-piuut´ *v* computar; calcular; **–er,** s ordenador *m.;* computadora *f.*

computer game, kompiuu-ta gueim s vídeojuego

comrade, kom´-reid s camarada *m.*

concave, kon´-keiv *a* cóncavo

conceal, kon-siil´ *v* esconder; ocultar; **–ment,** s escondite *m.;* secreto *m.*

concede, kon-siid´ *v*

conceder

conceit, kon-siit´ s vanidad *f.;* presunción *f.*

conceited*, kon-sii´-tid *a* presumido; vanidosa

conceive, kon-siiv´ *v* concebir; imaginar

concentrate, kon´-sentreit *v* concentrar

concept, kon´-sept s concepto *m.*

conception, kon-sep´-shon s concepción *f.*

concern, kon´-sĕrn s (interest) interés *m.;* (anxiety) preocupación *f.;* (firm) empresa *f.;* (disquiet) preocupación *f.; v* concernir; **to be –ed,** (anxious) estar inquieto; (involved, interested) estar mezclado

concert, kon´-sĕrt s concierto *m.*

concession, kon-sesh´-on s concesión *f.*

conciliate, kon-sil´-i-eit *v* conciliar

concise*, kon-sais´ *a* conciso

conclude, kon-kluud´ *v* concluir

conclusion, kon-kluu´-shon s conclusión *f.*

conclusive*, kon-kluu´-

siv *a* concluyente

concoct, kon-kokt´ *v* confeccionar; inventar´

concord, kon´-koard *s* concordia *f.*; *v* concordar

concordant, kon-koar´-dant *a* conforme

concourse, kŏn´-kórs *s* concurso *m.*; afluencia *f.*

concrete, kon´-kriit *s* hormigón *m.*; *a* concreto

concur, kon-kěr´ *v* concurrir; estar de acuerdo

concurrence, kon-kŏr´-ens *s* conformidad *f.*

concussion, kon-kŏsh´-on *s* concusión

condemn, kon-dem´ *v* condenar

condense, kon-dens *v* condensar

condescend, kon-di-send´ *v* condescender

condescension, kon-di-sen´-shon *s* condescendencia *f.*

condiment, kon´-di-ment *s* condimento *m.*

condition, kon-di´-shon *s* condición *f.*

conditional*, kon-di´-shon-al *a* condicional

condole, kon-doul´ *v*

condolerse; dar el pésame

condolence, kon-dou´-lens *s* pésame *m.*

condom, kon´-dom *s* condón *m.*; preservativo *m.*

condone, kon-doun´ *v* condonar

conduce, kon-diuus´ *v* conducir

conducive, kon-diuu´-siv *a* conducente

conduct, kon-dokt *s* conducta *f.*; proceder *m.*; *v* conducir; dirigir

conductor, kon-dŏkt´-a *s* (train) cobrador *m.*; (music) director de orquesta *m.*

conduit, kŏn´-dit *s* conducto *m.*; (pipe) caño *m.*

cone, koun *s* cono *m.*; (fir) piña *f.*

confabulate, kon-fAb´-iu-leit *v* confabular

confectioner, kon-fek´-sho-nA *s* confitero *m.*; (shop) confitería *f.*;– **y,** (candies) dulces *m. pl.*

confederate, kon-fed´-er-eit *s* confederado *m.*; cómplice *m.*

confederation, kon-fed´-er-ei-shon *s*

confederación *f.*

confer, kon-fěr´ *v* conferenciar; (bestow) conferir

confess, kon-fes´ *v* confesar; reconocer

confession, konfesh´-on *s* confesión *f.*

confide, kon´-faid *v* confiar

confidence, kon´-fi-dens *s* confianza *f.*; confidencia *f.*

confident*, kon´-fi-dent *a* seguro; (trustful) confiado

confidential*, kon-fi-den´-shal *a* confidencial

confine, kon-fain´ *v* limitar; (lock up) aprisionar; *s* confín *m.*; límite *m.*; **–ment,** prison *f.*

confirm, kon-fěrm´ *v* confirmar

confirmation, kon-fěr-mei´-shon *s* confirmación *f.*

confiscate, kon´-fis-keit *v* confiscar

conflagration, kon-fla-grei´-shon *s* incendio *m.*

conflict, kon´-flikt *s* conflicto *m.*; (combat) lucha *f.*; *v* contender; **–ing,** *a* contradictorio

confluent, kon´-flu-ent *a* confluente

conform, kon-foarm´ *v* conformar; **–to,** conformarse; **–able,** *a* conforme

confound, kon-faund´ *v* (confuse) consternar; (mistake) confundir; **–ed,** *a* maldito

confront, kon-frônt´ *v* confrontar

confuse, kon-fiuus´ *v* confundir

confusion, kon-fiuu´-shon *s* confusión *f.*

confutation, kon-fiu-tei´-shon *s* refutación *f.*

congeal, kon-CH iil´ *v* congelar

congenial, kon-CH ii´-ni-al *a* congenial; simpático

congenital, kon-CHen´-i-tl *a* congénito

congest, ko-CHest´ *v* aglomerar; congestionar; **–ion,** *s* acumulación *f.;* (med) congestión *f.*

congratulate, kon-grAt´-iu-leit *v* felicitar

congratulation, kon-grAt´-iu-lei´-shon *s* relicitación *f.;* enhorabuena *f.*

congregate, koñ´-gri-gueit *v* congregar; juntarse

congregation, koñ-gri-guei´-shon *s* asamblea *f.;* (eccl) congregación *f.*

congress, koñ-gres *s* congreso *m.*

congruous*, koñ´-gru-os *a* congruo

conjecture, kon-CHek´-tiur *v* conjeturar; *s* conjetura *f.*

conjointly, kon-CHoint´-li *adv* conjuntamente

conjugal, kon´-CHiuu-gal *a* conyugal

conjunct, kon-CHönkt´ *a* conjunto; unido

conjuncture, kon-CHönk´-tiur *s* coyuntura *f.*

conjure, kon´-CHer *v* hacer juegos de mano; conjurar

conjurer, kön´-CHer-a *s* prestidigitador *m.*

connect, ko-neet´ *v* juntar unir; (mech) acoplar; **–ion,** *s* conexión *f.;* relación *f.;* clientela *f.*

connive (at), ko-naiv´ (At) *v* hacer la vista gorda

connoisseur, kon-is-ěr´ *s* conocedor *m.*

conquer, koñ´-ker *v* conquistar; vencer; **–or,** *s* conquistador *m.;*

vencedor *m.*

conquest, koñ´-kuest *s* conquista *f.*

conscience, kon´-shens *s* conciencia *f.*

conscientious*, kon-shi´-en-shos *a* concienzudo

conscious*, kon´-shos *a* consciente

consciousness, kon´-shos-nes *s* conocimiento *m.*

conscript, kon´-skript *s* recluta *m.; a* conscripto; *v* reclutar

consecrate, kon´-si-kreit *v* consagrar

consecutive*, kon-sek´-iu-tiv *a* consecutivo

consent, kon-sent´ *v* consentir *s* consentimiento *m.*

consequence, kon´-si-küens *s* consecuencia *f.*

consequential*, kon-si-küen´-shal *a* importante

consequently, kon-si-küent´-li *adv* por consiguiente; consiguientemente

conservative, kon-sěr-va-tiv *s* conservador *m.; a* conservador

conservatory, kon-sěr´-va-to-ri *s* (plants) invernadero *m.;* (music) conservatorio *m.*

conserve, kon-sĕrv´ v conservar

consider, kon-sid´-a v (opinion) considerar; (ponder) reflexionar; **–ate,** a considerado, atento; **–ation,** s consideración f.; **in — ation of,** en consideración de; **–ing,** prep visto que, en atención; a considerando

considerable, kon-sid´-er-a-bl a considerable

consign, kon-sain´ v consignar; enviar; **–ee** s consignatario m.; **–ment,** consignación f.; envío m. ; expedición f.; **–or,** consignador m.

consist, kon-sist´ v consistir

consistency, kon-sis´-ten-si s consistencia f.

consistent*, kon-sis´-tent a consistente; compatible

consolation, kon-so-lei´-shon s consolación f.

console, kon-soul´ v consolar

consoler, kon-soul´-a s consolador m.

consolidate, kon-sol´-i-deit v consolidar

consonant, kon´-so-nant s consonante f.

consort, ko-ssoart s cónyuge m.; v asociarse

conspicuous*, kon-spik´-iu-os a (noticeable) visible; (distinguished) notable

conspiracy, kon-spir´-a-si s conspiración f.

conspirator, kon-spir´-ei-ta s conspirador m.

conspire, kon-spair´ v conspirar

constancy, kon´-stan-ci s constancia f.

constant*, kon´-stant a constante

constipated, kon-stip-eit-ed a estreñido

constipation, kon-sti-pei´-shon s estreñimiento m.

constituency, kon-stit´-iu-en-si s distrito electoral m.

constituent, kon-stit´-iu-ent s elector m.

constitute, kon´-sti-tiuut v constituir

constitution, kon-sti-tiuu´-shon s constitución f.

constrain, kon-strein´ v constreñir

constraint, kon-streint´ s constreñimiento m.

constriction, kon-strik´-shon s constricción f.

construct, kons-trŏkt´ v construir; edificar

construction, kons-trŏk´-shon s construcción f.; interpretación f.

construe, kon-struu v interpretar; construir

consul, kon´-sel s cónsul m.

consulate, kon´-siul-eit s consulado m.

consult, kon-sŏlt´ v consultar

consultation, kon-sel-tei´-shon s consulta f.

consume, kon-siuum´ v consumir

consumer, kon-siuu´-ma s consumidor m.

consummate, kon´-som-eit v consumar

consummation, kon-som-ei´-shon s consumación f.

consumption, kon-sŏm´-shon s (use) consumo m.; (med) tisis f.

consumptive, kon-sŏm´-tiv a tísico

contact, kon´-tAkt s contacto m.; **–lenses,** s pl lentes de contacto

contagious, kon-tei´-CH os a contagioso

contain, kon-tein´ v
contener

contaminate, kon-tAm´-i-
neit v contaminar

contemplate, kon´-tem-
pleit v contemplar

contemporary, kon-tem´-
po-ra-ri s
contemporáneo m.

contempt, kon-temt´ s
desprecio m.

contemptible, kon-tem´-
ti-bl a despreciable

contend, kon-tend´ v
contender; (maintain)
sostener

content, kon-tent´ v
contentar; a contento

contention, kon-ten´-shon
s contienda f.; disputa f.

contentious, kon-ten´-
shos a contencioso

contents, kon-tents´ s pl
contenido m.

contest, kon´-test s
contienda f.; disputa f.;
(competition) concurso
m.; v competir; disputar

contiguous*, kon-ti-guiu´-
os a contiguo

continent, kon´-ti-nent s
continente m.

contingency, kon-tin´-
CHen-si s eventualidad
f.; contigencia f.

contingent*, kon-tin´-

CHent a contingente;
casual

continual*, kon-tin´-iu-al
a continuo; incesante

continuation, kon-tin´-iu-
ei´-shon s continuación
f.

continue, kon-tin´-iuu v
continuar

continuous*, kon-tin´-iu-
os a continuo

contortion, kon-toar´-
shon s contorsión f.

contraband, kon´-tra-
bAnd s contrabando m.

contraceptive, kon-tra-
sep-tiv s & a
anticonceptivo m.;
contraceptivo m.

contract, kon-trAkt´ s
contrato m.; v contraer;
(marriage) contraer;
–for, contratar; –ion, s
contracción f.;
abreviación f.; –or,
contratante m.;
(builder) maestro de
obras m.

contradict, kon-tra-dikt´ v
contradecir

contradiction, kon-tra-
dik´-shon s
contradicción f.

contrary, kon´-tra-ri s
contrario m.

contrary, kon´-tra-ri a

opuesto

contrast, kon´-trAst s
contraste m.; v
contrastar

contravene, kon-tra-viin´
v contravenir; infringir

contravention, kon-tra-
ven´-shon s
contravención f.

contribute, kon-trib´-iut v
contribuir

contribution, kon-trib-
iuu´-shon s
contribución f.; (gift)
dádiva f.; (literary)
artículo m.

contrite, kon´-trait a
contrito

contrivance, kon-trai´-
vans s invención f.;
artificio m.; disposición
f.

contrive, kon-traiv´ v
imaginar; ingeniar

control, kon-troul´ v
dirigir; (feelings)
refrenar s dominio m.;
(authority) dirección f.

controller, kon-troul´-a s
director m.; inspector
m.

controls, kon-troul s´ s
(mech) mandos m. pl.

controversial, kon-tro-
vĕr´-shal a contovertido;
polémico

controversy, kon´-tro-ver-si s controversia *f.*

controvert, kon´-tro-ve rt *v* controvertir

conundrum, ko-nŏn´-drom s acertijo *m.*; adivinanza *f.*

convalescence, kon-va-les-´-ans s convalecencia *f.*

convalescent, kon-va-les´-ent *a* convaleciente

convene, kon-viin´ *v* convocar

convenience, kon-vii´-ni-ens s conveniencia *f.*

convenient*, kon-vii´-ni-ent *a* conveniente

convent, kon´-vent s convento *m.*

convention, kon-ven´-shon s convención *f.*; (assembly) asamblea *f.*

converge, kon-vĕr CH´ *v* converger

conversant, kon´-ver-sant *a* versado en; experto

conversation, kon-ver-sei´-shon s conversación *f.*

converse, kon-vĕrs´ *v* conversar

conversion, kon-ver´-shon s conversón *f.*

convert, kon-vĕrt´ *v* convertir; (alter)

cambiar; (religion) convertirse

convert, kon´-vĕrt s convertido *m.*

convex, kon´-veks *a* convexo

convey, kon-vei´ *v* transportar; (impart) transmitir; participar; –ance, s transporte *m.*; vehículo *m.*; (law) cesión *f.*

conveyancer, kon-vei´-ans-a s escribano *m.*

convict, kon´-vikt s convicto *m.*; presidiario *m.*; *v* condenar; –ion, s convicción *f.*; (crime) condenación *f.*

convince, kon-vins´ *v* convencer

convivial, kon-viv´-i-al *a* sociable; festivo

conviviality, kon-viv´-i-Al´-i-ti s jovialidad *f.*

convocation, kon-vou-kei´-shon s convocatoria *f.*; asamblea *f.*

convoy, kon-voi´ s convoy *m. v* convoyar

convulse, kon-vŏls´ *v* convulsionarse; (geological) sacudir

convulsion, kon-vŏl´-shon s convulsión *f.*; (geological) sacudida *f.*

convulsive*, kon-vŏl´-siv *a* convulsivo

coo, kuu, *v* arrullar

cook, kuk s cocinero *m.*; *v* hacer la comida; (in oil) guisar; (in water) cocer

cookery, kuk´-er-i s arte de cocina *m.*

cool, kuul *v* enfriar; *a** fresco; –ness, s frescura *f.*; indiferencia *f.*; sangre fría *f.*

coop, kuup *v* enjaular; s jaula *f.*

cooper, kuu´-pa s tonelero *m.*

cooperate, kou-op´-er-eit *v* cooperar

cooperator, kou-op´-er-ei-ta s cooperador *m.*

cope, koup *v* arreglárselas

copious*, kou´-pi-os *a* copioso; abundante

copper, kop-´a s cobre *m.*; *a* cobrizo

coppice, copse, kop´-is, kops s soto *m.*; bosquecillo *m.*

copy, kop´-i *v* copiar; s copia *f.*; ejemplar *m.*

copybook, kop´-i-buk s cuaderno de escribir *m.*

copyright, kop´-i-rait s derechos de autor *m.*

coquetry, kou-ket-ri s coquetería *f.*

coral, kor´-al s coral m.

cord, koard s cuerda f.; v encordelar

cordial*, koar´-di-al a cordial

corduroy, koar-diu-roi´ s pana f.

core, kó r s centro m.

cork, koark s corcho m.; (stopper) tapón m.; v tapar con corchos

corkscrew, koark´-scruu s sacacorchos m.

cormorant, koar´-mo-rant s cormoran m.

corn, koarn s maíz m.; grano m.; (foot) callo m.

corner, koar´-na s esquina f.; (of a room) rincón m.

cornflower, k arn´-flau-a s anciano m.

cornice, koar´-nis s cornisa f.

coronation, ko-ro-nei´-shon s coronación f.

coronary, kor-on-a-ri a coronario; s infarto m.; de miocardio; trombosis coronaria

coroner, kor´-o-na s oficial que hace la inspección jurídica de los cadaveres m.

coronet, kor´-o-net s corona de un título f.

corporal, koar´-po-ral s

cabo m.; a corporal

corporate, koar´-po-rit a incorporado

corporation, koar´-po-rei´-shon s corporación f.

corps, kó r s cuerpo militar m.

corpse, koarps s cadáver m.

corpulency, koar´-piu-len-si s corpulencia f.; gordura f.

corpulent, koar´-piu-lent a corpulento; gordo

corpuscle, koar´-pos-l s corpúsculo m.

correct, ´ko-rekt´ a* correcto; v corregir; (admonish) reprender; –ness, s exactitud f.; (manners) corrección f.

corrective, ko-rek´-tiv a correctivo

correspond, kor-i-spond´ v corresponder; –ence, s correspondencia f.; –ent, correspoudiente m.

corridor, kor´-i-doar s corredor m.; pasillo m.

corroborate, ko-rob´-o-reit v corroborar

corroboration, ko-rob´-o-rei´-shon s corroboración f.

corrode, ko-roud´ v

corroer

corrosive, ko-rou´-siv s corrosivo m.; a corroyente

corrugated, kor´-u-guei-tid a (iron) ondulado; (cardboard) acanalado

corrupt, ko-röpt´ v corromper; a* corrupto

corruption, ko-röp´-shon s corrupción f.

corsair, koar´-sé r s corsario m.

corset, koar´-set s corsé m.

cortege, koar-tesh´ s comitiva f.; séquito m.

corvette, koar-vet´ s corbeta f.

cost, kost s precio m.; –s, pl (law) costas f. pl.; v costar; –ly, a caro, costoso

cost-of-living, kost ov-liv´-ing s coste m.; de vida

costume, kos´-tiuum s traje m.; vestido m.

cot, kot s (hut) cabaña f. ; (child's) cuna f.

cottage, kot´-iCH s choza f.; casita de campo f.

cotton, kot´-n s algodón m.; (thread) hilo m.

cottonwool, kot´-n-uul s algodón en rama m.

couch, kauch s cama f.;

lecho m.

cough, koɑf s tos f.; v toser

could, kuud pp of **can**

council, kaun´-sil s
concejo m.; (state)
consejo m.

councillor, kaun´-sil-a s
concejal m.

counsel, kaun´-sl s
(lawyer) abogado
consejero m.; v
aconsejar

counselor, kaun´-sel-a s
consultor m.; (law)
consejero m.

count, kaunt v contar; --
less, a innumerable

countenance, kaun´-te-
nans s rostro m.; v
(tolerate) apoyar;
favorecer

counter, kaun´-ta s
mostrador m.; (games)
ficha f.; **--act,** v impedir,
frustrar; **--feit,** s
falsificación f.; v
falsificar; a falso; **--foil,** s
talón m.; **--mand,** v
contramandar; **--pane,** s
colcha f.; **--part,** s
contraparte f.; **--sign,** s
santo y seña m.

country, kŏn´-tri s (rural)
campo m.; (state) país
m.; **--man,** compatriota
m.; (rural) campesino

county, kaun´-ti s
condado m.

couple, kŏp´-l s par m.;
(people) pareja f.; v unir
m.

courage, kŏr´-iCH s valor
m.

courageous*, ko-rei´-CH
os a valiente

courier, kŏu-ri-a s
mensajero/a mf.; (for
tourist) guía mf.; (de
turismo)

course, kó rs s (direction)
curso m.; (tuition) serie
f.; (race) pista f.;
(ship's) rumbo m.;
(meal) plato m.; **of --,**
desde luego

court, kó rt s (royal) corte
f. ; (law) tribunal m.; v
cortejar; **--ier,** s
cortesano m.; **--martial,**
consejo de guerra m.;
--ship, corte f.; noviazgo
m.; **--yard,** patio m.

courteous*, kĕr´-ti-os a
cortés; afable

courtesy, kĕr´-ti-si s
cortesía f.

cousin, kŏ s ´-n s primo
m.; prima f.

cove, kouv s ensenada f.

covenant, kŏv´-i-nant s
convenio m.

cover, kŏv´-a s cubierta f.;

(lid) tapa f.; (shelter)
abrigo m.; v cubrir

cover-up, kŏv´-a ŏp v
(object) cubrir; tapar;
(truth) ocultar;
encubrir; (emotions)
disimular; s cubierta f.

covet, kŏv´-et v codiciar

cow, kau s vaca f.; v
intimidar; **--hide,** s cuero
vacuno m.

coward, kau´-uerd s
cobarde m.; **--ice,** s
cobardía f.

cowboy, kau-boi s vaquero
m.

cower, kau´-a v agacharse

cowl, kaul s (hood)
capucha f.; (chimney)
sombrerete m.

coxcomb, koks´-koum s
mequetrefe m.

coxswain, kok´-sn s
(steersman) timonero
m.

coy*, koi a tímido;
modesto; reservado

cozy, kou´zi a cómodó

crab, krAb s cangrejo m.;
--apple, manzana
silvestre f.; **--bed*,** a
aspero; (writing) ilegible

crack, krAk s hendedura
f.; grieta f.; (glass) raja
f.; (noise) crujido m.;
(of a whip) chasquido

m.; v (noise) crujir; (fissure) hender; agrietar; (whip) chasquear; (nuts) cascar

cracker, krAk´-er s (firework) carretilla f.; (nut) cascanueces m.; galleta de soda f.

crackle, krAk´-l v crujir; (fire) crepitar

cradle, krei´-dl s (crib) cuna f.

craft, kraaft s (trade) oficio m.; (ship) embarcación f.; (cunning) astucia f.

craftsman, kraafts´-man s artífice m.; artesano m.

crafty, kraaf´-ti a astuto

crag, krAg s risco escarpado m.

cram, krAm v apretar; (coach) preparar para examen

cramp, krAmp s calambre m.; v apretar

cranberry, krAn´-be-ri s arándano m.

crane, krein s (bird) grulla f.; (hoist) grúa f.; v extender

crank, krAnk s manivela f.; (fig) maniático m.

cranny, krAn´-i s grieta f.

crape, kreip s crespón m.

crash, krAsh v (collide)

chocar; (break) romper; (crash down) desplomarse; s choque m.; (noise) estrépito m.; (financial) quiebra f.

crater, kreit´-a s cráter m.

crave, kreív v suplicar; (desire) ansiar

craving, krei´-ving s deseo vehemente m.; antojo m.

crawfish, crayfish, kroa´-fish, krei´-fish s (river) cangrejo de río m.; (sea) cangrejo de mar m.; cigala f.

crawl, kroal v arrastrarse; –up, trepar

crayon, krei´-on s lápiz de color m.

craze, kreis s demencia f.; (mode) manía f.

crazy, krei´-si a demente

creak, kriik v crujir

cream, kriim s nata f.; (whipped) crema f.

creamy, krii´-mi a cremoso

crease, kriis s (press) pliegue m.; (crush) arruga f.; v plegar; arrugar

create, kri-eit´ v crear; causar; producir

creature, krii´-tiur s criatura f.

creche, kresh s nacimiento m.

credentials, kri-den´-shal s s pl credenciales f. pl.; (diplomatic) cartas credenciales f. pl.

credible, kred´-i-bl a creíble

credit, kred´-it s crédito m.; v acreditar; –able, a estimable; honorífico; –or, s acreedor m.

credit card, kred´-it kaard s tarjeta f.; de crédito

credulous, kred´-iu-los a crédulo

creed, kriid s credo m.

creep, kriip v deslizarse; (reptile) arrastrarse

creeper, krii´-pa s enredadera f.

cremate, krii-meit´ v incinerar

cremation, kri-mei´-shon s cremación f.

crematorium, krem-ator-iium s crematorio m.; horno m.; crematorio

creole, krii´-oul s criollo m.

crescent, kres´-ent s creciente m.

cress, kres s (watercress) berro m.

crest, krest s (bird's) cresta f.; (heraldry) cimera f.;

(hill) cima f.; **–fallen,** a abatido

crevice, krev´-is s hendedura f.; grieta f.

crew, kruu s tripulación f.

crick, krik s tortícolis m.

cricket, krik´-et s grillo m.; (game) criquet m.

crime, kraim s crimen m.

criminal, krim´-i-nal s criminal m.; delincuente m.; a criminal

crimson, krim´-son s carmesí m.; a carmesí

cringe, krinCH v rebajarse; humillarse

crinkle, kriñ´-kl v rizar; arrugarse; s arrugu f.

cripple, krip´-l s lisiado m.; v lisiar

crisis, krai´-sis s crisis f.

crisp, krisp a tostado; crespo; crujiente

criterion, krai-ti´-ri-on s criterio m.

critic, kri-tik s crítico/a mf.

critical*, krit´-i-kal a crítico; difícil

criticism, krit´-i-sis m s crítica f.

criticize, krit´-i-sais v criticar

croak, krouk v (crow) graznar; (frog) croar; s (crow) graznido m.;

(frog) canto m.

crochet, krou´-she s (needle) aguja de gancho f.; v hacer ganchillo

crockery, krok´-er-i s vajilla f.

crocodile, krok´-o-dail s cocodrilo m.

crook, kruuk s gancho m.; (rogue) estafador m.; ladron m.; **–ed*,** a curvo; deshonesto

crop, krop s cosecha f. v cosechar

cross, kros s cruz f.; a (vexed) mal humorado; v cruzar; **––examine,** repreguntar; **–ing,** s (railroad, road) cruce m.; (sea) travesía f.; **–out,** v rayer; **–over,** atravesar; **––road,** s encrucijada f.

crouch, krauch v agacharse

crow, krou s cuervo m.; v cacarear

crowbar, krou´baar s palanca f.; barra f.

crowd, kraud s (people) muchedumbre f.; (things) montón m.; v amontonar; (people) apiñarse

crown, kraun s corona f.;

(cranium) coronilla f.; v coronar

crucial, kruu´-shal a crucial; decisivo

crucible, kruu´-si-bel s crisol m

crucifix, kruu´-si-fiks s crucifijo m.

crucify, kruu´-si-fai v crucificar

crude*, kruud a (raw) crudo; (rough) tosco

cruel*, kruu´-el a cruel; **–ty,** s crueldad f.

cruet, kruu´-et s vinagrera f.

cruise, kruu s s viaje por mar m.; v navegar e corso

cruiser, kruu´-sa s crucero m.

crumb, krŏm s miga f.

crumble, krŏm´-bl v desmenuzar; desmigajar

crumple, krŏm´-pl v estrujar; arrugar

crunch, krŏnch v mascar

crush, krŏsh s apiñamiento m.; v aplastar

crust, krŏst s (bread) corteza f.; (pastry) pasta f.; (earth) capa f.; **–y,** a tostado

crutch, krŏch s muleta f.; horquilla f.

cry, krai s grito m.; v (call) gritar; (weep) llorar

cryptic, krip´-tik a escondido; secreto

crystal, kris´-tl s cristal m.

cub, kŏb s (dog) cachorro m.; (bear) osezno m.; (lion) leoncillo m.

cube, kiuub s cubo m.

cubicle, kiuu-bi-kal s caseta f.; cubículo m.

cuckoo, ku´-kuu s cuclillo m.; cuco m.

cucumber, kiuu´-kŏm-ba s pepino m.

cud, kŏd s rumia f.

cuddle, kŏd´-l v abrazar; abrazarse

cudgel, kŏ CH´-l s palo m.; v apalear

cue, kiuu s (acting) apunte m.; (billiard) taco m.

cuff, cŏf s puño m.; (slap) bofetada f.

culinary, kiuu´-li-na-ri a culinario

culminate, kŏl´-mi-neit v culminar

culpability, kŏl-pa-bil´-i-ti s culpabilidad f.

culpable, kŏl-pa-bl a culpable

culprit, kŏl-prit s reo m.; culpable m.

cult, kŏlt s culto m.

cultivate, kŏl´-ti-veit v cultivar

culture, kŏl´-tiur s cultura f.

cumbersome, kŏm´-ber-som a embarazoso; pesado

cunning, kŏn´-ing s astucia f.; a* astuto

cup, kŏp s taza f.; (trophy) copa f.

cupboard, kŏb´-erd s armario m.

cupola, kiuu´-po-la s cúpula f.; domo m.

cur, kĕr s perro de mala raza m.; hombre vil m.

curate, kiu´-reit s vicario m.

curb, kĕrb v refrenar; s freno m.; bordillo m.; cuneta f.; **–stone,** piedra que forma el reborde de la acera f.

curd, kĕrd s cuajada f.; requesón m.

curdle, kĕr´-dl v cuajar

cure, kiu r s (treatment) cura f.; (remedy) remedio m.; v curar; (meat, fish, etc) salar

curiosity, kiu-ri-os´-i-ti s curiosidad f.

curious*, kiu-ri-os a curioso; (peculiar) raro

curl, kĕrl s rizo m.; v rizarse

curlew, kĕr´-liuu s chorlito m.

curly, kĕr´-li a rizado

currant, kŏr´-ant s grosella f.; (dried) pasa de Corinto f.

currency, kŏr´-en-si s moneda f.

current, kŏr´-ent s corriente f.; a* corriente

curry, kŏr´-i s condimento de India m.

curse, kĕrs s maldición f.; v maldecir

cursory, kĕr´-so-ri a rápido; superficial

curt*, kĕrt a brusco; (brief) corto

curtail, ker-teil´ v acortar; (restrict) restringir

curtailment, ker-teil´-ment s acortamiento m.; abreviación f.

curtain, kĕr´-tin s cortina f.; (theater) telón m.

curtsy, kĕrt´-si s (obeisance) reverencia f.

curve, kĕrv s curva f.; v encorvar

cushion, kush´-on s cojín m.; almohada f.

custard, kŏs´-terd s natillas f. pl.

custody, kŏs´-to-di s

custodia m.; (care) cuidado m.

custom, kŏs´-tom s costumbre f.; (trade) parroquia f.; **--house,** aduana f.; **-s duty,** derechos de aduana m. pl.

customary, kŏs´-tom-a-ri a usual

customer, kŏs´-tom-a s ciente m.

customs, kŏs´-toms s aduana f.; (duty) derechos de aduana; **-officer** aduanero/a mf.

cut, kŏt s corte m.; (joint, etc) tajada f.; v cortar; separar; (cards) alzar; (snub) desairar; **-off,** amputar; decapitar; (phone) cortar

cuticle, kiuu´-ti-kl s cutícula f.

cutlass, kŏt´-las s cuchilla f.; espada ancha f.

cutler, kŏt´-la s cuchillero m.

cutlery, kŏt´-la-ri s cuchillería f.; cubiertos m.

cutlet, kŏt´-let s chuleta f.; costilla f.

cutter, kŏt´-a s (tailor) cortador m.; (ship) cúter m.

cuttlefish, kŏt´-l-fish s calamar m.

cyclamen, sik´-la-men s ciclamen m.

cycle, sai´-kl s ciclo m.; bicicleta f.

cylinder, sil´-in-da s cilindro m.

cynical, sin´-i-kal a cínico

cypress, sai´-pres s ciprés m.

dab, dAb s golpe ligero m.; toque m.; v golpear ligeramente; tocar ligeramente

daffodil, dAf´-o-dil s narciso atrompetado m.

dagger, dAg´-a s daga f.; puñal m.

dahlia, dAl´-i-a s dalia f.

daily, dei´-li adv diariamente; a cotidiano

dainty, dein´-ti s golosina f.; a delicado; elegante

dairy, dei´-ri s lechería f.

daisy, dei´-si s margarita f.; maya f.

dale, deil s valle m.

dam, dAm s dique m.; v estancar

damage, dAm´-iCH s daño m.; (average) avería f.; v dañar; averiar

damask, dAm´-ask s damasco m.

damn, dAm v maldecir; interj ¡maldito!

damnation, dAm-nei´-shon s condenación f.

damp, dAmp s humedad f.; a húmedo; v humedecer

damson, dAm´-sn s ciruela damascena f.

dance, daans s baile m.; danza f.; v bailar

dancer, daans´-a s bailador m.; bailarín m.

dandelion, dAn´-di-lai-on s diente de leon m.

dandruff, dAn´-drof s caspa f.

danger, dein´-CHa s peligro m.

dangerous*, dein´-CHer-os a peligroso

dangle, dAn´-gl v colgar

dapper, dAp´-a a apuesto

dare, dér v atreverse; (challenge) desafiar

daring, dé´-ring s audacia f.; a* audaz, osado

dark, daark a obscuro; **–ness,** s obscuridad f.

darling, daar´-ling s querido m.; a querido

darn, daarn v zurcir; s zurcido m.

dart, daart s dardo m.; v lanzar

dash, dAsh s (short line) raya f.; (small quantity) pequeña cantidad f.; v (throw) arrojar; (rush) lanzarse

dashing*, dAsh´-ing a fogoso; elegante

dastard, dAs´-tard s cobarde m.; a* cobarde

data, dei´-ta s pl datos m.; pl antecedentes m. pl.

date, deit s fecha f.; (fruit) dátil m.; v fechar

daughter, doa´-ta s hija f.; **–in-law,** nuera f.

dauntless*, doant´-les a intrépido

dawdle, doa´-dl v callejear; (lag) tardar

dawn, doan s alba m.; v amanecer

day, dei s día m.; **–break**

(see **dawn**)

daylight, dei´-lait s luz del día f.

dazzle, dʌs´-l v deslumbrar; (fig) ofuscar

deacon, dii´-kn s diácono m.

dead, ded a muerto

deaden, ded´-n v amortiguar

deadlock, ded´-lok s egar a un punto muerto m.; desacuerdo m.

deadly, ded´-li adv mortalmente a mortal

deaf, def a sordo

deafen, def´-n v ensordecer

deafness, def´-nes s sordera f.

deal, diil s (business) trato m.; (quantity) cantidad f.; v (trade) negociar; (treat, attend to) tratar; (cards) distribuir; **a great —,** mucho

dealer, diil´-a s negociante m.; (small) tratante m.; (cards) mano f.

dean, diin s deán m.; decano m.

dear, dir a* querido; (expensive) caro; costoso

dearth, dĕrz s escasez f.

death, dez s muerte f.

debar, di-baar´ v excluir; (deprive) privar

debase, di-beis´ v envilecer; degradar

debate, di-beit´ v debatir; s debate m.

debater, di-bei´-ta s orador m.; polemista m.

debauch, di-boach´ v corromper; pervertir

debauchery, di-boa´-cher-i s libertinaje m.

debenture, di-ben´-tiur s obligación f.

debility, di-bil´-i-ti s debilidad f.

debit, deb´-it s debe m.; v debitar

debt, det s deuda f.

debtor, det´-a s deudor m.

decade, de-keid s década f.; decenio m.

decadence, dek´-a-dens s decadencia f.

decaffeinated, di-kaf-in-eit-ed a descafeinado

decamp, di-kʌmp´ v escaparse

decant, di-kʌnt´ v trasegar

decanter, di-kʌn´-ta s garrafa f.

decarbonize, di-kaar´-bon-ai s v descarbonizar

decay, di-kei´ s (decline) decadencia f.; (rot) podredumbre f.; v

decaer; (rot) pudrirse; v (tooth) cariarse; a cariado

decease, di-siis´ v morir; s fallecimiento m.

deceased, di-siist´ s & a muerto m.; difunto m.

deceit, di-siit´ s engaño m.

deceitful*, di-siit´-ful a engañoso; falso

deceive, di-siiv´ v engañar; defraudar

December, di-sem´-ba s diciembre m.

decency, dii´-sen-si s decencia f.

decent*, dii´-sent a decente

deception, di-sep´-shon s decepción f.; (trick) engaño m.

deceptive, di-sep´-tiv a engañoso

decide, di-said´ v decidir; resolver

decided, di-sai´-did a resuelto; firme

decimal, des´-i-mal a decimal

decipher, di-sai´-fa v descifrar

decision, di-si´-s hon s decisión f.

decisive*, di-sai´-siv a decisivo

deck, dek v adornar; s

cubierta f.; (cards)
baraja f.
declaim, di-kleim´ v
declamar
declaration, dek-la-rei´-
shon s declaración f.
declare, di-klér´ v declarar
declension, di-klen´-shon
s (grammar) declinación
f.
decline, di-klain´ s
disminución f.; (values)
baja f.; (ground) declive
m.; (decadence)
decadencia f.; v decaer;
(reject) rehusar;
(grammar) declinar
decompose, di-kom-pou s´
v descomponer
decorate, dek´-o-reit v
decorar; adornar
decoration, dek-o-rei´-
shon s decoración f.
decorous*, dek´-o-ros a
decoroso; decente
decoy, di-koi´ s (thing)
seducción f.; (person)
entruchón m.; (bird)
señuelo m.; v entruchar
decrease, di-kriis´ v
disminuir; decrecer
decrease, dii´-kriis s
disminución f.
decree, di-krii´ v decretar;
s decreto m.
decry, di-krai´ v denigrar;

desacreditar
dedicate, ded´-i-keit v
dedicar; consagrar
deduct, di-dŏkt´ v rebajar;
deducir
deduction, di-dŏk´-shon s
deducción f.; rebaja f.
deed, diid s acto m.;
hecho m.; (valor)
hazaña f.; (document)
escritura f.
deem, diim v juzgar
deep, diip s piélago m.; a*
profundo; hondo
deepen, dii´-pn v
profundizar
deer, dir s venado m.;
ciervo m.
deface, di-feis´ v desfigurar
defamation, def-a-mei´-
shon s difamación f.
defame, di-feim´ v difamar
default, di-foalt´ s
(business) suspensión de
pagos f.; v dejar de
pagar; (law) estar en
rebeldía
defaulter, di-foalt´-a s
delicuente m.;
(payment) que no paga
defeat, di-fiit´ s derrota f.;
v derrotar; frustrar
defect, di-fekt´ s defecto
m.; imperfección f.
defective*, di-fek´-tiv a
defectuoso

defend, di-fend´ v
defender; proteger
defendant, di-fen´-dant s
demandado m.
defender, di-fen´-da s
defensor m.
defense, di-fens´ s defensa
f.; protección f.
defenseless, di-fens´-les a
indefenso
defensible, di-fen´-si-bl a
defendible
defensive*, di-fen´-siv a
defensivo
defer, di-fĕr´ v diferir
deference, def´-er-ens s
deferencia f.
defiance, di-fai´-ans s reto
m.; (challenge) desafío
m.
deficiency, di-fish´-en-si s
falta f.; (money) déficit
m.
deficient, di-fish´-ent a
deficiente
deficit, def´-i-sit s déficit
m.
defile, di-fail´ v (soil)
ensuciar; (moral)
manchar
define, di-fain´ v definirl;
determinar
definite*, def´-i-nit a
definidol; preciso
definition, def-i-ni´-shon s
definición f.

deflect, di-flekt´ v desviar; apartar; desviarse

deflection, di-flek´-shon s desviación f.

deform, di-foɑrm´ v deformar; desfigurar

defraud, di-froɑd´ v defraudar; estafar; frustrar

defray, di-frei´ v costear; pagar

deft*, deft a diestro; mañoso; hábil

defunct, di-föŋkt´ a difunto

defy, di-fai´ v desafiar; retar

degenerate, di-CHen´-er-et v degenerar; s degenerado m.

degradation, deg-ra-dei´-shon s degradación f.; envilecimiento m.

degrade, di-greid´ v degradar; envilecer

degree, di-grii´ s grado m.

dehydrated, di-jai-drei-ted a deshidratado; (milk) en polvo

deign, dein v dignarse; condescender

deject, di-CHekt´ v abatir; desalentar

dejection, di-CHek´-shon s abatimiento m.

delay, di-lei´ s dilación f.;

(late) retraso m.; v retardar; (linger) tardar

delectable, di-lek´-ta-bl a deleitable

delegate, del´-i-guet s delegado m.; v delegar

delete, di-liit´ v borrar

deleterious, di-li-tii´-ri-os a deletéreo; pernicioso

deletion, di-lii´-shon s tachadura f.; cancelación f.

deliberate, di-lib´-er-eit v deliberar; a circunspecto; prudente; premeditado

delicacy, del´-i-ka-si s delicadeza f.; (food) golosina f.

delicate*, del´-i-keit a delicado

delicious*, di-lish´-os a delicioso

delight, de-lait´ v deleitar; s deleite m.; delicia f.

delightful*, de-lait´-ful a delicioso

delineate, di-lin´-i-eit v delinear

delinquent, di-liñ´-kuent s & a delincuente mf.

delirious, di-lir´-i-os a delirante

delirium, di-lir´-i-om s delirio m.

deliver, di-liv´-a v (letters,

goods) entregar; (set free) libertar; (speech) pronunciar; **–y,** s entrega f.; (letters) distribución f.

delude, di-liuud´ v engañar; (mental) alucinar

delusion, di-liuu´-shon s ilusión f.; engaño m.

delve, delv v cavar

demand, di-maand´ s demanda f.; v demandar, exigir

demean (oneself), di-miin´ v rebajar

demeanor, di-mii´-nər s conducta f.; porte m.

demented, di-men´-tid a loco; demente

demise, di-mais ´ s muerte f.

democracy, dim-ok-ras-i s democracia f.

democrat, dem-ou-krɑt s demócrata mf.

democratic, dem-ou-krɑt´-ik a democrático

demolish, di-mol´-ish v demoler

demon, dii´-mon s demonio m.

demonstrate, dem´-on-streit v demostrar

demoralize, dii-mor´-a-lai s v desmoralizar

demote, di-mout v
degradar

demur, di-mĕr´ v
oponerse; s objeción f.

demure*, di-miuur a
reservado; modesto

den, den s antro m.;
(animal) cuchitril m.;
estudio m.

denial, di-nai´-al s
negativa f.; denegación
f.

denim, den-im s tela f.;
vaquera; –s pantalón m
vaquero m. pl.

denizen, den´-i-sn s
vecino m.; habitante
mf.

denomination, di-nom-i-
nei´-shon s
denominación f.;
(religion) secta f.

denote, di-nout´ v denotar

denounce, de-nauns´ v
denunciar; delatar

dense*, dens a espeso;
denso

density, dens´-i-ti s
densidad f.

dent, dent s abolladura f.;
v abollar

dentist, den´-tist s
dentista m.

dentistry, den´-tist-ri s
cirugía dental f.

denude, di-niuud´ v
desnudar; despojar

deny, di-nai´ v negar;
(refuse) rehusar

deodorant, di-ou´-der-ant
s desodorante m.

deodorizer, di-ou´-der-ai-
sa s desodorante m.

depart, di-paart´ v partir;
(decease) morir

department, di-paart´-
ment s departamento m.

department store, di-
paart´-ment stór s
grandes almacenes m. pl

departure, di-paar´-tiur s
partida f.; salida f.;
–platform, andén m.

depend (upon), di-pend´ v
(contingent) depender
de; (trust) confiar en

dependent, di-pen´-dant s
dependiente mf.

depict, di-pikt´ v pintar;
representar

deplete, di-pliit´ v agotar;
disipar

depletion, di-plii´-shon s
agotamiento m.

deplore, di-plór´ v
deplorar

deport, di-pórt v deportar

deportment, di-pórt´-
ment s porte m.;
conducta f.

depose, di-pous´ v
deponer

deposit, di-pos´-it s (bank,
sediment, on account,
etc) depósito m.; v
depositar

depositor, di-pos´-i-ta s
depositante mf.

depository, di-pos´-i-to-ri
s (store) almacén m.

depot, di´-pou s almacén
m.; (station) estación f.

deprave, di-preiv´ v
depravar; viciar

deprecate, dep´-ri-keit v
desaprobar

depreciate, di-prii´-shi-eit
v depreciar; rebajar

depredation, dep-ri-dei´-
shon s pillaje m.;
depredacioñ f.

depress, di-pres´ v
deprimir; desanimar

depression, di-presh´-on s
(trade) depresión f.;
(spirits) abatimiento m.;
(hollow) hondonada f.

deprivation, dep-ri-vei´-
shon s privación f.;
pérdida f.

deprive, di-praiv´ v privar;
despojar

depth, depz s profundidad
f.; hondo m.

deputation, di-piu-tei´-
shon s diputación f.

deputy, dep´-iu-ti s
substituto m.; delegado

m.

derailment, di-reil´-ment s
descarrilamiento m.

derange, di-reinCH´ v
desarreglar; **–ment,** s
desarreglo m.; trastorno
mental m.

derelict, der´-i-likt a
abandonado; s derrelicto
m.

deride, di-raid´ v mofar;
escarnecer

derision, di-rii´-shon s
mofa f.; escarnio m.

derisive*, di-rai´-siv a
irrisorio; burlesco

derive, di-raiv´ v derivar;
(knowledge) deducir

derogatory, di-rog´-a-to-ri
a despectivo

descend, di-send´ v bajar;
(lineage) descender

descendant, di-send´-ant s
descendiente m.

descent, di-sent´ s bajada
f.; (lineage)
descendencia f.

describe, di-skraib´ v
describir

description, di-skrip´-shon
s descripción f.

desecrate, des´-i-kreit v
profanar

desert, des ´-ert s
(wilderness) desierto m.

desert, di-sẽrt´ v

abandonar; (mil)
desertar

deserter, di-sẽrt´-a s
desertor m.

desertion, di-sẽr´-shon s
abandono m.; (mil)
deserción f.

deserve, di-sẽrv´ v
merecer

deservedly, di-sẽr´-ved-li
adv merecidamente

desiccate, di-sik´-eit v
desecar; secar

design, di-s ain´ s (sketch)
diseño m.; (intention)
intención m.; (pattern)
patrón m.; v (plan)
proyectar; (sketch)
diseñar

designing, di-s ai´-ning a
intrigante; artero

desirable, di-s ai´-ra-bl a
deseable

desire, di-sair´ s deseo m.;
v desear

desirous, di-sai´-ros a
deseoso

desist, di-sist´ v desistir;
cesar

desk, desk s pupitre m.;
escritorio m.

desolate, des´-o-leit a
desolado; v desolar

despair, di-sper´ v
desesperar; s
desesperación f.

desperate*, des´-per-eit a
desesperado

despicable, des´-pi-ka-bl a
despreciable

despise, di-spai s ´ v
despreciar

despite, di-spait´ prep a
pesar de

despoil, di-spoil´ v
despojar

despond, di-spond´ v
desalentarse

despondency, di-spon´-
den-si s desaliento m.

despot, des´-pot s déspota
m.; tirano m.

dessert, di-sẽrt´ s postres
m. pl.

destination, des-ti-nei´-
shon s destinación f.

destine, des´-tin v destinar

destiny, des-tin´-i s
destino m.; hado m.

destitute, des´-ti-tiuut a
destituído

destitution, des-ti-tiuu´-
shon s destitución f.;
privación f.

destroy, di-stroi´ v destruir

destruction, dis-trõk´-
shon s destrucción f.

destructive*, dis-trõk´-tiv
a destructivo

desultory, des´-ol-to-ri a
variable; inconstante

detach, di-tAch´ v separar;

(*mil*) destacar

detachable, di-tAch´-a-bl *a* movible

detail, di-teil´ *v* detallar

detail, dii´-teil *s* detalle *m.*; pormenor *m.*

detain, di-tein´ *v* detener

detect, di-tekt´ *v* descubrir; sorprender; detectar

detective, di-tek´-tiv *s* detective *m.*

detention, di-ten´-shon *s* detención *f.*

deter, di-těr´ *v* disuadir; acobardar

detergent, di-těr´-CHent *s* & *a* detergente *m.*

deteriorate, di-tii´-ri-ou-reit *v* deteriorar; desmejorar

determine, di-těr´-min *v* determinar; resolverse

detest, di-test´ *v* detestar

dethrone, di-zroun´ *v* destronar

detonation, di-to-nei´-shon *s* detonación *f.*

detour, di-túr´ *s* vuelta *f.*; rodeo *m.*; desvío *m.*

detract, di-trakt´ *v* detraer; (value) disminuir

detrimental, det-ri-men´-tal *a* perjudicial

deuce, diuus *s* (cards,

dice, two) dos *m.*; (equality) a patas *f. pl.*

devastate, dev´-as-teit *v* devastar

develop, di-vel´-op *v* desenvolver; desarrollar

development, di-vel´-op-ment *s* desarrollo *m.*

deviate, dii´-vi-eit *v* desviarse

device, di-vais´ *s* medio *m.*; invención *f.*

devil, dev´-l *s* diablo *m.*; demonio *m.*

devilry, dev´-il-ri *s* diablura *f.*

devise, di-vais´ *v* inventar; tramar; (law) disponer

devoid, di-void´ *a* falto; desprovisto

devote, di-vout´ *v* dedicar

devour, di-vaur´ *v* devorar

devout*, di-vaut´ *a* devoto; piadoso

dew, diuu *s* rocío *m.*

dexterous*, deks´-ter-os *a* diestro; hábil

diabetes, dai-a-bii´-tis *s* diabetes *f.*

diabolical*, dai-a-bol´-i-kal *a* diabólico

diagnose, dai-ag-nou´s´ *v* diagnosticar

diagonal, dai-ag´-o-nal *s* diagonal *m.*; *a** diagonal

diagram, dai´-a-gram *s*

diagrama *m.*

dial, dai´-al *s* (clock) esfera *f.*; (sun) reloj de sol *m.*; *v* marcar

dialect, dai´-a-lekt *s* dialecto *m.*

dialogue, dai´-a-log *s* diálogo *m.*

diameter, dai-am´-i-ta *s* diámetro *m.*

diamond, dai´-a-mond *s* diamante *f.*; (cards) oros *m. pl.*

diaper rash, nA-pi rAsh *s* escaldamiento *m.*; por pañales húmedos

diarrhea, dai-a-rii´-a *s* diarrea *f.*

diary, dai´-a-ri *s* diario *m.*; (business) agenda *f.*

dice, dais *s pl* dados *m. pl.*

dictate, dik-teit´ *v* dictar

dictator, dik-teit´-a *s* dictador *m.* -ora *f.*

dictionary, dik´-shon-a-ri *s* diccionario *m.*

die, dai *v* morir; fallecer; *s* (stamp) cuño *m.*; (mold) matriz *f.*

diesel, dii-sal *s* diesel *m*; gasóleo *m.*

diet, dai´-et *s* dieta *f.*; alimento *m.*; régimen *m.*; **to put on a –,** *v* poner a dieta; **to be on a –,** estar a dieta

differ, dif´-*a* v diferir; diferenciarse; (disagree) disentir

difference, dif´-er-ens s diferencia f.; disputa f.

different*, dif´-er-ent a diferente

difficult, dif´-ik-elt a difícil; **–y,** s dificultad f.

diffident*, dif´-id-ent a desconfiado; (fig) corto

diffuse, dif-iuus´ v difundir; a difuso

dig, dig v cavar; excavar

digest, di-CHest´ v digerir; s recopilación f.

digestion, di-CHes´-tion s digestión f.

dignified, dig´-ni-faid a grave; digno

dignitary, dig´-ni-ta-ri s dignatario m.

dignity, dig´-ni-ti s dignidad f.

digression, di-gresh´-on s digresión f.

dike, daik s dique m.; presa f.

dilapidated, di-lAp´-i-deit-id a dilapidado

dilapidation, di-lAp´-i-dei-shon s dilapidación f.

dilate, di-leit´ v dilatar; dilatarse

dilatory, dil´-a-to-ri a dilatorio; lento

dilemma, di-lem´-a s dilema m.

diligence, dil´-i-CHens s diligencia f.

diligent*, dil´-i-CHent a diligente

dilute, di-liuut´, dai-li-uut´; v diluir; aguar

dim, dim v obscurecer; a* obscuro; (sight) turbio

dimension, di-men´-shon s dimensión f.; medida f.

diminish, di-min´-ish v disminuir

dimness, dim´-nes s obscuridad f.

dimple, dim´-pel s hoyuelo m.

din, din v ensordecer; s estruendo m.; estrépito m.

dine, dain v comer

dingy, din´-CHi a deslustrado; deslucido

dinghy, ding-i or ding-gi s bote m.; lancha f.; neumática

dining car, dain´-ing-kaar s coche restaurante m.

dining room, dain´-ing-ruum s comedor m.

dinner, din´-a s comida f.; (supper) cena f.

dip, dip s inmersión f.; v sumergir; (moisten) mojar; (slope) bajar

diphtheria, dif-zii´-ri-a s difteria f.

diplomacy, di-plou´-ma-si s diplomacia f.

dire, dair a terrible; horrendo

direct, di-rekt´ v dirigir; a directo

direction, di-rek´-shon s dirección f.; (instruction) orden f.

directly, di-rekt´-li adv directamente; en seguida; conj luego que

director, di-rek´-ta s director m.; administrador m.

directory, di-rek´-to-ri s directorio m.; (small) guía f.

dirt, dërt s basura f.; lodo m.; suciedad f.

dirty, dër´-ti v ensuciar; a sucio

disability, dis-a-bil´-i-ti s inhabilidad f.; incapacidad f.

disable, dis-ei´-bl v mutilar; inutilizar

disabled, dis-ei´-bld a minusválido

disadvantage, dis-Ad-vaan´-tiCH s desventaja f.

disagree, dis-a-grii v disentir; discrepar;

incomodar

disagreeable, dis-*a*-grii´-*a*-bl *a* desagradable

disallow, dis-*a*-lau´ *v* desaprobar; rechazar

disappear, dis-*a*-pir´ *v* desaparecer

disappearance, dis-*a*-pi´-rans *s* desaparición *f*.

disappoint, dis-*a*-point´ *v* desengañar; desilusionar; frustrar; (promise) dar chasco; –ment, *s* desengaño *m*.; chasco *m*.; desilusión *f*.

disapprove, dis-*a*-pruuv´ *v* desaprobar

disarm, dis-aarm´ *v* desarmar

disaster, dis -aas´-ta *s* desastre *m*.

disastrous*, dis -aas-tros *a* desastroso

disavow, dis-*a*-vau´ *v* repudiar; desconocer

discard, dis-kaard´ *v* descartar; (cast off) desechar

discern, di-sěrn´ *v* discernir

discharge, dis-chaar CH´ *s* (dismissal) despedida *f*.; (gun) descarga *f*.; (merchandise) descargo *m*.; (med.) derrame *m*.; *v* despedir; descargar;

(fulfill) cumplir; (acquit) absolver; (release) poner en libertad

disciple, dis-ai´-pl *s* discípulo *m*.

discipline, dis´-i-plin *s* disciplina *f*.

disclaim, dis-kleim´ *v* renunciar; (deny) desconocer

disclose, dis-klous´ *v* revelar; descubrir

disclosure, dis-klou´-SHur *s* revelación *f*.

disco, diskod *s* disco *m*.

discolor, dis-kal´-a *v* descolorar; desteñir

discomfit, dis-kŏm´-fit *v* desconcertar; –ure, *s* desconcierto *m*.

discomfort, dis-kŏm´-fort *s* incomodidad *f*.

disconnect, dis-ko-nekt´ *v* desunir; desconectar

discontent, dis-kon-tent´ *s* descontento *m*.; –ed, *a* descontento

discontinue, dis-kon-tin´-iuu *v* interrumpir; (deter) aplazar; descontinuar

discord, dis-koard´ *s* discordia *f*.

discotheque, dis-ko-tek *s* discoteca *f*. ˙

discount, dis-kaunt *v* descontar; *s* descuento *m*.

discourage, dis-kŏr´-iCH *v* desalentar

discourse, dis-kórs´ *v* discurrir; conversar; *s* discurso *m*.; conversación *f*.

discourteous*, dis-koar´-ti-os *a* descortés

discover, dis-kŏv-*a* *v* descubrir

discovery, dis-kŏv´-er-i descubrimiento *m*.

discreet*, dis-kriit´ *a* discreto

discrepancy, dis-krep´-ans-i *s* discrepancia *f*.

discriminate, dis-krim´-i-neit *v* distinguir; discriminar

discuss, dis-kŏs´ *v* discutir

disdain, dis-dein´ *v* desdeñar *s* desdén *m*.

disdainful*, dis-dein´-ful *a* desdeñoso

disease, di-siis, enfermedad *f*.; dolencia *f*.

disembark, dis-em-baark *v* desembarcar

disengaged, dis-en-geiCH´ *a* libre; vacante

disentangle, dis-en-tAng´-gl *v* desenredar

disfigure, dis-fig´-*a* *v*
desfigurar

disgrace, dis-greis´ *s*
deshonra *f.*; *v* deshonrar

disguise, dis-gais´ *s* disfraz
m.; *v* disfrazar; (feelings)
ocultar

disgust, dis-gŏst´ *v*
disgustar; *s* repugnancia
f.

dish, dish *s* fuente *f.*;
(meal) plato *m.*; **–cloth,**
trapo *m.*; **–up,** *v* servir

dishearten, dis-jaar´-tn *v*
desalentar

disheveled, di-shev´-eld *a*
desgreñado

dishonest*, di-son´-ist *a*
deshonesto

dishonor, di-son´-a *v*
deshonrar; *s* deshonra *f.*

dishwasher, dish-uoash´-a
s lavaplatos *m.*;
lavavajillas *m.*; (person)
friegaplatos *mf.*

dishwashing liquid, dish-
uoash-ing lik´-uid *s*
líquido lavavajillas *m.*

disillusion, dis-i-liuu´-
shon *s* desilusión *f.*;
desengaño *m.*

disinclination, dis-in-klin-
ei´-shon *s* aversión *f.*

disinfect, dis-in-fekt´ *v*
desinfectar

disinherit, dis-in-jer´-it *v*

desheredar

disjoin, dis-CHoin´ *v*
descoyuntar; separar;
–ted, *a* dislocado;
separado; desarticulado

disk, disk *s* disco *m.*

disk jockey, disk CHok´-i
s pinchadiscos *mf.*

dislike, dis-laik´ *v* tener
aversión; *s* aversión *f.*

dislocate, dis´-lo-keit *v*
dislocar; (joint)
descoyuntar

disloyal, dis-loi´-al *a*
desleal; infiel

dismal*, dis´-mal *a* triste;
(gloomy) lúgubre

dismay, dis-mei´ *v*
aterrorizar; *s*
consternación *f.*

dismiss, dis-mis´ *v*
despedir; (mentally)
descartar

dismount, dis-maunt´ *v*
desmontar

disobedient*, dis-o-bii´-
di-ent *a* desobediente

disobey, dis-ou-bei´ *v*
desobedecer

disorder, dis-oar´-da *s*
desorden *m.*; *v*
desordenar

disorientated, dis-oar-
iien-teit-ed *a*
desorientado

disown, dis-oun´ *v*

repudiar; desconocer

disparage, dis-pAr´-iCH *v*
rebajar

dispatch, dis-pAch *s*
(message) despacho *m.*;
v despachar

dispel, dis-pel´ *v* dispersar;
disipar

dispensary, dis-pen´-*sa*-ri *s*
dispensario *m.*

dispensation, dis-pen-sei´-
shon *s* distribución *f.*;
(eccl) dispensa *f.*

disperse, dis-pĕrs´ *v*
dispersar

display, dis-plei´ *v* exhibir;
s exhibición *f.*

displease, dis-pliis´ *v*
desagradar

displeasure, dis-plesh´-er *s*
desagrado *m.*

disposable, dis-pous-abl *a*
desechable; de usar y
tirar; (income)
disponible

disposal, dis-pou´-sal *s*
disposición *f.*; venta *f.*

dispose, dis-pous´ *v*
disponer; vender

disprove, dis-pruuv´ *v*
refutar

disputable, dis-piuu´-*ta*-bl
a discutible

dispute, dis-piuut´ *v*
disputar; *s* disputa *f.*

disqualify, dis-kuou´-li-fai

v descalificar
disquiet, dis-kuai´-et *v*
inquietar; s inquietud *f*.
disregard, dis-ri-gaard´ *v*
desatender; s
desatención *f*.
disrepute, dis-ri-piuut´ s
descrédito *m*.
disrespect, dis-ri-spekt´ s
falta de respeto *f*.; **–ful***,
a irrespetuoso
disrupt, dis-rŏpt´ *v* (plans)
desbaratar; trastornar;
(conversation)
interrumpir
dissatisfy, di-sAt´-is-fai *v*
descontentar
dissect, dis-sekt´ *v* disecar
dissent, di-sent´ *v* disentir;
s disentimiento *m*.
dissimilar, di-sim´-i-lar *a*
diferente; disímil
dissipate, dis´-si-peit *v*
disipar; esparcir
dissociate, di-sou -shi-eit
v desunir; disociar
dissolute*, dis´-o-liuut *a*
disoluto; libertino
dissolve, di-solv´ *v*
disolver
dissuade, di-sueid´ *v*
disuadir
distance, dis´-tans s
distancia *f*.
distant*, dis´-tant *a*
distante; esquivo; frío

distasteful*, dis-teist´-ful
a desagradable
distemper, dis-tem´-pa s
(paint) destemple *m*.;
(veterinary) moquillo
m.; (peevish) mal
humor *m*.
distend, dis-tend´ *v*
distender; dilatar
distill, dis-til´ *v* destilar
distinct*, dis-tiñkt´ *a*
distinto; diferente
distinction, dis-tiñk´-shon
s distinción *f*.;
diferencia *f*.
distinguish, dis-tiñ´-güish
v distinguir
distort, dis-toart´ *v* falsear;
torcer
distract, dis-trAkt´ *v*
distraer; perturbar; **–ion**,
s distracción *f*.;
perturbación *f*.; locura *f*.
distress, dis-tres´ s pena *f*.;
angustia *f*.; *v* angustiar;
to be in –, (*naut*) estar
en apuros; **–ing**, *a*
penoso
distribute, dis-trib´-iuut *v*
distribuir; clasificar
distributor, dis-trib´-iuut-
a s (*mech*) mecanismo
distribuidor *m*.; (*comm*)
comerciante distribuidor
m.; concesionario *m*.
district, dis´-trikt s distrito

m.; región *f*.
distrust, dis-trŏst´ *v*
desconfiar s
desconfianza *f*.
disturb, dis-tĕrb´ *v*
perturbar; **–ance**, s
interrupción *f*.; disturbio
m.; (mob) tumulto *m*.
disuse, dis-iuus´ s desuso
m.
ditch, dich s zanja *f*.; foso
m.
ditto, dit´-oh *adv* idem
dive, daiv *v* zambullirse;
sumergirse; **–r**, s buzo *m*.
diverge, di-vĕrCH´ *v*
divergir
diverse, dai-vĕrs´ *a* varios;
diversos
diversion, di-vĕr´-shon s
desviación *f*.;
distracción *f*.
divert, dai-vĕrt´ *v* desviar;
(attention) distraer
divest, di-vest´ *v*
desnudar; (deprive)
despojar
divide, di-vaid´ *v* dividir;
separar; (distribute)
repartir
divine, di-vain´ *v*
adivinar; *a** divino
division, di´-vi-sh on s
división *f*.; partición *f*.
divorce, di-vórs´ *v*
divorciar; s divorcio *m*.

divulge, di-vŏlCH´ v
revelar

dizzy, dis´-i a vertiginoso;
(faint) desvanecido

do, duu, v hacer; servir;
bastar; cocer; hallarse

docile, dos´-il a dócil;
sumiso

dock, dok s dársena f.;
muelle m.; **dry-,** astillero
m.; **-yard,** astillero m.

doctor, dok -ta s médico
m.; v curar

doctrine, dok´-trin s
doctrina f.; dogma m.

document, dok´-iu-ment s
documento m.; **-ary,** s
(film) película
documental f.

dodge, doCH v evadir;
esquivar; s evasiva f.

dog, dog s perro m.; **-ged,**
a tenaz; terco

dole, doul v distribuir; s
distribución f.; dádiva f.;
imosna f.

doleful*, doul´-ful a
doloroso; lastimoso

doll, dol s muñeca f.

dollar, dol-a s dólar m.

domain, do-mein´ s
propriedad f.; dominio f.

dome, doum s cúpula f.;
domo m.

domestic, do-mes´-tik a
criado m.; doméstico m.;

a doméstico; **-ated,** a
domesticado

domicile, dom´-i-sail s
domicilio m.; v
domiciliar

dominate, dom´-i-eit v
dominar

domineer, dom-i-nir´ v
dominar; tiranizar

donate, do-neit v donar

donation, do-nei´-shon s
donación f.

donkey, dong´-ki s asno
m.; burro m.

donor, do´-na s donante
m.

doom, duum s sentencia
f.; destino m.; ruina f.; v
predestinar; **-sday,** s dia
del juicio final

door, dór s puerta f.; **--
keeper,** portero m.; **--
knocker,** picaporte m.;
--mat, tapete m.; **--
step,** escalera de entrada
f.

dormant, dor´-mant a
desuso; inactivo

dormitory, dor´-mi-to-ri s
dormitorio m.

dormouse, dor´-maus s
lirón m.

dose, dous s dosis f.; v
dosificar

dot, dot s punto m.; v
puntear

double, dób´-l s doble m.;
duplicado m.; v doblar

doubt, daut v dudar; s
duda f.; **-ful*,** a dudoso;
-less, adv sin duda

douche, dush s ducha f.

dough, dou s pasta f.;
masa f.

dove, dóv s paloma f.; **--
cote,** palomar m.

down, daun adv & prep
abajo; s plumón m.;
-cast, a abatido; **-fall,** s
caida f.; ruina f.; **-pour,**
aguacero m.; chaparrón
m.; **-wards,** adv hacia
abajo

dowry, dau´-ri s dote f.

doze, dous v dormitar;
sueño ligero m.

dozen, dŏs´-n s docena f.

drab, drAb a pardusco

draft, draaft s (money)
giro m.; (sketch) boceto
m.; (writing) borrador
m.; v redactar; (air)
corriente de aire f.

draftsman, draafts´man s
delineante m.

drag, drAg v arrastrar;
tirar; s red f.

dragon, drAg´-on s dragón
m.; **-fly,** libélula f.

drain, drein v desaguar; s
desaguadero m.;
(trench) zanja f.; **-age,**

desagüe m.

drake, dreik s pato m.

dram, drAm s dracma f.

dramatic, drAm-a´-tick a dramático

draper, drei´-pa s pañero m.

drastic, drAs´-tik a drástico

draw, droa v (pull) tirar; (attract) atraer; (sketch) dibujar; (bill) girar; (money) cobrar

drawback, droa´-bAk s desventaja f.

drawer, droa´-a s (furniture) cajón m.; (bill) girador m.; **–s,** pl calzoncillos m. pl.

drawing, droa´-ing s derechos de giro; (sketch) dibujo m.

drawl, droal v arrastrar las palabras

dray, drei s carromato m.

dread, dred s miedo m.; v temer

dreadful*, dred´-ful a terrible

dream, driim s sueño m.; v soñar

dreary, dri´-ri a triste; sombrío; fatigante

dredge, dreCH v dragar; **–r,** s draga f.

dregs, dregs s pl heces f.

pl.; sedimento m.

drench, drench v empapar; mojar

dress, dres s vestido m.; traje m.; v vestir; vestirse; (wounds) curar; (hair) peinar

dressing, dres´-ing s (med) vendajes m. pl.; (culinary) condimento m.; **–gown,** bata f.; **–room,** tocador m.

dressmaker, dres´-meik-a s modista f.

dribble, drib´-l v gotear

drift, drift s deriva f.; (snow, etc) torbellino m.; (tendency) tendencia f.; v derivar; impeler

drill, dril s (mil) ejercicio m.; (tool) taladro m.; v enseñar el ejercicio; taladrar

drink, dring-k s bebida f.; v beber

drip, drip v gotear; chorrear; s gotera f.

dripping, drip´-ing s (fat) pringue m.

drive, draiv v conducir; guiar; s (approach) calzada para coches f.; (outing) paseo en coche m.

driver, drai´-va s cochero

m.; chófer m.; (owner) conductor m.; (engine) maquinista m.

driver's license, draiv-ing lai-sens s carnet m.; de conducir

drizzle, dris´-l v lloviznar; s llovizna f.

droll, droul a jocoso; gracioso

drone, droun s zángano m.; v zumbar

droop, druup v inclinarse; (plants) marchitarse

drop, drop s caída f.; (liquid) gota f.; v caer; (let fall) dejar caer

dropsy, drop´-si s hidropesía f.

drought, draut s sequía f.; sequedad f.

drove, drouv s manada f.; rebaño m.

drown, draun v ahogar; ahogarse

drowsy, drau´-si a soñoliento; adormecido

drudge, drö CH s ganapán f.;esclavo del hagar o del trabajo m.; v afanarse

drudgery, drö CH-a-ri s faena f.

drug, drög v dragar s droga f.

druggist, drö´-guist s boticario m.;

farmaceútico m.

drum, drom s tambor m.;
(ear) tímpano m.;
(container) bidón m.;
–mer, tambor m.

drunk, drŏñg´-k a
borracho; **–ard** s
borrachón m.; **–enness,**
embriaguez f.

dry, drai v secar a * seco;
–ness, s sequedad f.

dubious*, diuu´-bi-os a
dudoso

duchess, dŏch´-es s
duquesa f.

duck, dŏk s pato m.; v
(immerse) zambullir;
(stoop) esquivar

due, diuu s (owing)
debido n.; a (owing)
debido; (bill) vencido

duel, diuu´-el s duelo m.

duet, diu-et´ s dúo m.

duke, diuuk s duque m.

dull, dŏl a (mind) lerdo;
(color) apagado;
(weather) cubierto;
(blunt) sin filo

duly, diuu´-li adv
oportunamente; a su
tiempo

dumb, dŏm a mudo

dumbfound, dŏm-faund´ v
dejar sin habla

dummy, dŏm´-i s (figure)
maniquí m.; (sham)

imitado m.; (cards)
mudo m.

dump, dŏmp s depósito
m.; estiba f.; v verter

dung, dŏñg s boñiga f.;
(manure) estiércol m.

dungeon, dŏn´-CHen s
calabozo m.

dupe, diuup s incauto m.;
v embaucar

duplicate, diuu´-pli-keit s
duplicado m.; doble m.;
v duplicar

durable, diu´-ra-bl a
durable; duradero

duration, diu-rei´-shon s
duración f.

during, diu´-ring prep
durante

dusk, dŏsk s obscuridad f.;
(evening) crepúsculo
m.; **–y,** a obscuro;
(color) moreno

dust, dŏst s polvo m.; v
quitar el polva

duster, dŏst´-a s plumero
m.; (cloth) trapo m.

dutiful*, diuu´-ti-ful s
obediente; respetuoso

duty, diuu´-ti s deber m.;
(customs) derechos m.
pl.; (service) servicio m.

dwarf, duoarf s & a enano
m.; v achicar

dwell, duel v habitar;
residir; **–er,** s habitante

m.; residente m.; **–ing,**
domicilio m.

dwindle, duin´-dl v
mermar; disminuirse

dye, dai s tinte m.;
colorante f.; v teñir

dynamite, dai´-na-mait s
dinamita f.

dynamo, dai´-na-mou s
dínamo m.

dysentery, dis´-n-tri s
disentería f.

each, iich, *pron* cada uno, todos; *a* cada todo; **–other,** *pron*el uno al otro; mutuamente

eager, ii´-g*A a* * deseoso; **–ness,** *s* ansia *f*.

eagle, ii´-gl *s* águila *m*.

ear, i r *s* oreja *f*.; (music) oído *m*.; (corn) espiga *f*.; **–mark,** *v* marcar; **–phone,** *s* auricular *m*.; **–ring,** pendiente *m*.; **–wig,** tijereta *f*.

earl, ěrl *s* conde *m*.

early, ěr´-li *adv* temprano; *a* matinal; primitivo

earn, ěrn *v* ganar; **–ings,** *s pl* sueldo *m*.

earnest*, ěr´-nest *a* serio; sincero

earring, ir-ing *s* pendiente *m*.; arete *m*.; zarcillo *m*.

earth, ěrz *s* tierra *f*.; suelo *m*.; **–enware,** *s* loza de barro *f*.; **–ly,** *a* terrestre; **–quake,** *s* terremoto *m*.

ease, iis *s* (comfort) comodidad *f*.; (relief) alivio *m*.; (facility) facilidad *f*.; *v* aliviar; **not at –,** mal a gusto

easel, ii´-sl *s* caballete de pintor *m*.

easily, ii´-si-li *adv* fácilmente

east, iist *s* este *m*.; oriente *m*.; **–erly,** *a* del este; **–ern,** oriental

Easter, iis´-ta *s* Pascua de Resurrección *f*.; semana santa *f*.

easy, ii´-si *a* fácil; cómodo; **–chair,** *s* sillón *m*.

eat, iit *v* comer; (worm; acid) roer

eatable, ii´-ta-bl *a* comestible; **–s,** *s pl* comestibles *m. pl.*

eavesdropper, iiv *s* ´-drop-*a s* el que escucha escondido; curioso

ebb, eb *v* menguar; *s* reflujo *m*.

ebony, eb´-o-ni *s* ébano *m*.

eccentric, ek-sen´-trik *a* excéntrico

echo, ek´-ou *s* eco *m*.

eclipse, i-klips´ *s* eclipse *m*.; *v* eclipsar

economic, ek-on-om-ik *a* económico; rentable

economize, i-kon´-o-mais *v* economizar

economy, i-kon´-o-mi *s* economía *f*.

ecstasy, ek´-sta-si *s* extasis *m*.

eczema, ek-sma *s* eccema *m*.; eczema *m*.

edge, eCH *v* (border) ribetear; *s* (knife) filo *m*.; (brink) borde *m*.

edible, ed´-i-bl *a* comestible

edify, ed´-i-fai *v* edificar

edit, ed´-it *v* redactar; editar; **–ion,** *s* edición *f*.; **–or,** editor *m*.; (press) director *m*.; **–orial,** *a* artículo de fondo m.

educate, ed´-iu-keit v educar; (rear) criar

education, ed-iu-kei´-shon s educación f.

eel, iil s anguila f.

efface, ef-eis´ v borrar

effect, ef-ekt´ v efectuar; s efecto m.

effective*, ef-ek´-tiv a eficaz; operativo

effeminate, ef-em´-i-neit a afeminado

effervescing, ef-er-ves´-ing a efervescente

effete, i´-fiit a estéril; agotado

efficacious*, ef-i-kei´-shos a eficaz

efficient, ef-i´-shent a competente; eficiente

effort, ef´-ert s esfuerzo m.

effusive*, ef-iuu´-siv a efusivo

egg, eg s huevo m.; --cup, huevera f.

egotism, eg´-ou-tism s egotismo m.

eiderdown, ai´-der-daun s edredón m.; colcha f.

eight, eit s & a ocho m.; --h, octavo m.; --een, s & a diez y ocho m.; --eenth, décimoctavo m.; --y, s & a ochenta m.

either, ai´-Da pron uno u

otro; cualquiera de los dos; adv tampoco

eject, i-CHekt´ v arrojar; expeler; despedir

elaborate, i-lAb´-o-reit v elaborar; a* elaborado

elapse, i-lAps´ v pasar; transcurrir

elastic, i-las´-tik s & a elástico m.

elate, i-leit´ v exaltar; elevar; a exaltado

elbow, el´-bou s codo m.; v codear

elder, el´-da s mayor m. & f.; (tree) saúco m.

elderly, el´-der-li a anciano

eldest, el´-dest a el mayor; primogénito a mayor

elect, i-lekt´ v elegir; s & a electo m.

election, i-lek´-shon s elección f.

electric (al*), i-lek´-trik(al) a eléctrico

electrician, i-lek-trish´-an s electricista m.

electricity, i-lek-tri´-si-ti s electricidad f.

electrify, i-lek´-tri-fai v electrizar

electronic*, i-lek-tron´-ik a electrónico

electroplate, i-lek´-troh-

pleit s artículo galvanizado m.; v galvanizar

elegance, el´-i-gans s elegancia f.

elegant*, el´-i-gant a elegante

element, el´-i-ment s elemento m.

elementary, el-i-men´-ta-ri a elemental; rudimentario

elephant, el´-i-fant s elefante m.

elevate, el´-i-veit v elevar; alzar; exaltar

elevated, el´-i-vei-tid a elevado; exaltado

eleven, il-ev´-n s & a once m.; --th, undécimo m.

elicit, il-is´-it v deducir; (draw out) sonsacar

eligible, el´-i-CHi-bl a elegible; apropiado

eliminate, i-lim´-i-neit v eliminar

elite, ei-liit´ s lo selecto m.; la flor f.

elk, elk s alce m.

elm, elm s olmo m.

elongate, ii-long´-eit v alargar

elope, i-loup´ v fugarse; --ment, s fuga f.

eloquent*, el´-o-kuent a

elocuente

else, els a otro; *adv* más
bién; **–where,** en otra
parte

elucidate, i-liuu´-si-deit *v*
aclarar

elude, i-liuud´ *v* eludir;
escapar

elusive*, i-liuu´-siv *a*
evasivo; esquivo

emaciate, i-mei´-shi-eit *v*
extenuar; adelgazar

E-mail, ii-meil *s* correo
electrónico *m.*

emanate, em´-a-neit *v*
emanar

emancipate, i-mAn´-si-
peit *v* emancipar

embalm, em-baam´ *v*
embalsamar

embankment, em-bang-
k´-ment *s* terraplén *m.*;
(water) malecón *m.*

embargo, em-baar´-gou *s*
embargo *m.*; *v* embargar

embark, em-baark´ *v*
embarcar; embarcarse

embarrass, em-bar-*ass v*
avergonzar; desconcerar;
turbar; apurar; **–ment,** *s*
turbación *f.*

embassy, em´-bAs-i *s*
embajada *f.*

embellish, em-bel´-ish *v*
embellecer; adornar

ember, em´-ber *s* ascua *f.*;

–s, *pl* rescoldo *m.*

embezzle, em-bes´-l *v*
desfalcar

embitter, em-bit´-a *v*
amargar; agriar

embody, em-bod´-i *v*
incorporar

embolden, em-boul´-dn *v*
animar; envalentonar

embrace, em-breis´ *v*
abrazar; *s* abrazo *m.*

embroider, em-broi´-da *v*
bordar; **–y,** *s* bordado *m.*

embroil, em-broil´ *v*
embrollar; confundir

emerald, em´-e-rald *s*
esmeralda *f.*

emerge, i-mĕrCH´ *v*
emerger; surgir; **–ncy,** *s*
emergencia *f.*; necesidad
urgente *f.*

emetic, i-met´-ik *s*
emético *m.*

emigrant, em´-i-grant *s*
emigrante *m.*

emigrate, em´-i-greit *v*
emigrar

eminence, em´-in-ens *s*
altura *f.*; eminencia *f.*

eminent*, em´-in-ent *a*
eminente

emissary, em´-is-a-ri *s*
emisario *m.*

emit, i-mit´ *v* emitir;
arrojar; exhalar

emotion, i-mou´-shon *s*

emoción *f.*; sensación *f.*

emperor, em´-per-a *s*
emperador *m.*

emphasis, em´-fa-sis *s*
énfasis *f.*

emphasize, em´-fa-sais *v*
acentuar; recalcar

emphatical*, em-fAt´-i-kl
a enfático

empire, em´-pai *r s*
imperio *m.*; dominio *m.*

employ, em-ploi´ *v*
emplear; **–er,** *s*
(principal) jefe *m.*;
(master) patrón *m.*;
–ment, empleo *m.*

emporium, em-pou´-ri-om
s emporio *m.*

empower, em-pau´-a *v*
autorizar; comisionar

empress, em´-pres *s*
emperatriz *f.*

empty, em´-ti *v* vaciar;
evacuar; *a* vacío

emulate, em´-iu-leit *v*
emular; imitar

emulation, em-iu-lei´-
shon *s* emulación *f.*

enable, en-ei´-bl *v*
habilitar; facilitar;
permitir

enact, en-Akt´ *v* decretar;
estatuir; efectuar

enamel, en-Am´-l *s*
esmalte *m.*; *v* esmaltar

enamored, en-Am´-erd *a*

enamorado

enchant, en-chaant´ *v* hechizar; (delight) encantar; **–ment,** *s* (fascination) encanto *m.*

encircle, en-sĕr´-kl *v* circundar; cercar; (round-up) rodear

enclose, en-klou s ´ *v* cercar; incluir

enclosure, en-klou´-shur *s* cercado *m.*; (in envelope, parcel, etc) contenido *m.*

encore, Ang-koar´ *v* pedir la repetición; *interj* ¡bis! ¡que se repita!

encounter, en-kann´-ta *s* encuentro *m.*; combate *m.*; *v* encontrar; batirse

encourage, en-kŏr´-ich *v* alentar; (spur) fomentar; **–ment,** *s* estímulo *m.*; fomento *m.*

encroach, en-krouch´ *v* abusar; usurpar; **–ment,** *s* abuso *m.*; usurpación *f.*

encumber, en-kŏm´-ba *v* estorbar; (law) gravar

encumbrance, en-kŏm´- brans *s* embarazo *m.*; (burden) estorbo *m.*; (legal) gravámen *m.*

encyclopedia, en-sai´-klo- pii´-di-a *s* enciclopedia

f.

end, end *s* fin *m.*; conclusión *f.*; final *f.*; extremo *m.*; *v* acabar; terminar; cesar

endanger, en-dein´-ch *a v* arriesgar; poner en peligro

endear, en-di r´ *v* hacerse querer; encarecer

endearment, en-di r´-ment *s* encarecimiento *m.*

endeavor, en-dev´-a *v* esforzarse; *s* esfuerzo *m.*

endive, en´-div *s* escarola *f.*

endless*, end´-les *a* sin fin; perpetuo; endibia

endorse, en-doars´ *v* endosar; (ratify) sancionar; **–ment,** *s* endoso *m.*; sanción *f.*

endow, en-dau´ *v* dotar; fundar

endurance, en-diúr´-ans *s* resistencia *f.*; paciencia *f.*

endure, en-diú r´ *v* soportar; tolerar

enema, en´-i-ma *s* lavativa *f.*

enemy, en´-i-mi *s* enemigo *m.*

energetic, en-er-chet´-ik *a* enérgico

energy, en´-er-chi *s*

energía *f.*

enervate, en´-er-veit *v* enervar; debilitar

enfeeble, en-fii´-bl *v* debilitar

enforce, en-fó rs *v* hacer observar; forzar

engage, en-gueich´ *v* (employ) emplear; (reserve) retener; (enemy) atacar; (bind) comprometerse

engaged, en-gueichd´ *a* (affianced) prometido; comprometido; (occupied) ocupado; (reserved) retenido

engagement, en-gueich´- ment *s* obligación *f.*; (mil) combate *m.*; (betrothal) esponsales *m. pl.*; (appointment) cita *f.*

engaging, en-guei´-ching *a* simpático; atractivo

engender, en-chen´-da *v* engendrar

engine, en´-chin *s* máquina *f.*; locomotora *f.*

engineer, en-chi-ni r´ *s* ingeniero *m.*

engineering, en-chi-ni r´- ing *s* ingeniería *f.*

England, ing-gland *s* Inglaterra *f.*

English, ing-glish *a* inglés/esa; *s* (language) inglés *m.*

engrave, en-greiv´ *v* grabar; **-r,** *s* grabador *m.*

engross, en-grous´ *v* absorber; copiar

engulf, en-gölf´ *v* engolfar

enhance, en-jaans´ *v* realzar; mejorar

enjoin, en-CHoin´ *v* ordenar; prescribir

enjoy, en-CHoi´ *v* gozar; **-oneself,** divertirse

enjoyment, en-CHoi´-ment *s* goce *m.*; placer *m.*

enlarge, en-laarCH´ *v* agrandar; dilatar

enlargement, en-laarCH´-ment *s* ampliación *f.*

enlighten, en-lai´-tn *v* iluminar; instruir

enlist, en-list´ *v* alistar; alistarse

enliven, en-lai´-vn *v* animar; alegrar

enmity, en´-mi-ti *s* enemistad *f.*; hostilidad *f.*

enormous*, i-noar´-mos *a* enorme

enough, i-nöf´ *adv* bastante; *interj* !basta¡

enrage, en-reiCH´ *v* exasperar; enfurecer

enrapture, en-rAp´-tiur *v* extasiar; arrobar

enrich, en-rich *v* enriquecer; (adorn) embellecer

enroll, en-roul´ *v* alistar; alistarse; registrar

ensign, en´-sain *s* (flag) bandera *f.*; (naval flag)¹ pabellón *m.*; (rank) alférez *m.*

enslave, en-sleiv´ *v* esclavizar

ensnare, en-sné r´ *v* tender un lazo; (*fig*) entrampar

ensue, en-siuu´ *v* seguir; sobrevenir

entail, en-teil´ ocasionar; (law) vincular

entangle, en-tAng´-l enmarañar; implicar

enter, en´-ta *v* entrar; **-up,** asentar

enterprise, en´-ter-prais *s* empresa *f.*; (originality, boldness) acometimiento *m.*

entertain, en-ter-tein´ *v* entretener; hospedar; **-ment,** *s* entretenimiento *m.*; hospitalidad *f.*; acogida *f.*

enthusiasm, en-ziuu´-si-Asm *s* entusiasmo *m.*

entice, en-tais´ *v* tentar; atraer

entire*, en-tai r´ *a* entero; íntegro; completo

entitle, en-tai´-tl *v* dar derecho; autorizar

entomb, en-tuum´ *v* enterrar; sepultar

entrance, en´-trans *s* entrada *f.*

entrance, en-traans´ *v* extasiar

entreat, en-triit´ *v* suplicar; implorar; exortar

entrench, en-trench´ *v* atrincherar

entrust, en-tröst *v* entregar; conflar

entry, en´-tri *s* entrada *f.*; (record) asiento *m.*

entwine, en-tuain´ *v* entrelazar

enumerate, i-niuu´-mer-eit *v* enumerar

envelop, en-vel´-op *v* envolver; cubrir

envelope, en´-vel-op *s* sobre *m.*; cubierta *f.*

envious*, en´-vi-os *a* envidioso

environment, en-vai´-ron-ment *s* medio ambiente *m.*

environs, en-vai´-ron *s s pl* alrededores *m. pl.*

envoy, en´-voi s enviado m.

envy, en´-vi v envidiar; s envidia f.

epicure, ep´-i-kiú r s epicúreo m.; gastrónomo m.

epidemic, ep-i-dem´-ik s epidemia f.

episode, ep´-i-soud s episodio m.

epistle, ep-is´-l s epístola f.; (letter) carta f.

epoch, ii´-pok, ep´-ok s época f.; era f.

equal, ii´-kual v igualar; a* igual; s igual m.

equality, i-kuol´-i-ti s igualdad f.

equalize, ii´-kua-lais v igualar

equator, i-kuei´-ta s ecuador m.

equilibrium, i-kui-lib´-ri-om s equilibrio m.

equip, i-kuip´ v equipar

equitable, ek´-ui-ta-bl a equitativo; imparcial

equity, ek´-ui-ti s equidad f.

equivalent, i-kui´-va-lent s & a equivalente m.

era, i´-ra s era f.; época f.

eradicate, i-rAd´-i-keit v desarraigar; extirpar

erase, i-reis´ v (delete) borrar

eraser, i-rei´-sa s (metal, etc) raspador m.; (rubber) goma para borrar f.

erect, i-rekt´ v erigir; a erguido; derecho

ermine, ĕr´-min s armiño m.

erode, e-roud v erosionar; desgastar; corroer

erotic, e-rot-ik a erótico

err, ĕr v errar; desviarse

errand, er´-and s recado m.

erratic, e-rat´-ik a errático

erroneous*, e-rou´-ni-os a erróneo

error, er´-or s error m.; yerro m.

erupt, i-rŏpt v entrar en erupción; estallar

eruption, i-rap´-shon s erupción f.

escalate, es-kal-eit v intensificarse; extenderse

escalator, es-kalpeit-a s escalera mecánica f.

escape, es-keip´ s escapada f.; escape m.; fuga f.; huída f.; v escapar, evitar

escort, es-koart´ v escoltar; s escolta f.

especially, es-pesh´-al-i adv especialmente

espionage, es-pii-on-aarCH s espionaje

espy, es-pai´ v divisar; observar

essay, es´-ei s ensayo m.

essential*, es-en´-shal a esencial

establish, es-tAb´-lish v establecer; –ment, s establicimiento m.

estate, es-teit´ s propiedades f. pl.; bienes m. pl.; (possessions) herencia f.; (status) rango m.

esteem, es-tiim´ v estimar; s estima f.

estimate, es´-ti-meit s (costs) estimación f.; v estimar; computar

estrange, es-treinCH´ v apartar

etching, ech´-ing s grabado m.

eternal*, i-tĕr´-nal a eterno

eternity, i-tĕr´-ni-ti s eternidad f.

ether, ii´-zer s éter m.

ethnic, ez-nik s ética.

euphony, iuu´-fo-ni s eufonía f.

Europe, iuu-rŏp s Europa f.

evacuate, -ivAk´-iu-eit *v* evacuar

evade, i-veid´ *v* evadir; eludir

evaporate, i-vAp´-or-eit *v* (*refl*) evaporarse

evasion, i-vei´-shon *s* evasión *f.*; evasiva *f.*

evasive*, i-vei´-siv *a* evasivo

eve, iiv *s* víspera *f.*; (evening) tarde *f.*

even, ii´-vn *adv* aun; *a** igual; (smooth) liso

evening, iiv´-ning *s* tarde *f.*; noche *f.*; **–dress,** traje de etiqueta *m.*; (ladies') vestido de noche *m.*

evensong, ii´-vn-song *s* vísperas *f. pl.*

event, i-vent´ *s* acontecimiento *m.*; caso *m.*; **–ful,** *a* memorable; **–ually,** *adv* al fin

ever, ev´-a *adv* siempre; (at any time) jamás; **–lasting*,** *a* perdurable; eterno

every, ev´-ri *a* cada; todo; todos; toda; todas; **–body,** *s* todo el mundo *m.*; **–thing,** todo *m.*; **–where,** *adv* en todas partes

evict, i-vikt´ *v* desposeer; **–ion** *s* desahucio *m.*

evidence, ev´-i-dens *s* evidencia *f.*; prueba *f.*; testimonio *m.*; **give –,** *v* dar testimonio

evident*, ev´-i-dent *a* evidente

evil, ii´-vl *s* mal *m.*; maldad *f.*; desgracia *f.*; *a* malo

evince, i-vins´ *v* probar; manifestar

evoke, i-vouk´ *v* evocar; llamar

evolution, iiv-o-luu-shon *s* evolución *f.*

evolve, i-volv´ *v* desenvolver; evolucionar

ewe, iuu *s* oveja *f.*

exact, eg-sAkt´ *a** exacto; *v* exigir; **–ing,** *a* exigente; **–itude,** *s* exactitud *f.*

exaggerate, eg-sACH´-er-eit *v* exagerar

exaggeration, eg-sACH´-er-e´-shon *s* exagera- ción *f.*

exalt, eg-soalt´ *v* exaltar

exam, eg-sAm´ *abbr* = **examination** *s* examen

examination, eg-sAm´-i-nei´-shon *s* examen *m.*; inspección *f.*; (legal) interrogatorio *m.*

examine, eg-sAm´-in *v* examinar; (excise) registrar

example, eg-saam´-pl *s* ejemplo *m.*

exasperate, eg-sAs´-per-eit *v* exasperar

excavate, eks´-ka-veit *v* excavar

exceed, ek-siid´ *v* exceder; **–ingly,** *adv* excesivamente; muy

excel, ek-sel´ *v* sobresalir; superar

excellent*, ek´-sel-ent *a* excelente

except, ek-sept´ *v* exceptuar; *prep* excepto; fuera de; **–ion,** *s* excepción *f.*; **take –ion,** *v* objetar a; **–ional,** *a* excepcional

excerpt, ek´-serpt *s* extracto *m.*; *v* extractar

excess, ek-sess´ *s* exceso *m.*; **–ive*,** *a* excesivo

exchange, eks-cheinCH´ *s* cambio *m.*; (telephone) central *f.*; (money) cambio *m.*; *v* cambiar

excise, ek´-sais *s* alcabala *f.*; impuestos

excitable, ek-sai´-ta-bl *a* excitable

excite, ek-sait´ *v* excitar; **–ment,** *s* excitación *f.*; conmoción *f.*; agitación

f.
exciting, ek-sai´-ting *a*
excitante; (thrilling)
conmovedo**r**
exclaim, eks-kleim´ *v*
exclamar
exclamation, eks-kla-
mei´-shon *s*
exclamación *f.*
exclude, eks-kluud´ *v*
excluir
exclusive*, eks-kluu´-siv
a exclusivo
excruciating, eks-kruu´-
shi-ei-ting *a* penosísimo;
atroz; horrible
excursion, eks-kĕr´-shon *s*
excursión *f.*
excuse, eks´-kiuus *s*
excusa *f.*
excuse, eks-kiuu *s´ v*
excusar; (pardon)
dispensar
execrate, eks´-si-kreit *v*
execrar
execute, ek´-si-kiuut *v*
ejecutar
executioner, ek-si-kiuu´-
shon-*a s* verdugo *m.*
executor, ek-sek´-iu-ta *s*
testamentario *m.*
exempt, eks-sempt´ *v*
eximir *a* exento
exemption, eg-s emp´-
shon *s* exención *f.*
exercise, eks´-er-sais *s*

ejercicio *m.; v*
ejercitarse; (mil) hacer
el ejercicio; (profession)
ejercer
exert, eg-sĕrt´ *v* esforzarse;
empeñarse
exertion, eg-sĕr´-shon *s*
esfuerzo *m.;* conato *m.*
exhale, eks-jeil´ *v* exhalar;
emitir
exhaust, eg-soast´ *s* escape
m.; v agotar; rendirse
exhaustive*, eg-soast´-iv
a completo
exhibit, eg-sib´-it *v*
exhibir; *s* objeto *m.*
exhibition, eks-i-bish´-on
s exposición *f.*
exhilarate, eg-sil´-a-reit *v*
regocijar; alegrar
exhilarating, eg-sil´-a-rei-
ting *a* vigorizante
exhort, eg-soart´ *v*
exhortar
exile, ek-sail´ *v* desterrar; *s*
destierro *m.;* (person)
desterrado *m.*
exist, eg-sist´ *v* existir
existence, eg-sis´-tens *s*
existencia *f.*
exit, ek´-sit *s* salida *f.;*
(departure) partida *f.*
exodus, ek´-so-dus *s* éxodo
m.; emigración *f.*
exonerate, eg-son´-er-eit *v*
exonerar; aliviar

exorbitant*, ek-soar´-bi-
tant *a* exorbitante
exotic, eg-s-ot-ik *a*
exótico
expand, eks-pAnd´ *v*
dilatar; **–ing,** *a* elástico
expansion, eks-pAn´-shon
s expansión *f.*
expect, eks-pekt´ *v* esperar
expectation, eks-pek-tei´-
shon *s* expectación *f.*
expedient, eks-pii´-di-ent
s expediente *m.; a**
conveniente; conveniente
expedite, eks´-pi-dait *v*
expedir; acelerar
expedition, eg-sped-i-shon
s expedición *f.*
expel, eks-pel´ *v* expeler;
expulsar
expend, eks´-pend *v*
gastar; **–iture,** *s* gasto
m.; desembolso *m.*
expense, eks-pens´ *s* gusto
m.; coste *m.*
expensive*, eks-pen´-siv *a*
caro; costoso
experience, eks-pi´-ri-ens
s experiencia *f.;* en- sayo
m.; v experimentar;
probar
experiment, eks-per-i-
ment *v* experimentar; *s*
experimento *m.*
expert, eks-pĕrt´ *s* experto
m.; perito *m.; a* experto;

perito

expire, eks-**pai** r´ v espirar;
caducar

explain, eks-**plein**´ v
explicar

explanation, eks-pla-**nei**´-
shon s explicación f.

explicit*, eks-**plis**´-it a
explícito; categórico

explode, eks-**ploud**´ v
estallar; explotar

exploit, eks-**ploit**´ s
hazaña f.; v explotar

explore, eks-**pló** r´ v
explorar; **–r,** s
explorador m.

explosion, eg-**splou**-shon s
explosión f.

explosive, eg-**splou**-siv s
& a explosivo m.

export, eks-**pó** rt´ v
exportar; **–er,** s
exportador m.; **–s,**
exportaciones f. pl.

expose, eks-**pou** s ´ v
exponer; (fraud)
desenmascarar; (plot)
revelar; (danger)
arriesgar

expostulate, eks-**pos**´-tiu-
leit v reconvenir

exposure, eks-**pou**-**sh** ur s
exposición f.; revelación
f.

expound, eks-**paund**´ v
exponer; explicar

express, eks-**pres**´ s
expreso m.; a expreso; v
expresar

expression, eks-**presh**´-on
s expresión f.

expulsion, eks-**pŏl**´-shon s
expulsión f.

exquisite*, eks´-**kui**-sit a
exquisito

extempore, eks-**tem**´-po-ri
a improvisado

extend, eks-**tend**´ v
extender; extenderse

extensive*, eks-**ten**´-siv a
extenso vasto

extent, eks-**tent**´ s
extensión f.; grado m.

extenuate, eks-**ten**´-iu-eit
v atenuar; extenuar

exterior, eks-**ti**´-ri-a s
exterior m.; a exterior

exterminate, eks-**tĕr**´-min-
eit v exterminar

external*, eks-**tĕr**´-nal a
externo; exterior

extinct, eks-**ting**´-kt a
extinto; (fire) apagado

extinguish, eks-**ting**´-uish
v extinguir; apagar

extort, eks-to**art** v
arrancar; **–ion,** s
extorsión f.

extra, eks-**trA** a adicional;
s suplemento m.;
–ordinary, a
extraordinario

extract, eks-**trAct**´ v
extraer; s extracto m.

extravagant*, eks-**trAv**´-a-
gant a extravagante;
pródigo

extreme, eks-**triim**´ s
extremo m.; a
extremado

extremely, eks-**triim**´-li
adv sumamente

extricate, eks´-**tri**-keit v
desembrollar

extrovert, eg-stro-**vĕrt** s &
a extrovertido/a mf.

eye, ai s ojo m.; **–ball,**
globo ocular m.; **–brow,**
ceja f.; **–glass,**
monóculo m.; **–glasses,**
lentes m. pl.; gafas f. pl.;
–lash, pestaña f.; **–let,**
ojete m.; **–lid,** párpado
m.; **–sight,** vista f.; **–
witness,** testigo ocular
m.

fable, féi´-bel s fábula f.

fabric, fAb´-rik s tejido m.; textura f.; (edifice) fábrica f.; **–ation,** fabricación f.; ficción f.

fabulous*, fAb´-iu-los a fabuloso; ficticio

facade, fa-seid´ s fachada f.

face, feis s cara f.; rostro m.; (clock) cuadrante m.; v afrontar; **–cream,** s crema facial f.; **–massage,** masaje facial m.

facetious*, fa-sii´-shos a chistoso; jocoso

facilitate, fa-sil´-i-teit v facilitar

facilities, fa-sil´-i-tiis s facilidades f. pl; servicios m. pl

facsimile, fA-si´-mi-li s facsímile m.

fact, fAkt s hecho m.; realidad f.

factory, fAk´-to-ri s fábrica f.

faculty, fAk´-ul-ti s facultad f.; aptitud f.

fade, feid v marchitarse; (color) descolorarse

fail, feil v (neglect) faltar a; (omit to) dejar de; (miscarry) fracasar; (examination) suspender; (insolvency) quebrar; **without –,** sin falta

failing, feil´-ing s falta f.

failure, feil´-iur s falta f.; (plans) fracaso m.; (insolvency) quiebra f.

faint, feint v desmayarse; s desmayo m.; a* lánguido; indistinto

fair, fé r a justo; (hair) rubio; (pleasing) bello; (weather) sereno; despejado; s feria f.; **–ness,** equidad f.; belleza f.

fairy, fé-ri s hada f.

faith, feiz s fe f.; confianza f.; fidelidad f.; **–ful,** a fiel; **–less,** infiel

fake, feik s falsificación f.; impostura f.; v falsificar; a falso; fingido

falcon, foal´-kn s halcón m.

fall, foal s decadencia f.; (tumble) caída f.; (prices) baja f.; (water) cascada f.; v caer; bajar

fallacy, fAl´-a-si s falacia f.; sofisma f.

false*, foals a falso; (artificial) postizo

falsehood, foals´-jud s falsedad f.

falsification, foal-si-fi-kei´-shon s falsificación f.

falsify, foal´-si-fai v falsificar

falter, foal´-ta v vacilar; (speech) titubear

fame, feim s fama f.; **–d,** a famoso; renombrado

familiar*, fa-mil´-ya *a* familiar

family, fAm´-i-li *s* familia *f.*

famine, fAm´-in *s* carestía *f.* hambre *f.*

famish, fAm´-ish *v* morir de hambre

famous*, fei´-mos *a* famoso

fan, fAn *s* abanico *m.*; ventilador *m.*; (admirer) aficionado *m.*; *v* abanicar

fanatic, fa-nAt´-ik *s* fanático *m. a* fanático

fanaticism, fa-nAt´-i-sis m *s* fanatismo *m.*

fancy, fAn´-si *s* imaginación *f.*; (liking) gusto *m.*; (preference) inclinación *f.*; *v* imaginar; desear; **-dress**, *s* disfraz *m.*

fang, fAng *s* colmillo *m.*

fantastic, fAn-tAs´-tik *a* fantástico

fantasy, fAn´-ta-si *s* fantasía *f.*

far, faa *r adv* lejos; *a* lejano; distante

farce, faa rs *s* farsa *f.*

fare, fé r *s* tarifa *f.*; (food) comida *f.*

farewell, fé r´-uel *interj* ¡adiós! *s* despedida *f.*

farm, faa rm *s* granja *f.*; cortijo *m.*; *v* cultivar

farmer, faa r´-ma *s* granjero *m.*; agricultor *m.*

farrier, fAr´-i-a *s* herrador *m.*

farther, faa r´-Da *adv* más lejos; además; *a* más lejano; otro; ulterior

fascinate, fAs´-in-eit *v* fascinar

fascinating, fAs´-in-eit-ing *a* fascinador

fashion, fAsh´-on *s* moda *f.*; *v* formar; **-able**, *a* de moda; **to be in –**, estar de moda

fast, faast *a* rápido; firme; (color) fijo; *s* ayuno *m.*; *v* ayunar

fast food, faast fuud *s* comida *f.*; rápida; platos *m. pl*; preparados

fasten, faas´-n *v* atar; (close) cerrar; (dress) abrochar

fastidious*, fAst-tid´-i-os *a* difícil; quisquilloso

fat, fAt *s* grasa *f.*; *a* grueso; gordo; **-ness**, *s* gordura *f.*; **-ten**, *v* engordar; **-ty**, *a* gordo

fatal*, fei´-tl *a* fatal; mortal

fate, feit *s* destino *m.*; suerte *f.*; **-d**, *a* predestinado

father, faa´-Da *s* padre *m.*; **–in-law**, suegro *m.*; **–ly** *a* paternal

fathom, fAD´-om *s* braza *f.*; *v* sondear

fatigue, fa-tig´ *v* fatigar; *s* fatiga *f.*

fault, foalt *s* culpa *f.*; (defect) falta *f.*; **-less**, *a* intachable; **-y**, defectuoso

favor, fei´-va *s* favor *m.*; **-able**, *a* favorable; **-ite**, *s* favorito *m.*; *a* favorito

fawn, foan *s* cervato *m.*; *v* halagar

fax, fAks *s* (document) fax *m.*; telefacsímil *m.*; (machine) (tele)fax *m.*; *v* mandar por (tele)fax

fear, fir *v* temer; recelar; *s* miedo *m.*; temor *m.*; **-ful**, *a** terrible; (timorous) temeroso; **-less***, audaz; valiente

feasible, fii´-si-bl *a* factible; practicable

feast, fiist *v* festejar; regalar; *s* fiesta *f.*; banquete *m.*

feat, fiit *s* hazaña *f.*; (skill) proeza *f.*

feather, feD´-a *s* pluma *f.*; *v* emplumar

feature, fii´-tiur s rasgo m.; **–s,** s pl facciones f. pl.

February, feb´-ru-a-ri s febrero m.

federation, fed-er-ei´-shon s confederación f.

fed up, fed-öp a **to be – (with)** estar harto (de)

fee, fii s honorarios m.; pl gajes m. pl.

feeble, fii´-bl a débil; enclenque

feed, fiid v alimentar; comer; (cattle) pastar

feel, fiil v (touch) palpar; tocar; (affect) sentir; **–ing,** s tacto m.; sentimiento m.; a tierno

feeler, fii´-la s antena f.; tentáculo m.; prueba f.

feign, fein v fingir; pretender

feint, feint s disimulación f.

fell, fel v (trees) cortar; (animals) derribar

fellow, fel´-ou s (member) compañero; socio m.; **–ship,** compañía f.; sociedad f.

felony, fel´-o-ni s felonía f.; traición f.

felt, felt s fieltro m.

female, fii´-meil s hembra f.; mujer f.

feminine, fem´-i-nin s femenino f.

fen, fen s pantano m.

fence, fens s valla f.; v (enclose) cercar; (swordsmanship) esgrimir

fencing, fen´-sing s esgrima f.

fender, fen´-da s guarda-fuegos m.; (ship) defensa; (car) parachoques m.

ferment, fer-ment´ v fermentar; s fermento m.

fern, fërn s helecho m.

ferocious*, fi-rou´-shos a feroz

ferret, fer´-et s hurón m.; v huronear

ferrule, fer´-ul s herrete m.

ferry, fer´-i s transbordador m.

fertile, fër´-tail a fértil

fertilize, fër-ta-lais´ v fertilizar

fervent*, fër´-vent a ferviente; ardiente

fester, fes´-ta v ulcerarse; amargarse

festival, fes´-ti-vl s fiesta f.; a festivo

festive, fes´-tiv a festivo; alegre

festoon, fes-tuun´ s festón m.; v festonear

fetch, fech v ir a buscar; traer; producir

fetter, fet´-a v encadenar; **–s,** s pl grillos m. pl.

feud, fiuud s feudo m.; **–al,** a feudal

fever, fii´-va s fiebre f.; **–ish,** a febril

few, fiuu a pocos; unos; a **–,** algunos

fiancé, fii-aan-sei s novio m; prometido m.; **-e** novia f.; prometida f.

fiber, fai´-ba s fibra f.

fickle, fik´-l a inconstante; variable

fiction, fik´-shon s ficción f.; literatura novelesca f.

fictitious*, fik-ti´-shos a ficticio; falso

fiddle, fid´-l s violín m.; v tocar el violín

fidelity, fi-del´-i-ti s fidelidad f.; lealtad f.

fidget, fiCH´-et v agitarse; molestar

fidgety, fiCH´-et-i a agitado; inquieto

field, fiild s campo m.

fiend, fiind s demonio m.; arpía f.; **–ish,** a diabólico

fierce*, firs a fiero; cruel; impetuoso; feroz

fiery, fai´-er-i a ardiente; fogoso

fife, faif s pífano m.

fifteen, fif-tiin´ s & a quince m.; **–th,** décimoquinto m.

fifth, fifz s & a quinto m.; (fraction) quinta parte f.

fiftieth, fif´-ti-iz s & a quincuagésimo m.; cincuentavo m.

fifty, fif´-ti s & a cincuenta m.

fig, fig s higo m.; **–tree,** higuera f.

fight, fait v pelear; combatir; s combate m.; lucha f.; pelea f.; **–er,** s (person) luchador m.; (plane) avión de caza m.

figure, fi´-guer s cuerpo m.; figura f. número m.; (number) cifra f.; v figurar; **–head,** s mascarón de proa m.

filbert, fil´-bert s avellana f.

filch, filch v ratear; sisar; hurtar

file, fail s (tool) lima f.; (office) carpeta m.; v limar; archivar; (mil) marchar en fila

fill, fil v llenar; satisfacer; (position) ocupar

filly, fil´-i s potra f.

film, film s (snapshots, etc) película f.; (cinema) film m.; (eye) membrana f.

filter, fil´-ta v filtrar; s filtro m.

filth, filz s basura f.; **–y,** a sucio; obsceno

fin, fin s aleta f.

final*, fai´-nal a final; último; decisivo

finalize, fain-a-lais v concluir; completar

finally, fain-a-li adv finalmente; por fin

finance, fi´-nAns s hacienda pública f.; ciencia financiera f.; v (loans) negociar; (undertaking) respaldar

financial*, fi-nAn´-shal a monetario; bancario

finch, finch s pinzón m.

find, faind v encontrar; descubrir; (law) fallar

fine, fain s (penalty) multa f.; v multar; a* fino; delicado; bello; sutil; excelente

finger, fing´-ga s dedo m.; v tocar

finish, fin´-ish v acabar; terminar; s fin m.

finite*, fai´-nait a finito; limitado

fir, fër s pino m.; abeto m.

fire, fair s fuego m.; (conflagration) incendio m.; v encender; (gun etc) tirar; **–alarm,** s alarma de incendio f.; **– department,** servicio de bomberos m.; **–engine,** bomba de incendios f.; **–escape,** aparato de salvamento m.; **–fly,** luciérnaga f.; **–man,** bombero m.; **–place,** hogar f.; chimenea f.; **–proof,** a incombustible; **–works,** s pl fuegos artificiales m. pl.

firm, fërm s firma f.; a* sólido; (resolute) firme

first, fërst adv primeramente; a primero

firth, fërz s estuario m.; brazo de mar m.

fish, fish v pescar; s (live) pez m.; (food) pescado m.; **–bone,** espina f.; **–erman,** pescador m.; **–hook,** anzuelo m.; **–monger,** pescadero m.

fishing, fish´-ing s pesca f.; **– rod,** caña de pescar f.

fissure, fish´-ur s grieta f.; hendedura f.

fist, fist s puño m.

fit, fit v ajustar; (clothes)

entallar; s convulsión f.;
*a** apto; propicio

fitting, fit´-ing *a*
conveniente; oportuno;
s pruebe f.; medida f.

five, faiv s & *a* cinco m.

fix, fiks *v* fijar; s apuro m.;
aprieto m.

fixture, fiks´-tiur s mueble
fijo m.; instalación f.

fizzy, fi-ssi *a* efervescente;
con gas

flabby, flAb´-i *a* fofo;
blando

flag, flAg s bandera f.;
pabellón m.; **—ship,**
buque almirante m.; **—
staff,** asta de la bandera
m.

flagon, flAg´-on s frasco
m.; botella f.

flagrant*, flei´-grant *a*
flagrante; enorme

flake, fleik s laminilla f.;
(snow, etc) copo m.

flaky, fleik´-i *a* (pastry)
hojaldrado

flame, fleim s llama f.; *v*
llamear

flaming, flei´,ming *a*
llameante; ardiente

flange, flAnCH s reborde
m.; pestaña f.; acoplo m.

flank, flang-k s (person)
costado m.; flanco m.;
(animal) ijada f.; *v*

flanquear

flannel, flAn´-l s franela f.

flap, flAp s (table) hoja f.;
(pocket) cartera f.;
(trap) trampa f.; (wings)
aleta f.; *v* aletear

flare, flé r s llamarada f.; *v*
brillar

flash, flAsh s (light)
resplandor m.;
(lightning) relámpago
m.; (gun, etc) fogonazo
m.; **—bulb,** s bombilla de
vidrio f.; **—light,** al
magnesio m.

flask, flaask s frasco m.;
redoma f.; (vacuum)
termos m.

flat, flAt s (music) bemol
m.; (dwelling) piso m.;
(land) llano m.; *a* llano,
insípido

flatten, flAt´-n *v* allanar

flatter, flAt´-ěr *v* lisonjear;
adular; **—ing,** *a*
halagüeño; **—y,** s lisonja
f.

flavor, flei´-va *v* sazonar; s
sabor m.; aroma m.

flaw, floa s defecto m.;
(crack) grieta f.

flax, flAks s lino m.

flea, flii s pulga f.

fledged, fleCHd *a* cubierto
de plumas

flee, flii *v* huir

fleece, fliis s vellón m.;
lana f.; *v* esquilar; (fig)
despojar

fleet, fliit s flota f.; *a* veloz

flesh, flesh s carne f.

flexible, fleks´-i-bl *a*
flexible

flicker, flik´-a *v* vacilar;
temblar; s vacilante m.;
tembleteo m.

flight, flait s huída f.;
(birds) vuelo m.; (stairs)
tramo m.

flimsy, flim´-si *a*
(material, paper) ligero;
delgado; (structure)
débil

flinch, flinch *v*
acobardarse; vacilar

fling, fling *v* lanzar; arrojar

flint, flint s pedernal m.

flippant*, flip´-ant *a*
ligero; petulante

flirt, flěrt s coqueta f.; *v*
coquetear

float, flout s (raft) balsa f.;
(angler's) corcho m.; *v*
flotar

flock, flok s (sheep)
rebaño m.; manada f.;
(birds) bandada f.; *v* ir
en tropel; congregarse

flog, flog *v* azotar

flood, flŏd *v* inundar; s
Diluvio m.; inundación
f.

floor, fló r s suelo m.; (story) piso m.

floppy disk, flo-pi disk s disco m flexible; disquete m.; floppy m.

florid*, flor´-id a florido; vivo

florist, flor´-ist s florista f.

flounce, flauns s (dress) volante m.

flour, flaur s harina f.

flourish, flôr´-ish s adorno m.; (signature) rúbrica f.; v (brandish) blandir; (prosper) prosperar

flout, flaut v mofar; burlarse

flow, flou v fluir; correr; s flujo m.; efusión f.

flower, flau´-a s flor f.; v florecer

flu, fluu s gripe

fluctuate, flŏk´-tiu-eit v fluctuar; vacilar

flue, fluu s cañon de chimenea m.

fluency, fluu´-en-si s fluidez f.; soltura f.

fluent*, fluu´-ent a fluente; fácil

fluffy, flŏf´-i a con plumón; con vello

fluid, fluu´-id s flúido m.; a flúido

fluke, fluuk s (chance) chiripa f.

flurry, flŏr´-i s ráfaga f.; v aturdir

flush, flŏsh v (redden) sonrojar; (rinse) fluir; chorrear; s rubor m.; a al ras de

fluster, flŏs´-ta v aturdir; s agitación f.

flute, fluut s flauta f.; v (groove) estriar

flutter, flŏt´,-a s aleteo m.; palpitación f.; emoción f.; v aletear

fly, flai s mosca f.; v volar; (flag) enarbolar

flyleaf, flai´-liif s guarda f.

flywheel, flai´-juil s volante m.

foal, foal s potro m.; v parir

foam, foum s espuma f.; v espumar

fob, fob s faltriquera del reloj f.

focal, fou´-kl a focal; céntrico; –**point,** s punto céntrico; punto focal

focus, fou´-kos s foco m.; v enfocar

fodder, fod´-a s forraje m.; pienso m.

foe, fou s enemigo m.

fog, fog s niebla f.; bruma f.; –**gy,** a brumoso; –**horn,** s sirena f.

foil, foil s (fencing) florete m.; (metal) hoja f.; v frustrar

foist, foist v imponer; meter

fold, fould s (cloth, etc) pliegue m.; (sheep) redil m.; v plegar

foliage, fou´-li-iCH s follaje m.

folk, fouk s gente f.

follow, fol´-ou v seguir; suceder; –**er,** s seguidor m.; discípulo m.; admirador m.

folly, fol´-i s locura f.; tontería f.

foment, fo-ment´ v fomentar

fond, fond a (affection) afectuoso; **to be –of,** v (affection) ser aficionado a; querer; (taste, recreation) gustar

fondle, fon´-dl v mimar; acariciar

fondness, fond´-nes s afecto m.; (inclination) afición f.

font, font s pila bautismal f.

food, fuud s alimento m.; comida f.; (fodder) pasto m.

fool, fuul s tonto m.; v embromar; –**ery,** s

tontería f.; **-hardy,** a temerario; **-ish*,** tonto; **-proof,** a a prueba de imprudencia

foot, fut s pie m.; **-ball,** balón m.; (game) fútbol m.; **--board,** (bus, train) plataforma f.; **-ing,** posición f.; **-man,** lacayo m.; **-path,** senda f.; (pavement) acera f.; **-step,** paso m.; (print) huella f.; **-stool,** escabel m.

fop, fop s pisaverde m.

for, for *prep* por; a causa de; para; en nombre de; *conj* porque; para que; como; pues

forage, for´-iCH s forraje m.; v forrajear

forbear, for-bé r´ v soportar; abstenerse

forbearance, for-bé r´-ans s indulgencia f.; paciencia f.; dominio m.

forbid, for´-bid v prohibir; **-ding,** a aborrecible

force, fó rs´ s fuerza f.; vigor m. v forzar

forceful, fó rs´-ful a fuerte; poderoso

forcible, fó rs´-i-bl a fuerte; concluyente

ford, fó rd v vadear; s vado m.

fore, fó r s proa f.; a delantero; *adv* delante

forearm, fó r´-aarm s antebrazo m.

forebode, fó r´boud v presagiar; pronosticar

foreboding, fó r-boud´-ing s presagio m.

forecast, fó r´-kaast s pronóstico m.

foreclose, fó r-klous´ v excluir

foredoom, fó r-duum v predestinar

forefather, fó r´-faa-Da s antepasado m.

forefinger, fó r´-fiñ-ga s dedo índice m.

forego, fó r-gou´ v renunciar; a abandonar

foregoing, fó r-gou´-ing s precedente

foregone, fó r-goun´ a anticipado

foreground, fó r´-graund s primer plano m.

forehead, fó r´-jed, fó r´-ed s frente f.

foreign, fó r´-in a extranjero; **-er,** s extranjero m.

foreman, fó r´-mn s capataz m.

foremost, fó r´-moust a primero; principal

forenamed, fó r´-neimd a susodicho

forenoon, fó r´-nuun s mañana f.

forerunner, fó r-rön´-a a precursor

foresee, fó r-sii´ v prever

foresight, fó r´-sait s previsión f.

forest, fó r´-est s bosque m.; selva f.

forestall, fó r-stoal´ v anticipar; prevenir

foretaste, fó r´-teist s goce anticipado m.

foretell, fó r-tel´ v predecir

forethought, fó r´-zoat s previsión f.; premeditación f.

forewarn, fó r-uoarn´ v prevenir

forfeit, fó r´-fit s multa f.; v perder

forge, fórCH v forjar; falsificar; s fragua f.; forja f.

forgery, fórCH´-er-i s falsificación f.

forget, for-guet´ v olvidar; **-ful,** a olvidadizo; **-fulness,** s olvido m.

forgive, for-guiv´ v perdonar; **-ness,** s perdón m.

fork, foark s tenedor m.; (tool) horca f.; (road) bifurcación f.; v bifurcarse

forlorn, for-loarn´ *a*
abandonado;
desesperado

form, foarm *s* forma *f.*;
(figure) figura *f.*; (a form
to fill up) formulario *m.*;
(seat) banco *m.*

formal*, foar´-mal *a*
formal; ceremonioso;
–ity, *s* formalidad *f.*;
etiqueta *f.*

formation, foar-mei´-shon
s formación *f.*

former, foar´-ma *a*
anterior; **–ly,** *adv* antes;
antiguamente

formula, foar´-miu-la *s*
fórmula *f.*; receta *f.*

forsake, for-seik´ *v* dejar;
abandonar

fort, fórt *s* fuerte *m.*;
–ress, fortaleza *f.*

forth, fórz *adv* adelante;
fuera; **–coming,** *a* futuro;
que viene; **–with,** *adv*
sin dilación

fortieth, foar´-ti-iz *s* & *a*
cuadragésimo *m.*;
cuarentavo *m.*

fortification, foar-ti-fi-
kei´-shon *s* fortificación
f.

fortify, foar´-ti-fai *v*
fortificar; (health)
fortalecer

fortitude, foar´-ti-tiuud *s*
firmeza *f.*; valor *m.*

fortnight, foart´-nait *s*
quincena *f.*; dos
semanas *f.* pl.

fortunate*, foar´-tiu-net *a*
afortunado; dichoso

fortune, foar´-tiun *s*
fortuna *f.*; (fate) suerte
f.

forty, foar´-ti *s* & *a*
cuarenta *m.*

forward, foar´-uard *v*
enviar; expedir; *adv*
adelante; *a* adelantado;
(pert) descarado; **–ness,**
descaro *m.*

fossil, fos´-il *s* fósil *m.*

foster, fost´-a *v* criar;
(encourage) fomentar;
–parents, *s pl* padres
adoptivos *m.* pl.

foul, faul *v* ensuciar; *a**
sucio; impuro; obsceno

found, faund *v* fundar;
(metal) fundir

foundation, faund-ei´-
shon *s* fundación *f.*;
(building, etc) cimiento
m.; (fig) fundamento *m.*

founder, faun´-da *v*
hundirse; *s* fundador *m.*

foundling, faund´-ling *s*
niño expósito *m.*

foundry, faun´-dri *s*
fundición *f.*

fountain, faun´-tin *s*
fuente *f.*

fountain pen, faun´-tin-
pen *s* pluma estilográfica
f.

four, fó r *s* & *a* cuatro *m.*;
–fold, *a* cuádruplo;
–teen, *s* & *a* catorce *m.*;
–th, cuarto *m.*

fowl, faul *s* ave *f.*;
(chicken) pollo *m.*

fox, foks *s* zorro *m.*;
–glove, dedalera *f.*;
–terrier, perro zorrero
m.

foyer, foi-ei *s* vestíbulo *m.*

fraction, frAk´-shon *s*
fracción *f.*; fragmento
m.

fracture, frAk´-tiur,
fractura *f.*; *v* fracturar

fragile, frACH´-il *a* frágil;
(health) delicado

fragment, frAg´-ment *s*
fragmento *m.*

fragrance, frei´-grans *s*
fragancia *f.*; perfume *m.*

fragrant*, frei´-grant *a*
fragante; perfumado

frail, freil *a* frágil; (health)
débil; endeble

frame, freim *s* marco *m.*; *v*
formar; (picture, etc)
enmarcar; **–work,** *s*
armazón *m.*

franchise, frAn´-chais *s*

sufragio *m*.

frank, frang-k *a* franco; **–ness,** *s* franqueza *f*.

frantic, frAn´-tik *a* frenético; furioso

fraternal*, fra-tĕr´-nal *a* fraternal

fraud, froad *s* fraude *m*.

fraudulent*, froa´-diu-lent *a* fraudulento

fray, frei *v* deshilachar; *s* riña *f*.; refriega *f*.

freak, friik *s* rareza *f*.; fenómeno *m*.

freckle, frek´-l *s* peca *f*.

free, frii *v* libertar; librar; *a** libre; gratuito; **–dom,** *s* libertad *f*.; **–hold,** dominio absoluto *m*.

freeze, friis *v* helar; congelarse

freezer, friis-*a s* congelador *m*.

freezing, frii´-sing *s* congelación *f*.; *a* glacial

freight, freit *s* carga *f*.; (cost) flete *m*.; *v* fletar

frenzy, fren´-si *s* frenesí *m*.

frequency, frii´-kuen-si *s* frecuencia *f*.

frequent*, frii´-kuent *a* frecuente; *v* frecuentar

fresh, fresh *a* fresco; puro

freshness, fresh´-nes *s* frescura *f*.; pureza *f*.

fret, fret *v* angustiarse; inquietarse; **–ful,** *a* irritable; enojadizo; **–saw,** *s* sierra de calados *f*.; **–work,** calados *m*.

friar, frai´-a *s* fraile *m*.

friary, frai´-er-i *s* convento de frailes *m*.

friction, frik´-shon *s* fricción *f*.; frotación *f*.

Friday, frai´-di *s* viernes *m*.; **Good –,** viernes santo *m*.

fridge, friCH *s* frigo *m*.; nevera *f*.; refrigerador *m*.

friend, frend *s* amigo *m*.; **–liness,** amistad *f*.; **–ly,** *a* amigable; **–ship,** *s* amistad *f*.

fright, frait *s* susto *m*.; terror *m*.

frighten, frai´-tn *v* espantar; aterrorizar

frightened, frai´-tnd *a* asustado/a

frightening, frai´-tn-ing *a* espantoso; aterrador

frightful*, frait´-ful *a* espantoso; horrible

frigid*, friCH´-id *a* frígido; indiferente

frill, fril *s* escarola *f*.; faralá *f*.; adorno *m*.; *v* escarolar

fringe, frinCH *s* franja *f*.; *v*

franjear

frisk, frisk *v* brincar; cabriolar

frisky, frisk´-i *a* juguetón; vivaracho

fritter, frit´-a *s* fritura *f*.; *v* desperdiciar; **–away,** malgastar

frivolous*, friv´-ol-os *a* frívolo

frizzle, friz´-l *v* rizar; (*fig*) achicharrar

fro, frou *adv* atrás; **to and –,** de un lado á otro

frock, frok *s* vestido *m*.

frog, frog *s* rana *f*.

frolic, frol´-ik *v* juguetear; *s* travesura *f*.

from, from *prep* de; desde; de parte de; según

front, front *s* frente *f*.; (*mil*) frente *m*.; *a* delantero

frontier, fron´-tir *s* frontera *f*.; *a* fronterizo

frost, froast *s* helada *f*.; *v* escarchar; **–bitten,** *a* helado; **–y,** helado

froth, froaz *s* espuma *f*.; *v* espumar

frown, fraun *s* ceño *m*.; *v* fruncir el ceño

frugal*, fruu´-gl *a* frugal; económico

fruit, fruut *s* fruta *f*.; fruto *m*.; **–erer,** frutero *m*.;

–**ful,** a fructífero; **–less*,** a infructuoso; estéril; **–tart,** s tarta de frutas f.

fruition, fru-ish´-on s fruición f.; goce m.

frustrate, frŏs-treit´ v frustrar

fry, frai v freír; **–ing pan,** s sartén f.

fuchsia, fluu´-shi-a s fucsia f.

fuel, flu´-el s combustible m.

fugitive, fluu´-CHi-tiv s fugitivo m.; a fugitivo

fugue, fluug s fuga f.

fulcrum, fŏl´-krom s fulcro m.

fulfill, ful-fil´ v cumplir; realizar; **–ment,** s realización f.; cumplimiento m.

full, ful a lleno; completo; saciado

fullness, ful´-nes s plenitud f.; abundancia f.

fulsome, ful´-som a repugnante; grosero; bajo

fume, fluum s humo m.; v humear

fun, fŏn s diversión f.; alegría f.; broma f.; (joke) chiste m.; **–ny,** a cómico; chistoso

function, fŏng-k´-shon s función f.; v funcionar

fund, fŏnd s fondo m.; v fundar

fundamental*, fŏnd-a-men´-tl a fundamental

funeral, fluu´-ner-al s entierro m.

funnel, fŏn´-l s embudo m.; (smoke) chimenea f.

fur, fĕr s piel f.; incrustación f.; v incrustarse; forrar con pieles

furbish, fĕr´-bish v acicalar; pulir

furious*, fluu´-ri-os a furioso

furlong, fĕr´-long s estadio m.

furlough, fĕr´-lou s licencia f.

furnace, fĕr´-nis s horno m.; (small) hornillo m.

furnish, fĕr´-nish v amueblar; equipar

furniture, fĕr´-ni-tiur s muebles m. pl.

furrier, fĕr´-i-a s peletero m.

furrow, fĕr´-ou v surcar s surco m.

further, fĕr´-Da a adicional; adv más allá v apoyar; **–ance,** s adelantamiento m.;

promoción f.

furtive*, fĕr´-tiv a furtivo

fury, flu´-ri s furor m.; furia f.

fuse, fluus s (slow match) mecha f.; (time) espoleta graduada f.; (electric) corta-circuitos m.; fusible m.; v fundirse

fuss, fŏs s barullo m.; v causar revuelo

futile, fluu´-tail a fútil; frívolo

future fluu´-tiur s porvenir m.; a futuro

gadfly, gAd´-flai s tábano m.

gag, gAg s mordaza f.; v amordazar

gaiety, gue´-i-ti s alegría f.

gaily, gue´-i-li adv alegremente

gain, guein s ganancia f.; v (win, earn) ganar; (attain) alcanzar; (watch) adelantar

gait, gueit s marcha f.; (horse) andadura f.

gaiter, guei´-ta s polaina f.

galaxy, gAl´-ak-si s (astronomical) galaxia f.; –of, grupo notable de

gale, gueil s ventarrón m.

gall, goal s (bile) bilis f.; hiel f.; v amargar; irritar; –stones, s cálculos biliarios m. pl.

gallant*, gAl´-ant a valeroso

gallantry, gAl´-ant-ri s valor m.; galantería f.

gallery, gAl´-ar-i s galería f.

gallop, gAl´-op s galope m.; v galopar

gallows, gAl´-ou s s horca f.; patíbulo m.

galoshes, ga-losh´-os s pl chanclos m. pl.

galvanism, gAl´-van-is m s galvanismo m.

gamble, gAm´-bl s jugada f.; v jugar

gambler, gAm´-bla s jugador m.; tahur m.

gambol, gAm´-bl s v brincar; saltar

game, gueim s juego m.; (animals) caza f.

gamekeeper, gueim-kiip´-a a guardabosque m.

gander, gAn´-da s ganso m.; ojeada f.

gang, gAng-g s cuadrilla f.; (robbers, etc) banda f.; –way, (passage) pasillo m.; (ship's) pasamano m.

gap, gAp s brecha f.; boquete m.; laguna f.

gape, gueip v abrir la boca; (open) abrirse

garage, gaa-riCH´ s garage m.

garb, gaarb s vestido m.

garbage, gaarb´-iCH s basura f.; desperdicios m. pl.

garden, gaar´-dn s jardín m.; (kitchen) huerto m.; –er, jardinero m.; –ing, jardinería f.

gargle, gaar´-gl v hacer gárgaras

garland, gaar´-land s guirnalda f.; v enguirnaldar

garlic, gaar´-lik s ajo m.

garment, gaar´-ment s prenda de vestir f.

garnish, gaar´-nish v aderezar; s aderezo m.

garret, gAr´-et s desván m.; buhardilla f.

garrison, gAr´-i-s´n s

guarnición f.

garrulity, ga-ruu´-li-ty s locuacidad f.

garrulous, gАr´-u-los a locuaz

garter, gaar´-ta s liga f.

gas, gАs s gas m.; **–burner,** mechero m.; **–eous,** a gaseoso; **→works,** s pl fábrica de gas f.

gas pump, pet´-rol pömp s (engine) bomba f.; de gasolina; (garage) surtidor m.; de gasolina

gas station, pet´-rol stei´-shon s gasolinera; estación de servicio

gash, gАsh s cuchillada f.; v acuchillar

gasket, gАs´-kit s junta elástica f.

gasp, gaasp s boqueada f.; v boquear

gastric, gАs´-trik a gástrico

gate, gueit s puerta f.; entrada f.; (field, etc) barrera f.

gather, gАD´-a, v reunir; (pluck) recoger; (infer) inferir; **–ing,** s reunión f.

gaudy, goa´-di a llamativo

gauge, gueiCH s (tool) calibrador m.; (rail) entrevía f.; (size) calibre m.; v mediar; estimar

gaunt, goаnt a enjuto; descarnado; demacrado

gauntlet, goаnt´-let s manopla f.; guante m.

gauze, goаs s gasa f.; (wire) tela metálica f.

gawky, goа´-ki a desgarbado

gay, guei a alegre; festivo; s & a gay mf.; homosexual mf.

gaze, gueis v mirar; contemplar

gazelle, ga-sel´ s gacela f.

gazette, ga-set´ s gaceta f.; v nombrar oficialmente

gear, guir s equip m.; herra f.; engranaje m.; **–box,** caja de engranajes f.

gelatin, CHel´-a-tin s gelatina f.; mientas f.

gem, CHem s joya f.; gema f.

gender, CHen´-da s género m.

general, CHen´-er-al s general m.; a general

generalize, CHen´-er-a-lais v generalizar

generally, CHen´-er-a-li adv generalmente

generate, CHen´-er-eit v engendrar; producir; generar

generation, CHen-er-ei´-shŏn s generación f.

generator, CHen´-er-eit-a s (elec) generador m.; alternador m.

generosity, CHen-er-os´-i-ti s generosidad f.

generous*, CHen´-er-os a generoso; liberal

genial*, CH ii´-ni-al a genial; cordial

genius, CH ii´-ni-os s genio m.

genteel, CHen-tiil´ a gentil; elegante; distinguido

Gentile, CHen´-tail s & a gentil m.; pagano m.

gentility, CHen-til´-i-ti s nobleza f.; gentileza f.

gentle, CHen´-tl a suave; dulce; **–man,** s caballero m.; **–ness,** suavidad f.

gently, CHen´-tli adv suavemente

gents, CHents s aseos m. pl (de caballeros)

genuine, CHen´-iu-in a genuino; auténtico; puro; sincero; **–ness,** s autenticidad f.; pureza f.

genus, CH iin´-os s género m.

geography, CHi-og´-ra-fi s geografía f.

geology, CHi-ol´-o-CHi s geología f.

geometry, CHi-om´-a-tri s

geometría f.

geranium, CHi-rei´-ni-om
s geranio m.

germ, CHĕrm s germen m.;
(disease) microbio m.

germinate, CHĕr´-mi-neit
v germinar

gesticulate, CHes-tik´-iu-
leit v gesticular

gesticulation, CHes-tik´-
iu-lei-shon s
gesticulación f.

gesture CHes´-tiur, s gesto
m.

get, guet, v obtener;
(earn) ganar; (attain)
llegar; (fetch) traer;
–away, escaparse;
–back; volver; (recover)
recobrar; **–down,** bajar;
–in, entrar; **–on,**
avanzar; **–out,** salir; **–up,**
levantarse

geyser, guii´-s a s
calentador de agua m.;
géiser m.

ghastly, gaast´-li a lívido;
(horrible) espantoso

gherkin, guĕr´-kin s
pepinillo m.

ghost, goust s fantasma
m.; espíritu m.

giant, CHai´-ant s gigante
m.; a gigantesco

gibberish, guib´-er-ish s
jerigonza f.

gibbet, CHib´-et s horca f.;
patíbulo m.

gibe, CHaib s mofa f.; burla
f.; v mofarse

giblets, CHib´-lets s pl
menudillos de ave m. pl.

giddiness, guid´-i-nes s
vertigo m.; mareo m.

giddy, guid´-i a
vertiginoso; mareado

gift, guift s regalo m.;
donación f.

gifted, guif´-tid a talentoso

gigantic, CHai-gAn´-tik a
gigantesco

giggle, guig´-l v reírse por
nada

gild, guild v dorar; **–ing,** s
doradura f.

gills, guils s pl branquias f.
pl.

gilt, guilt a dorado

gimlet, guim´-let s barrena
f.

gin, CHin s (spirit) ginebra
f.; (snare) trampa f.

ginger, CHin´-CHer s
jengibre m.; **–bread,** pan
de jengibre m.

giraffe, CHi-raf´ s jirafa f.

gird, guĕrd v ceñir;
(encompass) cercar

girder, guĕr´-da s viga f.

girdle, guĕr´-dl s faja f.;
cinturón m.; v ceñir

girl, guĕrl s muchacha f.;

–hood, doncellez f.

girth, guĕrz s cincha f.;
(measure) periferia f.

give, guiiv v dar; entregar;
–in, asentir; **–up,**
renunciar

giver, guiv´-a s donante
m.

gizzard, guis´-erd s
molleja de ave f.

glacier, glA´-si-a s glaciar
m.

glad*, glAd a contento;
alegre

gladden, glAd´-n v alegrar

glade, gleid s claro m.

gladness, glAd´-nes s
alegría f.; regocijo m.

glamorous, glAm-or-os a
encantador(a);
atractivo; hechicero

glamour, glAm-or s
encanto m.; hechizo m.

glance, glAns s ojeada f.; v
mirar de prisa

gland, glAnd s glándula f.

glare, glér s (sun) resol m.;
(light) deslumbramiento
m.; (stare) mirada
rencorosa f.; v
deslumbrar; (stare)
mirar con enojo

glaring*, glér´-ing a
deslumbrante; (striking)
manifiesto

glass, glaas s vidrio m.;

cristal m.; (vessel) vaso m.; (wine) copa f.; (mirror) espejo m.; **–es,** s pl gafas f.; **––ware,** s cristalería f.; **–y,** a vidrioso

glaze, gleis v vidriar; lustrar

glazed, gleisd a glaseado

glazier, glei´-sher s vidriero m.

gleam, gliim s (ray) rayo m.; destello; v destellar; brillar

gleaning, glii´-ning s rebusca f.

glee, glii s alegría f.

glen, glen s cañada f.; valle m.

glib,* glib a liso; voluble; poco sincero

glide, glaid s resbalón m.; deslizamiento m.; v resbalar; (air) planear; **–r,** s (aircraft) planeador m.

glimmer, glim´-a s vislumbre m.; v alborear

glimpse, glimps s vislumbre m.

glint, glint s destello m.; v destellar

glisten, glis´-n v relucir

glitter, glit´-a v brillar; centellear; s centelleo m.

gloat, glout v deleitarse

global, gloub-l a (world-wide) mundial; (sum) global; **–** **village** aldea f.; global

globe, gloub s globo m.

globular, gloub´-iu-la a esférico

gloom, gluum s obscuridad f.; (dismal) tristeza f.

gloomy, gluu´-mi a obscuro; sombrío; triste

glorify, glou´-ri-fai v glorificar; exaltar

glorious*, gló´-ri-os a glorioso; magnífico

glory, gló´-ri s gloria f.; v (in) gloriarse (de)

gloss, glos s lustre m.; brillo m.; v lustrar; **–y,** a lustroso

glove, glöv s guante m.; **–r,** guantero m.

glow, glou s brillo m.; (sky) fulgor m.; v brillar

glue, gluu s cola f.

glum, glöm a melancólico; pegamento m.; malhumorado

glut, glöt s exceso m.; v (market) inundar

glutton, glöt´-n s glotón m.

gnarled, naarld a nudoso

gnash, nAsh v crujir los

dientes; **–ing,** s rechinamiento m.

gnat, nAt s mosquito m.; cínife m.

gnaw, noa, v roer

go, gou v ir; (mech) andar; **–away,** irse; partir; marcharse; **–back,** volver; **–down,** bajar; **–off,** partir; (gun) dispararse; **–out,** salir; **–up,** subir; **–without,** pasarse de

goad, goud s aguijón m.; v aguijonear

goal, goul s objeto m.; (posts) meta f.; (score) tanto m.; gol m.

goalkeeper, goul kiip-a s guardameta mf.; portero/a mf.

goat, gout s cabra f.; cabrón m.

gobble, gob´-l v tragar; **–r,** s tragón m.

goblet, gob´-let s copa f.

goblin, gob´-lin s trasgo m.; duende m.

God, god s Dios m.; **––fearing,** a temeroso de Dios

god, god s ídolo m.; **––child,** ahijado m.; **–dess,** diosa f.; **––father,** padrino m.; **–less,** a impío, ateo; **–liness,** s

piedad *f.*; **–ly**, *a* piadoso;
––mother, *s* madrina *f.*

goggle-eyed, gog´-l-aid *a* de ojos saltones

goggles, gog´-ls *s pl* anteojos *m.*

going, gou´-ing *s* paso *m.*; (departure) ida *f.*; partida *f.*; (horse) andadura *f.*

goiter, goi´-ta *s* bocio *m.*

gold, gould *s* oro *m.*; *a* de oro; **–en**, en oro; **–finch**, *s* jilguero *m.*; **–fish**, pez de colores *m.*; **–leaf**, pan de oro *m.*; **–smith**, orfebre *m.*

golf, golf *s* golf *m.*

gone, gon *pp* ido; pasado; (dead) muerto

gong, gong *s* gongo *m.*

good, gud *s* bien *m.*; ventaja *f. a* bueno; válido; *adv* bien; **––bye**, *interj* ¡adiós!; **–ly**, *a* considerable; **– morning**, *interj* ¡buenos días!; **–natured**, *a* bonachón; **–ness**, *s* bondad *f.*; **–will**, buena voluntad *f.*; (business) clientela *f.*

Good Friday, gud-frai´-di *s* Viernes Santo *m*

goods, guds *s* mercancía *f.*

goose, guus *s* ganso *m.*;

gansa *f.*; oca *f.*; ánsar *m.*

gooseberry, guus´-be-ri *s* grosella *f.*

gore, gór *s* sangre cuajada *f.*; *v* cornear

gorge, goarCH *s* garganta *f.*; *v* hartarse

gorgeous*, goar´-CHos *a* suntuoso; esplenderoso

gorilla, go-ril´-la *s* gorila *m.*

gosling, gos´-ling *s* gansarón *m.*

gospel, gos´-pl *s* evangelio *m.*

gossamer, gos´-a-ma *s* telaraña *f.*

gossip, gos´-ip *s* chismoso *m.*; *v* chismear

gouge, gauCH *s* gubia *f.*; *v* escavar; sacar

gout, gaut *s* gota *f.*; **–y**, *a* gotoso

govern, gov´-ern *v* governar; **–ess**, *s* institutriz *f.*; **–ment**, gobierno *m.*; **–or**, gobernador *m.*; (*mech*) regulador *m.*

gown, gaun *s* vestido de mujer *m.*; (official) toga *f.*

grab, grAb, *v* asir; agarrar; *s* (*mech*) gancho *m.*

grace, greis *s* gracia *f.*; favor *m.*; **–ful***, *a*

gracioso; elegante; **–fulness**, *s* gracia *f.*; gentileza *f.*; **–less**, *a* desgarbado; descortés

gracious*, grei´-shos *a* gracioso; benévolo

gradation, gra-dei´-shon *s* gradación *f.*

grade, greid *s* grado *m.*; rango *m.*; *v* graduar

gradient, gre´-di-ent *s* rampa *f.*; pendiente *f.*

gradual*, grAd´-iu-al *a* gradual

graduate, grAd´-iu-eit *s* graduado *m.*; *v* graduarse

graft, graaft *s* corrupción *f.*; *v* (trees) injertar

grain, grein *s* grano *m.*; (wood, etc.) veta *f.*; (leather) flor *f.*; *v* (paint) vetear

gram(me), grAm´ *s* gramo *m.*

grammar, grAm´-a *s* gramática *f.*

granary, grAn´-a-ri *s* granero *m.*

grand*, grAnd *a* grandioso; magnífico; **–child**, *s* nieto *m.*; nieta *f.*; **–daughter**, nieta *f.*; **–father**, abuelo *m.*; **–mother**, abuela *f.*; **–son**, nieto *m.*

grange, greinCH *s* granja

f.; finca f.; (estate) quinta f.

grant, graant v conceder; (law) otorgar; s concesión f.; (gift) don m.

grape, greip s uva f.; — **fruit,** pomelo m.; — **shot,** metralla f.

graph, graaf s gráfica/o fm.

graphic*, grAf´-ik a gráfico

grapple, grAp´-l s v agarrar; –**with,** (confront boldly) luchar

grasp, graasp v empuñar; (mentally) comprender; s asimiento m.

grasping, graas´-ping a avaro

grass, graas s hierba f.; –**hopper,** saltamontes m.; –**y,** a herboso, herbáceo

grate, greit s (fire) parrilla f.; v raspar; irritar

grateful*, greit´-ful a agradecido

gratefulness, greit´-ful-nes s gratitud f.

gratification, grAt´-i-fi-kei´-shon s gratificación f.; recompensa f.

gratify, grAt´-i-fai, v gratificar; –**ing,** a agradable

grating, grei´-ting s reja f.; a (sound) chirriant

gratitude, grAt´-i-tiuud s gratitud f.

gratuitous*, gra-tiuu´-i-tos a gratuito

gratuity, gra-tiuu´-i-ti s recompensa f.; (tip) propina f.

grave, greiv s sepultura f.; tumba f.; a* grave; — **stone,** lápida sepulcral f.; –**yard,** cementerio m.

gravel, grAv´-l s gravilla f.

gravitate, grAv´-i-teit v gravitar

gravity, grAv´-i-ti s gravedad f.

gravy, grei´-vi s jugo m.; salsa f.

gray, grei a gris; pardo

graze, greis v rozar; (feed) pacer; pastar

grease, griis s grasa f.; v engrasar; lubricar

greasy, grii´-si a grasiento

great*, greit a gran; ilustre

greatness, greit´-nes s grandeza f.

greed, griid s voracidad f.; (avarice) codicia f.; –**ily,** adv vorazmente; –**iness,** s voracidad f.; avaricia f.; –**y,** a voraz; glotón; avaro

green, griin s verde m.; a verde; –**gage,** s ciruela claudia f.; –**house,** invernadero m.; –**ish,** a verdoso

greet, griit, v saludar

greeting, griit´-ing s saludo m.; salutación f.

grenade, gre-neid´ s granada f.; bomba f.

greyhound, grei´-jaund s galgo m.; galga f.

gridiron, grid´-ai-ern s parrilla f.

grief, griif s pena f.; dolor m.; aflicción f.

grievance, grii´-vans s agravio m.; perjuicio m.

grieve, griiv v afligir; afligirse; agraviar

grievous*, grii´-vos a penoso; doloroso; cruel

grill, grill s parrilla f.; v asar en parrilla

grim*, grim a ceñudo; horrendo

grimace, gri-meis´ s mueca f.; visaje m.

grime, graim s tizne m.; mugre f.

grin, grin s sonrisa burlona f.; v sonreír burlonamente

grind, graind v moler; (sharpen) afilar

grinder, grain´-da s (for

knives, etc) afilador m.;
(coffee, etc) molino m.

grip, grip s (action) presa
f.; agarro m.; (hand)
apretón m.; (handle)
mango m.; puño m.; v
agarrar; empuñar

gripe, graip, v (bowels)
dar cólico

grisly, gris´-li a espantoso;
horroroso

grist, grist s molienda f.

grit, grit s cascajo m.;
(particle) arena f.; v
rechinar

gritty, grit´-i a arenoso

groan, groun s gemido m.;
v gemir

groats, grouts s pl avena

grocer, grou´-sa s tendero
de ultramarinos m.

grocery, grou´-sa-ri s
tienda de ultramarinos f.

grog, grog s grog m.;
ponche m.

groggy, gro´-gui a
vacilante

groin, groin s ingle f.;
(arch) arista f.

groom, gruum s mozo de
cuadra m.; novio m.

groove, gruuv s ranura f.;
v acanalar

grope, group, v andar a
tientas

gross, grous s (12 dozen)

gruesa f.; (weight) bruto
m.; a* (coarse) grosero;
(flagrant) enorme

ground, graund v (vessel)
encallar; s tierra f.; suelo
m.; motivo m.; **—floor,**
piso bajo m.; **—less*,** a
infundado; **—s,** s pl (park,
etc) jardines m.pl.;
—work, s plan m.; base f.

group, gruup s grupo m.; v
agrupar

grouse, graus s gallina
silvestre f.

grove, grouv s arboleda f.;
alameda f.

grovel, grov´-l v
arrastrarse

grow, grou, v crecer;
cultivar; **—er,** s
cultivador m.;
productor m.; **—n up,**
adulto m.

growl, graul s gruñido m.;
v gruñir

growth, gruuz s
crecimiento m.; tumor
m.

grub, gröb s gorgojo m.;
larva f.

grudge, gröCH s ojeriza f.;
v envidiar

gruel, gruu´-el s avenate
m.

gruesome, gruu´-som a
horrendo

gruff, gröf a áspero; seco

grumble, gröm´-bl v
refunfuñar

grunt, grönt s gruñido m.;
v gruñir

guarantee, ga-ran-tii´ v
garantizar; s garantía f.

guard, gaard s guardia f.;
(railroad) conductor m.;
v guardar

guarded, gaar´-did a
circunspecto

guardian, gaar´-di-an s
guardián m.; (trustee)
tutor m.

gudgeon, gö CH´-n s gobio
m.

guess, gues v adivinar,
conjeturar; s conjetura
f.; **—work,** conjetura f.

guest, guest s (visitor;
lodger) huésped m.; (for
meals only) convidado
m.; (hotel) cliente m.

guidance, gai´-dans s
dirección f.; gobierno
m.

guide, gaid, v guiar; s guía
m.

guidebook, gaid´-buk s
guía de viajes f.

guild, guild s gremio m.;
corporación f.

guile, gail s engaño m.;
—less, a cándido

guilt, guilt s culpabilidad

f.; (moral) pecado *m*.

guilty, guil´-ti *a* culpable

guinea, guin´-i *s* guinea *f*.;
–fowl, pintada *f*.; **–pig,**
conejillo de Indias *m*.

guise, gais *s* manera *f*.;
apariencia *f*.

guitar, gui-taar´ *s* guitarra
f.

gulf, gŏlf *s* golfo *m*.;
abismo *m*.

gull, gŏl *s* gaviota *f*.; *v*
engañar

gullet, gŏl´-*et s* gaznate *m*.

gulp, gŏlp *s* trago *m*.; *v*
tragar

gum, gŏm *s* goma *f*.;
(teeth) encía *f*.;
(chewing) chicle *m*.; *v*
engomar

gun, gŏn *s* fusil *m*.;
(sports) escopeta *f*.;
(artillery) cañón *m*.;
–ner, artillero *m*.;
–powder, pólvora *f*.;
–smith, armero *m*.

gurgle, guĕr´-gl *v*
gorgotear; *s* gorgoteo *m*.

gush, gŏsh *v* borbotar; *s*
borbotón *m*.

gust, gŏst *s* ráfaga *f*.; racha
f.; **–y,** *a* rafagoso;
ventoso; borrascoso

gut, gŏt *s* tripa *f*.; *v*
destripar

gutter, gŏt´-*a s* (roof)

gotera *f*.; (street) arroyo
m.

guy, gai *s* mamarracho *m*.;
tío; tipo; sujeto

gymnasium, CHim-nei´-*s* -
om s gimnasio *m*.

gymnastics, CHim-nAs´-
tiks *s pl* gimnasia *f*.

gypsy, CHip´-si *s* gitano
m.; gitana *f*.; *a* gitanesco

gym, CHim *s* gimnasio *m*.

N.B.—La H debe
pronunciarse siempre,
excepto en las voces
marcadas §

habit, jAb´-it s hábito m.;
costumbre f.

habitable, jAb´-it-a-bl a
habitable

habitual*, ja-bit´-iu-al a
habitual; acostumbrado

hack, jAk s corte m.;
hachazo m.; v tajar;
cortar

hackneyed, jAk´-nid a
(subject) trillado

hag, jAg s bruja f.

haggard*, jAg´-ard a
(appearance) ojeroso

haggle, jAg´-l v regatear

hail, jeil s granizo m.; v
granizar; (call) llamar

hair, jér s pelo m.; cabello

m.; (horse) crin m.; —
brush, cepillo para el
pelo m.; —**dresser,**
peluquero m.; —**drier,**
s secador para el pelo m.;
—**pin,** horquilla f.; —**y,** a
peludo

hake, jeik s merluza f.

hale, jeil a sano; robusto

half, jaaf s mitad f.; a
medio; adv a medias

halibut, jAl´-i-bŏt s mero
m.; hipogloso m.

hall, joal s vestíbulo m.; —
mark, marca del
contraste f.

hallow, jAl´-ou v santificar

hallucination, ja-liu´-si-
nei´-shon s alucinación
f.

halo, jei´-lou s halo m.;
aureola f.

halt, joalt s parada f.; v
pararse interj ¡alto!

halter, joal´-ta s cabestro
m.

halve, jaav v partir en dos
mitades

ham, jAm s jamón m.

hamburger, jam-bĕr´-ga s
hamburguesa f.

hamlet, jAm´-let s aldea f.

hammer, jAm´-a s martillo
m.; v martillar

hammock, jAm´-ok s
hamaca f.

hamper, jAm´-pa s canasto
m.; v estorbar

hand, jAnd s (human,
clock, cards) mano; v
dar; —**bag,** s bolsa f.; —
bill, cartel m.; —**book,**
manual m.; —**cuffs,** s pl
esposas f. pl.; —**ful,** s
puñado m.; —**kerchief,**
pañuelo m.; —**made,** a
hecho á mano f.; —**rail,** s
barandal m.; **second—,**
de segundamano; —**y,** a
mañoso

handicapped, jAnd-ii-kApt
s deficiente mf (mental);
minusválido/a mf (físico,
-a)

handle, jAn´-dl s mango
m.; (bag) asa f.; (door)
botón m.; v manejar

handsome*, j An´-som a

bello; elegante; generoso

hang, jAng v (execute) ahorcar; **–er,** s colgadero m.; **–up,** v colgar

hangar, jAng´-ga s hangar m.

hang gliding, jAnd-glaiding s vuelo m.; libre

hangover, jAnd-ou´-va s (after drinking) resaca f.

hank, jAng-k s madeja f.

hanker, jAng´-ka v ansiar; apetecer

hapless, jAp´-les a desventurado

happen, jAp´-n v acontecer; ocurrir

happily, jAp´-i-li adv felizmente

happiness, jAp´-i-nes s felicidad f.; dicha f.

happy, jAp´-i a feliz; dichoso

harangue, ja-rAng´ s arenga f.; v arengar

harass, jAr´-as v acosar

harbinger, jaar´-bin-CH a s precursor m.

harbor, jaar´-br s puerto m.

hard, jaard a duro

harden, jaar´-dn v endurecer; (refl) endurecorse

hardly, jaard´-li adv apenas; severamente

hardness, jaard´-nes s dureza f.; dificultad f.

hardship, jaard´-ship s pena f.; privación f.

hardware, jaard´-uér s ferretería f.; quincallería f.

hardy, jaar´-di a robusto; atrevido

hare, jér s liebre f.

hark, jaark v escuchar; interj ¡oye!

harlequin, jaar´-li,-küin s arlequin m.

harm, jaarm s daño m.; v dañar; **–ful*,** a dañoso; **–less*,** inofensivo

harmonious*, jaar-mou´-ni-os a armonioso

harmonize, jaar´-mon-ais v armonizar

harness, jaar´-nes s (horses, armor) arnés m.; v enjaezar; (forces) acoplar

harp, jaarp s arpa f.

harpoon, jaar-puun´ s arpón m.

harrow, jAr´-ou s grada f.; v gradar (feelings) perturbar

harsh*, jaarsh a (sound) discordante; (severe) áspero; (color) duro

harvest, jaar´-vest s cosecha f.; v cosechar

hash, ⸗Ash s picadillo m.; salpicón m.; v picar

hassle, jAs´-ol s (quarrel) pelea f.; (difficulty) problema m.; dificultad f.; (bother) lío m.; follón m.; v molestar; fastidiar; dar la lata

hassock, jAs´-ok s cojín m.

haste, jeist s prisa f.; **–n,** v apresurarse

hastily, jeis´-ti-li adv precipitadamente

hat, jAt s sombrero m.; **–box,** sombrerera f.; **–pin,** alfiler de sombrero m.; **–stand,** percha f.; **–ter,** sombrerero m.

hatch, jAch s (naut) escotilla f.; v empollar; (plot) tramar

hatchback, jAch-bAk´ s (door) puerta f.; trasera; portón m; (vehicle) cincopuertas; coche m.; con pueta trasera

hatchet, jAch´-et s hacha f.

hate, jeit v odiar; s odio m.

hateful*, jeit´-ful a odioso; detestable

haughty, joa´-ti a altivo; soberbio

haul, joal s arrastre m.;

(catch) redada f.; v tirar de, arrastrar; **-age,** s tracción f.

haunch, joanch s anca f.

haunt, joant s (animal) guarida f.; v rondar; persiguir

have, jΛv v haber; tener; poseer; (to cause) hacer

haven, jei´-vn s puerto m.; (refuge) asilo m.

haversack, jΛv´-er-sΛk s mochila f.

havoc, jΛv´-ok s estrago m.; ruina f.

hawk, joak s halcón m.; v revender

hawker, joa´-ka s buhonero m.

hawthorn, joa´-zoαrn s espino m.

hay, jei s heno m.; **-- fever,** fiebre del heno f.; **--loft,** henil m.; **-making,** siega del heno f.; **--stack,** almiar m.

hazard, jΛs´-erd s azar m.; acaso m.; (risk) riesgo m.; v aventurar; **-ous*,** a arriesgado

haze, jeis s bruma f.; neblina f.

hazel, jei´-sl s avellano m.; **--nut,** avellana f.

hazy, jei´-si a brumoso

he, jii pron pers él

head, jed s cabeza f.; (chief) jefe m.; a (main) principal

headache, jed´-eik s dolor de cabeza m.

heading, jed´-ing s encabezamiento m.; título m.

headland, jed´-lAnd s cabo m.

headlights, jed´-laits s faros m. pl.

headline, jed´-lain s título m.; encabezamiento m.

headlong, jed´-long adv de cabeza; a temerario

headmaster, jed´-maas-ta s director de una escuela m.

headquarters, jed´-kuoar-tas s cuartel general m.

headstrong, jed´-strong a testarudo; terco

headwaiter, jed-uei´-ta s camarero principal m.

headway, jed´-uei s progreso m.

heady, jed´-i a temerario; fuerte

heal, jiil v sanar; curar

healing, jii´-ling s curación f.; a curativo

health, jelz s salud f.

healthy, jel´-zi a sano

heap, jiip s montón m.; v amontonar

hear, jir v oír; **-er,** s oyente m.; **-ing,** oído m.; (judicial) audiencia f.

hearsay, jir´-sei s rumor m.

hearse, jěrs s carro fúnebre m.; féretro m.

heart, jaart s corazón m.; (cards) copas m. pl.; **-- broken,** a transido de dolor; **--burn,** s acedía f.; **-ily,** adv cordialmente; **-iness,** s cordialidad f.; **-less,** a sin corazón; **-y,** cordial

hearth, jaarz s hogar m.

heat, jiit s calor m.; v calentar

heater, jiit´-a s calentador m.; calorífero m.

heath, jiiz s (land) brezal m.

heathen, jii´-Den s & a pagano m.; (fig) ateo m.

heather, jeD´-a s brezo m.

heating, jii´-ting s calefacción f.

heatstroke, jiit-strouk s insolación f.

heat wave, jiit-ueiv s hola f.; de calor

heave, jiiv v alzar; (naut) izar

heaven, jev´-n s cielo m.; firmamento m.

heavenly, jev´-n-li *a* celestial

heaviness, jev´-i-nes *s* pesadez *f.*

heavy, jev´-i *a* pesado

hedge, jeCH *s* seto *m.*; **–hog,** erizo *m.*

heed, jiid *v* atender; *s* atención *f.*

heedful*, jiid´-ful *a* atento; vigilante

heedless*, jiid´-les *a* descuidado; distraído

heel, jiil *s* talón *m.*; (shoe) tacón *m.*

heifer, jef´-a *s* ternera *f.*

height, jait *s* altura *f.*; (person) estatura *f.*

heighten, jai´-ten *v* elevar; realzar

heinous*, jei´-nos *a* atroz; odioso

§heir, ér *s* heredero *m.*

§heiress, ér´-es *s* heredera *f.*

§heirloom, ér´-lum *s* reliquia familiar *f.*

helicopter, jel´-i-kop-ta *s* helicóptero *m.*

hell, jel *s* infierno *m.*; **–ish,** *a* infernal

hello, jel-ou *interj* ¡hola!; (telephone, person answering) ¡diga!; **say –** to saludar

helm, jelm *s* timón *m.*;

–sman, timonero *m.*

helmet, jel´-met *s* yelmo *m.*; casco *m.*

help, jelp *s* ayuda *f.*; (in distress) socorro *m.*; *interj* ¡socorro!; *v* ayudar; socorrer; **–er,** *s* asistente *m.*; **–ful,** *a* útil; servicial; **–less,** desamparado; impotente; **–mate,** *s* compañero *m.*

hem, jem *s* dobladillo *m.*; **–in,** (surround) rodear

hemisphere, jem´-i-sfiir *s* hemisferio *m.*

hemorrhage, ji´-mor-iCH *s* hemorragia *f.*

hemp, jemp *s* cáñamo *m.*

hen, jen *s* gallina *f.*; **–pecked,** *a* marido que se deja mandar

hence, jens *adv* de aquí; por lo tanto

henceforth, jens´-fórz *adv* en adelante

her, jër, *pers pron* la; le; ella; a ella; *poss adj* su; sus (de ella)

herald, jer´-ald *s* heraldo *m.*; *v* anunciar

herb, jërb *s* hierba *f.*; **–alist,** herbolario *m.*

herd, jërd *s* manada *f.*; hato *m. v* reunir el ganado; ir en hatos; **–sman,** *s* vaquero *m.*

here, jir *adv* aquí; por aquí

hereabout(s), jir-a-baut´(s) *adv* por aquí cerca

hereafter, jir-aaft´-a *adv* en el futuro

hereby, jir-bai´ *adv* por éstas; por la presente

hereditary, ji-red´-i-ta-ri *a* hereditario

herein, jir-in´ *adv* aquí dentro; incluso

hereof, jir-ov´ *adv* de esto; de aquí

hereon, jir-on´ *adv* sobre esto

heresy, jer´-i-si *s* herejía *f.*

heretic, jer´-i-tik *s* hereje *m.*

hereto, ji-tuu´ *adv* a esto; a este fin

heretofore, jir-tuu-fó´r´ *adv* hasta ahora; hasta este momento

hereupon, jir-öp-on´ *adv* sobre esto; por consiguiente

herewith, jir-uiD´ *adv* con esto; adjunto

hermetic, jer´-met-ik *a* hermético

hermit, jër´-mit *s* ermitaño *m.*

hermitage, jër´-mi-tiCH *s* ermita *f.*

hernia, jër´-ni-a *s* hernia

f.

hero, ji´-rou s héroe m.;
(stage, etc) protagonista
m.

heroic, ji-rou´-ik a
heroico; épico

heroin, jer-ou-in s heroína
f.

heroine, ji´-ro-in s
heroína f.; (stage, etc)
protagonista f.

heroism, ji´-ro-ism s
heroísmo m.

herring, jer´-ing s arenque
m.

hers, jĕrs, pron f. suyo;
suya; de ella; el suyo; la
suya; los suyos; las suyas
(de ella)

herself, jĕr-self´ pron ella
misma

hesitate, jes´-i-teit v
vacilar; dudar; titubear

hesitation, jes-i-tei´-shon
s duda f.; indecisión f.

heterosexual, jet-ĕr-ou-
sek-shuu-l s & a
heterosexual mf.

hew, jiuu v tajar; (stone)
picar

hiatus, jai-ei´-tos s hiato
m.

hiccup, jik´-op s hipo m.

hide, jaid s cuero m.; piel
f.; v esconder

hideous*, jid´-i-os a

horrible; espantoso

hiding, jai´-ding s
(flogging) paliza f.; a (in
hiding) escondido;
–**place,** s escondite m.

hi-fi, jai´-fai abbr of high
fidelity s alta f.;
fidelidad

high*, jai a alto; (status)
eminente; (elevated)
elevado; (cost) caro;
–**est,** a el más alto;
supremo; –**ness,** s altura
f.; (title) Alteza f.

highbrow, jai´-brau s snob
intelectual m.; a docto;
erudito

highlight, jai´-lait s punto
sobresaliente m.; realce
m.; v poner de relieve

high-tech, jai-tek a de alta
tecnología

highway, jai´-uei s
carretera f.; camino real
m.

hijack, jai´-CHak v
piratear; secuestrar; s
secuestro m.; -**er** s
secuestrador m.

hilarious, jil-ér-iios a
divertido; regocijante;
alegre

hilarity, ji-lAr´-i-ti s
hilaridad f.

hill, jil s colina f.; (road)
cuesta f.; –**y,** montañoso

hilt, jilt s puño de espada
m.

him, jim, pers pron le; él; a
él

himself, jim-self´ pron él;
él mismo

hind, jaind s cierva f.; a
trasero

hinder, jin´-da v impedir;
estorbar

hindmost, jin´-der-moust
a postrero; último

hindrance, jin´-drans s
impedimento m.

hinge, jinCH s bisagra f.;
(door) gozne m.

hint, jint s indirecta f.;
sugestión f.; insinuación
f.; v sugerir; insinuar

hip, jip s cadera f.

hire, jair s alquiler m.; v
alquilar

his, jis, pron m.; suyo;
suya; de él; el suyo; la
suya; los suyos; las suyas
(de él); poss adj su; sus
(de él)

hiss, jis v (steam) silbar;
(derision) chiflar; s
silbido m.; (derision)
rechifla f.

historical*, jis-to´-rikal a
histórico

history, jis´-to-ri s historia
f.

hit, jit v pegar; (target,

etc) acertar; s golpe m.

hitch, jich s (pull) tirón m.; (obstacle) tropiezo m.; v enganchar; (naut) amarrar

hitchhike, jich-jaik v hacer autostop

hither, jiD´-a adv aquí; acá; por aquí; por acá

hitherto, jiD´-er-tu adv hasta ahora

hive, jaiv s colmena f.

hoard, jó rd v (money, jewels) atesorar; (food, etc) acaparar; s tesoro m.

hoarse*, jó rs a ronco; enronquecido

hoax, jouks s trampa f.; broma f.; v burlar; engañar

hobble, job´-l s cojera f. v (walk) cojear

hobby, job´-i s pasatiempo m.

hock, jok s vino del Rin m.; (animal) jarrete m.

hoe, jou s azada f.; v cavar

hog, jog s puerco m.; cerdo m.

hoist, joist v alzar; (flag) izar

hold, jould v tener; agarrar; (capacity) contener s presa f.; (ship) cala f.; **–back,** v

retener; **–on,** agarrarse; **–over,** aplazar

holder, joul´-da s tenedor m.; poseedor m.; (handle) mango m.; (receptacle) asa f.; (bracket) brazo m.; **share–,**accionista mf.

holding, joul´-ding s tenencia f.; (share) acción f.

hole, joul s agujero m.

holiday, jol´-i-dei s fiesta f.

holidays, jol´-i-deis s pl vacaciones f. pl.

holiness, jol´-i-nes s santidad f.

hollow, jol´-ou s hueco m.; a hueco; v ahuecar

holly, jol´-i s acebo m.

holocaust, jol-o-koust s holocausto m.

holy, jou´-li a santo; sagrado; **–water,** s agua bendita f.; **–week,** Semana Santa f.

homage, jom´-iCH s homenaje m.

home, joum s casa f.; hogar m.; (homeland) patria f.; **at –,** en casa; **–less,** sin hogar; **–ly,** a casero

homeopathic, jou´-mi-o-paz´-ik a homeopático

homesick, joum´-sik a nostálgico; tener morriño

homeward, joum´-uerd adv hacia casa; **–bound,** de regreso

homosexual, jom-o-sek-shuu-l s & a homosexual mf.

hone, joun s piedra de afilar f.; v (blades) afilar

§**honest*,** on´-est a honrado; honesto; sincero

§**honesty,** on´-est-i s honradez f.; honestidad f.

honey, jŏn´-i s miel f.; **–moon,** luna de miel f.; **–suckle,** madreselva f.

§**honor,** on´-a s honor m.

§**honorable,** on´-er-a-bl a honorable

§**honorary,** on´-er-a-ri a honorario

hood, jud s capucha f.; (vehicle) capota f.

hoodwink, jud´-uingk v enganar

hoof, juf s pezuña f.; (horse) casco m.

hook, juk s gancho m.; garfio m.; (fish) anzuelo m.; v enganchar; **–and eye,** s corchete m.; (hook) macho m.; (eye) hembra *f.*; **by – or by crook,** *adv* a tuertas o a derechas

hooligan, juu-li-gan *s* gamberro *m.*

hoop, jup *s* cerco *m.*; arco *m.*; aro *m.*

hoot, juut *s* (owl) grito *m.*; (motor) bocinazo *m.*; *v* gritar; (motor) bocinar

hop, jop *s* brinco *m.*; (plant) lúpulo *m.*; *v* brincar

hope, joup *s* esperanza *f.*; *v* esperar; **–ful*,** *a* prometedor; **–less*,** desesperado; irremediable

hopefully, joup-ful-i *a* (person) optimista; esperanzado; prometedor; *s* aspirante *mf.*; candidato *m.*

horizon, jo-rai´-son *s* horizonte *m.*

horizontal*, jo-ri-son´-tal *a* horizontal

hormone, jor-moun *s* hormona *f.*

horn, joarn *s* cuerno *m.*; asta *f.*; (motor) bocina *f.*; (hunt) cuerno de caza *m.*

hornet, joar´-net *s* avispón *m.*

horrible, jor´-i-bl *a* horrible

horrid*, jor´-id *a* horrible

horrify, jor´-i-fai *v* horrorizar

horror, jor´-or *s* horror *m.*; terror *m.*

hors d'oeuvre, or děr-v *s* entremés *m.*

horse, joars *s* caballo *m.*; **–back (on),** *adv* a caballo; **–hair,** *s* crin *f.*; **–man,** jinete *m.*; **–power,** caballos de fuerza *m. pl.*; **–radish,** rábano picante; **–shoe,** herradura *f.*

hose, jous *s* manga de riego *f.*; (stocking) media *f.*

hosier, jou´-sha *s* mediero *m.*; calcetero *m.*

hosiery, jou´-sher-i *s* calcetería *f.*

hospitable, jos´-pi-ta-bl *a* hospitalario

hospital, jos´-pi-tal *s* hospital *m.*

hospitality, jos-pi-tAl-iti *s* hospitalidad *f.*

host, joust *s* (inn) anfitrión *m.*; (friend) huésped *m.*; (sacrament) hostia *f.*

hostage, jos´-tiCH *s* (mil) rehén *m.*

hostelry, jos´-tel-ri *s* posada *f.*; hostelería *f.*

hostess, jous´-tes *s* huéspeda *f.*; anfitriona *f.*; (inn) posadera *f.*

hostile, jos´-tail *a* hostil; enemigo

hot*, jot *a* caliente; cálido; (condiment) picante

hotel, jo-tel´- *s* hotel *m.*; (inn) posada *f.*

hothouse, jot´-jaus *s* invernadero *m.*

hound, jaund *s* perro de caza *m.*; *v* cazar; perseguir

§hour, auer *s* hora *f.*; **–ly,** *adv* a cada hora

house, jaus *v* albergar; *s* casa *f.*; **–hold,** familia *f.*; **–holder,** amo de casa *m.*; **–keeper,** ama de llaves *f.*; **–maid,** criada *f.*

housewife, jaus-uaif *s* ama de casa *f.*

hovel, jov´-l *s* cabaña *f.*; choza *f.*

hover, jov´-a *v* revolotear; (fig.) perseguir

how, jau *adv* cómo; cuán; cuánto; por qué; **–ever,** como quiera que sea; *conj* sin embargo; **– far,** a qué distancia; **– much, many,** cuánto; cuánta;

cuántos; cuántas

howl, jaul *v* aullar; *s* aullido *m*.

hub, jŏb *s* cubo de la rueda *m*.

huddle, jŏd´-l *v* arrebujar; amontonar; *s* monton *m*.; grupo *m*.

hue, jiuu *s* color *m*.; tinte *m*.; **–and cry**, alarma *m*.

hug, jŏg *v* abrazar; *s* abrazo *m*.

huge, jiuCH *a* vasto; enorme; inmenso

hulk, jŏlk *s* casco *m*.

hull, jŏl *s* casco *m*.

hum, jŏm *v* (insect, engine) zumbar; (voice) tararear; *s* zumbido *m*.

human, jiuu´-man *a* humano; **–ity**, *s* humanidad *f*.

humane*, jiuu-mein´ *a* humano; humanitario

humble, jŏm´-bl *a* humilde; *v* humillar

humidity, jiuu-mid´-i-ti *s* humedad *f*.

humiliate, jiuu-mil´-i-eit *v* humillar

humiliation, jiuu-mi-li-ei´-shon *s* humillación *f*.

humor, jiuu´-ma *s* humor *m*.; *v* complacer

humorist, jiuu´-mer-ist *s* humorista *m*.

humorous*, jiuu´-mer-os *a* jocoso; cómico

hump, jŏmp *s* joroba *f*.; **–back**, jorobado *m*.

hunch, jŏnsh *s* giba *f*.; corazonada *f*.; sospecha *f*.; **–back**, joroba *f*.

hundred, jŏn´-dred *s* & *a* ciento *m*.; cien *m*.; **–fold**, *a* céntuplo; **–th**, centésimo

hunger, jŏn´-ga *s* hambre *m*.; *v* sufrir hambre

hungry, jŏn´-gri *a* hambriento

hunt, jŏnt *s* caza *f*.; *v* cazar; **–er**, *s* cazador *m*.

hurdle, jŏr´-dl *s* zarzo *m*.; valla *f*.

hurl, jĕrl *v* arrojar; precipitar

hurricane, jŏr´-i-kan *s* huracán *m*.

hurry, jŏr´-i *v* apresurarse; *s* prisa *f*.

hurt, jĕrt *v* herir; dañar; *s* mal *m*.

hurtful*, jĕrt´-ful *a* nocivo; perjudicial

husband, jŏs ´-band *s* marido *m*.; *v* economizar, ahorrar

hush, jŏsh *interj* ¡chitón! *v* **– up**, ocultar

husk, jŏsk *s* cáscara *f*.; vaina *f*.; **–y**, *a* ronco

hustle, jŏs´-l *v* darse prisa; (jostle) empujar

hut, jŏt *s* choza *f*.; cabaña *f*.

hutch, jŏch *s* (rabbit) conejera *f*.

hyacinth, jai´-a-sinz *s* jacinto *m*.

hydrant, jai´-drant *s* boca de riego *f*.; boca de incendio

hydraulic, jai´-drou-lik *a* hidráulico

hydro, jai´-drou, **–gen**, *s* hidrógeno *m*.; **–pathic**, *a* hidropático; **–phobia**, *s* rabia *f*.

hygiene, jai-CHii-n *n* higiene *f*.

hygienic, jai-CHi-en´-ik *a* higiénico

hymn, jim *s* himno *m*.

hyphen, jai´-fen *s* guión *m*.

hypocrisy, jip-ó-kri-si *s* hipocresía *f*.; disimulo *m*.

hypocrite, jip´-o-krit *s* hipócrita *mf*.

hysterical, jis-ter´-i-kal *a* histérico

I, ai *pron* yo

ice, ais *s* hielo *m.*; **–bound**, *a* aprisionado por el hielo; **–cream**, *s* helado *m.*

ice rink, ais-rink *s* pista de hielo *f.*; pista de patinaje

ice skating, ais-skeit-ing *s* patinaje *m.*; sobre hielo

icicle, ais´-i-kl *s* carámbano *m.*

icing, ais-ing *s* (sugar) azúcar glaseado *m.*; (ice) formación *f.*; de hielo

icy, ais´-i *a* helado

idea, ai-dii´-a *s* idea *f.*

ideal, ai-dii´-al *s* ideal *m.*; *a* ideal

idealize, ai-dii´-al-is *v* idealizar

identical*, ai-den´-ti-kl *a* idéntico

identify, ai-den´-ti-fai *v* identificar

identity, ai-den´-ti *s* identidad *f.*

idiom, id´-i-om *s* (phrase) modismo *m.*

idiot, id´-i-ot *s* idiota *mf.*

idiotic, id-i-ot´-ik *a* tonto; absurdo

idle, ai´-dl *a* ocioso; *v* holgazanear; **–ness**, *s* ociosidad *f.*; **–r**, holgazán *m.*

idol, ai´-dol *s* ídolo *m.*

idolize, ai´-dol-ais *v* idolatrar

if, if *conj* si; **even –**, aunque

ignite, ig-nait´ *v* encender

ignition, ig-ni´-shon *s* ignición *f.*

ignoble, ig-nou´-bl *a* innoble; vil

ignominious*, ig-no-min´-i-os *a* ignominioso

ignominy, ig´-no-min-i *s* ignominia *f.*

ignoramus, ig-nor-ei´-mos *a* ignorante

ignorance, ig´-nor-ans *s* ignorancia *f.*

ignorant, ig´-nor-ant *a* ignorante

ignore, ig-nó r´ *v* no hacer caso; pasar por alto

ill, il *a* enfermo; malo; (nausea) mareado; **–ness**, *s* enfermedad *f.*

illegal*, i-lii´-gal *a* ilegal

illegible, i-leCH´-i-bl *a* ilegible

illegitimate*, i-leCH-it´-i-met *a* ilegítimo

illiberal*, i-lib´-er-al *a* avaro; mezquino

illiterate, i-lit´-er-eit *s* & *a* analfabeto *m.*; ignorante *m.*

illness, il-nes *s* enfermedad *f.*; dolencia *f.*; indisposición *f.*

illogical*, i-loCH´-i-kl *a* ilógico

illuminate, i-liuu´-mi-neit *v* iluminar; **–d**, *adj* iluminado

illumination, i-liuu-mi-

374

nei´-shon s iluminación f.

illusion, i-liuu´-shon s ilusión f.

illusive*, i-liuu´-siv a ilusivo

illusory, i-liuu´-so-ri a ilusorio

illustrate, i-lus´-treit v (exemplify) ilustrar; (point) ejemplificar; demostrar; (subject) aclarar; (book) ilustrar

illustration, i-lus-trei´-shon s ilustración f.; n ejemplo m.; explicación f.; aclaración f.; (book) grabado m.; ilustración f.

illustrious*, i-lus´-tri-os a ilustre

image, im´-iCH s imagen f.

imaginary, i-maCH´-in-eri a imaginario

imagination, i-maCH´-in-ei´-shon s imaginación f.

imaginative, i-maCH´-in-a-tiv a imaginativo

imagine, i-maCH´-in v imaginar; figurarse

imbecile, im´-bi-sail a imbécil

imbibe, im-baib´ v beber; (absorb) embeber

imbue, im-biuu´ v imbuir; infundir

imitate, im´-i-teit v imitar; remedar

immaculate*, i-mAk´-iu-let a inmaculado

immaterial*, i-ma-tii´-ri-al a inmaterial; indiferente

immature, i-ma-tiúr´ a inmaduro; prematuro

immeasurable, i-mes h´-iu-ra-bl a inmensurable

immediately, i-mii´-di-et-li adv inmediatamente; en seguida

immense*, i-mens´ a inmenso

immensity, i-mens´-i-ti s inmensidad f.

immerse, i-mĕrs´ v sumergir

immigrant, i´-mi-grant s inmigrante m.

immigrate, i´-mi-greit v inmigrar

immigration, i´-mi-grei-shon s inmigración f.

imminent*, i´-mi-nent a inminente

immobilize, i-mo´-bi-lais v inmovilizar; paralizar

immoderate*, i-mod´-er-et a inmoderado

immodest*, i-mod´-ist a inmodesto; impúdico

immoral*, i-mor´-al a inmoral

immortal, i-mor´-tal a inmortal; –ize, v inmortalizar

immovable, i-muu´-va-bl a inmóvil; inamovible; inmueble

immune, i-miuun´ a inmune; exento

imp, imp s diablillo m.

impact, im´-pAkt s choque m.; impacto m.

impair, im-pé r´ v deteriorar; perjudicar

impale, im-peil´ v empalar

impanel, im-pAn´-l v nombrar los jurados

imparity, im-pAr´-i-ti s disparidad f.

impart, im-paart´ v comunicar; dar

impartial*, im-paar´-shal a imparcial

impassable, im-pass´-a-bl a itransitable

impassion, im-pAsh´-on v apasionar; conmover

impassive*, im-pAs´-iv a impasible

impatience, im-pei´-shens s impaciencia f.

impatient*, im-pei´-shent a impaciente

impeach, im-piich´ v acusar

impeachment, im-piich´-ment s acusación f.

impecunious, im-pi-kiuu´-ni-os *a* sin dinero; pobre

impede, im-piid´ *v* impedir

impediment *s* impedimento *m*.

impel, im-pel´ *v* impeler; incitar

impending, im-pen´-ding *a* inminente

imperative, im-per´-a-tiv *s* & *a* imperativo *m*.

imperfect*, im-pěr´-fekt *a* imperfecto

imperfection, im-pěr-fek´-shon *s* imperfección *f*.

imperial*, im-pi´-ri-al *a* imperial

imperil, im-per´-il *v* poner en peligro

imperious*, im-pi´-ri-os *a* imperioso; perentorio

imperishable, im-per´-i-sha-bl *a* imperecedero; indestructible

impermeable, im-pěr´-mi-a-bl *a* impermeable

impersonal*, im-pěr´-son-al *a* impersonal

impersonate, im-pěr´-son-eit *v* personificar; (stage) representar

impertinence, im-pěr´-ti-nens *s* impertinencia *f*.

impertinent*, im-pěr´-ti-nent *a* impertinente; (not pertaining to) fuera de propósito

impervious*, im-pěr´-vi-os *a* impenetrable

impetuosity, im-pet´-iu-os´-i-ti *s* impetuosidad *f*.

impetuous*, im-pet´-iu-os *a* impetuoso

impetus, im´-pi-tos *s* ímpetu *m*.; (fig) impulsión *f*.

impiety, im-pai´-et-i *s* impiedad *f*.

impious*, im´-pi-os *a* impío

implement, im´-pli-ment *s* instrumento *m*.; herramienta *f*.; **–ation,** *s* realización *f*.

implicate, im´-pli-keit *v* implicar

implicit*, im-plis´-it *a* implícito; absoluto

implore, im-pló r´ *v* implorar

imply, im-plai´ *v* implicar; denotar; insinuar

impolite*, im-po-lait´ *a* descortés

import, im-pórt´ *v* importar; *s* importación *f*.; **–duty,** derechos de entrada *m. pl.*; **–er,** importador *m*.

importance, im-pór´-tans *s* importancia *f*.

important, im-pór´-tant *a* importante

importunate, im-pór´-tiu-neit *a* importuno

impose, im-pous´ *v* imponer; **–upon,** abusar

imposing, im-pou´-sing *a* imponente

imposition, im-po-si´-shon *s* imposición *f*.; impostura *f*.; (tax) impuesto *m*.

impossibility, im-pos´-i-bil´-i-ti *s* imposibilidad *f*.

impossible, im-pos´-i-bl *a* imposible

impostor, im-pos´-tr *s* impostor *m*.

impotence, im´-po-tens *s* impotencia *f*.

impound, im-paund´ *v* encerrar; (judicial) depositar

impoverish, im-pov´-er-ish *v* empobrecer

imprecation, im-pri-kei´-shon *s* imprecación *f*.

impregnable, im-preg´-na-bl *a* inexpugnable

impregnate, im-preg´-neit *v* impregnar; (fertilize) empreñar

impress, im´-pres *v* imprimir; estampar;

(feelings) impresionar;
–ion, s impresión f.;
(stamp) marca f.; **–ive,** a
solemne; grandioso

imprint, im-print´s marca
f.; impresión f.; v
marcar; (mind) fijar

imprison, im-pris´-n v
encarcelar; **–ment,** s
encarcelación f.

improbable, im-prob´-a-bl
a improbable

improper*, im-prop´-a a
impropio; indecente

impropriety, im-pro-prai´-
i-ti s impropiedad f.

improve, im-pruuv´ v
mejorar; mejorarse;
–ment, s mejora f.;
progreso m.

improvident,* im-prov´-i-
dent a impróvido

improvise, im-pro-vais v
improvisar

imprudent*, im-pruu´-
dent a imprudente

impudence, im´-piu-dens s
descaro m.

impudent*, im´-piu-dent a
descarado

impulse, im´-pöls s
impulso m.

impure*, im-piú r´ a
impuro; (morally)
manchado

impurity, im-piú´-ri-ti s

impureza f.

impute, im-piuut´ v
imputar

in, in adv dentro; adentro;
prep en; por; sobre; a;
con; de; mientras

inability, in-a-bil´-i-ti s
incapacidad f.

inaccessible, in-ak-sess´-i-
bl a inaccesible

inaccuracy, in-Ak´-iu-ra-si
s inexactitud f.

inaccurate*, in-Ak´-iu-ret
a inexacto

inadequate*, in-Ad´-i-
kuet, a inadecuado

inadmissible, in-Ad-mi-si-
bl a inadmisible

inadvertent*, i-nAd-věr´-
tent a inadvertido

inane, i-nein´ a inepto,
fútil

inanimate i-nAn´-i-met a
inanimado

inapt, in-Apt´-t a inepto

inasmuch as, in-As-mŏch´
A s conj visto que

inaudible, in-oa´-di-bl a
inaudible

inaugurate, in-oa´-guiu-
reit v inaugurar

inborn, inbred, in´-boarn,
in´-bred a innato

incalculable, in-kAl´-kiu-
lei-bl a incalculable

incapable, in-kei´-pa-bl a

incapaz

incapacitate, in-ka-pAs´-i-
teit v incapacitar

incapacity, in-ka-pAs´-i-ti
s incapacidad f.

incarnation, in-kar-nei´-
shon s encarnación f.

incautious*, in-koa´-shos
a incauto

incense, in-sens´ s
incienso m. v (incite)
provocar; (anger)
encolerizar

incentive, in-sen´-tiv s
incentivo m.; estímulo
m.

incessant*, in-ses´-ant a
incesante

inch, inch s pulgada f.

incident, in´-si-dent s
incidente m.

incidental*, in-si-den´-tl a
incidental

incipient, in-sip´-i-ent a
incipiente

incision, in-sish´-on s
incisión f.

incite, in-sait´ v incitar

incivility, in-si-vil´-i-ti s
descortesía f.

inclination, in-kli-nei´-
shon s inclinación f.;
(disposition) tendencia
f.

incline, in-klain´ v
inclinar; inclinarse

incline, in´-klain s (slope)
declive m.

include, in-kluud´ v
incluir; encerrar

including, in-kluud´-ing
adv & a inclusive;
incluyendo

inclusive, in-kluu´-siv a
inclusivo

incoherent, in-ko-ji´-rent
a incoherente

income, in´-kom s
ingresos m. pl.; renta f.;
– tax, impuesto sobre la
renta m.

incoming, in´-kŏm-ing a
entrante

incommode, in-kom-oud´
v incomodar

incommodious*, in-kom-
ou´-di-os a incómodo

incomparable, in-kom´-
pa-ra-bl a incomparable

incompatible, in-kom-
pat´-i-bl a incompatible

incompetent, in-kom´-pi-
tent a incompetente

incomplete*, in-kom-
pliit´ a incompleto

incomprehensible, in-
kom´-pri-jen´-si-bl a
incomprensible

inconceivable, in-kon-sii´-
va-bl a inconcebible

inconclusive*, in-kon-
kluu´-siv a

inconcluyente

incongruous*, in-kon´-
gru-os a incongruo

inconsiderable, in-kon-
si´-de-ra-bl a
insignificante

inconsiderate, in-kon-si-
der-eit a poco
considerado

inconsistent*, in-kon-sis´-
tent a inconsistente;
inconsecuente;
contradictorio

inconsolable, in-kon-
soul´-a-bl a inconsolable

inconstant*, in-kon´-stant
a inconstante

inconvenience, in-kon-
vii´-ni-ens v perturbar
molestar; s
inconveniencia f.;
molestia f.

inconvenient, in-kon-vii´-
ni-ent a inconveniente

incorporate, in-kor´-po-
reit v incorporar

incorrect*, in-ko-rekt´ a
incorrecto; inexacto

incorrigible, in-kor´-i-
CHi-bl a incorregible

increase, in-kriis´ v
aumentar; crecer;
incremento m.

increase, in´-kriis s
aumento m.

incredible, in-kred´-i-bl a

increíble

incredulous, in-kred´-iu-
los a incrédulo

incriminate, in-krim´-i-
neit v incriminar

incumbent, in-kŏm´-bent
a obligatorio; (eccl)
beneficiado

incur, in-kĕr´ a incurrir

incurable, in-kiú´-ra-bl a
incurable

incursion, in-kĕr´-shon s
incursión f.

indebted, in-det´-id a
empeñado; reconocido;
adeudado

indecent*, in-dii´-sent a
indecente

indecision, in-di-si´-shon
s indecisión f.

indecisive*, in-di-sai´-siv
a indeciso; irresoluto

indecorous, in-di-kó´-ros
a indecoroso; indecente

indeed, in-diid´ adv
verdaderamente; de
veras

indefatigable, in-di-fAt´-i-
ga-bl a infatigable

indefensible, in-di-fen´-si-
bl a indefendible

indefinite, in-def´-i-nit a
indefinido

indelible, in-del´-i-bl a
indeleble

indelicacy, in-del´-i-ka-si s

indecoro m.

indemnify, in-dem´-ni-ai v indemnizar

indemnity, in-dem´-ni-ti s indemnización f.

indent, in-dent´ v (to dent) dentar; **–ation,** s indentación f.

independence, in-di-pen´-dens s independencia f.

independent*, in-di-pen´-dent a independiente

indescribable, in-di-skrai´-ba-bl a indescriptible

indestructible, in-di-strök´-ti-bl a indestructible

index, in´-dex s índice m.; **–finger,** dedo índice m.

indicate, in´-di-keit v indicar

indication, in-di-kei´-shon s indicación f.

indicator, in-di-kei-ta s indicador m.

indict, in-dait´ v procesar; encausar

indifference, in-dif´-er-ens s indiferencia f.

indifferent*, in-dif´-er-ent a indiferente; mediano

indigestible, in-di-CHes´-ti-bl a indigesto

indigestion, in-di-CHest´-ion s indigestión f.

indignant*, in-dig´-nant a indignado

indignity, in-dig´-ni-ti s indignidad f.

indirect*, in-di-rekt´ a indirecto

indiscreet*, in-dis-kriit´ a indiscreto

indiscriminate, in-dis-krim´-i-net a indistinto; **–ly,** adv indistintamente

indispensable, in-dis-pen´-sa-bl a indispensable

indisposed, in-dis-pous d´ a indispuesto

indisputable, in-dis´-piuu-ta-bl a indisputable

indistinct*, in-dis-tiñ-kt´ a indistinto

indistinguishable, in-dis-ting´-gui-sha-bl a indistinguible

indite, in-dait´ v redactar

individual, in-di-vid´-iu-al a* individual; s individuo m.

indolent, in´-do-lent a indolente

indoors, in-dórs adv en casa

induce, in-diuus´ v inducir; mover; **–ment,** s móvil m.; aliciente m.

indulge (in), in-dölCH´ v entregarse a; dar riende

suelta

indulgent*, in-döl´-CHent a indulgente

industrial, in-dös´-tri-al a industrial

industrious*, in-dös´-tri-os a industrioso; trabajador

industry, in´-dos-tri s industria f.

inebriated, in-ii´-bri-ei-tid a borracho

ineffective*, in-ef-ek´-tiv a ineficaz

ineffectual*, in-ef-ek´-tiu-al a ineficaz

inefficient*, in-ef-ish´-ent a ineficaz

inept*, i-nept´ a inepto; absurdo

inequality, in-i-kuol´-i-ti s desigualdad f.

inert*, in-ërt´ a inerte

inestimable, in-es´-ti-ma-bl a inestimable

inevitable, in-ev´-i-ta-bl a inevitable

inexact, in-eg-sAkt´ a inexacto; incorrecto

inexhaustible, in-eg-sous´-ti-bl a inagotable

inexpedient*, in-eks-pii´-di-ent a inoportuno

inexpensive*, in-eks-pen´-siv a barato

inexperience, in-eks-pii´-

ri-ens s inexperiencia f.

inexperienced, in-eks-
pii´-ri-enst a inexperto

inexplicable, in-eks´-pli-
ka-bl a inexplicable

inexpressible, in-eks-
press´-i-bl a indecible

infallible, in-fal´-i-bl a
infalible

infamous*, in´-fa-mos a
infame

infamy, in´-fa-mi s
infamia f.

infancy, in´-fan-si s
infancia f.; (law)
minoría f.

infant, in´-fant s infante
m.; niño m.; (law)
menor m.; a infantil

infantry, in-fan´-tri s
infantería f.

infatuation, in-fAt´-iu-ei´-
shon s
encaprichamiento m.

infect, in-fekt´ v infectar;
contagiar

infectious, in-fek´-shos a
infeccioso; contagioso

infer, in-fër´ v inferir;
–ence, s inferencia f.

inferior, in-fi´-ri-or s & a
inferior m.

infernal*, in-fër´-nal a
infernal

infest, in-fest´ v infestar;
(molest) plagar

infidel, in´-fi-del s & a
infiel m.

infinite*, in´-fi-nit a
infinito

infirm, in-fërm´ a
doliente; enfermizo;
inválido

infirmary, in-fër´-ma-ri s
enfermería f.

inflame, in-fleim´ v
inflamar

inflammable, in-flam´-a-bl
a inflamable

inflammation, in-fla-mei´-
shon s inflamación f.

inflate, in-fleit´ v inflar;
hinchar

inflexible, in-fleks´-i-bl a
inflexible

inflict, in-flikt´ v infligir;
imponer

influence, in´-flu-ens s
influencia f.; v influir

influential, in-flu-en´-shal
a influyente

influenza, in-flu-en´-sa s
gripe f.

inform, in-foarm´ v
informar; enterar;
comunicar; **–al,** a
informal; sin ceremonia;
–ality, s informalidad;
–ant, s informante m.;
denunciador m.; **–ation,**
s información f.

infrequent*, in-frii´-ku-

ent a infrecuente

infringe, in-frinCH´ v
infringir, contravenir;
–ment, s infracción f.;
contravención f.

infuriate, in-fiuu´-ri-eit v
enfurecer

infuse, in-fiuus´ v
infundir; (tea) poner en
infusión

ingenious*, in-CH ii´-ni-os
a ingenioso

ingenuity, in-CHin-iuu´-i-
ti s ingeniosidad f.

ingot, in´-got s lingote m.;
barra f.

ingratiate, in-grei´-shi-eit
v insinuarse

ingratitude, in-grAt´-i-
tiuud s ingratitud f.

ingredient, in-grii´-di-ent
s ingrediente m.

inhabit, in-jAb´-it v
habitar; **–able,** a
habitable; **–ant,** s
habitante m.

inhale, in-jeil´ v inhalar;
(smoke) tragar

inherent*, in-ji´-rent a
inherente

inherit, in-jer´-it v
heredar; **–ance,** s
herencia f.

inhibition, in-jib-i´-schon
s inhibición f.;
prohibición f.

inhospitable, in-jos´-pit-a-bl *a* inhospitable

inhuman, in-jiuu´-man *a* inhumano

iniquitous, in-ik´-ui-tos *a* inicuo

initial, in-ish´-al *s* letra inicial *f.*; *a* inicial

initiate, i-nish´-i-eit *v* iniciar

initiative, i-nish´-á-tiv *s* iniciativa *f.*

inject, in-CHekt´ *v* inyectar; **–ion,** *s* inyección *f.*

injudicious, in-CHiu-dish´-os *a* poco juicioso

injunction, in-CHongk´-shon *s* mandato *m.*; (law) entredicho *m.*

injure, in´-CHiú *r v* agraviar; (spoil) dañar; (bodily) lastimar

injurious*, in-CHiú´-ri-os *a* perjudicial; dañoso

injury, in´-CHer-i *s* daño *m.*; (bodily) lesión *f.*

injustice, in-CHŏs´-tis *s* injusticia *f.*

ink, ingk *s* tinta *f.*; **–stand,** tintero *m.*

inlaid, in-leid´ *a* incrustado

inland, in´-land *s & a* interior *m.*

in-laws, in-loas *s*

parientes *m. pl*; políticos; suegros *m. pl*

inlet, in´-let *s* entrada *f.*; ensenada *f.*

inmate, in´-meit *s* interno *m.*; acogido *m.*

inmost, in´-moust *a* recóndito; íntimo

inn, in *s* posada *f.*; fonda *f.*; **–keeper,** hospedero *m.*

inner, in´-a *a* interior

inner city, in´-a sit´-i *s* barrios *m. pl*; (deprimidos) del centro de una ciudad

innocent*, in´-o-sent *a* inocente

innocuous, in-o´-kiu-os *a* innocuo

innovation, in-o-vei´-shon *s* innovación *f.*

innumerable, in´-iu-mer-a-bl *a* innumerable

inoculate, in-o´-kiu-leit *v* inocular

inoffensive*, in-o-fen´-siv *a* inofensivo

inopportune, in-o´-por-tiuun *a* inoportuno

inquest, in´-kuest *s* pesquisa judicial *f.*

inquire, in-kuair´ *v* informarse; (ask) preguntar; (law) inquirir

inquiry, in-kuai´-ri *s*

investigación *f.*; (law) pesquisa *f.*

inquisitive*, in-kuis´-it-iv *a* curioso; inquisitivo

insane*, in-sein´ *a* loco; demente

insanity, in-san´-i-ti *s* locura *f.*; demencia *f.*

insatiable, in-sei´-shi-a-bl *a* insaciable

inscription, in-skrip´-shon *s* inscripción *f.*

insect, in´-sekt *s* insecto *m.*

insecure, in-si-kiú r´ *a* inseguro

insensible, in-sen´-si-bl *a* insensible; (unconscious) sin sentido

inseparable, in-sep´-a-ra-bl *a* inseparable

insert, in-sert´ *v* insertar; **–ion,** *s* inserción *f.*; (advertisement) anuncio *m.*

inside, in´-said *adv* en, dentro. *s* entrañas *f. pl.*; interior *m.*; *a* interior

insidious*, in-sid´-i-os *a* insidioso

insight, in´-sait *s* penetración *f.*; perspicacia *f.*

insignificant, in-sig-nif´-i-kant *a* insignificante

insincere, in-sin-sir´ *a* insincero; hipócritá

insinuate, in-sin´-iu-eit *v* insinuar

insipid, in-sip´-id *a* insípido; soso

insist, in-sist´ *v* insistir

insolence, in´-so-lens *s* insolencia *f.*

insolent*, in´-sou-lent *a* insolente

insolvency, in-sol´-ven-si *s* insolvencia *f.*

inspect, in-spekt´ *v* inspeccionar; **–ion**, *s* inspección *f.*; **–or**, *s* inspector *m.*

inspiration, in-spi-rei´-shon *s* inspiración *f.*

inspire, in-spair´ *v* inspirar; **–d**, *a* inspirado

install, in-stoal´ *v* instalar; montar; **–ation**, *s* instalación *f.*; (mech) montaje *m.*

installment, in-stoal´-ment *s* plazo *m.*; (books, serials) entrega *f.*

instance, in´-stans *s* caso *m.*; ejemplo *m.*

instant, in´-stant *s* instante *m.*; **–aneous***, *a* instantáneo; **–ly**, *adv* al instante

instead, in-sted´ *adv* en cambio; **–of**, en vez de

instep, in´-step *s* empeine *m.*

instigate, in´-sti-gueit *v* instigar

instill, in-stil´ *v* infundir

instinct, in´-sting-kt *s* instinto *m.*

institute, in´-sti-tiuut *s* instituto *m.*; *v* instituir

instruct, in-strökt´ *v* instruir; **–or**, *s* instructor *m.*; maestro *m.*; tutor *m.*; **–ion**, *s* instrucción *f.*

instrument, in´-stru-ment *s* instrumento *m.*

insubordinate, in-sub-or´-di-neit *a* insubodinado

insufferable, in-suf´-fer-a-bl *a* insufrible

insufficient*, in-suf-ish´-ent *a* insuficiente

insulation, in-siu-lei´-shon *s* aislamiento *m.*

insult, in-sölt´ *v* insultar; *s* insulto *m.*

insurance, in-shú r´-ans *s* seguro *m.*

insure, in-shú r´ *v* asegurar

insurrection, in-ser-rek´-shon *s* insurrección *f.*

integrate, in´-ti-greit *v* integrar; completar

intelligence, in-tel´-i-CHens *s* inteligencia *f.*; talento *m.*;

(information) informe *m.*

intact, in´-tAkt *a* íntegro; intacto; ileso; entero

intelligent*, in-tel´-i-CHent *a* inteligente

intemperate, in-tem´-per-et *a* inmoderado

intend, in-tend´ *v* querer; hacer

intense*, in-tens´ *a* intenso; vehemente

intensive care, in-tens-iv kér *s* unidad de vigilancia *f.* pl; intensiva; cuidados *m.* pl; intensivos

intent, in-tent´ *s* designio *m.*; **–ion**, intención *f.*; **–ional***, *a* intencional

inter, in-ter´ *v* enterrar; **–ment**, *s* entierro *m.*

intercept, in-ter-sept´ *v* interceptar

interchange, in´-ter-cheinCH, cambiar; *s* intercambio *m.*

intercourse, in´-ter-kó rs *s* comercio *m.*; relaciones *f.* pl.

interdict, in-ter-dikt´ *v* interdecir; prohibir

interest, in´-ter-rest *v* interesar; *s* interés *m.*; (money) rédito *m.*; **–ing**, *a* interesante

interfere, in-ter-fír′ v
mezclarse; meterse

interference, in-ter-fír′-
ens s intromisión f.;
interferencia f.

interior, in-tii′-ri-or s & a
interior m.

interlace, in-ter-leis′ v
entrelazar

interloper, in′-ter-lou-pa s
intruso m.

interlude, in′-ter-luud s
intermedio m.

intermediate, in-ter-mii′-
di-et a intermedio

intermingle, in-ter-ming′-
gl v mezclarse

intermission, in-ter-
mish′-on s interrupción
f.

intermittent*, in-ter-mit′-
ent a intermitente

intermix, in-ter-miks′ v
entremezclar

intern, in-tern′ v internar

internal*, in-ter′-nl a
interno

international, in-ter-
nAsh-o-nal a
internacional

internet, in-ter-net s
Internet

interpret, in-ter′-pret v
interpretar; –er, s
intérprete m.; traductor
m.

interrogate, in-ter′-o-gueit
v interrogar

interrupt, in-ter-rŏpt v
interrumpir

interval, in-ter-vl s
intervalo m.

intervene, in-ter-viin v
intervenir

intervention, in-ter-ven-
shon s intervención f.

interview, in-ter-viuu s
entrevista f.; v
entrevistarse con

intestate, in-tes′-tet a
intestado

intestine, in-tes′-tin s
intestino m.

intimacy, in′-ti-ma-si s
intimidad f.

intimate in′-ti-meit v
intimar; insinuar

intimate*, in′-ti-met a
íntimo

intimation, in-ti-mei′-
shon s intimación f.

intimidate, in-tim′-i-deit
v intimidar

into, in′-tu prep en;
dentro

intolerable, in-tol′-er-a-bl
a intolerable

intoxicate, in-tok′-si-keit
v embriagar

intrepid*, in-trep′-id a
intrépido

intricate*, in′-tri-ket a

intrincado

intrigue, in-triig′ s intriga
f.; v intrigar

intriguing, in-trii′-guing a
intrigante

intrinsic, in-trin′-sik a
intrínseco

introduce, in-tro-diuus′ v
introducir; presentar

introductory, in-tro-dŏk′-
to-ri a preliminar

intrude, in-truud′ v
ingerir; forzar; –r, s
intruso m.

intuition, in-tiu-ish′-on s
intuición f.

inundation, in-on-dei′-
shon s inundación f.

inure, in-iu r′ v habituar;
acostumbrar

invade, in-veíd′ v invadir;
–r, s invasor m.

invalid, in′-va-liid s
inválido m.

invalid, in-vAl′-id a
inválido; nulo

invaluable, in-vAl′-iu-a-bl
a inapreciable

invariable, in-véi′-ri-a-bl
a invariable

invasion, in-vei′-shon s
invasión f.

invent, in-vent′ v
inventar; –ion, s
invención f.; –or,
inventor m.

inventory, in´-ven-to-ri s inventario m.

inverse, in-věrs´ a inverso

invert, in-vě rt´ v invertir; (capital) invertir

invest, in-vest´ v investir; (capital) invertir

investigate, in-ves´-ti-gueit v investigar

investigation, in-ves-ti-guei-shon s investigación f.

investment, in-vest´-ment s inversión de fondos f.

inveterate*, in-vet´-er-eta a inveterado

invidious*, in-vid´-i-os a envidioso; odioso

invigorate, in-vig´-or-eit v vigorizar

invincible, in-vin´-si-bl a invencible

invisible, in-vis´-i-bl a invisible

invitation, in-vi-tei´-shon s invitación f.

invite, in-vait´ v invitar; convidar

invoice, in´-vois s factura f.

invoke, in-vouk´ v invocar

involuntary, in-vol´-ŏn-ta-ri a involuntario

involve, in-volv´ v implicar; complicar

inward, in´-uerd a

interior; interno; adv hacia dentro

iodine, ai´-o-din s yodo m.

I.O.U., ai ou yuu s vale m.; pagaré m.

ire, air s ira f.

iris, ai´-ris s flor de lis f.; (eye) iris m.

irksome*, ěrk-´-som a molesto; fastidioso

iron, ai´-ern v planchar; s hierro m.; (flat) plancha f.; (steam) plancha de vapor; –ware, ferretería f.

ironical*, ai-ron´-i-kl a irónico

irony, ai´-ron-i s ironía f.

irreconcilable, i-rek´-on-sai´-la-bl a irreconciliable

irregular*, i-re´-guiu-lar a irregular

irrelevant*, i-rel´-i-vant a inaplicable ajeno

irreproachable, i-re-prou´-cha-bl a irreprochable

irresistible, i-re-sis´-ti-bl a irresistible

irrespective (of), i-re-spek´-tiv a sin consideración de; independiente de

irresponsible, i-ri-spon´-si-bl a irresponsable

irretrievable, i-ri-trii´-va-

bl a irrecuperable

irreverent*, i-rev´-er-ent a irreverente

irrigate, i´-ri-gueit v irrigar

irritable, ir´-ri-ta-bl a irritable; irascible

irritate, i´-ri-teit v irritar

island, ai´-land s isla f.; –er, isleño m.

isle, ail s isla f.

islet, ai´-let s islote m.

isolate, ai´-sol-eit v aislar

isolation, ai-so-lei´-shon s aislamiento m.

issue, i´-shiuu s edición f.; progenie f.; (currency) emisión f.; v emitir; producir

isthmus, is´-mos s istmo m.

it, it pron él; ella; ello; lo; la; le

italic, i-tal´-ik s (type) letra cursiva f.

Italian, it-Aliian a italiano/a; s (language) italiano m.

Italy, it-a-li s Italia f.

itch, ich v picar; s comezón f.

item, ai´-tem s item f.; artículo m.; (news) noticia f.

itinerant, i-tin´-er-ant s viandante m.; a ambulante

its, its *pron* su; suyo; sus
itself, it-self´ *pron* el
    mismo; la misma; lo
    mismo; sí mismo
ivory, ai´-ver-i *s* marfil *m*.
ivy, ai´-vi *s* hiedra *f*.

J

jabber, CHAb´-*a v* charlar; *s* jerigonza *f.*

jack, CHAk *s* (mech) gato *m.*

jackal, CHAk´-*oal s* chacal *m.*

jacket, CHAk´-*et s* chaqueta *f.*

jackpot, CHAk-pot *s* bote *m;* premio *m.;* gordo

jade, CHeid *s* (stone) jade *m.;* –**d,** *a* cansado

jag, CHAg *s* mella *f.; v* mellar; dentar

jail, CHeil *s* cárcel *f.;* –**er,** carcelero *m.*

jam, CHAm *s* (conserve) confitura *f.; v* (lock) apretar

jangle, CHAng´-gl *v* rechinar; (quarrel) altercar

January, CHAn´-iu-*a*-ri *s* enero *m.*

jar, CHaar *s* tarro *m.;* –**ring,** *a* chirriante

jaundice, CHo*a*n´-dis *s* ictericia *f.*

jaunt, CHo*a*nt *s* excursión *f.;* –**y,** *a* ligero; alegre

jaw, CHo*a s* mandíbula *f.;* (animal) quijada *f.*

jay, CHei *s* arrendajo *m.*

jazz, CHAss *s* jazz; palabrería *f.;* disparates *m. pl*

jealous, CHel´-*os a* celoso; –**y,** *s* celos *m. pl.*

jeans, CHiins *s pl* (pantalones *m. pl*) vaqueros *m. pl;* tejanos *m. pl*

jeer, CHir *v* mofarse; *s* mofa *f.*

jelly, CHel´-i *s* jalea *f.;* –**fish,** medusa *f.*

jeopardize, CHep-*er*-dais´ *v* arriesgar

jeopardy, CHep´-*er*-di *s* riesgo *m.;* peligro *m.*

jerk, CHĕrk *v* sacudir; *s* sacudida *f.*

jersey, CHĕr´-si *s* jersey *m.*

jest, CHest *s* broma *f.; v* bromear

jester, CHes´-ta *s* bromista *m.;* (court) bufón *m.*

jet, CHet *s* (nozzle) caño de salida *m.;* (liquid) chorro *m.;* (engine) motor de chorro; propulsor de chorro; (plane) avión de retropropulsión a chorro; *v* brotar

jettison, CHet´-ti-son *v* arrojar

jetty, CHet´-i *s* muelle *m.*

Jew, CHiuu *s* judío *m.;* –**ess,** judía *f.*

jewel, CHiuu´-el *s* joya *f.;* –**ry,** joyas *f. pl.*

jeweler, CHiuu´-el-*a s* joyero *m.*

jig, CHig *s* baile alegre *m.*

jigsaw, CHig-sor *s* rompecabezas *m.*; puzle *m.*

jilt, CHilt *v* dar calabazas

jingle, CHing´-gl *v* retiñir; *s* retintín *m.*

job, CHob *s* empleo *m.*; (task) tarea *f.*

jobber, CHob´-ba *s* (stock) corredor de bolsa *m.*

jocular*, CHok´-iu-lar *a* jocoso; alegre

jog, CHog *s* empujoncito *m.*; codazo *m.*; *v* empujar; refrescar (memory); hacer footing

join, CHoin *v* juntar; unirse; (fit) encolar; (a club, etc) asociarse

joiner, CHoin´-a *s* ensamblador *m.*; carpintero *m.*

joint, CHoint *s* juntura *f.*; (anatomy) articulación *f.*; (meat) trozo de carne *m.*; *a* unido; colectivo

jointly, CHoint´-li *adv* conjuntamente; colectivamente

joke, CHouk *s* chiste *m.*; *v* bromear

jolly, CHol´-i *a* alegre; jovial

jolt, CHoult *s* sacudida *f.*; traqueteo *m.*

jostle, CHos-l *v* empujar; dar empellones

journal, CHěr´-nal *s* periódico *m.*; diario *m.*; **–ism,** periodismo *m.*; **–ist,** periodista *m.*

journey, CHěr´-ni *s* viaje *m.*; *v* viajar

jovial*, CHou´-vi-al *a* alegre; jovial

joy, CHoi *s* gozo *m.*; **–ful,** *a* gozoso; **–less,** sin alegría; triste; **–ous,** festivo

jubilant, CHuu´-bi-lant *a* alborozado

jubilee, CHuu´-bi-li *s* jubileo *m.*

judge, CHŏCH *s* juez *m.*; *v* juzgar

judgment, CHŏCH´-ment *s* discernimiento *m.*; sentencia *f.*

judicial*, CHu-dish´-al *a* judicial

judicious*, CHu-dish´-os *a* juicioso

jug, CHŏg *s* jarro *m.*; cántaro *m.*

juggle, CHŏg´-l *v* hacer juegos de mano

juggler, CHŏg´-la *s* prestidigitador *m.*

juice, CHuus *s* jugo *m.*; zumo *m.*

juicy, CHuu´-si *a* jugoso

jukebox, CHuuk-boks *s* tocadiscos *m.*

July, CHu-lai´ *s* julio *m.*

jumble, CHŏm´-bl *s* mezcla *f.*; *v* mezclar

jump, CHŏmp *v* saltar; *s* salto *m.*

jumper, CHŏmp´-a *s* saltador *m.*

junction, CHŏngk´-shon *s* unión *f.*; (rail) empalme *m.*

juncture, CHŏngk´-tiur *s* juntura *f.*; ocasión *f.*

June, CHuun *s* junio *m.*

jungle, CHŏng-gl *s* jungla *f.*; matorral *m.*

junior, CHuu´-ni-or *s* más joven *mf.*; (son) hijo *m.*

juniper, CHuu´-ni-pa *s* junípero *m.*

junk, CHŏngk *s* (cheap goods) baratijas *f. pl*; (rubbish) basura *f.*; (iron) chatarra; (lumber) trastos *m. pl* viejos

jurisdiction, CHú-ris-dik´-shon *s* jurisdicción *f.*

juror, CHú´-ror *s* jurado *m.*

jury, CHú´-ri *s* jurado *m.*

just, CHŏst *adv* justamente; apenas; *a** justo; exacto; **–ice** *s* justicia *f.*; (judge) juez *m.*; **–ification,** justificación *f.*; **–ify,** *v* justificar

jute, CHuut *s* yute *m.*

juvenile, CHuu´-vi-nail *a* juvenil

kale, keil s col rizada f.

kangaroo, kAn-ga-ruu´ s canguro m.

keel, kiil s quilla f.

keen*, kiin, a agudo; afilado; ansioso

keenness, kiin´-nes s agudeza f.; penetración f.

keep, kiip v guardar; tener; mantener; continuar; quedarse con; s mantenimiento m.; **–back,** v retener; **–off,** impedir; tener a distancia; **–to,** adherirse a; **–er,** s guardián m.; **–sake,** recuerdo m.

keg, keg s barrilito m.

kennel, ken´-l s perrera f.

kernel, kĕr´-nl s almendra f.; (pip) pepita f.

kettle, ket´-l s hervidor m.; **–drum,** timbal m.

key, kii s llave f.; (piano) tecla f.; **–board,** teclado m.; **–hole,** ojo de la cerradura m.

kick, kik s patada f.; coz f.; v dar puntapiés; (animal) cocear

kid, kid s cabrito m.; **–gloves,** guantes de cabritilla m. pl.; **–nap,** v secuestrar personas

kidney, kid´-ni s riñón m.

kill, kill v matar

kiln, kiln s horno m.

kilo, kii-lo s kilo m.

kin, kin s parentesco m.; **–sfolk,** parientes m. pl.; **–sman,** pariente m.; **–swoman,** parienta f.

kind, kaind a* bueno; benévolo; s especie f.

kindle, kin´-dl v encender

kindness, kaind´-nes s bondad f.

kindred, kind´-red s parentesco m.; a emparentado

king, king s rey m.; **–dom,** reino m.

kiosk, kii-osk s quiosco m.; **telephone –** cabina f.

kipper, kip´-a s arenque ahumado m.

kiss, kis s beso m.; v besar

kit, kit s equipo m.

kitchen, kit´-shin s cocina f.

kite, kait s cometa f.

kitten, kit´-n s gatito m.; gatita f.

knack, nAk s destreza f.; arte m.; maña f.

knapsack, nAp´-sAk s mochila f.

knave, neiv s bribón m.; (cards) sota f.

knead, niid v amasar

knee, nii s rodilla f.; **–cap,** rótula f.

kneel, niil v arrodillarse

knell, nel s toque de difuntos m.

knife, naif s cuchillo m.; **pocket–,** navaja f.

knight, nait s caballero m.; (chess) caballo m.

knit, nit *v* hacer punto

knitting, nit´-ing *s* trabajo
de punto *m*.

knob, nob *s* pomo *m*.; (of
a stick, etc) puño *m*.

knock, nok *s* golpe *m*.; *v*
(call) llamar; (strike)
golpear; **–against,**
tropezar contra; **–down,**
derribar; **–er,** *s* (door)
aldaba *f*.

knoll, noul *v* doblar las
campanas; *s* montecillo
m.

knot, not *s* nudo *m*.;
(*naut*) milla náutica *f*.; *v*
anudar; **–ty,** *a* nudoso;
(*fig*) intrincado

know, nou *v* conocer;
saber

knowledge, noul´-iCH *s*
conocimiento *m*.; saber
m.

knuckle, nok´-l *s* nudillo
m.

label, lei´-bl s etiqueta f.; rótulo m.; v rotular

labor, lei´-ba v trabajar; s trabajo m.

laboratory, lAb-o´-ra-to-ri s laboratorio m.

laborer, lei´-ba-ra s trabajador m.; obrero m.

laborious*, la-bó-ri-os a laborioso; penoso

laburnum, la-bĕr´-nom s laburno m.

lace, leis s encaje m.; (shoe, etc) cordón m.; v lazar

lacerate, lAs´-er-eit v lacerar

lack, lAk v faltar de; carecer de; s falta f.; carencia f.

lacquer, lAk´-a s laca f.; v laquear

lad, lAd s mozo m.; muchacho m.

ladder, lAd´-a s escalera f.

lading, lei´-ding s carga f.

ladle, leid´-l s cucharón m.; cacillo m.; v servir

lady, lei´-di s señora f.; – **bug**, mariquita f.

lag, lAg v remolonear; **–behind**, rezagarse

lagoon, la-guun´ s laguna f.

lair, lér s guarida f.

lake, leik s lago m.

lamb, lAm s cordero m.

lame, leim a* cojo; v lisiar; **–ness**, s cojera f.

lament, la-ment´ v lamentar; s lamento m.

lamp, lAmp s lámpara f.; (street lamp) farol m.; (electric bulb) bombilla eléctrica f.

lance, laans s lanza f.; v lancear; (surgery) abrir; **–r**, s lancero m.

land, lAnd v desembarcar; s tierra f.; (home) país m.; **–ing**, desembarco m.; (quay) desembarcadero m.; **–lady**, patrona f.; **–lord**, propietario m.; **–mark**, mojón m.; **–scape**, paisaje m.; **–slide**, derrumbamiento m.

lane, lein s (country) callejuela f.

language, lAng´-güiCH s lengua f.; idioma m.; lenguaje m.

languid*, lAng´-güid a lánguido

languish, lAng´-güish v languidecer; decaer

lank, lAngk a flaco; **–y**, alto y delgado

lantern, lAn´-tern s linterna f.

lap, lAp s regazo m.; v lamer

lapel, lA-pel´ s solapa f.

lapse, lAps v pasar; s curso m.; error m.

larceny, laar´-si-ni s hurto m.

lard, laard s manteca de cerdo f.

larder, laar´-da s despensa f.

large*, laarCH a grande; fuerte; considerable

lark, laark s alondra f.

laser, lei-sa s láser m.; **–printer** impresora f.; (por) láser

lash, lAsh s (whip) látigo m.; (stroke) latigazo m.; v (whip) azotar; (bind) amarrar

lass, lAs s mozuela f.; muchacha f.

lassitude, lAs-i-tiuud s cansancio m.

last, laast v durar; s (shoe) horma f.; a* último; **–ing*,** durable; permanente

latch, lAch s picaporte m.; v cerrar

latchkey, lAtch´-kii s llavín m.

late, leit adv tarde; a tardío; reciente; difunto

lately, leit´-li adv recientemente; hace poco

latent, lei´-tent a latente; oculto

lathe, leiD´-a s torno m.

lather, lAD´-a s jabonadura f.; v enjabonar

latitude, lAt´-i-tiuud s latitud f.

latter, lAt´-ta a último; adv recientemente

lattice, lAt´-is s celosía f.

laudable, loa´-da-bl a loable

laugh, laaf v reír; s risa f.; **–able,** a risible; **–ing-stock,** s hazmerreír m.; **–ter,** risa f.; hilaridad f.

launch, loanch s (boat) lancha f.; v botar al agua; (enter upon) lanzar

launderette, loam-dret s lavandería f. (automática)

laundry, loan´-dri s lavandería f.

laurel, loa´-rl s (tree) laurel m.; honor m.

lavatory, lAv´-a-to-ri s lavabo m.; servicios m.; excusado m.

lavender, lAv´-en-da s lavanda f.

lavish, lAv´-ish a* pródigo; v prodigar

law, loa s ley f.; **–ful*,** a legal; legítimo; lícito; **–less*,** a ilegal; **–suit,** a pleito m.; proceso m.; **–yer,** abogado m.; jurista m.

lawn, loan s césped m.

lax*, lAks a laxo; flojo

laxative, lAk´-sa-tiv s & a laxante m.; purgante m.

lay, lei v poner; (place) colocar; a lego; **–man,** s lego m.

layer, lei´-a s (strata) capa f.; estrato m.

layout, lei´-ant s trazado m.; disposición f.

laziness, lei´-si-nes s pereza f.

lazy, lei´-si a perezoso; holgazán

lead, led s plomo m.; (sounding) sondalesa f.; v emplomar

lead, liid v conducir; guiar; s (cards) salida f.; **–er,** conductor m.; jefe m.; **–ership,** dirección f.; **–ing,** a principal; primero; **–ing article,** s artículo de fondo m.

lead singer, liid sing-a s cantante mf.

leaf, liif s hoja f.; **–y,** a frondoso

leaflet, liif´-let s folleto m.

league, liig s liga f.; (measure) legua f.

leak, liik v gotear; hacer agua; s gotera f.

lean, liin a delgado; s (meat) magro m.; **–against,** v apoyarse

leap, liip v saltar; s salto

m.

leap year, liip´-yir *s* año bisiesto *m.*

learn, lĕrn *v* aprender; (news) saber

learned, lĕrn´-id *a* docto; erudito

learner, lĕrn´-a *s* estudiante *m.*; aprendiz *m.*

learning, lĕrn´-ing *s* estudio *m.*; (knowledge) saber *m.*

lease, liis *v* arrendar; *s* arriendo *m.*

leasehold, liis´-jould *s* arriendo *m.*

leash, liish *s* traílla *f.*; *v* atraillar

least, liist *adv* menos; *a* mínimo; **at–,** al menos

leather, leD´-a *s* cuero *m.*; **patent –,** charol *m.*

leave, liiv *s* permiso *m.*; (farewell) despedida *f.*; *v* partir marchar; dejar, abandonar; **–behind,** dejar atrás; **–off,** cesar; **–out,** omitir; **–to,** dejar a

lecture, lek´-tiur *v* dar una conferencia; sermonear; *s* conferencia *f.*; admonición *f.*

lecturer, lek´-tiur-a *s* conferenciante *m.*; profesor *m.*

ledge, leCH *s* (shelf) repisa *f.*; (mountain) borde *m.*

ledger, leCH´-a *s* libro mayor *m.*

leech, liich *s* sanguijuela *f.*

leek, liik *s* puerro *m.*

leer, lir *v* mirar de soslayo

left, left *a* izquierdo; **– handed,** zurdo

leg, leg *s* pierna *f.*; (furniture) pie *m.*; (animal) pata *f.*; **–ging,** polaina *f.*

legacy, leg´-a-si *s* legado *m.*; herencia *f.*

legal*, lii´-gal *a* legal; **–ize,** *v* legalizar

legation, li-gei´-shon *s* legación *f.*

legend, leCH´- end *s* leyenda *f.*

legible, leCH´-i-bl *a* legible

legion, lii´-CHon *s* legión *f.*

legislate, leCH´-is-leit *v* legislar

legislation, leCH-is-lei´- shon *s* legislación *f.*

legitimacy, leCH-it´-i-ma- si *s* legitimidad *f.*

legitimate*, leCH-it´-i-met *a* legítimo

leisure, lesh´-er *s* ocio *m.*; comodidad *f.*

leisurely, lesh´-er-li *adv* despacio

lemon, lem´-on *s* limón *m.*; **–ade,** limonada *f.*

lend, lend *v* prestar

length, leng´-gz *s* longitud *f.*; (time) duración *f.*

lengthen, leng-gzn *v* alargar; prolongar

lengthwise, leng´-uais *adv* a lo largo

lengthy, leng´-gzi *a* largo; difuso

leniency, lii´-ni-ens-i *s* indulgencia *f.*

lenient*, lii´-ni-ent *a* indulgente

lens, lens *s* lente *f.*

Lent, lent *s* cuaresma *f.*

lentil, len´-til *s* lenteja *f.*

leopard, lep´-ard *s* leopardo *m.*

leper, lep´-a *s* leproso *m.*

leprosy, lep´-ro-si *s* lepra *f.*

lesbian, les-bii-an *s* lesbiana *f.*; *a* lesbio

less, les *adv* menos; *a* menor

lessee, les´-ii *s* arrendatario *m.*

lessen, les´-n *v* disminuir; (pain) aliviar

lesson, les´-n *s* lección *f.*

let, let *v* dejar; permitir; (lease) arrendar

lethal, lii-zal *a* mortífero; (dose) mortal; fatal; atroz

letter, let´-a s carta f.; (alphabet) letra f.; **-of credit,** carta de crédito f.

lettuce, let´-is s lechuga f.

level, lev´-l s nivel m.; v nivelar; a llano; igual

lever, lii´-va s palanca f.; (watch) escape m.

levity, lev´-i-ti s levedad f.; ligereza f.

levy, lev´-i v (taxes) recaudar; s impuesto m.

lewd*, liuud a lascivo; **-ness,** s lascivia f.

liabilities, lai-a-bil´-i-tes s pl el pasivo m.; responsabilidades

liability, lai-a-bil´-i-ti s obligación f.; responsabilidad f.

liable, lai´-a-bl a expuesto; responsable

liaison, lii-eis-on s enlace m.; conexión f.; (affair) lío m; relaciones amorosas f. pl

liar, lai´-a s mentiroso m.; embustero m.

libel, lai´-bl s libelo m.; v difamar

libelous, lai´-bel-os a difamatorio

liberal, lib´-er-al s & a* liberal m.

liberate, lib´-er-eit v libertar

liberty, lib´-er-ti s libertad f.

librarian, lai-bré-ri-an s bibliotecario m.

library, lai´-bre-ri s biblioteca f.; librería f.

license, lai´-sens s licencia f.; v licenciar

licentious*, lai-sen´-shos a licencioso; libertino

lichen, lai´-ken s liquen m.

lick, lik v lamer

lid, lid s tapa f.; (eye) párpado m.

lie, lai s (untruth) mentira f.; v mentir; (in a place) estar; (situate) estar situado; **-about,** (disorder) estar esparcido; **-down,** (repose) acostarse

lieutenant, lef-ten´-ant s teniente m.

life, laif s vida f.; (vivacity) viveza f.; **-preserver,** salvavidas m.; **-boat,** lancha salvavidas f.; **-guard,** (mil) guardia de corps m.; vigilante m.; **-insurance,** seguro de vida m.; **-less,** a inanimado; muerto; **-like,** natural; **-long,** de toda la vida; **-size,** de tamaño natural; **-time,** s curso de la vida m.

lift, lift s ascensor m.; v levantar

light, lait s luz f.; claridad f.; a* ligero; claro; v encender; (illuminate) alumbrar; **-en,** aligerar; **-er,** s encendedor m.; (boat) gabarra f.; **-house,** faro m.; **-ing,** alumbrado m.; **-ness,** ligereza f.

lightbulb, lait-bölb s bombilla f.; foco m.

lightning, lait´-ning s relámpago m.; **-conductor,** pararrayos m.

like, laik v gustar; a (similar) semejante; parecido; (equal) igual

likelihood, laik´-li-jud s probabilidad f.

likely, laik´-li adv probablemente; a probable

likeness, laik´-nes s semejanza f.; parecido m.

likewise, laik´-uais adv también; asimismo

liking, lai´-king s gusto m.; inclinación f.

lilac, lai´-lak s lila f.

lily, lil'-i s lirio m.; –of
the valley, lirio de los
valles

limb, lim s (body)
miembro m. campo m.

lime, laim s cal f.;
(birdlime) liga f.; (fruit)
lima f.; (tree) tilo m.

lime juice, laim'-CHuus s
zumo de lima m.

limekiln, laim'-kiln s
calera f.

limelight, laim'-lait s luz
de calcio f.

limit, lim'-it s límite m.;
término m.; v limitar;
determinar

limp, limp v cojear; a flojo

limpet, lim'-pet s lapa f.

line, lain s línea f.;
(business) ramo m.;
(goods) renglón m m.;
(rope) cuerda f.;
(fishing) sedal m.;
cuerda f.; (railroad) riel
m.; v (garment) forrar

lineage, lin'-i-eCH s linaje
m.; genealogía f.

linen, lin'-en s hilo m.;
(laundry) ropa blanca f.

liner, lain'-a s
transatlántico m.; vapor
de línea m.

linger, ling'-guer v tardar;
languidecer

lingerie, langsh-ĕr-ei s

ropa f.; interior (de
mujer)

linguist, ling'-uist s
lingüista mf.

lining, lain'-ing s (of
clothes) forro m.

link, lingk v eslabonar;
unir; s eslabón m.; (cuff
links) gemelos m. pl.

linnet, lin'-net s pardillo
m.

linseed, lin'-siid s linaza f.

lint, lint s hilaza f.; hilas f.
pl.

lion, lai'-on s león m.;
–ess, leona f.

lip, lip s labio m.; –stick,
barra de labios f.

liquefy, lik'-ui-fai v
derretir; liquidar

liqueur, li-ker' s licor m.

liquid, lik'-uid s líquido
m.; a líquido

liquidate, lik'-ui-deit v
liquidar; (debts) saldar

liquidation, lik'-ui-dei'-
shon s liquidación f.

liquor, lik'-er s (alcoholic)
licor m.; (cooking) jugo
m

lisp, lisp v cecear; s ceceo
m.

list, list s lista f.; (naut)
bandeo m.; v catalogar;
alistar; registrar; (naut)
escorar

listen, lis'-n v escuchar;
–er, s oyente m.

liter, liit-a s litro m.

literal*, lit'-er-al a literal

literary, lit'-er-a-ri a
literario

literature, lit'-er-a-tiur s
literatura f.

lithograph, liz'-o-graf s
litografía f.; v litografiar

litigate, lit'-i-gueit v
litigar

litter, lit'-a s (stretcher)
camilla f.; (untidiness)
desorden m.; (bedding)
cama de paja f.; (young)
lechigada f.; v esparcir

little, lit'-l a (quantity,
time) poco; (size)
pequeño; adv poco

live, liv v vivir; habitar

live*, laiv a vivo; –ly,
animado

liver, liv'-a s hígado m.

livery, liv'-er-i s librea f.

livid, liv'-id a lívido

living, liv'-ing s vida f.;
(eccl) beneficio m.; a
vivo

lizard, lis '-erd s lagarto
m.

load, loud v cargar; s carga
f.

loaf, louf s (bread) pan m.;
vago m.

loafer, lou'-fa s (idler)

haragán m.

loam, loum s marga f.; **–y,** a margoso

loan, loun s (personal) préstamo m.; (public) empréstito m.; v prestar

loathe, louD v aborrecer; detestar

loathing, louD´-ing s repugnancia f.

loathsome, louD´-som a odioso; repugnante

lobby, lob´-i s vestíbulo m.

lobe, loub s lóbulo m.

lobster, lob´-sta s langosta f.

local*, lou´-kl a local; **–ity,** s localidad f.

locate, lou´-keit v situar; (find) encontrar

location, lou-kei-shon s (place) situación f.; posición f.; localización; (cinema) exteriores; rodaje fuera de estudio

lock, lok s cerradura f.; (hair) rizo m.; (canal) esclusa f.; v cerrar; **–et,** s medallón m.; **–in** (or up), v encerrar; **–jaw,** s tetano m.; **–out,** v dejar fuera; **–smith,** s cerrajero m.

locomotive, lou´-ko-mou-tiv s locomotora f.

locust, lou´-kust s

langosta f.

lodge, loCH s (inn) posada f.; (masonic) logia f.; v hospedarse

lodger, loCH´- a s huésped m.

lodging, loCH´-ing s alojamiento m.

loft, loft s desván m.; **–y,** a elevado; sublime

log, log s tronco m.; **– book,** diario de navegación m.

logic, loCH´-ik s lógica f.; **–al*,** a lógico

loin, loin s lomo m.

loiter, loi´-ta v holgazanear; **–er,** s holgazán m.

loll, lol v recostarse; (tongue) sacar la lengua

London, lŏn-dŏn s Londres m.

lone(ly), loun(ly) a & adv solo; solitario

loneliness, loun´-li-ness s soledad f.

long, long a largo; (time) mucho; **–for,** v suspirar por; **–ing,** s ansia f.; anhelo m.; **–to,** v ansiar

longitude, lon´-CHi-tiuud s longitud f.

long-term, long tĕrm a a largo plazo

look, luk s mirada f.; v

mirar; (seem) aparecer; **–after,** (take care of) cuidar de; **–at,** mirar; **–for,** buscar; **–out,** vigía f.; v asomarse; interj ¡cuidado! good **–ing,** a bien parecido

loom, lum s telar m.; v aparecer a lo lejos

loop, luup s lazo m.; **–hole,** tronera f.; **–the loop,** v describir círculos

loose*, luus a flojo; (morals) disoluto; **–n,** v aflojar; (to free) soltar; **–ning,** s aflojamiento m.

loot, luut s pillaje m.; v saquear

lop, lop v (prune) podar; **–off,** tajar; **–sided*,** a asimétrico; desequilibrado

loquacious*, lo-kuei´-shos a locuaz; hablador

Lord, loard s (Deity) el Señor m.; Dios m.

lose, luus v perder; (clock) atrasar

loser, luu´-sa s perdedor m.

loss, los s pérdida f.; (damage) daño m.

lot, lot s (auction) lote m.; (fate) suerte f.; (many) cantidad f.

lotion, lou´-shon s loción

f.

lottery, lot´-er-i *s* lotería *f.*

loud*, laud *a* alto; **—speaker,** *s* (radio) altavoz *m.*

lounge, launCH *v* holgazanear; *s* (room) salón *m.*

louse, laus *s* piojo *m.*

lout, laut *s* patán *m.*; rústico *m.*

love, lŏv *v* amar; querer; (like) gustar; *s* amor *m.*; **–liness,** hermosura *f.*; **–ly,** *a* hermoso; (charming) encantador; **–r,** *s* (illicit) amante *m.*

low, lou *v* mugir; *a** bajo; vil; **–er,** *v* bajar; humillar; (flag) arriar; (price) rebajar; **–land,** *s* tierra baja *f.*

loyal*, loi´-al *a* leal; fiel; **–ty,** *s* lealtad *f.*

lozenge, los´-enCH *s* pastilla *f.*; (geometry) rombo

lubricate, liuu´-bri-keit *v* lubricar

lubrication, liuu-bri-kei´-shon *s* lubricación *mf.*

lucid*, liuu´-sid *a* lúcido; claro

luck, lŏk *s* suerte *f.*; fortuna *f.*

lucky, lŏk´-i *a* afortunado;

dichoso; venturoso; (charm) para buena suerte

lucrative*, liuu-kra-tiv *a* lucrativo; provechoso

ludicrous, liuu´-di-kros *a* risible; ridículo

luggage, lŏg´-eCH *s* equipaje *m.*; **–rack,** *s* portaequipajes *m.*

lukewarm, liuuk´-uoarm *a* tibio

lull, lŏl *v* adormecer; (baby) arrullar; *s* calma *f.*

lullaby, lŏl´-a-bai *s* canción de cuna *f.*

lumbago, lom-bei´-gou *s* lumbago *m.*

lumber, lŏm´-ba *s* trastos *m.*; *pl* (timber) madera de construcción *f.*

luminous*, liuu´-mi-nos *a* luminoso

lump, lŏmp *s* pedazo *m.*; **–y,** *a* aterronado; grumoso

lunacy, luu´-na-si *s* locura *f.*

lunar, luu´-nar *a* lunar

lunatic, luu´-na-tik *s* lunático *m.*; loco *m.*

lunch(eon), lŏnch´(-n) *s* almuerzo *m.*; *v* almorzar

lung, lŏng-g *s* pulmón *m.*

lurch, lĕrCH *s* sacudida *f.*;

(ship) bandazo *m.*; **to leave in the –,** *v* dejar en la estancada

lure, liur *v* atraer; inducir; *s* señuelo *m.*

lurid, liu´-rid *a* (color) cárdeno

lurk, lĕrk *v* espiar; acechar; (hide) esconderse

luscious, lŏ´-shos *a* suculento

lust, lŏst *s* lujuria *f.*; (greed) codicia *f.*; *v* codiciar **–ful,** *a* lujurioso; sensual

luster, lŏs´-tr *s* brillo *m.*; (pendant) lustro *m.*

lute, liuut *s* laúd *m.*

luxurious*, lŏk-siu´-ri-os *a* lujoso; exuberante

luxury, lŏk´-sher-i *s* lujo *m.*; suntuosidad *f.*

lymph, limf *s* linfa *f.*

lynch, linch *v* linchar

lyrics, li-riks *s* *pl* (of songs) letra *f.*

macaroni, mAk-*a*-rou´-ni s macarrones m pl.

macaroon, mAk-*a*-ruun´ s almendrado m

mace, meis s maza f.

machine, m*a*-shiin´ s máquina f.

machine gun, m*a*-shiin´-gŏn s ametralladora f.

machinery, m*a*-shiin´-*er*-i s maquinaria f.

machinist, m*a*-shiin´-ist s maquinista m

mackerel, mAk´-*er*-el s escombro m.; caballa f.

mad, mAd *a* loco; (dogs) rabioso; **–man,** s loco m.; **–ness,** locura f.

madam, mAd´-m s señora f.; (unmarried) señorita f.

magazine, mA-g*a*-siin´ s (periodical) revista f.; (powder) polvorín m.; (gun) cámara f.

maggot, mAg´-ot s gusano m.; cresa f.

magic, mACH´-ik s magia f.; *a* mágico

magistrate, mACH´-is-treit s magistrado m.

magnanimity, mAg-nAn-im´-i-ti s magnanimidad f.

magnanimous*, mAg-nAn´-i-mos *a* magnánimo

magnesia, mAg-nii´-sh*a* s magnesia f.

magnesium, mAg-nii´-shi-om s magnesio m.

magnet, mAg´-net s imán m.; **–ic,** *a* magnético; **–ism,** s magnetismo m.;

–ize, *v* magnetizar

magneto, mAg-ni´-tou s magneto m.

magnificent*, mAg-nif´-i-sent *a* magnifico

magnify, mAg´-ni-fai *v* aumentar; ampliar

magnitude, mAg´-ni-tiuud s magnitud f.

magpie, mAg´-pai s urraca f.

mahogany, m*a*-jog´-A-ni s caoba f.

maid, meid s (young girl) doncella f.; (servant) sirvienta f.; **–en,** doncella f.; vírgen f.; **old –,** solterona f.

mail, meil s (post) correo m.; (armor) cota de malla f.; (mailbag) valija f.

maim, meim *v* mutilar

main, mein *a* principal; mayor; s (pipe) cañería maestra f.; **–land,** continente m.

maintain, mein-tein´ *v* mantener; er; sostener

maintenance, mein´-te-nans s mantenimiento m.

maize, meis s maíz m.

majestic, m*a*-CHes´-tik *a* majestuoso

majesty, mACH´-es-ti s

(His or Her) Su
Majestad *f.*

major, meiCH´-*or* s mayor
m.; (mil.) comandante
m.; *a* mayor

majority, mACH-o´-ri-ti s
mayoría *f.*

make, meik *v* hacer;
causar; (manufacture)
fabricar; s hechura *f.*;
(commercial) marca *f.*;
--**believe,** invención *f.*;
v fingir; **-r,** s fabricante
m.; constructor *m.*;
-shift, expediente *m.*;
-up, (face) maquillaje
m.; *v* maquillarse

malady, mAl´-*a*-di s
enfermedad *f.*

malaria, mAl-ei´-ri-*a* s
malaria *f.*

male, meil s varón *m.*;
(animal) macho *m.*

malevolent*, m*a*l-ev´-*o*-
lent *a* malévolo

malice, mAl´-is s malicia *f.*

malicious*, m*a*-lish´-*o*s *a*
malicioso

malign, m*a*-lain´ *v*
difamar; *a** maligno

malignant*, m*a*-lig´-n*a*nt
a maligno; nocivo

malinger, m*a*-ling´-*a* *v*
fingirse enfermo

mallet, mAl´et s mazo *m.*;
mallo *m.*

mallow, mAl´-ou s malva
f.

malnutrition, mAl´-niuu-
trish-*a*n s desnutrición

malt, moalt s malta *f.*

maltreat, mAl-triit´ *v*
maltratar

mammal, mAm´-*m*al s
mamífero *m.*

man, mAn *v* (a ship)
tripular; s hombre *m.*;
-hood, virilidad *f.*;
-kind, género humano
m.; **-ly,** *a* viril; **--**
servant, s criado *m.*

manacle, mAn´-*a*-kl s
manilla *f.*; *v* maniatar

manage, mAn´-iCH *v*
(business) administrar;
dirigir; (accomplish)
lograr; suceder;
(control) manejar;
gobernar; **-ment,** s
administración *f.*;
dirección *f.*

manager, mAn´-iCH-*a* s
gerente *m.*; director *m.*

mandate, mAn´-deit s
mandato *m.*; orden *f.*

mandolin, mAn´-dou-lin s
mandolina *f.*

mane, mEin s (of a horse,
lion) crin *m.*

maneuver, mA-nuu´-*ve*r s
maniobra *f.*; *v*
maniobrar

manger, mein´-CH*a* s
pesebre *m.*

mangle, mAng´-gl s
escurridor *m.*; *v*
clesrozar; mutilar

mania, mei´-ni-*a* s manía
f.

maniac, mei´-ni-Ak s
maniático *m.*

manicure, mAn´-i-kiur s
manicura *f.*; *v* hacer la
manicura

manifest, mAn´-i-fest s &
*a** manifesto *m.*; *v*
manifestar

manifesto, mAn-i-fest-o s
proclama *f.*; manifiesto
m.

manifold, mAn´-i-fould *a*
múltiple; diverso

manipulate, mAn-ip´-iuu-
leit *v* manipular

mankind, mAn-kaind s
humanidad; género *m.*;
humano

manner, mAn´-*a* s manera
f.; forma *f.*; modo *m.*;
costumbre *f.*; género *m.*;
-s, s *pl* modales *m. pl.*

manor, mAn´-*o*r s casa
solariega *f.* & *m.*

mansion, mAn´-shon s
mansión *f.*

manslaughter, mAn´-sloa-
t*a* s homicidio *m.*; sin
premeditación

mantle, mAn´-tl s manto m.; (gas) manguito incandescente m.

manual, mAn´-iu-al s manual m.; a* manual

manufacture, mAn-iu-fAk´-tiur s manufactura f.; fabricación f.; fabricar; –r, s fabricante m.

manure, ma-niú r s abono m.; estiércol m.; v abonar; engrasar

manuscript, mAn´-iu-skript s manuscrito m.

many, men´-i a muchos

map, mAp s mapa m.; (town) plan m.

maple, mei´-pl s arce m.

mar, maar v estropear; dañar; desfigurar

marathon, mA-r-a-zon s maratón m.

marble, maar´-bl s mármol m.; –s, (game) canicas f. pl.

march, maarch v marchar; s marcha f.

March, maarch s marzo m.

mare, meir s yegua f.

margarine, maar´-ga-rin s margarina f.

margin, maar´-CHin s margen mf. v marginar; –al note, s nota marginal f.

marigold, mAr´-i-gould s maravilla f.

marine, ma-riin´ s soldado de marina m.; a marino

mariner, maar´-in-a s marino m.; marinero m.

maritime, ma´-ri-tim a marítimo

mark, maark v marcar; s marca f.; **book--,** señal f.; **trade--,** marca de fábrica f.

market, maar´-ket s mercado m.

marmalade, maar´-ma-leid s mermelada de naranjas f.

marmot, maar´-mot s marmota f.

maroon, ma-ruun´ a marrón m.; v abandonar; aislar

marquee, maar-kii´ s marquesina f.

marriage, mAr´-iCH s matrimonio m.; boda f.

married, mAr´-id a (life) conyugal; –couple, s matrimonio m.

marrow, mAr´-ou s médula f.; tuétano m.; (vegetable) calabaza f.

marry, mAr´-i v casarse; (ceremony) casar

marsh, maarsh s pantano m.

marshal, maar´-shal s mariscal m.

mart, maart s mercado m.

marten, maar´-ten s marta f.

martial*, maar´-shal a marcial; militar; **court--,** s consejo de guerra m.; –law, ley marcial f.

martyr, maar´-ta v martirizar; s mártir mf.; –dom, martirio m.

marvel, maar´-vl s maravilla f.; v maravillarse; –lous, a maravilloso

marzipan, maars-i-pAn s mazapán m.

masculine, mAs´-kiu-lin a masculino

mash, mAsh v machacar; s (vegetable) masa f.

mask, mAsk s máscara f.; v enmascarar

mason, mei´-s´n s albañil f.; (stone worker) cantero m.; (Freemason) francmasón m.

Masonic, mei-son´-ik a masónico

masonry, mei´-son-ri s albañilería f.

masquerade, mAs-ker-eid´ v disfrazarse

mass, mAs s masa f.; (eccl) misa f.; v amontonar

massacre, mAs´-a-ker s matanza f.; carnicería f.

massage, ma-saaCH´ s masaje m.; v dar masaje

massive*, mas´-iv a macizo; impresionante

mast, maast s mástil m.; palo m.

master, maas´-ta v domar; vencer; s amo m.; (teacher) maestro m.; profesor m.; (teacher) maestro m.; profesor m.; **–ful**, a dominante; **–ly**, magistral; adv magistralmente; **––piece**, s obra maestra f.

masticate, mAs´-ti-keit v masticar

mastiff, mAs´-tif s mastín m.

mat, mAt s estera f.; esterilla f.

match, mAch s (safety) fósforo m.; (wax) cerilla f; (game) partido m.; (boxing) lucha f.; v igualar

matchless, mAch´-les a incomparable

mate, meit v aparear; s compañero m.

material, ma-tii´-ri-al s material m.; (cloth) paño m.; tela f.; **–ist**, s materialista

materialize, ma-tii´-ri-a-

lais v materializar

maternal*, ma-těr´-nl a materno

mathematics, mAz-i-mAt´-iks s matemáticas f. pl.

maths, mAzs s = **mathematics** mates; matemáticas f. pl

matrimony, mAt´-ri-mo-ni s matrimonio m.

matrix, mei´-trix s matriz f.; (mould) molde m.

matron, mei´-tron s matrona f.

matter, mAt´-a s materia f.; substancia f.; (pus) pus m.; (affair) asunto m.; (business) negocio m.; v importar

matting, mAt´-ing s estera f.

mattress, mAt´-res s colchón m.

mature, ma-tiúr´ v madurar; (bill) vencer; a maduro

maturity, ma-tiúr´-i-ti s madurez f.; vencimiento m.

maul, moal v aporrear; (claw) magullar

mauve, mouv s color de malva m.

maxim, mAk´-sim s máxima f.

maximum, mAk´-si-mom s

máximo m.

may, mei v poder; **–be**, adv acaso; quizás

May, mei s mayo m.; **––flower**, maya f.

maybe, mei-bi adv quizá(s); tal vez

mayor, mei´-or s alcalde m.; **–ess**, alcaldesa f.

mayonnaise, mei-on-eis s mayonesa f.

maze, meis s laberinto m.; confusión f.

me, mii pron me; mí; (to me) a mí

meadow, med´-ou s prado m.; pradera f.

meager, mii´-ga a magro; (scanty) insuficiente

meal, miil s harina f.; (repast) comida f.

mean, miin a* avaro; (action) bajo; v querer decir; **–ing**, s significado m.; (sense) sentido m.; **–ingless**, a sin sentido m.

means, miins s pl medios m. pl.; recursos m. pl.

meanwhile, miin´-uail adv entretanto; mientras tanto

measles, mii´-sls s pl sarampión m.

measure, mesh´-a s medida f.; (tape) metro

m.; v medir; **–d,** *a*
medido; **–ment,** *s*
medida *f.*

meat, miit *s* carne *f.*

mechanic, mi-kAn´-ik *s*
mecánico *m.;* **–al,** *a*
mecánico; **–s,** *s pl*
mecánica *f.*

mechanism, mek´an-is m
s mecanismo *m.*

mechanization, mek-*an*-
ais -ei´-shon *s*
mecanización *f.*

medal, med´-l *s* medalla *f.*

meddle, med´-l *v* meterse;
entremeterse

meddlesome, med´-l-som
a entrometido; intruso

media, mii´-dii-*a* spl
medios *mpl* de
comunicación; medios
de difusión

mediate, mii´-di-eit *v*
mediar; intervenir

medical, med´-i-kl *a*
médico

medication, med´-i-kei-
shon *s* medicación *f.*

medicine, med´-sin *s*
medicina *f.*

medieval, med-i-i´-vl *a*
medioeval

mediocre, mii´-di-ou´-kr *a*
mediocre; vulgar

meditate, med´-i-teit *v*
meditar; reflexionar

Mediterranean, med´-i-
tĕr-ein-ian *a*
mediterráneo; **– Sea**
Mar *m.;* Mediterráneo; *s*
Mediterráneo *m.*

medium, mii´-di-om *s*
medio *m.;* vía *f.; a*
mediano

meek*, miik *a* manso;
humilde

meet, miit *v* encontrar;
(obligations) honrar;
–ing, *s* encuentro *m.;*
reunión *f.;* (board) junta
f.

melancholy, mel´-an-kol-i
s melancolía *f.*

mellow, mel´-ou *a*
maduro; (tone) meloso

melodious*, mi-lou´-di-os
a melodioso

melody, mel´-o-di *s*
melodía *f.*

melon, mel´on *s* melón *m.*

melt, melt *v* derretir;
fundir; **–ing,** *s* fusión *f.*

member, mem´-ba *s*
miembro *m.;* (club)
socio *m.;* **–ship,** calidad
de socio *f.*

membrane, mem´-brein *s*
membrana *f.*

memento, mi-men´-tou *s*
recuerdo *m.;* memento
m.

memo, me-mou *s abbr* of

memorandum
memorandum *m.;* memo
m.

memoir, mem´-uaar *s*
memoria *f.*

memorandum, mem-or-
an´-dom *s* memorándum
m.

memorial, mi-mou´-ri-al *s*
monumento
conmemorativo *m.*

memory, mem´-o-ri *s*
memoria *f.*

menace, men´-as *v*
amenazar; *s* amenaza *f.*

menagerie, mi-nACH´-er-i
s colección de fieras *f.*

mend, mend *v* reparar;
corregirse

mendacious*, men-dei´-
shos *a* mendaz;
mentiroso

menial, mii´-ni-al *s* criado
m.; a servil

menstruation, men-struu-
ei-shon *s* menstruación
f.

mental*, men´-tl *a* mental

mention, men´-shon *v*
mencionar; *s* mención *f.*

menu, men´-iuu *s* menú
m.; lista de platos *f.*

mercantile, mĕr´-kan-tail
a mercantil; comercial

merchandise, mĕr´-chan-
dais *s* mercancía *f.*

merchant, měr´-chant s
comerciante m.;
mercader m.; a
comercial; (fleet)
mercante

merciful*, měr´-si-ful a
misericordioso;
clemente

mercury, měr´-kiu-ri s
mercurio m.

mercy, měr´-si s
misericordia f.; gracia f.

mere, mir a puro; mero; s
lago m.

merge, merCH v fundir;
absorber; **–er,** s unión f.;
consolidación f.

meridian, mi-ri´-di-an s
meridiano m.; a de
mediodía

merit, měr´-it s mérito m.;
v merecer

meritorious*, mer-i-tó´-ri-
os a meritorio

mermaid, měr´-meid s
sirena f.

merriment, mer´-i-ment s
alegría f.; júbilo m.

merry*, mer´-i a alegre; **–
go-round,** s caballitos
m. pl.; tiovivo m.

mesh, mesh s malla f.

mesmerize, mes´-mer-ais v
hipnotizar

mess, mes s (mil) rancho
de los oficiales m.; (dirt)

porquería f.; ló m.; v
manchar

message, mes´-iCH s
mensaje m.; recado m.

messenger, mes´-en-CH a s
mensajero m.

messy, me-si a (dirty)
sucio; (untidy)
desaliñado; desaseado;
(room) en desorden;
confuso

metal, met´-l s metal m.;
–lic, a metálico

meteor, mii´-ti-or s
meteoro m.

meter, mii´-ta s (gas, etc)
contador m.; (measure,
rhythm) metro m.

method, mez´-od s método
m.

metric, met-rik a métrico;
– system sistema m
métrico

metropolis, mi-trop´-o-lis
s metrópoli f.

mica, mai´-ka s mica f.

microphone, mai´-kro-
foun s micrófono m.

microscope, mai´-kros-
koup s microscopio m.

microwave, mai-kro-ueiv
s microonda f.; **– oven**
horno m. microondas

middle, mid´-l s medio m.;
centro m.; **–age,** edad
media f.; **–class,**

(people) clase media f.;
–man, intermediario m.

middling, mid´-ling a
mediano

midge, miCH s mosquito
m.

midget, miCH´-et s enano
m.

midnight, mid´-nait s
media noche f.

midshipman, mid´-ship-
man s guardia marina m.

midst, midst prep entre; en
medio de

midwife, mid´-uaif s
partera f.; comadrona f.

mien, miin s semblante
m.; facha f.

might, mait s fuerza f.;
poder m.

mighty, mait´-i a
poderoso; fuerte

mignonette, min-yon-et´ s
reseda f.

migraine, mii´-grein s
jaqueca f.

migrate, mai-greit´ v
emigrar

mild*, maild a suave;
benigno; templado

mildew, mil´-diuu s moho
m.; (plants) tizón m.

mile, mail s milla f.;
–stone, piedra miliaria f.

militant, mil´-i-tant a
militante; belicoso;

agresivo; s militante mf; activista mf

military, mil´-i-ta-ri a militar

milk, milk s leche f.; v ordeñar; **-y,** a lácteo

Milky Way, mil´-ki-uei s vía láctea f.

mill, mil v moler; s molino m.; **-er,** molinero m.

millinery, mil´-i-ner-i s modas f. pl.

million, mil´-yon s millón m.; **-aire,** millonario m.

mime, maim s pantomima; mímica; (actor) mimo m.; v representar con gestos; actuar de mimo

mimic, mim´-ik v remedar; s mimo m.; a mímico

mince, mins v (meat, etc) picar; (words) medir

mind, maind s mente f.; opinión f.; intención f.; v atender a; (nurse) cuidar; **-ful,** a atento

mine, main poss pron mío; mía; míos; mías

mine, main s mina f.; v minar; **-r,** s minero m.

mineral, min´-er-al s & a mineral m.

mineral water, min´-er-al uoa´-tr s agua f.; mineral

mingle, ming´-gl v mezclar; **-with,** mezclarse con

minimize, min´-i-mais v reducir; disminuir

minimum, min´-i-mŏm a mínimo

minister, min´-is-ta s clérigo m.; proveer

ministry, min´-is-tri s ministerio m.; gabinete m.

mink, mink s visón m.

minor, mai´-na s menor de edad m.; a menor

minority, mi-nor´-i-ti s minoría f.

minstrel, min´-strel s trovador m.

mint, mint s casa de la moneda f.; (plant) menta f.; v acuñar

minuet, min-iu-et´ s minueto m.; minué m.

minus, mai´-nos a & adv menos; prep sin

minute, min´-it s minuto m.; (records) minuta f.

minute*, mai-niuut´ a menudo; minucioso

miracle, mi´-ra-kl s milagro m.

miraculous*, mi-rAk´-iu-los a milagroso

mirage, mi-raash´ s espejismo m.

mire, mair s fango m.; lodo m.; cieno m.

mirror, mir´-or, s espejo m.; v reflejar

mirth, mĕrz s alegría f.; regocijo m.

mis, mis, **-adventure,** s desventura f.; **-apprehension,** equivocación f.; error m.; **-appropriate,** v malversar; **-behave,** portarse mal; **-believer,** s incrédulo m.; **-carriage,** aborto m.; **-carry,** v abortar; **-conduct,** s mala conducta f.; **-construction,** mala interpretación f.; error m.; **-count,** v contar mal; **-deed,** s fechoría f.; (law) delito m.; **-demeanor,** mala conducta f.; (law) delito m.; **-direct,** v dirigir erradamente; **-fit,** s lo que no ajusta bien; **-fortune,** desdicha f.; calamidad f.; **-giving,** recelo m.; **-govern,** v gobernar mal; **-guide,** descaminar; **-hap,** s accidente m.; contratiempo m.; **-inform,** v informar

mal; **–judge,** juzgar mal;
–lay, extraviar; perder;
–lead, descarriar; (fraud)
engañar; **–manage,**
administrar mal; **–place,**
extraviar; colocar mal;
–print, s errat f.;
–pronounce, v
pronunciar mal;
–represent, desfigurar;
pervertir; **–statement,** s
relación inexacta f.;
–take, v equivocarse; s
equivocación f.; **–taken,**
a erróneo; **–trust,** v
desconfiar; s
desconfianza f.;
–understand, v
entender mal;
–understanding, s
equivocación f.; mala
inteligencia f.; **–use,** v
abusar de

miscellaneous*, mis-el´-
ei´-ni-os a misceláneo

mischief, mis´-chif s daño
m.; perjuicio m.

mischievous*, mis´-chi-
vos a malicioso;
perjudicial

miscreant, mis´-krii-ant s
malandrín m.; bellaco
m.

miser, mai´-sa s avaro m.;
–ly, a avaricioso

miserable, mis ´-er-a-bl a

miserable; (sad)
angustiado

misery, miis ´-ri s miseria
f.; dolor m.

Miss, mis s señorita f.

miss- mis v perder;
(someone's absence)
echar de menos; **–ing,** a
extraviado; perdido

missile, mis´-il s proyectil
m.

mission, mish´-on s
misión f.

missionary, mish´-on-a-ri
s (eccl) misionero m.

mist, mist s bruma f.;
neblina f.

Mister (Mr) mis´-ta s
señor m.

mistletoe, mis-s'l-tou s
muérdago m.

mistress, mis´-tres s
(house) ama f.; dueña f.;
(school) maestra f.;
(kept) querida f.; (Mrs)
señora f.

misty, mis´-ti a brumoso

miter, mai´-ta s mitra f.;
(joint) inglete m.

mitigate, mit´-i-gueit v
mitigar; suavizar

mix, miks v mezclar;
(salad) aderezar; **–ed,** a
mezclado; **–er,** s
mezclador m.; **–ture,** s
mezcla f.

moan, moun v gemir; s
gemido m.

moat, mout s foso m.

mob, mob s chusma f.;
turba f.; v asaltar en
tropel; (enthusiasm)
cercar por la multitud

mobile, mou´-bil a móvil;
movible

mobilize, mo´-bi-lais v
movilizar

mock, mok v burlarse; a
falso; imitado; **–at,** v
burlarse de; **–ery,** s mofa
f.; buria f.; **–ingly,** adv
burlonamente

mode, moud s manera f.;
(fashion) moda f

model, mod´-l s modelo
m.; v modelar

moderate, mod´-er-eit v
moderar

moderate*, mod´-er-et a
moderado; mediocre

moderation, mod-er-ei´-
shon s moderación f.

modern, mod´-ern a
moderno

modest*, mod´-ist a
modesto

modify, mod´-i-fai v
modificar

Mohammedan, mou-
jAm´-me-dan s
mahometano m.*

moist, moist a húmedo;

–en, v humedecer

moisture, mois´-tiur s humedad f.

mold, mould v moldear; s molde m.; matriz f.; (mildew) moho m.; (earth) mantillo m.; **–er,** moldeador m.; **–ing,** moldura f.; **–y,** a mohoso

mole, moul s topo m.; (mark) lunar m.; **–hill,** topinera f.

molecule, mol´-e-kiuul s molécula f.

molest, mo-lest´ v molestar

mollify, mol´-i-fai v ablandar

molt, moult v mudar el pelo; (birds) desplumar

molten, moul´-tn a fundido

moment, mou´-ment s momento m.

momentous,* mou-men´-tos a importante; grave

momentum, mou-men´-tom s ímpetu m.; impulsión f.

monarch, mon´-ark s monarca m.

monarchy, mon´-ar-ki s monarquía f.

monastery, mon´-as-tri s monasterio m.

Monday, mon´-di s lunes m.

monetary, mon´-e-ta-ri a monetario

money, mon´-i s dinero m.; moneda f.; **–order,** libranza postal f.

monger, mong´-ga s traficante m.

mongrel, mong´-grel a mestizo

monk, mongk s monje m.; fraile m.

monkey, mong´-ki s mono m.

monocle, mon´-o-kl s monóculo m.

monogram, mon´-ou-gram s monograma m.

monopolize, mo-nop´-o-lais v monopolizar

monopoly, mo-nop´-o-li s monopolio m.

monotonous,* mon-ot´-o-nos a monótono

monster, mon´-sta s monstruo m.

monstrous,* mon´-stros a monstruoso

month, monz s mes m.; **–ly,** a mensual

monument, mon´-iu-ment s monumento m.

mood, muud s (temper) humor m.; (grammar) modo m.; **–y,** a caprichoso

moon, muun s luna f.; **–light,** luz de la luna f.

moor, muur s páramo m.; v amarrar

Moor, muur s moro m.; **–ish,** a morisco

moot, muut a discutible

mop, mop s estropajo m.; v limpiar

mope, moup v abatirse; atontarse

moral, mor´-al s (lesson) moraleja f.; a* moral; **–ity,** s moralidad f.; **–s,** s pl costumbres f. pl.

morale, mor-aal a moral; virtuoso; s moral f.; sentido m.; moral; ética f.; costumbres f. pl

morass, mo-rAs´ s ciénaga f.; marisma f.

moratorium, mou-ra-tou´-ri-om s moratoria f.

morbid,* moar´-bid a mórbido; enfermizo

more, mór adv más; **–over,** además

morning, moar´-ning s mañana f.; **early –,** madrugada f.; **good –,** buenos días

morocco, mo-rok´-ou s (leather) tafilete m.

morose, mo-rous´ a moroso

morrow, mor´-ou s
mañana m.

morsel, moar´-sl s bocado
m.

mortal, moar´-tl s & a*
mortal m.

mortality, mor-tal´-i-ti s
mortalidad f.

mortar, moar´-tr s mortero
m.

mortgage, moar´-guiCH s
hipoteca f.; **-e,** acreedor
hipotecario m.; **-r,**
deudor hipotecario m.

mortification, moar´-ti-fi-
kei´-shon s
mortificación f.

mortuary, moar´-tiu-a-ri s
depósito de cadáveres
m.

mosaic, mou-sei´-ik s & a
mosaico m.

mosque, mosk s mezquita
f.

mosquito, mos-kii´-tou s
mosquito m.

moss, mos s musgo m.

most, moust adv
sumamente; muy; más; s
la mayor parte f. a lo
más; **-ly,** adv
principalmente

moth, moz s polilla f.

mother, mŏD´-er s madre
f.; **-hood,** maternidad f.;
—in-law, suegra f.; **—of-**

pearl, nácar m.;
madreperla f.; **-ly,** adv
maternal

motion, mou´-shon s
movimiento m.

motionless, mou´-shon-les
a inmóvil

motive, mou´-tiv s motivo
m.; móvil m.; a motriz

motor, mou´-ta s motor
m.; **—cycle,** motocicleta
f.; **-ing,** automovilismo
m.; **-ist,** automovilista
mf.

mottled, mot´-ld a
moteado; abigarrado

motto, mot´-ou s divisa f.;
mote m.

mound, maund s
montículo m.; (mil)
terraplén m.; v
aterraplenar

mount, maunt s monte
m.; (horse) caballería f.;
(picture) marco m.;
(jewels) engaste m.; v
montar; subir; (jewels)
engastar; engarzar; **-ed,**
a (horseback) montado;
de a caballo

mountain, maun´-tin s
montaña f.; monte m.;
-eer, montañés m.;
-ous, a montañoso;
-range, s sierra f.

mountain bike, maun´-tin

baik s bicicleta f.; de
montaña

mountaineering, maun´-
tin-ir-ing s montañero/a
mf.; alpinista mf.; v
hacer alpinismo;
montañismo

mourn, moarn v lamentar,
llorar; **-er,** s miembro
del duelo m.; plañidero
m.; **-ful*,** a lúgubre;
triste; fúnebre; **-ing,** s
lamento m.; (apparel)
luto m.

mouse, maus s ratón m.;
—trap, ratonera f.

mousse, s mousse f.;
crema f.; batida

moustache, mus-taash´ s
bigote m.

mouth, mauz s boca f.;
(animal) hocico m.;
(river) desembocadura
f.; **-ful,** bocado m.; **—
piece,** boquilla f.; (fig)
intérprete m.

movable, muu´-va-bl a
móvil; mueble

move, muuv v mover;
(removal) mudarse;
(propose) proponer; s
movimiento m.; (fig)
golpe m.

movie, muu-vi s película
f.; **the —s** el cine

mow, mou v segar; **-er,** s

segadora f.

much, mŏch adv mucho;
muy; **how –?** ¿cuánto?

mud, mŏd s barro m.; **–dy,**
a barroso; fangoso;

muddle, mŏd´-l s desorden
m.; confusión f.

muff, mŏf s manguito m.

muffle, mŏf´-l v embozar;
(sound) amortiguar

muffler, mŏf´-la s bufanda
f.

mug, mŏg s tazór m.; jarra
f.

Muhammadan, mo-ham-
me-dan s mahometáno
m.

mulatto, miu-lAt´-ou s
mulato m.; mulata f.

mulberry, mŏl´-be-ri s
mora f; **–tree,** morera f.

mule, miuul s mulo m.;
mula f.

mullet, mŏl´-et s mújol
m.; **red –,** salmonete m.

multifarious*, mŏl-ti-fé´-
ri-os a variado; diverso

multiplication, mŏl´-ti-
pli-kei´-shon s
multiplicación f.

multiply, mŏl´-ti-plai v
multiplicar;
multiplicarse

multipurpose, mŏl´-ti-
pĕr´-pos a de
aplicaciones varias

multitude, mŏl´-ti-tiuud s
multitud f.

mummy, mŏm´-i s momia
f.

mumps, mŏmps s pl
paperas f.

munch, mŏnch v mascar

municipal, miu-nis´-i-pal
a municipal

munificent*, miu-nif´-i-
sent a munifico;
generoso

munition, miu-nish´-on s
municiones f. pl.

murder, mĕr´-da v
asesinar; s asesinato m.;
–er, asesino m.; **-ess,**
asesina f.; **-ous,** a
asesino

murky, mĕr´-ki a obscuro;
sombrio; lóbrego

murmur, mĕr´-mr v
murmurar; s murmullo
m.

muscle, mŏs´-l s músculo
m.

muse, miuu s v meditar; s
musa f.

museum, miu-zii´-om s
museo m.

mushroom, mŏsh´-rum s
seta f.

music, miuu´-sik s música
f.; **–al,** a musical

musician, miu-sish´-on s
músico m.

musk, mósk s almizcle m.

musket, mŏs´-ket s
mosquete m.; fusil m.

Muslim, mŏs-lim s & a
musulmán/ana mf.

muslin, mŏs´-lin s
muselina f.

mussel, mŏs´-l s mejillón
f.

must, mŏst v deber; haber
de; tener que; s (wine)
mosto m.; **-y,** a mohoso

mustard, mŏs´-tard s
mostaza f.

muster, mŏs´-ta v
congregar; (mil) pasar
lista

mute, miuut s mudo m.;
a* mudo

mutilate, miuu´-ti-leit v
mutilar

mutineer, miuu-ti-nir s
amotinador m.; rebelde
m.

mutinous, miuu´-ti-nos a
amotinado

mutiny, miuu´-ti-ni s
motín m.; v amotinarse

mutter, mŏt´-a v
murmurar

mutton, mŏt´-on s carne
de carnero f.

mutual, miuu´-tiu-al a
mutuo; mutual

muzzle, mŏ s ´-l s (for
dogs, etc) bozal m.;

(snout) hocico *m.*;
(gun) boca *f.*
my, mai *poss* mi, mis;
–**self,** *pron* yo mismo
myrtle, mĕr´-tl *s* mirto *m.*
mysterious*, mis-ti´-ri-os
a misterioso
mystery, mis´-ter-i *s*
misterio *m.*
mystify, mis´-ti-fai *v*
confundir
myth, miz *s* mito *m.*;
–**ology,** mitología *f.*

N

nag, nAg *v* regañar *s* (horse) jaca *f.*

nail, neil *s* clavo *m.*; (human) uña *f.*; *v* clavar; enclavar; **--brush,** *s* cepillo para las uñas *m.*; **--file,** lima para las uñas *f.*

naive*, ne´-iv *a* ingenuo

naked, nei´-kid *a* nudo; desnudo

name, neim *v* nombrar; llamar *s* nombre *m.*; **--less,** *a* anónimo; **--ly,** *adv* a saber; es decir; **--sake,** *s* tocayo *m.*; **Christian --,** nombre de bautismo *m.*; **sur--,**apellido *m.*

nanny, nA-ni *s* niñera *f.*

nap, nAp *s* siesta *f.*; (cloth) lanilla *f.*

nape, neip *s* nuca *f.*

naphtha, nAp´-*za* *s* nafta *f.*

napkin, nAp´-kin *s* servilleta *f.*

narcissus, nAr-sis´-os *s* narciso *m.*

narcotic, nAr-kot´-ik *s* & *a* narcótico *m.*

narrate, nAr-eit´ *v* narrar; relatar

narrative, nAr´-*a*-tiv *s* narrativa *f.*; relación *f.*

narrow*, nAr´-ou *a* estrecho; **--minded,** intolerant; **--ness,** *s* estrechura *f.*; estrechez *f.*

nasal*, nei´-s *al* *a* nasal

nasturtium, nas-tĕr´-shom *s* capuchina *f.*

nasty, naas´-ti *a* indecente; desagradable

nation, nei´-shon *s* nación *f.*

national, nAsh´-o-nal *a* nacional

nationality, nAsh-o-nal´-i-ti *s* nacionalidad *f.*

native, nei´-tiv *s* natural *mf.*; indígena *mf.*; *a* natal

natural*, nAt´-iu-ral *a* natural; **--ization,** *s* naturalización *f.*

nature, nei´-tiur *s* naturaleza *f.*; índole *f.*

naught, noat, nada; *s* cero *m.*

naughty, noa´-ti *a* travieso; revoltoso

nausea, noa´-sia *s* náusea *f.*; asco *m.*; repugnancia *f.*

nautical*, noa´-ti-kl *a* náutico

naval, nei´-val *a* naval; **--engagement,** *s* batalla naval *f.*; **--officer,** oficial de marina *m.*

navel, nei´-vel *s* ombligo *m.*

navigate, nAv´-i-gueit *v* navegar

navigation, nA-vi-guei´-shon *s* navegación *f.*

navigator, nA-vi-guei´-*ta* *s* navegante *m.*

navy, nei´-vi *s* marina de

guerra f.; armada f.

near, ni r a cercano; *prep* cerca de; *adv* cerca; v acercarse; **–ly,** *adv* casí; cerca de; **–ness,** s proximidad f.; **––side,** s lado cercano (in Spain); lado izquierdo (en Inglaterra) **––sighted,** a miope

neat, niit a (spruce) pulcro; (dainty) pulido; delicado; (tidy) aseado; (not diluted) puro; **–ness,** s pulcritud f.; delicadeza f.; aseo m.

necessarily, nes´-es-a-ri-li *adv* necesariamente

necessary, nes´-es-a-ri a necesario

necessitate, ne-ses´-i-teit v requerir; necesitar

necessity, ne-ses´-i-ti s necesidad f.; miseria f.

neck, nek s cuello m.; (bottle, etc) gollete m.; **–lace,** collar m.; **–tie,** corbata f.

need, niid v necesitar. s necesidad f.; **–ful*,** a necesario; **–less,** innecesario; inútil

needle, nii´-dl s aguja f.

needy, nii´-di a indigente; necesitado

negation, ni-guei´-shon s negación f.

negative, neg´-a-tiv s negativa f.; (photo) negativo m.; *a** negativo

neglect, nig-lekt´ v descuidar; s descuido m.; **–ful*,** a negligente; descuidado

negligence, neg´-liCH-ens s negligencia f.

negligent*, neg´-liCH-ent a negligente; descuidado

negotiate, ni-gou´-shi-eit v negociar

negotiation, ni-gou´-shi-ei´-shon s negociación f.

negro, nii´-grou s negro m.

neigh, nei v relinchar; s relincho m.

neighbor, nei´-ba s vecino m.; **–hood,** vecindad f.; vecindario m.; **–ly,** *adv* sociablemente; a sociable

neither, nai´-Da pron & a ni uno ni otro; ... **nor,** *conj* ni... ni; *adv* tampoco

neon, nii-on s neón m.

nephew, nev´-iu s sobrino m.

nerve, nĕrv s nervio m.; (pluck, etc) valor m.; sangre fría f.

nervous*, nĕr´-vos a nervioso; tímido

nest, nest s nido m.; v anidar

nestle, nes´-l v acogerse; (birds) anidar

net, net s red f.; a neto; **–work,** s red f.; cadena f. (radio, TV)

nettle, net´-l s ortiga f.

network, net-uĕrk s red; cadena

neuralgia, niu-rAl´-CHi-a s neuralgia f.

neuritis, niuu´-rai-tis s neuritis f.

neurotic*, niuu-rot´-ik s & a neurótico/a mf.

neuter, niuu´-ta s & a neutro m.

neutral*, niuu´-tral a neutral

never, nev´-a adv nunca; jamás; **–more,** nunca más; **–theless,** sin embargo

new*, niuu a nuevo; reciente; fresco; tierno; **–year,** s año nuevo m.

news, niuus s noticias f. pl; **––agent,** vendedor de periódicos m.; **–paper,** periódico m.; diario m.

next, nekst a próximo; siguiente; (beside) contiguo; de al lado; *adv* después

nib, nib s (pen) plumilla f.; pico m.

nibble, nib´-l v mordiscar; (rodents) roer

nice*, nais a amable; simpático; agradable; (good) bueno; exquisito; (pretty) lindo; bonito

nick, nik s muesca f.

nickel, nik´-l s níquel m.

nickname, nik´-neim s apodo m.; v apodar

nicotine, ni´-ko-tiin s nicotina f.

niece, niis s sobrina f.

night, nait s noche f.; –**club,** s cabaret m.; café cantante m.; –**dress,** camisón m.; –**fall,** anochecer m.; –**ingale,** ruiseñor m.; –**ly,** adv cada noche; –**mare,** s pesadilla f.

nightlife, nait-laif s vida f.; nocturna

nimble, nim´-bl a ágil; ligero; veloz

nine, nain s & a nueve m.; –**teen,** diez y nueve m.; –**teenth,** décimonono m.; –**tieth,** nonagésimo m.; –**ty,** noventa m.

ninth, nainz s & a nono; noveno m.

nip, nip v pellizcar; moreler; –**off,** desmochar

nipple, nip´-l s pezón m.

nitrate, nai´-treit s nitrato m.

nitrogen, nai´-trou-CH en s nitrogeno m.

no, nou adv no

nobility, no-bil´-i-ti s nobleza f.; aristocracia f.

noble, nou´-bl s & a noble m.

nobody, nou´-bod-i pron nadie; ninguno

nod, nod v cabecear; s cabeceo m.; saludo m.

noise, nois s ruido m.; –**less*,** a silencioso

noisily, noi´-si-li adv ruidosamente

noisy, noi´-s a ruidoso

nominal*, nom´-i-nal a nominal

nominate, nom´-i-neit v nombrar; elegir

nominee, nom-i-nii´ s nómino m.; candidato m.

none, nŏn pron & a ninguno; nadie

nonplussed, non´-plŏst a confundido

nonsense, non´-sens s disparate m.; tontería f.; ansurdo

nonskid, non´-skid a antirresbaladizo

nonsmoker, non-smouk-a s (person) no fumador/a mf.; (rail) departamento de no fumadores

nonstop, non´-stop a continuo; (train, etc) directo

nook, nuk s ángulo m.; (fig) rincón m.

noon, nuun s mediodía m.

no one, nou-uŏn pron = **nobody** nadie

noose, nuus s lazo corredizo m.

nor, noar, conj ni

normal*, noar´-m'l a normal

north, noarz s norte m.

northerly, noar´-Der-li a del norte; septentrional

nose, nous s nariz f.; (of a ship) proa f.

nostril, nos´-tr'l s ventana de la nariz f.

not, not adv no

notable, nou´-ta-bl a notable

notch, noch v hacer muescas; s muesca f.

note, nout v nótar; s nota f.; (currency) billete m.; –**book,** libreta f.; – **paper,** papel para cartas m.; –**d,** a afamado;

célebre

noteworthy, nout´-uĕr-Di *a* notable

nothing, nŏ´-zing *adv* nada; **for –,** de balde

notice, nou´-tis *v* notar. *s* aviso *m.*; (newspaper) noticia *f.*; (to quit) notificación *f.*

noticeable, nou´-tis-*a*-bl *a* notable; reparable

notify, nou´-ti-fai *v* notificar

notion, nou´-shon *s* noción *f.*; idea *f.*

notoriety, nou-to-rai´-i-ti *s* notoriedad *f.*

notorious*, no-tou´-ri-os *a* notorio

notwithstanding, not-uiD-stAn´-ding *prep* & *conj* a pesar de; no obstante; sin embargo

nought, nout, nada; *s* cero *m.*

noun, naun *s* nombre *m.*; substantivo *m.*

nourish, nŏr´-ish *v* nutrir; alimentar; **–ing,** *a* nutritivo; **–ment,** *s* alimento *m.*

novel, nov´-l *s* novela *f.*; *a* nuevo

novelist, nov´-el-ist *s* novelista *mf.*

novelty, nov´-el-ti *s* novedad *f.*

November, no-vem´-ba *s* noviembre *m.*

novice, nov´-is *s* novicio *m.*

now, nau *adv* ahora; **–and then,** de vez en cuando

nowadays, nau´-*a*-deis *adv* hoy día

nowhere, nou´-jué r *adv* en ninguna parte

noxious*, nok´-shos *a* nocivo; pernicioso

nozzle, nos ´-l *s* (of hose) boquilla de manguera *f.*

nuclear, niuu´-klir *a* nuclear

nucleus, niuu´-kli-os *s* núcleo *m.*

nude, niud *a* desnudo

nudge, nŏ CH *s* codazo *m.*; *v* dar codazos

nugget, nŏ´-guit *s* pepita *f.*

nuisance, niuu´-sens *s* (annoyance) fastidio *m.*; molestia *f.*; (bother) calamidad *f.*

null, nŏl *a* nulo; *v* anular

numb, nŏm *a* entumecido; (from cold) aterido; *v* entumecer; **–ness,** *s* entumecimiento *m.*

number, nŏm´-ba *s* número *m.*; *v* numerar

numberless, nŏm´-ber-les *a* innumerable; sin

número

numerous*, niuu´-mer-os *a* numeroso

nun, nŏn *s* monja *f.*; religiosa *f.*

nunnery, nŏn´-er-i *s* convento de monjas *m.*

nurse, nĕrs *s* enfermera *f.*; (male) enfermero *m.*; (maid) niñera *f.*; *v* cuidar; (suckle) criar

nursery, nĕrs´-er-i *s* cuarto de los niños *m.*; (plants) plantel *m.*; semillero *m.*; invernadero *m.*

nursery rhyme, nĕrs´-er-i-raim *s* cuento de niños *m.*

nut, nŏt *s* nuez *f.*; (hazel) avellana *f.*; (pea) cacahueate *m.*; (bolt) tuerca *f.*; **–cracker,** cascanueces *m.*; **–meg,** nuez moscada *f.*; **–shell,** cáscara de nuez *f.*

nutriment, niuu´-tri-ment *s* nutrimento *m.*; alimento *m.*

nutritious*, niuu-trish´-os *a* nutritivo

nylon, nai-lon *s* nilón *m.*; nailón *m.*; *a* de nilón; de nailón

oak, ouk s roble m.

oakum, ou´-kom s estopa f.

oar, ours remo m.

oarsman, ours´-mAn s remero m.

oasis, ou-ei´-sis s oasis m.

oat, out s avena f.; –meal, harina de avena f.

oath, ouz s juramento m.; maldición f.

obdurate*, ob´-diu-ret a obstinado; terco

obedience, o-bii´-di-ens s obediencia f.

obedient*, o-bii´-di-ent a obediente

obese, o-biis´ a obeso

obesity, o-bes´-i-ti s obesidad f.

obey, o-bei´ v obedecer

obfuscate, ob-fŏs´-keit v ofuscar

obituary, ob-it´-iuu-a-ri s obituario m.; a mortuorio

object, ob-CHekt´ v (resent) objetar; (oppose) oponerse

object, ob´-CHekt s objecto m.; (aim) propósito m.; (grammar) complemento m.; –ion, objeción f.; –ionable, a objectable; –ive, s & a objetivo m.

obligation, ob-li-guei´-shon s obligación f.

obligatory, ob´-li-guei-to-ri a obligatorio

oblige, ob-laiCH´ v obligar; complacer

obliging*, ob-laiCH´-ing a servicial;

condescendiente

obliterate, ob-lit´-er-eit v borrar; destruir

oblivion, ob-liv´-i-on s olvido m.

oblivious*, ob-liv´-i-os a olvidadizo

oblong, ob´-long a oblongo

obnoxious*, ob-nok´-shos a ofensivo; aborrecible

obscene*, ob-siin´ a obsceno

obscure, ob-skiúr´ v obscurecer; a* obscuro

observant, ob-sĕr´-vant a atento; observante

observation, ob-sĕr-vei´-shon s observación f.

observatory, ob-sĕr´-va-to-ri s observatorio m.

observe, ob-sĕrv´ v observar

obsess, ob-ses´ v obsesionar; –ion, s obsesión f.

obsolete, ob´-so-liit a anticuado; desusado

obstacle, ŏb´-sta-kl s obstáculo m.

obstinacy, ob´-sti-na-si s obstinación f.

obstinate*, ob´-sti-net a obstinado; terco

obstruct, ob-strŏkt´ v obstruir; impedir

413

obstruction, ob-strŏk´-shon s obstrucción f.

obtain, ob-tein´ v obtener; conseguir; alcanzar

obtrude, ob-truud´ v imponer; entrometerse

obtrusive, ob-truu´-siv a intruso; importuno

obviate, ob´-vi-eit v evitar; impedir

obvious*, ob´-vi-os a obvio; evidente; claro

occasion, o-kei´-shon v ocasionar; s ocasión f.; causa f.; **–al,** a ocasional; **–ally,** adv alguna vez; ocasionalmente

occult, ok-kŏlt´ a oculto; secreto

occupation, ok-kiu-pei´-shon s ocupación f.; empleo m.

occupier, o´-kiu-uai-a s ocupador m.; (tenant) inquilino m.

occupy, o´-kiu-pai v ocupar; (mil) apoderarse de; (oneself) ocuparse

occur, ok-ker´ v ocurrir; **–rence,** s ocurrencia f.

ocean, ou´-shan s océano m.; mar mf.

ocher, ou´-ker s ocre m.

o'clock, o-klok´ s ...hora f.

octagon, ok´-ta-guon s octágono m.

octagonal, ok-ta´-guon-al a octagonal

octave, ok´-teiv s octava f.

October, ok-tou´-ba s octubre m.

octopus, ok´-tou-pus s pulpo m.; pólipo m.

oculist, ok´-iu-list s oculista m.

odd, od a (number) impar; (single) suelto; (strange) extraño, **–ly,** adv extrañamente; **–s,** s pl (betting) ventaja f.; **–s and ends,** restos m. pl; despojos m. pl

odious*, ou´-di-os a odioso; detestable

odor, ou´-da s olor m.; (sweet) fragancia f.

of, ov prep de; en

off, of adv lejos; a distancia; a lo largo; **–hand,** adv improvisado; de repente; **–side,** s lado exterior (in Spain); a (games) fuera de juego; offside

offal, of´-l s desperdicios m. pl; bazofia f.

offend, o-fend´ v ofender; (law) delinquir

offense, o-fens´ s ofensa f.; (law) delito m.

offensive, o-fen´-siv a* ofensivo; s (mil) ofensiva f.

offer, of´-a v ofrecer; s oferta f.

offering, of´-er-ing s tributo m.; sacrificio m.

office, of´-is s oficio m.; (business) oficina f.

officer, of´-is-a s funcionario m.; (mil) oficial m.

official, o-fish´-l s funcionario m.; a* oficial

officious*, o-fish´-os a oficioso; solícito

off-peak, of-piik a (holiday) de temporada baja; (electricity) de banda económica

offspring, of´-spring s vástago m.; prole f.

oft, often, oft, of´-n adv a menudo; con frecuencia; muchas veces

ogle, ou´-gl v mirar al soslayo; guiñar

oil, oils s aceite m.; v lubricar; **–cloth,** s hule m.; **–y,** a aceitoso; oleoso

ointment, oint´-ment s ungüento m.

okay, ou´-kei = **OK** interj (all right)¡está bién!;

4 1 4

(yes) ¡sí!; *a* aprovado;
satisfactorio

old, ould *a* viejo; anciano;
antiguo

old-fashioned, ould-fÁsh-
nd *a* anticuado

olive, ol´-iv *s* aceituna *f.*;
–oil, aceite de oliva *m.*

Olympic Games, o-limp-
ik gueims *s* & *a* Juegos
m.pl; Olímpicos

omelet, om´-e-let *s* tortilla
f.; tortilla de huevos *f.*

omen, ou´-men *s* agüero
m.; presagio *m.*

ominous*, ou´-mi-nos *a*
ominoso; presagioso

omit, o-mit´ *v* omitir;
(neglect) descuidar

ommission, o-mish´-on *s*
omisión *f.*; (neglect)
descuido *m.*

omnibus, om´-ni-bos *s*
ómnibus *m.*

omnipotent, om-nip´-o-
tent *a* omnipotente

on, on *prep* (upon) en;
sobre; encima de; (date)
el; *adv* (onward)
adelante; **–foot,** a pie

once, uöns *adv* una vez;
(formerly) antes, en otro
tiempo; **at –,**
inmediatamente;
–more, otra vez

one, uön *s* uno *m.*; una *f.*;

(impersonal) uno *m.*;
una *f. a* un; uno; una;
–self, *pron* se; sí mismo

onerous*, on´-er-os *a*
oneroso; molesto

one-way, uön- uei *a*
(street) de sentido
único; (ticket) de ida

ongoing, on-gou-ing *a*
continuo; en marcha;
que sigue funcionando

onion, ŏn´-i-on *s* cebolla
f.

on-line, on-lain *a* & *adv*
comput on-line; en línea;
conectado

only, oun´-li *a* sólo; único;
adv sólo; solamente

onslaught, on´-slo *at s*
asalto *m.*

onto, on-tu *prep* on to

onward, on´-uerd *adv*
hacia; adelante

onyx, o´-lks *s* ónice *m.*;
ónix *m.*

ooze, uus *v* manar; fluir; *s*
fango *m.*

opal, ou´-pal *s* ópalo *m.*

opaque, o-peik´ *a* opaco

open, ou´-pn *v* abrir; *a**
abierto; **–er,** *s* (tool)
abridor *m.*; **–ing,**
abertura *f.*; oportunidad
f.

opera, op´-e-ra *s* ópera *f.*;
–glass, gemelos de

teatro *m. pl*; **–hat,**
sombrero de copa *m.*; **–
house,** teatro de la
ópera *m.*

operate, op´-er-eit *v*
funcionar; (med) operar

operation, op´-er-ei´-shon
s operación *f.*

operator, op´-e-rei-ta *s*
operario *m.*; (med)
operador *m.*

opinion, o-pin´-yon *s*
opinión *f.*

opium, ou´-pi-om *s* opio
m.

opossum, ou-pos´-som *s*
zarigüeya *f.*

opponent, o-pou´-nent *s*
adversario *m.*; rival *m.*

opportune*, o´-por-tiuun
a oportuno

opportunity, o-por-
tiuun´-i-ti *s* oportunidad
f.

oppose, o-pous´ *v* oponer;
combatir

opposite, op´-o-s it *a*
opuesto; (facing)
enfrente; adv opuesto *m.*

opposition, op-pou-si´-
shon *s* oposición *f.*

oppress, o-pres´ *v* oprimir

oppression, o-presh´-on *s*
opresión *f.*; pesadez *f.*

oppressive*, o-pres´-siv *a*
opresivo; tiránico

optical, op´-tik-al *a* óptico; relativo a la vista

optician, op-tish´-an *s* óptico *m*.

option, op´-shon *s* opción *f*.; **–al*,** *a* facultativo; opcional

opulence, op´-iu-lens *s* opulencia *f*.

opulent, op´-iu-lent *a* opulento

or, or *conj* o, u; sea, sea que; **–else,** o sino

oral*, ó´-ral *a* verbal

orange, or´-inCH *s* naranja *f*.

orator, or´-a-ta *s* orador *m*.

oratory, or´-a-to-ri *s* oratoria *f*.; elocuencia *f*.

orb, o arb *s* (sphere) globo *m*.; orbe *m*.; esfera *f*.

orbit, o arb´-it *s* órbita; *v* volar en círculo

orchard, oar´-cherd *s* huerta *f*.; (poetical) verjel *m*.

orchestra, oar´-kes-tra *s* orquesta *f*.

orchid, oar´-kid *s* orquídea *f*.

ordain, oar-dein´ *v* ordenar

ordeal, oar´-diil *s* dura prueba *f*.

order, oar´-da *s* orden *f*.; (goods) pedido *m*.; (command) orden *m*.; (decoration) condecoración *f*.; *v* ordenar; (goods) hacer un pedido

orderly, oar´-der-li *a** ordenado; (quiet) tranquilo; *s* ordenanza *f*.

ordinary, oar´-di-na-ri *a* ordinario

ordnance, oard´-nans *s* artillería *f*.

ore, ór *s* mineral *m*.

organ, oar´-gan *s* órgano *m*.

organic, oar-guan´-ik *a* orgánico

organization, oar-guan-ai-sei´-shon *s* organización *f*.

organize, oar´-gan-ai *s v* organizar

orgasm, oar-gua-sm *s* orgasmo *m*.

orgy, o ar´-CHi *s* orgía *f*.

orient, ó´-ri-ent *s* oriente *m*.

oriental, ou-ri-en´-tal *s &* *a* oriental *mf*.

origin, or´-i-CHin *s* origen *m*.; **–al*,** *a* original

originate, o-riCH´-in-eit *v* originar; originarse

ornament, oar´-na-ment *s* adorno *m*.; *v* adornar ornamento *m*.

ornamental, oar-na-men´-tal *a* decorativo

orphan, oar´-fan *s* huérfano *m*.; **–age,** asilo de huérfanos *m*.; orfanatorio *m*.

orthodox, or´-zo-doks *a* ortodoxo

orthography, or-zog´-ra-fi *s* ortografía *f*.

oscillate, os´-il-eit *v* oscilar

ostentatious*, os-ten-tei´-shos *a* ostentoso

ostrich, os´-trich *s* avestruz *m*.

other, ðD´-a *a* otro; **another time,** *adv* otra vez; **the other one,** *pron* el otro; **–wise,** *adv* de otro modo

otter, ot´-a *s* nutria *f*.

ought, oat *v* deber; convenir

ounce, auns *s* onza *f*. (28 gr. 35)

our, aúr *poss adj* nuestro

ours, aúrs *poss pron* el nuestro

ourselves, aúr-selvs ´ *pron* nosotros mismos

out, aut *adv* fuera; *a* (extinguish) apagado; (issue) publicado; **–bid,** *v* pujar más alto; **–break,**

s insurrección f.; epidemia f.; **–burst,** explosión f.; **–cast,** proscrito m.; **–come,** s resultado m.; fruto m.; **–cry,** clamor m.; alboroto m.; **–do,** v exceder; **–fit,** s equipo m.; **–fitter,** proveedor m.; (ship) armador m.; **–grow,** v crecer demasiado para; crecer más que; **–last,** durar más; **–law,** s bandido m.; v poner fuera de la ley; **–lay,** s desembolso m.; gasto m.; **–let,** salida f.; desagüe m.; **–line,** v bosquejar; s contorno m.; **–live,** v sobrevivir; **–look,** s aspecto m.; perspectiva f.; **–lying,** a distante; exterior; **–number,** v exceder en número; **–post,** s avanzada f.; **–put,** producción f.; **–rage,** ultraje m.; **–rageous*,** ultrajante; exagerado; **–right,** adv completamente; **–run,** v correr más que otro; pasar; **–side,** adv afuera; s & a exterior; **–sider,** s extraño m.; (racing) forastero m.; **–size,**

tamaño extra m.; **–skirts,** inmediaciones f. pl; **–spoken*,** a abierto; franco; **–standing,** a prominente; (debts) pendiente; **–ward,** adv fuera; a exterior; **–ward bound,** (shipping) en viaje de ida; **–wit,** v engañar

oval, ou´-vl s óvalo m.; a oval

ovation, ou-vei´-shon s ovación f.

oven, ŏ´-vn s horno m.

over, ou´-va adv sobre; por encima; prep sobre; encima de; **–alls,** s pl zahones m.pl; **–bearing,** a arrogante; **–board,** adv al mar; al agua; **–cast,** a nublado; **–charge,** s (price) extorsión f.; v sobrecargar; **–coat,** s sobretodo m.; **–come,** v triunfar de; **–do,** v excederse en; **–dose,** s dosis excesiva f.; **–draw,** v exceder el crédito; **–due,** a vencido y no pagado; **–flow,** v desbordar; **–grow,** crecer con exceso; **–hang,** sobresalir; suspender; completamente; **–haul,**

examinar; **–hear,** oir por casualidad; **–joy,** arrebatar de alegría; **–land,** a & adv por tierra; **–lap,** v trasla- par; **–load,** sobrecargar; **–look,** dominar; (forget) descuidar; (pardon) pasar por alto; **–power,** vencer; subyugar; **–rate,** encarecer; **–rule,** (set aside) denegar; **–run,** v invadir; infestar; **–seas,** a ultramar; **–see,** v inspeccionar; **–seer,** s superintendente m.; **–sight,** inadvertencia f.; **–sleep,** v dormir demasiado; **–step,** v exceder; **–take,** v alcanzar; **–throw,** (vanquish) vencer; **–time,** s (work) horas de trabajo extraordinarias f. pl; **–ture,** propuesta f.; (mus) obertura f.; **–turn,** v volcar; (deliberate) derribar; **–weight,** s exceso de peso m.; **–whelm,** v abrumar; **–work,** sobrecargar de trabajo

overnight, ou´-va-nait adv durante la noche; (fig) de la noche a la mañana; a de noche

owe, ou *v* deber; tener deudas

owing, ou´-ing *a* debido; **–owing,** ou´-ing; *a* debido; **–to,** debido a

owl, aul *s* buho *m.*; mochuelo *m.*

own, oun *v* poseer; *a* propio

owner, ou´-na *s* dueño *m.*; propietario *m.*

ox, ox *s* buey *m.*

oxygen, ok´-si-CHen *s* oxígeno *m.*

oyster, ois´-ta *s* ostra *f.*; **⁓ bed,** ostrero *m.*

ozone, ou-soun *s* ozono *m*; **– hole** agujero *m* de ozono; **– layer** capa *f* de ozono

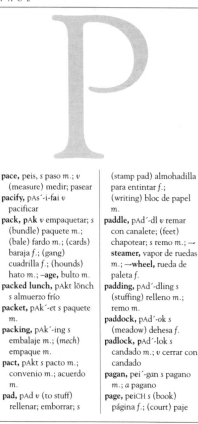

pace, peis, *s* paso *m.*; *v* (measure) medir; pasear

pacify, pʌs´-i-fai *v* pacificar

pack, pʌk *v* empaquetar; *s* (bundle) paquete *m.*; (bale) fardo *m.*; (cards) baraja *f.*; (gang) cuadrilla *f.*; (hounds) hato *m.*; **–age,** bulto *m.*

packed lunch, pʌkt lönch *s* almuerzo frío

packet, pʌk´-et *s* paquete *m.*

packing, pʌk´-ing *s* embalaje *m.*; (*mech*) empaque *m.*

pact, pʌkt *s* pacto *m.*; convenio *m.*; acuerdo *m.*

pad, pʌd *v* (to stuff) rellenar; emborrar; *s* (stamp pad) almohadilla para entintar *f.*; (writing) bloc de papel *m.*

paddle, pʌd´-dl *v* remar con canalete; (feet) chapotear; *s* remo *m.*; **–steamer,** vapor de ruedas *m.*; **–wheel,** rueda de paleta *f.*

padding, pʌd´-dling *s* (stuffing) relleno *m.*; remo *m.*

paddock, pʌd´-ok *s* (meadow) dehesa *f.*

padlock, pʌd´-lok *s* candado *m.*; *v* cerrar con candado

pagan, pei´-gan *s* pagano *m.*; *a* pagano

page, peiCH *s* (book) página *f.*; (court) paje *m.*

pageant, pʌCH´-ent *s* procesión *f.*; espectáculo *m.*

pail, peil *s* cubo *m.*

pain, pein *s* dolor *m.*; *v* doler; **–ful*,** *a* doloroso; **–less,** sin dolor.

paint, peint *v* pintar; *s* pintura *f.*; (art) color *m.*; **–brush,** brocha *f.*; (art) pincel *m.*; **–er,** pintor *m.*; **–ing,** cuadro *m.*; pintura *f.*

pair, pér *s* par *m.*; pareja *f.*

pajamas, pl-CHa´mas *s pl* pijamas *m. pl*

palace, pʌl´-is *s* palacio *m.*

palatable, pʌl´-a-ta-bl *a* sabroso

palate, pʌl´-et *s* paladar *m.*

pale, peil *a* pálido; *v* palidecer; **–ness,** *s* palidez *f.*

palette, pʌl´-et *s* paleta *f.*

paling, pei´-ling *s* (fence) palizada *f.*

palm, paam *s* palmera *f.*; (hand) palma *f.*; **–ist,** quiromántico *m.*; **–istry,** quiromancia *f.*; **–Sunday,** domingo de Ramos *m.*

palpitation, pʌl-pi-tei´-shon *s* palpitación *f.*

paltry, poal´-tri *a*

mezquino; vil; miserable

pamper, pAm´-pa *v*
(indulge) mimar

pamphlet, pAm´-flet *s*
folleto *m.*

pan, pAn *s* (frying) sartén
f.; –**cake,** buñuelo *m.*

pander, pAn´-da *v*
alcahuetear

pane, pein *s* vidrio *m.*;
cristal *m.*

panel, pAn´-l *s* entrepaño
m.; (persons) lista *f.*

pang, pAng *s* ansia *f.*;
dolor *m.*; angustia *f.*

panic, pAn´-ik *s* pánico *m.*

pansy, pAn´-si *s* (bot)
pensamiento *m.*

pant, pAnt *v* jadear

panther, pAn´-zer *s*
pantera *f.*

pantry, pAn´-tri *s*
despensa *f.*

pants, pAnts *s pl*
pantalones *m. pl*

pap, pAp *s* (food) papilla *f.*

papal, pei´-p'l *a* papal

paper, pei´-pa *s* papel *m.*;
news–,periódico *m.*;
diario *m.*; **wall**—, papel
de empapelar *m.*

par, paar *s* par *m.*

parable, pAr´-a-bl *s*
parábola *f.*

parachute, pAr´-a-shut *s*
paracaídas *m.*

parade, pa-reid´ *s* parada
f.; *v* ostentar; desfile *m.*

paradise, pAr´-a-dais *s*
paraíso *m.*

paraffin, pAr´-a-fin *s*
parafina *f.*

paragraph, pAr´-a-graaf *s*
párrafo *m.*; parágrafo *m.*

parallel, pAr´-a-lel *a*
paralelo

paralysis, pAr-a´-lai-sis *s*
parálisis *f.*

paralyze, pAr´-a-lais *v*
paralizar

parasite, pAr´-a-sait *s*
parásito *m.*

parcel, paar´-sl *s* paquete
m.

parched, paart´-sht *a*
reseco; mustio

parchment, paart´-shment
s pergamino *m.*

pardon, paar´-dn *v*
perdonar; *s* perdón *m.*;
(official) indulto *m.*

parents, pei´-rents *s pl*
padres *m. pl*

parish, pAr´-ish *s*
parroquia *f.*

park, paark *s* parque *f.*;
–**ing,** (motors)
estacionamiento *m.*;
–**ing place,** plaza de
estacionamiento *f.*

parley, paar´-li *v*
parlamentar;

conferenciar

parliament, paar´-li-ment
s parlamento *m.*

parlor, paar´-la *s* recibidor
m.

parochial, pa-rou´-ki-al *a*
parroquial

parrot, pAr´-ot *s* papagayo
m.

parry, pAr´-i *v* parar; *s*
quite *m.*; rechazo *m.*

parse, paars *v* (grammar)
analizar; (gramm)
construit

parsimonious*, paar´-si-
mou´-ni-os *a* tacaño

parsley, paar-sli *s* perejil *m.*

parsnip, paar´-snip *s*
chirivía *f.*

parson, paar´-sn *s* clérigo
m.; (parish) párroco *m.*

parsonage, paar´-son-icH *s*
rectoría *f.*; vicaría *f.*

part, paart *v* partir;
(separate) separar;
(hair) hacer la raya *s*
parte *f.*; (actor's) papel
m.; –**time,** *a* labor de
medio tiempo *f.*

partake, paar-teik´, –**in,** *v*
tomar parte en; –**of,**
participar

partial*, paar´-shal *a*
parcial; –**ity,** *s*
parcialidad *f.*; prejuicio

participate, paar-tis´-i-peit v participar

participle, paar´-ti-si-pl s participio m.

particle, paar´-ti-kl s partícula f.

particular*, par-tik´-iu-lr a particular; (fastidious) exigente; quisquilloso;. (exact) exacto; **-s,** s pl detalles m. pl

parting, paar´-ting s separación f.; (hair) raya f.

partition, paar-tish´-on s (wall) partición f.

partner, paart´-na s (business) socio m.; (cards) compañero m.; (dance) pareja f.

partnership, paart´-nership s sociedad f.

partridge, paar´-triCH s perdiz f.

part-time, paart - taim a & adv a tiempo parcial

party, paar´-ti s partido m.; (social) reunión f.; tertulia f.

pass, paas v pasar; (examination) aprobar s (mountain) puerto m.; pase m.; **--book,** libreta de banco f.; **-port,** pasaporte m.

m.; predilección f.

passage, pAs´-iCH s pasaje m.; (in a house) pasillo m.; (sea) travesía f.

passenger, pAs´-in-CHa s pasajero m.

passer-by, pAs´-r-bai s transeúnte m.

passion, pAsh´-on s pasión f.; (anger) cólera f.

passionate*, pAsh´-on-et a apasionado

past, paast s pasado m.; a pasado

paste, peist v engrudar; s engrudo m.; (cakes, gems, etc) pasta f.

pasteurized, pAs-tiĕr-aisd a paste(u)rizado

pastime, paas´-taim s pasatiempo m.

pastries, peis´-treis, s pl pastas f. pl; pasteles m.

pastry, peis´-tri s pastelería f.; **--cook's,** pastelería f.

pasture, paas´-tiur s pasto m.

pat, pAt v dar una palmadita

patch, pAch s remiendo m.; v remendar; parche m.

pâté, pA´-tei s paté m.; pastel (de carne, etc)

patent, pei´-tent a patente; visible;

manifesto; s patente f.; diploma f.; **-leather,** charol m.; hule m.

paternal*, pa-tĕr´-nal a paternal; paterno

path, paaz s senda f.; camino m.

pathetic, pa-ze´-tik a patético; conmovedor

patience, pei´-shens s paciencia f.

patient, pei´-shent a* paciente; s enfermo m.

patio, pAtiiou s patio m.

patriot, pei´-tri-ot s patriota m.

patriotic, pei-tri-ot´-ik a patriótico

patrol, pa-troul´ s patrulla f.; v patrullar

patronize, pAt´-ron-ais v patrocinar; proteger

pattern, pAt´-ern s modelo m.; (sample) muestra f.; (paper) patrón m.

paunch, poanch s panza f.

pauper, poa,-pr s pobre m.; limosnero m.

pause, poas s pausa f.; v pausar

pave, peiv v pavimentar

pavement, peiv´-ment s pavimento m.

pavilion, pa-vil´-yon s pabellón m.

paw, poa s garra f.; v (as a

horse) piafar

pawn, poan v empeñar; s prenda f.; (chess) peón m.; **–broker's shop,** casa de empeños f.

pay, pei v pagar; s paga f.; **–able,** a pagadero; **–er,** s pagador m.; **–load,** s carga rentable f.; carga explosiva f.; **–ment,** pago m.

payphone, pei-foun s teléfono m.; público

pea, pii s guisante m.; **–nut,** cacahuete m.

peace, piis s paz f.; **–ful*,** a pacífico; tranquilo

peach, piich s melocotón m.; durazno m.; **– tree,** melocotonero m.

peacock, pii-kok s pavo real m.

peak, piik s pico m.; cima f.

peal, piil v repicar; s (bells) repique m.; (thunder) tronido m.

pear, pér s pera f.; **–tree,** peral m.

pearl, pĕrl s perla f.

peasant, pes-ant s campesino m.

pebble, peb-l s guija f.; piedrecilla f.

peck, pek v picotear

peculiar*, pi-kiuu-li-a a

peculiar; **–ity,** s peculiaridad f.

pecuniary, pi-kiuu-ni-a-ri a pecuniario

pedal, ped-al s pedal m.

pedantic, pi-dan-tik a pedantesco

peddler, ped-la s buhonero m.

pedestal, ped-es-tal s pedestal m.

pedestrian, pi-des-tri-an s peatón m.; caminante m.

pedigree, ped-i-grii s genealogía f.

peel, piil v pelar; s corteza f.

peep, piip v atisbar; s ojeada f.

peer, pi r v escudriñar; s par m.; **–age,** dignidad de par f.

peerless, pir-les a sin par; incomparable

peevish*, pii-vish a quisquilloso

peg, peg s clavija f.; (for hats, etc) colgador m.; v enclavijar

pellet, pel-et s pelotilla f.; (shot) perdigón m.

pell-mell, pel-mel adv a trochemoche

pelt, pelt v pellejo m.; s (skin) piel f.

pen, pen v escribir; encerrar; s pluma f.; corral m.; (cattle, etc) corral m.; **–holder,** portapluma m.; **–knife,** navaja f.

penal, pii-nl a penal; **–servitude,** s presidio m.

penalty, pen-al-ti s castigo m.; (fine) multa f.

penance, pen-ans s penitencia f.

pencil, pen-sl s lápiz m.

pendant, pen-dant s medallón m.

pending, pen-ding a pendiente; prep durante

pendulum, pen-diu-lom s péndulo m.

penetrate, pen-i-treit v penetrar

penguin, pen-guin s pingüino m.

penicillin, pen-i-si-lin s penicilina f.

peninsula, pen-in-siu-la s península f.

penitent*, pen-i-tent a penitente

penniless, pen-i-les a sin dinero; indigente; pobre

penny, pen-i s penique m.

penpal, pen-pal s amigo/a mf.; por

correspondencia

pension, pen´-shon s
pensión f.; (mil) retiro
m.; v pensionar; **–er,** s
pensionado m.

pensive*, pen´-siv a
pensativo

people, pii´-pl s gente f.;
nación f.; v poblar

pepper, pep´-a s pimienta
f.; **–mint,** menta f.

per, per prep por; **–cent,**
por ciento; **–centage,** s
porcentaje m.

perceive, per-siiv´ v
percibir; comprender;
entender

perception, per-sep´-shon
s percepción f.

perch, pĕrch s percha f.;
(fish) perca f.

perchance, per-chaans´
adv acaso; tal vez; quizá

percolate, pĕr´-ko-leit v
colar; filtrar

peremptory, per-emp´-to-
ri a perentorio

perfect, pĕr´-fikt a*
perfecto; acabado; v
perfeccionar; **–ion,** s
perfección f.

perfidious*, per-fid´-i-os a
pérfido

perforate, per´-fo-reit v
perforar; horadar

perform, per-foarm´ v

hacer; ejecutar; (stage)
representar; **–ance,** s
ejecución f.; (stage)
representación f.

perfume, pĕr´-fiuum s
perfume m.; v perfumar

perhaps, per-jAps´ adv
quizá; acaso

peril, per´il s peligro m.;
–ous*, a peligroso

period, pi´-ri-od s periodo
m.; **–ical,** revista f.

periscope, pi´-ris-koup s
periscopio m.

perish, per´-ish v perecer;
(spoil) pasarse

perishable, per´-i-sha-bl a
perecedero

perjury, pĕr´-CHiu-ri s
perjurio m.

perk, pĕrk s beneficios m.
pl; adicionales; propinas
f. pl; v **to – up** reanimar

perm, pĕrm s permanente
f.; v abbr or **permute**
permutar

permanent*, pĕr´-ma-
nent a permanente

permeate, pĕr-mi-eit v
penetrar; (liquid) calar

permission, per-mish´-on
s permiso m.

permit, per-mit´ v permitir

permit, pĕr´-mit s permiso
m.

pernicious*, per-nish´os a

pernicioso

perpendicular, per-pen-
dik´-iu-la s & a*
perpendicular f.

perpetrate, pĕr´-pi-treit v
perpetrar; cometer

perpetual*, per-pet´-iu-al
a perpetuo

perplex, per-pleks´ v
confundir

persecute, pĕr´-si-kiuut v
perseguir

persecution, pĕr-si-kiuu´-
shon s persecución f.

perseverance, per-si-vii´-
rans s perseverancia f.

persevere, per-si-vir´ v
perseverar

persist, per-sist´ v persistir

person, pĕr´-son s persona
f.; **–al,** a personal; **–ality,**
s personalidad f.

personal computer, pĕr´-
son-al kom-piu-ta s
ordenador m.; personal

personify, per-son´-i-fai v
personificar

perspective, per-spek´-tiv
s perspectiva f.

perspicacity, pĕr-spi-kAs´-
i-ti s perspicacia f.

perspiration, pĕr-spi-rei´-
shon s sudor m.;
transpiración f.

perspire, pĕr-spair´ v
sudar; transpirar

persuade, per-sueid´ v
persuadir

persuasion, per-suei´-shon
s persuasión f.

pert*, pĕrt a petulante;
atrevido

pertain, per-tein´ v
pertenecer

pertinacity, per-ti-nAs´-i-
ti s pertinacia f.

pertinent*, pĕr´-ti-nent a
pertinente

perturb, per-tĕrb´ v
perturbar; agitar

perusal, pe-ruu´-sal s
examen m.

peruse, pe-ruus´ v
recorrer; examinar

perverse*, per-vĕrs´ a
perverso; depravado

pervert, per-vĕrt´ v
pervertir; falsear

pest, pest s peste f.;
pestilencia f.

pester, pes´-ta v molestar;
importunar

pet, pet s favorito m.;
(child) niño mimado
m.; v mimar; acariciar

petal, pet´-l s pétalo m.

petition, pi-tish´-on s
petición f.; memorial
m.; v pedir; dirigir un
memorial

petitioner, pi-tish´-on-a s
solicitante m.

petrify, pet´-ri-fai v
petrificar

petrol, pet´-rol s gasolina
f.; –guage, s indicador
de nivel de gasolina

petroleum, pi-trou´-li-om
s petróleo m.

petticoat, pet´-i-kout s
enaguas f. pl;
combinación f.

petty, pet-i a pequeño;
mezquino; despreciable

petulance, pet´-iu-lans s
petulancia f.

pew, piuu s banco de
iglesia m.

pewter, piuu´-ta s peltre
m.

phantom, fAn´-tom s
fantasma m.; espectro
m.

pharmacy, faarm-a-si s
farmacia f.

phase, fei s s fase f.

pheasant, fes ´-ant s faisán
m.

phenomenon, fi-nom´-i-
non s fenómeno m.

philosopher, fi-los´-o-fa s
filósofo m.

phlegm, flem s flema f.

phone, foun s = **telephone**
teléfono m.

phosphate, fos´-feit s
fosfato m.

phosphorus, fos´-fo-ros s
fósforo m.

photograph, fou´-to-grAf s
fotografía f.

photographer, fou-tog´-
raf-a s fotógrafo m.

phrase, freis s frase f.

physic, fis ´-ik s medicina
f.; –al*, a físico

physician, fi-sish´-an s
médico m.; físico m.

piano, pi-A´-nou s piano
m.; **grand** –, piano de
cola m.

pick, pik v picar; (choose)
escoger; (gather)
recoger; (teeth) mondar;
s pico m.; --**pocket**,
ratero m.; --**up**, v coger

pickle, pik´-l v encurtir;
–**s**, s pl encurtidos m. pl

picnic, pik´-nik s
merienda en el campo f.

picture, pik´-tiur s pintura
f.; cuadro m.; ilustración
f.; (portrait) retrato m.

pie, pai s pastel m.;
empanada f.

piece, piis s pedazo m.;
fragmento m.; (length)
pieza f.; (music, etc)
pieza f.; –**meal**, adv en
pedazos; --**work**, s obra
a destajo f.

pier, pir s muelle m.;
embarcadero m.

pierce, pirs v taladrar;

(ears) horadar

piercing, pir´-sing *a* penetrante; agudo

piety, pai´-i-ti *s* piedad *f.*; devoción *f.*

pig, pig *s* cerdo *m.*; puerco *m.*; --**iron,** hierro en lingotes, *m.*; --**sty,** pocilga *f.*

pigeon, piCH´-in *s* paloma *f.*; pichón *m.*

pigeonhole, piCH´-in-joul *s* casilla *f.*

pike, paik *s* pica *f.*; (fish) lucio *m.*

pilchard, pil´-cherd *s* sardina *f.*

pile, pail *s* estaca *f.*; (heap) montón *m.*; (carpet, etc) pelo *m.* *v* amontonar

piles, pail *s s pl* hemorroides *f. pl*

pileup, pail-öp *s aut* accidente *m.*; múltiple

pilfer, pil´-fa *v* ratear; hurtar

pilgrim, pil´-grim *s* peregrino *m.*

pilgrimage, pil´-gri-miCH *s* peregrinación *f.*

pill, pil *s* píldora *f.*

pillage, pil´-iCH *v* pillar; *s* pillaje *m.*

pillar, pil´-a *s* pilar *m.*; columna *f.*; --**box,**

buzón *m.*

pillory, pil´-o-ri *s* picota *f.*

pillow, pil´-ou *s* almohada *f.*

pillowcase, pil´-ou keis *s* funda *f.*; de almohada

pilot, pai´-lot *s* piloto *m.*; *v* pilotear

pimpernel, pim´-per-nel *s* pamplina *f.*

pimple, pim´-pl *s* grano *m.*; botón *m.*

pin, pin *s* alfiler *m.*; (safety) imperdible *m.*; *v* prender con alfileres

pinafore, pin´-a-fór *s* delantal *m.*

pincers, pin´-ser *s s pl* pinzas *f. pl*; tenazas *f. pl*

pinch, pinch *s* pellizco *m.*; *v* pellizcar; (press) apretar

pine, pain *v* languidecer; *s* (tree) pino *m.*

pineapple, pain´-Ap-el *s* piña *f.*; ananás *m.*

pinion, pin´-yon *s* piñón *m.*; *v* maniatar

pink, pingk *s* color de rosa *m.*

pinnacle, pin´-a-kl *s* pináculo *m.*

pint, paint *s* pinta *f.*

pioneer, pai-o-nir´ *s* colono *m.*; explorador *m.*; (mil) gastador *m.*

pious*, pai´-os *a* pío; devoto

pip, pip *s* pepita *f.*

pipe, paip *s* tubo *m.*; (water, gas, etc.) cañería *f.*; (tobacco) pipa *f.*; --**dream,** *s* sueño *m.*; ilusión *m.*

piquant*, pii´-kant *a* picante

pirate, pai´-ret *s* pirata *m.*

pistol, pis´-tl *s* pistola *f.*

piston, pis´-ton *s* émbolo *m.*; pistón *m.*

pit, pit *s* hoyo *m.*; (theater) platea *f.*; (mine) pozo *m.*

pitch, pich *s* pez *f.*; tono *m.*; *v* (naut) cabecear

pitcher, pich´-a *s* cántaro *m.*

pitchfork, pich´-foark *s* horca *f.*

piteous*, pi´-ti-os *a* lastimoso

pitfall, pit´-foal *s* trampa *f.*

pith, piz *s* (spinal) médula *f.*; (plant) meollo *m.*

pitiful*, pit´-i-ful *a* lastimoso

pitiless*, pit´-i-les *a* despiadado; cruel

pity, pit´-i *s* piedad *f.*; compasión *f.*

pivot, piv´-ot *s* pivote *m.*; eje *m.*

placard, plAk´-aard s
cartel m.; anuncio m.

place, pleis s lugar m.;
(locality) localidad f.; v
poner; colocar

placid*, plAs´-id a plácido;
apacible

plagiarism, plei´-CHi-a-ri s
m s plagio m.

plague, pleig s plaga f.;
peste f.; v molestar

plaice, pleis s platija f.

plain*, plein a (looks, etc)
ordinario; (simple)
sencillo; (clear) claro; s
llano m.; llanura f.; (in s
America) pampa f.

plaint, pleint s queja f.;
lamento m.; (legal)
alegato de quejas m.;
–iff, demandante m.;
–ive*, a (complaining)
quejoso; (sorrow)
dolorido

plait, plAt s trenza f.; v
trenzar; (fold) plegar

plan, plAn s plan m.;
proyecto m.; (drawing)
plano m.; v proyectar

plane, plein v cepillar; s
plano m.; (tool) cepillo
de carpintería m.; **–tree,**
plátano m.

planet, plAn´-et s planeta
m.

plank, plAngk s tabla f.

plant, plaant v plantar; s
planta f.; (mech)
maquinaria f.; **–ation,**
plantío m.; (coffee)
cafetal m.; (sugar)
ingenio m.; (tobacco)
tabacal m.

plaster, plaas´-ta v
enyesar; s yeso m.; (med)
emplasto m.; **sticking –,**
enyesar m.; **–of Paris,**
yeso mate m.

plastic, plAs´-tik s materia
plástica f.; a de plástico

plate, pleit v (chromium)
cromar; (nickel)
niquelar; (gold) dorar;
(silver) platear; s plato
m.; (family) vajilla de
plata f.; (photo) placa
f.; **–glass,** vidrio
cilindrado m.; luna f.

platform, plAt´-foarm s
plataforma f.; (station)
andén m.

platinum, plAt´-i-nom s
platino m.

play, plei v (game) jugar;
(music) tocar; s juego
m.; (theater)
representación f.; **–er,**
jugador m.; músico m.;
actor m.; actriz f.; **–ful,**
a juguetón; **–ground,** s
campo de juego m.; **–ing
cards,** naipes m. pl

plea, plii s proceso m.;
defensa f.; pretexto m.

plead, pliid v alegar; (law)
pleitear

pleasant*, ples´-ant a
agradable; placentero

please, pliis v agradar;
satisfacer; interj sírvase;
haga el favor; por favor;
to be –d, v complacerse;
estar contento

pleasing, pliis´-ing a
agradable; amable

pleasure, plesh´-er s
placer m.; gusto m.

pledge, pleCH s (pawn)
prenda f.; (oath)
promesa f.; v (pawn)
empeñar; (oath)
comprometerse a

plenty, plen´-ti s
abundancia f.

pleurisy, pliuu´-ri-si s
pleuresía f.

pliable, plai´-a-bl a
flexible; dócil; moldable

pliers, plai´-as, s pl alicates
m. pl

plight, plait s apuro m.;
aprieto m.

plod, plod v afanarse;
–along, (walk) andar
penosamente; **–der,** s
persona laboriosa f.

plot, plot v conspirar; s
intriga f.; (land) terreno

m., (story, etc) acción f.;
–ter, conspirador m.

plover, plŏv´-a s frailecillo m.

plow, plau v arar; s arado m.; **–man,** arador m.

pluck, plŏk v arrancar; desplumar; s valor m.

plug, plŏg v taponar. s tapón m.; obturador m.; (elec) enchufe m.; **spark –,** bujía (para tapón) f.

plum, plŏm s ciruela f.

plumage, plu´-meiCH s plumaje m.

plumb, plŏm v sondar; adv a plomo; s plomo m.

plumber, plŏm´-a s fontanero m.; plomero m.

plump, plŏmp a rollizo; (animal) gordo

plunder, plŏn´-da v saquear; s pillaje m.

plunderer, plŏn´-der-a s saqueador m.

plunge, plŏnCH v sumergirse, zambullirse; (dagger) hundir; s zambullida f.

plural, pluu´-ral s plural m.; a plural

plus, plŏs adv más

plush, plŏsh s felpa f.; peluche m.

ply, plai v (trade) ejercer;

s (plywood) madera de tres chapas f.; (plywool) lana de tres hilos f.; **–between,** v hacer el servicio entre…

pneumatic, niu-mAt´-ik a neumático

pneumonia, niu-mou´-ni a s pulmonía f.

poach, po ach v cazar en vedado; (eggs) escalfar; **–er,** s cazador furtivo m.

pocket, pok´-it v embolsar; s bolsillo m.

pod, pod s cápsula f.; (peas, etc) vaina f.

poem, pou´-em s poema m.

poet, pou´-et s poeta m.

poetry, pou´-et-ri s poesía f.; versos m. pl

point, point v indicar; apuntar; (sharpen) aguzar; s punto m.; (tip) punta f.; **–er,** apuntador m.; (dog) pachón m.

poise, pois v equilibrar. s (deportment) equilibro m.; (grace) donaire m.

poison, poi´-sn s veneno m.; v envenenar

poisonous, pois ´-nos a venenoso

poke, pouk s empujón m.; v empujar; (fire) atizar; **–r,** s atizador m.; (cards)

póker m.

pole, poul s pértiga f.; (geographical) polo m.; palo m.

police, po-lis´ s policía f.; **–man,** policía m.; guardia m.; **– station,** comisaría f.; puesto de guardia m.

policewoman, polis´-uu´-man s mujer f.; policía; agente f.

policy, pol´-i-si s política f.; (insurance) póliza f.

polish, pol´-ish s (gloss) brillo m.; (for shoes) betún m.; (furniture, etc) barniz m.; v pulir; (shoes) limpiar

polite*, po-lait a cortés; **–ness,** s cortesía f.

political, po-lit´-i-kal a político

politician, pol-i-tish´-an s político m.

politics, pol´-i-tiks s política f.

poll, poul s elección f.; v votar

pollen, pol-en s polen m.

pollute, po-liuut´ v manchar; contaminar; corromper

pollution, pol-uu-shon s polución f.; contaminación f.

polyester, pol-ii-est-*a* s
poliéster m.

polythene, pol-i-ziin s
poliétileno m.

pomade, pou-meid´ s
pomada f.

pomegranate, pŏm´-grA-net s granada f.

pomp, pomp s pompa f.;
–ous*, a pomposo

pond, pond s estanque m.

ponder, pon´-da v
ponderar; –ous*, a
ponderoso

pontiff, pon´-tif s
Pontífice m.

pony, pou´-ni s haca f.;
jaco m.; poney m.

poodle, puu´-dl s perro de
lanas m.

pool, puul s (water) balsa
f.; v (funds)
mancomunar intereses

poop, puup s (naut) popa
f.

poor*, púr a pobre. s los
pobres m. pl

pop, pop s (of a cork)
taponazo m.; v saltar

Pope, poup s Papa m.

poplar, pop´-la s álamo m.

poppy, pop´-i s amapola f.

populace, pop´-iu-las s
pueblo m.

popular*, pop´-iu-lr a
popular

populate, pop´-iu-leit v
poblar

population, po-piu-lei´-
shon s población f.

populous, pop´-iu-los a
populoso

porcelain, pórs´-lin s
porcelana f.

porch, pórch s pórtico m.;
porche m.

porcupine, por´-kiu-pain s
puerco espín m.

pore, pór s poro m.; –over,
v estudiar

pork, pŏrk s carne de
puerco f.

porous, pó´-ros a poroso

porpoise, póar´-pos s
puerco marino m.

porridge, por´-iCH s
gachas de avena f. pl

port, pórt s (wine) oporto
m.; (harbor) puerto m.;
(naut) babor m.; –hole,
babor m.; porta f.

portable, pór´-ta-bl a
portátil

portend, poar-tend´ v
pronosticar

portentous*, por-ten´-tos
a portentoso

porter, pór´-ta s (door)
portero m.; (luggage)
mozo m.; –age, porte m.

portfolio, pórt-fou´-li-ou s
cartera porta papeles m.;

(government)
ministerio m.

portion, pór´-shon s
porción f.; (share) parte
f.

portly, pórt´-li a
corpulento; majestuoso

portmanteau, pórt-mAn´-
tou s maleta f.

portrait, pór´-tret s retrato
m.

portray, pór-trei´ v
retratar; (describe)
describir

pose, pou s s postura f.; v
colocar; –as, pasar por

position, po-sish´-on s
posición f.; (job)
colocación f.

positive*, pos´-i-tiv a
positivo; (certain) cierto

possess, po-ses´ v poseer;
–ion, s posesión f.

possessor, po-ses´-er s
poseedor m.

possibility, pos-i-bil´-i-ti s
posibilidad f.

possible, pos´-i-bl a
posible

possibly, pos´-i-bli adv
posiblemente

post, poust s correo m.;
(wood, etc) poste m.;
(job) empleo m.; v echar
al correo; –age, s
franqueo m.; –card,

tarjeta postal f.; **–date,** v posfechar; **–er,** s cartel m.; **–paid,** a franco de porte; **–man,** s cartero m.; **––master,** administrador de correos m.; **––mortem,** autopsia f.; **––office,** correos m. pl; **–pone,** v diferir, posponer; **–script,** s posdata f.

posterior, post-i´-ri-a a posterior

posterity, pos-těr´-i-ti s posteridad f.

posture, pos´-tiur s postura f.

pot, pot s pote m.; (flower) tiesto m.; (cooking) olla f.

potash, pot´-Ash s potasa f.

potato, pou-tei´-tou s patata f.

potent*, pou´-tent a potente; eficaz; **–ial,** s potencial m.; a potencial; eficaz

potion, pou´-shon s poción f.

pottery, pot´-er-i s alfarería f.

pouch, pauch s bolsillo m.; (tobacco) tabaquera f.

poulterer, poul´-ter-a s

pollero m.; gallinero m.

poultice, poul´-tis s cataplasma f.

poultry, poul´-tri s aves de corral f. pl

pounce, pauns v (on, upon) echarse sobre

pound, paund s libra esterlina f.; (weight) libra f.; (animals) corral m.; v (pulverize) machacar

pour, pór v verter; (rain) llover a cántaros

pour out, póraut v echar; (serve) servir

pout, paut v enfurruñarse

poverty, pov´-er-ti s pobreza f.

powder, pau´-da s polvo m.; (gun) pólvora f.; (face) polvos m. pl; v pulverizar; (face) darse polvos

power, pau´-a s poder m.; (mech) fuerza f.; (state) potencia f.; **–ful*,** a poderoso; **–less*,** impotente

pox, poks, **small––,** s viruelas f. pl; **chicken––,** viruelas locas f. pl

practicability, prAk´-ti-ka-bil´-i-ti s posibilidad f.

practical*, prAk´-ti-kl a practico

practice, prAk´-tis s práctica f.; (custom) costumbre f.; (professional) clientela f.; (exercise) ejercicio m.; v ejercitarse; (profession) ejercer

practitioner, prAk-tish´-on-a s médico m.

praise, preis v alabar; s alabanza f.; elogio m.

praiseworthy, preis ´-uěr-Di a digno de alabanza

prance, praans v cabriolar; (fig) pavonearse

prank, prAngk s travesura f.; jugarreta f.

prattle, prAt´-l v charlar; s charla f.

prawn, proan s langostino m.

pray, prei v orar; rezar

prayer, preir s oración f.; **–book,** devocionario m.; **Lord's Prayer,** Padre Nuestro m.

preach, priich v predicar; **–er,** s predicador m.

preamble, prii´-Am-bl s preámbulo m.

precarious*, pri-ké´-ri-os a precario

precaution, pri-koa´-shon s precaución f.

precede, pri-siid´ v preceder

precedence, prii-sii´-dens *s* precedencia *f*.

precedent, pres´-ii-dent *s* (example) precedente *m*.

precept, pri´-sept *s* precepto *m*.

preceptor, pri-sep´-ta *s* preceptor *m*.

precinct, prii´-singkt *s* recinto *m*.; distrito electoral *m*.

precious*, presh´-os *a* precioso

precipice, pres´-i-pis *s* precipicio *m*.

precise*, pri-sais´ *a* exacto; preciso; **–ness,** *s* exactitud *f*.

precision, pri-sish´-on *s* precisión *f*.

preclude, pri-kiuud´ *v* excluir; impedir

precocious*, pri-kou´-shos *a* precoz

predatory, pred´-a-to-ri *a* de rapiña; rapaz

predecessor, prii-dii-ses´-a *s* predecesor *m*.

predicament, pri-dik´-a-ment *s* predicamento *m*.

predicate, pred´-i-ket *s* (grammar) atributo *m*.; predicar

predict, pri-dikt´ *v* predecir

prediction, pri-dik´-shon *s* predicción *f*.

predominant*, pri-dom´-i-nant *a* predominante

preeminent*, prii-em´-i-nent *a* preeminente

preface, pref´-is *s* prefacio *m*.

prefect, prii´-fekt *s* prefecto *m*.

prefer, pri-fër´ *v* preferir

preferable, pref´-er-a-bl *a* preferible

preference, pref´-er-ens *s* preferencia *f*.

prefix, prii-fiks´ *v* anteponer; *s* prefijo *m*.

pregnancy, preg´-nan-si *s* preñez *f*.; embarazo *m*.

pregnant, preg´-nant *a* embarazada; encinta; (animals) preñada

prejudice, pre´-CHiu-dis *v* perjudicar; predisponer; *s* perjuicio *m*.; **without –,** sin prejuicio

prejudicial*, preCH-u-dish´-al *a* perjudicial

prelate, prel´-et *s* prelado *m*.

preliminary, prii-lim´-i-na-ri *s* & *a* preliminar *m*.

prelude, pre´-liuud *v* preludiar; *s* preludio *m*.

premature*, prem´-a-tiúr

a prematuro

premeditate, pri-med´-i-teit *v* premeditar

premier, prii´-mi-a *s* primer ministro *m*.; *a* primero

premises, prem´-i-sis *s pl* posesiones *f. pl*; edificio *m*.; predio *m*.

premium, prii´-mi-om *s* premio *m*.; prima *f*.

preparation, prep-a-rei´-shon *s* preparación *f*.

prepare, pri-pér´ *v* preparar

prepay, pri-pei´ *v* pagar adelantado

prepossessing, pri-po-ses´-ing *a* simpático; atractivo

preposterous*, pri-pos´-ter-os *a* absurdo

prerogative, prii-rog´-a-tiv *s* prerrogativa *f*.

prescribe, pri-skraib´ *v* prescribir

prescription, priis-krip´-shon *s* prescripción *f*.

presence, pres´-ens *s* presencia *f*.; **–of mind,** presencia de ánimo *f*.

present, pri-sent´ *v* presentar; (gift) regalar

present, pres´-ent *s* regalo *m*.; *a* presente; **–ation,** *s* presentación *f*.; **–ly,** *adv* luego; en seguida

presentiment, pri-sen´-ti-ment s presentimiento m.

preservation, pre s-er-vei´-shon s (state, condition) preservación f.

preserve, pri-sĕrv´ v preservar; conservar; guardar; (fruit) confitar; **-s,** s pl; confitura f.

preside, pri-said´ v presidir

president, pres´-i-dent s presidente m.

press, pres s prensa f.; v apretar; (fruit) exprimir; (clothes) prensar; **-ing,** a urgente

pressman, pres´-mAn s periodista m.

pressure, presh´-er s presión f.; urgencia f.

presume, pri-siuum v presumir; (dare) atreverse

presumption, pri-sŏmp´-shon s presunción f.

pretend, pri-tend´ v pretender

pretense, pri-tens´ s pretencia f.; pretexto m.

pretentious*, pri-ten´-shos a presuntuoso

pretext, pri-text´ s

pretexto m.

pretty, pri´-ti a lindo; bonito

prevail, pri-veil´ v prevalecer; **-upon,** persuadir

prevalent*, prev´-a-lent a prevaleciente

prevaricate, pri-vAr´-i-keit v prevaricar; mentir

prevent, pri-vent´ v impedir; **-ion,** s prevención f.; **-ive*,** a preventivo

preview, prii-viuu n (of film) preestreno m.; (fig) anticipo; vista f.; anticipada

previous*, prii´-vi-os a previo; anterior

prevision, pri-vi´-shon s previsión f.

prey, prei s presa f.; víctima f.; v robar; s botín m.

price, prais s precio m.; **-less,** a inapreciable

prick, prik v picar; s picadura f.; **-le,** espina f.; **-ly,** a espinoso

pride, praid s orgullo m.; v enorgullecerse

priest, priist s sacerdote m.

priggish, prig´-ish a afectado; petulante

prim, prim a afectado; (dress) peripuesto

primary, prai´-ma-ri a primario; fundamental

primary school, prai´-ma-ri skuul s escuela f.; primaria

primate, prai´-met s primado m.

prime, praim s (of life) flor f.; a (quality) selecto; v preparar; **-minister,** s primer ministro m.; premier m.

primer, praim´-a-s s libro de prima instrucción m.

primitive, prim´-i-tiv a primitivo

primrose, prim´-rous s primavera f.

prince, prins s príncipe m.

princely, prins´-li a grande; noble; regio; principesco

princess, prin´-ses s princesa f.

principal, prin-si-pal s director m.; jefe m.; (funds) principal m.; a* principal

principle, prin-si-pl s principio m.

print, print v imprimir; s impresión f.; (photo) positiva f.; **-er,** impresor m.; **-ing,** impresión f.

prior, prai´-or *s* prior *m*.; *a* anterior; *adv* antes de; **–ity**, *s* prioridad *f*.; **–y**, priorato *m*.

prism, prism *s* prisma *m*.; **–atic**, *a* prismático

prison, pri-sn *s* prisión *f*.; cárcel *f*.

prisoner, prii´-son-a *s* prisionero *m*.; preso *m*.

privacy, prai´-va-si *s* retraimiento *m*.

private*, prai-vet *a* privado; personal; secreto

privation, prai-vei´-shon *s* privación *f*.

privilege, priv´-i-liCH *s* privilegio *m*.; *v* privilegiar

prize, prais *s* premio *m*.; *v* apreciar

probable, prob´-a-bl *a* probable

probate, prou´-beit *s* rerificación de un testamento *f*.

probation, prou-bei´-shon *s* probación *f*.; prueba *f*.; **–er**, meritorio *m*.; (*eccl*) novicio *m*.

probe, proub *v* sondar; *s* sonda *f*.

probity, prob´-i-ti *s* probidad *f*.

problem, prob´-lem *s*

problema *m*.

procedure, pro-sii´-diú *r s* proceder *m*.; (law) procedimiento *m*.

proceed, pro-siid´ *v* proceder; continuar; **–ings**, *s pl* procedimiento *m*.; (law) proceso *m*.; rédito *m*.

proceeds, pro´-siids *s pl* producto *m*.

process, prou´-ses *s* proceso *m*.; curso *m*.

procession, pro-sesh´-on *s* procesión *f*.

proclaim, pro-kleim´ *v* proclamar; publicar

proclamation, prok-la-mei´-shon *s* proclamación *f*.

proclivity, pro-kliv´-i-ti *s* propensión *f*.; inclinación *f*.

procrastination, pro-krAsti-nei´-shon *s* dilación *f*.

proctor, prok´-ta *s* (university) censor *m*.; juéz escolástico *m*.

procurable, pro-kiú´-ra-bl *a* asequible

procure, pro-kiúr´ *v* conseguir; procurar

prod, prod *v* aguijonear; *s* aguijón *m*.

prodigal*, prod´-i-gal *a* pródigo

prodigious*, pro-diCH´-os *a* prodigioso

prodigy, prod´-iCH-i *s* prodigio *m*.

produce, pro´-diuus´ *s* producto *m*.; producción *f*.

produce, pro-diuus´ *v* producir. *s* producto *m*.; **–r**, productor *m*.; (stage) director *m*.

product, prod´-ŏkt *s* producto *m*.; **–ion**, producción *f*.; (stage) representación *f*.

profane, pro-fein´ *v* profanar; *a** profano

profess, pro-fes´ *v* profesar; declarar; **–ion**, *s* profesión *f*.; carrera *f*.; **–ional**, *a* profesional

professor, pro-fess´-a *s* profesor *m*.

proficiency, pro-fish´-en-si *s* adelanto *m*.; abilidad *f*.

proficient*, pro-fish´-ent *a* adelantado; versado; proficiente

profile, prou´-fail *s* perfil *m*.

profit, prof´-it *s* ganancia *f*.; utilidad *f*.; *v* ganar; **–able**, *a* provechoso; **–eer**, *s* acaparador *m*.

profligate, prof´-li-guet *a* licencioso; disoluto;

perdido

profound*, pro-faund´ *a* profundo

profuse*, pro-fiuus´ *a* profuso

prognosticate, prog-nos´-ti-keit *v* pronosticar

program, prou´-grAm *s* programa *m.*

programmer, prou´-grAm-a *s* programador *m.*

progress, pro-gres´ *v* progresar; adelantar

progress, prou´-gres *s* progreso *m.*; curso *m.*

prohibit, prou-jib´-it *v* prohibir

prohibition, prou-jib-i´-shon *s* prohibición *f.*

project, pro-CHekt´ *v* proyectar; sobresalir; *s* proyecto *m.*; –ile, proyectil *m.*; –ion, proyección *f.*; –or, proyector *m.*

proletarian, prou-li-té´-ri-an *s* & *a* proletario *m.*

prologue, prou´-log *s* prólogo *m.*

prolong, prou-long´ *v* prolongar

promenade, prom-i-naad´ *s* paseo *m.*; *v* pasearse

prominent*, prom´-i-nent *a* prominente

promiscuous*, pro-mis´-

kiu-os *a* promiscuo

promise, pro´-mis *s* promesa *f.*; *v* prometer

promissory note, prom´-is-o-ri nout *s* pagaré *m.*

promote, pro-mout´ *v* promover; fomentar

promoter, pro-mou´-ta *s* promotor *m.*

promotion, pro-mou´-shon *s* promoción *f.*

prompt, prompt *a* pronto; *v* sugerir; (stage) apuntar; –er, *s* apuntador *m.*; –ly, *adv* en punto

promulgate, pro´-mul-gueit *v* promulgar; publicar

prone, proun *a* propenso; inclinado

prong, prong *s* púa *f.*; punta *f.*

pronoun, prou´-naun *s* pronombre *m.*

pronounce, pro-nauns´ *v* pronunciar; (sentence) dar

pronunciation, pro-nŏn-si-ei´-shon *s* pronunciación *f.*

proof, pruuf *s* prueba *f.*; *a* a prueba de

prop, prop *s* apoyo *m.*; puntal *m.*; *v* sostener

propaganda, prop-a-

guan´-da *s* propaganda *f.*

propagate, prop´-a-gueit *v* propagar

propel, pro-pel´ *v* impeler; –lent, *s* propulsor *m.*; *a* propulsante; –ler, *s* hélice *mf.*

proper*, prop´-a *a* propio; apto; decoroso; decente

property, prop´-er-ti *s* propiedad *f.*; bienes *m. pl*

prophecy, prof´-i-si, profecía *f.*

prophesy, prof´-i-sai *v* profetizar

prophet, prof´-et *s* profeta *m.*; profetisa *f.*

propitious*, pro-pish´-os *a* propicio

proportion, pro-pór´-shon *s* proporción *f.*

proposal, pro-pou´-sal *s* propuesta *f.*; (marriage) declaración *f.*

propose, pro-pous´ *v* proponer; declararse

proposition, pro-pos-ish´-on *s* proposición *f.*

proprietor, pro-prai´-e-ta *s* propietario *m.*; dueño *m.*

propriety, pro-prai´-e-ti *s* propiedad *f.*; decoro *m.*

propulsion, pro-pŏl´-shon *s* propulsión *f.*; impulso

m.

proscribe, pro-skraib´ *v*
proscribir

prose, prous *s* prosa *f.*

prosecute, pros´-i-kiut *v*
(law) procesar

prosecution, pros-i-kiu´-
shon *s* prosecución *f.*

prosecutor, pros´-i-kiu-*ta*
s acusador *m.*

prospect, pros´-pekt *s*
perspectiva *f.; v* explorar

prospective*, pros-pek´-
tiv *a* en perspectiva

prospectus, pros-pek´-tos *s*
prospecto *m.*

prosper, pros´-*pa v*
prosperar; **–ity,** *s*
prosperidad *f.;* **–ous*,** *a*
próspero

prostitute, pros´-ti-tiuut *s*
prostituta *f.*

prostrate, pros-treit´ *v*
prosternarse; *a* postrado;
postrarse

prostration, pros-trei´-
shon *s* postración *f.*

protect, pro-tekt´ *v*
proteger

protection, pro-tek´-shon
s protección *f.*

protest, pro-test´ *v*
protestar; *s* protesto *m.*

protract, pro-trAkt´ *v*
prolongar; diferir

protrude, pro-truud´ *v*

sobresalir

proud*, praud *a* orgulloso

prove, pruuv *v* probar

proverb, prov´-*erb s*
proverbio *m.*

provide, pro-vaid´ *v*
proveer; estipular

providence, prov´-i-dens *s*
providencia *f.*

provident*, prov´-i-dent *a*
providente

provider, pro-vai´-*da s*
proveedor *m.*

province, prov´-ins *s*
provincia *f.;* (sphere)
incumbencia *f.*

provision, pro-vish´-on *s*
provisión *f.;*
estipulación *f.;* **–al,** *a**
provisorio;
provisionalmente

provisions, pro-vish´-on *s*
s pl comestibles *m. pl;*
provisiones

provocation, prov-o-kei´-
shon *s* provocación *f.*

provoke, pro-vouk´ *v*
provocar

provost, prov´-ost *s*
preboste *m.*

prowl, praul *v* rondar;
rastrear

proximity, prok-sim´-i-ti *s*
proximidad *f.*

proxy, prok´-si *s*
apoderado *m.;* **by –,** por

poder

prude, pruud *s* mojigata
f.; **–nce,** prudencia *f.;*
–nt, *a* prudente; **–ry,** *s*
mojigatería *f.*

prudish*, pruu´-dish *a*
remilgado; mojigato *m.*

prune, pruun *s* ciruela
pasa *f.; v* (trees) podar

pry, prai *v* escudriñar;
acechar

psalm, saam *s* salmo *m.*

pseudonym, siuu´-do-nim
s seudónimo *m.*

psychiatrist, sai-kai-*a*-trist
s psiquiatra *mf.*

psychiatry, sai-kai-*a*-tri *s*
psiquiatría *f.*

psychoanalyst, sai-ko-A´-
nal´-ist *s* psicoanalista
mf.

psychological, sai-kol-o-
CH-ik-*al a* psicológico

psychology, sai-kol´-*o*-CHi
s psicología *f.*

psychopath, sai-kou-pAz *s*
psicópata *mf.*

public, pŏb´-lik *s* el
público *m.; a** público;
–an, *s* publicano *m.;*
tabernero *m.*

publication, pŏb-li-kei´-
shon *s* publicación *f.;*
(notification)
promulgación *f.*

publicity, pŏb-li´-sit-i *s*

publicidad f.

publish, pŏb´-lish v publicar; (books) editar

publisher, pŏb´-lish-a s editor m.; editorial f.

pucker, pŏk´-a v fruncir; s pliegue m.

pudding, pud´-ing s pudín m.

puddle, pŏd´-l s charco m.

puerile, piu´-er-ail a pueril

puff, pŏf v soplar; s (breath) soplo m.; (of wind) ráfaga f.; **powder** –, polvera f.; polvearse f.

puffy, pŏf-i a hinchado; inflado

pug, pŏg s (dog) perro faldero m.; –**nacious,** a pugnaz; –**nosed,** nacho

pull, pul s tirón m.; (tension) nariz respingona f.; v tirar; –**down,** derrumbar; (lower) bajar; –**out,** sacar; extraer; –**up,** levantar; alzar

pullet, pul´-et s pollito m.; pollita f.

pulley, pul´-i s polea f.; garrucha f.

pullover, pul-ou´-va s jersey m.; suéter m.

pulp, pŏlp s wood––, pulpa de madera f.

pulpit, pul´-pit s púlpito m.

pulse, pŏls s pulso m.

pumice, pŏm´-is-ston s piedra pómez f.

pump, pŏmp s bomba f.

pumpkin, pŏmp´-kin s calabaza f.

pun, pŏn s juego de palabras m.

punch, pŏnch v puñetazo m.; perforar; s metido m.; perforador m.; (drink) ponche m.

punctilious*, pŏng-ktil´-i-os a puntilloso

punctual*, pŏng´-ktiu-al a puntual

punctuate, pŏng´-ktiu-eit v puntuar

punctuation, pŏng-ktiu-ei´-shon s puntuación f.

puncture, pŏng-ktiur s punción f.; (tire) pinchazo m.; v punzar; (tire) pinchar

pungency, pŏn´-CHen-si s picante m.; acerbidad f.

pungent*, pŏn´-CHent a picante; acre; mordaz

punish, pŏn´-ish v castigar; –**able,** a punible

punishment, pŏn´-ish-ment s castigo m.; pena

f.

punitive, piuu´-ni-tiv a penal; punitivo

punt, pŏnt s lancha de fondo plano f.

puny, piuu´-ni a insignificante; débil

pupil, piuu´-pil s alumno m.; (eye) pupila f.

puppet, pŏp´-et s muñeco m.; títere m.

puppy, pŏp´-i s cachorro m.

purchase, pėr´-chis v comprar; s compra f.

purchaser, pėr´-chis-a s comprador m.

pure*, piú r a puro; (chaste) casto

purgative, pėr´-ga-tiv s purgante m.

purgatory, pėr´-ga-to-ri s purgatorio m.

purge, pėrCH v purgar; purificar; (med) purgar

purify, piú´-ri-fai v purificar

purity, piú´-ri-ti s pureza f.

purloin, pėr-loin´ v hurtar; robar

purple, pėr´-pl s púrpura f.; a purpúreo; morado

purport, pėr´-port s sentido m. v significar

purpose, pėr´-pos s

intención *f.*; *v*
proponerse; *s* objetivo *f.*
purposely, pĕr´-pos-li *adv*
a propósito
purr, pĕr *v* ronronear
purse, pĕrs *s* bolsa *f.*;
porta-monedas *m.*;
monedero *m.*
purser, pĕr´-*sa s*
sobrecargo *m.*
pursue, pĕr-siuu´ *v*
perseguir; continuar
pursuit, pĕr-siuut´ *s*
persecución *f.*; **–s,** tareas
f. pl
purveyor, pĕr-vei-*a s*
proveedor *m.*
pus, pŏs *s* pus *m.*; materia
f.
push, push *s* empujón *m.*;
v empujar
pushing, push´-ing *a*
(enterprising)
emprendedor
puss, pus *s* micho *m.*
put, put *v* poner; colocar;
–off, posponer; **–on,**
ponerse
putrefy, piuu´-tri-fai *v*
pudrirse; corromperse
putrid, piuu´-trid *a*
podrido; pútrido
putty, pŏt´-i *s* masilla *f.*
puzzle, pŏs ´-l *v*
confundir; *s* problema
m.; (pastime)

rompecabezas *m.*;
crossword –, crucigrama
m.
pyramid, pir´-*a*-mid *s*
pirámide *f.*
python, pai´-zŏn *s* boa *f.*;
pitón *m.*

quack, kuAk *v* graznar; *s* curandero *m.*; charlatán *m.*; **–ing,** graznido *m.*

quadrant, kuod´-rant *s* cuadrante *m.*

quadrille, kua-dril´ *s* contradanza *f.*

quadruped, kuod´-ru-ped *s* cuádrúpedo *m.*

quadruple, kuod´-ru-pl *a* cuádruplo

quagmire, kuAg´-mair *s* tremedal *m.*

quail, kueil *s* codorniz *f.*

quaint*, kueint *a* curioso; agradable; **–ness,** *s* singularidad *f.*

quake, kueik *v* temblar; *s* temblor *m.*; **earth- –,**

terremoto *m.*

quaker, kuei´-ka *s* cuáquero *m.*

qualification, kuol´-i-fi-kei´-shon *s* calificación *f.*; requisito *m.*

qualified, kuol´-i-faid *a* apto; competente; capacitado; cualificado

qualify, kuol´-i-fai *v* calificar; habilitarse; (degree) obtener un grado

qualities, kuol´-i-tes, *s pl* cualidades *f. pl*; (things) propiedades *f. pl*

quality, kuol´-i-ti *s* calidad *f.*; (nobility) distinción *f.*

quandary, koun´-da-ri *s* perplejidad *f.*

quantity, koun´-ti-ti *s* cantidad *f.*

quarantine, kour´-an-tiin *s* cuarentena *f.*

quarrel, kour´-el *s* riña *f.*; pendencia *f.*; *v* reñir

quarrelsome, kuor´-el-som *a* pendenciero

quarry, kuor´-i *s* cantera *f.*; (prey) presa *f.*

quart, kuoart *s* cuarto de galón *m.*

quarter, kuoar´-ta *v* hacer cuartos; *s* cuarto *m.*; cuartel *m.*; (period) trimestre *m.*; **–ly,** *a* trimestral; (naut) cabo de brigadas *m.*

quartet, kuoar´-tet *s* cuarteto *m.*

quartz, kuoarts *s* cuarzo *m.*

quash, kuosh *v* exprimir; (a verdict) anular

quaver, kuei´-va *v* gorjear; *s* (mus) corchea *f.*

quay, kii *s* muelle *m.*

queen, kuiin *s* reina *f.*

queer*, ukir *a* raro; extraño

quell, kuel *v* reprimir; (allay) aquietar

quench, kuench *v* apagar; (thirst) calmar

querulous*, kuer´-u-los *a*

querelloso; quejoso
query, (see **question**)
quest, kuest s busca f.;
investigación f.; informe
m.
question, kues´-tyon v
interrogar; (doubt)
dudar; s pregunta f.;
–able, a cuestionable; –
mark, s punto de
interrogación m.
queue, kiuu s cola f.; fila
f.
quibble, kui´-bl v hacer
uso de argucias; s
subterfugio m.; evasiva
f.
quick*, kuik a rápido;
(wit, etc) vivo; **–en,** v
animar; (hasten)
apresurar; **–lime,** s cal
viva f.; **–ness,** rapidez f.;
–sand, arena movediza
f.; **–silver,** azogue m.;
mercurio m.
quiet, kuai´-et s quietud f.;
a* quieto; tranquilo
quill, kuil s (pen) pluma
de ave f.
quilt, kuilt s colcha f.
quince, kuins s membrillo
m.
quinine, kuiin´-in s
quinina f.
quit, kuit v salir de; **–s,**
adv en paz; desistir

quite, kuait adv
enteramente;
totalmente
quiver, kuiv´-a v temblar;
s (sheath) aljaba f.
quiz, kuis s
(interrogation)
interrogatorio; examen;
(inquiry) enquesta; v
interrogar; **– show**
concurso de preguntas y
respuestas
quota, kuou´-ta s cuota f.
quotation, kuou-tei´-shon
s citación f.; (price)
cotización f.
quote, kuout v citar;
(price) cotizar

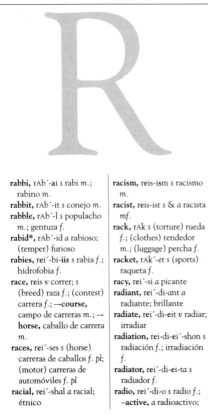

rabbi, rAb´-ai s rabi m.; rabino m.

rabbit, rAb´-it s conejo m.

rabble, rAb´-l s populacho m.; gentuza f.

rabid*, rAb´-id a rabioso; (temper) furioso

rabies, rei´-bi-iis s rabia f.; hidrofobia f.

race, reis v correr; s (breed) raza f.; (contest) carrera f.; **–course,** campo de carreras m.; **– horse,** caballo de carrera m.

races, rei´-ses s (horse) carreras de caballos f. pl; (motor) carreras de automóviles f. pl

racial, rei´-shal a racial; étnico

racism, reis-ism s racismo m.

racist, reis-ist s & a racista mf.

rack, rAk s (torture) rueda f.; (clothes) tendedor m.; (luggage) percha f.

racket, rAk´-et s (sports) raqueta f.

racy, rei´-si a picante

radiant, rei´-di-ant a radiante; brillante

radiate, rei´-di-eit v radiar; irradiar

radiation, rei-di-ei´-shon s radiación f.; irradiación f.

radiator, rei´-di-ei-ta s radiador f.

radio, rei´-di-o s radio f.; **–active,** a radioactivo;

–activity, s radioactividad f.; **–– active waste** residuos radioactivos

radio station, rei´-di-o stei´-shon s emisora f.

radish, rAd´-ish s rábano m.; **horse –,** rábano picante m.

radium, rei´-di-om s radium m.

radius, rei´-di-os s radio m.

raffle, rAf´-l s rifa f.; sorteo m.; v rifar

raft, raaft s balsa f.; almadía f.

rafter, raaf´-ta s cabrio m.; viga f., traviesa f.

rag, rAg s trapo m.; **–ged,** a harapiento

rage, reiCH s rabia f.; furor m.; v enfurecerse

raid, reid v invadir; s incursión f.

rail, reil v injuriar; s (railroad) riel m.; (stair) baranda f.; **–lery,** chocarrería f.

raiment, rei´-ment s ropa f.

rain, rein v llover; s lluvia f.; **–bow,** arco iris m.; **–coat,** impermeable m.; **–fall,** aguacero m.; (measure) caída de agua

f.; **–water,** agua de lluvia
f.; **–y,** a lluvioso

raise, reis v (pick up)
recoger; (heighten)
elevar; (pull up)
levantar; (crops)
cultivar

raisin, rei´-sin s pasa f.

rake, reik s rastrillo m.;
libertino m.; v rastrillar;
(fire) atizar

rally, rAl´-i v reunir;
reanimar

ram, rAm v meter afuerza
m.; (battering) ariete
m.; v apisonar

ramble, rAm´-bl s paseo
m.; correteo m.; v
pasearse

rampant, rAm´-pant a (fig)
exuberante

rampart, rAm´-paart s
terraplén m.; muralla f.

rancid, rAn´-sid a rancio

rancor, rAng´-ka s rencor
m.

random, rAn´-dom, **at –,**
adv al azar

range, reinCH s (kitchen)
cocina f.; (extent)
extensión f.;
(mountain) cordillera f.;
(practice) campo de tiro
m.; (projectile) alcance
m.; v arreglar, ordenar;
–finder, s (photog)

telémetro m.; **–r,** s
guardabosque m.

rank, rAngk a (taste,
smell) rancio. s grado
m.; (row) fila f.; **–and
file,** la tropa f.

ransack, rAn´-sAk v
saquear; escudriñar

ransom, rAn´-som s
rescate m.; v rescatar

rap, rAp s golpe seco m.; v
(hit) golpear; (knock)
llamar; tocar

rape, reip s rapto m.;
violación f.; v violar

rapid*, rAp´-id a rápido;
(stream) raudo; **–ity,** s
rapidez f.; **–s,** rabión m.

rapier, rei´-pi-a s espadin
m.

rapture, rAp´-tiur s rapto
m.; éxtasis m.

rare*, rér a raro;
(precious) valioso;
(thin) ralo

rarefy, rei´-fai v enrarecer;
enralar

rarity, ré´-ri-ti s rareza f.

rascal, raas´-kl s pícaro m.;
bribón m.

rash, rAsh s (skin)
sarpullido m. a
temerario; **–er,** s magra
f.; lonja f.; **–ness,**
temeridad f.

rasp, raasp s raspador m.; v

raspar

raspberry, raas´-ber-i s
frambuesa f.

rat, rAt s rata f.; **–trap,**
ratonera f.

rate, reit s (proportion)
razón f.; taza f.;
(exchange) tipo m.;
(tax) contribución f.;
(price) precio m.;
(speed) razón f.; v
(value) tasar

rather, raaD´-a adv dicho;
(prefer) más bien; mejor

ratify, rAt´-i-fai v ratificar

ratio, rei´-shi-ou s
proporción f.

ration, rei´-shon s ración
f.

rational*, rAsh´-on-al a
racional; razonable

rattle, rAt´-l v matraquear;
s matraqueo m.;
(instrument) matraca f.;
(toy) sonajero m.

rattlesnake, rAt´-l-sneik s
culebra de cascabel f.

ravage, rAv´-iCH s saqueo
m.; v saqueat

rave, reiv v enfurecerse;
–about, entusiasmarse
locamente

raven, reiv´-n s cuervo m.

ravenous, rAv´-en-os a
voraz

ravine, rA-viin´ s barranca

f.; cañada f.

raving, rei´-ving *a* delirante; **–mad,** loco rematado

ravish, rʌv´-ish *v* arrebatar; violar; (charm) encantar; **–ing,** *a* encantador

raw, roɑ *a* crudo; (wound) en carne viva

ray, rei *s* rayo *m*.

raze, reis *v* arrasar

razor, rei´-sɑ *s* navaja de afeitar *f*.; (safety –) navajade afeitar *f*.; (electric –) maquina de afeitar; **–blade,** hoja de afeitar *f*.

reach, riiCH *v* (extend to) alcanzar; (arrive) llegar

react, rii-Akt´ *v* reaccionar; **–ion,** *s* reacción *f*.; **–or,** *s* reactor

read, riid *v* leer; estudiar; **–er,** *s* lector *m*.; corrector *m*.; **–ing,** lectura *f*.; interpretación *f*.

readily, red´-i-li *adv* prontamente; de buena gana

readiness, red´-i-nes *s* prontitud *f*.; buena voluntad *f*.

ready, red´-i *a* listo;

pronto; **–made,** ya hecho

real*, rii´-ɑl *a* real; verdadero

reality, rii´-ɑ-li-ti *s* realidad *f*.

realize, rii´-ɑ-lais *v* darse cuenta; (cash) realizar

realm, relm *s* reino *m*.; dominio *m*.

ream, riim *s* resma *f*.

reap, riip *v* segar; recoger; **–er,** *s* segador *m*.; **–ing machine,** segadora mecánica *f*.

reappear, rii-a-pir´ *v* reaparecer

rear, riir *v* criar; (prance) encabritarse; *s* (mil.) retaguardia *f*.; (background) fondo *m*.

rear admiral, riir-Ad´-mi-ral *s* contralmirante *m*.

reason, rii´-sn *v* razonar; *s* razón *f*.

reasonable, rii´-sn-a-bl *a* razonable

reassure, rii-a-shúr´ *v* tranquilizar

rebate, rii-beit´ *v* rebajar; *s* rebaja *f*.

rebel, reb´-l *s* rebelde *m*.

rebel, ri-bel´ *v* rebelarse; **–lion,** *s* rebelión *f*.

rebound, ri-baund´ *v* rebotar; *s* rebote *m*.

rebuff, ri-böf´ *v* desairar; *s* repulsa *f*.; rechazo *m*.

rebuke, ri-biuuk´ *v* reprender; *s* reprensión *f*.; regaño *m*.

recall, ri-koal´ *v* revocar; recordar

recant, ri-kAnt´ *v* retractarse

recapitulate, ri-ka-pit´-iu-leit *v* recapitular

recede, ri-siid´ *v* retroceder; cejar

receipt, ri-siit´ *s* recibo *m*.; *v* dar recibo

receipts, ri-siits´ *s pl* (business) ingresos *m*. *pl*; recibos *m*. *pl*

receive, ri-siiv´ *v* recibir; **–r,** *s* receptor *m*.; (bankruptcy) síndico *m*.

recent*, rii´-sent *a* reciente

receptacle, ri-sep´-ta-kl *s* receptáculo *m*.

reception, ri-sep´-shon *s* recepción *f*.

recess, ri-ses´ *s* nicho *m*.; vacaciones *f*. *pl*; recreo *m*.

recipe, res´-i-pi *s* receta *f*.

reciprocate, ri-sip´-ro-keit *v* reciprocar

recital, ri-sai´-tl *s* relato *m*.; recital *m*.

recite, ri-sait´ *v* recitar;

relatar; declamar

reckless*, rek´-les *a* temerario; descuidado

reckon, rek´-n *v* contar; calcular; computar

reclaim, ri-klaim´ *v* reclamar; (land) rellenar

recline, ri-klain´ *v* reclinarse; recostarse

recluse, ri-kluus´ s & *a* recluso *m.*

recognition, rek-og-nish´-on s reconocimiento *m.*

recognize, rek-og-nais´ *v* reconocer

recoil, ri-koil´ *v* recular; retroceder; s retroceso *m.*

recollect, rek-o-lekt´ *v* recordar; acordarse

recollection, rek-o-lek´-shon s recuerdo *m.*

recommence, rii-ko-mens´ *v* empezar de nuevo

recommend, rek-o-mend´ *v* recomendar; –ation, s recomendación *f.*

recompense, rek´-om-pens *v* recompensar; s recompensa *f.*

reconcile, rek´-on-sail *v* reconciliar

reconsider, rii-kon-siid´-a *v* considerar de nuevo

record, ri-koard´ *v* registrar; (tape, disk)

grabar

record, rek´-oard s registro *m.*; (phonograph) disco *m.*

recourse, ri-kórs´ s recurso *m.*; remedio *m.*

recover, ri-kŏv´-a *v* (retrieve) recuperar; (health) restablecerse; –y, s recuperación *f.*; restablecimiento *m.*

re-cover, ri-kŏv´-a *v* volver a cubrir

recreation, rek-rii-ei´-shon s recreo *m.*, diversión *f.*

recruit, ri-kruut´ s recluta *m.*; *v* reclutar

rectangular, rek-tang´-iuu-lar *a* rectangular

rectify, rek´-ti-fai *v* rectificar; refinar

rector, rek´-ta s rector *m.*; –y, rectoría *f.*

recumbent, ri-kŏm´-bent *a* recostado; reclinado

recuperate, ri-kiuu´-per-eit *v* restablecerse

recur, ri-kĕr´ *v* repetirse; volver; recurrir

red, red *a* rojo; –breast, s petirrojo *m.*; –den, *v* enrojecer; (blush) ruborizarse; –dish, *a* rojizo; –hot, candante; –ness, s rojez *f.*

redeem, ri-diim´ *v* (promise) cumplir; (bonds, etc) amortizar; (pledge) desempeñar; (soul) redimir

redemption, ri-demp´-shon s redención *f.*; (commercial) amortización *f.*

red-light district, red-lait dis´-trikt s zona de prostitution *m.*

redouble, ri-dŏb´-l *v* redoblar

redress, ri-dres´ s reparación *f.*; reparar

reduce, ri-diuus´ *v* reducir; (disgrace) degradar

reduction, ri-dŏk´-shon s reducción *f.*; rebaja *f.*

redundant, ri-dŏn-dant *a* excesivo; superfluo; redundante

reed, riid s caña *f.*

reef, riif s arrecife *m.*; (sail) rizo *m.*; *v* arrizar

reek, riik s vapor *m.*; humo *m.*; *v* humear

reel, riil s (cotton, film, fishing) carrete *m.*; (yarn) devanadera *f.*; *v* (sway) tambalear

refer, ri-fĕr´ *v* referir; consultar

referee, ref-er-ii´ s árbitro

m.

reference, ref´-er-ens s
referencia f.;
(testimonial)
recomendación f.

referendum, ref-ĕr-en-
dŏm s referéndum f.

refine, ri-fain´ v refinar;
–d*, a refinado; culto;
–ment, s cultura f.

reflect, ri-flekt´ v reflejar;
meditar; –ion, s reflejo
m.; (thought) reflexión
f.; (blame) reproche m.;
–or, reflector m.

reflex, rii´-fleks s reflejo
m.

reform, ri-foarm´ v
reformar; reformarse;
–ation, s reformación f.;
(church) Reforma f.

refrain, ri-frein´ v
abstenerse

refresh, ri-fresh´ v
refrescar

refreshment, ri-fresh´-
ment s refrescos m. pl;
refrigerio m.

refrigerator, ri-friCH´- a-
rei-ta s refrigerador m.;
(icèbox) nevera f.

refuel, rii-fiu-el v
reaprovisionar; poner
nuero combstible

refuge, ref´-iuu CH s
refugio m.; asilo m.

refugee, ref´-iuu-CHi s
refugiado m.

refund, ri-fŏnd´ v
reembolsar; restituir

refusal, ri-fiuu´- sl s
negativa f.

refuse, ri-fiuus ´ v rehusar;
negar

refuse, ref´-iuus s basura f.

refute, ri-fiuut´ v refutar

regain, ri-guein´ v
recuperar

regal*, ri´-gl a real; regio

regale, ri-gueil´ v agasajar;
regalar

regard, ri-gaard´ v
observar; considerar; s
consideración f.; –less, a
indiferente; negligente

regards, ri-gaards ´ s pl
(greetings) expresiones
f. pl

regenerate, ri-CHen´-er-eit
v regenerar

regent, ri´-CHent s regente
m. & f.

regiment, reCH´-i-ment s
regimiento m.

region, rii´-CHon s región
f.; territorio m.;
provincia f.

register, reCH´-is-ta s
registro m.; v registrar;
(letters) certificar

registrar, reCH´-is-traar s
registrador m. & f.

registration, reCH-is-trei´-
shon s registro m.;
inscripción f.

registry, reCH´-is-tri s
oficina de registros f.

regret, ri-gret´ v sentir;
arrepentirse; s
sentimiento m.;
remordimiento m.

regrettable, ri-gret´-a-bl a
lamentable

regular*, re´-guiu-la a
regular

regulate, reg´-iu-leit v
regularizar; regular

regulation, re-guiu-lei´-
shon s regulación f.;
regla f.; (official)
reglamento m.

rehearsal, ri-jĕr´-sl s
ensayo m.

rehearse, ri-jĕrs´ v
ensayar; repetir

reign, rein s reinar m.; s
reino m.

reimburse, rii-im-bĕrs´ v
reembolsar

rein, rein s rienda f.

reindeer, rein´-dir s reno
m.

reinforce, rii-in-fórs´ v
reforzar

reinstate, rii-in-steit´ v
reintegrar

reject, ri-CHekt´ v
rechazar; (spurn)

desechar; despreciar

rejoice, ri-CHois´ v regocijarse; alegrarse

rejoicings, ri-CHois´-ings s pl (public) fiestas f. pl

rejuvenate, ri-CHuu´-veneit v rejuvenecer

relapse, ri-lAps´ s recaída f.; v recaer

relate, ri-leit´ v relatar; –d, a relacionado

relation, ri-lei´-shon s relación f.; pariente m.

relative, rel´-a-tiv s pariente m.; familiar mf; a relativo; respectivo

relax, ri-lAks´ v relajar; –ing, a enervante

relay, ri-lei´ v (radio) transmitir; s trasmisión f.

release, ri-liis´ v soltar; libertar; s libertad f.; hacer público

relent, ri-lent´ v aplacarse; –less*, a implacable

relevant*, rel´-i-vant a aplicable; apropiado

reliable, ri-lai´-a-bl a seguro; veraz

reliance, ri-lai´-ans s confianza f.

relic, rel´-ik s reliquia f.; resto m.

relief, ri-liif´ s (anxiety, pain) alivio m.; (help) socorro m.; (raised) relieve m.

relieve, ri-liiv´ v aliviar; socorrer; consolar

religion, ri-liCH´- on s religión f.

religious*, ri-liCH´- os a religioso

relinquish, ri-ling´-kuish v abandonar; ceder

relish, rel´-ish v saborear; s sabor m.

reluctance, ri-lŏk´-tans s repugnancia f.; disgusto

reluctant*, ri-lŏk´-tant a recalcitrante; renuente

rely, ri-lai´ v confiar

remain, ri-mein´ v quedar; permanecer; –der, s residuo m.; –s, restos m. pl

remand, ri-maand´ v (law) devolver a la cárcel; al lugar de procedencia

remark, ri-maark´ s observación f.; v observar

remarkable, ri-maark´-a-bl a notable

remedy, rem´-i-di s remedio m.; v remediar

remember, ri-mem´-ba v acordarse de; recordar

remembrance, ri-mem´-brans s recuerdo m.; memoría f.

remind, ri-maind´ v recordar

remit, ri-mit´ v remitir; –tance, s remisa f.

remnant, rem´-nAnt s resto m.; –s, retazos m. pl; retal m.

remonstrate, ri-mon´-streit v reconvenir; objetar

remorse, ri-moars´ s remordimiento m.

remote*, ri-mout´ a remoto; distante

removal, ri-muu´-val s mudanza f.; v acción de quitar

remove, ri-muuv´ v mudar; mudarse; remove; quitar

remunerate, ri-miuu´-nereit v remunerar

remunerative*, ri-miuu´-ner-ei-tiv a lucrativo

rend, rend v rasgar; –er, (aid, service) prestar; (account) presentar; –ing, v presentando

renegade, ren´-i-gueid s renegado m.

renew, ri-niuu´ v renovar

renewal, ri-niuu´-al s renovación f.

renounce, ri-nauns´ v renunciar

renovate, ren´-o-veit v

renovar

renown, ri-naun´ s
renombre m.; fama f.

rent, rent s renta f.; (tear)
rasgón m.; v alquilar

renunciation, ri-nŏn-si-
ei´-shon s renunciación
f.

repair, ri-pér´ s reparación
f.; v reparar

reparation, rep-a-rei´-shon
s reparación f.

repartee, rep-ar-tii´ s
réplica f.

repeal, ri-piil´ v revocar; s
revocación f.

repeat, ri-piit´ v repetir

repel, ri-pel´ v repeler;
–lent, a repulsivo

repent, ri-pent´ v
arrepentirse

repetition, rep-i-tish´-on s
repetición f.

replace, ri-pleis´ v
reponer; reemplazar

replenish, ri-plen´-ish v
volver a llenar; rellenar

reply, ri-plai´ s respuesta
f.; v responder

report, ri-pórt s informe
m.; (school) notas f. pl;
(noise) estampido m.; v
informar; denunciar

reporter, ri-pór´-ta s
(journalist) reportero m.

repose, ri-pous´ v reposar

repository, ri-pos´-i-to-ri
s depósito m.

represent, rep-ri-sent´ v
representar; –ation, s
representación f.;
–ative, representate m.

reprieve, ri-priiv´ v
indultar; s indulto m.;
demorar un castigo

reprimand, rep-ri-maand´
v reprender; s
reprimenda f.

reprint, ri-print´ v
reimprimir; s
reimpresión f.

reprisal, ri-prais´-al s
represalia f.

reproach, ri-prouch´ v
reprochar; s reproche m.

reprobate, rep´-ro-bet s
réprobo m.

reproduce, rii-pro-diuus´ v
reproducir

reproduction, rii-pro-
dŏk´-shon s
reproducción f.

reproof, ri-pruuf´ s
reprobación f.

reprove, ri-pruuv´ v
reprobar; reprender

reptile, rep´-tail s reptil m.

republic, ri-pŏb´-lik s
república f.

repudiate, ri-piuu´-di-eit v
repudiar

repugnant*, ri-pŏg´-nant;

a repugnante

repulse, ri-pŏls´ v repulsar;
repeler; rechazar

repulsive*, ri-pŏl´-siv a
repulsivo

reputable, rep´-iuu-ta-bol
a acreditado; de
confianza; formal

reputation, rep-iu-tei´-
shon s reputación f.

repute, ri-piuut´ s fama f.

request, ri-kuest´ s ruego
m.; petición f.; solicitud
f.; v rogar

require, ri-kuair´ v
necesitar; requerir;
–ment, s necesidad f.;
requerimiento m.

requisite, rek´-ui- sit s
requisito m.; a necesario

rescind, ri-sind´ v
rescindir; anular

rescue, res´-kiuu v salvar;
rescatar; s salvación f.

research, ri-sěrch´ s
investigación f.

resemble, ri- sem´-bl v
parecerse

resent, ri- sent´ v
resentirse; –ful*, a
resentido; –ment, s
resentimiento m.

reservation, res-ěr-vei-
shon s reservación f.;
reserva f.; (on road)
mediana f.; franja

central

reserve, ri- sŏrv´ s reserva f.; v reservar

reservoir, res´-ŏr-voar s depósito m.; tanque m.

reside, ri- said´ v residir

residence, res´-i-dens s residencia f.

resident, res´-i-dent a residente; s habitante m.

resign, ri- sain´ v abandonar; (a post) dimitir; (oneself) resignarse

resin, res´-in s resina f.; (violin) colofonia f.

resist, ri- sist´ v resistir; –ance, s resistencia f.

resolute*, res´-o-liuut a resoluto; determinado

resolution, res -o-liuu´-shon s resolución f.

resolve, ri- solv´ v resolver; decidir

resort, ri- soart´ v recurrir

resound, ri- sound´ v resonar; retumbar

resource, ri-sórs s recurso m.; –s, recursos m. pl

respect, ri-spekt´ v respetar; s respeto m.; –ability, respetabilidad f.; –able, a respetable; –ful*, respetuoso; –ive*, respectivo

respire, ri-spair´ v respirar

respite, res´-pit s tregua f.

respond, ri-spond´ v responder

respondent, ri-spon´-dent s demandado m.; defensor m.

response, ri-spons´ s respuesta f.

responsible, ri-spon´-si-bl a responsable

rest, rest s descanso m.; (sleep) reposo m.; (remainder) resto m.; v descansar; –ful, a tranquilo; –ive, impaciente; –less, inquieto

restaurant, res´-tou-rant s restaurante m.

restore, ri-stór´ v restituir; (health) restaurar

restrain, ri-strein´ v refrenar; restringir; (law) prohibir; –t, s refrenamiento m.; sujeción f.

restrict, ri-strikt´ v restringir; limitar

restriction, ri-strik´-shon s restricción f.

result, ri- sŏlt´ v resultar; s resultado m.

resume, ri-siuum´ v resumir; continuar

resumption, ri- sŏmp´-shon s reasunción f.

resurrection, res -er-rek´-shon s resurrección f.

retail, ri-teil´ v vender al por menor; s venta al por menor f.; –er, revendedor m.

retain, ri-tein´ v retener; (keep) guardar

retaliate, ri-tAl´-i-eit v desquitarse; vengarse

retard, ri-taard´ v retardar; demorar

reticent*, ret´-i-sent a reservado

retinue, ret´-i-niuu s comitiva f.; séquito m.

retire, ri-tair´ v retirarse; retirar; –ment, s retiro m.; retraimiento m.

retort, ri-toart´ v replicar; s réplica f.

retract, ri-trAkt´ v retractar; retractarse

retreat, ri-triit´ v retirarse; s retreta f.

retrospect, ret´-ros-pekt s mirada retrospectiva f.; n reflexion de lo pasado

return, ri-tĕrn´ v volver; (give back) devolver; s vuelta f.; –s, ganancia f.; – ticket, billeto de ida y vuelta m.

reveal, ri-viil´ v revelar

revel, rev´-l v parrandear; s orgía

revenge, ri-venCH´ v vengarse; s venganza f.

revenue, rev´-i-niuu s renta f.; ingreso m.

revere, ri-vir´ v reverenciar

reverend, rev´-er-end a reverendo

reverse, ri-věrs´ v invertir; (engine) hacer marcha atrás; s reverso m.; (defeat) revés m.; a contrario

revert, ri-věrt´ v volver; retroceder

review, ri-viuu´ v (consider) revisar; (inspect) revistar; (books, etc) criticar; s revista f.; (books) crítica f.

revile, ri-vail´ v injuriar; ultrajar; denigrar

revise, ri-vais´ v revisar

revision, ri-vish´-on s revisión f.

revive, ri-vaiv´ v avivar; reanimarse; resucitar; restablecer

revoke, ri-vouk´ v revocar s (cards) renuncio m.

revolt, ri-volt´ v rebelarse; s revuelta f.

revolve, ri-volv´ v revolver; girar

revolver, ri-vol´-va s

revólver m.

reward, ri-uoard´ v remunerar; s premio m.; recompensa f.

rheumatism, ruu´-ma-tism s reumatismo m.

rhinoceros, rai-nos´-e-ros s rinoceronte m.

rhubarb, ruu´-baarb s ruibarbo m.

rhyme, raim v rimar; s rima f.

rib, rib s costilla f.; varilla (de paraguas) f.

ribbon, rib´-on s cinta f.; listón m.; (medal) condecoración f.

rice, rais s arroz m.

rich*, rich a rico; –es, s pl riqueza f.

rickets, rik´-ets s raquitismo m.

rickety, rik´-et-i a (shaky) desvencijado

rid, rid v desembarazar; librar

riddle, rid´-l s enigma m.; v acribillar; juego de palabras m.

ride, raid v ir a caballo; ir en auto; ir en bicicleta; s paseo m.

ridge, riCH s (mountain) cumbre f.

ridicule, rid´-i-kiuul v ridiculizar; s ridículo m.

ridiculous*, ri-dik´-iu-los a ridículo; risible

rifle, rai´-fl v robar; pillar. s fusil m.

rift, rift s (crack) grieta f.; (cleft) hendidura f.

rig, rig v (naut) aparejar; s (ship) aparejo m.

right, rait s derecho m.; v enderezar; a* derecho; justo; recto; honesto

rigid*, riCH´-id a rígido; tieso

rigor, rig´-a s rigor m.; orilla f.

rigorous*, rig´-or-os a riguroso; duro

rim, rim s borde m.; (wheel) llanta f.

rind, raind s corteza f.; (bacon) pellejo m.

ring, ring v tocar; s anillo m.; (circus) redondel m.

ringleader, ring´-lii-da s cabecilla m.

rinse, rins v enjuagar

riot, rai´-ot s tumulto m.; motín m.; v amotinarse

rip, rip v hender; (cloth) rasgar

ripe, raip a maduro; –n, v madurar

ripple, rip´-l s onda f.; susurro m.

rise, rais v subir; (stand up, revolt, etc)

levantarse; (river) crecer; (sun) salir. s subida f.

risk, risk s riesgo m.; peligro m.; v arriesgar

rite, rait s ríto m.; **–s,** (funeral) exequias f. pl

rival, rai´-vl a rival; s rival m.; competidor m.

river, riv´-a s río m.

rivet, riv´-et s remache m.; v remachar

road, roud s camino m.; ruta f.; carretera f.

road map, roud-mAp s mapa f.; de carreteras

roam, roum v vagar

roar, rór v rugir; s rugido m.

roast, roust v asar. s asado m.

rob, rob v robar; hurtar; **–ber,** s ladrón m.

robbery, rob´-er-i s robo m.; hurto m.

robe, roub s traje m.; (eccl) vestimenta f.

robin, rob´-in s petirrojo m.

robust*, ro-bŏst´ a robusto; vigoroso

rock, rok v (roll) bambolear; (cradle) mecer; s roca f.; **–y,** a peñascoso

rock and roll, rok-nd-roul s rocanrol m.

rocket, rok´-et s cohete m.

rod, rod s vara f.; (fishing) caña de pescar f.

roe, rou s (deer) corzo m.; (fish) hueva f.

rogue, roug s bribón m.; **–ry,** bribonada f.

roll, roul v rodar; (-up) enrollar. s rollo m.; (bread) bollo m.; **–call,** acto de pasar lista m.; **–er,** rodillo m.; **–erskate,** patín de ruedas m.

romance, rou-mAns´ s romance m.; novela f.

romantic, rou-mAn´-tik s & a romántico/a mf.

romp, romp v retozar

roof, ruuf s tejado m.; (mouth) paladar m.

rook, ruk s corneja f.

room, ruum s cuarto m.; (space) espacio m.

room-service, ruum sĕr´-vis s servicio f.; de habitación

roost, ruust v descansar en una percha

root, ruut s raíz f.; v arraigarse

rope, roup s cuerda f.; (naut.) cordaje m.

rosary, rou´-sa-ri s rosario m.; jardin de rosales m.

rose, rous s rosa f.; **–bush,** rosal m.

rosemary, rous ´-ma-ri s romero m.

rosy, rou´-si a rosado; sonrosado

rot, rot v pudrirse; s putrefacción f.

rotate, rou´-teit v girar

rotten, rot´-n a podrido; putrefacto

rouge, ruush, s colorete m.

rough*, rŏf a (coarse) áspero; (manners) grosero; (crude) tosco; (sea, wind) borrascoso; (bumpy) escabroso; **–ness,** a aspereza f.; groseria f.; tosquedad f.

round, raund a* redondo; circular; v redondear; s círculo m.; **–about,** a indirecto; s tiovivo m.; **–ness,** redondez f.

rouse, raus v provocar; (awaken) despertar

rout, raut v (mil) derrotar; s derrota f.

route, ruut s ruta f.; via f.

routine, ru-tiin´ s rutina f.

rove, rouv v errar; vagar

row, rou v remar; s hilera f.; fila f.

row, rau s riña f.

royal*, roi´-al a real; **–ty,** s

realeza f.; (payment) derechos de autor m. pl

rub, rŏb v frotar; s frotamiento m.; **–off**, limpiar; **–out**, borrar; **–ber**, s caucho m.; (eraser) goma de borrar f.

rubbish, rŏb´-ish s escombro m.; basura f.; (nonsense) disparate m.

ruby, ruu´-bi s rubí m.; (color) carmín m.

rucksack, rŏk-sAk s mochila f.

rudder, rŏd´-a s timón m.

rude*, ruud a descortés; (manner) brusco

rudiment, ru´-di-ment s rudimento m.

rue, ruu v lamentar; **–ful**, a lamentable

ruffian, rŏf´-i-an s rufián m.

ruffle, rŏf´-l v desordenar; incomodar

rug, rŏg s manta f.; (mat) tapete m.

rugby, rŏg-bi s rugby m.

rugged*, rŏ´-guid a (scenery) escarpado; áspero; tosco

ruin, ruu´-in v arruinar; s ruina f.

rule, ruul v gobernar; (lines) reglar. s

(regulation) regla f.; reglamento

ruler, ruu´-la s (drawing) regla f.; mandatario m.

rum, rŏm s rón m.

rumble, rŏm´-bl s ruido sordo m.

rummage, rŏm´-eCH v revolver

rumor, ruu´-ma s rumor m.

run, rŏn v correr; (colors) extenderse; **–away**, huir; s (horse) caballo desbocado m.

runway, rŏn-uei s pista f.

rupture, rŏp´-tiur s hernia f.; ruptura

rural*, ru´-rl a campestre; rural; rústico

rush, rŏsh s carrera precipitada f.; (water) torrente m.; (people) agolpamiento m.; (reed) junco m.; v precipitarse; agolparse; **–hour**, s hora punta; hora de afluencia f.

rust, rŏst v oxidarse; s orín m.; **–y**, a oxidado

rustic, rŏs´-tik s & a rústico m.

rustle, rŏs´-l v susurrar; (silk) crujir; s susurro m.; crujido m.

rusty, rŏs´-ti a oxidado;

mohoso; (fig) falta de práctica

rut, rŏt s rodada f.; surco m.; costumbre f.; rutina f.

rye, rai s centeno m.

sable, sei´-bl s marta f.; cebellina f.

sachet, sA-shei s sobrecito m.; bolsita f.

sack, sAk s saco m.; v (mil) saquear

sacrament, sAk´-ra-ment s sacramento m.

sacred*, sei´-krid a sagrado; consagrado

sacrifice, sAk´-ri-fais v sacrificar; s sacrificio m.

sacrilege, sAk´-ri-liCH s sacrilegio m.

sad*, sAd a triste; **–ness,** s tristeza f.

saddle, sAd´-l s silla de montar f.; v ensillar

saddler, sAd´-la s sillero m.

safe, seif a seguro; s caja fuerte f.; **–guard,**

salvaguardia f.; v proteger; **–ty,** s seguridad f.

safety pin, seif-ti-pin s imperdible m.

sag, sAg v combarse; doblegarse

sagacious*, sa-guei´-shos a sagaz

sage, seiCH s sabio m.; (herb) salvia f.; a sabio

sail, seil v navegar; (leave) zarpar s vela f.

sailor, seil´-a s marinero m.

saint, seint s santo m.; santa f. a santo; san

sake, seik s causa f.; consideración f.; amor m.

salad, sAl´-ad s ensalada f.

salad dressing, sAl´-ad-

dres-ing s aliño m.

salary, sAl´-a-ri s salario m.; sueldo m.; paga f.

sale, seil s venta f.; liquidación f.; **–able,** a vendible; **–sman,** s vendedor m.

salient, sei´-li-ent a saliente; saledizo

saliva, sa-lai´-va s saliva f.

sallow, sAl´-ou a cetrino; pálido

salmon, sAm´-on s salmón m.

saloon, sa-luun´ s salón m.

salt, soalt s sal m.; sabor m.; gracia f.; a salado; **–shaker,** salero m.

salty, soal-ti a salado

salute, sa-luut´ v saludar; s saludo m.

salvage, sAl´-viCH s salvamento m.; v salvar

salvation, sAl-vei´-shon s salvación f.; **–army,** Ejército de Salvación m.

salver, sAl´-va s bandeja f.

same, seim a & pron mismo

sample, saam´-pl v probar; s muestra f.

sanctimonious*, sAngk-ti-mou´-ni-os a devoto

sanction, sAngk´-shon s sanción f.; v sancionar

sanctity, sAngk´-ti-ti s santidad f.

sanctuary, sAngk´-tiu-a-ri s santuario m.

sand, sAnd s arena f.; **-y,** a arenoso; de arena

sandal, sAn´-dl s sandalia f.

sandwich, sAnd´-uich s bocadillo m.; emparedado m.

sane*, sein a cuerdo; sano

sanguine*, sAng´-guin a sanguíneo; vehemente

sanitary, sAn´-i-ta-ri a sanitario; **-towel,** s toalla higiénica f.

sanity, sAn´-i-ti s cordura f.

sap, sAp, v zapar. s savia f.; **-per,** zapador m.

sapphire, saf´-air s zafiro m.

sarcasm, saar´-kAsm s sarcasmo m.

sarcastic, sAr-kas´-tik a sarcástico

sardine, saar-diin´ s sardina f.

sash, sAsh s (belt) faja f.

satchel, sAtsh´-l s mochila f.; (school) bolsa f.

satellite, sAt´-e-lait s satélite m.

satiate, sei´-shi-eit, v saciar; hartar

satin, sAt´-in s raso m.; a de raso

satire, sAt´-air s sátira f.

satisfaction, sAt-is-fAk´-shon s satisfacción f.

satisfactory, sAt-is-fAk´-to-ri a satisfactorio

satisfy, sAt´-is-fai, v satisfacer

satsuma, sAt´-suu-ma s satsuma f.; mandarina f.

saturate, sAt´-iu-reit v saturar

Saturday, sAt´-er-di s sábado m.

satyr, sAt´-er s sátiro m.

sauce, soas s salsa f.; **-pan,** cacerola f.

saucer, soa´-sa s plato pequeño m.

saucy, soa´-si a (fam.) descarado; atrevido

sauna, soa´-na s sauna f.

saunter, soan´-ta v vagar; andar sin rumbo

sausage, so´-siCH s salchicha f.

savage*, sAv´-iCH a salvaje; feroz; s salvaje m.

save, seiv v salvar; (economize) ahorrar; (keep) guardar

saving, sei´-ving a ecónomico; frugal. s ahorro m.; economía f.

savior, sei´-vi-a s salvador m.

savor, sei´-va s sabor m.; v saborear

savory, sei´-va-ri s entremés m.; a sabroso

saw, soa s sierra f.; v serrar

say, sei, v decir

saying, sei´-ing s dicho m.; proverbio m.

scabbard, skAb´-erd s (sword) vaina de espada f.

scaffold, skAf´-old s (building) andamio m.; (execution) patíbulo m.; **-ing,** andamiada f.

scald, skoald v escaldar; quemar

scale, skeil v escamar; (climb) escalar; s (fish) escama f.; (measure) escala f.; (music) gama f.

scales, skeils s pl balanza f.

scallop, skAl´-op s (fish) venera f.

scalp, skAlp s cuero cabelludo m.; cráneo m.

scamp, skAmp s bribón m.; pícaro m.

scamper, skAm´-pa v escaparse

scan, skAn v escudriñar

scandal, skAn´-dl s escándalo m.

scandalous*, skAn´-dal-os *a* escandaloso

scanty, skAn´-ti *a* escaso

scapegoat, skeip´-gout *s* víctima propiciatoria *f.*

scar, skaar *s* cicatriz *f.*; *v* cicatrizar

scarce*, ské rs *a* escaso

scarcity, ské r´-si-ti *s* escasez *f.*; carestía *f.*

scare, ské r *s* susto *m.*; *v* asustar; espantar; **–away**, *s* espantar; **–crow**, *s* espantajo *m.*

scarf, skaarf *s* bufanda *f.*; chalina *f.*

scarlet, skaar´-let *a* de color escarlata; *s* escarlata *f.*; **– fever**, escarlatina *f.*

scathing*, skei´-Ding *a* dañoso

scatter, skAt´-a *v* esparcir; (wealth) disipar; **–brained**, *a* atolondrado

scavenger, skAv´-en-CH *s* basurero *m.*; animal que se alimenta de carroña *m.*

scene, siin *s* escena *f.*

scenery, sii´-ner-i *s* paisaje *m.*; vista *f.*; (theater) decoraciones *f. pl*

scent, sent *s* perfume *m.*; (flowers) fragancia *f.*; (track) pista *f.*; *v* perfumar; olfato *m.*

scepter, sep´-ta *s* cetro *m.*

schedule, shed´-iuul *s* cédula *f.*; anexo *m.*; horario *m.*

scheme, skiim *s* proyecto *m.*; plan *m.*; *v* proyectar

schism, sism *s* cisma *m.*

schist, shist *s* esquisto *m.*

scholar, skol´-a *s* escolar *m.*; (pupil) alumno *m.*; erudito *m.*

scholarship, skol´-er-ship *s* (prize) beca *f.*

school, skuul *s* escuela *f.*; **–teacher**, maestro de escuela *m.*; maestra de escuela *f.*

schooner, skuun´-a *s* goleta *f.*

sciatica, sai-At´-i-ka *s* ciática *f.*

science, sai´-ens *s* ciencia *f.*

scientific, sai´-en-ti-fik *a* científico

scion, sai´-on *s* vástago *m.*; descendiente *m.*

scissors, sis´-ers *s pl* tijeras *f. pl*

scoff, skof *v* burlarse

scold, skould, *v* regañar; reñir

scoop, skuup *s* cucharón *m.*; *v* ahuecar

scope, skoup *s* esfera *f.*; (aim) objeto *m.*; alcauce

m.

scorch, skoarch *v* chamuscar; (sun) abrasar

score, skór *s* (number) veintena *f.*; cuenta *f.*; (games) puntos *m. pl*; *v* ganar; (cut) hacer muescas; (record) marcar

scorn, skoarn *s* desdén *m.*; *v* desdeñar

scornful, skoarn´-ful *a* desdeñoso

scoundrel, skaun´-drel *s* pícaro *m.*; bribón *m.*

scour, skaur *v* fregar; estregar; rascar

scourge, skĕr CH *v* azotar; *s* azote *m.*

scout, skaut *s* escucha *m.*; (boy) explorador *m.*; *v* explorar

scowl, skaul *v* mirar con ceño *m.*

scraggy, skrA´-gui *a* (thin) flaco

scramble, skrAm´-bl *s* (struggle) arrebatiña *f.*; *v* (climb) trepar; **–for**, arrebatarse

scrap, skrAp *s* fragmento *m.*; (cloth) retal *m.*; migaja *f.*

scrape, skreip, *v* raspar; *s* raspadura *f.*

scraper, screi´-pa s
raspador m.

scratch, skrAch s arañazo
m.; rasguño m.; (sport)
línea de partida f.; v
arañar; (rub oneself)
rascar; (glass) rayar;
(sports) abandonar

scream, skriim v chillar; s
chillido m.

screen, skriin s (fire,
movie, light) pantalla f;
(wind) biombo m.;
(partition) tabique m.; v
proteger

screw, skruu s tornillo m.;
v atornillar; -- **driver**, s
destornillador m.

scribble, skrib´-l v
borrajear; garabatear s
garabatos m. pl

scrip, skrip s cédula f.;
certificado provisional
m.; esquela f.

scripture, skrip´-tiur s
Sagrada Escritura f.

scroll, skroul s rollo de
papel pergamino m.;
lista f.

scrounge, skraunCH v ir
de gorra; gorronear;
obtener sin pagar

scrub, skrób, v fregar;
frotar

scruple, skruu´-pl, v tener
escrúpulos; s escrúpulo

m.

scrupulous*, skruu´-piu-
los a escrupuloso

scrutinize, skruu´-ti-nais v
escudriñar

scuffle, sköf´-l v pelear;
pelea f.; riña f.

scull, sköl v bogar con
espadilla; s remo de
espadilla m.

scullery, sköl´-er-i s
fregadero m.

sculptor, skölp´-ta s
escultor m.

sculpture, skölp´-tiur s
escultura f.

scum, sköm s espuma f.; v
espumar

scurf, skö rf s tiña f.;
costra de una herida f.

scurrilous*, skör´-i-los a
grosero; injurioso

scurvy, skö r´-vi s
escorbuto m.; a vil, ruín

scuttle, sköt´-l s (coal)
cubo para carbón m.; v
echar a pique

scythe, saiD s guadaña f.

sea, sii s mar m. & f.;
--**man**, marino m.; --
sick, a mareado; --**side**,
s costa f.; playa f.; --
weed, alga marina f.; --
worthy, a capaz de
navegar

seal, siil, v sellar; s sello

m.; (animal) f.; --**ing**
wax, lacre m.; --**skin**,
piel de foca f.

seam, siim v coser; s
costura f.; (mine) vena
f.; filón m.; --**stress**,
costurera f.

sear, sir v (dry up) agostar;
(burn) quemar; (brand)
herrar a fuego;
cauterizar; a (withered)
marchito

search, sërch v buscar;
examinar; s busca f.;
(customs) examen m.;
--**light**, reflector m.

season, sii´-sn, v sazonar;
(timber) secar; s
estación f.;
(fashionable) temporada
f.; --**able**, del tiempo; --
ticket, s abono m.

seasoning, sii´-son-ing s
condimento m.

seat, siit s asiento m.;
(bench) banco m.;
(country estate) quinta
f.; v sentar

secluded, si-kluu´-did a
retirado

seclusion, si-kluu´-sh on s
reclusión f.; retiro m.;
aislamiento m.

second, sek´-ond v
(support) secundar; s
(time; number) segundo

m.; (duel, etc) padrino
m.; *a* segundo; **--hand,**
de ocasión

secrecy, sii´-kri-si s secreto
m.; reserva f.

secret, sii´-krit s secreto
m.; *a** secreto

secretary, sek´-ri-ta-ri s
secretario m.

secrete, si-kriit´ v
esconder; (separate)
secretar

secretion, si-krii´-shon s
secreción f.

sect, sekt s secta f.

section, sek´-shon s
sección f.; (cross) corte
transversal m.

secular, sek´-iuu-la a
secular; seglar

secure, si-kiú r´ v
asegurar; *a** seguro

securities, si-kiú r´-i-tis s
pl valores m. pl

security, si-kiú r´-i-ti s
seguridad f.; garantía f.

sedate, si-deit´ a sosegado;
formal

sedative, sed´-a-tiv s
calmante m.; sedativo
m.

sedentary, sed´-en-ta-ri a
sedentario

sediment, sed´-i-ment s
sedimento m.; hez f.

sedition, si-dish´-on s

sedición f.

seditious, si-dish´-os a
sedicioso

seduce, si-diuus´ v seducir

see, sii v ver; **--through,**
ver a través; (fig)
penetrar; **--to,** cuidar

seed, siid s semilla f.;
simiente f.

seek, siik v buscar; (strive)
ambicionar

seem, siim v parecer; **--ly,**
a* decente

seethe, siiD v hervir;
bullir; (unrest)
fermentar

seize, siis v asir; tomar;
(law) embargar

seizure, sii´-sh er s
asimiento m.; (law) em-
bargo m.; (stroke)
ataque m.; secuestro m.

seldom, sel´-dm adv
raramente

select, si-lekt´ v escoger;
seleccionar; a selecto;
escogido

selection, si-lek´-shon s
selección f.

self, self a mismo; **one--,**
pron sí mismo; **--ish,** a
egoísta; **--ishness,** s
egoísmo m.; **--starter,**
(motor) arranque
automático m.

self-service, self-sër´-vis a

de autoservicio

sell, sel, v vender; **--er,** s
vendedor m.

semblance, sem´-blans s
semejanza f.; aparíencia
f.

semi, sem´-i *prefix* semi;
medio; **--circle,** s semi-
círculo m.; **--colon,**
punto y coma m.

semolina, sem-o-li´-na s
sémola f.

senate, sen´-et s senado m.

send, send v enviar;
despachar; **--away,**
(dismiss) despedir;
--back, devolver; **--er,** s
remitente m.; **--for,** v
enviar por; **--in advance,**
enviar por adelantado

senile, sii´-nail a senil;
caduco

senior, sii´-ni-a a mayor; s
mayor m.; **-- partner,**
socio principal m.

sensation, sen-sei´-shon s
sensación f.

sense, sens s sentido m.;
--less, a sin sentido

sensible, sen´-si-bl a
sensato

sensitive, sen´-si-tiv a
sensitivo

sensual*, sen´-shu-al a
sensual

sentence, sen´-tens s frase

f.; oración f.; (law) sentencia f.; v condenar

sentiment, sen´-ti-ment s sentimiento m.; opinión f.

sentry, sen´-tri s centinela m.; **–box,** garita f.

separable, sep´-a-ra-bl a separable

separate, sep´-a-reit, v separar; dividir

separation, sep-a-rei´-shon s separación f.; (law) separación judicial f.

September, sep-tem´-ba s septiembre m.

septic, sep´-tik a séptico

sequel, sii´-kuel s secuela f.; consecuencia f.

sequence, sii´-kuens s serie f.; orden de sucesión m.; continuación f.

serenade, ser-i-neid´ s serenata f.

serene*, si-riin´ a sereno; tranquilo

serge, ser CH s sarga f.; estameña f

sergeant, saar´-CH ent s sargento m.

serial, si´-ri-al a consecutivo; s folletín m.; serial m.

series, si´-riis s serie f.

serious*, si-ri-os a serio;

grave; seriamente

sermon, ser´-mon s sermón m.

serpent, ser´-pent s serpiente f.

serum, sir´-um s suero m.

servant, ser´-vant s criado m.; (maid) criada f.

serve, serv v servir; (law) ejecutar

service, ser´-vis s servicio m.; (divine) oficio m.

serviceable, ser´-vis-a-bl a serible

servile, ser´-vail a servil

servitude, ser´-vi-tiuud s servidumbre f.; (penal) trabajo forzado m.

session, sesh´-on s sesión f.

set, set v (type, music) componer; (clock) regular; (trap) tender; (task) imponer; (example) dar; (tools) asentar; (fracture) entablar; (solidify) cuajar; (jewels) engastar; s colección f.; serie f.; (buttons, etc) juego m.; (china) servicio m.; colocar; fijar; **–on fire,** pegar fuego a

settee, set´-ii s sofá m.

settle, set´-l v (accounts)

ajustar; liquidar; (finish) poner fin a; (decide) resolver; (assign) asignar; (in a place) establecerse; **–ment,** s colonia f.; establecimiento m.; (dowery) dote f.; (agreement) convenio m.; (accounts) liquidación f.; **–r,** colono m.

seven, sev´-n s & a siete m.; **–teen,** diecisiete m.; **–th,** séptimo m.; **–ty,** setenta m.

sever, sev´-a v separar; (cut) cortar

several, sev´-er-al a diversos; varios

severe*, si-vir´ a severo; riguroso; violento

severity, si-ver´-i-ti s severidad f.

sew, sou v coser; **–ing,** s costura f.; **–ing thread,** hilo de coser m.; **–ing machine,** máquina de coser f.

sewage, siuu´-e CH s aguas de alcantarillado m. pl

sewer, siuu´-a s albañal m.; cloaca f.

sex, seks s sexo m.; **–ual,** a sexual

sexist, sek´-sist s & a

sexista *mf*.

sexy, sek´-si *a* (person) sexy; cachondo; (dress) provocativo; sexy; (film, joke) verde; escabroso

shabbiness, shAb´-i-nes *s* desaseo *m*.; miseria *f*.

shabby, shAb´-i *a* raído; (unkempt) desaseado; destartalado

shackle, shAk´-l *s* (feet) grillete *m*.; (hands) esposas *f. pl*; *v* encadenar

shade, sheid *s* sombra *f*.; (of colors) matiz *m*.; (lamp) pantalla *f*.; (eyes) visera *f*.; *v* sombrear

shadow, shAd´-ou *s* sombra *f*.; *v* (follow) seguir; protección *f*.

shady, shei´-di *a* umbroso; (fig) sospechoso

shaft, shaaft *s* (arrow) asta *f*.; (mech.) eje *m*.; (mine) pozo de mina *m*.

shaggy, shAg´-gui *a* lanudo; hirsuto; afelpado

shake, sheik, *v* agitar; (quake) sacudir; (tremble) temblar; (hands) estrechar; *s* sacudida *f*.; (hands) apretón de manos *m*.

shaky, she-ki *a* trémulo; vacilante; inseguro; tembloroso

shall, shAl *aux v* (use to form future tenses) – **I help you?** ¿quieres que te ayude?; **I'll buy three, – I?** compro tres, ¿no te parece?

shallow, shAl´-ou *a* somero; superficial

sham, shAm *s* ficción *f*.; fingimiento *m*.; *v* fingir; engañar; *a* fingido

shame, sheim *s* vergüenza *f*.; (modesty) pudor *m*.; *v* avergonzar; **–ful,** *a* vergonzoso; **–less,** desvergonzado

shampoo, shAm´-puu *s* champú *m*.

shamrock, shAm-rok *s* trébol *m*.

shape, sheip *s* forma *f*.; *v* dar forma; modelar

share, shé r *s* participación *f*.; (stock) acción *f*.; *v* repartir; participar; **–holder,** *s* accionista *m*.

shark, shaark *s* tiburón *m*.

sharp, shaarp *a* afilado; (point) puntiagudo; (mind) agudo; (taste) picante; **–en,** *v* afilar; **–ness,** *s* agudeza *f*.

sharper, shaar´-pa *s* estafador *m*.; (cards) tramposo *m*.

shatter, shAt´-a *v* estrellar; quebrantar

shave, sheiv, *v* afeitar; afeitarse

shaving, shei´-ving, **–brush,** *s* brocha de afeitar *f*.; **–s,** (wood) raspaduras *f. pl*

shawl, shoal *s* chal *m*.; toquilla *f*.; mantón *m*.

she, shii *pers pron* ella

sheaf, shiif *s* haz *m*.; (corn) gavilla *f*.; (papers) legajo *m*.

shear, shir, *v* esquilar; **–s,** *pl* tijeras *f. pl*

sheath, shiiz *s* (scabbard) vaina *f*.

shed, shéd *s* cobertizo *m*.; *v* (tears, blood) derramar; (hair, feathers) pelechar; (leaves) perder

sheen, shiin *s* brillo *m*.; lustre *m*.

sheep, shiip *s* carnero *m*.; oveja *f*.

sheer, shir *a* puro; (steep) escarpado; transparente

sheet, shiit *s* (bed) sábana *f*.; (paper) hoja *f*.; cuartilla *f*.; (metal) plancha *f*.; **–lightning,**

relampagueo *m.*

shelf, shelf *s* anaquel *m.*; estante *m.*; (a set) estantería *f.*

shell, shel *s* (hard) cascara *f.*; (soft) pellejo *m.*; (fish) concha *f.*; (artillery) bomba *f.*; *v* descascarar; bombardear; **–fish,** *s* marisco *m.*

shelter, shel´-ta *s* abrigo *m.*; albergue *m.*; guarida *f.*; *v* resguardarse, refugiarse

shepherd, shep´-erd *s* pastor *m.*

sheriff, sher´-if *s* alguacil mayor *m.*

sherry, sher´-i *s* vino de Jerez *m.*

shield, shiild *s* escudo *m.*; *v* escudar

shift, shift *s* (working) tanda *f.*; turno *m.*; *v* mudar; remover

shin, shin *s* canilla *f.*; tibia *f.*

shine, shain *s* lustre *m.*; brillo *m.*; *v* brillar, lucir

shingle, shing´-gl *s* ripia *f.*; *v* (hair) rapar

ship, ship *s* buque *m.*; barco *m.*; *v* embarcar; **–ment,** embarque *m.*; cargamento *m.*; **–owner,**

naviero *m.*; armador *m.*; **–ping,** (traffic) navegación *f.*; **–wreck,** naufragio *m.*; **–yard,** astillero *m.*; arsenal *m.*

shirk, shěrk *v* esquivar; evadir; **–er,** *s* tumbón *m.*

shirt, shěrt *s* camisa *f.*

shiver, shiv´-a, *v* tiritar; temblar; *s* estremecimiento *m.*; (fever) escalofrío *m.*

shoal, shoal *s* multitud *f.*; (fish) cardume *m.*; (shallows) bajío *m.*

shock, shok *s* (jolt) choque *m.*; (electric, etc) sacudida *f.*; (fright) susto *m.*; (med) postración *f.*; *v* (disgust) ofender; **– absorber,** *s* amortiguador *m.*; **–ing,** *a* espantoso; ofensivo

shoddy, shod´-i *s* paño burdo *m.*; *a* burdo; aguijeta *f.*

shoe, shuu, *s* zapato *m.*; (horse) herradura *f.*; *v* (horse) herrar; **–horn,** calzador *m.*; **–lace,** cordón *m.*; **–maker,** zapatero *m.*; **–-polish,** bétún *m.* lustre *m.*

shoot, shuut *v* disparar; (kill) matar; (execute) fusilar; (grow) brotar; *s*

caza *f.*; (growth) retoño *m.*; **–ing,** tiro *m.*; **–ing star,** estrella fugaz *f.*

shop, shop *s* tienda *f.*; (stores) almacenes *m. pl*; *v* ir de compras; **–keeper,** *s* tendero *m.*

shop assistant, shop *a*-sist´-ant *s* dependiente/a *mf.*

shoplifting, shop-lift-ing *s* ratería *f.*; hurto *m.*; (en las tiendas)

shopping, shop´-ing *s* compras *f. pl*

shore, shó r *s* costa *f.*; orilla *f.*; (land) tierra *f.*; (support) puntal *m.*; *v* apuntalar

shorn, sho rn *a* mocho; (deprived) espojado

short, shoart *a* corto; (persons) pequeño; (need) escaso; **–age,** *s* déficit *m.*; **–circuit,** *s* cortocircuito *m.*; **–en,** *v* acortar; abreviar; **–hand,** *s* taquigrafía *f.*; **–ly,** *adv* dentro de poco; pronto; **–ness,** *s* cortedad *f.*; brevedad *f.*; deficiencia *f.*; **–sighted,** *a* miope

shot, shot *s* tiro *m.*; (marksman) tirador *m.*; (pellet) perdigones *m. pl*

should, shŏd *aux v* (use to

form conditional tense)
I – go debería ir; **I – go
if I were you** yo en tu
lugar me iría; **if he –
come** si viniese

shoulder, shoul´-da s
hombro m.; v cargar al
hombro; **–blade,** s
omoplato m.

shout, shaut s grito m.; v
gritar

shove, shǒv s empujón m.;
v empujar

shovel, shǒv´-l s pala f.; v
traspalar

show, shou s espectáculo
m.; exposición f.; v
mostrar; (teach)
enseñar; **–room,** s sala
de exposición f.; **–y,** a
(gaudy) vistoso

shower, shau´-a s
chaparrón m.; **–y,** a
lluvioso

shred, shred s triza f.;
(tatter) harapo m.; v
picar; rallar

shrew, shruu s arpía f.;
–d*, a astuto

shriek, shriik, v chillar; s
chillido m.

shrill, shril a agudo;
penetrante

shrimp, shrimp s camarón
m.

shrine, shrain s relicario

m.; santuario m.

shrink, shringk v
encogerse

shrivel, shriv´-l v
arrugarse; encogerse

shroud, shraud s mortaja
f.; sudaríum; v amortajar

Shrove Tuesday, shrouv-
tiuus ´-di s martes de
carnaval m.

shrub, shrŏb s arbusto m.

shrug, shrŏg v encogerse
de hombros

shudder, shŏd´-a v
estremecerse; s
estremecimiento m.

shuffle, shŏf´-l v (gait)
arrastrar los pies; (cards)
barajar

shun, shŏn v rehuir;
esquivar; evitar

shunt, shŏnt v (trucks,
etc) desviar

shut, shŏt v cerrar; **–ter,** s
persiana f.; (camera)
obturador m.

shuttle, shŏt´-l s (sewing)
lanzadera f.

shy, shai a* tímido;
reservado; vergonzoso; v
asustarse

shyness, shai´-nes s
timidez f.; reserva f.

sick, sik a enfermo;
mareado; **–en,** v
enfermar; **–ly,** adv

enfermizo; **–ness,** s
enfermedad f.; náusea f.

sickle, sik´-l s hoz f.

side, said,s., lado m.; (hill)
falda f.; (river) orilla f.;
v tomar parte; **–board,** s
aparador m.

side effect, said ef-ekt´ s
efecto f.; secundario

sideways, said´-uei s adv
de lado

siding, sai´-ding s
desviadero m.; cobertura
de una casa

siege, sii CH s de
maderasitio m.; asedio
m.

sieve, siiv tamiz m.; criba
f.

sift, sift v tamizar; cribar;
investigar; (mil) cernir

sigh, sai s suspiro m.; v
suspirar

sight, sait v avistar; s (eye)
vista f.; (spectacle)
espectáculo m.; (gun)
mira f.; **at –,** a la vista;
by –, de vista

sign, sain, v firmar; s
señal f.; (board) muestra
de establecimiento f.;
–post, poste de guía m.

signal, sig´-nal s señal f.; v
señalar

signature, sig´-na-tiur s
firma f.

significant*, sig-nif´-i-kant *a* significante

signification, sig-ni-fi-kei´-shon *s* significación *f.*

signify, sig´-ni-fai *v* significar; manifestar

silence, sai´-lens *s* silencio *m.*; (quiet) sosiego *m.*; *interj* !silencio!; *v* hacer callar

silencer, sai´-len-sa *s* (engine) silencioso *m.*; silenciador *m.*

silent*, sai´-lent *a* silencioso; callado; taciturno

silhouette, sil´-luu-et *s* silueta *f.*

silicon, sil´-i-kon *s* silicio *m.*

silk, silk *s* seda *f.*; (thread) hilo de seda *m.*; **–en**, *a* de seda; **–worm**, *s* gusano de seda *m.*; **–y**, *a* sedoso

sill, sill *s* (door) umbral *m.*; (window) antepecho *m.*

silly, sil´-i *a* tonto; bobo

silver, sil´-va *s* plata *f.*; *a* de plata; *v* platear

silversmith, sil´-ver-smiz *s* platero *m.*

similar*, sim´-i-la *a* semejante; **–ity**, *s*

semejanza *f.*

simile, sim´-i-li *s* comparación *f.*

simmer, sim´-a *v* hervir a fuego lento

simple, sim´-pl *a* simple; **–ton**, *s* simplón *m.*

simplicity, sim-plis´-i-ti *s* sencillez *f.*

simplify, sim´-pli-fai *v* simplificar

simultaneous*, si-mol-tei´-ni-os *a* simultáneo

sin, sin *v* pecar; *s* pecado *m.*; culpa *f.*; **–ful**, *a* pecaminoso; **–less**, sin pecado; **–ner**, *s* pecador *m.*

since, sins *prep* desde; *adv* desde entonces; *conj* desde que; después que; ya que; puesto que

sincere*, sin-sir´ *a* sincero

sinew, sin´-iuu *s* tendón *m.*; músculo *m.*; nervio *m.*

sing, sing *v* cantar; **–er**, *s* cantor *m.*; cantante *m.* or *f.*

singe, sinCH, *v* chamuscar

single, sing´-gl *a* solo; (unmarried) soltero

single-handed, sing´-gl-jAn-did *a* solo

single room, sing´-gl ruum *s* habitación *f.*;

individual

singly, sing´-gli *adv* uno a uno

singular*, sing´-guiu-lr *a* singular; peculiar

sinister, sin´-is-ta *a* siniestro

sink, singk *s* vertedero *m.*; fregadero *m.*; (drain) albañal *m.*; *v* hundir; (scuttle) echar a pique; (shaft) fijar

sip, sip, *v* sorber; libar; *s* sorbo *m.*

siphon, sai´-fn *s* sifón *m.*

siren, sai´-ren *s* sirena *f.*

sirloin, sẽr´-loin *s* lomo *m.*; solomillo *m.*

sister, sis´-ta *s* hermana *f.*; **–in-law**, cuñada *f.*

sit, sit *v* sentarse; (incubate) empollar; **–down**, *s* sentarse; **–ting**, *a* sentado; *s* sesión *f.*

site, sait *s* sitio *m.*; (building) solar *m.*

situated, sit´-iu-ei-tid *a* situado

situation, sit-iu-ei´-shon *s* situación *f.*; (post) colocación *f.*

six, six *s* & *a* seis *m.*; **–teen**, dieciséis *m.*; **–teenth**, décimosexto *m.*; **–th**, sexto *m.*;

–tieth, sexagésimo *m.*;
–ty, sesenta *m.*

size, sai *s* tamaño *m.*;
talla *f.*; (measure)
medida *f.*; (glue) cola *f.*;
v encolar

skate, skeit, *v* patinar; *s*
patín *m.*; (fish) raya *f.*

skateboard, skeit-bórd *s*
monopatín *m.*

skating, skei-ting *s*
patinaje *m.*

skating rink, skei-ting
rink *s* pista *f.*; de
patinaje

skein, skein *s* madeja *f.*

skeleton, skel´-*e*-ton *s*
esqueleto *m.*

skeptical, skep´-ti-kal *a*
escéptico

sketch, skech *v* bosquejar;
s boceto *m.*

skewer, skiuu´-*a s* espetón
m.; boceto *m.*; pequeño
estoque

ski, skii *s* esquí; *v* esquiar

skid, skid *v* patinar;
deslizar

skiff, skif *s* esquife *m.*

skiing, skii-ing *s* esquí; -
resort estación *f.*; de
esquí

ski lift, skii-lift *s* remonte
m.; telesquí *m.*; telesilla
m.

skill, skil *s* habilidad *f.*;

destreza *f.*; (natural)
maña *f.*

skillful*, skil´-f*u*l *a*
diestro; hábil

skim, skim *v* rasar;
espumar; (cream)
desnatar

skimmed milk, skimd
milk *s* leche *f.*;
desnatada

skin, skin *s* piel *f.*; cutis
m.; (hide) cuero *m.*;
(peel) pellejo *m.*; *v*
desollar; (fruit) pelar

skip, skip *v* omitir; saltar

skipper, skip´-*a s* patrón
de buque *m.*

skirmish, skĕr´-mish *s*
escaramuza *f.*

skirt, skĕrt *s* falda *f.*;
(border) borde *m.*; *v*
faldear; bordear

ski slope, skii-sloup *s* pista
f.; de esquí

skull, skŏl *s* cráneo *m.*

skunk, skŏnk *s* mofeta *f.*;
zorillo *m.*

sky, skai *s* cielo *m.*;
firmamento *m.*; claraboya *f.*

skyscraper, skai-skrei´-pa
s rascacielos *m.*

slab, slAb *s* losa *f.*; (large)
lastra *f.*

slack, slAk *s* escoria *f.*; *a*
flojo; **–en,** *v* aflojar

slander, slaan´-da *v*
calumniar; *s* calumnia *f.*

slanderer, slaan´-da-rer *s*
calumniador *m.*

slang, slAng *s* argot *m.*;
jerga *f.*

slant, slaant *v* sesgarse;
oblicuar; *s* sesgo *m.*;
oblicuidad *f.*; **–ing,** *a*
sesgado; oblícuo

slap, slAp *v* dar una
manotada; *s* manotada
f.; bofetada *f.*

slash, slAsh *s* (cut)´corte
m.; *v* cortar

slate, sleit *v* empizarrar; *s*
pizarra *f.*

slaughter, sloa´-ta *v*
matar; (massacre)
degollar; *s* matanza *f.*;
–er, matador *m.*

slave, sleiv *v* trabajar
como un esclavo; *s*
esclavo *m.*; **–ry,**
esclavitud *f.*

slay, slei *v* matar

sledge, sleCH *s* trineo *m.*;
–hammer, macho *m.*;
mandarria *f.*

sleek*, sliik *a* liso;
(manners) suave

sleep, sliip *v* dormir. *s*
sueño *m.*; **–ing car,**
coche cama *m.*; **–less,** *a*
insomne; desvelado;
–lessness, *s* insomnio

m.; –y, a soñoliento

sleeping bag, sliip-ing bAg s saco m.; de dormir

sleeping pill, sliip-ing pil s somnífero m.

sleet, sliit s aguanieve f.

sleeve, sliiv s manga f.

sleigh, slei s trineo m.

sleight, slait s maña f.; astucia f.; **–of hand,** juego de manos m.

slender*, slen´-da a delgado; (means) escaso

slice, slais s tajada f.; (bread) rebanada f.; v cortar en lonchas

slide, slaid s resbalón m.; (microscopic, photographic, etc.) placa f.; diapositiva f.; v resbalar

slight, slait s desaire m.; a ligero; a leve; v desairar

slim, slim a delgado; v adelgazar

slime, slaim s limo m.; (mud) fango m.

slimy, slai´-mi a viscoso; fangoso

sling, sling s (med) cabestrillo m.; v (throw) lanzar

slink, slingk v escabullirse; escaparse

slip, slip v resbalar s caída f.; **-pery,** a resbaladizo

slipper, slip´-a s zapatilla f.; chinela f.

slit, slit v rajar; s raja f.

slop, slop s agua sucia f.; **--pail,** cubo para agua sucia m.

slope, sloup v sesgarse; s declive m.; ladera f.

slot, slot s muesca f.; ranura f.; **–machines,** s máquina de servicios automáticos f.

sloth, slouz s pereza f.; (animal) perezoso m.

slouch, slauch v andar cabizbajo; a joroba f.

slovenly, slŏv´-n-li a desaliñado; sucio

slow*, slou a lento; despacio; v (clock, etc.) atrasar

slug, slŏg s babosa f.; (missile) posta f.; zángano m.

sluggish, slŏ´-guish a perezoso; indolente

sluice, sluus s (gate) compuerta f.

slum, slŏm s barrio bajo m.

slumber, slŏm´-ba v dormitar; s sueño ligero m.

slump, slŏmp s baja repentina en los valores f.; hundimiento m.

slur, slër s mancha f.; v manchar; afrenta f.

slush, slŏsh s lodo m.; fango m.

sly*, slai a astuto; furtivo

smack, smAk s (hand) cachete f.; (lips) rechupete m.; (kiss) beso sonado m.; (boat) queche m.; v (beat) pegar; (lips) rechuparse

small, smoal a pequeño; **–ness,** s pecȳeñez f.

smallpox, smoal´-poks s viruelas f. pl

smart, smaart a vivo; (clever) listo; (spruce) elegante; v escocer

smash, smAsh s colisión f.; (commercial) fracaso m.; v romper; destrozar

smattering, smAt´-er-ing s conocimiento superficial m.

smear, smir v untar; s mancha f.

smell, smel v oler; s olor m.; **-ing salts,** sales aromáticas f. pl

smelt, smelt v fundir; s eperlano m.

smile, smail v sonreírse; s sonrisa f.

smite, smait v herir; afligir

smith, smiz s forjador m.; herrero m.; **-y,** forja f.

ligero; v desairar

slim, slim a delgado; v adelgazar

slime, slaim s limo m.; (mud) fango m.

slimy, slai´-mi a viscoso; fangoso

sling, sling s (med) cabestrillo m.; v (throw) lanzar

slink, slingk v escabullirse

slip, slip v resbalar; s caída f.; **–pery,** a resbaladizo

slipper, slip´-a s zapatilla f.

slit, slit v rajar; s raja f.

sloe, slou s endrina f.

slop, slop s agua sucia f.; **–pail,** cubo para agua sucia m.

slope, sloup v sesgarse; s declive m.

slot, slot s muesca f.; ranura f.; **–machines,** s máquina de servicios automáticos f.

sloth, slouz s pereza f.; (animal) perezoso m.

slouch, slauch v andar cabizbajo

slough, slau s (fig) abismo m.

slovenly, slŏv´-n-li a desaliñado

slow*, slou a lento; despacio; v (clock, etc) atrasar

slug, slŏg s babosa f.; (missile) posta f.

sluggish, slŏ´-guish a perezoso; indolente

sluice, sluus s (gate) compuerta f.

slum, slŏm s barrio bajo m.

slumber, slŏm´-ba v dormitar; s sueño ligero m.

slump, slŏmp s baja repentina en los valores f.

slur, slĕr s mancha f.; v manchar

slush, slŏsh s lodo m.; fango m.

sly*, slai a socarrón

smack, smAk s (hand) cachete m.; (lips) rechupete m.; (kiss) beso sonado m.; (boat) queche m.; v (beat) pegar; (lips) rechuparse

small, smoal a pequeño; **–ness,** s pequeñez f.

small-pox, smoal´-poks s viruelas f. pl

smart, smaart a vivo; (clever) listo; (spruce) elegante; v escocer

smash, smAsh s colisión f.; (commercial) fracaso m.; v romper; destrozar

smattering, smAt´-er-ing s

conocimiento superficial m.

smear, smir v untar; s mancha f.

smell, smel v oler; s olor m.; **–ing-salts,** sales aromáticas f. pl

smelt, smelt v fundir; s eperlano m.

smile, smail v sonreírse; s sonrisa f.

smite, smait v herir; afligir

smith, smiz s forjador m.; **–y,** forja f.

smoke, smouk s humo m. v fumar; **–less,** a sin humo; **–r,** s fumador m.

smoky, smouk´-i a ahumado

smooth, smuuD a* suave; liso; v alisar

smother, smŏD´-a v sofocar

smoulder, smoul´-da v arder en rescoldo

smudge, smŏ CH s tiznón m.; v tiznar

smug, smŏg a pimpante; presumido

smuggle, smŏg´-l v hacer contrabando

smuggler, smŏg´-gla s contrabandista m.

smut, smŏt s tiznón m.

snack, snAk s piscolabis

m.; taco *m.*; bocadillo *m.*

snail, sneil *s* caracol *m.*

snake, sneik *s* serpiente *f.*; culebra *f.*

snap, snAp *s* chasquido *m.*; (bite) dentellada *f.*; *v* chasquear; (break) romperse; (fingers) castañetear; (animal) dentellear

snapshot, snAp´-shot *s* instantánea *f.*

snare, sné *r s* lazo *m.*; trampa *f.*; *v* poner trampas

snarl, snaarl *v* gruñir

snatch, snAch **–from,** *v* arrebatar; **–at,** echar mano

sneak, sniik *s* soplón *m.*; *v* (steal) ratear; **–away,** escabullirse

sneer, snir *v* mofarse; *s* mofa *f.*

sneeze, sniis, *v* estornudar; *s* estornudo *m.*

sniff, snif *v* husmear; (smell) olfatear

snip, snip *s* tijeretada *f.*; *v* tijeretear

snipe, snaip *s* agachadiza *f.*; **–r,** tirador *m.*

snore, snór *v* roncar

snorkel, snór-kl *s* esnórquel *m*; respirador;

v nadar respirando por un tubo

snort, snoart *v* resoplar; *s* resoplido *m.*

snout, snaut *s* hocico *m.*; (pig) jeta *f.*

snow, snou *v* nevar; *s* nieve *f.*; **–bound,** *a* sitiado por la nieve; **–drop,** campanilla blanca *f.*; **–storm,** nevada *f.*

snub, snöb *s* desaire *m.*; *v* desairar

snub-nose, snöb´-nous *s* nariz chata *f.*

snuff, snöf *s* rapé *m.*; tabaco en polvo *m.*

snug, snög *a* cómodo; abrigado

so, sou *adv* así; así pues; por tanto; tan

soak, souk *v* remojar; empapar

soap, soup *s* jabón *m.*

soar, sór *v* remontarse; cernerse

sob, sob *s* sollozo *m.*; *v* sollozar

sober*, sou´-ba *a* sobrio; moderado

sociable, sou´-sha-bl *a* sociable

social*, sou´-shal *a* social; **–ism,** *s* socialismo *m.*; **–ist,** socialista *m.*

society, so-sai´-i-ti *s* sociedad *f.*

sock, sok *s* calcetín *m.*

socket, sok´-it *s* encaje *m.*; (eyes) cuenca *f.*; (teeth) alvéolo *m.*

sod, sod *s* témpano *m.*

soda, sout´-da *s* sosa *f.*; **–water,** agua de soda *f.*

sofa, sou-fa *s* sofá *m.*

soft*, soft *a* blando; muelle; **–en,** *v* ablandar

soft drink, soft dring-k *s* bebida *f.*; no alcohólica; bebida *f.*; refrescante

softness, soft´-nes *s* blandura *f.*

software, soft-uer *s* software *m.*; elementos de programación

soil, soil *s* tierra *f.*; *v* manchar; ensuciar

sojourn, söCH´-ern *s* estancia *f.*; *v* morar

solace, sol´-as *s* consuelo *m.*; *v* consolar

solder, sol´-da *v* soldar; *s* soldadura *f.*

soldier, soul´-CH *a s* soldado *m.*

sole, soul *s* suela *f.*; (fish) lenguado *m.*; *v* echar suelas; *a** único; solo

solemn*, sol´-em *a* solemne

solicit, so-lis´-it *v* solicitar

source, só rs s fuente f.;
origen m.

south, sauz s sur m., sud
m.

southerly, soz´-er-li a del
sur; meridional

souvenir, su-vi-niir´ s
recuerdo m.

sovereign, sov´-er-in s
soberano m.; a supremo;
(remedy) eficaz

sow, sau s cerda f.; puerca
f.

sow, sou v sembrar; **–er,** s
sembrador m.

space, speis s espacio m.;
período m.; **–craft,** s
nave espacial f.

spacious*, spei´-shos a
espacioso

spade, speid s azada f.;
(cards) espadas f. pl;
espada f.

span, spAn s palmo m.;
(architecture) tramo m.;
v extenderse sobre

spangle, spAng´-gl s
lentejuela f.

spaniel, spAn´-yel s perro
de aguas m.

spar, spaar v boxear; s
(naut) mástil m.

spare, spé r v perdonar;
evitar; (grant) hacer el
favor de

sparing*, spé´-ring a

frugal; económico

spark, spaark v chispear; s
chispa f.

sparkle, spaar´-kl v
centellear; (wine)
espumar

sparrow, spAr´-ou s
gorrión m.

spasm, spa s m s espasmo
m.; **–odic,** a
espasmódico

spatter, spAt´-a v salpicar

spawn, spoan s huevas f.
pl; v desovar

speak, spiik, v hablar; **–er,**
s orador m.

spear, spir s lanza f.; arpón
m.; v alancear

special*, spesh´-al a
especial

speciality, spesh-i-al´-i-ti s
especialidad f.

specie, spii´-shii s moneda
f.; dinero m.

species, spii´-shii-es s
especie f.; género m.

specific, spe-si-fik s
específico m.; aspectos
m. pl; concretos; a
específico; expreso;
explícito

specification, spes-i-fi-
kei´-shon s
especificación f.

specify, spes´-i-fai v
especificar; detallar

specimen, spes´-i-men s
espécimen m.; ejemplar
m.; muestra f.

specious*, spii´-shos a
especioso; plausible

speck, spek s mota f.;
mancha f.

spectacle, spek´-ta-kl s
espectáculo m.

spectacles, spek´-ta-kls s
(optical) gafas f. pl;
anteojos m. pl

spectator, spek´-tei´-ta s
espectador m.

specter, spek´-tr s espectro
m.; fantasma m.

speculate, spek´-iu-leit v
especular; reflexionar

speech, spiich s habla m.;
(discourse) discurso m.;
–less, a (fig) mudo

speed, spiid s rapidez f.;
velocidad f.; **–ometer,** s
velocímetro m.; **–y,** a
veloz

speed limit, spiid lim´-it s
velocidad f.; máxima;
límite f.; de velocidad

spell, spel s hechizo m.; v
deletrear

spend, spend v gastar;
–thrift, s pródigo m.

sphere, sfir s esfera f.

spice, spais s especia f.; v
condimentar

spicy, spai´-si a aromático;

(*fig*) picante

spider, spai´-da s araña f.

spike, spaik s alcayata f.; clavo m.; v clavar con alcayatas

spill, spil v derramar

spin, spin v hilar; (turn) girar; **–ning,** s hilado m.

spinach, spin´-iCH s espinaca f.

spinal, spai´-nl a espinal; vertebral

spindle, spin´-dl s huso m.; (axle) eje m.

spine, spain s espina dorsal f.

spinster, spin´-sta s soltera f.

spiral, spai´-rl a espiral; s espira f.

spire, spair s chapitel m.; (deunatorre) aguja f.

spirit, spir´-it s espíritu m.; alcohol m.; (animation) brío m.; **–ed,** a brioso; (bold) valiente; **–ual,** espiritual; **–ualist,** s espiritista m.

spit, spit v escupir; s saliva f.; (roasting) asador m.

spite, spait, v despechar; vejar. s despecho m.; **–ful*,** a despechado, rencoroso; **in –of,** a pesar de

splash, splAsh v salpicar; (play) chapotear

splendid*, splen´-did a espléndido; magnífico

splendor, splen´-dr s esplendor m.

splint, splint s (surgical) tablilla f.

splinter, splin´-ta s astilla f.; v hacer astillas

split, split v hender; s hendedura f.

spoil, spoil v echar a perder; (child, etc) mimar

spoke, spouk s rayo de rueda m.

spokesman, spouks´-mAn s portavoz m.

sponge, spônCH s esponja f.; v esponjar

sponsor, spon´-sr s fiador m.; (baptism) padrino m.; persona responsable de f.

spontaneous*, spon-tei´-ni-os a espontáneo

spool, spuul s canilla f.; carrete m.; bobina f.; v devanar

spoon, spuun s cuchara f.; **–ful,** cucharada f.

sport, spó rt s deporte m.; **–ive,** a deportivo

sportsman, spó rts´-mAn s deportista m.

spot, spot v manchar; s mancha f.; (place) sitio m.; lugar m.; **–less,** a sin mancha

spouse, spaus s esposo m.; esposa f.

spout, spaut s (outlet) canalón m.; (jug or pot) pico m. caño m.; v brotar; borbotar

sprain, sprein v torcer; discolarse; s torcedura f.

sprat, sprAt s arenque m.

sprawl, sproal v despatarrar

spray, sprei s (branch) ramita f.; (water) rociada f.; v rociar; (med.) pulverizar

sprayer, sprei´-a s pulverizador m.

spread, spred v extender; (on bread, etc) untar; (news) divulgar; **–out,** desplegar

sprig, sprig s ramito m.; (offshoot) vástago m.

sprightly, sprait´-li a alegre; vivo; despierto

spring, spring s primavera f.; (leap) salto m.; (water) manantial m.; (metal) resorte m.; muelle m.; v saltar

sprinkle, spring´-kl v espolvorear; (water)

rociar; salpicar

sprout, spraut *v* brotar; *s* brote *m.*

spruce, spruus *s* abeto *m.*; *a* elegante

spur, spёr *s* espuela *f.*; *v* espolear

spurious*, spiu´-ri-*o*s *a* falso

spurn, spёrn *v* desdeñar; despreciar

spy, spai *s* espía *m.*; *v* espiar

squabble, skuob´-l *s* riña *f.*; *v* reñir; disputar

squad, skuod *s* (*mil*) pelotón *m.*; **–ron,** (*mil*) escuadrón *m.*; (*naval*) escuadrilla *f.*

squalid*, skuol´-id *a* escuálido

squall, skuoal *s* (wind) chubasco *m.*; *v* (scream) chillar

squalor, skuoal´-r *s* escualidez *f.*; suciedad *f.*

squander, skuon´-da *v* derrochar; malgastar

square, skuér *s* cuadrado *m.*; (public) plaza *f.*; *a** cuadrado

squash, skuosh *v* aplastar; (*fig*) apretar; *s* presión *m.*; calabaza *f.*

squat, skuot *v* ponerse en cuclillas; agacharse; *a*

rechoncho

squeak, skuiik *v* chillar; (bearings, etc) chirriar

squeeze, skuii *s v* estrujar; (cuddle) apretar; exprimir

squid, skuid *s* calamar *m.*

squint, skuint *v* bizquear; mirar de reojo; *s* bizco *m.*

squirrel, skuir´-l *s* ardilla *f.*

squirt, skuёrt *v* jeringar; *s* jeringa *f.*

stab, stAb *v* apuñalar; *s* puñalada *f.*

stability, sta-bil´-i-ti *s* estabilidad *f.*

stable, stei´-bl *s* caballeriza *f.*; establo *m.*; *a* estable; fijo

stack, stAck *s* (wood) pila *f.*; (hay) niara *f.*; (chimney) chimenea *f.*; *v* amontonar

stadium, steii-di-um *s* estadio *m.*

staff, staaf *s* cayado *m.*; bastón corvo *m.*; (employees) personal *m.*; (*mil*) estado mayor *m.*; **flag—,** asta *f.*

stag, stAg *s* ciervo *m.*

stage, steiCH *s* escenario *m.*; escena *f.*; (hall) tablado *m.*; (period) fase

f.; *v* poner en escena

stagger, stAg´-a *v* tambalearse; (*fig*) asombrar; alternar

stagnate, stAg´-neit *v* estancarse

staid*, steid *a* grave; sosegado

stain, stein, *v* teñir; (soil) manchar; *s* tinte *m.*; mancha *f.*; **–less,** *a* (steel) inoxidable

stair, ster *s* peldaño *m.*; escalón *m.*; **–s,** escalera *f.*

stake, steik *s* estaca *f.*; (wager) apuesta *f.*; *v* estacar; (wager) apostar

stale, steil *a* (bread, etc) viejo; rancio; (beer) pasada

stalk, stoalk *s* tallo *m.*; *v* acechar

stall, stoal *s* (market) puesto *m.*; (theater) butaca *f.*

stalwart, stoal´-uert *a* fornido; vigoroso

stamina, stAm´-i-na *s* vigor *m.*; resistencia *f.*

stammer, stAm´-a *v* tartamudear

stamp, stAmp *s* (rubber, etc, seal) estampador *m.*; (postage) sello de correo *m.*; *v* estampar;

(postage) timbrar; (foot) patear

stampede, stAm-piid´ s estampida f.

stand, stAnd v estar de pie; (place) colocar; (endure) soportar; s tribuna f.; pedestal m.; (market) puesto m.; (resistance) resistencia f.; **–still,** parada f.

standard, stAn´-dard s estandarte m.; norma f.; a de ley; clásico; **–ize,** v uniformar; unificar; tipificar

standing, stAn´-ding a permanente; s posición f.; **–room,** sitio para estar de pie m.

staple, stei´-pl s armella f.; a corriente; artículo de primera necesidad

star, staar s estrella f.; **–ry,** a estrellado

starboard, staar´-bó rd s (naut) estribor m.

starch, staarch s almidón m.; v almidonar

stare, stér v fijar la vista; s mirada fija f.

starling, staar´-ling s estornino m.

start, staart s comienzo m. principio m.; (shock) sobresalto m.; v

(commence) comenzar; principiar; (mech) poner en marcha; (leave) salir

startle, staar´-tl v asustar

starvation, staar-vei´-shon s muerte por hambre f.; inanición f.

starve, staarv v morir de hambre

state, steit, v declarar; s estado m.; (condition) condición f.; (pompa) pompa f.; **–ly,** a majestuoso; **–ment,** s declaración f.; (account) estado de cuentas m.

statesman, steits´-man s estadista m.

station, stei´-shon s estación f.; (position) posición f.; v apostar

stationary, stei´-shon-a-ri a estacionario

stationer, stei´-shon-a s papelero m.

stationery, stei´-shon-a-ri s papelería f.

statistics, stA-tis´-tiks s estadística f.

statue, stAt´-iu s estatua f.

statute, stAt´-iuut s estatuto m.; ley f.

staunch, stoanch a* constante; v estancar

stave, steiv s duela f.

stay, stei s estancia f.; v permanecer; quedarse

stays, steis s corsé m.

stead, sted s lugar m.; sitio m.; **in–of,** adv en lugar de

steadfast, sted´-fast a constante; determinado

steady, sted´-i a firme; (reliable) formal; estable; (markets) firme

steak, steik s (beef) biftec m.

steal, stiil v robar; hurtar

stealth, stelz s hurto m.; cautela f.; **by –,** a hurtadillas

steam, stiim s vapor m.

steamer, stii´-ma s buque de vapor m.

steel, stiil s acero m.

steep, stiip v empapar; a empinado

steeple, stii´-pl s campanario m.; torre f.

steer, stir v gobernar; (motor) conducir; s novillo m.; **–age,** proa f.; entrepuente m.

stem, stem s tallo m.; (glass) pie m.; v contrarrestar

stench, stench s hedor m.

stenographer, sten-og´-raf-a s taquígrafa f.; estenógrafa f.

step, step *v* dar un paso; *s* paso *m*.; (stair) peldaño *m*.; **--father,** padrastro *m*.; **--mother,** madrastra *f*.

stepbrother, step-bröD´-a *s* hermanastro *m*.

stepladder, step-lAd´-a *s* escalera doble o de tijera

stepsister, step-sis´-ta *s* hermanastra *f*.

stereo, ste-rii-o *abbr* of **stereophonic** estéreo

stereophonic*, ster-rio-fon´-ik *a* estereofónico

sterile, ster´-il *a* estéril

sterilize, ster´-i-lais *v* esterilizar

sterling, stěr´-ling *s* esterlina *f*.; *a* genuino; puro

stern, stěrn *s* (naut) popa *f*.; *a** austero, severo

stevedore, stii´-vi-dor *s* estibador *m*.

stew, stiuu *s* estofado *m*.; guisado *m*.; *v* estofar

steward, stiuu´-erd *s* camarero *m*.; (estate) mayordomo *m*.; **--ess,** camarera *f*.

stewardess, stiuu´-erd-es *s* auxiliar *mf*.; de vuelo; azafata *f*.; camarera *f*.

stick, stik *v* (affix) pegar; *s* palo *m*.; (walking) bastón *m*.; **--y,** *a* pegajoso

stiff, stif *a* tieso; yerto; **--en,** *v* atiesar

stifle, stai´-fl *v* sofocar; ahogar

stigmatize, stig´-ma-tais *v* estigmatizar

stile, stail *s* portillo *m*.; **turn--,** torniquete *m*.

still, stil *s* (distill) alambique *m*.; *v* (to calm) calmar; *a* quieto; *adv* aún; todavía; *conj* (yet) sin embargo

stimulate, stim´-iu-leit *v* estimular

sting, sting *v* picar; (nettle) ortigar; *s* aguijón *m*.

stingy, stin´-CHi *a* avaro; mezquino

stink, stink *v* heder; apestar; *s* hedor *m*.

stint, stint *v* limitar; restringir; escatimar

stipend, stai´-pend *s* (eccl) estipendio *m*.; salario *m*.

stipulate, stip´-iu-leit *v* estipular

stipulation, stip-iu-lei´-shon *s* estipulación *f*.

stir, stěr *v* revolver; agitar; moverse; *s* alboroto *m*.

stirrup, stěr-op *s* estribo *m*.

stitch, stich *v* dar puntadas; *s* puntada *f*.; (pain) punzada *f*.

stock, stok *v* vender; poner en surtido; *s* (tree) tronco *m*.; (gun) caja *f*.; (flower) alelí *m*.; (goods) existencias *f*. *pl*; (live) ganado *m*.; **--broker,** corredor de bolsa *m*.; **-- exchange,** bolsa *f*.; **--s,** (securities) acciones *f*. *pl*; valores *m*. *pl*; (pillory) cepo *m*.; **-- taking,** inventario *m*.

stocking, stok´-ing *s* media *f*.; calceta *f*.

stoke, stouk *v* atizar el fuego; **--r,** *s* fogonero *m*.

stolid,* stol´-id *a* estólido; impasible

stomach, stŏm´-ak *s* estómago *m*.; **--ache,** dolor de estómago *m*.

stone, stoun *v* apedrear; *s* piedra *f*.; (pebble) guijo *m*.

stool, stuul *s* banqueta *f*.; (med.) bacín *m*.; eracuación *f*.

stoop, stuup *v* agacharse; (fig) humillarse

stop, stop *s* parada *f*.; (interruption) pausa *f*.; (punctuation) punto *m*.; *v* parar; pararse;

(payment) suspender; (cease) cesar; **–up,** cegar

stopper, stop´-*a* s tapón m.; obturador m.

storage, stou´-reiCH s almacenaje m.

store, stór s (shop) tienda f.; (department) almacén m.; v almacenar

stork, stoark s cigüeña f.

storm, stoarm v asaltar; s tempestad f.

stormy, stoar´-mi *a* tempestuoso

story, stó´-ri s cuento m.; historia f.; (floor) piso m.

stout*, staut *a* corpulento; (strong) fuerte

stove, stouv s estufa f.; (range) fogón m.

stow, stou v hacinar; (naut) estivar; ordenar

stowaway, stou´-*a*-uei s polizón m.

straggle, strAg´-l v desparramarse

straight*, streit *a* derecho; directo; **–en,** v enderezar; **–forward,*** *a* recto; sincero

strain, strein s esfuerzo m.; (music) acorde m.; (pull) tirantez f.; v esforzarse; (stretch)

estirar; (tendon) torcer; (liquid) colar

strainer, strei´-na s colador m.

straits, streits s pl (channel) estrecho m.

strand, strAnd v (naut) encallar; s playa f.; (hair) trenza f.

strange*, streinCH *a* extraño; (peculiar) raro

stranger, strein´-CH *a* s forastero m.; extraño m.

strangle, strAng´-gl v estrangular

strap, strAp v atar con correas; s correa f.

strategy, strAt-*a*-CHi s estrategia f.

straw, stroa s paja f.

strawberry, stroa´-ber-i s fresa f.

stray, strei v extraviarse; descarriarse; *a* (animal) extraviado

streak, striik s raya f.; v rayar; veta f.

streaky, striik´-i *a* rayado

stream, striim v correr; s corriente f.; (small) arroyo m.

street, striit s calle f.

street plan, striit-plAn s plano m.

streetwise, striit-uais *a* pícaro; experimentado

en la vida callejera

strength, strengz s fuerza f.; **–en,** v fortificar; reforzar; (health) fortalecer

strenuous*, stren´-iu-os *a* estrenuo; enérgico

stress, stres s (pressure) fuerza f.; (urge) urgencia f.; v acentuar

stretch, strech v estirar; s extensión f.; distancia f.

stretcher, strech´-*a* s camilla f.; tendedor m.

strew, struu v esparcir; desparramar

strict*, strikt *a* estricto; riguroso

stride, straid v andar a trancos; s tranco m.; avance m.

strife, straif s contienda f.; riña f.; disputa f.

strike, straik v (work) declararse en huelga; (smite) pegar; golpear; (lightning) herir; (match) encender; s huelga f.; paro m.; **–off,** **–out,** v (delete) borrar

striker, straik´-*a* s (work) huelguista m.

string, string s cordel m.; hilo m.; (thin) bramante m.; (violin) cuerda f.; v (beads) ensartar

stringency, strin´-CHen-si s rigor m.; aprieto m.

strip, strip s tira f.; v desnudar

stripe, straip s raya f.; (mil) galón m.; v rayar

strive, straiv v esforzarse; contender

stroke, strouk s toque m.; (med.) ataque m.; (piston) carrera f.; (pen) trazo m.; v acariciar

stroll, stroul v pasearse; s paseo m.

strong*, strong a fuerte; robusto; sólido; (light) brillante

structure, strŏk´-tiur s construcción f.; estructura f.; edificio m.

struggle, strog´-l v luchar; s lucha f.; conflicto m.

strut, strŏt v pavonearse; s (brace) riostra f.

stubborn*, stŏb´-ern a testarudo; obstinado

stud, stŏd s tachón m.; (collar) botón m.; (breeding) yeguada f.; v tachonar

student, stiuu´-dent s estudiante m.

studio, stiuu´-di-ou s estudio m.

studious*, stiuu´-di-os a

estudioso

study, stŏd´-i s estudio m.; (room) escritorio m.; v estudiar

stuff, stŏf v rellenar; (preserve) empajar; s (cloth) tela f.; (suiting) paño m.

stuffing, stŏf´-ing s relleno m.

stumble, stŏm´-bl v dar un traspié; tropezar

stump, stŏmp s tocón m.; (arm, leg) muñón m.; (tooth) raigón m.

stun, stŏn v aturdir; –ning, a (fig) pasmoso

stunt, stŏnt s maniobra sensacional f.

stunted, stŏnt´-id a achaparrado

stupefy, stiuu´-pi-fai v causar estupor

stupendous*, stiu-pen´-dos a estupendo

stupid*, stiuu´-pid a tonto; estúpido

stupidity, stiuu-pi´-di-ti s estupidez f.

stupor, stiuu´-pr s estupor m.

sturdy, stěr´-di a fuerte; vigoroso

sturgeon, stěr´-CH on s esturión m.

stutter, stŏt´-a v

tartamudear

sty, stai s pocilga f.; (med) orzuelo m.

style, stail s estilo m.; moda f.

stylish, štai´-lish a elegante; a la moda

subdue, sŏb-diuu´ v sojuzgar; (tame) amansar; rendir

subject, sŏb-CHekt´ v sujetar; obligar

subject, sŏb´-CHekt s sujeto m.

subjection, sŏb-CHek´-shon s sujeción f.

subjunctive, sŏb-CHŏngk´-tiv s subjuntivo m.

sublime, sŏb-laim´ a sublime

submarine, sŏb-ma-riin´ s & a submarino m.

submerge, sŏb-měr CH´ v sumergir

submission, sŏb-mish´-on s sumisión f.

submit, sŏb´-mit´ v someter; someterse

subordinate*, sŏb-or´-di-neit a subordinado

subscribe, sŏb-skraib´ v subscribir; (papers) abonarse; –r, s subscriptor m.; abonado m.

subscription, sŏb-skrip´-shon s subscripción f.; abono m.

subsequent*, sŏb´-si-kuent a subsecuente

subservient, sŏb-sĕr´-vi-ent a subordinado

subside, sŏb-said´ v hundirse; (water) bajar; apaciguarse

subsidy, sŏb´-si-di s (grant) subvención f.

subsist, sŏb-sist´ v subsistir

substance, sŏb´-stance s sustancia f.; esencia f.

substantial*, sŏb-stan´-shal a substancial

substantiate, sŏb-stan´-shi-eit; v verificar; comprobar

substitute, sŏb´-sti-tiuut s substituto m.; (proxy) suplente m.; v substituir

subterranean, sŏb-ter-rei´-nii-an a subterráneo

subtitle, sŏb-tai´-tl s subtítulo m.; v subtitular

subtle, sŏt´-l a sutil

subtract, sŏb-trAkt´ v substraer; restar

suburb, sŏb´-ĕrb s suburbio m.

subversive, sŏb-ver´-siv a subversivo

subway, sŏb´-uei s metro

m.; subterráneo m.; túnel m.; ferrocarril m.

succeed, sŏk-siid´ v suceder; (achieve) lograr; **–to,** (inherit) heredar

success, sŏk-ses´ s éxito m.; acierto m.; **–ful*,** a eficaz; próspero; **–ion,** s sucesión f.

successor, sŏk-ses´-a s sucesor m.

succor, sŏk´-er s socorro m.; v socorrer

succumb, sŏk-ŏm´ v sucumbir

such, sŏch a tal; igual; **–a,** tal; igual

suck, sŏk v chupar; **–le,** amamantar

suction, sŏk´-shon s succión f.

sudden*, sŏd´-n a repentino; súbito

sue, siuu v demandar en justicia

suede, sui-eid s ante m.; gamuza f.

suffer, sŏf-a v sufrir; soportar; **–ing,** s sufrimiento m.; a paciente; **on –ance,** con tolerancia

suffice, sŏ-fais´ v bastar; ser suficiente

sufficient*, sŏ-fish´-ent a

suficiente

suffocate, sŏf´-o-keit v sofocar

sugar, shu´-ga s azúcar m.

suggest, sŏ-CHest´ v sugerir; (advise) aconsejar; **–ion,** s sugestión f.; idea f.; **–ive,** a sugestivo

suicide, siuu´-i-said s suicidio m.

suit, siuut, v convenir; (dress, climate) sentar bien; s traje m.; (law) pleito m.; **–able,** a apropiado; **–or,** s (wooer) pretendiente m.

suitcase, suut-keis s maleta f.; valija f.

suite, suiit s (retinue) séquito m.; apartamento m.; (furniture) juego m.

sulfur, sŏl´-fr s azufre m.

sulk, sŏlk v amurriarse; **–y,** a murriático; ponerse de mal humor

sullen*, sŏl´-n a sombrío; hosco

sultry, sŏl´-tri a bochornoso; sofocante; húmedo

sum, sŏm s suma f.; **–up,** v resumir

summary, sŏm´-a-ri s resumen m.; a (law) sumario

summer, sŏm´-a s verano m.

summit, sŏm´-it s cima f.; cumbre f.

summon, sŏm´-n v citar; (call) llamar

summons, sŏm´-n s s (legal) citación f.

sumptuous*, sŏmp´-tiu-os a suntuoso

sun, sŏn s sol m.; **–beam,** rayo de sol m.; **–dial,** reloj de sol m.; **–ny,** a soleado; **–rise,** s salida del sol f.; amanecer m.; **–set,** puesta del sol f.; **–shine,** luz del sol f.; **–stroke,** insolación f.

sunbathe, sŏn´-beiD v tomar el sol

sunblock, sŏn´-blok s filtro m.; solar

sunburn, sŏn´-bĕrn s quemadura f.; de sol

Sunday, són-di s domingo m.

sundries, sŏn´-dris s pl géneros varios m. pl; varias cosas

sundry, sŏn´-dri a vario; diverso

sunglasses, sŏn´-glaas-es s pl gafas f. pl; de sol

sunken, sŏng´-kn a hundido

sunlight, sŏn´-lait s sol

m.; luz f.; del sol; luz f.; solar

sunstroke, sŏn´-strouk s insolación f.

suntan, sŏn´-tAn s bronceado m.

suntan lotion, sŏn-tAn lou´-shons crema f.; bronceadora; bronceador

sup, sŏp v cenar; **–per,** s cena f.; sorber

super, siuu´-per s (theatrical) comparsa m. & f.; cosa de superior calidad; **–annuation,** s pensión f.; **–cillious,** a arrogante; **–ficial,** superficial; **–fine,** superfino; **–intend,** v vigilar; **–intendent,** s superintendente m.; **–natural,** lo sobrenatural n.; **–sede,** v reemplazar; **–vise,** inspeccionar; **–vision,** s vigilancia f.

superb*, siu-pĕrb´ a soberbio

superfluous*, siuu-pĕr´-flu-os a superfluo

superior*, siuu-pi´-ri-a a superior

superlative, siuu-pĕr´-la-tiv s & a* superlativo m.

supermarket, suu-pĕr-

maar´-ket s supermercado m.

superstitious*, siuu-pĕr-stish´-os a supersticioso

supplant, so-plaant´ v suplantar

supple, sŏp´-l a flexible; blando

supplement, sŏp´-li-ment s suplemento m.

supplicant, sŏp´-li-kant s & a suplicante m. & f.

supplier, sŏp´-lai-a s proveedor m.; suministrador m.

supply, so-plai´ v proveer; s provisión f.

support, so-pó rt´ s (prop) puntal m.; (moral) sostén m.; (maintenance) manutención f.; v apuntalar; sostener; mantener

suppose, so-pous´ v suponer

supposition, so-pous -i´-shon s suposición f.

suppress, so-pres´ v suprimir; (conceal) ocultar

supremacy, siu-prem´-a-si s supremacía f.

supreme*, siu-priim´ a supremo

surcharge, ser-chaardCH´,

(postal) recargo m.; v recargar

sure*, shú r a seguro cierto

surety, shú r´-ti s (bail) fianza f.; (person) fiador m.

surf, sĕrf s oleaje m.; resaca f.

surface, sĕr´-fis s superficie f.

surfboard, sĕrf´-bórd s tabla f. (de surf)

surfing, sĕrf´-ĭng s surf m.

surge, sĕr CH v embravecerse; s oleaje m.

surgeon, sĕr´-CH on s cirujano m.

surgery, sĕr´-CH er-i s cirugía f.

surgical, sĕr´-CHi-kal a quirúrgico

surly, sĕr´-li a rudo; (dog) arisco

surmise, ser-mais ´ v conjeturar; sospedar; s conjetura f.

surmount, ser-maunt´ v (overcome) vencer; superar

surname, sĕr´-neim s apellido m.

surpass, ser-pass´ v superar; aventajar

surplus, sĕr´-plos s

sobrante m.; excedente m.

surprise, ser-prais ´ v sorprender; s sorpresa f.

surrender, se-ren´-da s (mil) rendición f.; v rendirse; (cede) ceder

surround, se-raund´ v rodear; (mil) cercar

surroundings, se-raund´-ings s alrededores m. pl

survey, sĕr´-vei s (land, etc) medición f.;inspección f.; v medir; (look at) inspeccionar; –or, s topógrafo m.

survival, ser-vai´-vl s supervivencia f.

survive, ser-vaiv´ v sobrevivir

survivor, ser-vai´-vr s sobreviviente m.

susceptible, so-sep´-ti-bl a susceptible

suspect, sos-pekt´ v sospechar; s sospechosa f.

suspend, sos-pend´ v suspender; (defer) aplazar

suspenders, sos-pen´-ders s pl ligas f. pl; tirantes m. pl

suspense, sos´-pens s incertidumbre f.;

suspenso m.

suspension, sos-pen´-shon s suspensión f.; – **bridge,** puente colgante m.

suspicion, sos-pish´-on s sospecha f.

suspicious*, sos-pish´-os a sospechoso

sustain, sos-tein´ v sostener; mantener; sufrir

sustenance, sos´-ten-ans s sustento m.

swagger, suAg´-a v fanfarronear

swallow, suol´-ou s trago m.; sorbo m.; (bird) golondrina f.; v tragar

swamp, suomp s pantano m.; v (boat) echar a pique

swan, suon s cisne m.

swarm, suoarm s nube f.; (bees) enjambre m.; (people) multitud f.; v enjambrar; hormiguear

sway, suei v oscilar; dominar; influir; (reel) tambalear; s (power) poder m.; (influence) influjo m.

swear, suér v jurar; (curse) blasfemar

sweat, suet s sudor m.; v sudar

sweep, suiip v barrer;

(chimney) deshollinar *s* (chimney) deshollinador *m.*; **–er,** barrendero *m.*; (carpet) escoba mecánica *f.*

sweet, suiit *a* dulce; *s* (confection) golosina *f.*; (dinner, etc.) dulces *m. pl*; **––bread,** lechecillas de ternera *f. pl*; **–en,** *v* endulzar; **–heart,** *s* novio *m.*, novia *f.*; **–ness,** dulzura *f.*; (smell) fragancia *f.*; **––pea,** guisante de olor *m.*

swell, suel *s* (sea) oleaje *m.*; *v* hinchar

swelling, suel´-ing *s* hinchazón *f.*

swerve, suěrv *v* desviarse; apartarse

swift, suift *a* veloz; rápido

swim, suim *v* nadar; *s* natación *f.*

swimmer, suim´-ma *s* nadador *m.*

swimming, suim´-ing *n* natación *f.*

swimsuit, suim-suut *s* traje *m.*; de baño; bañador *m.*

swimming pool, suim´-ing puul *s* piscina *f.*

swimming trunks, suim´-ing trŏngks *s* pantalón

m.; de baño; bañador *m.*

swindle, suin´-dl *v* estafar; *s* estafa *f.*

swindler, suin´-dla *s* estafador *m.*

swine, suain *s* cerdo *m.*; puerco *m.*

swing, suing *s* oscilación *f.*; (child's) columpio *m.*; *v* oscilar; balancear; columpiarse; (whirl) remolinar

switch, suich *s* (riding) latiguillo *m.*; (electric) conmutador *m.*; (*elec*) interruptor; *v* (train) desviar; **–off,** (electric) cortar; **–on,** poner

swivel, sui´-vel *s* eslabón giratorio *m.*

swoon, swuun *v* desmayarse; *s* desmayo *m.*

swoop, swuup *v* precipitarse; (bird) arrebatar

sword, só rd *s* espada *f.*

sworn, suó rn *a* juramentado

syllable, sil´-a-bl *s* sílaba *f.*

syllabus, sil´-a-bos *s* sílabo *m.*; horario *m.*

symbol, sim´-bol *s* símbolo *m.*

symmetry, sim´-et-ri *s* simetría *f.*

sympathetic, sim-pa-zet´-ik *a* simpático

sympathize, sim-pa-zais ´ *v* simpatizar

sympathy, sim´-pa-zi *s* simpatía *f.*

symptom, simp´-tom *s* síntoma *m.*

synchronize, sin´-kro-nais *v* sincronizar

syndicate, sin´-di-keit *s* sindicato *m.*

synonymous*, si-non´-i-mos *a* sinónimo

syringe, sir´-inCH *s* jeringa *f.*; *v* jeringar

syrup, sir´-op *s* jarabe *m.*; **fruit –,** jarabe de frutas *m.*

system, sis´-tem *s* sistema *m.*

T

tabernacle, tAb´-er-nak´l s
tabernáculo m.

table, tei´-bl s mesa f.;
(list) cuadro m.; tabla f.;
—cloth, mantel m.; **—
land,** meseta f.

tablespoon, tei´-bl-spuun
s cuchara f.

tablet, tab´-let s tableta f.;
placa f.; pastilla f.

table tennis, tei´-bl ten´-is
s tenis m.; de mesa;
ping-pong m.

tack, tAk s tachuela f.; v
clavar; (sew) hilvanar;
(naut) virar

tackle, tAk´-l s (fishing)
avíos de pescar m. pl;
(naut) aparejo m.; v
(attack) atajar

tact, takt s tacto m.;
—ful*, a diplomático;

—less, falto de tacto;
—ics, s táctica f.

tadpole, tAd´-poul s
renacuajo m.

tail, teil s rabo m.;
(comet) cola f.; (dress)
faldón m.

tailor, tei´-lr s sastre m.

taint, teint v manchar;
infeccionar s mancha f.

take, teik v tomar; coger;
(medicine) tomar;
(accept) aceptar;
(along) llevar; **—away,**
llevar; **—care of,** cuidar
de; **—off,** quitarse; (aero)
elevarse

takings, tei´-kings s pl
ingresos m. pl

talcum powder, tAl´-kŏm
pau´-da s (polvos mpl
de) talco m.

tale, teil s narración f.;
(fairy) cuento m.

talent, tAl´-ent s talento
m.

talk, toak v hablar;
conversar; s
conversación f.

talkative, toak´-a-tiv a
locuaz; charlatán

tall, toal a alto; elevado

tallow, tAl´-ou s sebo m.

tally, tAl´-i v (agree)
concordar; s cuenta f.

talon, tAl´-on s garra f.

tame, teim a*
domesticado; manso; v
domesticar; (animals)
domar; **—ness,** s
mansedumbre f.; **—r,**
domador m.

tamper, tAm´-pa **—with,** v
entremeterse en

tampon, tAm´-pon s med
tampón m.

tan, tAn v curtir; (sun)
tostar; s casca f.; **—ner,**
curtidor m.; **—nery,**
tenería f.

tangerine, tAn´-CHe-rin s
mandarina f.

tangible, tAn´-CHi-bl a
tangible, palpable

tangle, tAng´-gl s enredo
m.; embrollo m.; v
enredar

tank, tAngk s aljibe m.;

(mil) tanque m.

tankard, tAng´-kerd s pichel m.; cántaro con tapadera m.

tantalize, tAn´-ta-lais v atormentar

tantamount, tAn´-ta-maunt a equivalente

tap, tAp s golpecito m.; (on shoulder, etc) palmada f.; (cock) grifo m.; (barrel) espita f.; v llamar; (tree) sangrar; (barrel) horadar

tape, teip s cinta f.; (adhesive) cinta adhesiva; (magnetic) cinta magnética; v (record) registrar cinta magnética; **––measure,** s cinta métrica; **––worm,** solitaria f.; **red –,** (fig) formalismo m.

taper, tei´-pa v hacer punta; s cirio m.

tapestry, tAp´-es-tri s tapicería f.; (piece) tapiz m.

tar, taar s brea f.; alquitrán m.; v embrear

tardiness, taar´-di-nes s lentitud f.; tardanza f.

tardy, taar´-di a tardo; (late) tardío

tare, tè r s (plant) cizaña f.; (weight) tara f.

target, taar´-guet s blanco m.

tariff, tAr´-if s tarifa f.

tarnish, taar´-nish v deslustrar; empañar

tarpaulin, taar´-poa´-lin s lienzo empegado m.; toldo m.

tart, taart s tarta f.; a* ácido

task, taask s tarea f.; faena f.; quehacer m.

tassel, tAs´-el s borla f.

taste, teist v gustar; s gusto m.; sabor m.; **–ful,** a de buen gusto; **–less,** insípido; soso

tasty, teis´-ti a sabroso

tatter, tAt´-a s andrajo m.; harapo m.

tattered, tAt´-erd a andrajoso

tattoo, ta-tuu´ s (mil) retreta f.; tatuaje m.; v (the skin) tatuar

taunt, toant v vituperar; s vituperio m.; burla f.

tavern, tAv´-ern s taberna f.

tawdry, toa´-dri a charro; chillón

tax, tAks v poner impuestos; s impuesto m.; contribución f.; **–– payer,** contribuyente m.

taxi, tAks´-i s taxi m.

tea, tii s té m.; **––pot,** tetera f.

teach, tiich v enseñar; **–er,** s maestro m.; profesor m.

teaching, tiich´-ing s enseñanza f.

team, tiim s (sport) equipo m.; (horses) tronco m.; (oxen) yunta f.

tear, tér v (rend) rasgar; s rasgón m.

tear, tir s lágrima f.

tease, tiis v molestar; (joke) embromar

teat, tiit s teta f.; (dummy) chupete m.

technical*, tek´-ni-kl a técnico

technique, tek-niik´ s técnica f.

technology, tek-nol´-o-CHi s technología f.

tedious*, tii´-di-os a aburrido; pesado

tedium, tii´-di-ŏm s tedio m.; fastidio m.

teem, tiim v abundar; producir

teenager, tiin-eiCH-a s quinceañero/a mf.; adolescente mf.; joven mf.

teething, tii´-Ding s dentición f.

teetotaler, tii´-tou-t'la s

abstemio m.

telegram, tel´-i-grAm s
telegrama f.

telegraph, tel´-i-grAf v
telegrafiar; s telégrafo m.

telephone, tel´-i-foun v
telefonear; s teléfono m.

telephone booth, tel´-i-
foun booD s cabina f.;
de teléfono; locutorio
m.

telephone call, tel´-i-foun
koal s llamada f.
(telefónica)

telephone number, tel´-i-
foun nŏm´-ba s número
de teléfono m.

telephoto, tel´-i-fou-to s
telefoto m.

telescope, tel´-i-skoup s
telescopio m.

television, tel´-i-vish-on s
televisión f.

television set, tel´-i-vish-
on set s aparato de
televisión m.; televisor
m.

tell, tel v decir; (relate)
contar; informar

temper, tem´-pa s humor
m.; (steel) temple m.; v
templar; temperamento
m.

temperance, tem´-per-ans
s moderación f.;
sobriedad f.; a sobrio

temperate, tem´-per-et a
moderado; (habits)
morigerado; sobrio

temperature, tem´-per-a-
tiur s temperatura f.;
(fever) calentura f.

tempest, tem´-pest s
tempestad f.; tormenta
f.

temple, tem´-pl s templo
m.; (head) sien f.

temporary, tem´-po-ta-ri a
temporario; provisional

tempt, tempt v tentar;
–ation, s tentación f.

ten, ten s & a diez m.;
–th, décimo m.

tenable, ten´-a-bl a
defendible

tenacious*, ti-nei´-shos a
tenaz

tenacity, ti-nAs´-i-ti s
tenacidad f.

tenancy, ten´-an-si s
tenencia f.; inquilinato
m.

tenant, ten´-ant s
inquilino m.

tend, tend v guardar;
(nurse) cuidar

tendency, ten´-den-si s
tendencia f.

tender, ten´-da v ofrecer; s
oferta f.; (public)
sumisión f.; a* tierno;
(sensitive) sensitivo; →

hearted, compasivo;
–ness, s (affection)
ternura f.

tenement, ten´-i-ment s
habitación f.; vivienda
f.

tennis, ten´-is s tenis m.

tennis court, ten´-is kórt s
pista f.; de tenis; cancha
f.; de tenis

tennis racket, ten´-is
rAk´-et s raqueta de
tenis f.

tenor, ten´-or s tenor m.;
(purport) substancia f.

tense, tens a* tenso;
tirante; s (grammar)
tiempo m.

tension, ten´-shon s
tensión f.; tirantez f.

tent, tent s tienda de
campaña f.

tentative*, ten´-ta-tiv a
tentativo

tenure, ten´-iur s tenencia
f.

tepid, tep´-id a tibio

term, tĕrm s término m.;
(time) período m.

terminal, tĕr´-mi-nal a
(disease) mortal;
terminal; s comput
terminal m.; (coach)
(estación f.) terminal f.;
(air) terminal

terminate, tĕr´-mi-neit v

terminar; limitar

terminus, tĕr´-mi-nos *s* estación terminal *f.*

terms, tĕrms *s pl* condiciones *f. pl;* (instalments) plazos *m. pl;* términos *m. pl*

terrace, ter´-is *s* terraplén *m.;* terraza *f.*

terrible, ter´-i-bl *a* terrible

terrific, ter-if´-ik *a* terrífico; formidable

terrify, ter´-i-fai *v* aterrar

territory, ter´-i-to-ri *s* territorio *m.*

terror, ter´-or *s* terror *m.;* espanto *m.*

terrorist, ter´-or-ist *s* terrorista *mf.*

terrorize, ter´-or-ais *v* aterrorizar

terse*, tĕrs *a* conciso; breve

test, test *v* probar; ensayar; *s* prueba *f.;* ensayo *m.;* examen *m.;* **–ify,** *v* testificar; **–imonial,** *s* recomendación *f.;* (presentation) testimonial *m.;* **–imony,** *s* testimonio *m.*

testicle, tes´-ti-kl *s* testículo *m.*

tether, teD´-a *s* traba *f.; v* estacar

text, text *s* texto *m.;* **–**

book, libro de texto *m.*

textile, tex´-tail *a* textil

texture, tex´-tiur *s* tejido *m.;* textura *f.*

than, DAn *conj* que; de

thank, zAngk *v* agradecer; **–you!** *interj* ¡gracias! **–ful*,** a agradecido; **–less,** desagradecido; **–s,** *s pl* gracias *f. pl;* **–s to,** gracias a

thanksgiving, zAngks´-guiv-ing *s* acción de gracias *f.*

that, DAt *a* ese *m.;* esa *f.;* aquel *m.,* aquella *f.; pron* ése *m.;* ésa *f.;* eso *n.;* aquel *m.;* aquella *f.;* aquello *n.; relative pron* que; *conj* que, para que; **–is,** es decir; **–one,** aquel; aquella

thatch, zAch *s* techo de paja *m.*

thaw, zoa *s* deshielo *m.; v* deshelar; descongelar

the, De *art* el; la; lo; los; las

theater, zii´-a-ta *s* teatro *m.*

theft, zeft *s* robo *m.;* (petty) hurto *m.*

their, Dér *poss adj* su; suyo; suya; de ellos; de ellas

theirs, Dérs *pron* el suyo; la suya; los suyos; las

suyas

them, Dem *pron* los; las; les; ellos; ellas

theme, ziim *s* tema *m.;* motivo *m.*

themselves, Dem-selvs ´ *pron* ellos mismos; ellas mismas; sí mismos

then, Den *adv* entonces; luego; *conj* pues

thence, Dens *adv* desde allí

thenceforth, Dens-fórz´ *adv* desde entonces

theology, zi-ol´-o-CHi *s* teología *f.*

theoretical*, zi-o-ret´-i-kal *a* teórico

theory, zii´-o-ri *s* teoría *f.*

therapy, ze´-ra-pi *s* terapia *f.*

there, Dér *adv* allí; allá; ahí; **–about,** por allí; **–after,** después; **–by,** de este modo; **–fore,** por consiguiente; **–from,** de allí; de allá; **–in,** en eso; en esto; **–upon,** en consecuencia; **–with,** con eso

thermal, zĕr´-ml *a* termal

thermometer, zĕr-mom´-i-ter *s* termómetro *m.*

thermostat, zĕr-mou-stAt *s* termostato *m.*

these, Diis *pron* & *a* estos;

estas

thesis, zi´-sis s tesis f.; disertación f.

they, Dei pers pron ellos m.; ellas f.

thick*, zik a grueso; denso; (liquids) espeso; **–en,** v espesar; **–et,** s matorral m.; **–ness,** grosor m.; espesura f.; densidad f.

thief, ziif s ladrón m.

thieve, ziiv v (theft) hurtar; (robbery) robar

thigh, zai s muslo m.

thimble, zim´-bl s dedal m.

thin, zin a delgado; (sparse) ralo; escaso; v adelgazar; (plants, etc) enralecer; **–ness,** s delgadez f.; raleza f.

thine, Dain pron & a tuyo; tuya

thing, zing s cosa f.; (business) asunto m.

think, zingk v pensar; (believe) creer; **–of,** pensar en; (opinion) pensar de; **–over,** pensarlo

third, zërd s tercio m.; a tercero

thirdly, zërd´-li adv en tercer lugar

thirst, zërst s sed f.; **to be**

–y, tener sed

thirteen, zër´-tiin s & a trece m.

thirteenth, zër´-tiinz s & a décimotercero m.

thirtieth, zër´-ti-iiz s & a trigésimo m.

thirty, zër´-ti s & a treinta m.

this, Dis pron éste, ésta, esto; a este, esta

thistle, zis´-l s cardo m.

thither, DiD´-a adv allí; allá

thong, zong s correa f.

thorn, zoarn s espina f.; **–y,** a espinoso

thorough*, zör´-o a entero; perfecto; real; **–bred,** de pura raza; **–fare,** s vía pública f.; (main street) calle principal f.; **no –fare,** prohibido el paso

those, Dous pron & a esos m.; esas f.; aquellos m.; aquellas f.

though, Dou conj aunque; sin embargo

thought, zoat s pensamiento m.; **–ful*,** a pensativo; considerado; atento; **–less*,** atolondrado; inconsiderado; descuidado

thousand, zau´- sand s & a mil m.

thousandth, zau´- sands s & a milésimo m.

thrall, zróal s esclavo m.; esclavitud f.

thrash, zrAsh v trillar; (flog) azotar; **–ing,** s trilla f.; (flogging) zurra f.

thread, zred s hilo m.; v enhebrar; **–bare,** a raído

threat, zret s amenaza f.; **–en,** v amenazar

threatening, zret´-ning a amenazador

three, zrii s & a tres m.; **–fold,** a triple

threshold, zresh´-jould s umbral m.

thrice, zrais adv tres veces

thrift, zrift s economía f.; frugalidad f.; **–less,** a pródigo

thrifty, zrift´-i a económico

thrill, zril v causar una emoción; estremecerse; s conmoción f.

thrive, zraiv v prosperar; (plants; physically) medrar

throat, zrout s garganta f.

throb, zrob v vibrar; (heart) latir

throes, zrous s dolores m.

pl; agonía *f*.; (*fig*)
congojas *f. pl*

throne, zroun *s* trono *m*.

throng, zrong *s* tropel *m*.;
multitud *f*.; *v* apiñarse

throttle, zrot'-l *s* (*mech*)
gaznate *m*.; *v* (kill)
ahogar

through, zruu *prep* por, a
través de; a causa de;
-out, por entre; todo;
adv (everywhere) en
todas partes; – **train,** *s*
tren directo *m*.

throw, zrou *v* echar;
lanzar; *s* toro *m*.; echada
f.

thrush, zrŏsh *s* tordo *m*.

thrust, zrŏst *v* empujar;
(sword) embestir *s*
empuje *m*.; (sword)
estocada *f*.

thud, zŏd *s* sonido sordo
m.

thumb, zŏm *s* pulgar *m*.

thump, zŏmp *s* porrazo *m*.;
v aporrear; golpe *m*.

thunder, zŏn'-da *v* tronar;
s trueno *m*.;– **bolt,** rayo
m.; **-storm,** tronada *f*.

Thursday, zěrs'-di *s*
jueves *m*.

thus, Dŏs *adv* así; de ese
modo

thwart, zuo*art v* frustrar;
desbaratar

thyme, taim *s* tomillo *m*.

tick, tik *v* (clock) hacer
tic-tac; (check)
contramarcar; *s* (cattle)
garrapata *f*.; (cover)
terliz *m*.; **-ing,** tic-tac
m.

ticket, tik'-et *s* billete *m*.;
(label) etiqueta *f*.;
boleto *m*.; **season-,**
abono *m*.

ticket office, tik'-et of'-is
s taquilla *f*.

tickle, tik'-l *v* hacer
cosquillas

ticklish, tik'-lish *a*
cosquilloso

tidal, tai'-dl *a* de marea

tide, taid *s* marea *f*.; **high
–,** marea alta *f*.; **low
–,** bajamar *f*.; marea
meguante *f*.

tidings, tai'-dings *s pl*
noticias *f. pl*; nuevas *f.
pl*

tidy, tai'-di *a* ordenado;
(neat) pulcro; *v* poner
en orden

tie, tai *s* (bow) lazo *m*.;
(neck) corbata *f*.; *v* atar;
liar; unir; (surgery) ligar

tier, tir *s* fila *f*.; (theater)
fila de palcos *f*.

tiff, tif *s* pique *m*.; disgusto
m.

tiger, tai'-ga *s* tigre *m*.

tight*, tait *a* cerrado;
(garments) estrecho;
apretado; **air-,**
hermético, **-en,** *v*
estrechar; (a screw)
apretar; **water-,** *a*
estanco

tights, taits *s pl* calzas
ajustadas *f. pl*

tile, tail *s* (roof) teja *f*.;
(glazed) azulejo *m*.;
(floor) baldosa *f*.; *v* tejar

till, til *s* gaveta *f*.; *v* (land)
labrar; *conj* hasta que;
prep hasta; ahora

tiller, til'-a *s* (*naut*) caña
del timón *f*.

tilt, tilt *v* inclinar; ladear

timber, tim'-ba *s* madera
de construcción *f*.

time, taim *v* medir el
tiempo; *s* tiempo *m*.;
(occasion) vez *f*.; (hour)
hora *f*.; (music; in
marching) compás *m*.;
-keeper, marcador de
tiempo *m*.; **-ly,** *a* & *adv*
oportuno

timetable, raim-tei'-bl *s*
horario *m*.; itinerario *m*.

timid*, tim-id *a* tímido;
temeroso

tin, tin *v* estañar; *s*
(metal) estaño *m*.; lata
f.; **-box,** caja de lata *f*.;
-foil, hoja de estaño *f*.;

–ned, (food) enlatado;
--plate, hoja de lata f.

tincture, tingk´-tiur s
tintura f.

tinder, tin´-da s mecha f.

tinge, tinCH v colorar; s
tinte m.; (fig.) dejo m.

tingle, ting´-l v sentir
hormigueo

tinkle, tingk´-l v retiñir; s
retintín m.

tinsel, tin´-sl s oropel m.;
brocadillo m.

tint, tint s tinte m.; v teñir

tiny, tai´-ni a minúsculo;
pequeño; chico

tip, tip v (cart, etc) volcar;
(give) dar propina. s
propina f.; (point)
punta f.; información f.;
on --toe, adv de
puntillas

tire, tair s (rim) llanta f.; v
cansar; fatigar; **–d,** a
cansado; **–of,** v cansarse
de

tiresome, tair´-som a
fastidioso; cansado

tissue, tish´-iu s tejido m.;
(veiling) gasa f.

tissue paper, tish´-iu-pei´-
pa s papel de seda m.

tithe, taiD s diezmo m.

title, tai´-tl s título m.;
–deed, título de
propiedad m.; **–page,**

portada f.

titter, tit´-a v reír entre
dientes

to, tu prep a; en; de; por;
hasta; con

toad, toud s sapo m.

toast, toust s (bread)
tostada f.; v tostar

toast, toust v (propose
health) brindar; s
brindis m.

tobacco, to-bʌk´-ou s
tabaco m.; **–nist,**
tabaquero m.; **– pouch,**
bolsa para tabaco f.

toboggan, to-bog´-an s
tobogán m.

today, tu-dei adv hoy

toddler, tod´-la s niño/a
mf.; que empieza a andar

toe, tou s dedo del pie m.

toffee, tof´-i s caramelo m.

together, to-gueD´-a adv
juntos; juntamente

toil, toil v afanarse; s faena
f.; trabajo penoso m.

toiler, toi´-la s trabajador
m.

toilet, toi´-let s tocado m.;
excusado m.

toilet paper, toi´-let pei´-
pa s papel higiénico m.

token, tou´-kn s señal f.;
(gift) recuerdo m.

tolerable, tol´-er-a-bl a
tolerable; pasadero

tolerance, tol´-er-ans s
tolerancia f.

tolerant*, tol´-er-ant a
tolerante

tolerate, tol´-er-eit v
tolerar

toll, toul s (coll)
marimacho m.; (due)
portazgo m.; (bell)
tañido m.; v doblar

tomato, to-maa´-tou s
tomate m.

tomb, tuum s tumba f.;
–stone, lápida sepulcral
f f.

tomboy, tom´-boi s moza
retozona f.

tomcat, tom´-kʌt s gato
m.

tomfoolery, tom-fuul´-er-i
s mentecatada f.

tomorrow, tu-mor´-ou adv
mañana

tomtit, tom´-tit s paro m.

ton, tŏn s tonelada f.;
–nage, tonelaje m.

tone, toun s tono m.

tongs, tong s s pl tenazas f.
pl

tongue, tŏng s lengua f.;
–tied, a con frenillo

tonic, ton´-ik s & a tónico
m.

tonight, tu-nait´ adv esta
noche

tonsil, ton´-sil s tonsila f.;

amídgala f.; **–itis,** tonsilitis f.

too, tuu adv demasiado; (also) también; **–much,** demasiado

tool, tuul s herramienta f.

tooth, tuuz s diente m.; **– ache,** dolor de muelas m.; **––brush,** cepillo de dientes m.; **––paste,** pasta dentífrica f.; **–pick,** mondadientes m.; palillo m.; **–– powder,** polvos dentífricos m. pl

top, top s (upper part) parte de arriba f.; (mountain) cumbre f.; (of tree) copa f.; (school) primero m.; (spinning) peonza f.; **– hat,** chistera f.; **on –,** encima

topic, top´-ik s tópico m.; tema m.

topless, top-les a top-less

topple (over), top´-l v volcarse

topsy-turvy, top´-si-tĕr´-vi adv transtornado

torch, toarch s antorcha f.; hacha f.

torment, toar´-ment s tormento m.; v atormentar

tornado, toar-ne´-dou s

tornado m.; huracán m.

torpedo, toar-pii´-dou s torpedo m.; **–** boat, torpedero m.

torpid, toar´-pid a entorpecido; aletargado

torpor, toar´-pr s torpor m.; estupor m.

torque, toark s (mech) fuerza f.; de torsión m.; (necklace) collar m.

torrent, toar´-ent s torrente m.

torrid, toar´-id a tórrido

tortoise, toar´-tos s tortuga f.; **––shell,** concha de carey f.

torture, toar´-tiur v torturar. s tortura f.

toss, tos s sacudida f.; v lanzar; (coin) echar a cara o cruz; (bull, etc.) revolcar; **–about,** revolverse

total, tou´-tl s total m.; a* total; completo; v sumar; totalizar; **–izator,** s totalizador m.

totter, tot´-a v bambolear; **–ing,** a ruinoso

touch, tŏch s contacto m.; toque m.; v tocar; (emotion) conmover; **–ing,** a commovedor

touchy, tŏch´-i a susceptible; quisquilloso

tough*, tŏf a duro; correoso

tour, túr s excursión f.; v viajar por **–ist,** s turista m. & f.; **–nament,** torneo m.

tourist office, tur-ist of´-is s oficina de turismo f.

tout, taut a tieso; tirante

tow, tou v (haul) remolcar; s (flax) estopa f.; **–ing,** remolque m.; **– line,** sirga f.

towards, tou´-erd s prep con; para con; (direction) hacia

towel, tau´-el s toalla f.; paño de manos m.

tower, tau´-a s torre f.

town, taun s ciudad f.; pueblo m.; villa f.; **– hall,** ayuntamiento m.

town center, taun-sen´-tr s centro m.; urbano

toy, toi s juguete m.; v juguetear

trace, treis s (track) huella f.; rastro m.; (harness) jaez n.; v seguir la pista; (draw) trazar

tracing, treis´-ing s trazo m.; **–paper,** papel de calcar m.

track, trAk s rastro m.; (race) pista f.; (railroad)

via *f*.; *v* seguir la pista

tract, trAkt *s* trecho *m*.

traction, trAk´-shon *s* arrastre *m*.

tractor, trAkt-*a s* tractor *m*.

trade, treid *v* comerciar; *s* comercio *m*.; (craft) oficio *m*.; **—mark**, marca de fábrica *f*.; **—sman**, tendero *m*.; **–s union**, sindicato *m*.

trading, tre´-ding *s* comercio *m*.; *a* mercantil

tradition, tra-di´-shon *s* tradición *f*.

traditional*, tra-dish´-on al *a* tradicional

traffic, trAf´-ik *s* circulación *f*.; trafico *m*.; (trade) intercambio *m*.; **– jam**, — CHAm *s* embotellamiento *m*.; atasco *m*.; **– lights**, — laits *s* semáforo *m*.

tragedian, tra-CHii´-di-an *s* trágico *m*.

tragedy, trACH´-i-di *s* tragedia *f*.

tragic, trACH´-ik *a* trágico

trail, treil *v* seguir el rastro; (drag) arrastrar *s* rastro *m*.; pista *f*.; **–er**, (van) remolque *m*.

train, trein *s* tren *m*.; (dress) cola *f*.; (retinue)

séquito *m*.; *v* instruir; educar; disciplinar; (animals) amaestrar; (sport) entrenar; **–ing**, *s* instrucción *f*.; (sport) entrenamiento *m*.

traitor, trei´-ta *s* traidor *m*.

tram, trAm *s* tranvía *m*.

tramp, trAmp *s* vagabundo *m*.; *v* ir a pie

trample, trAm´-pl *v* hollar; pisotear

trance, traans *s* síncope *m*.; éxtasis *m*.; estado hipnótico *m*.

tranquil*, trAng´-kuil *a* tranquilo

tranquilizer, trAng´-luil-lais-*a s* tranquilizante *f*.

transact, trAn-sAkt´ *v* tramitar

transaction, trAn-sAkt´-shon *s* negociación *f*.

transcribe, trAn-skraib´ *v* transcribir

transfer, trAns-fêr´ *v* transferir; *s* traspaso *m*.

transform, trAns-foarm´ *v* transformar

tranship, trAn-ship´ *v* transbordar

transit, trAn´-sit *s* tránsito *m*.; trámite *m*.

translate, trAns-leit´ *v* traducir

translation, trAns-lei´-shon *s* traducción *f*.

translator, trAns-lei´-ta *s* traductor *m*.

transmit, trAns-mit´ *v* negociar; transmitir

transparent*, trAns-pé´-rent *a* transparente

transpire, trAns-pair´ *v* transpirar

transport, trAns-pórt´ *v* transportar *s* transporte *m*.

transpose, trAns-pous´ *v* transponer

trap, trAp *v* atrapar; *s* trampa *f*.

trapdoor, trAp´-dór *s* escotillón *m*.

trash, trAsh *s* basura *f*.; (fig) desperdicios *m. pl*; hojarasca *f*.; **–y**, *a* hojarascoso

travel, trAv´-l *v* viajar; **–er**, *s* viajero *m*.

traveler's check, trAv´-l-as chek *s* cheque de viaje *m*.

travel sickness, trAv´-l sik-nes *s* mareo

travel agent, trAv´-l ei´-CHent *s* agente de viajes *mf*.

traverse, trAv´-ers *v* atravesar; *a* transversal

trawler, trou´-la *s* (ship)

buque para la pesca a la rastra f.

tray, trei s bandeja f.

treacherous*, trech´-er-os a traidor

treachery, trech´-er-i s traición f.

tread, tred v pisar; s paso m.; (stair) escalón m.

treason, trii´- sn s traición f.

treasure, tresh´-er s tesoro m.; v atesorar

treasurer, tresh´-er-a s tesorero m.

treasury, tresh´-er-i s tesorería f.

treat, triit, s (entertainment) festín m.; (outing) excursión campestre f.; v (negotiate) tratar

treatise, trii´-tis s tratado m.; memoria f.

treatment, triit´-ment s trato m.; tratamiento m.

treaty, trii´-ti s tratado m.; pacto m.

treble, treb´-l a triple; v triplicar; s (mus) tiple f.

tree, trii s árbol m.; **family –,** árbol genealógico m.

trellis, trel´-is s enrejado m.

tremble, trem´-bl v temblar

tremendous*, tri-men´-dos a tremendo

tremulous*, trem´-iu-los a trémulo

trench, trench s zanja f.; (mil) trinchera f.

trend, trend s curso m.; v inclinarse; tendencia f.

trespass, tres´-pas v traspasar; infringir

trespasser, tres´-pas-a s transgresor m.

trestle, tres´-l s caballete m.

trial, trai´-al s prueba f.; (law) juicio m.

triangle, trai´-Ang-gl s triángulo m.

triangular, trai-Ang´-giuu-la a triangular

tribe, traib s tribu f.

tribunal, trai-biuu´-nal s tribunal m.

tributary, trib´-iu-ta-ri s & a tributario m.

tribute, trib´-iuut s tributo m.

trick, trik s (fraud) engaño m.; timo m.; (dexterity) juego de manos m.; (cards) baza f.; (joke) broma f.; v engañar; timar; **–ery,** s engaño m.; **–ster,** trapacero m.

trickle, trik´-l v (drip)

gotear; (flow) escurrir

trifle, trai´-fl s bagatela f.; pequeñez f.; **–with,** v jugarse de

trifling, trai´-fling a insignificante

trigger, trig´-a s gatillo m.

trill, tril v trinar; s trinio m.

trim, trim v (hat; dress) guarnecer; (hair, etc) recortar; (ship; sails) orientar; a aseado

trimming, trim´-ing s (garments) guarnición f.

trinity, trin´-i-ti s trinidad f.

trinket, tring´-ket s chuchería f.; (jewel) joya f.

trio, trii´-ou s trío m.; (music) terceto m.

trip, trip s excursión f.; viaje corto m.; v (stumble) tropezar; **–up,** v echar una zancadilla

tripe, traip s tripas f. pl

triple, trip´-l a triple

triplets, trip´-lets s pl trillizos m. pl

tripod, trai´-pod s trípode m.

triumph, trai´-omf s triunfo m.; v triunfar

trivial*, triv´-i-al a trivial; insignificante

trolley, trol´-i s tranvía
m.; omnibus eléctrico
m.

trombone, trom´-boun s
trombón m.

troop, truup s tropa f.;
–**ship**, buque transporte
m.

trooper, truu´-pa s
soldado de caballería m.

trophy, trou´-fi s trofeo m.

tropical, trop´-i-kal a
tropical

tropics, tro´-piks s pl
trópicos m. pl

trot, trot v trotar; s trote
m.

trouble, trŏb´-l v molestar;
(perturb) perturbar; s
(cares) afanes m.; pl
inquietudes f. pl;
(inconvenience)
molestia f.;
(disturbance) distrubio
m.; alboroto m.;
(difficulty) dificultad f.;
–**some**, a molesto;
(difficult) difícil

trough, trŏf a continuo;
de un lado a otro

trounce, trauns v zurrar;
apalear

trousers, trau´- sers s pl
pantalones m. pl

trout, traut s trucha f.

trowel, trau´-el s

(mason's) llana f.; paleta
f.; (garden)
desplantador m.

truant, truu´-ant, play –,v
hacer novillos; s
holgazán m.

truce, truus s tregua f.

truck, trŏk s camión m.;
carreta f.; (railroad)
furgón de andén m.

truculent*, trŏk-i´-iu-lent
a truculento; cruel

trudge, trŏ CH v afanarse;
cierto; arrastrarse;
–**along**, andar
penosamente

true, truu a verdadero;
(faithful) fiel

truffle, trŏf´-l s trufa f.

truism, truu´-ism s verdad
evidente f.; axioma m.

trump, trŏmp v jugar
triunfo; s triunfo m.

trumpery, trŏm´-per-i s
oropel m.; a de
relumbrón

trumpet, trŏm´-pet s
trompeta f.

truncheon, trón´-shon s
porra f.; garrote m.

trunk, trŏngk s (tree)
tronco m.; (elephant)
trompa f.; (traveling)
baúl m.; cofre m.;
(body) tronco m.

truss, trŏs s baz m.;

(surgical) braguero m.; v
ligar; (poultry) espetar

trust, trŏst s confianza f.;
(combine) trust m.; v
confiar en; fiarse de;
(rely) contar con

trustee, trŏs´-tii s (public)
fideicomisario m.;
(bankruptcy) síndico m.

trustworthy, trŏst´-uĕr-Di
a fidedigno; fiable; digno
de confianza

truth, truuz s verdad f.;
–**ful***, a veraz

try, trai v procurar; tratar
de; (taste) probar; (law)
procesar, juzgar; –**ing**, a
penoso; –**on**, v probarse

T-shirt, tii´-shĕrt s
camiseta f.

tub, tŏb s tina f.; cuba f.;
(bath) bañera f.

tube, tiuub s tubo m.;
caño m.; **inner**, s cámara
de aire f.

tuck, tŏk s pliegue m.; v
plegar; –**in**, (rug, etc)
arropar; –**up**, v
arremangar

Tuesday, tiuus ´-di s
martes m.

tuft, tŏft s copete m.;
(feathers) penacho m.

tug, tŏg v tirar de; (boats)
remolcar; s tirón m.

tugboat, tŏg´-bout s

remolcador m.

tuition, tiu-ish´-on s instrucción f.; enseñanza f.

tulip, tiuu´-lip s tulipán m.

tumble, tóm´-bl v (fall) desplomarse

tumbler, tŏm´-bla s vaso sin pie m.

tumor, tiuu´-mor s tumor m.

tumult, tiuu´-molt s tumulto m.; (riot) motín m.

tuna, tiuu-na s atún

tune, tiuun v afinar; s aire m.; tonada f.; v sintonizar

tuneful, tiuun´-ful a melodioso

tunic, tiuu´-nik s túnica f.; (mil) guerrera f.

tuning fork, tiuu´-ning-foark s horquilla tónica f.

tunnel, tŏn´-l s túnel m.; v horadar

turbine, těr´-bain s turbina f.

turbot, těr´-bot s (pez) rodaballo m.

turbulence, těr´-biu-lens s turbulencia f.; desorden m; disturbios m. pl

turbulent*, těr´-biu-lent a

turbulento

tureen, tiu-riin´ s (soup) sopera f.; (sauce) salsera f.

turf, těrf s césped m.; (peat) turba f.

turkey, těr´-ki s pavo m.

turmoil, těr´-moil s alboroto m.; disturbio m.

turn, těrn s vuelta f.; (duty) servicio m.; (order of succession) turno m.; v volver; volverse; –about, girar; –aside, desviar; –back, retroceder; –ing, s (corner) vuelta f.; –ing point, punto decisivo m.; –into, v convertir; –off, cerrar; apagar; –on, abrir; prender; –out, (expel) echar; –over, volver; volverse s (trade) cifra total f.; –to, v acudir

turner, těr´-na s (artisan) tornero m.

turnip, těr´-nip s nabo m.

turnstile, těrn´-stail s torniquete m.

turpentine, těr´-pen-tain s trementina f.

turret, těr´-et s torrecilla f.; (naval) torre blindada f.

turtle, těr´-tl s tortuga f.; –dove, tórtola f.

tusk, tŏsk s colmillo m.

tussle, tŏs´-l v luchar; s agarrada f.

tutor, tiuu´-ta s tutor m.; v enseñar

TV, ti-vi abbr of television

twang, tuAgn s tono nasal m.; (sound) estridor m.; (string) punteado m.; (taste) dejo m.

tweezers, tuii´- sas s pl pinzas f. pl; (hair) tenacillas f. pl

twelfth, tuelfz s & a duodécimo m.

twelve, tuelv s & a doce m.

twentieth, tuen´-ti-iz s & a vigésimo m.

twenty, tuen´-ti s & a veinte m.

twice, tuais adv dos veces

twig, tuig s ramita f.

twilight, tuai´-lait s crepúsculo m.

twin, tuin s & a gemelo m.; mellizo m.

twin beds, tuin-beds s camas gemelas f. pl

twine, tuain v enroscarse; torcer; s guita f.; pita f.

twinge, tuinCH s punzada f.; v punzar

twinkle, tuing´-kl *v*
centellear; (eyes)
parpadear

twirl, tuĕrl *v* voltear; girar;
s vuelta *f*.

twist, tuist *v* torcer; *s*
(turn) vuelta *f*.

twitch, tuich *s*
crispamiento *m*.; *v*
crisparse

twitter, tuit´-*a v* gorjear;; *s*
gorjeo *m*.

two, tuu *s* & *a* dos *m*.;
–fold, *a* doble

type, taip *s* tipo *m*.; *v*
escribir; *a* máquina

typewriter, taip´-rai-ta *s*
máquina de escribir *f*.

typhoid, tai´-fo-id *s* fiebre
tifoidea *f*.

typical*, tip´-i-kal *a* típico

typist, tai´-pist *s*
mecanografa *f*. & *m*.

typography, taip-o´-gra-fi *s*
tipografía *f*.

tyrannical*, ti-rAn´-i-kl *a*
tiránico

tyrannize, tir´-an-ais *v*
tiranizar

tyrant, tai´-rant *s* tirano
m.

U

ubiquitous, iuu-bik´-ui-tos *a* ubicuo

udder, ŏd´*-a s* ubre *f.*

ugliness, ŏg´-li-nes *s* fealdad *f.*

ugly, ŏg´-li *a* feo

ulcer, ŏl´-sa *s* úlcera *f.*

ulcerate, ŏl´-ser-eit *v* ulcerar

ulterior, ŏl-ti´-ri-*or a* ulterior

ultimate*, ŏl´-ti-met *a* último; fundamental

ultimatum, ŏl-ti-mei´-tŏm *s* ultimátum *m.*

ultimo, ŏl´-ti-mou, *adv* del mes próximo pasado

ultra, ŏl´-tra, ultra, extremo

umbrella, ŏm-brel´-*a s* paraguas *m.*; – **stand,** paragüero *m.*

umpire, ŏm-pair *s* árbitro *m.*

unabashed, ŏn-a-basht´ *a* descocado; desenvuelto

unabated, ŏn-*a*-bei´-tid *a* completo; cabal

unable, ŏn-ei´-bl *a* incapaz; **to be –,** *v* no poder

unacceptable, ŏn-Ak-sep´-ta-bl *a* inaceptable

unaccountable, ŏn-*a*-kaun´-ta-bl *a* inexplicable; extraño

unacquainted, ŏn-*a*-kuen´-tid *a* desconocido; **to be – with,** *v* desconocer

unaffected*, ŏn-*a*-fek´-tid *a* inafectado; (unmoved) impasible

unaided, ŏn-ei´-did *a* sin ayuda

unalterable, ŏn-oal´-ter-*a*-bl *a* inalterable

unaltered, ŏn-oal´-terd *a* inalterado

unanimity, iuu-na-ni´-mi-ti *s* unanimidad *f.*

unanimous*, iuu-nAn´-i-mos *a* unánime

unanswerable, ŏn-aan´-ser-*a*-bl *a* incontestable

unapproachable, ŏn-*a*-prouch´-*a*-bl *a* inaccesible

unarmed, ŏn-aarmd´ *a* desarmado

unashamed*, ŏn-*a*-sheimd´ *a* desvergonzado

unassailable, ŏn-*a*-sei´-la-bl *a* inatacable

unattainable, ŏn-*a*-tei´-na-bl *a* inasequible

unattended, ŏn-*a*-ten´-did *a* solo; desatendido

unattractive, ŏn-*a*-trAkt´-iv *a* poco atractivo

unavoidable, ŏn-*a*-voi´-da-bl *a* inevitable

unaware, ón-*a*-uér´ *a* ignorante

unawares, ŏn-*a*-uérs ´ *adv* desprevenido

unbearable, ŏn-bér´-*a*-bl *a* intolerable

unbecoming*, ŏn-bi-

unbelievable, ŏn-bi-liiv´-a-bl *a* increíble

unbeliever, ŏn-bi-liiv´-a *s* incrédulo *m*.

unbend, ŏn-bend´ *v* enderezar

unbending, ŏn-ben´-ding *a* inflexible

unbiased, ŏn-bai´-ast *a* imparcial

unbleached, ŏn-bliicht´ *a* sin blanquear; sin teñir

unblemished, ŏn-blem´-isht *a* sin tacha; puro

unbounded, ŏn-baun´-did *a* ilimitado

unbreakable, ŏn-breik´-a-bl *a* irrompible

unburden, ŏn-bĕr´-dn *v* descargar

unbutton, ŏn-bŏt´-ŏn *v* desabotonar; desabrochar

uncalled for, ŏn-koald´-fór *a* immerecido; (remark) gratuito

uncanny, ŏn-kAn´-i *a* misterioso

uncared for, ŏn-kérd´-for *a* abandonado

unceasing*, ŏn-siis´-ing *a* incesante

uncertain*, ŏn-sĕr´-tin *a* incierto

unchangeable, ŏn-chein´-CHa-bl *a* invariable

uncivil, ŏn-siv´-il *a* incivil; descortés

unclaimed, ŏn-kleimd´ *a* no reclamado

uncle, oug´-kl *s* tío *m*.

unclean*, ŏn-kliin´ *a* sucio; impuro

uncomfortable, ŏn-kom´-for-ta-bl *a* incómodo

uncommon*, ŏn-kom´-on *a* raro; extraordinario

unconcern, ŏn-kón-sĕrn´ *s* indiferencia *f*.

unconditional*, ŏn-kon-dish´-o-nl *a* incondicional

uncongenial*, ŏn-kon-CHii´-ni-al *a* antipático

unconscious, ŏn-kon´-shos *a* inconsciente; sin sentido; ignorante

uncontrollable, ŏn-kon-trou´-la-bl *a* incontrolable; indomable

unconventional*, ŏn-kon-ven´-shon-l *a* informal

uncork, ŏn-koark´ *v* descorchar

uncouth*, ŏn-kuuz´ *a* (manners) grosero; tosco

uncover, ŏn-kŏv´-a *v* descubrir

uncultivated, ŏn-kŏl´-ti-vei-tid *a* inculto

undated, ŏn-dei´-tid *a* sin fecha

undaunted*, ŏn-doan´-tid *a* atrevido; impávido

undecided, ŏn-di-sai´-did *a* indeciso

undefiled, ŏn-di-faild´ *a* impoluto; puro

undelivered, ŏn-di-liv´-erd *a* sin entregar

undeniable, ŏn-di-nai´-a-bl *a* innegable

under, ŏn´-da, *adv* debajo; *prep* bajo; debajo de; **–age**, *a* menor de edad

undercarriage, ŏn´-da-kAr-iCH *s* bastidor *m*.; tren de aterrizaje(de un aeroplano) *m*.

underclothing, ŏn´-da-klouD-ing *s* ropa interior *f*.

underdone, ŏn´-da-dŏn *a* poco cocido

underfed, ŏn´-da-fed *v* mal alimentado

undergo, ŏn´-da-gou *v* sufrir; sostener

underground, ŏn´-da-graund *a* subterráneo; *s* (railroad) metro *m*.

undergrowth, ŏn´-da-grouz *s* maleza *f*.

underhand, ŏn´-da-jAnd *a* clandestino

underline, ŏn´-da-lain *v*

subrayar

undermine, ŏn´-da-main v
minar

underneath, ŏn´-da-niiz´
adv debajo; prep bajo

under-proof, ŏn´-da-pruuf
a de baja graduación

underrate, ŏn-da-reit´ v
menospreciar

undersell, ŏn-da-sel´ v
vender más barato

undersigned, ŏn´-da-saind
a suscrito m. & f.

undersized, ŏn-da-saisd´ a
achaparrado; (children)
raquítico

understand, ŏn-da-stAnd´
v entender; –ing, s
entendimiento m.;
inteligencia f.

understate, ŏn-da-steit´ v
quedarse corto

understudy, ŏn´-da-stŏd-i
s sustituto; ta a un actor
en el teatro

undertake, ŏn´-da-teik v
emprender; encargárse
de

undertaker, ŏn´-da-teik-a
s director de pompas
fúnebres m.

undertaking, ŏn´-da-teik-
ing s empresa f.

undertone, ŏn´-da-toun s
tono bajo m.; voz baja f.

underwear, ŏn´-da-uér s

ropa interior f.

underwriter, ŏn´-da-rai-ta
s asegurador m.

undeserved,* ŏn-di-
sĕrvd´ a inmerecido;
injusto

undesirable, ŏn-di- sai´-
ra-bl a indeseable

undignified, ŏn-dig´-ni-
faid a sin dignidad

undiminished, ŏn-di-mi´-
nisht a íntegro

undisclosed, ŏn-dis-
klousd´ a no revelado

undismayed, ŏn-dis-meid´
a impávido; sereno

undisturbed, ŏn-dis-
tĕrbd´ a sereno;
tranquilo

undo, ŏn-duu´ v deshacer;
(untie) desatar

undoubted, ŏn-dau´-tid a
fuera de duda

undress, ŏn-dres´ v
desnudar; desnudarse

undue, ŏn-diuu´ a
indebido; excesivo

unearned, ŏn-ernd´ a
desmerecido; (money)
no ganado

unearthly, ŏn-ĕrz´-li a
sobrenatural

uneasy, ŏn-ii´- si a
inquieto; ansioso

uneducated, ŏn-ed´-iuu-
kei-tid a indocto;

ignorante; inculto

unemployed, ŏn-em-
ploid´ a sin empleo

unemployment, ŏn-em-
ploi´-ment s falta de
trabajo f.

unequaled, ŏn-ii´-kuald a
sin igual; sin par

unerring, ŏn-ĕr´-ing a
infalible

uneven*, ŏn-ii´-vn a
desigual; disparejo

unexpected*, ŏn-eks-
pek´-tid a inesperado

unfailing*, ŏn-fei´-ling a
infalible; seguro

unfair*, ŏn-fér´ a injusto

unfaithful*, ŏn-feiz´-ful a
infiel; desleal

unfaltering*, ŏn-foal´-ter-
ing a firme

unfasten, ŏ n-fAs´-n v
desatar; (dress)
desabrochar

unfathomable, ŏn-fAD´-
om-a-bl a insondable

unfavorable, ŏn-fei´-vor-
a-bl a desfavorable

unfeeling*, ŏn-fii´-ling a
insensible; cruel

unfit, ŏn-fit´ a
incapacitado;
incompetente

unflagging*, ŏn-flA´-guing
a infatigable

unflinching*, ŏn-flinch´-

ing *a* firme; resuelto

unfold, ŏn-fould´ *v* desplegar; revelar

unforeseen, ŏn-foar-sin´ *a* imprevisto

unfortunate*, ŏn-foar´-tiu-net *a* desgraciado; desafortunado

unfounded*, ŏn-faoun´-did *a* infundado

unfriendly, ŏn-frend´-li *a* poco amistoso; hostil

unfulfilled, ŏn-ful-fild´ *a* incumplido

unfurl, ŏn-fĕrl´ *v* desplegar; (naut.) desaferrar

unfurnished, ŏn-fer´-nisht *a* desamueblado

ungainly, ŏn-guein´-li *a* desgarbado; sin gracia; desmañado

ungrateful*, ŏn-greit´-ful *a* ingrato; malagradecido

unguarded*, ŏn-gaar´-did *a* (uncontrolled) desprevenido

unhappily, ŏn-jap´-i-li, *adv* desdichadamente

unhappiness, ŏn-jap´-i-nes *s* infelicidad *f*.; desgracia *f*.; desdicha *f*.

unhappy, ŏn-jap´-i *a* desdichado infeliz; triste

unharness, ŏn-jaar´-nes *v* desenjaezar

unhealthy, ŏn-jelz´-i *a* enfermizo; insalúbre

unheard, ŏn-jĕrd´ *a* inaudito; –of, sin ejemplo; no imaginado

unheeded, ŏn-jii´-did *a* desatendido

unhinge, ŏn-jincH´ *v* desgoznar

unhinged, ŏn-jincHd´ *a* (mind) turbado

unhurt, ŏn-jĕrt´ *a* ileso; indemne

unification, iuu-ni-fi-kei´-shon *s* unificación *f*.

uniform, iuu´-ni-foarm *s* & *a* uniforme *m*.

uniformity, iuu-ni-foarm´-i-ti *s* uniformidad *f*.

unilateral* uu-ni-lAt´-te-ral *a* unilateral

unimaginable, ŏn-im-ACH´-i-na-bl *a* inimaginable

unimaginative, ŏn-im-ACH´-i-na-tiv *a* sin imaginación

unimpaired, ŏn-im pèrd´ *a* intacto; inalterado

unimpeachable, ŏn-im-piich´-a-bl *a* irreprensible

unimportant, ŏn-im-por´-tant *a* sin importancia

uninhabitable, ŏn-in-jAb´-i´ta-bl *a*

inhabitable

unintelligible, ŏn-in-tel´-iCH-i-bl *a* ininteligible

unintentional, ŏn-in-ten´-shon-al *a* sin intención

uninviting, ŏn-in-vai´-ting *a* poco atrayente

union, yuu´-ni-on *s* unión *f*.

unique, yu-niik´ *a* único

unit, yuu´-nit *s* unidad *f*.

unite, yu-nait´ *v* unir; juntar

unity, yuu´-ni-ti *s* unidad *f*.; concordia *f*.

universal*, yuu-ni-vĕr´-sl *a* universal

universe, yuu´-ni-vĕrs *s* universo *m*.

university, yuu-ni-ver´-si-ti *s* universidad *f*.; escuela superior *f*.

unjust*, ŏn-cHŏst´ *a* injusto

unkind, ŏn-kaind´ *a* poco amable; desatento

unknown, ŏn-noun´ *a* desconocido; ignorado

unlawful*, ŏn-loa´-ful *a* ilegal; ilícito

unleaded, ŏn-le-ded *s* gasŏlina sin plomo *f*.; *a* (petrol) sin plomo

unless, ŏn-les´ *conj a* menos que; como no sea; excepto

unlike, ŏn-laik´ a
desemejante

unlikely, ŏn-laik´-li a
improbable

unlimited, ŏn-lim´-i-tid a
ilimitado

unload, ŏn-loud´ v
descargar

unlock, ŏn-lok´ v abrir ina
cerradura; (fig) revelar

unlooked for, ŏn-lukt´ fór
a inesperado

unlucky, ŏn-lŏk-i a
desdichado; desgraciado;
(portend) de mal
agüero; desafortunado

unmannerly, ŏn-mAn´-er-
li a descortés; grosero

unmarried, ŏn-mar´-id a
célibe; soltero

unmerciful*, ŏn-mŏ r´-si-
ful a inclemente; cruel

unmistakable, ŏn-mis-
tei´-ka-bl a inequívoco

unmoved, ŏn-muuvd´ a
impasible; inmovido

unnatural, ŏn-nAt´-iu-rl a
desnaturalizado;
inhumano

unnecessary, ŏn-nes´-ses-
a-ri a innecesario;
superfluo

unnerve, ŏn-nĕrv´ v
amedrentar; enervar

unnoticed, ŏn-nou´-tist a
inadvertido

unobtainable, ŏn-ob-tei´-
na-bl a inasequible

unoccupied, ŏn-ok´-iu-
paid a vacante;
desocupado

unofficial, ŏn-o-fish´-l a
no oficial

unopposed, ŏn-o-possd´ a
sin oposición

unorthodox, ŏn-or´-zo-
doks a no ortodoxo

unpack, ŏn-pAk´ v
desembalar;
desempaquetar

unpardonable, ŏn-paar´-
dŏn-a-bl a imperdonable

unpleasant*, ŏn-ples ´-ant
a desagradable

unpopular, ŏn-pop´-iu-la
a impopular

unprecedented, ŏn-pres´-
i-den-tid a sin
precedente

unprepared, ŏn-prii-peird´
a sin preparación;
desprevenido

unproductive*, ŏn-pro-
dŏk´-tiv a improductivo;
infructuoso

unprofitable, ŏn-prof´-i-
ta-bl a no provechoso;
improductivo; que no
rinde utilidad

unpromising, ŏn-prom´-
is-ing a que no promete

unprotected, ŏn-pro-tek´-

tid a desamparado

unprovided, ŏn-pro-vai´-
did a desprovisto;
destituido

unpunctual, ŏn-pŏngk´-
tiu-al a falto de
puntualidad

unquestionable, ŏn-kues´-
tion-a-bl a indisputable

unravel, ŏn-rAv´-l v
desenredar; (solve)
resolver

unread, ŏn-red´ a sin leer;
(person) inculto

unreadable, ŏn-rii´-da-bl a
ilegible

unreasonable, ŏn-rii´-
son-a-bl a irracional

unrelated, ŏn-ri-lei´-tid a
sin conexión

unrelenting, ŏn-ri-len´-
ting a inexorable

unreliable, ŏn-ri-lai´-a-bl
a inseguro; poco
confiable

unremitting, ŏn-ri-mit´-
ing a perseverante

unreserved, ŏn-ri- sĕrvd´
a sin reserva

unrest, ŏn-rest´ s
inquietud f.; desasosiego
m.

unrestrained, ŏn-ri-
streind´ a desenfrenado;
ilimitado

unrestricted, ŏn-ri-strik´-

tid a sin restricción

unripe, ŏn-raipŏ a verde

unroll, ŏn-roul´ v
desenrollar

unruly, ŏn-ruu´-li a
ingobernable;
turbulento

unsafe, ŏn-seif´ a poco
seguro; inseguro

unsalable, ŏn-seil-a-bl a
invendible

unsatisfactory, ŏn-sAt-is-
fAk´-to-ri a poco
satisfactorio

unscrew, ŏn-skruu´ v
destornillar

unscrupulous, ŏn-skruu´-
piu-los a sin escrúpulo

unseasonable, ŏn-sii-sn-a-
bl a intempestivo

unseemly, ŏn-siim´-li a
indecente

unseen, ŏn-siin´ a
invisible

unselfish*, ŏn-sel´-fish a
desinteresado; generoso

unsettled, ŏn-set´-ld a
inestable; pendiente

unshaken, ŏn-shei´-kn a
inmovible; firme;
estable

unshrinkable, ŏn-
shringk´-a-bl a que no se
encoge

unshrinking, ŏn-shringk´-
ing a intrépido

unsightly, ŏn-sait´-li a feo;
disforme; deforme

unskilled, ŏn-skild´ a
inexperto

unskillful*, ŏn-skil´-ful a
inhábil; inexperto

unsociable, ŏn-sou´-sha-bl
a insociable

unsold, ŏn-sould´ a no
vendido

unsolicited, ŏn-so-lis´-i-
tid a no solicitado

unsolved, ŏn-solvd´ a no
resuelto

unsound, ŏn-saund´ a
defectuoso; enfermo;
erróneo; (credit) poco
sólido; (mind) demente

unsparing*, ŏn-spé´-ring a
pródigo

unsteady, ŏn-sted´-i a
inseguro

unstinted, ŏn-stin´-tid a
liberal

unsuccessful, ŏn-sŏk-ses´-
ful a infructuoso;
(person) sin éxito

unsuitable, ŏn-siuu´-ta-bl
a impropio; incapaz

unsuited, ŏn-siuu´-tid a
no apropiado

unsupported, ŏn-so-por´-
tid a sin apoyo

unsurpassed, ŏn-sor-
paast´ a insuperable

unsuspecting, ŏn-sos-

pek´-ting a confiado

unsympathetic*, ŏn-sim-
pa-zet´-ik a indiferente;
sin conmiseración

untamed, ŏn-teimd´ a
indómito

untarnished, ŏn-taar´-
nisht a limpio

untenable, ŏn-ten´-a-bl a
insostenible

untenanted, ŏn-ten-an-tid
a desalquilado

unthankful*, ŏn-zAngk´-
ful a desagradecido

unthinking, ŏn-zingk´-ing
a descuidado; desatento

untidy, ŏn-tai´-di a
desarreglado

untie, ŏn-tai´ v desatar

until, ŏn-til´ prep hasta;
conj hasta que

untimely, ŏn-taim´-li adv
prematuramente

untiring, ŏn-tai´-ring a
incansable

untold, ŏn-tould´ a no
narrado; (vast)
incalculable

untouched, ŏn-tŏcht´ a
intacto

untranslatable, ŏn-trans-
lei´-ta-bl a intraducible

untried, ŏn-traid´ a no
ensayado

untrodden, ŏn-trŏd´-n a
no pisado

untrue, ŏn-truu´ *a* falso; infiel

untrustworthy, ŏn-trŏst´-uerD-i *a* indigno de confianza

untruth, ŏn-truuz´ *s* falsedad *f.*; mentira *f.*

untwist, ŏn-tuist´ *v* destorcer; desenroscar

unusual*, ŏn-iuu´-shu-al *a* inusitado; extraño

unvaried, ŏn-vé´-rid *a* invariable

unveil, ŏn-veil´ *v* descubrir; levantar el velo

unwarrantable, ŏn-uor´-an-ta-bl *a* injustificable; inexcusable

unwavering, ŏn-uei´-ver-ing *a* firme; determinado

unwelcome, ŏn-uel´-kom *a* mal acogido; inoportuno

unwell, ŏn-uel´ *a* indispuesto; malo

unwholesome, ŏn-joul´-sŏm *a* malsano; dañino

unwieldly, ŏn-uii´l´-di *a* pesado

unwilling, ŏn-uil´-ing *a* renuente; mal dispuesto

unwind, ŏn-uaind´ *v* desenredar

unwise, ŏn-uais´ *a* imprudente; indiscreto

unwittingly, ŏn-uit´-ing-li *adv* inconscientemente

unworthy, ŏn-uŏrD´-i *a* indigno; desmerecedor

unwrap, ŏn-rAp´ *v* desenvolver; descubrir

unwritten, ŏn-rit´-n *a* oral; verbal

unyielding, ŏn-yiil´-ding *a* inflexible; rígido

up, ŏp *adv* arriba; hacia arriba; *prep* (up on) sobre; *pp* (risen) levantado; **–and down,** *adv* arriba y abajo; **–here,** (position) aquí arriba; **–there,** allá arriba; **–to,** *prep* (until) hasta

upbraid, ŏp-breid´ *v* echar en cara

upheaval, ŏp-jii´-vl *s* (geological) cataclismo *m.*; alzamiento

uphill, ŏp-jiil´, *adv* cuesta arriba; (fig) penoso

uphold, ŏp-jould´ *v* sostener; mantener

upholsterer, ŏp-joul´-ster-a *s* tapicero *m.*

upholstery, ŏp-joul´-ster-i *s* tapicería *f.*

upkeep, ŏp-kiip´ *s* mantenimiento *m.*; (expenses) gastos *m. pl*

upland, ŏp-land´ *s* tierras

altas *f. pl*

uplift, ŏp-lift´ *v* levantar; elevar

upon, ŏp-on´ *prep* sobre

upper, ŏp´-a, superior; de encima; **–hand,** *s* ventaja *f.*; **–most,** *a* predominante

upperpart, ŏp´-a-paart *s* parte superior *f.*

upright, ŏp´-rait *a* derecho; (honest) honrado *s* montante *m.*

uprising, ŏp-rai´- *sing s* levantamiento *m.*

uproar, ŏp-rór´ *s* tumulto *m.*; alboroto *m.*

uproot, ŏp-ruut´ *v* desarraigar

upset, ŏp-set´ *v* volcar; trastornar; mortificar; *a* (perturbed) perturbado

upside, ŏp´-said, **–down,** *adv* al revés; (fig) en confusión

upstairs, ŏp´-stérs, *adv* arriba; en el piso de arriba; **go –,** *v* subir

upstart, ŏp´-staart *s* advenedizo *m.*

upwards, ŏp´-uerds *adv* hacia arriba

uranium, yú-rein-i-om *s* uranio *m.*

urban, ĕr´-bn *a* urbano

urchin, ĕr´-chin *s* (zool)

erizo; granuja m.;
pilluelo m.
urge, ĕrCH s impulso m.; v
impeler; incitar
urgency, ĕr´-CHen-si s
urgencia f.
urgent*, ĕr´-CHent a
urgente
urinate, yu´-rin-eit v
orinar (se)
urine, yú´-rain s orina f.
urn, ĕrn s urna f.
us, ŏs pron nos; nosotros
use, iuus v usar; emplear; s
uso m.; utilidad f.; **–up,**
v consumir; utilizar
useful*, iuus´-ful a útil
useless*, iuus´-les a inútil
usher, ŏsh´-a s ujier m.;
conserje m.; (cinema,
theater) acomodador;
–in,
v anunciar
usual*, yuu´-shu-al a
usual; habitual;
ordinario
usually, yuu´-shu-al-i adv
por lo general; por regla
general
usurer, yuu´-shúr-a s
usurero m.; logrero m.
usurp, yu- sĕrp´ v usurpar
usury, yuu´-shú-ri s usura
f.
utensil, yu-ten´-sil s
utensilio m.

utility, yuu-til´-i-ti s
utilidad f.
utilize, yuu-til´-ais v
utilizar
utmost, ŏt´-moust a
mayor; sumo; adv lo
más; s lo mayor
utter, ŏt´-a v pronunciar;
emitir; a total; entero
utterance, ŏt´-er-ans s
expresión f.;
pronunciación f.; habla
f.
uttermost, (see **utmost**)

V

vacancy, vei´-kan-si *s* vacancia *f.*; (lack) vacío *m.*

vacant, vei´-kant *a* vacante; (empty) vacío; (free) desocupado; (mind) vago

vacate, va-keit´ *v* dejar vacante; (mil.) evacuar

vacation, va-kei´-shon *s* (holidays) vacación *f*

vaccinate, vAk´-si-neit *v* vacunar

vaccination, vAk´-si-nei-shon *s* vacunación *f*

vacillate, vAs´-i-leit *v* vacilar

vacuum, vAk´-iuu-om *s* vacío *m.*; – **cleaner,** aspirador de polvo *m.*

vagabond, vAg´-a-bŏnd *s* vagabundo *m.*

vague*, veig *a* vago

vain*, vein *a* vanidoso; **in –,** *adv* en vano

vale, veil *s* valle *m.*

valet, vAl´-et *s* criado *m.*; lacayo *m.*

valiant*, vAl´-i-ant *a* valiente

valid*, vAl´-id *a* válido

valley, vAl´-i *s* valle *m.*

valor, vAl´-r *s* valor *m.*; fortaleza

valorous*, vAl´-o-ros *a* valeroso

valuable, vAl´-iu-a-bl *a* valioso

valuables, vAl´-iu-a-bls *s pl* objetos de valor *m. pl*

valuation, vAl´-iu-ei´-shon *s* valuación *f.*; valía *f*

value, vAl´-iu *v* valorar; estimar; *s* valor *m.*

valuer, vAl´-iu-a *s* tasador *m.*; valuador *m.*

valve, vAlv *s* válvul a *f.*; (radio) lámpara *f*

vamp, vAmp *s* pala de zapato *f.*; *v* (*mus*) improvisar

vampire, vAm-pair *s* vampiro *m.*

van, vAn *s* camión *m.*; (train) furgón *m.*; (*mil*) vanguardia *f*

vandalism, vAn-dal-ism *s* vandalismo *m.*

vane, vein *s* veleta *f*; (windmill) aspa *f*

vanilla, va-nil´-a *s* vainilla *f*

vanish, vAn´-ish *v* desvanecerse; desaparecer

vanity, vAn´-i-ti *s* vanidad *f*

vanquish, vAng´-kuish *v* vencer

vapor, vei´-pr *s* vapor *m.*

vaporize, vei´-por-ais *v* vaporizar

variable, vei´-ri-a-bl *a* variable

variation, vei-ri-ei´-shon *s* variación *f*

varicose vein, vei´-ri-kous vein *s* varice *f.*

varied, vè´-rid *a* variado;

ameno

variegated, vè´-ri-guei-tid *a* abigarrado

variety, va-rai´-i-ti *s* variedad *f.*; – **theater,** teatro de variedades *m.*

various*, vé´-ri-os *a* vario; diverso; diferente

varnish, vaar´-nish *v* barnizar; *s* barniz *m.*

vary, vè´-ri *v* variar; cambiar

vase, vaas *s* jarrón *m.*; florero *m.*

vast*, vaast *a* vasto; inmenso

vat, vAt *s* cuba *f.*; tina *f.*; (tannery) noque *m.*

Vatican, vAt´-i-kan *s* Vaticano *m.*

vault, voalt *s* bóveda *f.*; (church, etc) cripta *f.*; (burial) tumba *f.*; *v* (jump) voltear

veal, viil *s* ternera *f.*

veer, vir *v* virar; (wind) cambiar

vegetable, veCH´-i-ta-bl *a* vegetal; verdura; legumbre

vegetables, veCH´-i-ta-b'ls *s pl* legumbres *f. pl*

vegetarian, veCH-i-tei´-ri-an *s* vegetariano *m.*

vegetation, veCH-i-tei´-shon *s* vegetación *f.*

vehement, vii´-ji-ment *a* vehemente

vehicle, vii´-ji-kl *s* vehículo *m.*

veil, veil *s* velo *m.*; *v* velar; esconder

vein, vein *s* vena *f.*

vellum, vel´-m *s* vitela *f.*; pergamino *m.*

velocity, vi-los´-i-ti *s* velocidad *f.*

velvet, vel´-vet *s* terciopelo *m.*

velveteen, vel-ve-tiin´ *s* terciopelo de algodón *m.*

vending machine, ven´-ding mashiin´ *s* vendedora *f.*; automática; distribuidor *m.*; automático

vendor, ven´-dr *s* vendedor *m.*

veneer, vi-nir´ *s* chapa *f.*; *v* chapear; enchapar

venerable, ven´-er-a-bl *a* venerable

veneration, ven-er-ei´-shon *s* veneración *f.*

venereal, vi-ni-ri-al *a* venéreo

vengeance, ven´-CHans *s* venganza *f.*

venial*, vii´-ni-al *a* venial

venison, ven´-sn *s* carne de venado *f.*

venom, ven´-m *s* veneno *m.*

venomous*, ven´-om-os *a* venenoso; ponzoñoso

vent, vent *s* salida *f.*; (cask) venteo *m.*; **give –to,** *v* desahogar

ventilate, ven´-ti-leit *v* ventilar

ventilator, ven´-ti-lei-ta *s* ventilador *m.*

ventriloquist, ven-tril´-o-kuist *s* ventrílocuo *m.*

venture, ven´-tiúr *v* aventurar; (dare) osar; *s* ventura *f.*; riesgo *m.*; **–some,** *a* arriesgado; (individual) emprendedor

veracity, vi-rAs´-i-ti *s* veracidad *f.*

veranda, vi-ran´-da *s* pórtico *m.*; galería *f*

verb, vërb *s* verbo *m.*

verbal*, vër´-bl *a* verbal; oral

verbatim, vër-bei´-tim *adv* palabra por palabra

verbose, vër-bous´ *a* verboso; abundante en palabras

verdant, vër´-dant *a* verde; verdoso

verdict, vër´-dikt *s* opinión *f.*; (legal) fallo *m.*; veredicto *m*

verdigris, vĕr´-di-gris s verdete m.

verge, vĕrCH v aproximarse; s borde m.

verify, vé r´-i-fai v verificar

vermilion, vĕr-mil´-yŏn s bermellón m.

vermin, vĕr´-min s sabandija f.; (fig) piojos m. pl

vernacular, vĕr-nАk´-iu-lar; s idioma vernáculo m.

versatile, vĕr´-sa-tail a versátil

verse, vĕrs s verso m.; poesía f.

versed, vĕrst a versado

version, vĕr´-shon s versión f.; traducción f

versus, vĕr´-sos prep contra

vertical*, vĕr´-ti-kal a vertical

vertigo, vĕr´-ti-gou s vértigo m.

very, ver´-i adv muy; mucho; sumamente; a mismo; verdadero; idéntico

vessel, ves´-l s vasija f.; (naut.) buque m.

vest, vest v vestir; s chaleco m.

vested, ves´-tid a

investidor; (rights) poseído; (interest) creado

vestige, ves´-tiCH s vestigio m.; (sign) señal f

vestment, vest´-ment s vestidura f.; (eccl) vestimenta f

vestry, ves´-tri s sacristía f.

vet, vet s abbr of **veterinary surgeon, veterinarian** veterinario/a mf.; v revisar; repasar; examinar

veteran, vet´-i-ran s & a veterano m.

veterinary, vet´-e-ri-na-ri a veterinario; –ian, s veterinario m.

veto, vii´-tou s veto m.; v poner el veto

vex, veks v vejar

vexation, veks-ei´-shon s vejación f

vexatious, veks-ei´-shos a vejatorio; molesto

via, vai´-a prep por vía de

viaduct, vaí-a-dŏkt s viaducto m.

vibrate, vai´-breit v vibrar

vibration, vai-brei´-shon s vibración f

vicar, vik´-a s vicario m.

vicarage, vik´-er-iCH s vicaría f.

vice, vais s vicio m.; (mech) tornillo de carpintero m.; (prefix) vice-

vice versa, vais vĕr-sa adv vice versa; a la inversa

viceroy, vis´-roi s virrey m.

vicinity, vi-sin´-i-ti s vecindad f.; proximidad f.

vicious*, vish´-os a vicioso

viciousness, vish´-os-ness s depravación f.; vicio m.

victim, vik´-tim s víctima f

victimize, vik´-tim-ais v hacer víctima

victor, vik´-to s vencedor m.

victorious*, vik-tó´-ri-os a victorioso

victory, vik´-to-ri s victoria f.

victual, vit´-l v avituallar; abastecer

victuals, vit´-ls s pl vitualla f.; víveres m. pl

video, vid-i-ou s vídeo m.; v hacer un vídeo de

vie, vai v rivalizar; competir

view, viuu s vista f.; opinión f.; perspectiva f.; – **finder**, s (photog) visor m.

vigil, viCH´-il s vigilia f.

vigilance, viCH´-i-lans s vigilancia f

vigilant*, viCH´-i-lant a vigilante

vigor, vig´-r s vigor m.; fuerza f.

vigorous*, vig´-or-os a vigoroso; fuerte

vile*, vail a vil; bajo

vilify, vil´-i-fai v envilecer; difamar

village, vil´-iCH s aldea f.

villager, vil´-iCH-a s aldeano m.

villain, vil´-in s villano m.

villainous*, vil´-a-nos a vil; infame

villainy, vil´-a-ni s villanía f.

vindicate, vin´-di-keit v vindicar; vengar

vindication, vin-di-kei´-shon s vindicación f.; venganza f.

vindictive*, vin-dik´-tiv a vengativo; –**ness**, s caracter vengativo m.

vine, vain s vid f.; parra f.

vinegar, vin´-i-ga s vinagre m.

vineyard, vin´-yaard s viña f.; viñedo m.

vintage, vin´it-CH s vendimia f.

violate, vai´-o-leit v violar; (law) infringir

violence, vai´-o-lens s violencia f.

violent*, vai´-o-lent a violento

violet, vai´-o-let s violeta f.; a (color) violado m.

violin, vai´-o-lin s violín m.

violinist, vai-ou´-li-nist s violinista m.

viper, vai´-pa s víbora f.

virgin, věr´-CHin s virgen f.

virile, vir´-ail, vir´-il a viril; varonil

virtual*, věr´-tiu-al a virtual

virtue, věr´-tiuu s virtud f.

virtuous*, věr´-tiu-os a virtuoso

virulent*, vir´-u-lent a virulento; venenoso

virus, vai-rŏs s virus m.

visa, vii-sa s visado m; visa f.; v visar

visibility, vis-i-bil´-i-ti s visibilidad f

visible, vis´-i-bl a visible

vision, vish´-on s visión f.; fantasma m.

visit, vis´-it v visitar; s visita f.

visitor, vis´-i-ta s visita f.

visual*, vish´-iu-al a visual

vital*, vai´-tl a esencial; vital

vitality, vai-ta´-li-ti s vitalidad f.

vitals, vai´-tals s pl órganos; vitales m. pl

vitamin, vit´-a-min s vitamina f.

vitriol, vit´-ri-ol s vitriolo m.

vivacious*, vi-vei´-shos a vivaz; animado

vivacity, vi-vAs´-i-ti s vivacidad f

vivid*, viv´-id a vívido; (color) brillante

vivify, viv´-i-fai v vivificar

vixen, vik´-sen s zorra f.; raposa f.; mujer regañona f.

vocabulary, vou-kAb´-iu-la-ri s vocabulario m.

vocal, vou´-kal a vocal; – **chords**, s pl cuerdas vocales f pl

vocalist, vou´-kal-ist s cantor m.; cantante m.

vocation, vou-kei´-shon s vocación f.; profesión f.

vociferous, vo-sif´-er-os a vociferador; vocinglero

vogue, voug s moda f

voice, vois s voz f

void, void a vacío; (null) nulo; s vacío m.

volatile, vol´-a-tail a volátil

volcano, vol-kei´-nou s volcán m.

volley, vol´-i s descarga f.; (salute) salva f

volt, volt s voltio m.; –age, s voltaje m.

voluble, vol´-iu-bl a voluble

volume, vol´-ium s volumen m.; (book) tomo m.

voluminous*, vol-iuu´-mi-nos a voluminoso

voluntary, vol´-on-ta-ri a voluntario

volunteer, vol-on-tir´ s voluntario m.; v ofrecerse

voluptuous*, vo-lŏp´-tiu-os a voluptuoso

vomit, vom´-it v vomitar

voracious, vo-rei´-shos a voraz; devorador

vortex, voar´-teks s vórtice m.; remolino m.

vote, vout v votar s voto m.

voter, vout´-a s votante m. & f.

vouch, vauch v garantizar; –for, responder de

voucher, vauch´-a s (document) resguardo m.; documento m.; comprobante

vow, vau s voto m.; v hacer votos

vowel, vau´-l s vocal f

voyage, voi´-iCH s viaje por mar m.

vulgar*, vŏl´-gar a vulgar; grosero

vulnerable, vŏl-ner-a-bl a vulnerable

vulture, vŏl´-tiur s buitre m.

W

wad, uod *s* (cartridge) taco *m.*; (cotton wool, etc) borra *f.*; guata *f.*; **–ding,** *s* guata; (padding) entretela

waddle, uod´-l *v* andar como un pato

wade, ueid *v* vadear

wafer, uei´-fa *s* (thin biscuit) barquillo *m.*; (eccl) hostia *f.*

wag, uAg *v* menear; *s* chancero *m.*; bromista *m.*

wager, uei´-CHa *s* apuesta *f.*; *v* apostar

wages, uei´-CHis *s* salario *m.*; (daily) jornal *m.*

waggle, uAg´-l *v* menearse

wagon, uAg´-n *s* carretón *m.*; (train) vagón *m.*

waif, ueif *s* niño

abandonado *m.*; granuja *m.*

wail, ueil *v* lamentarse; *s* lamentación *f.*

waist, ueist *s* cintura *f.*; talle *m.*

wait, ueit *v* esperar; aguardar; (at table) servir; **–er,** *s* mozo *m.*; camarero *m.*; **–for,** *v* esperar a; **–ing,** *s* espera *f.*; (service) servicio *m.*; **–ing room,** sala de espera *f.*; (professional) antesala *f.*; **–ress,** camarera *f.*; moza *f.*; **–upon,** *v* servir; atender a

waive, ueiv *v* renunciar; (a un derecho) abandonar

wake, ueik *v* (to awake)

despertar; (to be called) llamar; *s* (ship's) estela *f.*

walk, uoak *v* andar; (stroll) pasearse; *s* paseo *m.*; caminata *f.*; **–er,** caminante *m.*; peatón *m.*; (stroller) paseante *m.*

wall, uoal *s* muro *m.*; (inside) pared *f.*; **– flower,** alelí doble *m.*; **– paper,** papel tapiz *m.*

wallet, uol´-it *s* (note case) cartera *f.*

wallow, uol´-ou *v* revolcarse

walnut, uoal´-nŏt *s* nuez *f.*; (wood) nogal *m.*

walrus, uoal´-ros *s* morsa *f.*

waltz, uoalts *s* vals *m.*; *v* valsar

wan, uoan *a* pálido

wander, uoan´-da *v* vagar; extraviarse; (mentally) delirar

wane, uein *v* menguar; decaer

want, uoant *s* (lack) falta *f.*; (shortage) carencia *f.*; (distress) indigencia *f.*; *v* querer, desear

wanton*, uon´-ton *a* (wicked) perverso; (lustful) lascivo; (waste) extravagante

war, uoar v guerrear. s guerra f.; **–fare,** hostilidades f. pl; conflicto; **–like,** a belicoso

warble, uoar´-bl v trinar; gorjear

ward, uoard s (minor) menor en tutela m.; (hospital) sala de hospital f.; **–en,** (guard) guardián m.; **–er,** carcelero m.; **–off,** v desviar; evitar; **–robe,** guardarropa m.; **–room,** (naval) cuadro de oficiales m.

ware, uèr s mercadería f.

warehouse, uèr´-jaus s depósito m.; almacén m.; v almacenar

warily, uè´-ri-li adv cautelosamente

wariness, uè´-ri-nes s cautela f.; precaución f.

warm*, uoarm a caliente; v calentarse

warmth, uoarmz s calor m.

warn, uoarn v advertir; notificar; avisar

warning, uoarn´-ing s advertencia f.

warp, uoarp v (wood) combar; torcer; pervertir

warrant, uor´-ant s (authority) autoridad f.;

(for arrest) orden de arresto f.; (voucher) autorización f.; **–y,** garantía f.

warrior, uor´-i-a s guerrero m.

wart, uoart s verruga f.

wary, ué´-ri a cauto; prudente

wash, uoash v lavar; lavarse; **–bowl,** s jofaina f.; **–ing,** lavandería f.

washer, uoash´-a s (mech) arandela f.

washing detergent, uoash-ing di-tër´-CHent s detergente m.

washing machine, uoash-ing ma-shiin´ s lavadora f.

wasp, uoasp s avispa f.

waste, ueist s derroche m.; (refuse) desperdicios m. pl; (land) tierra baldía f.; v derrochar; (extravagance) desperdiciar; **–away,** irse consumiendo

wasteful, ueist´-ful a pródigo; ruinoso

watch, uoch v vigilar; observar; s reloj m.; (naut) guardia f.; **– maker,** relojero m.; **–man,** (night) sereno

m.; **–over,** v custodiar; **–word,** s consigna f.

water, uoa´-tr v regar; (cattle, etc) abrevar; agua f.; **hot –bottle,** bolsa para agua caliente f.; **–color,** acuarela f.; **–cress,** berros m. pl; **–fall,** cascada f.; **–lily,** nenúfar m.; **–line,** línea de flotación f.; **–logged,** a anegado en agua; **–proof,** s & a impermeable m.; **– tight,** a estanco; **–y,** aguanoso

watering, uoa´-ter-ing s riego m.; irrigación f.; **– can,** regadera f.; **– place,** balneario m.

waterskiing, uoa´-tr ski-ing s esquí acuático m.

wave, ueiv s ola f.; onda f.; v (flags) agitar; (to somebody) hacer señas; (sway) balancearse; (hair) ondear

waver, uei´-va v vacilar

wavering, uei´-ver-ing a vacilante

wax, uaks v encerar; s cera f.; **–works,** exposición de figuras de cera f.

way, uei s camino m.; (manner) manera f.; forma f.; **–in,** entrada f.;

–lay, v acechar; –out, s salida f.; –side, cuneta f.; borde de camino m.; –through, pasaje m.; –ward, a voluntarioso

we, uii pron pers nosotros m.; nosotras f.

weak*, uiik a débil; flojo; –en, v debilitar; flaquear; –ening, a debilitación; –ling, s encanijado m. & f.; –ly, a enfermizo; –ness, s debilidad f.; flojedad f.

weal, uiil s prosperidad f.; (wale) verdugón m.

wealth, uelz s riqueza f.

wealthy, uel'-zi a rico; opulento

wean, uiin v destetar; (fig) enajenar

weapon, uep'-n s arma f.

wear, uér s (by use) desgaste m.; v (carry) llevar; usar; (last) durar; –out, gastar; (clothes) ponerse; (fatigue) rendir

weariness, ui'-ri-nes s cansancio m.

weary, ui'-ri v cansado; fatigado

weasel, uii'-sl s comadreja f.

weather, ueD'-a s tiempo m.; v aguantar; –bound, a

detenido por el mal tiempo; –cock, s veleta f.; –report, boletín metereológico m.

weave, uiiv v tejer; trenzar; –r, s tejedor m.

web, ueb s (spider) telaraña f.

web-footed, ueb-fut'-id a palmípedo

webbing, ueb'-ing s cincha f.

wed, ued v casarse; (perform ceremony) casar

wedding, ued'-ing s boda f.; – ring, anillo nupcial m.

wedge, ueCH s cuña f.; acuñar; –in, meter por fuerza

wedlock, ued'-lok s matrimonio m.

Wednesday, uens '-di s miércoles m.

weed, uiid v escardar. s mala yerba f.; cizaña f.

week, uiik s semana f.; – day, día laborable f.; – end, fin de semana m.; –ly, a semanal

weep, uiip v llorar; lamentar; –ing, s llanto; dolor; lágrimas; –ing willow, s sauce llorón m.

weevil, uii'-v'l s gorgojo

m.

weigh, uei v pesar; (mentally) ponderar

weight, ueit s peso m.

weighty, uei'-ti a pesado; (serious) grave

weir, uir s presa f., esclusa f.

weird, uird a misterioso; (odd) raro

welcome, uei'-kom s bienvenida f.; a bienvenido; v dar la bienvenida; recibir bien

weld, ueld v soldar

welfare, uel'-fér s bienestar m.; prosperidad f.

well, uel s (water) pozo m. adv bien. a bueno; – being, s bienestar m.; – bred, a bien educado; –done, (meat, etc) bien cocido

well-known, uel noun a (person) conocido

wend, uend v encaminarse

west, uest s oeste m.; –erly, a del oeste

wet, uet s humedad f.; a húmedo; mojado; v mojar; humedecer

wetsuit, uet-suut s traje m.; (iso)térmico

whack, uAck v golpear; s golpe m.

whale, ueil *s* ballena *f.*; –**bone,** barba de ballena *f.*; –**r,** ballenero *m.*

wharf, uoarf *s* muelle *m.*; malecón *m.*; embarcadero *m.*

what, uot *relative pron* lo que; *interrogative pron* qué; *interrogative a* qué; cuál

whatever, uot-ev´-a, *pron & a* cuanto; cualquiera cosa que; todo lo que; sea lo que fuere

wheat, uiit *s* trigo *m.*

wheedle, uii´-dl *v* halagar; (obtain) sonsacar

wheel, uiil *s* rueda *f.*; *v* hacer rodar; **spinning** – *s* torno para hilar *m.*; –**barrow,** carretilla *f.*; –**wright,** carrero *m.*

wheelchair, uiil-chér *s* silla de ruedas *f.*

wheezy, uii´-si *a* resollante

when, uen *adv* cuándo; *conj* cuando; luego que; –**ce,** *adv* de donde; –**ever,** *conj* siempre que; cuando quiera que; todas las veces que

where, uér *adv* donde; ora que; –**about (s),** donde; –**as,** *conj* mientras que; –**at,** *adv* a lo cual; –**by,** por lo cual; –**fore,** por

eso; –**in,** en donde; en que; –**on,** sobre lo cual

wherever, uér-ev´-a *adv* donde quiera que

whet, uet *v* afilar; amolar; (appetite) abrir

whether, ueD´-a *conj* si; sea que

which, uich *interrogative pron* cuál; qué; *relative pron* que; el cual; la cual; lo cual; el que; la que; lo que

whichever, uich-ev´-a *pron* cualquiera; quienquiera

while, uail *v* pasar; *conj* mientras; *s* rato *m.*; momento *m.*

whim, uim *s* capricho *m.*; antojo *m.*; –**sical,** *a* caprichoso

whimper, uim´-pa *s* lloriqueo *m.*; *v* lloriquear

whine, uain *v* gemir; lloriquear

whip, uip *s* látigo *m.*; *v* azotar; fustigar

whirl, uërl *v* girar; –**pool,** *s* remolino de agua *m.*; –**wind,** torbellino *m.*

whisk, uisk *s* (brush) escobilla *f.*; (cookery) batidor *m.*; *v* (sweep) barrer; (cookery) batir

whiskers, uis´-kers *s pl* patillas *f. pl*; (cat) bigotes *m. pl*

whiskey, uis´-ki *s* whisky *m.*

whisper, uis´-pa *v* cuchichear; *s* cuchicheo *m.*

whistle, uis´-l *s* pito *m.*; (sound) silbido *m.*; *v* silbar

white, uait *a* blanco; *s* blanco *m.*; –**ness,** blancura *f.*; –**of egg,** clara de huevo *f.*

whitewash, uait´-uoash *s* blanqueo *m.*

whither, uiD´-a *adv* adonde; a que parte

whiting, uai´-ting *s* (fish) merlán *m.*; fice *m.*

whiz, uis *v* zumbar; silbar

who, juu *interrogative pron* quién; *relative pron* quien que; el cual; la cual; el que, la que

whoever, juu-ev´-a *pron* quienquiera que

whole, joul *s* total *m.*; el todo *m.*; *a* total, todo, entero; –**sale,** al por mayor; –**some,** sano; saludable

wholewheat, joul-juiit *s* harina integral *f.*

wholly, joul´-i *adv*

enteramente;
totalmente

whom, juum *interrogative pron* a quién; *relative pron* a quien; al cual; al que; que

whoop, juup *s* alarido *m.*; *v* huchear

whooping cough, juu´-ping-koaf *s* tosferina *f.*

whose, juus *interrogative pron* de quién; *relative pron* a cuyo; cuya

whosoever, juu-so-ev´-a *pron* quienquiera que

why, uai *adv* por qué; ¡por qué?

wick, uik *s* mecha *f.*

wicked*, uik´-id *a* malvado; inicuo; perverso

wickedness, uik´-id-nes *s* maldad *f.*; iniquidad *f.*; perversidad *f.*

wicker, uik´-a *s* mimbre *m.*

wide, uaid *a* ancho; vasto; **—awake,** (*fig*) despabilado; **-ly,** *adv* extensivamente; **—n,** *v* ensanchar; **—spread,** *a* esparcido

widow, uid´-ou *s* viuda *f.*

widower, uid´-ou-a *s* viudo *m.*

width, uidz *s* ancho *m.*;

anchura *f.*

wield, uiild *v* manejar; (power) gobernar

wife, uaif *s* mujer *f.*; esposa *f.*

wig, uig *s* peluca *f.*

wild*, uaild *a* salvaje; feroz; (*fig*) loco

wilderness, uil´-der-nes *s* desierto *m.*; soledad *f.*; selva *f.*

wildlife, uaild´-laif *s* fauna *f.* (y flora *f.*)

wile, uail *s* ardid *m.*; engaño *m.*

will, uil *s* voluntad *f.*; testamento *m.*; *v* querer; (bequeath) legar

willful*, uil´-ful *a* voluntarioso; (act) premeditado

willing*, uil´-ing *a* dispuesto; gustoso

willingness, uil´-ing-nes *s* buena voluntad *f.*

will-o'-the-wisp, uil-o-Di-uisp´ *s* fuego fatuo *m.*

willow, uil´-ou *s* sauce *m.*

wily, uai´-li *a* astuto; mañoso

win, uin *v* ganar; **—ner,** *s* ganador *m.*; vencedor *m.*; **—ning,** *a* (manners) encantador; **—nings,** ganancias *f. pl*

wince, uins *v* retroceder;

respingar

winch, uinch *s* manubrio *m.*; cigüeña *f.*

wind, uaind *v* ovillar; (road, river, etc) serpentear; **—ing,** *a* serpentino; **—up,** *v* ovillar; (clock) dar cuerda; (business) liquidar

wind, uind *s* viento *m.*; flatulencia *f.*; **—fall,** fortuna *f.*; **—mill,** molino de viento *m.*; **—pipe,** tráquea *f.*; **—shield,** *s* parabrisas *m. pl*; **—shield wipers,** *s* limpiaparabrisas *m. pl*; **—ward,** *adv* a barlovento; **—y,** *a* ventoso

windlass, uind´-lass *s* cabrestante *m.*; montacargas *m.*

window, uin´-dou *s* ventana *f.*; (shop) escaparate *m.*

wine, uain *s* vino *m.*; **— glass,** copa para vino *f.*

wine list, uain-list *s* lista *f.*; de vinos

wing, uing *s* ala *f.*; (theater) bastidor *m.*; (mil) flanco *m.*

wink, uingk *v* guiñar; *s* guiño *m.*

winkle, uin´-kl s (shellfish) bígaro m.

winsome, uin´-som a mono; simpático; alegre

winter, uin´-ta s invierno m.; v invernar

winter sports, uin´-ta spórts s deportes de invierno m. pl

wipe, uaip v limpiar; (to dry) secar

wire, uair s alambre m.

wireless, uair´-les s radio m.; radiotelegrafía f.; (apparatus) radio m.; (message) radiotelegrama m. v radiotelegrafiir

wiring, uair´-ing s instalación eléctrica f.; alumbrado m.

wisdom, uis´-dm s sabiduría f.; prudencia f.

wise*, uais a sabio; prudente

wish, uish s deseo m.; anhelo m.; v desear; anhelar

wishful, uish´-ful a deseoso; anheloso

wisteria, uis-té-ri-a s glicina f.

wistful*, uist´-ful a pensativo

wit, uit s ingenio m.; to –, a saber; es decir

witch, uich s bruja f.

witchcraft, uich´-kraaft s brujería f.

with, uiD prep con, de, a; –draw, v retirarse; (money) retirar; (apologize) retractarse; –hold, detener; (sanction) rehusar; –in, prep dentro; adv (outside) fuera; –stand, v resistir a

wither, uiD´-a v marchitarse

witness, uit´-nes s testigo m.; v atestiguar

wits, uits s sentido m.; aqudeza f.; ingenios m. pl; to live by one's –, vivir de gorra

witticism, uit´-sis m s rasgo de ingenio m.

witty, uit´-i a ingenioso

wizard, uis ´-erd s brujo m.; hechicero m.; mago m.

wobble, uou´-bl v bambolearse; vacilar

woe, nou s pena f.; infortunio m.; –to him, interj ¡ay de él! –ful, a triste; afligido

wolf, uulf s lobo m.; female –, loba f.

woman, uu´-man s mujer f.; –ly, a mujeril

womanhood, uu´-man-jud s la mujer en general f.

womb, uum s matriz f.; útero m.

wonder, uŏn´-da s maravilla f.; v extrañarse; maravillarse de; (doubt) preguntarse

wonderful*, uŏn´-der-ful a maravilloso; estupendo

woo, uu v cortejar; –er, s cortejador m.

wood, uud s madera f.; (forest) bosque m.; –bine, madreselva f.; –cock, chochaperdiz f.; –pecker, pájaro carpintero m.

wooden, uud´-n a de madera

woody, uud´-i a (trees) arbolado

wool, uul s lana f.

woolen, uul´-en a de lana

woolly, uul´-i a lanudo

word, uĕrd s palabra f.; (news) nuevas f. pl; v expresar; (written) redactar; – of honor, s palabra de honor f.

wording, uĕrd´-ing s redacción f.; estilo m.

work, uĕrk v trabajar; (mine) explotar; (mech) funcionar; s trabajo m.; ocupación f.;

(achievement) obra *f.*; **–er,** obrero *m.*; **–ing,** (*mech*) funcionamiento *m.*; (mine) explotación *f.*; **–ing expenses,** gastos de funcionamiento *m. pl*; **–man,** obrero *m.*; **–manship,** mano de obra *f.*; **–shop,** taller *m.*

works, ueřks *s pl* fábrica *f.*; (*mech*) mecanismo *m.*

world, ueřld *s* mundo *m.*; universo *m.*

worldly, ueřld´-li *a* mundano; mundanal

worm, ueřm *s* gusano *m.*; (intestinal) lombriz *f.*; (screw) rosca *f.*; **–eaten,** *a* carcomido

worry, ueř´-i *s* cuidado *m.*; (anxiety) ansiedad *f.*; *v* atormentarse; (bother) molestar

worse, ueřs *adv* peor; *a* peor; pésimo

worship, ueř´-ship *v* adorar; *s* adoración *f.*; (divine) culto *m.*

worst, ueřst *adv* pésimamente; *s* lo peor *n.*

worsted, ueř´-stid *s* (yarn) estambre *m.*

worth, ueřz *s* valor *m.*; mérito *m.*; *a* que vale; **–ily,** *adv* dignamente;

–less, *a* sin valor; **–while,** valer la pena; **–y,** *a* digno

would, uud´ *v aux* (conditional tenses) **if you asked him he – do it** si se lo pidieras, lo haría; (in offers) **– you like a biscuit?** ¿quieres una galleta?; (conjeture) **it – have been midnight** sería medianoche; (indicating habit) **he – go there on Mondays** iba allí los lunes; (in indirect speech) **I said I – do it** dije que lo haría

would-be, uud´-bii *a* pretendiente; supuesto

wound, uund *s* herida *f.*; *v* herir

wrangle, rAng´-gl *v* contender; *s* riña *f.*; contienda *f.*

wrap, rAp *s* manto *m.*; *v* envolver; **–up,** (oneself) arroparse

wrapper, rAp´-a *s* envoltura *f.*; (postal) faja *f.*

wrapping paper, rAp-ing pei´-pa *s* papel de envolver *m.*; papel de regalo *m.*

wrath, roaz *s* ira *f.*; furor *m.*

wreath, riiz *s* corona *f.*; coronar

wreathe, riiD *v* entrelazar

wreck, rek *s* buque naufragado *m.*; (*fig*) ruina *f.*; *v* naufragar; (*fig*) arruinar; **–age,** *s* despojos *m. pl.*

wrecked, rekt *a* naufragado; arruinado

wren, ren *s* reyezuelo *m.*

wrench, rench *s* tirón *m.*; (sprain) torcedura *f.*; (tool) llave inglesa *f.*; destornillador *m.*; *v* torcer; (pull) arrancar

wrestle, res´-l *v* luchar; **–r,** *s* luchador *m.*

wretch, rech *s* miserable *m.* & *f.*; **–ed,** *a* triste; (person) miserable; **–edness,** *s* miseria *f.*

wriggle, rig´-l *v* retorcerse

wring, ring *v* torcer; retorcer

wrinkle, ring´-kl *s* arruga *f.*; *v* arrugar; (brow) fruncir

wrist, rist *s* muñeca *f.*

writ, rit *s* escrito *m.*

write, rait *v* escribir

writer, rai´-ta *s* escritor *m.*; autor *m.*

writhe, raiD *v* retorcerse

writing, rai´-ting *s* escritura *f.*; **hand–,** letra

f.; **in –,** *adv* porescrito;
–**paper,** papel de cartas
m.; –**desk,** escritorio *m.*
written, rit´-n *a* escrito
wrong, rong *s* agravio *m.*;
injusticia *f.*; *v* agraviar. *a*
falso; errado; malo;
inoportuno; injusto;
ilegal; –**side,** *s*
(material) revés *m.*; **to
be –,** *v* no tener razón
wroth, ro*a*z *a* enojado;
irritado
wrought iron, to*a*t ai´-*e*rn
s hierro forjado *m.*
wry, rai *a* torcido; –**face,** *s*
mueca *f.*; (bird)
torcecuello *m.*

Xmas, (=**Christmas**),
kris´-mas *s* Navidad *f*.
X-ray, eks´-rei *s* rayo X
m.; (X-ray photograph)
fotografía por los rayos
X *f*.
xylophone, sai´-lo-foun *s*
xilófono *m*.; especie de
marimba *f*.

yacht, yŏt, s yate m.; **–ing,** navegación en yate f.

yard, yaard s patio m.; (farm) corral m.; (measure) yarda f.; **ship–,** astillero m.; **lumber–,** depósito de madera m.

yarn, yaarn s hilo m.; estambre m.

yawn, yoan v bostezar; s bostezo m.

yawning, yoan´-ing a (chasm, etc) abierto

year, yir s año m.

yearling, yir´-ling s aimal de un año de edad

yearly, yir´-li a * anual

yearn, yĕrn v anhelar; ansiar; **–ing,** s anhelo m.; ansia f.; **–ingly,** adv anhelantemente

yeast, yiist s levadura f.; fermento m.

yellow, yel´-ou a amarillo

yelp, yelp v latir; gañir; ladrar; gañido m.

yes, yes adv sí

yesterday, yes´-ter-di adv ayer

yet, yet adv aún; todavía; conj sin embargo

yew, yuu s (bot.) tejo m.

yield, yiild v ceder; producir; s producto m.

yogurt, yog-ĕrt s yogur m.

yoke, youk v uncir; sujetar; s yugo m.; opresión f.

yokel, youk´-l s patán m.

yolk, youk s yema de huevo f.

yonder, yon´-da adv allí; allá; a aquel; aquella

you, yuu pron vosotros; usted, ustedes; (fam) tú

young, yŏng a joven

younger, yŏng´-a a más joven; menor

youngster, yŏng´-sta s jovencito m.

your, yúr a vuestro; vuestra; vuestros; vuestras; su; sus; de usted; de ustedes; (fam) tu; tus

yours, yúrs pron el vuestro, la vuestra; los vuestros; las vuestras; el suyo; la suya; los suyos; las suyas; el de usted; la de usted; los de usted; las de usted; el de ustedes; la de ustedes; los de ustedes; las de ustedes; (fam) el tuyo; la tuya; los tuyos; las tuyas

youth, ´yuuz s juventud f.; (lad) joven m.; **–ful*,** a juvenil; **–fulness,** s mocedad f.

youth hostel s alberge m.; para jóvenes

yuletide, yuul´-taid s pascua de Navidad m.

zeal, s**ii**l s celo m.; ardor m.; ahinco

zealous*, s**el**´-os a celoso; entusiasta

zebra, s**ii**´-bra s cebra f.

zenith, s**en**´-iz s cénit m.

zephyr, s**ef**´-r s céfiro m.

zero, s**i**´-rou s cero m.

zest, s**e**st s gusto m.; deleite m.

zinc, s**ing**k s cinc m.; v recubrir de cinc

zone, s**ou**n s zona f.

zoo s parque m.; zoológico

zoological, s**ou**-o-loCH-i-kl a zoológico

zoology, s**ou**-ol´-o-CHi s zoología f.